ALL · IN · ONE

CompTIA

Network+®

Certification

EXAM GUIDE

Seventh Edition

(Exam N10-007)

ALL·IN·ONE

CompTIA

Network+®

Certification

EXAM GUIDE
Seventh Edition

(Exam N10-007)

Mike Meyers

Mc
Graw
Hill
Education

New York   Chicago   San Francisco
Athens   London   Madrid   Mexico City
Milan   New Delhi   Singapore   Sydney   Toronto

Library of Congress Cataloging-in-Publication Data

Names: Meyers, Mike, 1961– author. | Jernigan, Scott, author. | Computing Technology Industry Association.
Title: CompTIA network+ certification all-in-one exam guide / Mike Meyers, Scott Jernigan.
Description: Seventh edition. | New York : McGraw-Hill Education, [2018] | Includes bibliographical references and index.
Identifiers: LCCN 2018021046 | ISBN 9781260122381 (hard cover : alk. paper)
Subjects: LCSH: Computer networks—Examinations—Study guides. | Telecommunications engineers—Certification. | Electronic data processing personnel—Certification.
Classification: LCC TK5105.5 .M483 2018 | DDC 004.6076—dc23
LC record available at https://lccn.loc.gov/2018021046

CompTIA Network+® Certification All-in-One Exam Guide, Seventh Edition (Exam N10-007)

2 3 4 5 6 7 8 9 LCR 21 20 19

ISBN   978-1-260-12238-1
MHID   1-260-12238-7

Sponsoring Editor Tim Green	**Technical Editor** Jonathan S. Weissman	**Production Supervisor** James Kussow
Editorial Supervisor Janet Walden	**Copy Editor** Bill McManus	**Composition** Cenveo® Publishing Services
Project Editor LeeAnn Pickrell	**Proofreader** Claire Splan	**Illustration** Cenveo Publishing Services
Acquisitions Coordinator Claire Yee	**Indexer** Jack Lewis	**Art Director, Cover** Jeff Weeks

To Dr. Anthony Brown: Thank you for keeping me alive and healthy, despite my best efforts to the contrary!

ABOUT THE AUTHOR

Michael Meyers is the industry's leading authority on CompTIA Network+ certification. He is the president and founder of Total Seminars, LLC, a member of CompTIA, and a major provider of IT fundamentals, PC and network repair, and computer security training and training materials for thousands of organizations throughout the world.

Mike has written numerous popular textbooks, including the best-selling *CompTIA A+® Certification All-in-One Exam Guide*, *Mike Meyers' CompTIA Network+® Guide to Managing and Troubleshooting Networks*, and *Mike Meyers' CompTIA Security+® Certification Guide*.

Mike has attained numerous industry certifications, including CompTIA A+, CompTIA Network+, CompTIA Security+, CompTIA Cybersecurity Analyst (CySA+), and Microsoft Certified Professional.

About the Contributor

Scott Jernigan wields a mighty red pen as Editor in Chief for Total Seminars. With a Master of Arts degree in Medieval History, Scott feels as much at home in the musty archives of London as he does in the crisp IPS glow of Total Seminars' Houston HQ. After fleeing a purely academic life, he dove headfirst into IT, working as an instructor, editor, and writer.

Scott has written, edited, and contributed to dozens of books on computer literacy, hardware, operating systems, networking, security, and certification, including *Computer Literacy—Your Ticket to IC³ Certification*, and co-authoring with Mike Meyers the *CompTIA IT Fundamentals® All-in-One Exam Guide* and *Mike Meyers' CompTIA Security+® Certification Guide*.

Scott has taught computer classes all over the United States, including stints at the United Nations in New York and the FBI Academy in Quantico. Practicing what he preaches, Scott is a CompTIA A+, CompTIA Network+, and CompTIA Security+ certified technician, a Microsoft Certified Professional, a Microsoft Office User Specialist, and Certiport Internet and Computing Core Certified.

About the Technical Editor

Jonathan S. Weissman is an associate professor and IT program coordinator (Department of Computing Sciences) at Finger Lakes Community College. He is also a senior lecturer (Department of Computing Security) at Rochester Institute of Technology and teaches part-time at Syracuse University (Department of Electrical Engineering and Computer Science) and Nazareth College (School of Management).

Jonathan is the co-author of *Mike Meyers' CompTIA Network+® Certification Passport, Sixth Edition* and *Mike Meyers' CompTIA Network+® Guide to Managing and Troubleshooting Networks Lab Manual, Fifth Edition*, and also serves as technical editor for many industry textbooks. Jonathan also developed three courses for the edX RITx Cybersecurity MicroMasters program, which he has taught to more than 50,000 students worldwide. In addition to teaching, Jonathan is a networking and cybersecurity consultant for local businesses and individuals.

Jonathan has a master's degree in Computer Science from Brooklyn College and holds 34 industry certifications, including CCNP® Routing and Switching, CCNA® Security, CompTIA Security+, CompTIA Network+, CompTIA A+, Certified Ethical Hacker, Computer Hacking Forensic Investigator, and IPv6 Certified Network Engineer (Gold), among others.

LinkedIn: https://www.linkedin.com/in/jonathan-s-weissman-058b649b

Twitter: https://twitter.com/cscprof

Becoming a CompTIA Certified
IT Professional Is Easy

It's also the best way to reach greater professional opportunities and rewards.

Why Get CompTIA Certified?

Growing Demand

Labor estimates predict some technology fields will experience growth of more than 20% by the year 2020. (Source: CompTIA 9th Annual Information Security Trends study: 500 U.S. IT and Business Executives Responsible for Security.) CompTIA certification qualifies the skills required to join this workforce.

Higher Salaries

IT professionals with certifications on their resume command better jobs, earn higher salaries, and have more doors open to new multi-industry opportunities.

Verified Strengths

Ninety-one percent of hiring managers indicate CompTIA certifications are valuable in validating IT expertise, making certification the best way to demonstrate your competency and knowledge to employers. (Source: CompTIA Employer Perceptions of IT Training and Certification.)

Universal Skills

CompTIA certifications are vendor neutral—which means that certified professionals can proficiently work with an extensive variety of hardware and software found in most organizations.

Learn

Learn more about what the exam covers by reviewing the following:

- Exam objectives for key study points.

- Sample questions for a general overview of what to expect on the exam and examples of question format.

- Visit online forums, like LinkedIn, to see what other IT professionals say about CompTIA exams.

Certify

Purchase a voucher at a Pearson VUE testing center or at CompTIAstore.com.

- Register for your exam at a Pearson VUE testing center.

- Visit pearsonvue.com/CompTIA to find the closest testing center to you.

- Schedule the exam online. You will be required to enter your voucher number or provide payment information at registration.

- Take your certification exam.

Work

Congratulations on your CompTIA certification!

- Make sure to add your certification to your resume.

- Check out the CompTIA Certification Roadmap to plan your next career move.

Learn More: Certification.CompTIA.org

CompTIA Disclaimer

CONTENTS AT A GLANCE

CONTENTS

ACKNOWLEDGMENTS

I'd like to acknowledge the many people who contributed their talents to make this book possible:

To Tim Green, my sponsoring editor at McGraw-Hill: I love what you bring to the table with every book—the encouragement, the joy, the witty banter, and the grammar hammer. Always a pleasure to work with you!

To my in-house Editor-in-Chief, Scott Jernigan: I couldn't have done it without you, amigo. Truthfully, has there ever been a better combo than a wizard and a paladin?

To Jonathan S. Weissman, technical editor: Wait, how many more certifications did you get since the last edition? No wonder you keep me honest (and accurate)! Still, tossing in smiley faces after telling me, in perfect New Yorker, "you're totally wrong here!" doesn't actually stop the sting much. Ha!

To Bill McManus, copy editor: So wonderful to work with you again. You are the best!

To Michael Smyer, Total Seminars' resident tech guru and photographer: Your contributions continue to shine, from superb photographs to excellent illustrations and, in this edition, some nicely styled writing. Well done!

To Dave Rush, crack technologist and ridiculously talented person: How can I list the many contributions you've made to make this book—and all the crazy products that go with it—so awesome? Researching, writing, arguing, filming, arguing, researching some more … and the final product. All fun!

To Travis Everett, Internet guru and writer: You bring the "A" game every time and your contributions to this book in writing and as a technologist were both lasting and timely. Thank you!

To Dudley Lehmer, my partner at Total Seminars: As always, thanks for keeping the ship afloat while I got to play on this book!

To Claire Yee, acquisitions coordinator at McGraw-Hill: Another stellar effort from you keeping us on task, on yet another book that is better by far because of your participation. Thank you!

To LeeAnn Pickrell, project editor: So fun working with you again. Not a rollercoaster this time, but just smooth sailing!

To Claire Splan, proofreader: You did a super job, thank you!

To Cenveo Publishing Services, compositors: The layout was excellent, thanks!

INTRODUCTION

By picking up this book, you've shown an interest in learning about networking. But be forewarned. The term *networking* describes a vast field of study, far too large for any single certification, book, or training course to cover. Do you want to configure routers and switches for a living? Do you want to administer a large Windows network at a company? Do you want to install wide area network connections? Do you want to set up Web servers? Do you want to secure networks against attacks?

If you're considering a CompTIA Network+ certification, you probably don't yet know exactly what aspect of networking you want to pursue, and that's okay! You're going to *love* preparing for the CompTIA Network+ certification.

Attaining CompTIA Network+ certification provides you with four fantastic benefits. First, you get a superb overview of networking that helps you decide what part of the industry you'd like to pursue. Second, it acts as a prerequisite toward other, more advanced certifications. Third, the amount of eye-opening information you'll gain just makes getting CompTIA Network+ certified plain old *fun*. Finally, you'll significantly enhance your opportunity to get a job. Everything seems to be networked today, putting network techs in demand.

Nothing comes close to providing a better overview of networking than CompTIA Network+. The certification covers local area networks (LANs), wide area networks (WANs), the Internet (the world's largest WAN), security, cabling, and applications in a wide-but-not-too-deep fashion that showcases the many different parts of a network and hopefully tempts you to investigate the aspects that intrigue you by looking into follow-up certifications.

The process of attaining CompTIA Network+ certification will give you a solid foundation in the whole field of networking. Mastering the competencies will help fill in gaps in your knowledge and provide an ongoing series of "a-ha!" moments of grasping the big picture that make being a tech so much fun.

Ready to learn a lot, grab a great certification, and have fun doing it? Then welcome to CompTIA Network+ certification!

Who Needs CompTIA Network+? I Just Want to Learn about Networks!

Whoa up there, amigo! Are you one of those folks who either has never heard of the CompTIA Network+ exam or just doesn't have any real interest in certification? Is your goal only to get a solid handle on networks and a jump start on the basics? Are you looking for that "magic bullet" book that you can read from beginning to end and then start installing and troubleshooting a network? Do you want to know what's involved with running network cabling in your walls or getting your new wireless network working? Are you tired of not knowing enough about TCP/IP and how it works? If these types of questions are running through your mind, then rest easy—you have the right book. Like every book with my name, you'll get solid concepts without pedantic details or broad, meaningless overviews. You'll look at real-world networking as performed by real techs. This is a book that understands your needs and goes well beyond the scope of a single certification.

If the CompTIA Network+ exam isn't for you, you can skip the rest of this Introduction, shift your brain into learn mode, and dive into Chapter 1. But then, if you're going to have the knowledge, why *not* get the certification?

What Is CompTIA Network+ Certification?

CompTIA Network+ certification is an industry-wide, vendor-neutral certification program developed and sponsored by the Computing Technology Industry Association (CompTIA). The CompTIA Network+ certification shows that you have a basic competency in the physical support of networking systems and knowledge of the conceptual aspects of networking. To date, many hundreds of thousands of technicians have become CompTIA Network+ certified.

CompTIA Network+ certification enjoys wide recognition throughout the IT industry. At first, it rode in on the coattails of the successful CompTIA A+ certification program, but it now stands on its own in the networking industry and is considered the obvious next step after CompTIA A+ certification. (CompTIA A+ is the certification for PC technicians.)

What Is CompTIA?

CompTIA is a nonprofit, industry trade association based in Oakbrook Terrace, Illinois, on the outskirts of Chicago. Tens of thousands of computer resellers, value-added resellers, distributors, manufacturers, and training companies from all over the world are members of CompTIA.

CompTIA was founded in 1982. The following year, CompTIA began offering the CompTIA A+ certification exam. CompTIA A+ certification is now widely recognized as the *de facto* requirement for entrance into the PC industry. Because the CompTIA A+ exam initially covered networking only lightly, CompTIA decided to establish a vendor-neutral test covering basic networking skills. So, in April 1999, CompTIA unveiled the CompTIA Network+ certification exam.

CompTIA provides certifications for a variety of areas in the computer industry, offers opportunities for its members to interact, and represents its members' interests to government bodies. CompTIA certifications include CompTIA A+, CompTIA Network+, and CompTIA Security+, to name a few. Check out the CompTIA Web site at www.comptia.org for details on other certifications.

CompTIA is *huge*. Virtually every company of consequence in the IT industry is a member of CompTIA: Microsoft, Dell, Cisco … Name an IT company and it's probably a member of CompTIA.

The Current CompTIA Network+ Certification Exam Release

CompTIA constantly works to provide exams that cover the latest technologies and, as part of that effort, periodically updates its certification objectives, domains, and exam questions. This book covers all you need to know to pass the N10-007 CompTIA Network+ exam released in 2018.

How Do I Become CompTIA Network+ Certified?

To become CompTIA Network+ certified, you simply pass one computer-based exam. There are no prerequisites for taking the CompTIA Network+ exam, and no networking experience is needed. You're not required to take a training course or buy any training materials. The only requirements are that you pay a testing fee to an authorized testing facility and then sit for the exam. Upon completion of the exam, you will immediately know whether you passed or failed.

Once you pass, you become CompTIA Network+ certified for three years. After three years, you'll need to renew your certification by taking the current exam or completing approved Continuing Education activities. By completing these activities, you earn credits that (along with an annual fee) allow you to keep your CompTIA Network+ certification. For a full list of approved activities, check out CompTIA's Web site (www.comptia.org) and search for **CompTIA Continuing Education Program**.

 NOTE The American National Standards Institute (ANSI) has accredited the CompTIA Network+ certification as compliant with the ISO 17024 Standard. That makes it special.

Now for the details: CompTIA recommends that you have at least nine to twelve months of networking experience and CompTIA A+ knowledge, but this is not a requirement. Note the word "recommends." You may not need experience or CompTIA A+ knowledge, but each helps! The CompTIA A+ certification competencies have a degree of overlap with the CompTIA Network+ competencies, such as types of connectors and how networks work.

As for experience, keep in mind that CompTIA Network+ is mostly a practical exam. Those who have been out there supporting real networks will find many of the questions reminiscent of the types of problems they have seen on LANs. The bottom line is that you'll probably have a much easier time on the CompTIA Network+ exam if you have some CompTIA A+ experience under your belt.

What Is the Exam Like?

The CompTIA Network+ exam contains 100 questions, and you have 90 minutes to complete the exam. To pass, you must score at least 720 on a scale of 100–900.

CompTIA uses two types of questions: multiple-choice and performance-based. *Multiple-choice questions* offer four or five answer options; you select the correct answer and proceed to the next question. The majority of the questions follow this format.

Performance-based questions require you to do something. You might need to arrange a wireless access point in an office for maximum coverage, for example, or properly align the colored wires on a network connector. You need to have appropriate command-line skills to respond at a command prompt. These are all things that good network techs should be able to do without blinking. I'll cover all the topics in the book, and you'll get practical experience as well in the various extra design elements and labs.

The exam questions are divided into five areas that CompTIA calls domains. This table lists the CompTIA Network+ domains and the percentage of the exam that each represents.

CompTIA Network+ Domain	Percentage
1.0 Network Concepts	23%
2.0 Infrastructure	18%
3.0 Network Operations	17%
4.0 Network Security	20%
5.0 Network Troubleshooting and Tools	22%

The CompTIA Network+ exam is extremely practical. Questions often present real-life scenarios and ask you to determine the best solution. The CompTIA Network+ exam loves troubleshooting. Let me repeat: many of the test objectives deal with direct, *real-world troubleshooting*. Be prepared to troubleshoot both hardware and software failures and to answer both "What do you do next?" and "What is most likely the problem?" types of questions.

A qualified CompTIA Network+ certification candidate can install and configure a PC to connect to a network. This includes installing and testing a network card, configuring drivers, and loading all network software. The exam will test you on the different topologies, standards, and cabling.

Expect conceptual questions about the Open Systems Interconnection (OSI) seven-layer model. You need to know the functions and protocols for each layer to pass the CompTIA Network+ exam. You can also expect questions on most of the protocol suites, with heavy emphasis on the TCP/IP suite. If you've never heard of the OSI seven-layer model, don't worry! This book will teach you all you need to know.

NOTE CompTIA occasionally makes changes to the content of the exam, as well as the score necessary to pass it. Always check the Web site of my company, Total Seminars (www.totalsem.com), before scheduling your exam.

How Do I Take the Test?

To take the test, you must go to an authorized testing center. You cannot take the test over the Internet. Pearson VUE administers the actual CompTIA Network+ exam. You'll find thousands of Pearson VUE testing centers scattered across the United States and Canada, as well as in over 75 other countries around the world. You may take the exam at any testing center. To locate a testing center and schedule an exam, call Pearson VUE at 877-551-7587. You can also visit their Web site at https://home.pearsonvue.com/.

NOTE Although you can't take the exam over the Internet, Pearson VUE provides easy online registration. Go to https://home.pearsonvue.com/ to register online.

How Much Does the Test Cost?

CompTIA fixes the price, no matter what testing center you use. The cost of the exam depends on whether you work for a CompTIA member. At press time, the cost for non-CompTIA members is $302 (U.S.).

If your employer is a CompTIA member, you can save money by obtaining an exam voucher. In fact, even if you don't work for a CompTIA member, you can purchase a voucher from member companies (like mine) and take advantage of significant member savings. You simply buy the voucher and then use the voucher to pay for the exam. Vouchers are delivered to you on paper and electronically via e-mail. The voucher number is the important thing. That number is your exam payment, so protect it from fellow students until you're ready to schedule your exam.

If you're in the United States or Canada, you can visit www.totalsem.com or call 800-446-6004 to purchase vouchers. As I always say, "You don't have to buy your voucher from us, but for goodness' sake, get one from somebody!" Why pay full price when you have a discount alternative?

You must pay for the exam when you schedule, whether online or by phone. If you're scheduling by phone, be prepared to hold for a while. Have your Social Security number (or the international equivalent) ready and either a credit card or a voucher number when you call or begin the online scheduling process. If you require any special accommodations, Pearson VUE will be able to assist you, although your selection of testing locations may be a bit more limited.

International prices vary; see the CompTIA Web site for international pricing. Of course, prices are subject to change without notice, so always check the CompTIA Web site for current pricing!

How to Pass the CompTIA Network+ Exam

The single most important thing to remember about the CompTIA Network+ certification exam is that CompTIA designed it to test the knowledge of a technician with as little as nine months of experience—so keep it simple! Think in terms of practical knowledge. Read this book, answer the questions at the end of each chapter, take the practice exams on the media accompanying this book, review any topics you missed, and you'll pass with flying colors.

Is it safe to assume that it's probably been a while since you've taken an exam? Consequently, has it been a while since you've had to study for an exam? If you're nodding your head yes, you'll probably want to read the next sections. They lay out a proven strategy to help you study for the CompTIA Network+ exam and pass it. Try it. It works.

Obligate Yourself

The first step you should take is to schedule the exam. Ever heard the old adage that heat and pressure make diamonds? Well, if you don't give yourself a little "heat," you might procrastinate and unnecessarily delay taking the exam. Even worse, you may end up not taking the exam at all. Do yourself a favor. Determine how much time you need to study (see the next section), and then call Pearson VUE and schedule the exam, giving yourself the time you need to study—and adding a few extra days for safety. Afterward, sit back and let your anxieties wash over you. Suddenly, turning off the television and cracking open the book will become a lot easier!

Set Aside the Right Amount of Study Time

After helping thousands of techs get their CompTIA Network+ certification, we at Total Seminars have developed a pretty good feel for the amount of study time needed to pass the CompTIA Network+ exam. Table 1 will help you plan how much study time you must devote to the exam. Keep in mind that these are averages. If you're not a great student or if you're a little on the nervous side, add another 10 percent. Equally, if you're the type who can learn an entire semester of geometry in one night, reduce the numbers by 10 percent. To use this table, just circle the values that are most accurate for you and add them up to get the number of study hours.

Type of Experience	Amount of Experience			
	None	**Once or Twice**	**On Occasion**	**Quite a Bit**
Installing a SOHO wireless network	4	2	1	1
Installing an advanced wireless network (802.1X, RADIUS, etc.)	2	2	1	1
Installing structured cabling	3	2	1	1
Configuring a home router	5	3	2	1
Configuring a Cisco router	4	2	1	1
Configuring a software firewall	3	2	1	1
Configuring a hardware firewall	2	2	1	1
Configuring an IPv4 client	8	4	2	1
Configuring an IPv6 client	3	3	2	1
Working with a SOHO WAN connection (DSL, cable)	2	2	1	0
Working with an advanced WAN connection (Tx, OCx, ATM)	3	3	2	2
Configuring a DNS server	2	2	2	1
Configuring a DHCP server	2	1	1	0
Configuring a Web application server (HTTP, FTP, SSH, etc.)	4	4	2	1
Configuring a VLAN	3	3	2	1
Configuring a VPN	3	3	2	1
Configuring a dynamic routing protocol (RIP, EIGRP, OSPF)	2	2	1	1

Table 1 Determining How Much Study Time You Need

A complete neophyte may need 120 hours or more of study time. An experienced network technician already CompTIA A+ certified should only need about 24 hours.

Study habits also come into play here. A person with solid study habits (you know who you are) can reduce the number by 15 percent. People with poor study habits should increase that number by 20 percent.

The total hours of study time you need is _____.

Study for the Test

Now that you have a feel for how long it's going to take to study for the exam, you need a strategy for studying. The following has proven to be an excellent game plan for cramming the knowledge from the study materials into your head.

This strategy has two alternate paths. The first path is designed for highly experienced technicians who have a strong knowledge of PCs and networking and want to concentrate on just what's on the exam. Let's call this group the Fast Track group. The second path, and the one I'd strongly recommend, is geared toward people like me: the ones who want to know why things work, those who want to wrap their arms completely around a concept, as opposed to regurgitating answers just to pass the CompTIA Network+ exam. Let's call this group the Brainiacs.

To provide for both types of learners, I have broken down most of the chapters into two parts:

- **Historical/Conceptual**   Although not on the CompTIA Network+ exam, this knowledge will help you understand more clearly what is on the CompTIA Network+ exam.

- **Test Specific**   These topics clearly fit under the CompTIA Network+ certification domains.

The beginning of each of these areas is clearly marked with a large banner that looks like the following.

Historical/Conceptual

If you consider yourself a Fast Tracker, skip everything but the Test Specific section in each chapter. After reading the Test Specific sections, jump immediately to the Chapter Review questions, which concentrate on information in the Test Specific sections. If you run into problems, review the Historical/Conceptual sections in that chapter. After going through every chapter as described, take the free online practice exams on the media that accompanies the book. First, take them in practice mode, and then switch to final mode. Once you start scoring in the 80–85 percent range, go take the test!

Brainiacs should first read the book—the whole book. Read it as though you're reading a novel, starting on page 1 and going all the way through. Don't skip around on the first read-through, even if you are a highly experienced tech. Because there are terms and concepts that build on each other, skipping around might confuse you, and you'll just end up closing the book and firing up your favorite PC game. Your goal on this first read is to understand concepts—to understand the whys, not just the hows.

Having a network available while you read through the book helps a lot. This gives you a chance to see various concepts, hardware, and configuration screens in action as you read about them in the book. Plus, you'll need some gear to do all the hands-on exercises sprinkled throughout the book. Nothing beats doing it yourself to reinforce a concept or piece of knowledge!

You will notice a lot of historical information—the Historical/Conceptual sections—that you may be tempted to skip. Don't! Understanding how some of the older stuff worked or how something works conceptually will help you appreciate the reason behind current networking features and equipment, as well as how they function.

After you have completed the first read-through, cozy up for a second. This time, try to knock out one chapter per sitting. Concentrate on the Test Specific sections. Get a highlighter and mark the phrases and sentences that make major points. Look at the pictures and tables, noting how they illustrate the concepts. Then, answer the end of chapter questions. Repeat this process until you not only get all the questions right, but also understand *why* they are correct!

Once you have read and studied the material in the book, check your knowledge by taking the online practice exams included on the media accompanying the book. The exams can be taken in practice mode or final mode. In practice mode, you are allowed to check references in the book (if you want) before you answer each question, and each question is graded immediately. In final mode, you must answer all the questions before you are given a test score. In each case, you can review a results summary that tells you which questions you missed, what the right answer is to each, and where to study further.

Use the results of the exams to see where you need to bone up, and then study some more and try them again. Continue retaking the exams and reviewing the topics you missed until you are consistently scoring in the 80–85 percent range. When you've reached that point, you are ready to pass the CompTIA Network+ exam!

If you have any problems or questions, or if you just want to argue about something, feel free to send an e-mail to me at michaelm@totalsem.com or to my editor, Scott Jernigan, at scottj@totalsem.com.

For additional information about the CompTIA Network+ exam, contact CompTIA directly at its Web site: www.comptia.org.

Good luck!

—Mike Meyers

Network Models

The CompTIA Network+ certification exam expects you to know how to

- 1.2 Explain devices, applications, protocols and services at their appropriate OSI layers
- 1.3 Explain the concepts and characteristics of routing and switching

To achieve these goals, you must be able to

- Describe how models such as the OSI seven-layer model and the TCP/IP model help technicians understand and troubleshoot networks
- Explain the major functions of networks with the OSI seven-layer model
- Describe the major functions of networks with the TCP/IP model

The CompTIA Network+ certification challenges you to understand virtually every aspect of networking—not a small task. Networking professionals use one of two methods to conceptualize the many parts of a network: the *Open Systems Interconnection (OSI) seven-layer model* and the *Transmission Control Protocol/Internet Protocol (TCP/IP) model.*

These models provide two tools that make them essential for networking techs. First, the OSI and TCP/IP models provide powerful mental tools for diagnosing problems. Understanding the models enables a tech to determine quickly at what layer a problem can occur and helps him or her zero in on a solution without wasting a lot of time on false leads. Second, these models provide a common language techs use to describe specific network functions. Figure 1-1 shows product information for a Cisco-branded advanced networking device. Note the use of the terms "L3" and "layer 7." These terms directly reference the OSI seven-layer model. Techs who understand the OSI model understand what those numbers mean, giving them a quick understanding of what the device provides to a network.

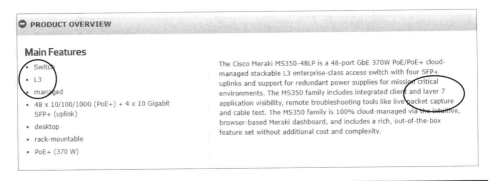

Figure 1-1   Using OSI terminology in device documentation

This chapter looks first at models in general and how models help conceptualize and troubleshoot networks. The chapter then explores both the OSI seven-layer model and the TCP/IP model to see how they help clarify network architecture for techs.

Cisco and Certifications

Cisco Systems, Inc. is famous for making many of the "boxes" that interconnect networks all over the world. It's not too far of a stretch to say that Cisco helps power a huge portion of the Internet. These boxes are complicated to configure, requiring a high degree of technical knowledge.

To address this need, Cisco offers a series of certifications. The entry-level certification, for example, is the Cisco Certified Entry Networking Technician (CCENT). The next step is the Cisco Certified Network Associate (CCNA) Routing and Switching.

Go to Cisco's certification Web site and compare the objectives for the two certifications with what you learned about CompTIA Network+ in the "Introduction" of this book. Ask yourself this question: could you study for CCENT or CCNA R&S and CompTIA Network+ simultaneously?

Historical/Conceptual

Working with Models

Networking is hard. It takes a lot of pieces, both hardware and software, all working incredibly quickly and in perfect harmony, to get anything done. Just making Google appear in your Web browser requires millions of hours in research, development, and manufacturing to create the many pieces to successfully connect your system to a server somewhere in Googleland and to enable them to communicate. Whenever we encounter highly complex technologies, we need to simplify the overall process by breaking it into discrete, simple, individual processes. We do this using a network *model*.

Biography of a Model

What does the word "model" mean to you? Does the word make you think of a beautiful woman walking down a catwalk at a fashion show or some hunky guy showing off the latest style of blue jeans on a huge billboard? Maybe it makes you think of a plastic model airplane? What about those computer models that try to predict weather? We use the term "model" in a number of ways, but each use shares certain common themes.

All models are a simplified representation of the real thing. The human model ignores the many different types of body shapes, using only a single "optimal" figure. The model airplane lacks functional engines or the internal framework, and the computerized weather model might disregard subtle differences in wind temperatures or geology (Figure 1-2).

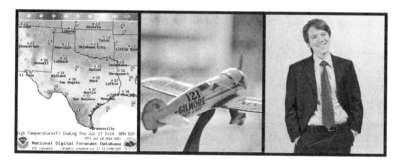

Figure 1-2   Types of models (images from left to right courtesy of NOAA, Mike Schinkel, and Michael Smyer)

Additionally, a model must have at least all the major functions of the real item, but what constitutes a major rather than a minor function is open to opinion. Figure 1-3 shows a different level of detail for a model. Does it contain all the major components of an airplane? There's room for argument that perhaps the model should have landing gear to go along with the propeller, wings, and tail.

Figure 1-3
Simple model
airplane

Network Models

Network models face similar challenges. What functions define all networks? What details can you omit without rendering the model inaccurate? Does the model retain its usefulness when describing a network that does not employ all the layers?

In the early days of networking, different manufacturers made unique types of networks that functioned well. Part of the reason they worked was that every network manufacturer made everything. Back then, a single manufacturer provided everything for a customer when the customer purchased a network solution: all the hardware and all the software in one complete and expensive package. Although these networks worked fine as stand-alone networks, the proprietary nature of the hardware and software made it difficult—to put it mildly—to connect networks of multiple manufacturers. To interconnect networks and therefore improve the networking industry, someone needed to create a guide, a model, that described the functions of a network. Using this model, the people who made hardware and software could work together to make networks that worked together well.

Two models tend to stand out: the OSI model and the TCP/IP model. The OSI model is covered on the CompTIA Network+ exam. The TCP/IP model is not on the exam but it is common and important and you should know it. Let's look at both.

NOTE The International Organization for Standardization (ISO) created the OSI seven-layer model. ISO may look like a misspelled acronym, but it's actually a word, derived from the Greek word *isos,* which means "equal." The International Organization for Standardization sets standards that promote *equality* among network designers and manufacturers, thus ISO.

The best way to learn the OSI and TCP/IP models is to see them in action. For this reason, I'll introduce you to a small network that needs to copy a file from one computer to another. This example goes through each of the OSI and TCP/IP layers needed to copy that file, and I explain each step and why it is necessary. By the end of the chapter, you should have a definite handle on using either of these models as a tool to conceptualize networks. You'll continue to build on this knowledge throughout the book and turn your OSI and TCP/IP model knowledge into a powerful troubleshooting tool.

The OSI Seven-Layer Model in Action

Each layer in the OSI seven-layer model defines an important function in computer networking, and the protocols that operate at that layer offer solutions to those functions. *Protocols* are sets of clearly defined rules, regulations, standards, and procedures that enable hardware and software developers to make devices and applications that function properly at a particular layer. The OSI seven-layer model encourages modular design in networking, meaning that each layer has as little to do with the operation of other layers as possible. Think of it as an automobile assembly line. The guy painting the car doesn't care about the gal putting doors on the car—he expects the assembly line process to make sure the cars he paints have doors. Each layer on the model trusts that the other layers on the model do their jobs.

The OSI seven layers are

- **Layer 7** Application
- **Layer 6** Presentation
- **Layer 5** Session
- **Layer 4** Transport
- **Layer 3** Network
- **Layer 2** Data Link
- **Layer 1** Physical

The OSI seven layers are not laws of physics—anybody who wants to design a network can do it any way he or she wants. Although many protocols fit neatly into one of the seven layers, others do not.

 EXAM TIP Be sure to memorize both the name and the number of each OSI layer. Network techs use OSI terms such as "Layer 4" and "Transport layer" synonymously. Students have long used mnemonics for memorizing such lists. One of my favorites for the OSI seven-layer model is "Please Do Not Throw Sausage Pizza Away." Yum! Another great mnemonic that helps students to memorize the layers from the top down is "All People Seem To Need Data Processing." Go with what works for you.

Now that you know the names of the layers, let's see what each layer does. The best way to understand the OSI layers is to see them in action. Let's see them at work at the fictional company of MHTechEd, Inc.

 NOTE This section is a conceptual overview of the hardware and software functions of a network. Your network may have different hardware or software, but it will share the same functions.

Welcome to MHTechEd!

Mike's High-Tech Educational Supply Store and Post Office, or MHTechEd for short, has a small network of PCs running Windows, a situation typical of many small businesses today. Windows runs just fine on a PC unconnected to a network, but it also comes with all the network software it needs to connect to a network. All the computers in the MHTechEd network are connected by special network cabling.

As in most offices, virtually everyone at MHTechEd has his or her own PC. Figure 1-4 shows two workers, Janelle and Dana, who handle all the administrative functions at MHTechEd. Because of the kinds of work they do, these two often need to exchange data between their two PCs. At the moment, Janelle has just completed a new employee handbook in Microsoft Word, and she wants Dana to check it for accuracy. Janelle could transfer a copy of the file to Dana's computer by the tried-and-true Sneakernet method—saving the file on a flash drive and walking it over to her—but thanks to the wonders of computer networking, she doesn't even have to turn around in her chair. Let's watch in detail each piece of the process that gives Dana direct access to Janelle's computer, so she can copy the Word document from Janelle's system to her own.

Figure 1-4
Janelle and Dana, hard at work

Long before Janelle ever saved the Word document on her system—when the systems were first installed—someone who knew what they were doing set up and configured all the systems at MHTechEd to be part of a common network. All this setup activity resulted in multiple layers of hardware and software that can work together behind the scenes to get that Word document from Janelle's system to Dana's. Let's examine the different pieces of the network, and then return to the process of Dana grabbing that Word document.

Test Specific

Let's Get Physical—Network Hardware and Layers 1–2

Clearly the network needs a physical channel through which it can move bits of data between systems. Most networks use a cable like the one shown in Figure 1-5. This cable, known in the networking industry as *unshielded twisted pair (UTP)*, usually contains four pairs of wires that can transmit and receive data.

Figure 1-5
UTP cabling

Another key piece of hardware the network uses is a special box-like device that handles the flow of data from each computer to every other computer (Figure 1-6). This box is often tucked away in a closet or an equipment room. (The technology of the central box has changed over time. For now, let's just call it the "central box." I'll get to variations in a bit.) Each system on the network has its own cable that runs to the central box. Think of the box as being like one of those old-time telephone switchboards, where operators created connections between persons who called in wanting to reach other telephone users.

Figure 1-6
Typical central box

Layer 1 of the OSI model defines the method of moving data between computers, so the cabling and central box are part of the *Physical layer* (Layer 1). Anything that moves data from one system to another, such as copper cabling, fiber optics, even radio waves, is part of the OSI Physical layer. Layer 1 doesn't care what data goes through; it just moves the data from one system to another system. Figure 1-7 shows the MHTechEd network in the OSI seven-layer model thus far. Note that each system has the full range of layers, so data from Janelle's computer can flow to Dana's computer. (I'll cover what a "hub" is shortly.)

Figure 1-7
The network
so far, with
the Physical
layer hardware
installed

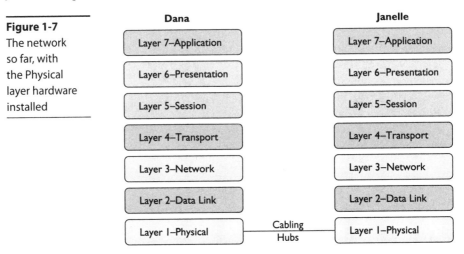

The real magic of a network starts with the *network interface card*, or *NIC* (pronounced "nick"), which serves as the interface between the PC and the network. While NICs come in a wide array of shapes and sizes, the ones at MHTechEd look like Figure 1-8.

Figure 1-8
Typical NIC

On older systems, a NIC truly was a separate card that snapped into a handy expansion slot, which is why they were called network interface *cards*. Even though they're now built into the motherboard, they are still called NICs.

When installed in a PC, the NIC looks like Figure 1-9. Note the cable running from the back of the NIC into the wall; inside that wall is another cable running all the way back to the central box.

Figure 1-9
NIC with cable
connecting the
PC to the wall
jack

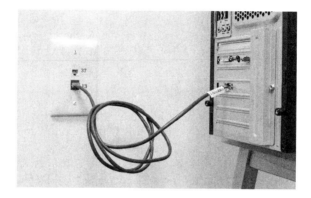

Cabling and central boxes define the Physical layer of the network, and NICs provide the interface to the PC. Figure 1-10 shows a diagram of the network cabling system. I'll build on this diagram as I delve deeper into the network process.

Figure 1-10
The MHTechEd
network

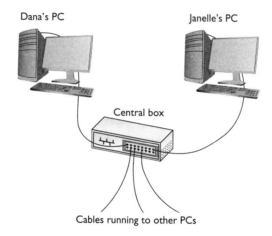

Dana's PC   Janelle's PC

Central box

Cables running to other PCs

You might be tempted to categorize the NIC as part of the Physical layer at this point, and you'd have a valid argument. The NIC clearly is necessary for the physical connection to take place. Many authors put the NIC in OSI Layer 2, the Data Link layer, though, so clearly something else is happening inside the NIC. Let's take a closer look.

The NIC

To understand networks, you must understand how NICs work. The network must provide a mechanism that gives each system a unique identifier—like a telephone number—so data is delivered to the right system. That's one of the NIC's most important jobs. Inside every NIC, burned onto some type of ROM chip, is special firmware containing a unique identifier with a 48-bit value called the *media access control address*, or *MAC address*.

No two NICs ever share the same MAC address—ever. Any company that makes NICs must contact the Institute of Electrical and Electronics Engineers (IEEE) and request a block of MAC addresses, which the company then burns into the ROMs on its NICs. Many NIC makers also print the MAC address on the surface of each NIC, as shown in Figure 1-11. Note that the NIC shown here displays the MAC address in hexadecimal notation. Count the number of hex characters—because each hex character represents 4 bits, it takes 12 hex characters to represent 48 bits. MAC addresses are always written in hex.

Hexadecimal Aside

A hexadecimal numbering system uses base 16 for representing numbers—that would be 0–15 (in base 10 values). Contrast this with the more common decimal numbering system, numbered 0–9. Just as with decimal, people who work with hexadecimal need a single character to represent each number for the 16 values. Using 0–9 makes sense, but then hex is represented in letter form for the values 10–15 (A, B, C, D, E, F).

Hexadecimal works great with binary. Four bits provide the values of 0–15. 0001, for example, is the value 1; 1000 in binary is 8; 1111 is 15. When we work with MAC addresses, it's far easier to break each 4-bit section of the 48-bit address and translate that into hex. Humans work better that way!

Back to MAC Addresses

The MAC address in Figure 1-11 is 004005-607D49, although in print, we represent the MAC address as 00–40–05–60–7D–49. The first six digits, in this example 00–40–05, represent the number of the NIC manufacturer. Once the IEEE issues those six hex digits to a manufacturer—referred to as the *Organizationally Unique Identifier (OUI)*—no other manufacturer may use them. The last six digits, in this example 60–7D–49, are the manufacturer's unique serial number for that NIC; this portion of the MAC is often referred to as the *device ID*.

Figure 1-11
MAC address

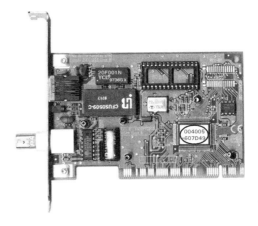

Would you like to see the MAC address for your NIC? If you have a Windows system, type `ipconfig /all` from a command prompt to display the MAC address (Figure 1-12). Note that `ipconfig` calls the MAC address the *physical address*, which is an important distinction, as you'll see a bit later in the chapter. (For macOS, type `ifconfig` from a terminal; for Linux, type `ip a` from a terminal to get similar results.)

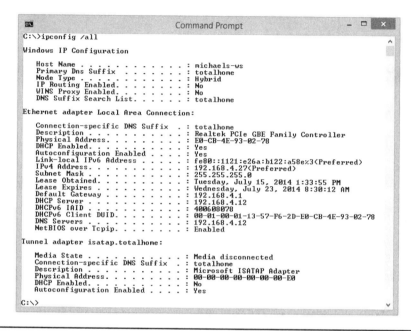

Figure 1-12   Output from `ipconfig /all`

MAC-48 and EUI-48

The IEEE forms MAC addresses from a numbering name space originally called *MAC-48*, which simply means that the MAC address will be 48 bits, with the first 24 bits defining the OUI, just as described here. The current term for this numbering name space is *EUI-48*. EUI stands for *Extended Unique Identifier*. (IEEE apparently went with the new term because they could trademark it.)

Most techs just call them MAC addresses, as you should, but you might see MAC-48 or EUI-48 on the CompTIA Network+ exam.

Okay, so every NIC in the world has a unique MAC address, but how is it used? Ah, that's where the fun begins! Recall that computer data is binary, which means it's made up of streams of ones and zeroes. NICs send and receive this binary data as pulses of electricity, light, or radio waves. The NICs that use electricity to send and receive data were the originals, so let's consider that type of NIC. The specific process by which a NIC uses electricity to send and receive data is exceedingly complicated but, luckily for you, not necessary to understand. Instead, just think of a *charge* on the wire as a *one* and *no charge* as a *zero*. A chunk of data moving in pulses across a wire might look something like Figure 1-13.

Figure 1-13
Data moving
along a wire

Try This!

What's Your MAC Address?
You can readily determine your MAC address on a desktop computer.

1. On macOS systems, open a terminal, type **ifconfig**, and press the ENTER key.

2. On Linux systems, open a terminal, type **ip a**, and press the ENTER key.

3. In Windows, type **cmd** at the Start screen and press ENTER when the Command Prompt option appears on the right. At the command prompt, type the command **ipconfig /all** and press the ENTER key.

If you put an oscilloscope on the wire to measure voltage, you'd see something like Figure 1-14. An oscilloscope is a powerful tool that enables you to see electrical pulses.

Figure 1-14
Oscilloscope
of data

Now, remembering that the pulses represent binary data, visualize instead a string of ones and zeroes moving across the wire (Figure 1-15).

Figure 1-15
Data as ones
and zeroes

1 0 1 0 1 1 1 0 1 1

Once you understand how data moves along the wire, the next question is, how does the network get the right data to the right system? All networks transmit data by breaking whatever is moving across the Physical layer (files, print jobs, Web pages, and so forth) into discrete chunks called frames. A *frame* is basically a container for a chunk of data moving across a network. A frame *encapsulates*—puts a wrapper around—information and data for easier transmission. (More on this later in the chapter.) The NIC creates and sends, as well as receives and reads, these frames.

> **NOTE** The unit of data specified by a protocol at each layer of the OSI seven-layer model is called a *protocol data unit (PDU)*. A frame is the PDU for Layer 2.

I like to visualize an imaginary table inside every NIC that acts as a frame creation and reading station. I see frames as those pneumatic canisters you see when you go to a drive-in teller at a bank. A little guy inside the network card—named Nick, of course—builds these pneumatic canisters (the frames) on the table and then shoots them out on the wire to the central box (Figure 1-16).

Figure 1-16
Inside the NIC

> **NOTE** Different frame types are used in different networks. All NICs on the same network must use the same frame type, or they will not be able to communicate with other NICs.

Here's where the MAC address becomes important. Figure 1-17 shows a representation of a generic frame, a simplified version of the most common wired network technology, called *Ethernet*. (Chapter 3 covers Ethernet in great detail. For now just go with the frame described here as a generic wired thing.)

Even though a frame is a string of ones and zeroes, we often draw frames as a series of rectangles, each rectangle representing a part of the string of ones and zeroes. You will see this type of frame representation used quite often, so you should become comfortable with it (even though I still prefer to see frames as pneumatic canisters).

Figure 1-17
Generic frame

Recipient's MAC address	Sender's MAC address	Type	Data	FCS

Note that the frame begins with the MAC address of the NIC to which the data is to be sent, followed by the MAC address of the sending NIC. Next comes the *Type* field, which indicates what's encapsulated in the frame. Then comes the *Data* field that contains what's encapsulated, followed by a special bit of checking information called the *frame check sequence (FCS)*. The FCS uses a type of binary math called a *cyclic redundancy check (CRC)* that the receiving NIC uses to verify that the data arrived intact.

You can think of a frame in a different way as having three sections. The *header* (MAC addresses and Type) starts, followed by the *payload* (whatever is encapsulated in the frame); this is followed by the *trailer* (the FCS).

So, what's inside the data part of the frame? You neither know nor care. The data may be a part of a file, a piece of a print job, or part of a Web page. NICs aren't concerned with content! The NIC simply takes whatever data is passed to it via its device driver and addresses it for the correct system. Special software will take care of *what* data gets sent and what happens to that data when it arrives. This is the beauty of imagining frames as little pneumatic canisters (Figure 1-18). A canister can carry anything from dirt to diamonds—the NIC doesn't care one bit (pardon the pun).

Figure 1-18

Frame as a
canister

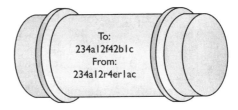

To:
234a12f42b1c
From:
234a12r4er1ac

Like a canister, a frame can hold only a certain amount of data. Different types of networks use different sizes of frames, but the frames used in most wired networks hold at most 1500 bytes of data. This raises a new question: what happens when the data to be sent is larger than the frame size? Well, the sending system's software must chop the data up into nice, frame-sized chunks, which it then hands to the NIC for sending. As the receiving system begins to accept the incoming frames, the receiving system's software recombines the data chunks as they come in from the network. I'll show how this disassembling and reassembling is done in a moment—first, let's see how the frames get to the right system!

Into the Central Box

When a system sends a frame out on the network, the frame goes into the central box. What happens next depends on the technology of the central box.

In the early days of networking, the central box was called a *hub*. A hub was a dumb device, essentially just a repeater. When it received a frame, the hub made an exact copy of that frame, sending a copy of the original frame out of all connected ports except the port on which the message originated.

The interesting part of this process was when the copy of the frame came into all the other systems. I like to visualize a frame sliding onto the receiving NIC's "frame assembly table," where the electronics of the NIC inspected it. (This doesn't exist; use your imagination!) Here's where the magic took place: only the NIC to which the frame was addressed would process that frame—the other NICs simply dropped it when they saw that it was not addressed to their MAC address. This is important to appreciate: with a hub, *every* frame sent on a network was received by *every* NIC, but only the NIC with the matching MAC address would process that frame (Figure 1-19).

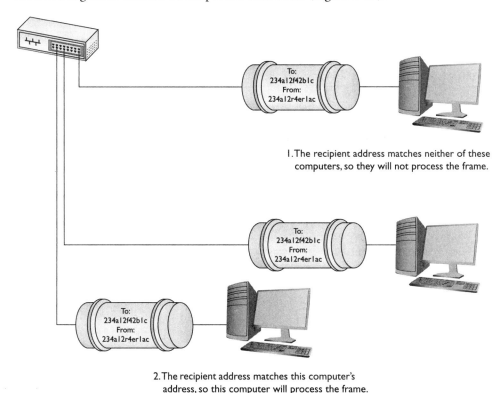

1. The recipient address matches neither of these computers, so they will not process the frame.

2. The recipient address matches this computer's address, so this computer will process the frame.

Figure 1-19 Incoming frame!

Later networks replaced the hub with a smarter device called a *switch*. Switches, as you'll see in much more detail as we go deeper into networking, filter traffic by MAC address. Rather than sending all incoming frames to all network devices connected to it, a switch sends the frame only to the interface associated with the destination MAC address.

FCS in Depth

All FCSs are only 4 bytes long, yet the wired frame carries at most 1500 bytes of data. How can 4 bytes tell you if all 1500 bytes in the data are correct? That's the magic of the math of the CRC. Without going into the grinding details, think of the CRC as just the remainder of a division problem. (Remember learning remainders from division back in elementary school?) The NIC sending the frame does a little math to make the CRC. Using binary arithmetic, it works a division problem on the data using a divisor called a *key*. The result of this division is the CRC. When the frame gets to the receiving NIC, it divides the data by the same key. If the receiving NIC's answer is the same as the CRC, it knows the data is good; if it's not good, the frame is dropped.

Getting the Data on the Line

The process of getting data onto the wire and then picking that data off the wire is amazingly complicated. For instance, what would happen to keep two NICs from speaking at the same time? Because all the data sent by one NIC is read by every other NIC on the network, only one system could speak at a time in early wired networks. Networks use frames to restrict the amount of data a NIC can send at once, giving all NICs a chance to send data over the network in a reasonable span of time. Dealing with this and many other issues requires sophisticated electronics, but the NICs handle these issues completely on their own without our help. Thankfully, the folks who design NICs worry about all these details, so we don't have to!

Getting to Know You

Using the MAC address is a great way to move data around, but this process raises an important question. How does a sending NIC know the MAC address of the NIC to which it's sending the data? In most cases, the sending system already knows the destination MAC address because the NICs had probably communicated earlier, and each system stores that data. If it doesn't already know the MAC address, a NIC may send a *broadcast* onto the network to ask for it. The MAC address of FF-FF-FF-FF-FF-FF is the Layer 2 *broadcast address*—if a NIC sends a frame using the broadcast address, every single NIC on the network will process that frame. That broadcast frame's data will contain a request for a system's MAC address. Without knowing the MAC address to begin with, the requesting computer will use an IP address to pick the target computer out of the crowd. The system with the MAC address your system is seeking will read the request in the broadcast frame and respond with its MAC address. (See "IP—Playing on Layer 3, the Network Layer" later in this chapter for more on IP addresses and packets.)

The Complete Frame Movement

Now that you've seen all the pieces used to send and receive frames, let's put these pieces together and see how a frame gets from one system to another. The basic send/receive process is as follows.

First, the sending system's operating system hands some data to its NIC. The NIC builds a frame to transport that data to the receiving NIC (Figure 1-20).

Figure 1-20
Building the
frame

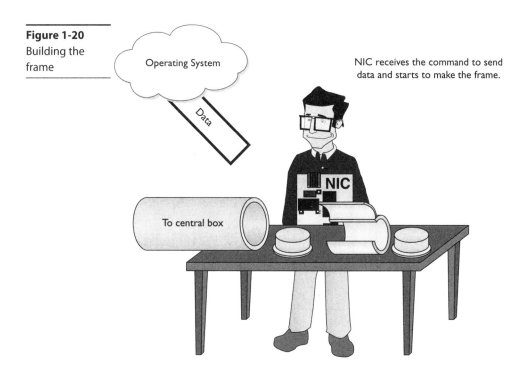

Figure 1-21
Adding the data
and FCS to the
frame

After the NIC creates the frame, it adds the FCS, and then dumps it and the data into the frame (Figure 1-21).

Next, the NIC puts both the destination MAC address and its own MAC address onto the frame. It then sends the frame through the cable to the network (Figure 1-22).

Figure 1-22
Sending the frame

NIC sends the frame when
no one else is using the wire.

To central box

To:
234a12f42b1c
From:
234a12r4er1ac

NIC

NOTE Any frame addressed specifically to another device's MAC address is called a *unicast frame*. The one-to-one addressing scheme is called *unicast addressing*; you'll see it in other layers as well as Layer 2.

The frame propagates down the wire into the central box. The switch sends unicast frames to the destination address and sends broadcast frames to every system on the network. The NIC receives the frame (Figure 1-23). The NIC strips off all the framing information and sends the data to the software—the operating system—for processing. The receiving NIC doesn't care what the software does with the data; its job stops the moment it passes on the data to the software.

Figure 1-23
Reading an incoming frame

The frame has the
MAC address for this NIC.

To central box

To:
234a12r4er1ac
From:
234a12f42b1c

NIC

Any device that deals with a MAC address is part of the OSI *Data Link layer*, or Layer 2 of the OSI model. Let's update the OSI model to include details about the Data Link layer (Figure 1-24).

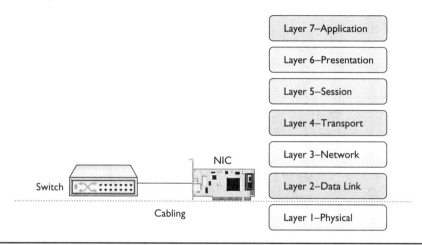

Figure 1-24 Layer 1 and Layer 2 are now properly applied to the network.

Note that the cabling and hubs are in the Physical layer. Switches handle traffic using MAC addresses, so they operate at Layer 2. That's the way modern wired networks work. The NIC is in the Data Link layer and the Physical layer.

The Two Aspects of NICs

Consider how data moves in and out of a NIC. On one end, frames move into and out of the NIC's network cable connection. On the other end, data moves back and forth between the NIC and the network operating system software. The many steps a NIC performs to keep this data moving—sending and receiving frames over the wire, creating outgoing frames, reading incoming frames, and attaching MAC addresses—are classically broken down into two distinct jobs.

The first job is called the *Logical Link Control (LLC)*. The LLC is the aspect of the NIC that talks to the system's operating system (usually via device drivers). The LLC handles multiple network protocols and provides flow control.

EXAM TIP The CompTIA Network+ exam tests you on the details of the OSI seven-layer model, so remember that the Data Link layer is the only layer that has sublayers.

The second job is called the *Media Access Control (MAC)*, which creates and addresses the frame. It adds the NIC's own MAC address and attaches MAC addresses to the frames. Recall that each frame the NIC creates must include both the sender's and recipient's MAC addresses. The MAC sublayer adds or checks the FCS. The MAC also ensures that the frames, now complete with their MAC addresses, are then sent along the network cabling. Figure 1-25 shows the Data Link layer in detail.

Figure 1-25
LLC and MAC, the two parts of the Data Link layer

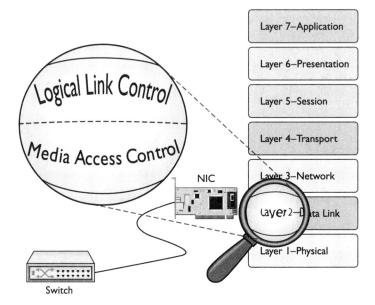

NIC and Layers

Most networking materials that describe the OSI seven-layer model put NICs squarely into the Data Link layer of the model. It's at the MAC sublayer, after all, that data gets encapsulated into a frame, destination and source MAC addresses get added to that frame, and error checking occurs. What bothers most students with placing NICs solely in the Data Link layer is the obvious other duty of the NIC—putting the ones and zeroes on the network cable for wired networks and in the air for wireless networks. How much more physical can you get?

Many teachers will finesse this issue by defining the Physical layer in its logical sense—that it defines the rules for the ones and zeroes—and then ignore the fact that the data sent on the cable has to come from something. The first question when you hear a statement like that—at least to me—is, "What component does the sending?" It's the NIC, of course, the only device capable of sending and receiving the physical signal.

Network cards, therefore, operate at both Layer 2 and Layer 1 of the OSI seven-layer model. If cornered to answer one or the other, however, go with the more common answer, Layer 2.

Beyond the Single Wire—Network Software and Layers 3–7

Getting data from one system to another in a simple network (defined as one in which all the computers connect to one switch) takes relatively little effort on the part of the NICs. But one problem with simple networks is that computers need to broadcast to get MAC addresses. It works for small networks, but what happens when the network gets big, like the size of the entire Internet? Can you imagine millions of computers all broadcasting? No data could get through.

Equally important, data flows over the Internet using many technologies, not just Ethernet. These technologies don't know what to do with Ethernet MAC addresses. When networks get large, you can't use the MAC addresses anymore.

Large networks need a *logical addressing* method, like a postal code or telephone numbering scheme, that ignores the hardware and enables you to break up the entire large network into smaller networks called *subnets*. Figure 1-26 shows two ways to set up a network. On the left, all the computers connect to a single switch. On the right, however, the LAN is separated into two five-computer subnets.

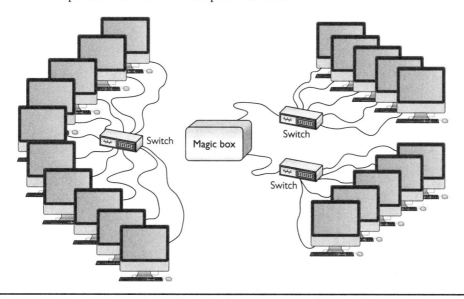

Figure 1-26   Large LAN complete (left) and broken up into two subnets (right)

To move past the physical MAC addresses and start using logical addressing requires some special software called a *network protocol*. Network protocols exist in every operating system. A network protocol not only has to create unique identifiers for each system, but also must create a set of communication rules for issues like how to handle data chopped up into multiple packets and how to ensure those packets get from one subnet to another. Let's take a moment to learn a bit about the most famous network protocol—TCP/IP—and its unique universal addressing system.

   EXAM TIP   MAC addresses are also known as *physical addresses.*

To be accurate, TCP/IP is really several network protocols designed to work together—better known as a *protocol suite*—but two protocols, TCP and IP, do so much work that the folks who invented all these protocols named the whole thing TCP/IP. *TCP* stands for *Transmission Control Protocol*, and *IP* stands for *Internet Protocol*. IP is the network protocol I need to discuss first; rest assured, however, I'll cover TCP in plenty of detail later.

IP—Playing on Layer 3, the Network Layer

At the *Network layer*, Layer 3, containers called *packets* get created and addressed so they can go from one network to another. The Internet Protocol is the primary logical addressing protocol for TCP/IP. IP makes sure that a piece of data gets to where it needs to go on the network. It does this by giving each device on the network a unique numeric identifier called an *IP address*. An IP address is known as a *logical address* to distinguish it from the physical address, the MAC address of the NIC.

NOTE   A packet is the PDU for Layer 3.

IP uses a rather unique dotted decimal notation (sometimes referred to as a dotted-octet numbering system) based on four 8-bit numbers. Each 8-bit number ranges from 0 to 255, and the four numbers are separated by periods. (If you don't see how 8-bit numbers can range from 0 to 255, don't worry—by the end of this book, you'll understand these numbering conventions in more detail than you ever believed possible!) A typical IP address might look like this:

192.168.4.232

NOTE   TCP/IP dominates networking today, and although it might be fun to imagine that it had humble beginnings in someone's garage lab, that's not the case. In the early 1970s, two researchers at the U.S. Defense Advanced Research Projects Agency (DARPA), Bob Kahn and Vint Cerf, worked out the basic parameters of what would become TCP/IP. TCP/IP offered amazing robustness in its design and eventual implementation. Government research at its most profound and world shaping!

No two systems on the same network share the same IP address; if two machines accidentally receive the same address, unintended side effects may occur. These IP addresses don't just magically appear—they must be configured by the network administrator.

What makes logical addressing powerful is another magic box—called a *router*—that connects each of the subnets, as in Figure 1-26, earlier. Routers use the IP address, not the MAC address, to forward data. This enables networks to connect across data lines that don't use Ethernet, like the telephone network. Each network type (such as Ethernet, SONET, and others that we'll discuss later in the book) uses a unique frame. Figure 1-27 shows a typical router.

Figure 1-27
Typical small router

In a TCP/IP network, each system has two unique identifiers: the MAC address and the IP address. The MAC address (the physical address) is literally burned into the chips on the NIC, whereas the IP address (the logical address) is simply stored in the system's software. MAC addresses come with the NIC, so you don't configure MAC addresses, whereas you must configure IP addresses using software. Figure 1-28 shows the MHTechEd network diagram again, this time with the MAC and IP addresses displayed for each system.

NOTE Try to avoid using redundant expressions. Even though many techs will say "IP protocol," for example, you know that "IP" stands for "Internet Protocol." It wouldn't be right to say "Internet Protocol protocol" in English, so it doesn't work in network speak either. (Also, don't say "NIC card" for the same reason!)

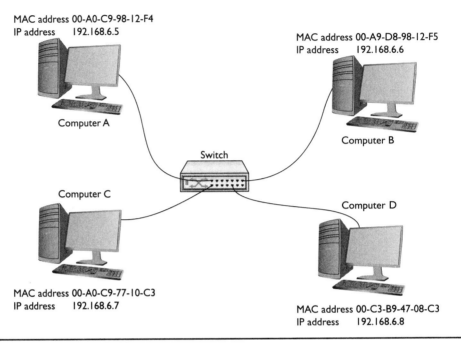

MAC address 00-A0-C9-98-12-F4
IP address   192.168.6.5

Computer A

MAC address 00-A9-D8-98-12-F5
IP address   192.168.6.6

Computer B

Switch

Computer C

Computer D

MAC address 00-A0-C9-77-10-C3
IP address   192.168.6.7

MAC address 00-C3-B9-47-08-C3
IP address   192.168.6.8

Figure 1-28   MHTechEd addressing

Packets Within Frames

For a TCP/IP network to send data successfully, the data must be wrapped up in two distinct containers. A frame of some type enables the data to move from one device to another. Inside that frame are both an IP-specific container that enables routers to determine where to send data—regardless of the physical connection type—and the data itself. In TCP/IP, that inner container is the *packet*.

Figure 1-29 shows a typical IP packet; notice the similarity to the frames you saw earlier.

Figure 1-29
IP packet

Destination IP address	Source IP address	Data

NOTE This is a highly simplified IP packet. I am not including lots of little parts of the IP packet in this diagram because they are not important to what you need to understand right now—but don't worry, you'll see them later in the book!

But IP packets don't leave their PC home without any clothes on! Each IP packet is handed to the NIC, which then encloses the IP packet in a regular frame, creating, in essence, a *packet within a frame*. I like to visualize the packet as an envelope, with the envelope in the pneumatic canister frame, as depicted in Figure 1-30. A more conventional drawing would look like Figure 1-31.

Figure 1-30
IP packet
in a frame
(as a canister)

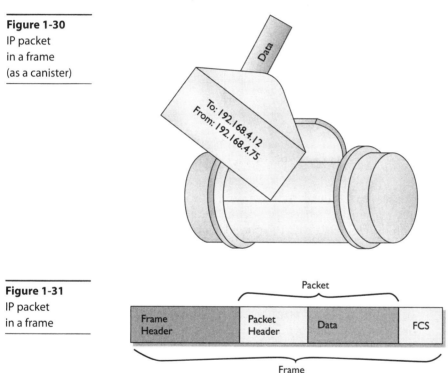

Figure 1-31
IP packet
in a frame

When you send data from one computer to another on a TCP/IP network such as the Internet, that data can go through many routers before it reaches its destination. Each router strips off the incoming frame, determines where to send the data according to the IP address in the packet, creates a new frame, and then sends the packet within a frame on its merry way. The new frame type will be the appropriate technology for whatever connection technology connects to the next router. That could be a cable or DSL network connection, for example (Figure 1-32). The IP packet, on the other hand, remains unchanged.

Figure 1-32
Router removing network frame and adding one for the outgoing connection

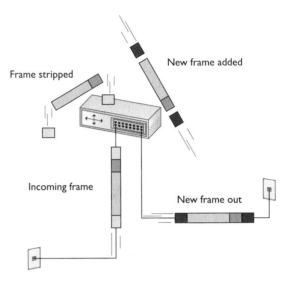

Frame stripped

New frame added

Incoming frame

New frame out

Once the packet reaches the destination subnet's router, that router will strip off the incoming frame—no matter what type—look at the destination IP address, and then add a frame with the appropriate destination MAC address that matches the destination IP address.

NOTE Not all networks are Ethernet networks (although all wired networks at home or work always use Ethernet). Ethernet may dominate, but IP packets fit in all sorts of other connectivity options. Cable modems, for example, use a type of frame called DOCSIS. The beauty of IP packets is that they can travel unchanged in many frame types. For more about these technologies, check out Chapter 13, "Remote Connectivity."

The receiving NIC strips away the Ethernet frame and passes the remaining packet off to the software. The networking software built into your operating system handles all the rest of the work. The NIC's driver software is the interconnection between the hardware and the software. The NIC driver knows how to communicate with the NIC to send and receive frames, but it can't do anything with the packet. Instead, the NIC driver hands the packet off to other services that know how to deal with all the separate packets and turn them into Web pages, e-mail messages, files, and so forth.

Segmentation and Reassembly—Layer 4, the Transport Layer

Because most chunks of data are much larger than a single packet, they must be chopped up before they can be sent across a network. When a serving computer receives a request for some data, it must be able to chop the requested data into chunks that will fit into a packet (and eventually into the NIC's frame), organize the packets for the benefit of the receiving system, and hand them to the NIC for sending. This is called *segmentation*. The receiving system does the *reassembly* of the packets. It must recognize a series of incoming packets as one data transmission, reassemble the packets correctly based on information included in the packets by the sending system, and verify that all the packets for that piece of data arrived in good shape.

This part is relatively simple—the transport protocol breaks up the data into chunks called *segments* or *datagrams* (depending on the specific transport protocol used) and gives each segment some type of sequence number. (Datagrams are simpler and don't get sequence numbers.)

I like to compare this sequencing process to the one that my favorite international shipping company uses. I receive boxes from UPS almost every day; in fact, some days I receive many, many boxes from UPS. To make sure I get all the boxes for one shipment, UPS puts a numbering system, like the one shown in Figure 1-33, on the label of each box. A computer sending data on a network does the same thing. Embedded into the data of each packet containing a segment is a sequencing number. By reading the sequencing numbers, the receiving system knows both the total number of segments and how to put them back together.

Figure 1-33
Labeling the boxes

The MHTechEd network just keeps getting more and more complex, doesn't it? And the Word document still hasn't been copied, has it? Don't worry; you're almost there—just a few more pieces to go!

Layer 4, the *Transport layer* of the OSI seven-layer model, has a big job: it's the segmentation/reassembly software. As part of its job, the Transport layer also initializes requests for packets that weren't received in good order (Figure 1-34).

 NOTE A lot of things happen on a TCP/IP network at the Transport layer. I'm simplifying here because the TCP/IP model does a way better job describing what happens with each TCP/IP-specific Transport layer protocol than does the OSI model.

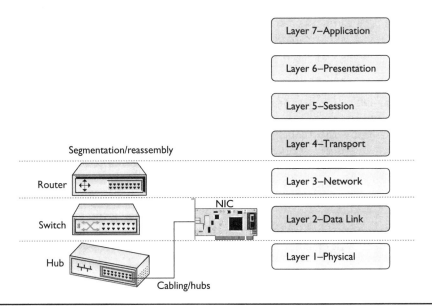

Figure 1-34 OSI updated

Talking on a Network—Layer 5, the Session Layer

Now that you understand that the system uses software to segment and reassemble data packets, what's next? In a network, any one system may be talking to many other systems at any given moment. For example, Janelle's PC has a printer used by all the MHTechEd systems, so there's a better than average chance that, as Dana tries to access the Word document, another system will be sending a print job to Janelle's PC (Figure 1-35).

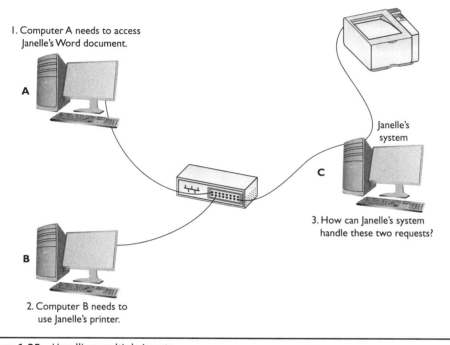

1. Computer A needs to access Janelle's Word document.

A

Janelle's system

C

3. How can Janelle's system handle these two requests?

B

2. Computer B needs to use Janelle's printer.

Figure 1-35   Handling multiple inputs

Janelle's system must direct these incoming files, print jobs, Web pages, and so on, to the right programs (Figure 1-36). Additionally, the operating system must enable one system to make a connection to another system to verify that the other system can handle whatever operation the initiating system wants to perform. If Bill's system wants to send a print job to Janelle's printer, it first contacts Janelle's system to ensure that it is ready to handle the print job. The *session software* handles this part of networking, connecting applications to applications.

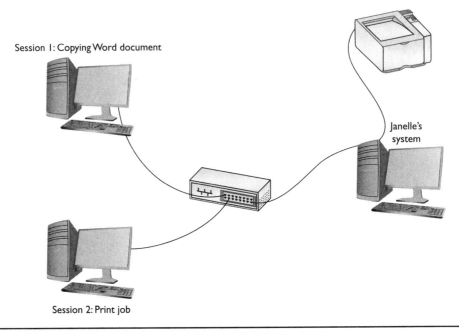

Session 1: Copying Word document

Janelle's system

Session 2: Print job

Figure 1-36 Each request becomes a session.

Try This!

See Your Sessions

How many sessions does a typical system have running at one time? Well, if you have a TCP/IP network (and who doesn't these days), you can run the netstat program from a command prompt to see all of them. Open a command prompt and type the following:

```
netstat -a
```

Then press the ENTER key to see your sessions. Don't worry about trying to interpret what you see—Chapter 8, "TCP/IP Applications," covers netstat in detail. For now, simply appreciate that each line in the netstat output is a session. Count them!

Layer 5, the *Session layer* of the OSI seven-layer model, handles all the sessions for a system (Figure 1-37). The Session layer initiates sessions, accepts incoming sessions, and opens and closes existing sessions.

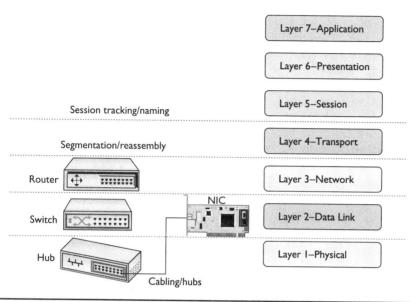

Figure 1-37   OSI updated

Translation—Layer 6, the Presentation Layer

The *Presentation layer* translates data from lower layers into a format usable by the Application layer, and *vice versa* (Figure 1-38). This manifests in several ways and isn't necessarily clear cut. The messiness comes into play because TCP/IP networks don't necessarily map directly to the OSI model.

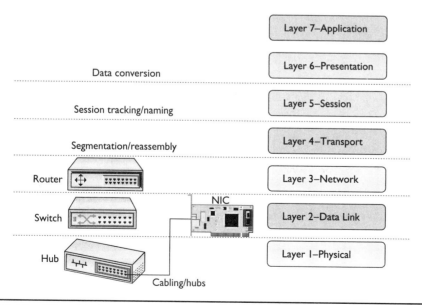

Figure 1-38   OSI updated

A number of protocols function on more than one OSI layer and can include Layer 6, Presentation. The encryption protocols used in e-commerce, SSL/TLS, for example, seem to initiate at Layer 5, then encrypt and decrypt at Layer 6. But even one of the authors of SSL disputes that SSL/TLS should even be included in any OSI chart! It makes for some confusion. Modern network discussions, therefore, work better using the TCP/IP model where the OSI Layers 5 through 7 are lumped together as the Application layer. We'll get there shortly.

Network Applications—Layer 7, the Application Layer

The last and most visible part of any network is the software applications that use it. If you want to copy a file residing on another system in your network, you need an application like Network in Windows 10 that enables you to access files on remote systems. If you want to view Web pages, you need a Web browser like Google Chrome or Mozilla Firefox. The people who use a network experience it through an application. A user who knows nothing about all the other parts of a network may still know how to open an e-mail application to retrieve mail (Figure 1-39).

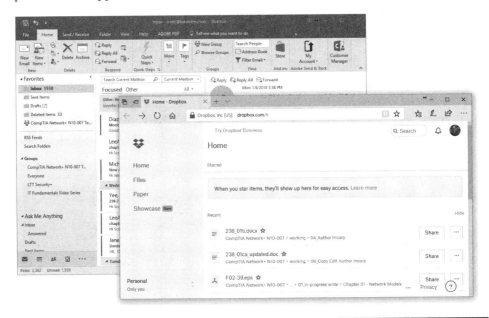

Figure 1-39 Network applications at work

Applications may include additional functions, such as encryption, user authentication, and tools to control the look of the data. But these functions are specific to the given applications. In other words, if you want to put a password on your Word document, you must use the password functions in Word to do so.

The *Application layer* is Layer 7 in the OSI seven-layer model. Keep in mind that the Application layer doesn't refer to the applications themselves. It refers to the code built into all operating systems that enables network-aware applications. All operating systems have *Application Programming Interfaces (APIs)* that programmers can use to make their programs network aware (Figure 1-40). An API, in general, provides a standard way for programmers to enhance or extend an application's capabilities.

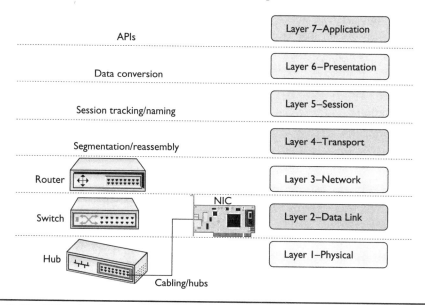

Figure 1-40 OSI updated

Encapsulation and De-Encapsulation

The term *encapsulation* encompasses the entire process of preparing data to go onto a network. This includes all the steps from the application to the Application, Presentation, Session, Transport, Network, and Data Link layers. Each layer adds more information so that the data gets to the correct recipient and the recipient knows what to do with the data.

The receiving computer reverses the process, stripping all the extra header information out as the data goes up the stack. This reverse process is called *de-encapsulation*.

The Transport layer creates a segment or datagram and hands it down to the Network layer. (See "The Transport Layer" later in this chapter for more details.) That layer adds IP information, encapsulating the segment or datagram. The Data Link layer wraps all that goodness up, encapsulating the packet in a frame for delivery over the network.

The TCP/IP Model

The OSI model was developed as a reaction to a world of hundreds, if not thousands, of different protocols made by different manufacturers that needed to play together. ISO declared the OSI seven-layer model as the tool for manufacturers of networking equipment to find common ground between multiple protocols, enabling them to create standards for interoperability of networking software and hardware.

The OSI model is extremely popular and very well known to all networking techs. Today's world, however, is a TCP/IP world. The complexity of the OSI model doesn't always make sense in a world with one protocol suite. Given its dominance, the aptly named TCP/IP model shares some popularity with the venerable OSI model.

The TCP/IP model consists of four layers:

- Application
- Transport
- Internet
- Link/Network Interface

It's important to appreciate that the TCP/IP model doesn't have a standards body to define the layers. Because of this, there are a surprising number of variations on the TCP/IP model.

A great example of this lack of standardization is the Link layer. Without a standardizing body, we can't even agree on the name. While "Link layer" is extremely common, the term "Network Interface layer" is equally popular. A good tech knows both of these terms and understands that they are interchangeable. Notice also that, unlike the OSI model, the TCP/IP model does not identify each layer with a number.

The version I use is concise, having only four layers, and many important companies, like Cisco and Microsoft, use it as well. The TCP/IP model gives each protocol in the TCP/IP protocol suite a clear home in one of the four layers.

The clarity of the TCP/IP model shows the flaws in the OSI model. The OSI model couldn't perfectly describe all the TCP/IP protocols.

The TCP/IP model fixes this ambiguity, at least for TCP/IP. Because of its tight protocol-to-layer integration, the TCP/IP model is a *descriptive* model, whereas the OSI seven-layer model is a *prescriptive* model.

The Link Layer

The TCP/IP model lumps together the OSI model's Layer 1 and Layer 2 into a single layer called the *Link layer* (or *Network Interface layer*), as seen in Figure 1-41. It's not that the Physical and Data Link layers are unimportant to TCP/IP, but the TCP/IP protocol suite really begins at Layer 3 of the OSI model. In essence, TCP/IP techs count on other techs to handle the physical connections in their networks. All of the pieces that you learned in the OSI model (cabling, physical addresses, NICs, and switches) sit squarely in the Link layer.

Figure 1-41
TCP/IP Link layer
compared to OSI
Layers 1 and 2

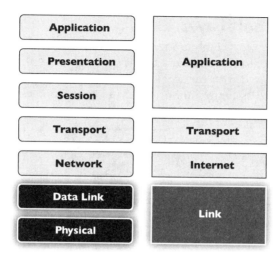

A nice way to separate layers in the TCP/IP model is to think about packets and frames. Any part of the network that deals with complete frames is in the Link layer. The moment the frame information is stripped away from an IP packet, we move out of the Link layer and into the Internet layer.

The Internet Layer

The *Internet layer* should really be called the "IP packet" layer (Figure 1-42). Any device or protocol that deals with pure IP packets—getting an IP packet to its destination—sits in the Internet layer. IP addressing itself is also part of the Internet layer, as are routers and the magic they perform to get IP packets to the next router. IP packets are created at this layer.

Figure 1-42
TCP/IP Internet
layer compared
to OSI Layer 3

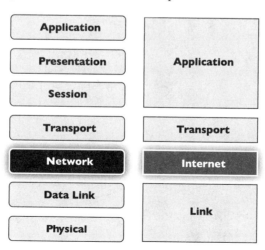

The Internet layer doesn't care about the type of data an IP packet carries, nor does it care whether the data gets there in good order or not. Those jobs are for the next layer: the Transport layer.

The Transport Layer

The *Transport layer* combines features of the OSI Transport and Session layers with a dash of Application layer just for flavor (Figure 1-43). While the TCP/IP model is certainly involved with the segmentation and reassembly of data, it also defines other functions, such as connection-oriented and connectionless communication.

Figure 1-43
TCP/IP Transport
layer compared
to OSI Layers 4, 5,
and part of 7

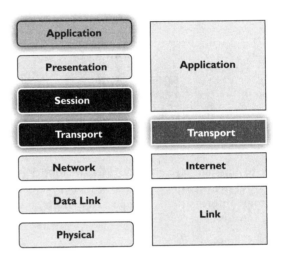

Connection-Oriented vs. Connectionless Communication

Some protocols, like the Internet Message Access Protocol (IMAP) used for sending e-mail messages, require that the e-mail client and server verify that they have a good connection before a message is sent (Figure 1-44). This makes sense because you don't want your e-mail message to be a corrupted mess when it arrives.

Figure 1-44
Connection
between e-mail
client and server

Alternatively, a number of TCP/IP protocols simply send data without first waiting to verify that the receiving system is ready (Figure 1-45). When using Voice over IP (VoIP), for example, the call is made without verifying first whether another device is there.

Figure 1-45
Connectionless
communication

The connection-oriented protocol is Transmission Control Protocol (TCP). The connectionless protocol is *User Datagram Protocol (UDP)*.

NOTE Chapter 6, "TCP/IP Basics," covers TCP, UDP, and all sorts of other protocols in detail.

Everything you can do on the Internet, from Web browsing to Skype phone calls to playing World of Warcraft, is predetermined to be either connection-oriented or connectionless. It's simply a matter of knowing your applications.

Segments Within Packets

To see the Transport layer in action, strip away the IP addresses from an IP packet. What's left is a chunk of data in yet another container called a *TCP segment*. TCP segments have many other fields that ensure the data gets to its destination in good order. These fields have names such as Destination port, Source port, Checksum, Flags, and Acknowledgement. Figure 1-46 shows a typical (although simplified) TCP segment.

Destination port	Source port	Sequence number	Checksum	Flags	Acknowledgement	Data

Figure 1-46 TCP segment

Chapter 6 goes into more detail on TCP segments, but let's look at Destination and Source ports as an example. You saw physical ports earlier in the chapter, but this use of the word "port" means something completely different. In this context, a *port*—a number between 1 and 65,536—is a logical value assigned to specific applications or services. A quick example will make this clear. Many TCP segments come into any computer. The computer needs some way to determine which TCP segments go to which applications. A Web server, for example, sees a lot of traffic, but it "listens" or looks for TCP segments with the Destination port number 80, grabs those segments, and processes them. Equally, every TCP segment contains a second port number—the Source port—so the client knows what to do with returning information.

Data comes from the Application layer. The Transport layer breaks that data into chunks, adding port numbers and sequence numbers, creating the TCP segment. The Transport layer then hands the TCP segment to the Internet layer, which, in turn, creates the IP packet.

Although a lot of traffic on a TCP/IP network uses TCP at the Transport layer, like Yoda said in *The Empire Strikes Back*, "There is another," and that's UDP. UDP also gets data from the Application layer and adds port and length numbers plus a checksum to create a container called a *UDP datagram*. A UDP datagram lacks most of the extra fields found in TCP segments, simply because UDP doesn't care if the receiving computer gets its data. Figure 1-47 shows a UDP datagram.

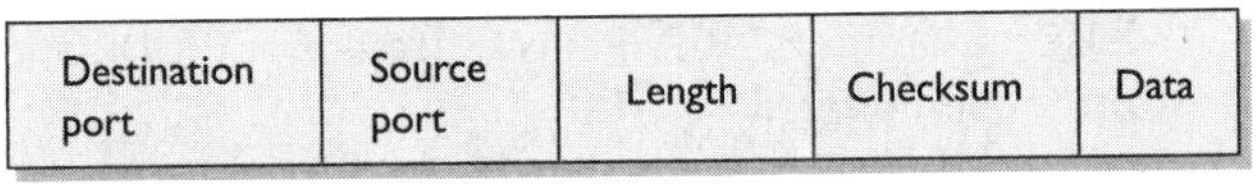

Figure 1-47
UDP datagram

Destination port	Source port	Length	Checksum	Data

Sessions

The TCP model makes the idea of a session easier to see as compared to the OSI model. Many operating systems represent a session using the combination of the IP address and port numbers for both sides of a TCP or UDP communication. You can see a Web browser's session connecting to a Web server, for example, by running the netstat command that you ran earlier in the chapter. This time, run it as netstat -n. It'll return many lines like this:

```
TCP    192.168.4.34:45543        11.12.13.123:80        Established
```

The numbers describe the session. A Web client with the IP of 192.168.4.34, using port number 45543, is in a TCP session with a Web server (we know it's a Web server because port 80 is dedicated to Web servers) using IP address 11.12.13.123.

The Application Layer

The TCP/IP *Application layer* combines features of the top three layers of the OSI model (Figure 1-48). Every application, especially connection-oriented applications, must know how to initiate, control, and disconnect from a remote system. No single method exists for doing this. Each TCP/IP application uses its own method.

Figure 1-48

TCP/IP Application layer compared to OSI Layers 5–7

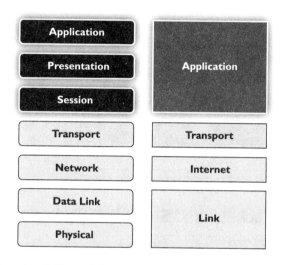

Although we can say that the OSI model's Presentation layer fits inside the TCP/IP model's Application layer, no application requires any particular form of presentation as seen in the OSI model. Standard formats are part and parcel with TCP/IP protocols. For example, all e-mail messages use an extremely strict format called MIME. All e-mail servers and clients read MIME without exception.

In the OSI model, we describe the API—the smarts that make applications network-aware—as being part of the Application layer. While this is still true for the TCP/IP model, all applications designed for TCP/IP are, by definition, network-aware. There is no such thing as a "TCP/IP word processor" or a "TCP/IP image editor" that requires the added ability to know how to talk to a network—all TCP/IP applications can talk to the network, as long as they are part of a network. And every TCP/IP application must be a part of a network to function: Web browsers, e-mail clients, multiplayer games, and so on.

Don't think that the TCP/IP model is any simpler than the OSI model just because it only uses four layers. With the arguable exception of the Presentation layer, everything you saw in the OSI model is also found in the TCP/IP model (Figure 1-49).

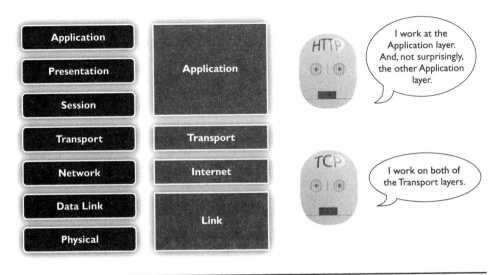

Figure 1-49   OSI model and TCP/IP model side by side

Frames, Packets, and Segments/Datagrams, Oh My!

The TCP/IP model shows its power in its ability to describe what happens at each layer to the data that goes from one computer to another. The Application layer programs create the data. The Transport layer breaks the data into chunks, putting those chunks into TCP segments or UDP datagrams. The Internet layer adds the IP addressing and creates the IP packets. The Link layer wraps the IP packet into a frame, with the MAC address information and a frame check sequence (FCS). Now the data is ready to hit the wire (or airwaves, if you're in a café). Figure 1-50 shows all this encapsulating goodness relative to the TCP/IP model.

Figure 1-50
Data
encapsulation
in TCP/IP

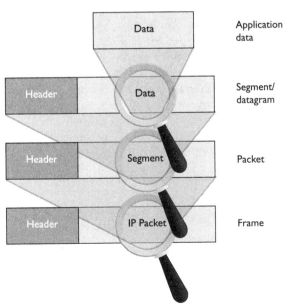

Knowing the layer at which each encapsulation takes place can assist in your troubleshooting. Table 1-1 shows the layers and the corresponding data structure.

TCP/IP Model Layer	Data Structure
Link	Frame
Internet	IP packet
Transport	TCP segment/UDP datagram
Application	(The data, or *payload*, starts and ends here)

Table 1-1 TCP/IP Model Layers and Corresponding Data Structures

 SIM Check out the "Network Models" Chapter 1 sim at **totalsem.com/007**. It's an excellent Challenge! game.

The Tech's Troubleshooting Tools

The OSI seven-layer model and TCP/IP model provide you with a way to conceptualize a network to determine what could cause a specific problem when the inevitable problems occur. Good techs always use a model to troubleshoot their networks.

If Jane can't print to the networked printer, for example, a model can help solve the problem. If her NIC shows activity, then, using the OSI model, you can set aside both the Physical layer (Layer 1) and Data Link layer (Layer 2). If you're a TCP/IP model tech, you can look at the same symptoms and eliminate the Link layer. In either case, you'll find yourself moving up the layer ladder to the OSI model's Network layer (Layer 3) or the TCP/IP model's Internet layer. If her computer has a proper IP address, then you can set that layer aside too, and you can move on up to check other layers to solve the problem.

Understanding both the OSI and TCP/IP models is important. They are the primary diagnostic tools for troubleshooting networks and also the communication tools for talking with your fellow techs.

Chapter Review

Questions

1. Where does a hub send data?

   A. Only to the receiving system

   B. Only to the sending system

   C. To all the systems connected to the hub

   D. Only to the server

2. What uniquely identifies every NIC?

   A. IP address

   B. Media access control address

   C. ISO number

   D. Packet ID number

3. What Windows utility do you use to find the MAC address for a system?

   A. `ipconfig /all`

   B. `ipcfg /all`

   C. `ping`

   D. `mac`

4. A MAC address is known as a(n) _____ address.

   A. IP

   B. logical

   C. physical

   D. OEM

5. A NIC sends data in discrete chunks called _____.

   A. segments

   B. sections

   C. frames

   D. layers

6. Which MAC address begins a frame?

   A. Receiving system

   B. Sending system

   C. Network

   D. Router

7. A frame ends with a special bit called the frame check sequence (FCS). What does the FCS do?

   A. Cycles data across the network

   B. Verifies that the MAC addresses are correct

   C. Verifies that the data arrived correctly

   D. Verifies that the IP address is correct

8. Which of the following is an example of a MAC address?

   A. 0–255

   B. 00–50–56–A3–04–0C

   C. SBY3M7

   D. 192.168.4.13

9. Which layer of the TCP/IP model controls the segmentation and reassembly of data?

   A. Application layer

   B. Presentation layer

   C. Session layer

   D. Transport layer

10. Which layer of the OSI seven-layer model keeps track of a system's connections to send the right response to the right computer?

    A. Application layer

    B. Presentation layer

    C. Session layer

    D. Transport layer

Answers

1. **C.** Data comes into a hub through one wire and is then sent out through all the other wires. A hub sends data to all the systems connected to it.

2. **B.** The unique identifier on a network interface card is called the media access control (MAC) address.

3. **A.** All versions of Windows use `ipconfig /all` from the command line to determine the MAC address.

4. **C.** The MAC address is a physical address.

5. **C.** Data is sent in discrete chunks called frames. Networks use frames to keep any one NIC from hogging the wire.

6. **A.** The frame begins with the MAC address of the receiving NIC, followed by the MAC address of the sending NIC, followed, in turn, by type of encapsulated data, the data, and FCS.

7. **C.** The data is followed by a special bit of checking information called the frame check sequence, which the receiving NIC uses to verify that the data arrived correctly.

8. **B.** A MAC address is a 48-bit value, and no two NICs ever share the same MAC address—ever. 00–50–56–A3–04–0C is a MAC address. Answer D (192.168.4.13) is an IP address.

9. **D.** The Transport layer controls the segmentation and reassembly of data.

10. **C.** The Session layer keeps track of a system's connections to ensure that it sends the right response to the right computer.

Cabling and Topology

The CompTIA Network+ certification exam expects you to know how to

- 1.5 Compare and contrast the characteristics of network topologies, types and technologies
- 2.1 Given a scenario, deploy the appropriate cabling solution

To achieve these goals, you must be able to

- Explain the different types of network topologies
- Describe the different types of network cabling and connectors
- Describe the IEEE networking standards

Every network must provide some method to get data from one system to another. In most cases, this method consists of some type of cabling running between systems, although many networks skip wires and use wireless methods to move data. Stringing those cables brings up a number of critical issues you need to understand to work on a network. How do all these cables connect the computers? Does every computer on the network run a cable to a central point? Does a single cable snake through the ceiling, with all the computers on the network connected to it? These questions need answering!

Furthermore, manufacturers need standards so they can make networking equipment that works well together. While we're talking about standards, what about the cabling itself? What type of cable? What quality of copper? How thick should it be? Who defines the standards for cables so they all work in the network?

This chapter answers these questions in three parts. First, you will learn about the *network topology*—the way that cables and other pieces of hardware connect to one another. Second, you will tour the most common standardized cable types used in networking. Third, you will learn about the IEEE committees that create network technology standards.

Test Specific

Network Topologies

Computer networks employ many different *topologies*, or ways of connecting computers together. This section looks at both the historical topologies—bus, ring, and star; all long dead—and the modern topologies—hybrid and mesh. In addition, we will look at what parameters are used to make up a network topology.

NOTE Wireless networks employ topologies too, just not with wires. We'll cover the common wireless topologies—infrastructure and ad hoc—in Chapter 14.

Bus and Ring

The first generation of wired networks used one of two topologies, both shown in Figure 2-1. A *bus topology* network used a single cable (i.e., the *bus*) that connected all the computers in a line. A *ring topology* network connected all computers on the network with a ring of cable.

 NOTE Note that topologies are diagrams, much like an electrical circuit diagram. Real network cabling doesn't go in perfect circles or perfect straight lines.

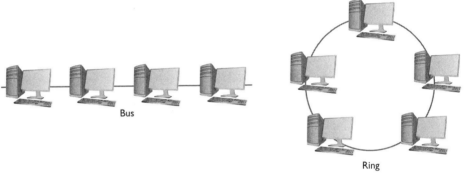

Figure 2-1 Bus and ring topologies

Data flowed differently between bus and ring networks, creating different problems and solutions. In bus topology networks, data from each computer simply went out on the whole bus. A network using a bus topology needed termination at each end of the cable to prevent a signal sent from one computer from reflecting at the ends of the cable, quickly bringing the network down (Figure 2-2).

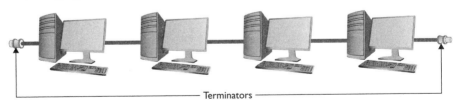

Figure 2-2 Terminated bus topology

In a ring topology network, in contrast, data traffic moved in a circle from one computer to the next in the same direction (Figure 2-3). With no end to the cable, ring networks required no termination.

Figure 2-3
Ring topology
moving in a
certain direction

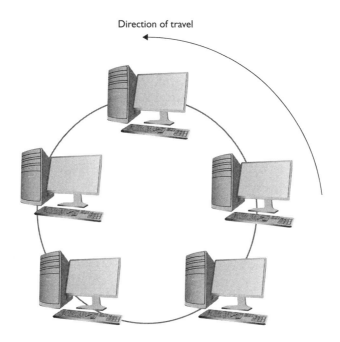

Bus and ring topology networks worked well but suffered from the same problem: the entire network stopped working if the cable broke at any point (Figure 2-4). The broken ends on a bus topology network didn't have the required termination, which caused reflection between computers that were still connected. A break in a ring topology network simply broke the circuit, stopping the data flow.

Figure 2-4
Nobody is
talking!

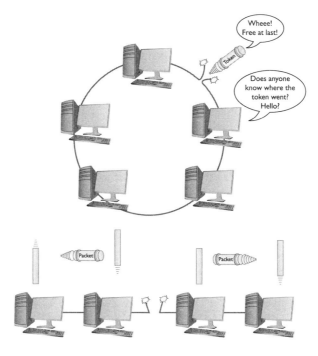

Star

The *star topology* used a central connection box for all the computers on the network (Figure 2-5). Star topologies had a huge benefit over ring and bus topologies by offering *fault tolerance*—if one of the cables broke, all of the other computers could still communicate. Bus and ring topology networks were popular and inexpensive to implement, however, so the old-style star topology networks weren't very successful. Network hardware designers couldn't easily redesign their existing networks to use a star topology.

Figure 2-5
Star topology

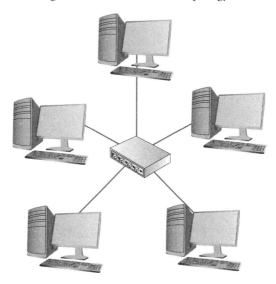

Hybrid

Even though network designers couldn't easily use a star topology, the benefits of star topologies were overwhelming, motivating smart people to come up with a way to use star topologies without requiring a major redesign—and the way they did so was ingenious. The ring topology network designers struck first by taking the entire ring and shrinking it into a small box, as shown in Figure 2-6.

Figure 2-6
Shrinking
the ring

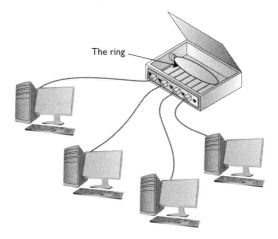

The ring

This was quickly followed by the bus topology folks, who, in turn, shrunk their bus (better known as the *segment*) into their own box (Figure 2-7).

Figure 2-7
Shrinking
the segment

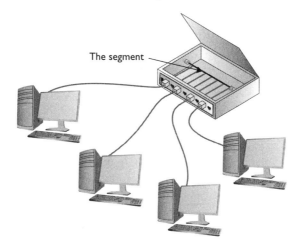

The segment

Physically, both of these hybrid designs looked like a star, but if you examined them as an electronic schematic, the signals acted like a ring or a bus. Clearly the old definition of topology needed a little clarification. When we talk about topology today, we separate how the cables physically look (the *physical topology*) from how the signals travel electronically (the signaling topology or *logical topology*).

EXAM TIP Most techs refer to the signaling topology as the logical topology today. That's how you'll see it on the CompTIA Network+ exam as well. Look for a question on the exam that challenges you on logical versus physical topology.

Any form of networking technology that combines a physical topology with a signaling topology is called a *hybrid topology*. Hybrid topologies have come and gone since the earliest days of networking. Only two hybrid topologies, *star-ring topology* and *star-bus topology*, ever saw any amount of popularity. Eventually, star-ring lost market share, and star-bus reigns as the undisputed "star" (pun intended) of wired network topologies.

NOTE The most successful of the star-ring topology networks was called Token Ring, manufactured by IBM.

Mesh

Topologies aren't just for wired networks. Wireless networks also need topologies to get data from one machine to another, but using radio waves instead of cables involves somewhat different topologies. Wireless devices can connect in a *mesh topology* network, where every computer connects to every other computer via two or more routes. Some of the routes between two computers may require traversing through another member of the mesh network. (See Chapter 14 for the scoop on wireless network types.)

There are two types of meshed topologies: partially meshed and fully meshed (Figure 2-8). In a *partially meshed topology* network, at least two machines have redundant connections. Every machine doesn't have to connect to every other machine. In a *fully meshed topology* network, every computer connects directly to every other computer.

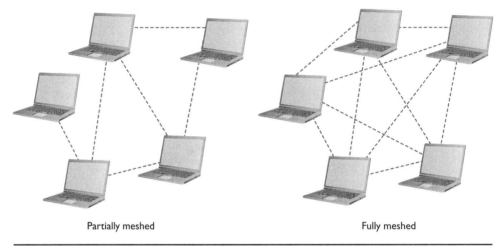

Partially meshed　　　　　　　　　　Fully meshed

Figure 2-8　Partially and fully meshed topologies

Parameters of a Topology

Although a topology describes the method by which systems in a network connect, the topology alone doesn't describe all of the features necessary to enable those networks. The term *bus topology*, for example, describes a network that consists of machines connected to the network via a single linear piece of cable. Notice that this definition leaves a lot of questions unanswered. What is the cable made of? How long can it be? How do the machines decide which machine should send data at a specific moment? A network based on a bus topology can answer these questions in several ways—but it's not the job of the topology to define issues like these. A functioning network needs a more detailed standard.

 EXAM TIP　Make sure you know the topologies: bus, ring, star, hybrid, and mesh.

Over the years, manufacturers and standards bodies have created network technologies based on different topologies. A *network technology* is a practical application of a topology and other critical technologies that provides a method to get data from one computer to another on a network. These network technologies have names like 100BaseT, 1000BaseLX, and 10GBaseT. You will learn all about these in the next two chapters.

SIM Check out the excellent Chapter 2 "Topology Matching" Challenge! over at **http://totalsem.com/007**. It's a good tool for reinforcing the topology variations.

Cabling and Connectors

Most networked systems link together using some type of cabling. Different types of networks over the years have used different types of cables—and you need to learn about all these cables to succeed on the CompTIA Network+ exam. This section explores scenarios where you would use common network cabling.

All cables used in the networking industry can be categorized in two distinct groups: copper and fiber-optic. All styles of cables have distinct connector types that you need to know.

Copper Cabling and Connectors

The most common form of cabling uses copper wire wrapped up in some kind of protective sheathing, thus the term *copper cables*. The two primary types of copper cabling used in the industry are coaxial and twisted pair.

Both cable types sport a variety of connector types. I'll cover the connector types as I discuss the cable varieties.

Coaxial Cable

Coaxial cable contains a central conductor wire (usually copper) surrounded by an insulating material, which, in turn, is surrounded by a braided metal shield. The cable is referred to as coaxial (coax for short) because the center wire and the braided metal shield share a common axis or centerline (Figure 2-9).

Figure 2-9
Cutaway view of coaxial cable

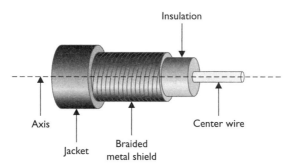

Coaxial cable shields data transmissions from interference. Many devices in the typical office environment—including lights, fans, copy machines, and refrigerators—generate magnetic fields. When a metal wire encounters these magnetic fields, electrical current is generated along the wire. This extra current, called *electromagnetic interference (EMI)*, can shut down a network because it is easily misinterpreted as a signal by devices like NICs.

To prevent EMI from affecting the network, the outer mesh layer of a coaxial cable shields the center wire (on which the data is transmitted) from interference (Figure 2-10).

Figure 2-10
Coaxial cable
showing braided
metal shielding

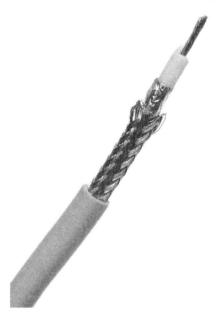

Early bus topology networks used coaxial cable to connect computers together. Back in the day, the most popular cable used special bayonet-style connectors called *BNC connectors* (Figure 2-11). Even earlier bus networks used thick cable that required vampire connections—sometimes called *vampire taps*—that literally pierced the cable.

Figure 2-11
BNC connector
on coaxial cable

NOTE Techs all around the globe argue over the meaning of BNC. A solid percentage says with authority that it stands for "British Naval Connector." An opposing percentage says with equal authority that it stands for "Bayonet Neill-Concelman," after the stick-and-twist style of connecting and the purported inventors of the connector. The jury is still out, though this week I'm leaning toward Neill and Concelman and their bayonet-style connector.

You'll find coaxial cable used today primarily to enable a cable modem to connect to an Internet service provider (ISP). That's the typical scenario for using coaxial cable: connecting a computer to the cable modem enables that computer to access the Internet. This cable is the same type used to connect televisions to cable boxes or to satellite receivers. These cables use an *F connector* (or *F-type connector*) that screws on, making for a secure connection (Figure 2-12).

Figure 2-12
F-type connector
on coaxial cable

 EXAM TIP Coaxial cabling is also very popular with satellite dishes, over-the-air antennas, and even some home video devices. This book covers cable and other Internet connectivity options in great detail in Chapter 13, "Remote Connectivity."

Cable modems connect using one of two coaxial cable types. *RG-59* was used primarily for cable television rather than networking. Its thinness and the introduction of digital cable motivated the move to the more robust *RG-6*, the predominant cabling used today (Figure 2-13).

Figure 2-13
RG-6 cable

All coax cables have a *Radio Guide (RG) rating*. The U.S. military developed these ratings to provide a quick reference for the different types of coax. The only important measure of coax cabling is its *Ohm rating*, a relative measure of the resistance (or more precisely, characteristic impedance) on the cable. You may run across other coax cables that don't have acceptable Ohm ratings, although they look just like network-rated coax. Fortunately, most coax cable types display their Ohm ratings on the cables themselves (see Figure 2-14). Both RG-6 and RG-59 cables are rated at 75 Ohms.

Figure 2-14
Ohm rating (on an older, RG-58 cable used for networking)

 NOTE The Ohm rating of a piece of cable describes the impedance of that cable. *Impedance* describes a set of characteristics that define how much a cable resists the flow of electricity. This isn't simple resistance, though. Impedance is also a factor in such things as how long it takes the wire to get a full charge—the wire's *capacitance*—and more.

Given the popularity of cable for television and Internet in homes today, you'll run into situations where people need to take a single coaxial cable and split it. Coaxial handles this quite nicely with coaxial splitters like the one shown in Figure 2-15. You can also connect two coaxial cables together easily using a barrel connector when you need to add some distance to a connection (Figure 2-16). Table 2-1 summarizes the coaxial standards.

Figure 2-15
Coaxial splitter

Figure 2-16
Barrel connector

	Rating	Ohms	Use	Connector
Table 2-1 Coaxial Cables	RG-58	50	Networking	BNC
	RG-59	75	Cable TV	F Type
	RG-6	75	Cable TV	F Type

Twisted Pair

The most common type of cabling used in networks consists of twisted pairs of cables, bundled together into a common jacket. Each pair in the cable works as a team either transmitting or receiving data. Using a pair of twisted wires rather than a single wire to send a signal reduces a specific type of interference, called *crosstalk*. The more twists per foot, the less crosstalk. Two types of twisted-pair cabling are manufactured: shielded and unshielded.

Shielded Twisted Pair   *Shielded twisted pair (STP)* consists of twisted pairs of wires surrounded by shielding to protect them from EMI. There are six types, differentiated by which part gets shielding, such as the whole cable or individual pairs within the cable. Table 2-2 describes the six types. Figure 2-17 shows a typical piece of STP with the cladding partly removed so you can see the internal wiring.

Name	Description
F/UTP	Foil shields the entire cable; inside, the wires are just like UTP.
S/UTP	A braid screen shields the entire cable; inside, the wires are just like UTP.
SF/UTP	A braid screen and foil shield the entire cable; the wires inside are just like UTP.
S/FTP	A braid screen shields the entire cable; foil shields each wire pair inside.
F/FTP	A foil screen shields the entire cable; foil shields each wire pair inside.
U/FTP	No overall shielding; each pair inside is shielded with foil screens.

Table 2-2   STP Standards

Figure 2-17
Shielded twisted
pair

 EXAM TIP You don't need to memorize the STP variations for the CompTIA
Network+ exam. You will, however, see them in the field once you become a
network tech. The typical scenario in which you'd deploy STP over UTP is in
high-EMI environments.

Unshielded Twisted Pair *Unshielded twisted pair (UTP)* consists of twisted pairs of
wires surrounded by a plastic jacket (Figure 2-18). This jacket does not provide any protection from EMI, so when installing UTP cabling, you must be careful to avoid interference from fluorescent lights, motors, and so forth. UTP costs much less than STP but,
in most cases, performs just as well.

Figure 2-18
Unshielded
twisted pair

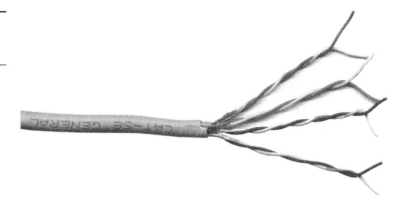

Twisted-pair cabling has been around since the 1970s and evolving technologies
demanded higher speeds. Over the years, manufacturers increased the number of twists
per foot, used higher gauge cable, and added shielding to make twisted pair able to
handle higher data speeds. To help network installers get the right cable for the right

network technology, the cabling industry developed a variety of grades called *category (Cat) ratings*. Cat ratings are officially rated in *megahertz (MHz)*, indicating the highest frequency the cable can handle. Table 2-3 shows the most common categories along with their status with the TIA (see the Note below for more information).

Cat Rating	Max Frequency	Max Bandwidth	Status with TIA
Cat 3	16 MHz	16 Mbps	Recognized
Cat 4	20 MHz	20 Mbps	No longer recognized
Cat 5	100 MHz	100 Mbps	No longer recognized
Cat 5e	100 MHz	1 Gbps	Recognized
Cat 6[1]	250 MHz	10 Gbps	Recognized
Cat 6a[2]	500 MHz	10 Gbps	Recognized
Cat 7	600 MHz	10+ Gbps	Not recognized
Cat 7a[3]	1000 MHz	40–100 Gbps	Not recognized
Cat 8	2000 MHz	25–40 Gbps	Not recognized

[1] Cat 6 cables can use the full 100-meter length when used with 10/100/1000BaseT networks. With 10GBaseT networks, Cat 6 is limited to 55 meters.
[2] Cat 6a cables can use the full 100-meter length with networks up to 10GBaseT.
[3] Cat 7a cables can theoretically support 40 Gbps at 50 meters; 100 Gbps at 15 meters.

Table 2-3   Cat Ratings for Twisted Pair

NOTE   Several international groups set the standards for cabling and networking in general. Ready for alphabet soup? At or near the top is the International Organization for Standardization (ISO). The American National Standards Institute (ANSI) is both the official U.S. representative to ISO and a major international player. ANSI checks the standards and accredits other groups, such as the Telecommunications Industry Association (TIA).

UTP cables handle a certain frequency or cycles per second, such as 100 MHz or 1000 MHz. You could take the frequency number in the early days of networking and translate that into the maximum throughput for a cable. Each cycle per second (or hertz) basically accounted for one bit of data per second. A 10 million cycle per second (10 MHz) cable, for example, could handle 10 million bits per second (10 Mbps). The maximum amount of data that goes through the cable per second is called the *bandwidth*.

EXAM TIP   The CompTIA Network+ exam is only interested in your knowledge of Cat 3, Cat 5, Cat 5e, Cat 6, Cat 6a, and Cat 7 cables. Further, you'll see the abbreviation for category in all caps, so CAT 5e or CAT 6a. (In the field you'll see category represented in both ways.)

For current networks, developers have implemented *bandwidth-efficient encoding schemes*, which means they can squeeze more bits into the same signal as long as the cable can handle it. Thus, the Cat 5e cable can handle a throughput of up to 1000 Mbps, even though it's rated to handle a frequency of only up to 100 MHz.

Because most networks can run at speeds of up to 1000 MHz, most new cabling installations use Category 6 (Cat 6) cabling, although a large number of installations use Cat 6a or Cat 7 to future-proof the network.

Make sure you can look at twisted pair and know its Cat rating. There are two places to look. First, twisted-pair is typically sold in boxed reels, and the manufacturer will clearly mark the Cat level on the box (Figure 2-19). Second, look on the cable itself. The category level of a piece of cable is usually printed on the cable (Figure 2-20).

Figure 2-19
Cat level marked on box of twisted-pair cabling

Figure 2-20
Cat level on twisted-pair cabling

Try This!

Shopping Spree!

Just how common has Cat 6a or Cat 7 become in your neighborhood? Take a run down to your local hardware store or office supply store and shop for UTP cabling. Do they carry Cat 6a? Cat 7? What's the difference in price? If it's not much more expensive to go with the better cable, the expected shift in networking standards has occurred and you might want to upgrade your network.

The old landline telephones plugged in with a *registered jack (RJ)* connector. Telephones used *RJ-11* connectors, designed to support up to two pairs of UTP wires. Current wired networks use the four-pair *8 position 8 contact (8P8C)* connectors that most techs (erroneously) refer to as *RJ-45* connectors (Figure 2-21). (A true *RJ45S* connector has slightly different keying and won't plug into a standard network port. They look very similar to the 8P8C connectors, though, so that is the name that stuck.)

Figure 2-21
RJ-11 (left) and
8P8C/"RJ-45"
(right)
connectors

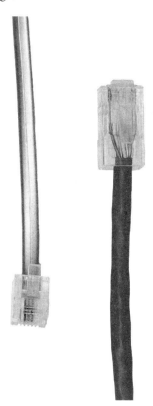

EXAM TIP CompTIA follows the common usage for networking cable connectors. You will *not* see 8P8C on the exam; you will *only* see RJ-45.

Fiber-Optic Cabling and Connectors

Fiber-optic cable transmits light rather than electricity, making it attractive for both high-EMI areas and long-distance transmissions. Whereas a single copper cable cannot carry data more than a few hundred meters at best, a single piece of fiber-optic cabling will operate, depending on the implementation, for distances of up to tens of kilometers. A fiber-optic cable has four components: the glass fiber itself (the *core*); the *cladding*, which is the part that makes the light reflect down the fiber; *buffer* material to give strength; and the *insulating jacket* (Figure 2-22).

Figure 2-22
Cross section
of fiber-optic
cabling

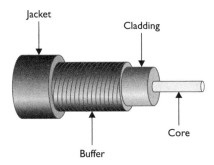

You might see the term *fiber cables* on the CompTIA Network+ exam to describe the two varieties of fiber-optic cables discussed in this section. Just as copper cables don't have copper connectors, fiber cables don't have *fiber connectors*, but that's the term used in the CompTIA Network+ Spare Parts list. I'll discuss cables and connector types shortly.

 NOTE For those of you unfamiliar with it, the odd little u-shaped symbol describing fiber cable size (μ) stands for *micro,* or 1/1,000,000.

Fiber-optic cabling is manufactured with many different diameters of core and cladding. Cable manufacturers use a two-number designator to define fiber-optic cables according to their core and cladding measurements. The most common fiber-optic cable size is 62.5/125 μm. Almost all network technologies that use fiber-optic cable require pairs of fibers. One fiber is used for sending, the other for receiving. In response to the demand for two-pair cabling, manufacturers often connect two fibers together to create *duplex* fiber-optic cabling (Figure 2-23).

Figure 2-23

Duplex fiber-
optic cable

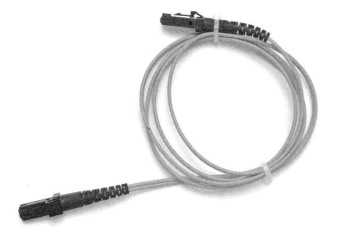

Light can be sent down a fiber-optic cable as regular light or as laser light. The two types of light require totally different fiber-optic cables. Most network technologies that use fiber optics use LEDs (light emitting diodes) to send light signals. A fiber-optic cable that uses LEDs is known as *multimode fiber (MMF)*.

A fiber-optic cable that uses lasers is known as *single-mode fiber (SMF)*. Using laser light and single-mode fiber-optic cables prevents a problem unique to multimode fiber optics called *modal distortion* (signals sent at the same time don't arrive at the same time because the paths differ slightly in length) and enables a network to achieve phenomenally high transfer rates over incredibly long distances.

NOTE A *nano*—abbreviated as *n*—stands for 1/1,000,000,000, or one-billionth of whatever. Here you'll see it as a nanometer (nm), one-billionth of a meter. That's one tiny wavelength!

Fiber optics also defines the wavelength of light used, measured in nanometers (nm). Almost all multimode cables transmit 850-nm wavelengths, whereas single-mode transmits either 1310 nm or 1550 nm, depending on the laser.

Fiber-optic cables come in a broad choice of connector types. There are over one hundred different connectors, but the four you need to know for the CompTIA Network+ exam are ST, SC, LC, and MT-RJ. Figure 2-24 shows the first three; Figure 2-25 shows an MT-RJ connector.

Figure 2-24
From left to right: ST, SC, and LC fiber-optic connectors

Figure 2-25
MT-RJ fiber-optic connector

Although all fiber connectors must be installed in pairs, the ST and SC connectors traditionally have unique ends. The LC and MT-RJ connectors are always duplex, meaning both the send and receive cables are attached. You can certainly find SC connectors or sleeves to make them duplex too, so don't get too caught up with which can be which. We'll revisit fiber-optic connectors in Chapter 4 when we discuss implementation of specific networking standards.

 NOTE Most technicians call common fiber-optic connectors by their initials—such as ST, SC, or LC—perhaps because there's no consensus about what words go with those initials. ST probably stands for *straight tip*, although some call it *snap and twist*. But SC and LC? How about *subscriber connector*, *standard connector*, or *Siemon connector* for the former, and *local connector* or *Lucent connector* for the latter? If you want to remember the connectors for the exam, try these: *snap and twist* for the bayonet-style ST connectors; *stick and click* for the straight push-in SC connectors; and *little connector* for the … little … LC connector.

Other Cables

Fiber-optic and UTP make up almost all network cabling, but a few other types of cabling appear on the CompTIA Network+ exam: the ancient serial and parallel cables from the earliest days of PCs. These cables were used for networking, but have not been in use for many years.

Classic Serial

Serial cabling predates both networking and the personal computer. *RS-232*, the *recommended standard (RS)* upon which all serial communication took place on a PC, dates from 1969 and hasn't substantially changed in around 50 years. When IBM invented the PC way back in 1980, serial connections were just about the only standard input/output technology available, so IBM included two serial ports on every PC. The most common serial port at the end of the technology was a 9-pin, male D-subminiature (or *DB-9*) connector, as shown in Figure 2-26.

Figure 2-26
Serial port

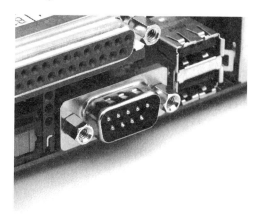

Serial ports offered a poor option for networking, with very slow data rates—only about 56,000 bps (note, that's *bits* per second!)—and only point-to-point connections. Serial ports were last used decades ago for connecting to networking devices, such as high-end switches, for configuration purposes only.

Parallel

Parallel connections are as ancient as serial ports. Parallel ran up to around 2 Mbps, although when used for networking, they tended to be much slower. Parallel was also limited to point-to-point topology, meaning directly connecting two devices with a single cable. They used a 25-pin female—rather than male—DB type connector called a *DB-25* (Figure 2-27). The *IEEE 1284* committee set the standards for parallel communication. (See the section "Networking Industry Standards—IEEE," later in this chapter.)

Figure 2-27
Parallel
connector

EXAM TIP   Concentrate on UTP—that's where the hardest CompTIA Network+ exam questions come into play. Don't forget to give coax, STP, and fiber-optic a quick pass, and make sure you understand the reasons for picking one type of cabling over another. Even though the CompTIA Network+ exam does not test too hard on cabling, this is important information that you will use in real networking.

Fire Ratings

Did you ever see the movie *The Towering Inferno?* Don't worry if you missed it—*The Towering Inferno* was one of the better disaster movies of the 1970s, although it was no *Airplane!* Anyway, Steve McQueen stars as the fireman who saves the day when a skyscraper goes up in flames because of poor-quality electrical cabling. The burning insulation on the wires ultimately spreads the fire to every part of the building. Although no cables made today contain truly flammable insulation, the insulation is made from plastic, and if you get any plastic hot enough, it will create smoke and noxious fumes. The risk of burning insulation isn't fire—it's smoke and fumes.

To reduce the risk of your network cables burning and creating noxious fumes and smoke, Underwriters Laboratories and the National Electrical Code (NEC) joined forces to develop cabling *fire ratings*. The two most common fire ratings are PVC and plenum. Cable with a *polyvinyl chloride (PVC)* rating has no significant fire protection. If you burn a *PVC-rated cable*, it creates lots of smoke and noxious fumes. Burning *plenum-rated cable* creates much less smoke and fumes, but plenum-rated cable costs about three to five times as much as PVC-rated cable. Most city ordinances require the use of plenum cable for network installations. The bottom line? Get plenum!

The space between the acoustical tile ceiling in an office building and the actual concrete ceiling above is called the *plenum*—hence the name for the proper fire rating of cabling to use in that space. A third type of fire rating, known as *riser*, designates the proper cabling to use for vertical runs between floors of a building. Riser-rated cable provides less protection than plenum cable, though, so most installations today use plenum for runs between floors.

EXAM TIP   Look for a question on the CompTIA Network+ exam that asks you to compare plenum versus PVC cable best use.

Networking Industry Standards—IEEE

The *Institute of Electrical and Electronics Engineers (IEEE)* defines industry-wide standards that promote the use and implementation of technology. In February 1980, a committee called the 802 Working Group took over from the private sector the job of defining network standards. (Get it? 02/80?) The IEEE 802 committee defines frames, speeds, distances, and types of cabling to use in a network environment. Concentrating on cables, the IEEE recognizes that no single cabling solution can work in all situations and, therefore, provides a variety of cabling standards.

IEEE committees define standards for a wide variety of electronics. The names of these committees are often used to refer to the standards they publish. The IEEE 1284 committee, for example, set standards for parallel communication, so you would see parallel cables marked "IEEE 1284–compliant," as in Figure 2-28.

Figure 2-28
Parallel cable
marked IEEE
1284–compliant

The IEEE 802 committee sets the standards for networking. Although the original plan was to define a single, universal standard for networking, it quickly became apparent that no single solution would work for all needs. The 802 committee split into smaller subcommittees, with names such as IEEE 802.3 and IEEE 802.11. Table 2-4 shows the currently recognized IEEE 802 subcommittees and their areas of jurisdiction. The missing numbers, such as 802.2 and 802.12, were used for committees long-ago disbanded. Each subcommittee is officially called a Working Group, except the few listed as a Technical Advisory Group (TAG) in the table.

IEEE 802.1	Higher Layer LAN Protocols (with many subcommittees, like 802.1X for port-based network access control)
IEEE 802.3	Ethernet (with a ton of subcommittees, such as 802.3ae for 10-Gigabit Ethernet)
IEEE 802.11	Wireless LAN (WLAN); specifications, such as Wi-Fi, and many subcommittees
IEEE 802.15	Wireless Personal Area Network (WPAN)
IEEE 802.18	Radio Regulatory Technical Advisory Group
IEEE 802.19	Wireless Coexistence Working Group
IEEE 802.20	Mobile Broadband Wireless Access (MBWA); (in hibernation)
IEEE 802.21	Media Independent Handover Services
IEEE 802.22	Wireless Regional Area Networks

Table 2-4   Some IEEE 802 Subcommittees

Chapter Review

Questions

1. Which of the following topologies required termination?

    A. Star

    B. Bus

    C. Mesh

    D. Ring

2. Star-bus is an example of a _____ topology.

    A. transitional

    B. system

    C. hybrid

    D. rampant

3. Of the topologies listed, which one is the most fault-tolerant?

    A. Point-to-point

    B. Bus

    C. Star

    D. Ring

4. What term is used to describe the interconnectivity of network components?

    A. Segmentation

    B. Map

    C. Topology

    D. Protocol

5. Coaxial cables all have a(n) _____ rating.

    A. resistance

    B. watt

    C. speed

    D. Ohm

6. Which of the following is a type of coaxial cable?

    A. RJ-45

    B. RG-59

    C. BNC

    D. Barrel

7. Which network topology connected nodes with a ring of cable?

   A. Star

   B. Bus

   C. Ring

   D. Mesh

8. Which network topology is most commonly seen only in wireless networks?

   A. Star

   B. Bus

   C. Ring

   D. Mesh

9. Which of the following is a duplex fiber-optic connection?

   A. LC

   B. RJ-45

   C. ST

   D. SC

10. What is the most common category of UTP used in new cabling installations?

   A. Cat 3

   B. Cat 5e

   C. Cat 6

   D. Cat 7

Answers

1. **B.** In a bus topology, all computers connected to the network via a main line. The cable had to be terminated at both ends to prevent signal reflection.

2. **C.** Star-bus is a hybrid topology because it uses a star physical topology and a bus signal topology.

3. **C.** Of the choices listed, only star topology has any fault tolerance.

4. **C.** *Topology* is the term used to describe the interconnectivity of network components.

5. **D.** All coaxial cables have an Ohm rating. RG-59 and RG-6 both are rated at 75 Ohms.

6. **B.** RG-59 is a type of coaxial cable.

7. **C.** The aptly named ring topology connected nodes with a central ring of cable.

8. **D.** Mesh is, for the most part, unique to wireless networks.

9. **A.** Of the options given, only the LC connector is designed for duplex fiber-optic.

10. **B.** Cat 6 is the most common cabling category used today, although Cat 6a and Cat 7 are gaining in popularity.

Ethernet Basics

The CompTIA Network+ certification exam expects you to know how to

- 2.1 Given a scenario, deploy the appropriate cabling solution
- 2.2 Given a scenario, determine the appropriate placement of networking devices on a network and install/configure them
- 4.6 Explain common mitigation techniques and their purposes

To achieve these goals, you must be able to

- Define and describe Ethernet
- Explain early Ethernet implementations
- Describe ways to enhance and extend Ethernet networks

In the beginning, there were no networks. Computers were isolated, solitary islands of information in a teeming sea of proto-geeks who banged out binary messages with wooden clubs and wore fur pocket protectors. Okay, maybe it wasn't that bad, but if you wanted to move a file from one machine to another, you had to use *Sneakernet*, which meant you saved the file on a disk, laced up your tennis shoes, and hiked over to the other system.

All that walking no doubt produced lots of health benefits, but frankly, proto-geeks weren't all that into health benefits—they were into speed, power, and technological coolness in general. (Sound familiar?) It's no wonder, then, that geeks everywhere agreed on the need to replace walking with some form of networking technology that connects computers together to transfer data at very high speeds.

This chapter explores the networking technology that eventually took control of the industry, Ethernet. We'll start with basic terminology, then look at two early forms of Ethernet. The chapter finishes with a discussion on enhancing and expanding Ethernet networks.

Historical/Conceptual

Ethernet

In 1973, Xerox answered the challenge of moving data without sneakers by developing *Ethernet*, a networking technology standard based on a bus topology. The original Ethernet used a single piece of coaxial cable to connect several computers, enabling them to transfer data at a rate of up to three million bits per second (Mbps). Although slow by today's standards, this early version of Ethernet was a huge improvement over manual transfer methods and served as the foundation for all later versions of Ethernet.

Ethernet remained a largely in-house technology within Xerox until 1979, when Xerox decided to look for partners to help promote Ethernet as an industry standard. Xerox worked with Digital Equipment Corporation (DEC) and Intel to publish what became known as the Digital/Intel/Xerox (DIX) standard. The DIX Ethernet standard improved on the original Ethernet standard, increasing speed to a screaming 10 Mbps.

These companies then did something visionary: they transferred (one might also say gave away) control of the Ethernet standard to the Institute of Electrical and Electronics Engineers (IEEE), which, in turn, created the *802.3 (Ethernet)* committee that continues to control the Ethernet standard to this day. By transferring control to IEEE, Ethernet became an open standard, enabling anyone to make interchangeable Ethernet equipment. Making Ethernet an open standard made Ethernet much cheaper than any alternative technology and certainly contributed to Ethernet winning the marketplace.

802.3 Standards

The 802.3 committee defines wired network standards that share the same basic frame type and network access method. Each of these variants is under the IEEE 802.3 standard, each with its own identifier. Here's a small selection of 802.3 standards:

- **802.3i**   10 Mbps Ethernet using twisted pair cabling (1990)
- **802.3ab**   Gigabit Ethernet over twisted pair (1999)
- **802.3by**   25 Gigabit Ethernet over fiber (2016)

Because the technologies share essential components, you can communicate among them just fine. The implementation of the network might be different, but the frames remain the same.

 NOTE   There have been four different Ethernet frame types defined over the years, but only one, the Ethernet II frame type, is used today. Every version of 802.3 Ethernet uses the same Ethernet II frame.

Ethernet's designers faced the same challenges as the designers of any network: how to send data across the wire, how to identify the sending and receiving computers, and how to determine which computer should use the shared cable at what time. The engineers resolved these issues by using data frames that contain MAC addresses to identify computers on the network and by using a process called CSMA/CD (discussed shortly) to determine which machine should access the wire at any given time. You saw some of this in action in Chapter 1, "Network Models," but now I need to introduce you to a bunch of additional terms.

> **NOTE**   The source for all things Ethernet is but a short click away on the Internet. For starters, check out www.ieee802.org.

Test Specific

Ethernet Frames

All network technologies break data transmitted between computers into smaller pieces called *frames*, as you'll recall from Chapter 1. Using frames addresses two networking issues. First, frames prevent any single machine from monopolizing the shared bus cable. Second, they make the process of retransmitting lost data more efficient.

> **EXAM TIP**   The terms *frame* and *packet* are sometimes used interchangeably, but this book uses the terms strictly. You'll recall from Chapter 1 that frames at Layer 2 are based on MAC addresses; packets are associated with data assembled by the IP protocol at Layer 3 of the OSI seven-layer model.

The process you saw in Chapter 1 of transferring a word processing document between two computers illustrates these two issues. First, if the sending computer sends the document as a single huge frame, the frame will monopolize the cable and prevent other machines from using the cable until the entire file gets to the receiving system. Using relatively small frames enables computers to share the cable easily—each computer listens on the *segment*, sending a few frames of data whenever it detects that no other computer is transmitting. Second, in the real world, bad things can happen to good data. When errors occur during transmission, the sending system must retransmit the frames that failed to get to the receiving system in good shape. If a word processing document were transmitted as a single massive frame, the sending system would have to retransmit the entire frame—in this case, the entire document. Breaking the file up into smaller frames enables the sending computer to retransmit only the damaged frames. Because of these benefits—shared access and more efficient retransmission—all networking technologies use frames.

In Chapter 1, you saw a generic frame. Let's take what you know of frames and expand on that knowledge by inspecting the details of an Ethernet frame. A basic Ethernet frame contains five fields: the *destination*—the MAC address of the frame's recipient; the *source*—the MAC address of the sending system; the *type* of the data; the *data* itself; and a *frame check sequence*. Figure 3-1 shows these components. Transmission of a frame starts with a *preamble* and can also include some extra filler called a *pad*. Let's look at each piece.

Figure 3-1
Ethernet frame

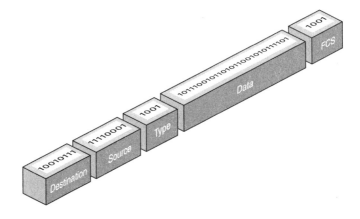

Preamble

A *preamble*, a 7-byte series of alternating ones and zeroes followed by a 1-byte *start frame delimiter*, always precedes a frame. The preamble gives a receiving NIC time to realize a frame is coming and to know exactly where the frame starts. The preamble is added by the sending NIC.

MAC Addresses

Each NIC on an Ethernet network must have a unique identifying address. Ethernet identifies the NICs on a network using special 48-bit (6-byte) binary addresses known as *MAC addresses*.

 EXAM TIP The CompTIA Network+ exam might describe MAC addresses as 48-bit binary addresses or 6-byte binary addresses.

In a bus network, all the connected computers could see all traffic. The *destination* address in the frame enabled NICs to examine each frame and process only frames intended for them. The *source* address in the frame enabled the recipient to respond accurately.

Type

An Ethernet frame may carry one of several types of data. The *type* field helps the receiving computer interpret the frame contents at a very basic level. This way the receiving computer can tell if the frame contains IPv4 data, for example, or IPv6 data. (See Chapter 6 for more details on IPv4; I cover IPv6 in Chapter 12.)

The type field does *not* tell you if the frame carries higher-level data, such as an e-mail message or Web page. You have to dig deeper into the data section of the frame to find that information.

Data

The *data* part of the frame contains whatever payload the frame carries. If the frame carries an IP packet, that packet will include extra information, such as the IP addresses of both systems.

Pad

The minimum Ethernet frame is 64 bytes in size, but not all of that has to be actual data. If an Ethernet frame has fewer than 64 bytes of data to haul, the sending NIC will automatically add extra data—a *pad*—to bring the data up to the minimum 64 bytes. A pad is not a regular field and is rarely added in modern networking.

Frame Check Sequence

The *frame check sequence (FCS)* enables Ethernet nodes to recognize when bad things happen to good data. Machines on a network must be able to detect when data has been damaged in transit. To detect errors, the computers on an Ethernet network attach a special code to each frame. When creating an Ethernet frame, the sending machine runs the data through a special mathematical formula called a *cyclic redundancy check (CRC)* and attaches the result, the frame check sequence, to the frame. The receiving machine opens the frame, performs the same calculation, and compares its answer with the one included with the frame. If the answers do not match, the receiving machine drops the frame.

Early Ethernet Standards

Contemplating the physical network brings up numerous questions. What kind of cables should you use? What should they be made of? How long can they be? For these answers, turn to the IEEE 802.3 standard, both true bus and star-bus versions.

Bus Ethernet

The original Ethernet networks employed a true bus topology, meaning every computer on a network connected to the same cable, the bus. Every version of Ethernet invented since the early 1990s uses a hybrid star-bus topology. At the center of these early networks was a *hub*. A hub was nothing more than an electronic *repeater*—it interpreted the ones and zeroes coming in from one port and repeated the same signal out to the other connected ports. Hubs did not send the same signal back down the port that originally sent it (Figure 3-2). Any scenario involving these early networks found the placement of a hub at the center of the network.

10BaseT

In 1990, the IEEE 802.3 committee created a version of Ethernet called *10BaseT* that rapidly became the most popular network technology in the world, replacing competing and now long-gone competitors with names like Token Ring and AppleTalk. The classic 10BaseT network consisted of two or more computers connected to a central hub. The NICs connected with wires as specified by the 802.3 committee.

The name 10BaseT follows roughly the same naming convention used for earlier Ethernet cabling systems. The number *10* refers to the speed: 10 Mbps. The word *Base* refers to the signaling type: baseband. (*Baseband* means that the cable only carries one type of signal. Contrast this with *broadband*—as in cable television—where the cable carries multiple signals or channels.) The letter *T* refers to the type of cable used: twisted-pair. 10BaseT used unshielded twisted-pair (UTP) cabling.

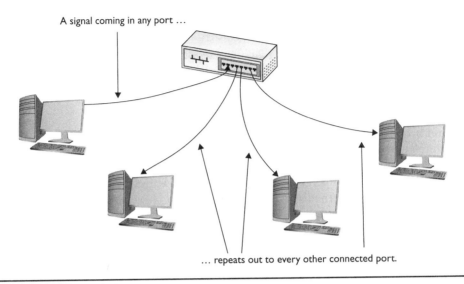

A signal coming in any port ...

... repeats out to every other connected port.

Figure 3-2   Ethernet hub

UTP

Officially, 10BaseT required the use of Cat 3 (or higher), two-pair, unshielded twisted-pair (UTP) cable. One pair of wires sent data to the hub while the other pair received data from the hub. Even though 10BaseT only required two-pair cabling, everyone installed four-pair cabling to connect devices to the hub as insurance against the possible requirements of newer types of networking (Figure 3-3). Not surprisingly, this came in handy very soon. See Chapter 4, "Modern Ethernet," for more details.

Figure 3-3
A typical four-pair Cat 5e unshielded twisted-pair cable

Most UTP cables (then and now) come with stranded Kevlar fibers to give the cable added strength, which, in turn, enables installers to pull on the cable without excessive risk of literally ripping it apart.

10BaseT also introduced the networking world to the *RJ-45 connector* (Figure 3-4). Each pin on the RJ-45 connects to a single wire inside the cable; this enables devices to put voltage on the individual wires within the cable. The pins on the RJ-45 are numbered from 1 to 8, as shown in Figure 3-5.

Figure 3-4

Two views of an RJ-45 connector

Figure 3-5

The pins on an RJ-45 connector are numbered 1 through 8.

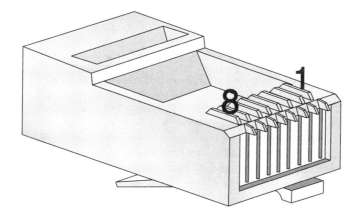

The 10BaseT standard designates some of these numbered wires for specific purposes. As mentioned earlier, although the cable has four pairs, 10BaseT used only two of the pairs. 10BaseT devices used pins 1 and 2 to send data, and pins 3 and 6 to receive data. Even though one pair of wires sent data and another received data, a 10BaseT device connected to a hub could not send and receive simultaneously. See "CSMA/CD" later in this chapter for details about collisions and using a shared bus.

NICs that can communicate in only one direction at a time run in *half-duplex* mode. Later advances (as you'll see shortly) enabled NICs to send and receive at the same time, thus running in *full-duplex* mode.

An RJ-45 connector is usually called a *crimp*, and the act (some folks call it an art) of installing a crimp onto the end of a piece of UTP cable is called *crimping*. The tool used to secure a crimp onto the end of a cable is a *crimper*. Each wire inside a UTP cable must connect to the proper pin inside the crimp. Manufacturers color-code each wire within a piece of four-pair UTP to assist in properly matching the ends. Each pair of wires consists of a solid-colored wire and a striped wire: blue/blue-white, orange/orange-white, brown/brown-white, and green/green-white (Figure 3-6).

Figure 3-6
Color-coded
pairs (note the
alternating solid
and striped
wires)

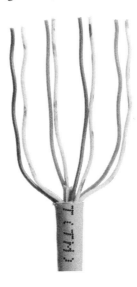

 NOTE As noted in Chapter 2, the real name for RJ-45 is *8 position 8 contact (8P8C)* modular plug. The term RJ-45 is so prevalent, however, that nobody but the nerdiest of nerds calls it by its real name. Stick to RJ-45.

The Telecommunications Industry Association/Electronics Industries Alliance (TIA/EIA) defines the industry standard for correct crimping of four-pair UTP. You'll find two standards mentioned on the CompTIA Network+ exam: *TIA/EIA 568A* and *TIA/EIA 568B*. (CompTIA uses lower-case letters in the objectives, at least as we go to press—568a and 568b—though the industry uses upper-case.) Figure 3-7 shows the TIA/EIA 568A and TIA/EIA 568B color-code standards. Note that the wire pairs used by 10BaseT (1 and 2, 3 and 6) come from the same color pairs (green/green-white and orange/orange-white). Following an established color-code scheme, such as TIA/EIA 568A, ensures that the wires match up correctly at each end of the cable.

 EXAM TIP TIA/EIA 568C, the current standard, includes the same wiring standards as TIA/EIA 568A and TIA/EIA 568B. It's all just wrapped up in a slightly different name: *ANSI/TIA-568-C*. When the EIA left the planet in 2011, the names of the standards changed. CompTIA continues to use the older names on exams.

The ability to make your own Ethernet cables is a real plus for a network tech. With a reel of Cat 5e, a bag of RJ-45 connectors, a moderate investment in a crimping tool, and a little practice, you can kiss those mass-produced cables goodbye! You can make cables to

Figure 3-7
The TIA/EIA
568A and 568B
standards

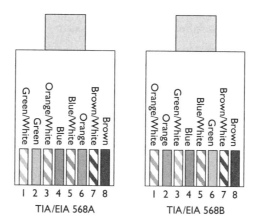

TIA/EIA 568A   TIA/EIA 568B

your own length specifications, replace broken RJ-45 connectors that would otherwise mean tossing an entire cable—and, in the process, save your company or clients time and money.

EXAM TIP   An easy trick to remembering the difference between 568A and 568B is the word "GO." The green and orange pairs are swapped between 568A and 568B, whereas the blue and brown pairs stay in the same place!
   For the CompTIA Network+ exam, you will be tested on the TIA/EIA 568a or 568b color codes. Memorize them. You'll see the standards listed as EIA/TIA 568A, TIA/EIA568A, T568A, or just 568A. Know the A and B and you'll be fine.

10BaseT Limits and Specifications

Like any other Ethernet standard, 10BaseT had limitations, both on cable distance and on the number of computers. The key distance limitation for 10BaseT was the distance between the hub and the computer. The twisted-pair cable connecting a computer to the hub could not exceed 100 meters in length. A 10BaseT hub could connect no more than 1024 computers, although that limitation rarely came into play. It made no sense for vendors to build hubs that large—or more to the point, that *expensive*.

10BaseT Summary

- **Speed**   10 Mbps
- **Signal type**   Baseband
- **Distance**   100 meters between the hub and the node
- **Node limit**   No more than 1024 nodes per hub
- **Topology**   Star-bus topology: physical star, logical bus
- **Cable type**   Cat 3 or better UTP cabling with RJ-45 connectors

SIM   Check out the Chapter 3 Challenge! sim "T-568B" here:

http://totalsem.com/007

It's a great tool for getting the colors set in your head.

10BaseFL

Just a few years after the introduction of 10BaseT, a fiber-optic version, called *10BaseFL*, appeared. As you know from the previous chapter, fiber-optic cabling transmits data packets using pulses of light instead of using electrical current. Using light instead of electricity addresses the three key weaknesses of copper cabling. First, optical signals can travel much farther. The maximum length for a 10BaseFL cable was up to 2 kilometers, depending on how you configured it. Second, fiber-optic cable is immune to electrical interference, making it an ideal choice for high-interference environments. Third, the cable is much more difficult to tap into, making fiber a good choice for environments with security concerns. 10BaseFL used *multimode* fiber-optic and employed either an SC or an ST connector.

NOTE   10BaseFL is often simply called "10BaseF."

Figure 3-8 shows a typical 10BaseFL card. Note that it uses two fiber connectors—one to send and one to receive. All fiber-optic networks use at least two fiber-optic cables. Although 10BaseFL enjoyed some popularity for a number of years, most networks today are using the same fiber-optic cabling to run far faster network technologies.

Figure 3-8
Typical 10BaseFL
card

10BaseFL Summary

- **Speed** 10 Mbps
- **Signal type** Baseband
- **Distance** 2000 meters between the hub and the node
- **Node limit** No more than 1024 nodes per hub
- **Topology** Star-bus topology: physical star, logical bus
- **Cable type** Multimode fiber-optic cabling with ST or SC connectors

So far you've seen two different flavors of star-bus Ethernet, 10BaseT and 10BaseFL. Even though these used different cabling and hubs, the actual packets were still Ethernet frames. As a result, interconnecting flavors of Ethernet were (and still are) common. Because 10BaseT and 10BaseFL used different types of cable, you could use a *media converter* (Figure 3-9) to interconnect different Ethernet types.

Figure 3-9
Typical copper-
to-fiber Ethernet
media converter
(photo courtesy
of TRENDnet)

CSMA/CD

One of the issues with bus communication is that devices essentially share the same cable. This applies to pure bus networks and hybrid star-bus networks as well. The NICs need some way to determine which machine should send data at which time. Ethernet designers came up with a clever way to handle the issue of potential collisions.

Ethernet networks use a system called *carrier sense multiple access/collision detection (CSMA/CD)* to determine which computer should use a shared cable at a given moment. *Carrier sense* means that each node using the network examines the cable before sending a data frame (Figure 3-10). If another machine is using the network, the node detects traffic on the segment, waits a few milliseconds, and then rechecks. If it detects no traffic—the more common term is to say the cable is "free"—the node sends out its frame.

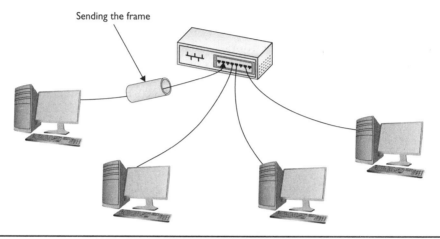

Sending the frame

Figure 3-10 No one else is talking—send the frame!

 EXAM TIP CSMA/CD is a network access method that maps to the IEEE 802.3 standard for Ethernet networks.

Multiple access means that all machines have equal access to the wire. If the line is free, any Ethernet node may begin sending a frame. From Ethernet's point of view, it doesn't matter what function the node is performing: it could be a desktop system running Windows 10 or a file server running Windows Server or Linux. As far as Ethernet is concerned, a node is a node is a node and access to the cable is assigned strictly on a first-come, first-served basis.

So what happens if two machines, both listening to the cable, simultaneously decide that it is free and try to send a frame? A collision occurs, and both of the transmissions are lost (Figure 3-11). A collision resembles the effect of two people talking at the same time: the listener hears a mixture of two voices and can't understand either one.

When two NICs send at the same time, they'll sense the overlapping signals, and immediately know that a collision has occurred. When they detect a collision, both nodes stop transmitting.

They then each generate a random number to determine how long to wait before trying again. If you imagine that each machine rolls its magic electronic dice and waits for that number of seconds, you wouldn't be too far from the truth, except that the amount of time an Ethernet node waits to retransmit is much shorter than one second (Figure 3-12).

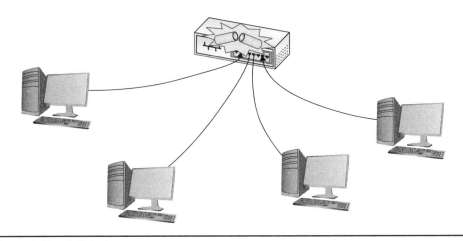

Figure 3-11 Collision!

Whichever node generates the lowest random number begins its retransmission first, winning the competition to use the wire. The losing node then sees traffic on the wire and waits for the wire to be free again before attempting to retransmit its data.

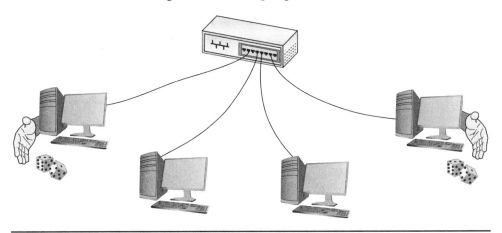

Figure 3-12 Rolling for timing

Collisions were a normal part of the operation of early Ethernet networks, because every device shared a bus. A group of nodes that have the capability of sending frames at the same time as each other, resulting in collisions, is called a *collision domain*. Better technology today makes collisions very rare.

Enhancing and Extending Ethernet Networks

While plain-vanilla 10BaseT Ethernet performed well enough for first-generation networks (which did little more than basic file and print sharing), by the early 1990s networks used more-demanding applications, such as Lotus Notes, SAP business management software, and Microsoft Exchange, which quickly saturated a 10BaseT network. Fortunately, those crazy kids over at the IEEE kept expanding the standard, giving the network tech in the trenches a new tool that provided additional bandwidth—the switch.

Additionally, more companies and organizations adopted Ethernet, leading to a demand for larger networks, both geographically and in the number of nodes that could interconnect. Hubs were cranky and creaky; switches brought much better scalability.

The Trouble with Hubs

A classic 10BaseT network with a hub could only have one message on the wire at any time. When two computers sent at the same time, the hub dutifully repeated both signals. The nodes recognized the collision and, following the rules of CSMA/CD, attempted to resend. Add in enough computers and the number of collisions increased, lowering the effective transmission speed for the whole network. A busy network became a slow network because all the computers shared the same collision domain.

 EXAM TIP Adding another hub or two to an early Ethernet network enabled you to add more devices, but also compounded the problem with collisions. In such a scenario, you could connect networks using a bridge. A *bridge* acted like a repeater to connect two networks, but then went a step further—filtering and forwarding traffic between those segments based on the MAC addresses of the computers on those segments. This placement between two segments preserved bandwidth, making larger Ethernet networks possible. You'll see the term "bridge" applied to modern devices, primarily in wireless networking. The interconnectedness of network segments is similar, but the devices are fundamentally different. See Chapter 14 for the scoop on wireless.

Switches to the Rescue

An Ethernet *switch* looks like a hub, because all nodes plug into it (Figure 3-13). But switches don't function like hubs inside. Switches come with extra smarts that enable them to take advantage of MAC addresses, effectively creating point-to-point connections between two conversing computers. This gives every conversation between two computers the full bandwidth of the network.

Figure 3-13
Hub (top) and switch (bottom) comparison

To see a switch in action, check out Figure 3-14. When you first turn on a switch, it acts like a hub, passing all incoming frames right back out to all the other ports. As it forwards all frames, however, the switch copies the source MAC addresses and quickly creates a table of the MAC addresses of each connected computer, called a *source address table (SAT)*.

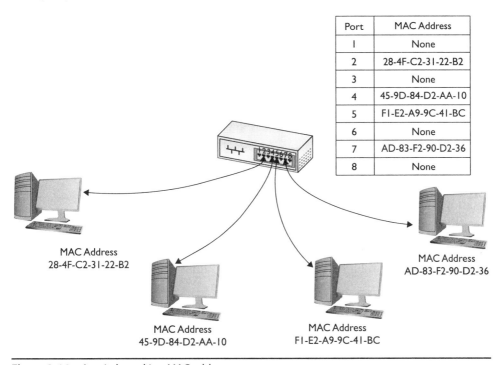

Port	MAC Address
1	None
2	28-4F-C2-31-22-B2
3	None
4	45-9D-84-D2-AA-10
5	F1-E2-A9-9C-41-BC
6	None
7	AD-83-F2-90-D2-36
8	None

MAC Address
28-4F-C2-31-22-B2

MAC Address
45-9D-84-D2-AA-10

MAC Address
F1-E2-A9-9C-41-BC

MAC Address
AD-83-F2-90-D2-36

Figure 3-14   A switch tracking MAC addresses

EXAM TIP   One classic difference between a hub and a switch is in the repeating of frames during normal use. Although it's true that switches initially forward all frames, they filter by MAC address in regular use. Hubs never learned and always forwarded all frames.

As soon as this table is created, the switch begins to do something amazing. When a computer sends a frame into the switch destined for another computer on the same switch, the switch acts like a telephone operator, creating an on-the-fly connection between the two devices. While these two devices communicate, it's as though they are the only two computers on the network. Figure 3-15 shows this in action. Because the switch handles each conversation individually, each conversation runs at the full network speed.

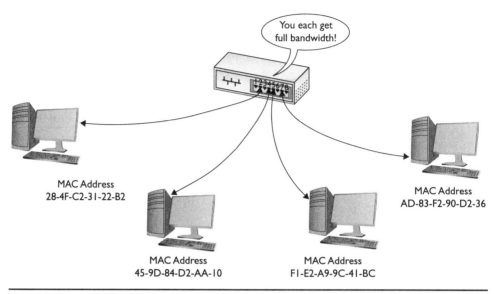

Figure 3-15 A switch making two separate connections

Each port on a switch is in its own collision domain, plus the switch can buffer incoming frames. That means that two nodes connected to the switch can send data at the same time and the switch will handle it without any collision.

 NOTE Because a switch filters traffic on MAC addresses (and MAC addresses run at Layer 2 of the OSI seven-layer model), they are sometimes called *Layer 2 switches*.

Unicast messages always go only to the intended recipient when you use a switch. The switch will send all broadcast messages to all the ports (except the port on which the frame originated). You'll commonly hear a switched network called a *broadcast domain* to contrast it to the ancient hub-based networks with their collision domains.

Connecting Ethernet Segments

Sometimes, one switch is just not enough. Once an organization uses every port on its existing switch, adding more nodes requires adding switches. Even fault tolerance can motivate an organization to add more switches. If every node on the network connects to the same switch, that switch becomes a single point of failure—if it fails, everybody drops off the network. You can connect switches in two ways: via an uplink port or a crossover cable.

Uplink Ports

Uplink ports enable you to connect two switches using a *straight-through* cable. They're clearly marked on older switches, as shown in Figure 3-16. To connect two switches, insert one end of a cable in the uplink port and the other end of the cable in any one of the regular ports on the other switch.

Figure 3-16
Typical uplink
port

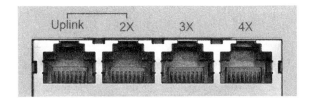

Modern switches do not have a dedicated uplink port, but instead auto-sense when another switch is plugged in. You can plug into any port.

Crossover Cables

Switches can also connect to each other via special twisted-pair cables called crossover cables. A *crossover cable* reverses the sending and receiving pairs on one end of the cable. One end of the cable is wired according to the TIA/EIA 568A standard, whereas the other end is wired according to the TIA/EIA 568B standard (Figure 3-17). With the sending and receiving pairs reversed, the switches can hear each other; hence the need for two standards for connecting RJ-45 jacks to UTP cables.

Figure 3-17
A crossover
cable reverses
the sending and
receiving pairs.

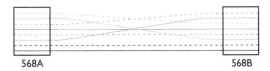

A crossover cable connects to a regular port on each switch. Modern switches with auto-sensing ports don't require a crossover cable.

In a pinch, you can use a crossover cable to connect two computers together using Ethernet NICs with no switch between them at all. This is handy for quickie connections, although not used much anymore because we mostly go wireless now.

Spanning Tree Protocol

Because you can connect switches together in any fashion, you can create redundant connections in a network. These are called *bridging loops* or *switching loops* (Figure 3-18).

 EXAM TIP   The CompTIA Network+ exam refers to STP, BPDU guard, and root guard as *mitigation techniques*. That's a fancy term for "making bad things not as destructive."

In the early days of switches, making a bridging loop in a network setup would bring the network crashing down. A frame could get caught in the loop, so to speak, and not reach its destination.

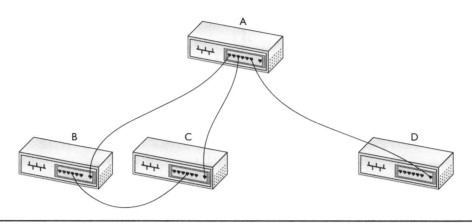

Figure 3-18 A bridging loop

The Ethernet standards body adopted the *Spanning Tree Protocol (STP)* to eliminate the problem of accidental bridging loops. For decades, switches have had STP enabled by default, and can detect potential loops before they happen. Using special STP frames known as *bridge protocol data units (BPDUs)*, switches communicate with other switches to prevent loops from happening in the first place.

Configuration BPDUs establish the topology, where one switch is elected *root bridge* and acts as the center of the STP universe. Each switch then uses the root bridge as a reference point to maintain a loop-free topology. There will be redundant links, for fault tolerance, that would ordinarily cause a bridging loop, but certain ports will be placed in a "blocking" state and will not send or receive data frames. Ports in the blocking state will still hear the configuration BPDUs, which are sourced by the root bridge and forwarded downstream to the other switches every 2 seconds.

If a link or device goes down, STP springs into action with another type of BPDU, called a *topology change notification (TCN) BPDU*, that enables the switches to rework themselves around the failed interface or device. The blocked ports, listening to the BPDUs, will realize they're needed and eventually move to a forwarding state.

Administrators can manually change STP settings for a switch. A switch port directly connected to a PC, for example, should never participate in STP, and could be configured with a setting called *PortFast* that enables the interface to come up right away, without the normal latency introduced by STP. Another reason to configure switch ports with PortFast is to prevent TCN BPDUs being sent out of that switch every time a PC is powered on and off, which has severe side effects, like causing all switches to flush their source address table, and relearn MAC addresses.

BPDU guard will move a port configured with PortFast into an errdisable state (i.e., error occurred, disabled) if a BPDU is received on that port. This requires an administrator to manually bring the port back up.

Ports configured with PortFast should never receive a BPDU, and if they do, it could start a bridging loop. Another mechanism, *root guard*, will move a port into a root-inconsistent state if BPDUs coming from a certain direction indicate another switch is trying to become the root bridge. The root-inconsistent port will automatically return to its forwarding state once these BPDUs stop. This helps define locations where the root bridge should never be located.

The original Spanning Tree Protocol, introduced by IEEE as 802.1d, was replaced a long time ago (2001) by the Rapid Spanning Tree Protocol (RSTP), 802.1w. RSTP offers significantly faster convergence time following some kind of network change. STP could take up to 50 seconds to get back to a steady state, for example, whereas an RSTP network could return to convergence in 6 seconds.

Troubleshooting Switches

The simple switches described in this chapter generally function flawlessly for years without any need for a tech to do more than wipe dust off the top. Very occasionally you'll run into a switch that has problems. These problems fall into two categories:

- Obvious physical damage
- Dead ports

Diagnosing any of these problems follows a similar pattern. First, you recognize that a switch might have problems because a device you've plugged in can't connect to the network. Second, you examine the switch for obvious damage. Third, you look for link lights. If they're not flashing, try a different port. Fourth, you look at your cables. If anything looks bent, broken, or stepped on, you should replace it. A bad cable or improper cable type can lead to problems that point to a "failed" switch when the true culprit is really the cable. Finally, you use the tried and true method of replacing the switch or the cable with a known-good device.

 NOTE When we get to modern higher-end switches in Chapter 11, "Advanced Networking Devices," you'll need to follow other procedures to do proper diagnostic work. We'll get there soon enough!

Chapter Review

Questions

1. Ethernet hubs take an incoming packet and _____ it out to the other connected ports.

    A. amplify

    B. repeat

    C. filter

    D. distort

2. What is appended to the beginning of the Ethernet frame?

　　A. MAC address

　　B. Length

　　C. Preamble

　　D. CRC

3. What type of bus does 10BaseT use?

　　A. Bus

　　B. Ring

　　C. Star bus

　　D. Bus ring

4. What is the maximum distance that can separate a 10BaseT node from its hub?

　　A. 50 meters

　　B. 100 meters

　　C. 185 meters

　　D. 200 meters

5. When used for Ethernet, unshielded twisted pair uses what type of connector?

　　A. RG-58

　　B. RJ-45

　　C. RJ-11

　　D. RS-232

6. What is the maximum number of nodes that can be connected to a 10BaseT hub?

　　A. 1024

　　B. 500

　　C. 100

　　D. 185

7. Which of the following is not true of crossover cables?

　　A. They are a type of twisted-pair cabling.

　　B. They reverse the sending and receiving wire pairs.

　　C. They are used to connect hubs.

　　D. Both ends of a crossover cable are wired according to the TIA/EIA 568B standard.

8. Which of the following connectors are used by 10BaseFL cable? (Select two.)

   A. SC

   B. RJ-45

   C. RJ-11

   D. ST

9. Which networking devices can use the Spanning Tree Protocol (STP)?

   A. Hubs

   B. Media converters

   C. UTP cables

   D. Switches

10. What device directs packets based on MAC addresses?

   A. Router

   B. Hub

   C. Repeater

   D. Switch

Answers

1. B. Hubs are nothing more than multiport repeaters.

2. C. Appended to the front of the Ethernet frame is the preamble.

3. C. 10BaseT uses a star-bus topology.

4. B. The maximum distance between a 10BaseT node and its hub is 100 meters.

5. B. UTP cable uses an RJ-45 connector when used for Ethernet. RG-58 is the type of coaxial cable used with 10Base2. RJ-11 is the standard four-wire connector used for regular phone lines. RS-232 is a standard for serial connectors.

6. A. A 10BaseT hub can connect no more than 1024 nodes (computers).

7. D. One end of a crossover cable is wired according to the TIA/EIA 568B standard; the other is wired according to the TIA/EIA 568A standard. This is what crosses the wire pairs and enables two hubs to communicate without colliding.

8. A, D. 10BaseFL uses two types of fiber-optic connectors called SC and ST connectors.

9. D. The Spanning Tree Protocol is unique to switches.

10. D. A switch uses MAC addresses to direct traffic only to the appropriate recipient.

Modern Ethernet

The CompTIA Network+ certification exam expects you to know how to
- 1.5 Compare and contrast the characteristics of network topologies, types and technologies
- 2.1 Given a scenario, deploy the appropriate cabling solution
- 2.2 Given a scenario, determine the appropriate placement of networking devices on a network and install/configure them

To achieve these goals, you must be able to
- Describe the varieties of 100-megabit Ethernet
- Discuss copper- and fiber-based Gigabit Ethernet
- Discover and describe Ethernet varieties beyond Gigabit

Within a few years of its introduction, 10BaseT proved inadequate to meet the growing networking demand for speed. As with all things in the computing world, bandwidth is the key. Even with switching, the 10-Mbps speed of 10BaseT, seemingly so fast when first developed, quickly found a market clamoring for even faster speeds. This chapter looks at the improvements in Ethernet since 10BaseT. You'll read about the 100-megabit standards and the Gigabit Ethernet standards. The chapter finishes with a look at Ethernet that exceed Gigabit speeds.

Test Specific

100-Megabit Ethernet

The quest to break 10-Mbps network speeds in Ethernet started in the early 1990s. By then, 10BaseT Ethernet had established itself as the most popular networking technology (although other standards, such as IBM's Token Ring, still had some market share). The goal was to create a new speed standard that made no changes to the actual Ethernet frames themselves. By doing this, the 802.3 committee ensured that different speeds of Ethernet could interconnect, assuming you had something that could handle the speed differences and a media converter if the connections were different.

Two of the defining characteristics of Ethernet—the frame size and elements, and the way devices share access to the bus (carrier sense multiple access [CSMA])—stay precisely the same when going from 100-megabit standards to 1000-megabit (and beyond). This standardization ensures communication and scalability.

The CompTIA Network+ exam objectives refer to only five Ethernet standards by name or by category: 100BaseT, 1000BaseT, 1000BaseLX, 1000BaseSX, and 10GBaseT. This chapter starts with the first four as named, adding a fiber variation called 100BaseFX, but then breaks the 10-gigabit standards out into distinct subsets for fiber and copper because, if you get a job in a data center, you'll need a deeper understanding of the faster standards.

100BaseT

If you want to make a lot of money in the technology world, create a standard and then get everyone else to buy into it. For that matter, you can even give the standard away and still make tons of cash if you have the inside line on making the hardware that supports the standard.

When it came time to come up with a new standard to replace 10BaseT, network hardware makers forwarded a large number of potential standards, all focused on the prize of leading the new Ethernet standard. As a result, two twisted-pair Ethernet standards appeared: *100BaseT4* and *100BaseTX*. 100BaseT4 used Cat 3 cable, whereas 100BaseTX used Cat 5 and Cat 5e. By the late 1990s, 100BaseTX became the dominant 100-megabit Ethernet standard. 100BaseT4 disappeared from the market and today has been forgotten. As a result, we never say 100BaseTX, simply choosing to use the term *100BaseT*.

NOTE 100BaseT was at one time called *Fast Ethernet*. The term still sticks to the 100-Mbps standards even though there are now much faster versions of Ethernet.

100BaseT Summary

- **Speed**   100 Mbps
- **Signal type**   Baseband
- **Distance**   100 meters between the hub/switch and the node
- **Node limit**   No more than 1024 nodes per hub/switch
- **Topology**   Star-bus topology: physical star, logical bus
- **Cable type**   Cat 5 or better UTP or STP cabling with RJ-45/8P8C connectors

EXAM TIP   A *baseband* network means that only a single signal travels over the wires of the network at one time, occupying the lowest frequencies. Ethernet networks are baseband. Contrast this with *broadband*, where you can get multiple signals to flow over the same wire at the same time, modulating to higher frequencies. The latter is how cable television and cable Internet work.

Upgrading a 10BaseT network to 100BaseT was not a small process. First, you needed Cat 5 cable or better. Second, you had to replace all 10BaseT NICs with 100BaseT NICs. Third, you needed to replace the 10BaseT hub or switch with a 100BaseT hub or switch. Making this upgrade cost a lot in the early days of 100BaseT, so people clamored for a way to make the upgrade a little easier and less expensive. This was accomplished via multispeed, auto-sensing NICs and hubs/switches.

Figure 4-1 shows a typical multispeed, auto-sensing 100BaseT NIC from the late 1990s. When this NIC first connected to a network, it negotiated automatically with the hub or switch to determine the other device's highest speed. If they both did 100BaseT, then you got 100BaseT. If the hub or switch only did 10BaseT, then the NIC did 10BaseT. All of this happened automatically (Figure 4-2).

NOTE   If you want to sound like a proper tech, you need to use the right words. Techs don't actually say, "multispeed, auto-sensing," but rather "10/100/1000." As in, "Hey, is that a 10/100/1000 NIC you got there?" Now you're talking the talk!

Figure 4-1
Typical 100BaseT
NIC

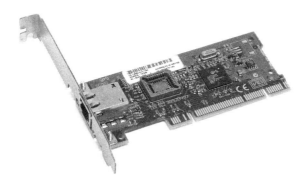

Figure 4-2
Auto-negotiation
in action

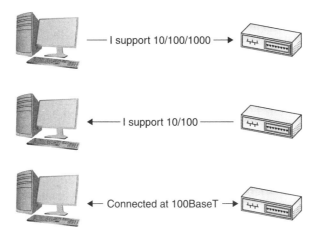

Distinguishing a 10BaseT NIC from a 100BaseT NIC without close inspection was impossible. You had to look for something on the card to tell you its speed. Some NICs had extra link lights to show the speed (see Chapter 5, "Installing a Physical Network," for the scoop on link lights). Of course, you could always simply install the card, as shown in Figure 4-3, and see what the operating system says it sees.

Figure 4-3
Typical
100BaseT NIC in
Windows 8.1

You'll also have trouble finding a true 10BaseT or 100BaseT NIC any longer because multispeed NICs have been around long enough to have replaced any single-speed NIC. All modern NICs are multispeed and auto-sensing.

100BaseFX

Most Ethernet networks use unshielded twisted pair (UTP) cabling, but quite a few use fiber-based networks instead. In some networks, using fiber simply makes more sense.

UTP cabling cannot meet the needs of every organization for three key reasons. First, the 100-meter distance limitation of UTP-based networks is inadequate for networks covering large buildings or campuses. Second, UTP's lack of electrical shielding makes it a poor choice for networks functioning in locations with high levels of *electromagnetic interference (EMI)*—disturbance in electrical signals caused by electrical radiation coming from nearby devices. Finally, the Jason Bournes and James Bonds of the world find UTP cabling (and copper cabling in general) easy to tap, making it an inappropriate choice for high-security environments. To address these issues, the IEEE 802.3 standard provides for a flavor of 100-megabit Ethernet using fiber-optic cable, called 100BaseFX.

The *100BaseFX* standard saw quite a bit of interest for years, as it combined the high speed of 100-megabit Ethernet with the reliability of fiber optics. Outwardly, 100BaseFX looked exactly like its predecessor, 10BaseFL (introduced in Chapter 3). 100BaseFX uses the multimode fiber-optic cabling, and SC or ST connectors. 100BaseFX offers improved data speeds over 10BaseFL, of course, and equally long cable runs, supporting a maximum cable length of 2 kilometers.

100BaseFX Summary

- **Speed**   100 Mbps
- **Signal type**   Baseband
- **Distance**   Two kilometers between the hub/switch and the node
- **Node limit**   No more than 1024 nodes per hub/switch
- **Topology**   Star-bus topology: physical star, logical bus
- **Cable type**   Multimode fiber-optic cabling with ST or SC connectors

 EXAM TIP   There is no scenario today where you would install 100Base networking components, except perhaps to make use of donated equipment. You will definitely find 100Base gear installed and functioning in many organizations.

Full-Duplex Ethernet

Early 100BaseT NICs, just like 10BaseT NICs, could send and receive data, but not at the same time—a feature called *half-duplex* (Figure 4-4). The IEEE addressed this characteristic shortly after adopting 100BaseT as a standard. By the late 1990s, most 100BaseT cards could auto-negotiate for full-duplex. With *full-duplex*, a NIC can send and receive at the same time, as shown in Figure 4-5.

Figure 4-4
Half-duplex;
sending at the
top, receiving at
the bottom

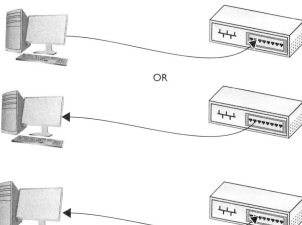

OR

Figure 4-5
Full-duplex

 NOTE   Full-duplex doesn't increase network speed directly, but it doubles network bandwidth. Imagine a one-lane road expanded to two lanes while keeping the speed limit the same. It also prevents those cars from crashing (colliding) into each other!

All NICs today run full-duplex. The NIC and the attached switch determine full- or half-duplex during the auto-negotiation process. The vast majority of the time you simply let the NIC do its negotiation. Every operating system has some method to force the NIC to a certain speed/duplex, as shown in Figure 4-6.

Figure 4-6
Forcing speed
and duplex in
Windows 10

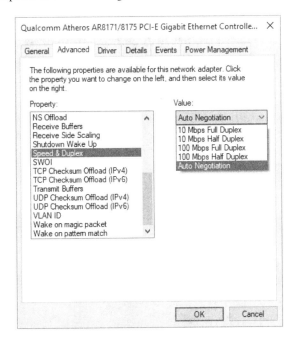

Fast Ethernet at 100 Mbps makes sense for simple networks where you share small data, like documents and spreadsheets. Plenty of local area networks (LANs) around the world continue to soldier on at 100-megabit speeds. A lot of network-connected devices, such as printers, function just fine on Fast Ethernet as well. Still, Fast Ethernet is dead in new installations, so let's turn to the current standard.

SIM Check out the two excellent Chapter 4 Sims over at **http:// totalsem.com/007**. Both the Show and the Challenge titled "Manage Duplex Settings" help reinforce the concepts of full-duplex and half-duplex.

Gigabit Ethernet

By the end of the 1990s, the true speed junkie needed an even more powerful version of Ethernet. In response, the IEEE created *Gigabit Ethernet*, which today is the most common type of Ethernet found on new NICs.

The IEEE approved two different versions of Gigabit Ethernet. The most widely implemented solution, published under the IEEE *802.3ab* standard, is called *1000BaseT*. The other version, published under the *802.3z* standard and known as *1000BaseX*, is divided into a series of standards, with names such as 1000BaseSX and 1000BaseLX.

1000BaseT uses four-pair UTP or STP cabling to achieve gigabit performance. Like 10BaseT and 100BaseT, 1000BaseT has a maximum cable length of 100 meters on a segment. 1000BaseT connections and ports look exactly like the ones on a 10BaseT or 100BaseT network. 1000BaseT is the dominant Gigabit Ethernet standard.

NOTE The term *Gigabit Ethernet* is more commonly used than *1000BaseT*.

The 802.3z standards require a bit more discussion. Let's look at each of these solutions in detail to see how they work.

EXAM TIP The vast majority of network rollouts in offices use a base of 1000BaseT connections (or *drops*, as you'll hear them called). You can imagine any number of appropriate scenarios for using 1000BaseT. Many offices also add in wireless today. We'll get there in Chapter 14.

1000BaseSX

Many networks upgrading to Gigabit Ethernet use the *1000BaseSX* standard. 1000BaseSX uses multimode fiber-optic cabling to connect systems, with a generous maximum cable length of 220 to 500 meters; the exact length is left up to the various manufacturers. 1000BaseSX uses an 850-nm (nanometer) wavelength LED to transmit light on the fiber-optic cable. 1000BaseSX devices look similar to 100BaseFX devices, and although both standards can use several types of connectors, 1000BaseSX devices commonly use LC, while 100BaseFX devices frequently use SC. (See "SFF Fiber Connectors" later in the chapter for the scoop on LC connectors.)

EXAM TIP The *wavelength* of a particular signal (laser, in this case) refers to the distance the signal has to travel before it completes its particular shape and starts to repeat. The different colors of the laser signals feature different wavelengths.

1000BaseLX

1000BaseLX is the long-distance carrier for Gigabit Ethernet. 1000BaseLX uses lasers on single-mode cables to shoot data at distances up to 5 kilometers—and some manufacturers use special repeaters to increase that to distances as great as 70 kilometers! The Ethernet folks are trying to position this as the Ethernet backbone of the future, and already some large carriers are beginning to adopt 1000BaseLX. You may live your whole life and never see a 1000BaseLX device, but odds are good that you will encounter connections that use such devices in the near future. 1000BaseLX connectors look like 1000BaseSX connectors.

SFF Fiber Connectors

Around the time that Gigabit Ethernet first started to appear, two problems began to surface with ST and SC connectors. First, ST connectors are relatively large, twist-on connectors, requiring the installer to twist the cable when inserting or removing it. Twisting is not a popular action with fiber-optic cables, as the delicate fibers may fracture. Also, big-fingered techs have a problem with ST connectors if the connectors are too closely packed: they can't get their fingers around them.

SC connectors snap in and out, making them much more popular than STs. SC connectors are also large, however, and the folks who make fiber networking equipment wanted to pack more connectors onto their boxes.

This brought about two new types of fiber connectors, known generically as *small form factor (SFF)* connectors. The first SFF connector—the *Mechanical Transfer Registered Jack (MT-RJ)*, shown in Chapter 2—gained popularity with important companies like Cisco and is still quite common.

You read about the second type of popular SFF connector, the *LC*, in Chapter 2, "Cabling and Topology"—it's shown in Figure 4-7. LC-type connectors are very popular, particularly in the United States, and many fiber experts consider the LC-type connector to be the predominant fiber connector.

Figure 4-7
LC-type
connector

LC and MT-RJ are the most popular types of SFF fiber connectors, but many others exist, as outlined in Table 4-1. The fiber industry has no standard beyond ST and SC connectors, which means that different makers of fiber equipment may have different connections.

Standard	Cabling	Cable Details	Connectors	Length
1000BaseSX	Multimode fiber	850 nm	Variable, commonly LC	220–500 m
1000BaseLX	Single-mode fiber	1300 nm	Variable, commonly LC and SC	5 km
1000BaseT	Cat 5e/6 UTP	Four-pair/full-duplex	RJ-45	100 m

Table 4-1 Gigabit Ethernet Summary

Mechanical Connection Variations

Aside from the various connection types (LC, MT-RJ, and so on), fiber connectors vary in the connection point. The standard connector type today is called a *Physical Contact (PC) connector* because the two pieces of fiber touch when inserted. These connectors replace the older *flat-surface connector* that left a little gap between the connection points due to imperfections in the glass. PC connectors are highly polished and slightly spherical, reducing the signal loss at the connection point.

Two technologies have dropped in price and have replaced PC connectors in some implementations: UPC and APC. *Ultra Physical Contact (UPC) connectors* are polished extensively for a superior finish. These reduce signal loss significantly over PC connectors. *Angled Physical Contact (APC) connectors* add an 8-degree angle to the curved end, lowering signal loss further. Plus, their connection does not degrade from multiple insertions, unlike earlier connection types.

EXAM TIP As of this writing, the CompTIA Network+ Acronyms list incorrectly identifies the "P" in UPC and APC as "Polished." It's "Physical" as indicated here, but don't get thrown off on the exam.

So, note that when you purchase fiber cables today, you'll see the connector type and the contact type, plus the type of cable and other physical dimensions. A typical patch cable, for example, would be an SC/UPC single-mode fiber of a specific length.

Implementing Multiple Types of Gigabit Ethernet

Because Ethernet frames don't vary among the many flavors of Ethernet, network hardware manufacturers have long built devices capable of supporting more than one flavor right out of the box.

You can also use dedicated *media converters* to connect any type of Ethernet cabling together. Most media converters are plain-looking boxes with a port or dongle on either side with placement between two segments. They come in all flavors:

- Single-mode fiber (SMF) to UTP/STP
- Multimode fiber (MMF) to UTP/STP
- Fiber to coaxial
- SMF to MMF

Eventually, the Gigabit Ethernet folks created a standard for modular ports called a *gigabit interface converter (GBIC)*. With many Gigabit Ethernet switches and other hardware, you can simply pull out a GBIC *transceiver*—the connecting module—that supports one flavor of Gigabit Ethernet and plug in another. You can replace an RJ-45 port GBIC, for example, with an SC GBIC, and it'll work just fine. In this kind of scenario, electronically, the switch or other gigabit device is just that—Gigabit Ethernet—so the physical connections don't matter. Ingenious!

Many switches and other network equipment use a much smaller modular transceiver, called a *small form-factor pluggable (SFP)*. Hot-swappable like the GBIC transceivers, the SFPs take up a lot less space and support all the same networking standards.

Ethernet Evolutions

The vast majority of wired networks today feature Gigabit Ethernet, which seems plenty fast for current networking needs. That has not stopped developers and manufacturers from pushing well beyond those limits. This last section looks at high-speed Ethernet standards: 10/40/100 gigabit.

10 Gigabit Ethernet

Developers continue to refine and increase Ethernet networking speeds, especially in the LAN environment and in backbones. *10 Gigabit Ethernet (10 GbE)* offers speeds of up to 10 gigabits per second, as its name indicates.

10 GbE has a number of fiber standards and two copper standards. While designed with fiber optics in mind, copper 10 GbE can still often pair excellent performance with cost savings. As a result, you'll find a mix of fiber and copper in data centers today.

Fiber-Based 10 GbE

When the IEEE members sat down to formalize specifications on Ethernet running at 10 Gbps, they faced an interesting task in several ways. First, they had to maintain the integrity of the Ethernet frame. Data is king, after all, and the goal was to create a network that could interoperate with any other Ethernet network. Second, they had to figure out how to transfer those frames at such blazing speeds. This second challenge had some interesting ramifications because of two factors. They could use the traditional Physical layer mechanisms defined by the Ethernet standard. But a perfectly usable ~10-Gbps fiber network, called *Synchronous Optical Network (SONET)*, was already in place and being used for wide area networking (WAN) transmissions. What to do?

 NOTE Chapter 13 covers SONET in great detail. For now, think of it as a data transmission standard that's different from the LAN Ethernet standard.

The IEEE created a whole set of 10 GbE standards that could use traditional LAN Physical layer mechanisms, plus a set of standards that could take advantage of the SONET infrastructure and run over the WAN fiber. To make the 10-Gbps jump as easy as possible, the IEEE also recognized the need for different networking situations. Some implementations require data transfers that can run long distances over single-mode fiber, for example, whereas others can make do with short-distance transfers over multimode fiber. This led to a lot of standards for 10 GbE.

The 10 GbE standards are defined by several factors: the type of fiber used, the wavelength of the laser or lasers, and the Physical layer signaling type. These factors also define the maximum signal distance.

The IEEE uses specific letter codes with the standards to help sort out the differences so you know what you're implementing or supporting. All the standards have names in the following format: "10GBase" followed by two other characters, what I'll call xy. The x stands for the type of fiber (usually, though not officially) and the wavelength of the laser signal; the y stands for the Physical layer signaling standard. The y code is always either R for LAN-based signaling or W for SONET/WAN-based signaling. The x differs a little more, so let's take a look.

10GBaseSy uses a short-wavelength (850 nm) signal over multimode fiber. The maximum fiber length is 300 meters, although this length will vary depending on the type of multimode fiber used. *10GBaseSR* is used for Ethernet LANs, and *10GBaseSW* is used to connect to SONET devices.

Standard	Fiber Type	Wavelength	Physical Layer Signaling	Maximum Signal Length
10GBaseSR	Multimode	850 nm	LAN	26–300 m
10GBaseSW	Multimode	850 nm	SONET/WAN	26–300 m

10GBaseLy uses a long-wavelength (1310 nm) signal over single-mode fiber. The maximum fiber length is 10 kilometers, although this length will vary depending on the type of single-mode fiber used. *10GBaseLR* connects to Ethernet LANs and *10GBaseLW* connects to SONET equipment. 10GBaseLR is the most popular and least expensive 10 GbE media type.

Standard	Fiber Type	Wavelength	Physical Layer Signaling	Maximum Signal Length
10GBaseLR	Single-mode	1310 nm	LAN	10 km
10GBaseLW	Single-mode	1310 nm	SONET/WAN	10 km

10GBaseEy uses an extra-long-wavelength (1550 nm) signal over single-mode fiber. The maximum fiber length is 40 kilometers, although this length will vary depending on the type of single-mode fiber used. *10GBaseER* works with Ethernet LANs and *10GBaseEW* connects to SONET equipment.

Standard	Fiber Type	Wavelength	Physical Layer Signaling	Maximum Signal Length
10GBaseER	Single-mode	1550 nm	LAN	40 km
10GBaseEW	Single-mode	1550 nm	SONET/WAN	40 km

The 10 GbE fiber standards do not define the type of connector to use and instead leave that to manufacturers (see the upcoming section "10 GbE Physical Connections").

The Other 10 GbE Fiber Standards

Manufacturers have shown both creativity and innovation in taking advantage of both existing fiber and the most cost-effective equipment. This has led to a variety of standards that are not covered by the CompTIA Network+ exam objectives, but that you should know about nevertheless. The top three as of this writing are 10GBaseL4, 10GBaseRM, and 10GBaseZR.

The *10GBaseL4* standard uses four lasers at a 1300-nanometer wavelength over legacy fiber. On multimode cable, 10GBaseL4 can support up to 300-meter transmissions. The range increases to 10 kilometers over single-mode fiber.

The *10GBaseLRM* standard uses the long-wavelength signal of 10GBaseLR but over legacy multimode fiber. The standard can achieve a range of up to 220 meters, depending on the grade of fiber cable.

Finally, some manufacturers have adopted the *10GBaseZR* "standard," which isn't part of the IEEE standards at all (unlike 10GBaseL4 and 10GBaseLRM). Instead, the manufacturers have created their own set of specifications. 10GBaseZR networks use a 1550-nanometer wavelength over single-mode fiber to achieve a range of a whopping 80 kilometers. The standard can work with both Ethernet LAN and SONET/WAN infrastructure.

Copper-Based 10 GbE

It took until 2006 for IEEE to come up with a standard for 10 GbE running on twisted pair cabling—called, predictably, 10GBaseT. *10GBaseT* looks and works exactly like the slower versions of UTP Ethernet. The only downside is that 10GBaseT running on Cat 6 has a maximum cable length of only 55 meters. The Cat 6a standard enables 10GBaseT to run at the standard distance of 100 meters. Table 4-2 summarizes the 10 GbE standards.

Standard	Cabling	Wavelength/ Cable Details	Connectors	Length
10GBaseSR/SW	Multimode fiber	850 nm	Not defined	26–300 m
10GBaseLR/LW	Single-mode fiber	1310 nm	Variable, commonly LC	10 km
10GBaseER/EW	Single-mode fiber	1550 nm	Variable, commonly LC and SC	40 km
10GBaseT	Cat 6/6a UTP	Four-pair/ full-duplex	RJ-45	55/100 m

Table 4-2 10 GbE Summary

10 GbE Physical Connections

This hodgepodge of 10 GbE types might have been the ultimate disaster for hardware manufacturers. All types of 10 GbE send and receive the same signal; only the physical medium is different. Imagine a single router that had to come out in seven different versions to match all these types! Instead, the 10 GbE industry simply chose not to define the connector types and devised a very clever, very simple concept called *multisource agreements (MSAs)*: agreements among multiple manufacturers to make interoperable devices and standards. A transceiver based on an MSA plugs into your 10 GbE equipment, enabling you to convert from one media type to another by inserting the right transceiver. Figure 4-8 shows a typical module called XENPAK.

Figure 4-8
XENPAK
transceiver

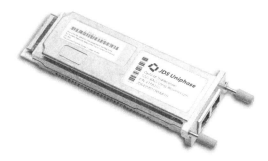

NOTE At the time of this writing, the CompTIA Network+ Acronyms list incorrectly identifies MSA as Master Service Agreement. This chapter uses the correct identification as multisource agreements. You're unlikely to see either term on the exam.

One of the most popular transceivers currently used in 10 GbE is called the *enhanced small form-factor pluggable (SFP+)*, shown in Figure 4-9.

Figure 4-9
SFP+ transceiver
(Photo courtesy
of D-Link)

Characteristics of Fiber Transceivers

Up to this point, the book has described the most common forms of fiber-optic networking, where fiber is installed in pairs, with one cable to send and the other to receive. This is still the most common fiber-based networking solution out there. All the transceivers used in these technologies have two connectors, a standard *duplex* format.

Manufacturers have developed technology that relies on *wave division multiplexing (WDM)* to differentiate wave signals on a single fiber, creating *single strand fiber transmission. Bidirectional (BiDi) transceivers* (Figure 4-10) have only a single optical port designed inside to send on one wavelength, such as 1310 nm, and receive on a different wavelength, such as 1550 nm. A corresponding BiDi transceiver must be installed on the other end of the fiber for this to work.

Figure 4-10
Cisco BiDi
transceiver

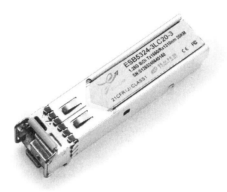

BiDi technology has a couple of notable advantages over its dual-fiber predecessors. First, it costs less to deploy in a new network. You can establish the same level of network performance using half the number of fiber runs. Second, you can use existing fiber runs to rapidly double the capacity of a network. Replace the duplex transceivers with twice the number of BiDi transceivers and plug in the fiber.

Gigabit BiDi transceivers typically use SFP optics. Most 10GBase BiDi transceivers use SFP+ connectors. 40GBase BiDi transceivers use *quad small form-factor pluggable (QSFP)* optics. (See "Beyond Network+" for the scoop on 40-gigabit Ethernet.)

Backbones

The beauty and the challenge of the vast selection of Ethernet flavors is deciding which one to use in your network. The goal is to give your users the fastest network response time possible while keeping costs reasonable. To achieve this balance, most network administrators find that a multispeed Ethernet network works best. In a multispeed network, a series of high-speed (relative to the rest of the network) switches maintain a backbone network. No computers, other than possibly servers, attach directly to this backbone. Figure 4-11 shows a typical backbone network. Each floor has its own switch that connects to every node on the floor. In turn, each of these switches also has a separate high-speed connection to a main switch that resides in the office's computer room.

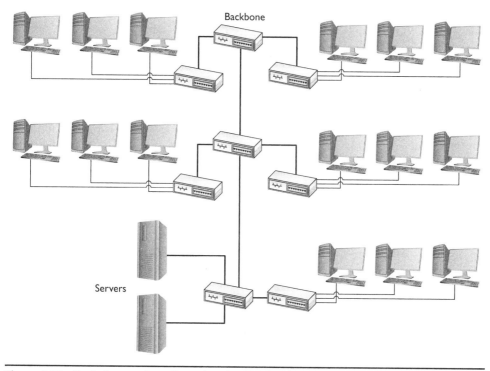

Figure 4-11   Typical network configuration showing backbone (pun intended)

To make this work, you need switches with separate, dedicated, high-speed ports like the ones shown in Figure 4-12. The ports (often fiber) on the switches run straight to the high-speed backbone switch.

Figure 4-12
Switches with
dedicated, high-
speed ports

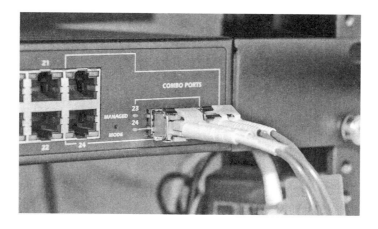

Try This!

Shopping for Switches

Cisco, one of the industry leaders for Ethernet switches, has a great Web site for its products. Imagine that you are setting up a network for your school or business (keep it simple and pick a single building if you're in a large organization). Decide what type of switches you'd like to use, including both the backbone and local switches. If you're really motivated, decide where to locate the switches physically. Don't be afraid to try a fiber backbone—almost every Cisco switch comes with special ports to enable you to pick the type of Ethernet you want to use for your backbone.

Beyond Network+

IEEE 802.3ba

Way back in 2010, the IEEE 802.3ba committee approved standards for 40- and 100-Gb Ethernet, *40 Gigabit Ethernet (40 GbE)* and *100 Gigabit Ethernet (100 GbE)*, respectively. Both standards, in their many varieties, use the same frame as the slow-by-comparison earlier versions of Ethernet, so with the right switches, you've got perfect interoperability. Various committees are currently at work on expanding the 40 GbE and 100 GbE offerings, none of which you'll see on the CompTIA Network+ exam.

The 40 GbE and 100 GbE standards are primarily implemented in backbones and machine-to-machine connections. These standards aren't something you'll see in a LAN . . . yet.

Chapter Review

Questions

1. With 100BaseT, what is the maximum distance between the hub (or switch) and the node?

   A. 1000 meters

   B. 400 meters

   C. 100 meters

   D. 150 meters

2. What type of cable and connector does 100BaseFX use?

    A. Multimode fiber with ST or SC connectors

    B. STP Cat 6 with RJ-45 connectors

    C. Single-mode fiber with MT-RJ connectors

    D. UTP Cat 5e with RJ-45 connectors

3. How many pairs of wires do 10BaseT and 100BaseT use?

    A. 4

    B. 1

    C. 3

    D. 2

4. What standard does IEEE 802.3ab describe?

    A. 1000BaseLX

    B. 1000BaseT

    C. 100BaseT

    D. 1000BaseSX

5. What is the big physical difference between 1000BaseSX and 100BaseFX?

    A. 1000BaseSX uses the SC connector exclusively.

    B. 1000BaseSX is single-mode, whereas 100BaseFX is multimode.

    C. 1000BaseSX uses the ST connector exclusively.

    D. There is no difference.

6. What is the maximum distance for 1000BaseLX without repeaters?

    A. 1 mile

    B. 2500 meters

    C. 20,000 feet

    D. 5000 meters

7. What is a big advantage to using fiber-optic cable?

    A. Fiber is common glass; therefore, it's less expensive.

    B. Fiber is not affected by EMI.

    C. Making custom cable lengths is easier with fiber.

    D. All that orange fiber looks impressive in the network closet.

8. How many wire pairs does 1000BaseT use?

    A. 1

    B. 2

    C. 3

    D. 4

9. What is the standard connector for the 10 GbE fiber standard?

   A. ST

   B. SC

   C. MT-RJ

   D. There is no standard.

10. What is the maximum cable length of 10GBaseT on Cat 6?

   A. 55 meters

   B. 100 meters

   C. 20 meters

   D. 70 meters

Answers

1. **C.** The maximum distance is 100 meters.

2. **A.** 100BaseFX uses multimode fiber with either ST or SC connectors.

3. **D.** 10BaseT and 100BaseT use two wire pairs.

4. **B.** IEEE 802.3ab is the 1000BaseT standard (also known as Gigabit Ethernet).

5. **A.** While 1000BaseSX looks similar to 100BaseFX, the former does not allow the use of the ST connector.

6. **D.** 1000BaseLX can go for 5000 meters (5 kilometers).

7. **B.** Because fiber uses glass and light, it is not affected by EMI.

8. **D.** 1000BaseT uses all four pairs of wires.

9. **D.** There is no standard connector; the 10 GbE committee has left this up to the manufacturers.

10. **A.** With Cat 6 cable, 10GBaseT is limited to 55 meters.

Installing a Physical Network

The CompTIA Network+ certification exam expects you to know how to

- 2.1 Given a scenario, deploy the appropriate cabling solution
- 3.1 Given a scenario, use appropriate documentation and diagrams to manage the network
- 3.2 Compare and contrast business continuity and disaster recovery concepts
- 5.3 Given a scenario, troubleshoot common wired connectivity and performance issues

To achieve these goals, you must be able to

- Recognize and describe the functions of basic components in a structured cabling system
- Explain the process of installing structured cable
- Install a network interface card
- Perform basic troubleshooting on a structured cable network

Armed with the knowledge of previous chapters, it's time to start going about the business of actually constructing a physical network. This might seem easy; after all, the most basic network is nothing more than a switch with a number of cables snaking out to all of the PCs on the network (Figure 5-1).

Figure 5-1
What an orderly
looking network!

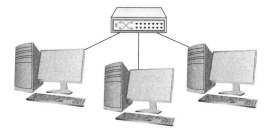

On the surface, such a network setup is absolutely correct, but if you tried to run a network using only a switch and cables running to each system, you'd have some serious practical issues. In the real world, you need to deal with physical obstacles like walls and ceilings.

You also need to deal with those annoying things called *people*. People are incredibly adept at destroying physical networks. They unplug switches, trip over cables, and rip connectors out of NICs with incredible consistency unless you protect the network from their destructive ways. Although the simplified switch-and-a-bunch-of-cables type of network can function in the real world, the network clearly has some problems that need addressing before it can work safely and efficiently (Figure 5-2).

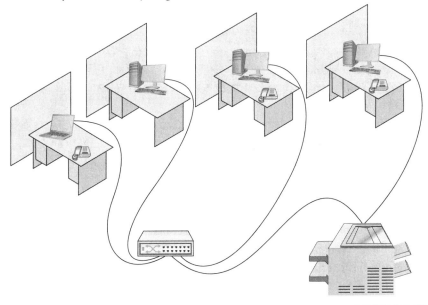

Figure 5-2   A real-world network

This chapter takes the abstract discussion of network technologies from previous chapters into the concrete reality of real networks. To achieve this goal, it marches you through the process of installing an entire network system from the beginning. The chapter starts by introducing you to *structured cabling*, the critical set of standards used all over the world to install physical cabling in a safe and orderly fashion. It then delves into the world of larger networks—those with more than a single switch—and shows you some typical methods used to organize them for peak efficiency and reliability. Next, you'll take a quick tour of the most common NICs used in PCs and see what it takes to install them. Finally, you'll look at how to troubleshoot cabling and other network devices, including an introduction to some fun diagnostic tools.

Historical/Conceptual

Understanding Structured Cabling

If you want a functioning, dependable, real-world network, you need a solid understanding of a set of standards, collectively called *structured cabling*. These standards, defined by the Telecommunications Industry Association/Electronic Industries Alliance

(TIA/EIA)—yup, the same folks who tell you how to crimp an RJ-45 onto the end of a UTP cable—give professional cable installers detailed standards on every aspect of a cabled network, from the type of cabling to use to the position of wall outlets.

NOTE EIA ceased operations in 2011, but various groups (like TIA) maintain the standards. Expect to see EIA on the CompTIA Network+ exam.

The CompTIA Network+ exam requires you to understand the basic concepts involved in designing a network and installing network cabling and to recognize the components used in a real network. The CompTIA Network+ exam does not, however, expect you to be as knowledgeable as a professional network designer or cable installer. Your goal is to understand enough about real-world cabling systems to communicate knowledgeably with cable installers and to perform basic troubleshooting. Granted, by the end of this chapter, you'll have enough of an understanding to try running your own cable (I certainly run my own cable), but consider that knowledge a handy bit of extra credit.

The idea of structured cabling is to create a safe, reliable cabling infrastructure for all of the devices that may need interconnection. Certainly this applies to computer networks, but also to telephone, video—anything that might need low-power, distributed cabling.

NOTE A structured cabling system is useful for more than just computer networks. You'll find structured cabling defining telephone networks and video conferencing setups, for example.

You should understand three issues with structured cabling. Cable basics start the picture, with switches, cabling, and PCs. You'll then look at the components of a network, such as how the cable runs through the walls and where it ends up. This section wraps up with an assessment of connections leading outside your network.

NOTE Many networks today have a wireless component in addition to a wired infrastructure. The switches, servers, and workstations rely on wires for fast networking, but the wireless component supports workers on the move, such as salespeople.

This chapter focuses on the wired infrastructure. Once we get through Wi-Fi in Chapter 14, "Wireless Networking," I'll add that component to our networking conversation.

Cable Basics—A Star Is Born

This exploration of the world of connectivity hardware starts with the most basic of all networks: a switch, some UTP cable, and a few PCs—in other words, a typical physical star network (Figure 5-3).

Figure 5-3
A switch
connected by
UTP cable to
two PCs

No law of physics prevents you from installing a switch in the middle of your office and running cables on the floor to all the computers in your network. This setup works, but it falls apart spectacularly when applied to a real-world environment. Three problems present themselves to the network tech. First, the exposed cables running along the floor are just waiting for someone to trip over them, damaging the network and giving that person a wonderful lawsuit opportunity. Possible accidents aside, simply moving and stepping on the cabling will, over time, cause a cable to fail due to wires breaking or RJ-45 connectors ripping off cable ends. Second, the presence of other electrical devices close to the cable can create interference that confuses the signals going through the wire. Third, this type of setup limits your ability to make any changes to the network. Before you can change anything, you have to figure out which cables in the huge rat's nest of cables connected to the switch go to which machines. Imagine *that* troubleshooting nightmare!

"Gosh," you're thinking (okay, I'm thinking it, but you should be, too), "there must be a better way to install a physical network." A better installation would provide safety, protecting the star from vacuum cleaners, clumsy coworkers, and electrical interference. It would have extra hardware to organize and protect the cabling. Finally, the new and improved star network installation would feature a cabling standard with the flexibility to enable the network to grow according to its needs and then to upgrade when the next great network technology comes along.

As you have no doubt guessed, I'm not just theorizing here. In the real world, the people who most wanted improved installation standards were the ones who installed cable for a living. In response to this demand, the TIA/EIA developed standards for cable installation. The TIA/EIA 568 standards you learned about in earlier chapters are only part of a larger set of TIA/EIA standards all lumped together under the umbrella of structured cabling.

 NOTE Installing structured cabling properly takes a startlingly high degree of skill. Thousands of pitfalls await inexperienced network people who think they can install their own network cabling. Pulling cable requires expensive equipment, a lot of hands, and the ability to react to problems quickly. Network techs can cost employers a lot of money—not to mention losing their good jobs—by imagining they can do it themselves without the proper knowledge.

If you are interested in learning more details about structured cabling, an organization called the Building Industry Consulting Service International (BICSI; www.bicsi.org) provides a series of widely recognized certifications for the cabling industry.

Test Specific

Structured Cable—Network Components

Successful implementation of a basic structured cabling network requires three essential ingredients: a telecommunications room, horizontal cabling, and a work area. Let's zero in on one floor of Figure 4-11 from the previous chapter. All the cabling runs from individual PCs to a central location, the *telecommunications room* (Figure 5-4). What equipment goes in there—a switch or a telephone system—is not the important thing. What matters is that all the cables concentrate in this one area.

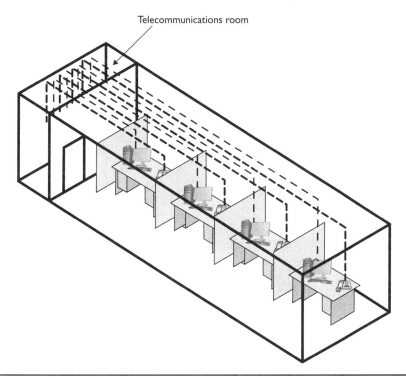

Figure 5-4 Telecommunications room

All cables run horizontally (for the most part) from the telecommunications room to the PCs. This cabling is called, appropriately, *horizontal cabling*. A single piece of installed horizontal cabling is called a *run*. At the opposite end of the horizontal cabling from the telecommunications room is the work area. The *work area* is often simply an office or cubicle that potentially contains a PC and a telephone. Figure 5-5 shows both the horizontal cabling and work areas.

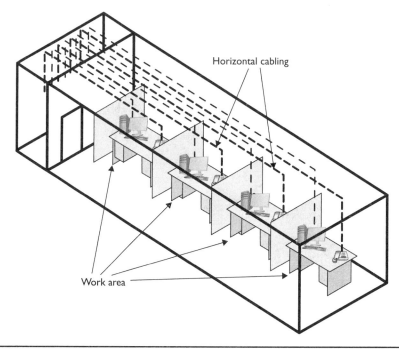

Figure 5-5   Horizontal cabling and work area

Each of the three parts of a basic star network—the telecommunications room, the horizontal cabling, and the work area(s)—must follow a series of strict standards designed to ensure that the cabling system is reliable and easy to manage. The cabling standards set by TIA/EIA enable techs to make sensible decisions on equipment installed in the telecommunications room, so let's tackle horizontal cabling first, and then return to the telecommunications room. We'll finish up with the work area.

Horizontal Cabling

A horizontal cabling run is the cabling that goes more or less horizontally from a work area to the telecommunications room. In most networks, this cable is Cat 5e or better UTP, but when you move into structured cabling, the TIA/EIA standards define a number of other aspects of the cable, such as the type of wires, number of pairs of wires, and fire ratings.

EXAM TIP   A single piece of cable that runs from a work area to a telecommunications room is called a *run*.

Solid Core vs. Stranded Core   All UTP cables come in one of two types: solid core or stranded core. Each wire in *solid core* UTP uses a single solid wire. With *stranded core*, each wire is actually a bundle of tiny wire strands. Each of these cable types has its benefits and downsides. Solid core is a better conductor, but it is stiff and will break if handled too often or too roughly. Stranded core is not quite as good a conductor, but it will stand up to substantial handling without breaking. Figure 5-6 shows a close-up of solid and stranded core UTP.

Figure 5-6
Solid and
stranded core
UTP

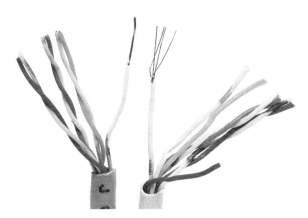

TIA/EIA specifies that horizontal cabling should always be solid core. Remember, this cabling is going into your walls and ceilings, safe from the harmful effects of shoes and vacuum cleaners. The ceilings and walls enable you to take advantage of the better conductivity of solid core without the risk of cable damage. Stranded core cable also has an important function in a structured cabling network, but I need to discuss a few more parts of the network before I talk about where to use stranded core UTP cable.

Number of Pairs   Pulling horizontal cables into your walls and ceilings is a time-consuming and messy business, and not a process you want to repeat, if at all possible. For this reason, most cable installers recommend using the highest Cat rating you can afford. Many years ago, I would also mention that you should use four-pair UTP, but today, four-pair is assumed. Four-pair UTP is so common that it's difficult, if not impossible, to find two-pair UTP.

NOTE   Unlike previous Cat standards, TIA/EIA defines Cat 5e and later as four-pair-only cables.

You'll find larger bundled UTP cables in higher-end telephone setups. These cables hold 25 or even 100 pairs of wires (Figure 5-7).

Choosing Your Horizontal Cabling   In the real world, network people only install Cat 5e or Cat 6 UTP, although Cat 6a is also starting to show up as 10GBaseT begins to see acceptance. Installing higher-rated cabling is done primarily as a hedge against new network

Figure 5-7
25-pair UTP

technologies that may require a more advanced cable. Networking *caveat emptor* (buyer beware): many network installers take advantage of the fact that a lower Cat level will work on most networks and bid a network installation using the lowest-grade cable possible.

The Telecommunications Room

The telecommunications room is the heart of the basic star. This room—technically called the *intermediate distribution frame (IDF)*—is where all the horizontal runs from all the work areas come together. The concentration of all this gear in one place makes the telecommunications room potentially one of the messiest parts of the basic star. Even if you do a nice, neat job of organizing the cables when they are first installed, networks change over time. People move computers, new work areas are added, network topologies are added or improved, and so on. Unless you impose some type of organization, this conglomeration of equipment and cables decays into a nightmarish mess.

NOTE   The telecommunications room is also known as the *intermediate distribution frame (IDF)*, as opposed to the main distribution frame (MDF), which we will discuss later in the chapter.

Fortunately, the TIA/EIA structured cabling standards define the use of specialized components in the telecommunications room that make organizing a snap. In fact, it might be fair to say that there are too many options! To keep it simple, we're going to stay with the most common telecommunications room setup and then take a short peek at some other fairly common options.

Equipment Racks   The central component of every telecommunications room is one or more equipment racks. An *equipment rack* provides a safe, stable platform for all the different hardware components. All equipment racks are 19 inches wide, but they vary in height from two- to three-foot-high models that bolt onto a wall (Figure 5-8) to the more popular floor-to-ceiling models, free-standing racks (Figure 5-9).

Figure 5-8
A short
equipment rack

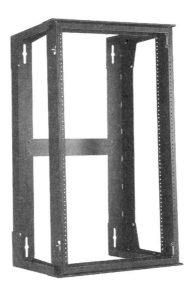

 NOTE Equipment racks evolved out of the railroad signaling racks from the 19th century. The components in a rack today obviously differ a lot from railroad signaling, but the 19-inch width has remained the standard for well over a hundred years.

You can mount almost any network hardware component into a rack. All manufacturers make rack-mounted switches that mount into a rack with a few screws. These switches are available with a wide assortment of ports and capabilities. There are even rack-mounted servers, complete with slide-out keyboards, and rack-mounted uninterruptible power supplies (UPSs) to power the equipment (Figure 5-10).

Figure 5-9
A free-standing
rack

Figure 5-10
A rack-mounted
UPS

All rack-mounted equipment uses a height measurement known simply as a *unit (U)*. A U is 1.75 inches. A device that fits in a 1.75-inch space is called a 1U; a device designed for a 3.5-inch space is a 2U; and a device that goes into a 7-inch space is called a 4U. Most rack-mounted devices are 1U, 2U, or 4U. The rack in Figure 5-10 is called a 42U rack to reflect the total number of Us it can hold.

The key when planning a rack system is to determine what sort of rack-mounted equipment you plan to have and then get the rack or racks for your space. For example, if your rack will only have patch panels (see the next section), switches, and routers, you can get away with a *two-post rack*. The pieces are small and easily supported.

If you're going to install big servers, on the other hand, then you need to plan for a *four-post rack* or a *server rail rack*. A four-post rack supports all four corners of the server. The server rail rack enables you to slide the server out so you can open it up. This is very useful for swapping out dead drives for new ones in big file servers.

When planning how many racks you need in your rack system and where to place them, take proper air flow into consideration. You shouldn't cram servers and gear into every corner. Even with good air conditioning systems, bad air flow can cook components.

Finally, make sure to secure the telecommunications room. Rack security is a must for protecting valuable equipment. Get a lock!

Patch Panels and Cables Ideally, once you install horizontal cabling, you should never move it. As you know, UTP horizontal cabling has a solid core, making it pretty stiff. Solid core cables can handle some rearranging, but if you insert a wad of solid core cables directly into your switches, every time you move a cable to a different port on the switch, or move the switch itself, you will jostle the cable. You don't have to move a solid core cable many times before one of the solid copper wires breaks, and there goes a network connection!

Luckily for you, you can easily avoid this problem by using a patch panel. A *patch panel* is simply a box with a row of female ports in the front and permanent connections in the back, to which you connect the horizontal cables (Figure 5-11).

Figure 5-11
Typical patch
panels

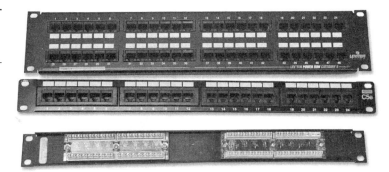

The most common type of patch panel today uses a special type of connector called a *110 block*, or sometimes called a *110-punchdown block*. UTP cables connect to a 110 block using a *punchdown tool*. Figure 5-12 shows a typical punchdown tool, and Figure 5-13 shows the punchdown tool punching down individual strands.

Figure 5-12
Punchdown tool

Figure 5-13
Punching down
a 110 block

The punchdown block has small metal-lined grooves for the individual wires. The punchdown tool has a blunt end that forces the wire into the groove. The metal in the groove slices the cladding enough to make contact.

NOTE Make sure you insert the wires according to the same standard (TIA/EIA 568A or TIA/EIA 568B) on both ends of the cable. If you don't, you might end up swapping the sending and receiving wires (known as *TX/RX reversed*) and inadvertently creating a crossover cable.

At one time, the older 66-punchdown block patch panel (a *66 block*), found in just about every commercial telephone installation (Figure 5-14), saw some use in PC networks. The 110 block introduces less crosstalk than 66 blocks, so most high-speed network installations use the former for both telephone service and LANs. Given their large installed base, it's still common to find a group of 66-block patch panels in a telecommunications room separate from the network's 110-block patch panels.

Figure 5-14
66-block patch
panels

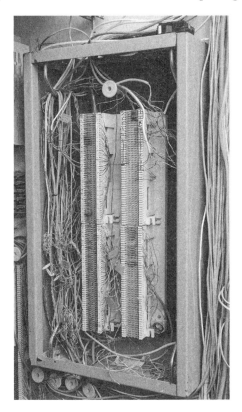

EXAM TIP The CompTIA Network+ exam uses the terms *110 block* and *66 block* exclusively to describe the punchdown blocks common in telecommunication. In the field, in contrast, and in manuals and other literature, you'll see the punchdown blocks referred to as *110-punchdown blocks* and *66-punchdown blocks* as well. Some manufacturers even split punchdown into two words: *punch down*. Be prepared to be nimble in the field, but expect 110 block and 66 block on the exam.

Not only do patch panels prevent the horizontal cabling from being moved, but they are also your first line of defense in organizing the cables. All patch panels have space in the front for labels, and these labels are the network tech's best friend! Simply place a tiny label on the patch panel to identify each cable, and you will never have to experience that sinking feeling of standing in the telecommunications room of your nonfunctioning network, wondering which cable is which. If you want to be a purist, there is an official, and rather confusing, TIA/EIA naming convention called *TIA/EIA 606*, but a number of real-world network techs simply use their own internal codes (Figure 5-15).

Figure 5-15
Typical patch panels with labels

NOTE   The ANSI/TIA-606-C standard covers proper labeling and documentation of cabling, patch panels, and wall outlets. If you want to know how the pros label and document a structured cabling system (and you've got some cash to blow), check out the ANSI/TIA-606-C naming conventions from TIA.

Patch panels are available in a wide variety of configurations that include different types of ports and numbers of ports. You can get UTP, STP, or fiber ports, and some manufacturers combine several different types on the same patch panel. Panels are available with 8, 12, 24, 48, or even more ports.

UTP patch panels, like UTP cables, come with Cat ratings, which you should be sure to check. Don't blow a good Cat 6 cable installation by buying a cheap patch panel—get a Cat 6 patch panel! A Cat 6 panel can handle the 250-MHz frequency used by Cat 6 and offers lower crosstalk and network interference. A higher-rated panel supports earlier standards, so you can use a Cat 6 or even Cat 6a rack with Cat 5e cabling. Most manufacturers proudly display the Cat level right on the patch panel (Figure 5-16).

Figure 5-16
Cat level on a
patch panel

Once you have installed the patch panel, you need to connect the ports to the switch through *patch cables*. Patch cables are short (typically two- to five-foot) straight-through UTP cables. Patch cables use stranded core rather than solid core cable, so they can tolerate much more handling. Even though you can make your own patch cables, most people buy premade ones. Buying patch cables enables you to use different-colored cables to facilitate organization (yellow for accounting, blue for sales, or whatever scheme works for you). Most prefabricated patch cables also come with a reinforced (booted) connector specially designed to handle multiple insertions and removals (Figure 5-17).

Figure 5-17
Typical patch
cable

A telecommunications room doesn't have to be a special room dedicated to computer equipment. You can use specially made cabinets with their own little built-in equipment racks that sit on the floor or attach to a wall, or you can use a storage room if the equipment can be protected from the other items stored there. Fortunately, the demand for telecommunications rooms has been around for so long that most office spaces have premade telecommunications rooms, even if they are no more than closets in smaller offices.

At this point, the network is taking shape (Figure 5-18). The TIA/EIA horizontal cabling is installed and the telecommunications room is configured. Now it's time to address the last part of the structured cabling system: the work area.

Figure 5-18
Network taking
shape, with
racks installed
and horizontal
cabling runs

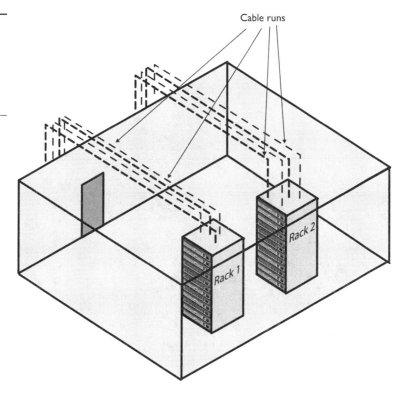

Cable runs

Rack 2

Rack 1

EXAM TIP   Some mission-critical networks require specialized electrical hardware. Although the CompTIA Network+ exam objectives don't refer to these boxes by name—*rack-mounted AC distribution boxes*—they dance around some of the features. Notably, an AC distribution system can supply multiple *dedicated AC circuits* to handle any challenging setups. If you install such a box in your rack, make sure to add labels to both systems and circuits. Proper system labeling and circuit labeling can make life much easier in the event of problems later on.

The Work Area

From a cabling standpoint, a work area is nothing more than a wall outlet that serves as the termination point for horizontal network cables: a convenient insertion point for a PC and a telephone. (In practice, of course, the term "work area" includes the office or cubicle.) A wall outlet itself consists of one or two female jacks to accept the cable, a mounting bracket, and a face-plate. You connect the PC to the wall outlet with a patch cable (Figure 5-19).

Figure 5-19
Typical work area outlet

The female RJ-45 jacks in these wall outlets also have Cat ratings. You must buy Cat-rated jacks for wall outlets to go along with the Cat rating of the cabling in your network. In fact, many network connector manufacturers use the same connectors in the wall outlets that they use on the patch panels. These modular outlets significantly increase ease of installation. Make sure you label the outlet to show the job of each connector (Figure 5-20). A good outlet will also have some form of label that identifies its position on the patch panel. Proper documentation of your outlets will save you an incredible amount of work later.

Figure 5-20
Properly labeled outlet

The last step is connecting the PC to the wall outlet. Here again, most folks use a patch cable. Its stranded core cabling stands up to the abuse caused by moving PCs, not to mention the occasional kick.

You'll recall from Chapter 4, "Modern Ethernet," that 10/100/1000BaseT networks specify a limit of 100 meters between a hub or switch and a node. Interestingly, though, the TIA/EIA 568 specification allows only UTP cable lengths of 90 meters. What's with the missing 10 meters? Have you figured it out? Hint: the answer lies in the discussion we've just been having. Ding! Time's up! The answer is … the patch cables! Patch cables add extra distance between the switch and the PC, so TIA/EIA compensates by reducing the horizontal cabling length.

The work area may be the simplest part of the structured cabling system, but it is also the source of most network failures. When a user can't access the network and you suspect a broken cable, the first place to look is the work area.

Structured Cable—Beyond the Star

Thus far you've seen structured cabling as a single star topology on a single floor of a building. Let's now expand that concept to an entire building and learn the terms used by the structured cabling folks, such as the demarc and NIU, to describe this much more complex setup.

 NOTE Structured cabling goes beyond a single building and even describes methods for interconnecting multiple buildings. The CompTIA Network+ certification exam does not cover interbuilding connections.

You can hardly find a building today that isn't connected to both the Internet and the telephone company. In many cases, this is a single connection, but for now, let's treat them as separate connections.

As you saw in the previous chapter, a typical building-wide network consists of a high-speed backbone that runs vertically through the building and connects to multispeed switches on each floor that, in turn, service the individual PCs on that floor. A dedicated telephone cabling backbone that enables the distribution of phone calls to individual telephones runs alongside the network cabling. While every telephone installation varies, most commonly you'll see one or more 25-pair UTP cables running to the 66 block in the telecommunications room on each floor (Figure 5-21).

Demarc

Connections from the outside world—whether network or telephone—come into a building at a location called a *demarc*, short for *demarcation point*. The term "demarc" refers to the physical location of the connection and marks the dividing line of responsibility for the functioning of the network. You take care of the internal functioning; the person or company that supplies the upstream service to you must support connectivity and function on the far side of the demarc.

In a private home, the DSL or cable modem supplied by your ISP is a *network interface unit (NIU)* that serves as a demarc between your home network and your ISP, and most homes have a network interface box, like the one shown in Figure 5-22, that provides the connection for your telephone.

Figure 5-21
25-pair UTP cables running to local 66 block

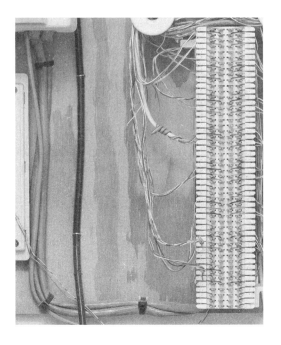

 NOTE The terms used to describe the devices that often mark the demarcation point in a home or office get tossed about with wild abandon. Various manufacturers and technicians call them network interface units, network interface boxes, or network interface devices. (Some techs call them demarcs, just to muddy the waters further, but we won't go there.) By name or by initial—NIU, NIB, or NID—it's all the same thing, the box that marks the point where your responsibility begins on the inside.

Figure 5-22
Typical home network interface box

In an office environment, the demarc is usually more complex, given that a typical building simply has to serve a much larger number of telephones and computers. Figure 5-23 shows the demarc for a midsized building, showing both Internet and telephone connections coming in from the outside.

Figure 5-23
Typical office
demarc

 NOTE   The best way to think of a demarc is in terms of responsibility. If something breaks on one side of the demarc, it's your problem; on the other side, it's the ISP/phone company's problem.

One challenge to companies that supply ISP/telephone services is the need to diagnose faults in the system. Most of today's NIUs come with extra "smarts" that enable the ISP or telephone company to determine if the customer has disconnected from the NIU. These special (and very common) NIUs are known as *smart jacks*. Smart jacks also have the very handy capability to set up a remote loopback—critical for loopback testing when you're at one end of the connection and the other connection is blocks or even miles away.

Connections Inside the Demarc

After the demarc, network and telephone cables connect to some type of box, owned by the customer, that acts as the primary distribution tool for the building. That box is called the *customer-premises equipment (CPE)*. Any cabling that runs from the NIU to whatever CPE is used by the customer is the *demarc extension*. For telephones, the cabling might connect to special CPE called a *multiplexer* and, on the LAN side, almost certainly to a powerful switch. This switch usually connects to a patch panel. This patch panel, in turn, leads to every telecommunications room in the building. This main patch panel is called a *vertical cross-connect*. Figure 5-24 shows an example of a *fiber distribution panel* (or fiber patch panel) acting as a vertical cross-connect for a building.

Figure 5-24
LAN vertical cross-connect

Telephone systems also use vertical cross-connects. Figure 5-25 shows a vertical cross-connect for a telephone system. Note the large number of 25-pair UTP cables feeding out of this box. Each 25-pair cable leads to a telecommunications room on a floor of the building.

Figure 5-25
Telephone vertical cross-connect

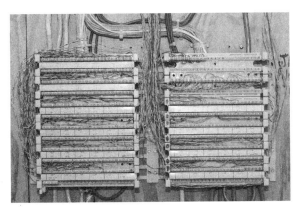

The combination of demarc, telephone cross-connects, and LAN cross-connects needs a place to live in a building. The room that stores all of this equipment is known as a *main distribution frame (MDF)* to distinguish it from the multiple IDF rooms (a.k.a., telecommunications rooms) that serve individual floors.

The ideal that every building should have a single demarc, a single MDF, and multiple IDFs is only that—an ideal. Every structured cabling installation is unique and must adapt to the physical constraints of the building provided. One building may serve multiple customers, creating the need for multiple NIUs each serving a different customer. A smaller building may combine a demarc, MDF, and IDF into a single room. With structured cabling, the idea is to appreciate the terms while, at the same time, appreciating that it's the actual building and the needs of the customers that determine the design of a structured cabling system.

Installing Structured Cabling

A professional installer always begins a structured cabling installation by first assessing your site and planning the installation in detail before pulling a single piece of cable. As the customer, your job is to work closely with the installer. That means locating floor plans, providing access, and even putting on old clothes and crawling along with the installer as he or she combs through your ceilings, walls, and closets. Even though you're not the actual installer, you must understand the installation process to help the installer make the right decisions for your network.

Structured cabling requires a lot of planning. You need to know if the cables from the work areas can reach the telecommunications room—is the distance less than the 90-meter limit dictated by the TIA/EIA standard? How will you route the cable? What path should each run take to get to the wall outlets? Don't forget that just because a cable looks like it will reach, there's no guarantee that it will. Ceilings and walls often include hidden surprises like firewalls—big, thick, concrete walls designed into buildings that require a masonry drill or a jackhammer to punch through. Let's look at the steps that go into proper planning.

Getting a Floor Plan

First, you need a blueprint of the area. If you ever contact an installer and he or she doesn't start by asking for a floor plan, fire them immediately and get one who does. The floor plan is the key to proper planning; a good floor plan shows you the location of closets that could serve as telecommunications rooms, alerts you to any firewalls in your way, and gives you a good overall feel for the scope of the job ahead.

If you don't have a floor plan—and this is often the case with homes or older buildings—you'll need to create your own. Go get a ladder and a flashlight—you'll need them to poke around in ceilings, closets, and crawl spaces as you map out the location of rooms, walls, and anything else of interest to the installation. Figure 5-26 shows a typical do-it-yourself floor plan.

Mapping the Runs

Now that you have your floor plan, you need to map the cable runs. Here's where you survey the work areas, noting the locations of existing or planned systems to determine where to place each cable drop. A *cable drop* is the location where the cable comes out of the wall in the workstation. You should also talk to users, management, and other

Figure 5-26
Network floor
plan

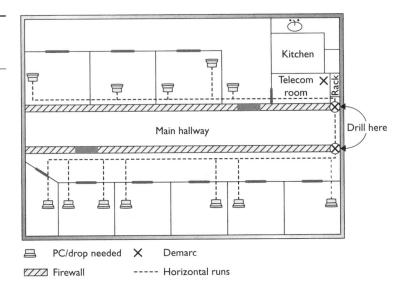

Symbol	Meaning	Symbol	Meaning
🖳	PC/drop needed	✕	Demarc
▨	Firewall	-----	Horizontal runs

interested parties to try to understand their plans for the future. Installing a few extra drops now is much easier than installing them a year from now when those two unused offices suddenly find themselves with users who immediately need networked computers!

EXAM TIP Watch out for the word *drop*, as it has more than one meaning. A single run of cable from the telecommunications room to a wall outlet is often referred to as a "drop." The word "drop" is also used to define a new run coming through a wall outlet that does not yet have a jack installed.

At this point, cost first raises its ugly head. Face it: cables, drops, and the people who install them cost money! The typical price for a network installation is around US $50–150 per drop. Find out how much you want to spend and make some calls. Most network installers price their network jobs by quoting a per-drop cost.

While you're mapping your runs, you have to make another big decision: Do you want to run the cables in the walls or outside them? Many companies sell wonderful external *raceway* products that adhere to your walls, making for a much simpler, though less neat, installation than running cables in the walls (Figure 5-27). Raceways make good sense in older buildings or when you don't have the guts—or the rights—to go into the walls.

Figure 5-27
A typical raceway

Determining the Location of the Telecommunications Room

While mapping the runs, you should decide on the location of your telecommunications room. When deciding on this location, keep five issues in mind:

- **Distance**   The telecommunications room must be located in a spot that won't require cable runs longer than 90 meters. In most locations, keeping runs under 90 meters requires little effort, as long as the telecommunications room is placed in a central location.

- **Power**   Many of the components in your telecommunications room need power. Make sure you provide enough! If possible, put the telecommunications room on its own dedicated circuit; that way, when someone blows a circuit in the kitchen, it doesn't take out the entire network.

- **Humidity**   Electrical components and water don't mix well. (Remind me to tell you about the time I installed a rack in an abandoned bathroom and the toilet that later exploded.) Remember that dryness also means low humidity. Avoid areas with the potential for high humidity, such as a closet near a pool or the room where the cleaning people leave mop buckets full of water. Of course, any well air-conditioned room should be fine—which leads to the next big issue …

- **Cooling**   Telecommunications rooms tend to get warm, especially if you add a couple of server systems and a UPS. Make sure your telecommunications room has an air-conditioning outlet or some other method of keeping the room cool. Figure 5-28 shows how I installed an air-conditioning duct in my small equipment closet. Of course, I did this only after I discovered that the server was repeatedly rebooting due to overheating!

Figure 5-28   An A/C duct cooling a telecommunications room

- **Access**   Access involves two different issues. First, it means preventing unauthorized access. Think about the people you want and don't want messing around with your network, and act accordingly. In my small office, the equipment closet literally sits eight feet from me, so I don't concern myself too much with unauthorized access. You, on the other hand, may want to consider placing a lock on the door of your telecommunications room if you're concerned that unscrupulous or unqualified people might try to access it.

One other issue to keep in mind when choosing your telecommunications room is expandability. Will this telecommunications room be able to grow with your network? Is it close enough to be able to service any additional office space your company may acquire nearby? If your company decides to take over the floor above you, can you easily run vertical cabling to another telecommunications room on that floor from this room? While the specific issues will be unique to each installation, keep thinking "expansion" or *scalability* as you design—your network will grow, whether or not you think so now!

So, you've mapped your cable runs and established your telecommunications room—now you're ready to start pulling cable!

Pulling Cable

Pulling cable is easily one of the most thankless and unpleasant jobs in the entire networking world. It may not look that hard from a distance, but the devil is in the details. First of all, pulling cable requires two people if you want to get the job done quickly; having three people is even better. Most pullers like to start from the telecommunications room and pull toward the drops. In an office area with a drop ceiling, pullers will often feed the cabling along the run by opening ceiling tiles and stringing the cable via hooks or *cable trays* that travel above the ceiling (Figure 5-29). Professional cable pullers have an arsenal of interesting tools to help them move the cable horizontally, including telescoping poles, special nylon pull ropes, and even nifty little crossbows and pistols that can fire a pull rope long distances!

Figure 5-29

Cable trays over a drop ceiling

Cable trays are standard today, but a previous lack of codes or standards for handling cables led to a nightmare of disorganized cables in drop ceilings all over the world. Any cable puller will tell you that the hardest part of installing cables is the need to work around all the old cable installations in the ceiling (Figure 5-30).

Figure 5-30
Messy cabling
nightmare

Local codes, TIA/EIA, and the National Electrical Code (NEC) all have strict rules about how you pull cable in a ceiling. A good installer uses either hooks or trays, which provide better cable management, safety, and protection from electrical interference (Figure 5-31). The faster the network, the more critical good cable management becomes.

Figure 5-31
Nicely run cables

Running cable horizontally requires relatively little effort, compared to running the cable down from the ceiling to a pretty faceplate at the work area, which often takes a lot of skill. In a typical office area with sheetrock walls, the installer first decides on the position for the outlet, generally using a stud finder to avoid cutting on top of a stud. Once the worker cuts the hole (Figure 5-32), most installers drop a line to the hole using a weight tied to the end of a nylon pull rope (Figure 5-33). They can then attach the network cable to the pull rope and pull it down to the hole. Once the cable is pulled through the new hole, the installer puts in an outlet box or a low-voltage *mounting bracket* (Figure 5-34). This bracket acts as a holder for the faceplate.

Figure 5-32
Cutting a hole

Figure 5-33
Locating a dropped pull rope

Figure 5-34
Installing a mounting bracket

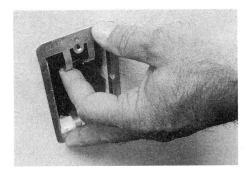

Back in the telecommunications room, the many cables leading to each work area are consolidated and organized in preparation for the next stage: making connections. A truly professional installer takes great care in organizing the equipment closet. Figure 5-35 shows a typical installation using special cable guides to bring the cables down to the equipment rack.

Figure 5-35
End of cables
guided to rack

Making Connections

Making connections consists of connecting both ends of each cable to the proper jacks. This step also includes the most important step in the entire process: testing each cable run to ensure that every connection meets the requirements of the network that will use it. Installers also use this step to document and label each cable run—a critical step too often forgotten by inexperienced installers, and one you need to verify takes place!

Connecting the Work Areas

In the work area, the cable installer connects a cable run by crimping a jack onto the end of the wire and mounting the faceplate to complete the installation (Figure 5-36). Note the back of the jack shown in Figure 5-36. This jack uses the popular 110-punchdown

Figure 5-36
Crimping a jack

connection, just like the one shown earlier in the chapter for patch panels. All 110 connections have a color code that tells you which wire to punch into which connection on the back of the jack.

Rolling Your Own Patch Cables

Although most people prefer simply to purchase premade patch cables, making your own is fairly easy. To make your own, use stranded core UTP cable that matches the Cat level of your horizontal cabling. Stranded core cable also requires specific crimps, so don't use crimps designed for solid core cable. Crimping is simple enough, although getting it right takes some practice.

Figure 5-37 shows the two main tools of the crimping trade: an RJ-45 crimper with built-in wire stripper and a pair of wire snips. Professional cable installers naturally have a wide variety of other tools as well.

Figure 5-37
Crimper and
snips

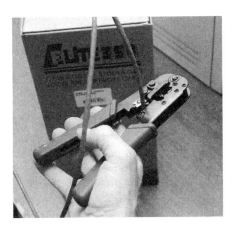

Here are the steps for properly crimping an RJ-45 onto a UTP cable. If you have some crimps, cable, and a crimping tool handy, follow along!

1. Cut the cable square using RJ-45 crimpers or scissors.

2. Strip off ½ inch of plastic jacket from the end of the cable (Figure 5-38) with a dedicated wire stripper or the one built into the crimping tool.

Figure 5-38
Properly stripped
cable

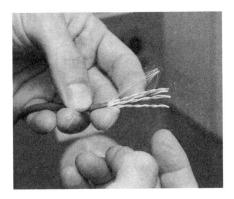

3. Slowly and carefully insert each individual wire into the correct location according to either TIA/EIA 568A or B (Figure 5-39). Unravel as little as possible.

Figure 5-39
Inserting the
individual
strands

4. Insert the crimp into the crimper and press (Figure 5-40). Don't worry about pressing too hard; the crimper has a stop to prevent you from using too much pressure.

Figure 5-40
Crimping the
cable

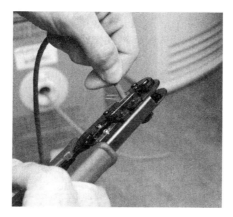

Figure 5-41 shows a nicely crimped cable. Note how the plastic jacket goes into the crimp.

Figure 5-41
Properly crimped
cable

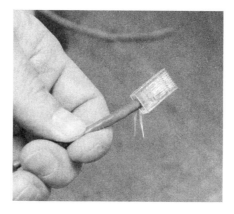

A good patch cable should include a boot. Figure 5-42 shows a boot being slid onto a newly crimped cable. Don't forget to slide each boot onto the patch cable *before* you crimp both ends!

Figure 5-42
Adding a boot

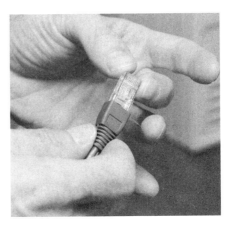

After making a cable, you need to test it to make sure it's properly crimped. Read the section on testing cable runs later in this chapter to see how to test them.

Try This!

Crimping Your Own Cable

If you've got some spare CAT 5 lying around (and what tech enthusiast doesn't?) as well as a cable crimper and some crimps, go ahead and use the previous section as a guide and crimp your own cable. This skill is essential for any network technician. Remember, practice makes perfect!

Connecting the Patch Panels

Connecting the cables to patch panels requires you to deal with three issues. The first issue is patch cable management. Figure 5-43 shows the front of a small network's equipment rack—note the complete lack of cable management!

Managing patch cables means using the proper cable management hardware. Plastic D-rings guide the patch cables neatly along the sides and front of the patch panel. Finger boxes are rectangular cylinders with slots in the front; the patch cables run into the open ends of the box, and individual cables are threaded through the fingers on their way to the patch panel, keeping them neatly organized.

Creativity and variety abound in the world of cable-management hardware—there are as many different solutions to cable management as there are ways to screw it up. Figure 5-44 shows a rack using good cable management—these patch cables are well

Figure 5-43
Bad cable
management

secured using cable-management hardware, making them much less susceptible to damage from mishandling. Plus, it looks much nicer!

The second issue to consider when connecting cables is the overall organization of the patch panel as it relates to the organization of your network. Organize your patch panel so it mirrors the layout of your network. You can organize according to the physical layout, so the different parts of the patch panel correspond to different parts

Figure 5-44
Good cable
management

of your office space—for example, the north and south sides of the hallway. Another popular way to organize patch panels is to make sure they match the logical layout of the network, so the different user groups or company organizations have their own sections of the patch panel.

Finally, proper patch panel cable management means documenting everything clearly and carefully. This way, any competent technician can follow behind you and troubleshoot connectivity problems. Good techs draw diagrams!

Testing the Cable Runs

Well, in theory, your horizontal cabling system is now installed and ready for a switch and some systems. Before you do this, though, you must test each cable run. Someone new to testing cable might think that all you need to do is verify that each jack has been properly connected. Although this is an important and necessary step, the interesting problem comes after that: verifying that your cable run can handle the speed of your network.

Copper- and fiber-based network runs have different issues and potential problems, and thus require different tools to resolve. Let's look at copper, then fiber.

Before I go further, let me be clear: a typical network admin/tech cannot properly test a new cable run. TIA/EIA provides a series of incredibly complex and important standards for testing cable, requiring a professional cable installer. The testing equipment alone totally surpasses the cost of most smaller network installations. Advanced network testing tools easily cost over $5,000, and some are well over $10,000! Never fear, though—a number of lower-end tools work just fine for basic network testing.

 NOTE The test tools described here also enable you to diagnose network problems.

Copper Challenges

Most network admin types staring at a scenario with a potentially bad copper cable want to know the following:

- How long is this cable? If it's too long, the signal will degrade to the point that it's no longer detectable on the other end.

- Are any of the wires broken or not connected in the crimp (open)? If a wire is broken or a connection is open, it no longer has *continuity* (a complete, functioning connection). Are there bent pins on the RJ-45 or in the jack?

- Is there any place where two bare wires touch? This creates a *short*. Shorts can take place when cables are damaged, but you can also get a short when improperly crimping two cables into the same place on a crimp.

- If there is a break, where is it? It's much easier to fix if the location is detectable.

- Are all of the wires terminated in the right place in the plug or jack? Does each termination match to the same standard? In other words, am I looking at an *incorrect pin-out* scenario?

- Is there electrical or radio interference from outside sources? UTP is susceptible to electromagnetic interference (EMI), as introduced in Chapter 4.

- Is the signal from any of the pairs in the same cable interfering with another pair? This common problem in UTP installations is called a *split pair*.

To answer these questions, you must verify that both the cable and the terminated ends are correct. Making these verifications requires a *cable tester*. Various models of cable testers can answer some or all of these questions, depending on the amount of money you are willing to pay. At the low end of the cable tester market are devices that only test for continuity. These inexpensive (under $100) testers are often called *continuity testers* (Figure 5-45). Many of these testers require you to insert both ends of the cable into the tester. Of course, this can be a bit of a problem if the cable is already installed in the wall!

Figure 5-45
Continuity tester

Better testers can run a *wiremap* test that goes beyond mere continuity, testing that all the wires on both ends of the cable connect to the right spot. A wiremap test will pick up shorts, crossed wires, and more.

NOTE   Many techs and network testing folks use the term *wiremap* to refer to the proper connectivity for wires, as in, "Hey Joe, check the wiremap!"

A multimeter works perfectly well to test for continuity, assuming you can place its probes on each end of the cable. Set the multimeter (Figure 5-46) to its continuity setting if it has one or to Ohms. With the latter setting, if you have a connection, you get zero Ohms, and if you don't have a connection, you get infinite Ohms.

Medium-priced testers (~$400) certainly test continuity and wiremap and include the additional capability to determine the length of a cable; they can even tell you where a break is located on any of the individual wire strands. This type of cable tester

Figure 5-46
Multimeter

(Figure 5-47) is generically called a *time domain reflectometer (TDR)*. Most medium-priced testers come with a small loopback device to insert into the far end of the cable, enabling the tester to work with installed cables. This is the type of tester you want to have around!

Figure 5-47
A typical
medium-priced
TDR called a
MicroScanner

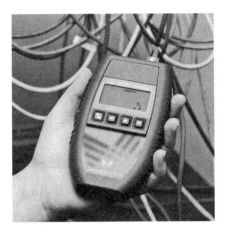

If you want a device that fully tests a cable run to the very complex TIA/EIA standards, the price shoots up fast. These higher-end testers can detect things the lesser testers cannot, such as crosstalk and attenuation.

Crosstalk poses a threat to properly functioning cable runs. Today's UTP cables consist of four pairs of wires, all squished together inside a plastic tube. When you send a signal down one of these pairs, the other pairs pick up some of the signal, as shown in Figure 5-48. This is called *crosstalk*.

Every piece of UTP in existence generates crosstalk. Worse, when you crimp the end of a UTP cable to a jack or plugs, crosstalk increases. A poor-quality crimp creates so much crosstalk that a cable run won't operate at its designed speed. To detect crosstalk, a normal-strength signal is sent down one pair of wires in a cable. An electronic detector,

Figure 5-48
Crosstalk

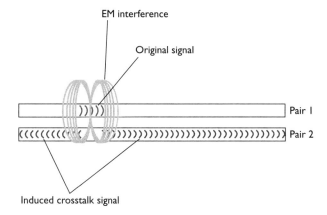

connected on the same end of the cable as the end emanating the signal, listens on the other three pairs and measures the amount of interference, as shown in Figure 5-49. This is called *near-end crosstalk (NEXT)*.

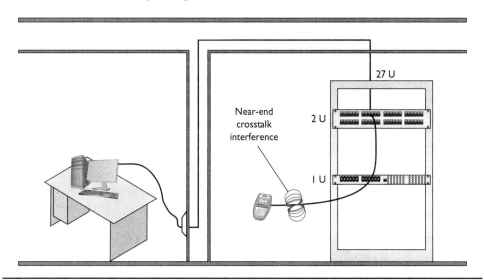

Figure 5-49   Near-end crosstalk

If you repeat this test, sending the signal down one pair of wires, but this time listening on the other pairs on the far end of the connection, you test for *far-end crosstalk (FEXT)*, as shown in Figure 5-50.

NOTE   Both NEXT and FEXT are measured in decibels (dB).

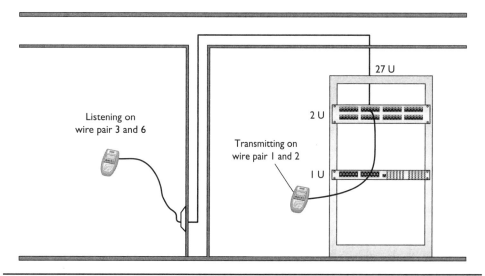

Figure 5-50   Far-end crosstalk

As if that's not bad enough, as a signal progresses down a piece of wire, it becomes steadily weaker: this is called *attenuation*. As a cable run gets longer, the attenuation increases, and the signal becomes more susceptible to crosstalk. A tester must send a signal down one end of a wire, test for NEXT and FEXT on the ends of every other pair, and then repeat this process for every pair in the UTP cable.

EXAM TIP   Every network—copper or otherwise—experiences data loss or lag over distances and with enough traffic. Ethernet network frame traffic has *latency*, a delay between the time the sending machine sends a message and the time the receiving machine can start processing those frames.

Add in a lot of machines and the network will also experience *jitter*, a delay in completing a transmission of all the frames in a message. This is perfectly normal and modern network technologies handle jitter fine. The only time it becomes a serious problem is in real-time voice communication. Excessive jitter generally sounds like, "Dude, you're totally breaking up." We'll explore voice communication in Chapter 13, "Remote Connectivity," in some detail.

Measuring Signal Loss

Signal loss in networking is measured in a unit called a decibel (dB). This applies to both electrical signals in copper wires and light signals in fiber cables. Unfortunately for a lot of network techs, a decibel is tough to grasp without a lot of math. I'm going to skip the technical details and give you a shorthand way to understand the numbers.

When referring to a signal traveling from one end of a cable to another, you really care about how much information on that signal gets to the end, right? In a simple sense, if you have some interference, some imperfections in the cable or fiber, you'll get some loss from beginning to end. Most people think about that loss in terms of percentage or even in more common terms, like "a little" or "a lot of" loss. No problem, right?

The problem when you take that same concept to networking is that the percentages lost can be gigantic or really, really small. When you start talking about a 10,000 percent loss or a .00001 percent loss, most folks eyes glaze over. The numbers are simply too big or small to make intuitive sense.

Technicians use the term "decibel" to describe those numbers in a more digestible format. When a tech looks at a signal loss of 3 dB, for example, he or she should be able to know that that number is a lot smaller than a signal loss of 10 dB.

This process of verifying that every cable run meets the exacting TIA/EIA standards requires very powerful testing tools, generally known as *cable certifiers* or just certifiers. Cable certifiers can both do the high-end testing and generate a report that a cable installer can print out and hand to a customer to prove that the installed cable runs pass TIA/EIA standards.

Figure 5-51 shows an example of this type of scanner made by Fluke Networks (www .flukenetworks.com) in its Microtest line. Most network techs don't need these advanced testers, so unless you have some deep pockets or find yourself doing serious cable testing, stick to the medium-priced testers.

Figure 5-51
A typical cable certifier—a Microtest OMNIScanner (photo courtesy of Fluke Networks)

Fiber Challenges

Fiber cable runs offer similar challenges to copper cable runs, but there are also some very specific differences. Just like with copper, signal loss is important and measured in decibels. But the causes of loss can differ a lot. Also, the many competing standards can catch techs running fiber by surprise.

Signal Loss/Degradation   Just like with copper wire, various imperfections in the media—the glass fiber, in this case—cause signal loss over distance. A lot of factors come into play.

Damaged cables or *open connections* obviously stop signals. The typical small form-factor pluggable (SFP) or gigabit interface converter (GBIC) can have problems. When you're checking for a *bad SFP/GBIC*, you'll need to check both the connector and the cable going into that connector. Either or both could cause the signal loss.

A *dirty connector* can cause pretty serious signal loss with fiber. It's important not to smudge the glass!

When you think about fiber-optic cables, you need to remember that the part that carries the signal is really tiny, only a few microns. When you're connecting two pieces of fiber, even a small *connector mismatch* in either the cladding (the outside) or the core (the inside) can cause serious losses.

Attenuation is the weakening of a signal as it travels long distances. *Dispersion* is when a signal spreads out over long distances. Both attenuation and dispersion are caused when wave signals travel too far without help over fiber-optic media.

Every piece of fiber has a certain *bend radius limitation.* If you bend a fiber-optic cable too much, you get *light leakage*, as shown in Figure 5-52. Light leakage means that part of the signal goes out the cable rather than arriving at the end. That's not a good thing.

Figure 5-52
Light leakage—
the arrows show
the light leaking
out at the bends.

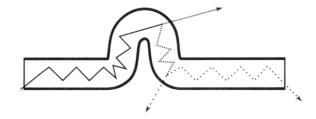

Physical or Signal Mismatch

Fiber networks have a relatively small number of connectors but offer a pretty wide variety of signal types that use those connectors. These variations come into play in several ways. First, just because you can connect to a particular SFP or GBIC, that doesn't mean the signal will work. Plugging a generic SFP into a Cisco switch might work in a physical sense, but if the switch won't play with anything but Cisco technology, you'll get a *transceiver mismatch.*

Likewise, you can find fiber connectors like SC or LC that will attach to single-mode or multimode fiber. Plugging a single-mode cable into a switch that expects multimode? Such a *cable mismatch* or *fiber mismatch*—an *incorrect cable type*—means your network—at least that portion of it—won't work.

Finally, different runs of fiber use different wavelength signals. You might be able to plug an LC connector into a switch just fine, for example, but if the signal starts at 1310 nm and the switch expects 1530 nm, that sort of *wavelength mismatch* will stop the transmission cold.

Fiber Tools   A fiber technician uses a large number of tools (Figure 5-53) and an almost artistic amount of skill. Over the years, easier terminations have been developed, but putting an ST, SC, LC, or other connector on the end of a piece of fiber is still very challenging.

Figure 5-53
Older fiber
termination kit

A fiber-optic run has problems that are both similar to and different from those of a UTP run. Fiber-optic runs don't experience crosstalk or interference (as we usually think of it) because they use light instead of an electrical current.

Fiber-optic cables still break, however, so a good tech always keeps an *optical time domain reflectometer (OTDR)* handy (Figure 5-54) for just such scenarios. OTDRs determine continuity and, if there's a break, tell you exactly how far down the cable to look for the break.

TIA/EIA has very complex requirements for testing fiber runs, and the cabling industry sells fiber certifiers to make sure a fiber will carry its designed signal speed.

The three big issues with fiber are attenuation, light leakage, and modal distortion. The amount of light propagating down the fiber cable diffuses over distance, which causes attenuation or *dispersion* (when the light signal spreads).

The process of installing a structured cabling system is rather involved, requires a great degree of skill, and should be left to professionals. By understanding the process, however, you can tackle most of the problems that come up in an installed structured cabling system. Most importantly, you'll understand the lingo used by the structured cabling installers so you can work with them more efficiently.

Figure 5-54
An optical
time domain
reflectometer
(photo courtesy
of Fluke
Networks)

NICs

Now that the network is completely in place, it's time to turn to the final part of any physical network: the NICs. A good network tech must recognize different types of NICs by sight and know how to install and troubleshoot them. Let's begin by reviewing the differences between UTP and fiber-optic NICs.

All UTP Ethernet NICs use the RJ-45 connector. The cable runs from the NIC to a switch (Figure 5-55).

Figure 5-55
Typical UTP NIC

NOTE Many motherboards these days include an onboard NIC. This, of course, completely destroys the use of the acronym "NIC" to represent network interface card because no card is actually involved. But heck, we're nerds and, just as we'll probably never stop using the term "RJ-45" when the correct term is "8P8C," we'll keep using the term "NIC." I know! Let's just pretend it stands for network interface connection!

Fiber-optic NICs come in a wide variety; worse, manufacturers use the same connector types for multiple standards. You'll find a 100BaseFX card designed for multimode cable with an SC connector, for example, and an identical card designed for single-mode cable, also with an SC connector. You simply must see the documentation that comes with the two cards to tell them apart. Figure 5-56 shows a typical fiber-optic network card.

Figure 5-56
Typical fiber NIC (photo courtesy of 3Com Corp.)

Buying NICs

Some folks may disagree with me, but I always purchase name-brand NICs. For NICs, I recommend sticking with big names, such as Intel. The NICs are better made, have extra features, and are easy to return if they turn out to be defective.

Plus, replacing a missing driver on a name-brand NIC is easy, and you can be confident the drivers work well. The type of NIC you should purchase depends on your network. Try to think about the future and go for multispeed cards if your wallet can handle the extra cost. Also, where possible, try to stick with the same model of NIC. Every different model you buy means another set of driver disks you need to haul around in your tech bag. Using the same model of NIC makes driver updates easier, too.

NOTE Many people order desktop PCs with NICs simply because they don't take the time to ask if the system has a built-in NIC. Take a moment and ask about this!

Physical Connections

I'll state the obvious here: If you don't plug the NIC into the computer, the NIC won't work! Many users happily assume some sort of quantum magic when it comes to computer communications, but as a tech, you know better. Fortunately, most PCs come with built-in NICs, making physical installation a nonissue. If you're buying a NIC, physically inserting the NIC into one of the PC's expansion slots is the easiest part of the job. Most PCs today have two types of expansion slots. The older, but still common, expansion slot is the Peripheral Component Interconnect (PCI) type (Figure 5-57).

Figure 5-57
PCI NIC

The newer PCI Express (PCIe) expansion slots are now more widely adopted by NIC suppliers. PCIe NICs usually come in either one-lane (×1) or two-lane (×2) varieties (Figure 5-58).

Figure 5-58
PCIe NIC

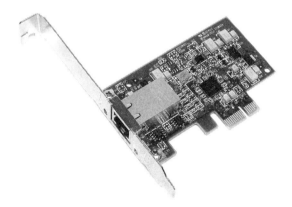

If you're not willing to open a PC case, you can get NICs with USB connections (Figure 5-59). USB NICs are handy to keep in your toolkit. If you walk up to a machine that might have a bad NIC, test your suspicions by inserting a USB NIC and moving the network cable from the potentially bad NIC to the USB one.

Figure 5-59
USB NIC

Drivers

Installing a NIC's driver into a Windows, macOS, or Linux system is easy: just insert the driver CD when prompted by the system. Unless you have a very offbeat NIC, the operating system will probably already have the driver preinstalled, but there are benefits to using the driver on the manufacturer's CD. The CDs that come with many NICs, especially the higher-end, brand-name ones, include extra goodies such as enhanced drivers and handy utilities, but you'll only be able to access them if you install the driver that comes with the NIC.

Every operating system has some method to verify that the computer recognizes the NIC and is ready to use it. Windows systems have the Device Manager; Ubuntu Linux users have the Network applet under the Administration menu; and macOS users get the Network utility in System Preferences. Actually, most operating systems have multiple methods to show that the NIC is in good working order. Learn the various ways to verify the NIC for your OS, as this is the ultimate test of a good NIC installation.

Bonding

Most switches enable you to use multiple NICs for a single machine, a process called *bonding* or *link aggregation.* Bonding effectively doubles (or more) the speed between a machine and a switch. In preparing for this book, for example, I found that the connection between my graphics development computer and my file server was getting pounded by my constant sending and receiving of massive image files, slowing down everyone else's file access. Rather than upgrading the switches and NICs from Gigabit to 10 Gigabit Ethernet, I found that simply doubling the connections among those three machines—graphics computer, switch, and file server—increased performance all around. If you want to add link aggregation to your network to increase performance, use identical NICs and switches from the same companies to avoid incompatibility.

EXAM TIP The *Link Aggregation Control Protocol (LACP)* controls how multiple network devices send and receive data as a single connection.

Link Lights

All UTP NICs made today have some type of light-emitting diodes (LEDs) that give information about the state of the NIC's link to whatever is on the other end of the connection. Even though you know the lights are actually LEDs, get used to calling them *link lights*, as that's the term all network techs use. NICs can have between one and four different link lights, and the LEDs can be any color. These lights give you clues about what's happening with the link and are one of the first items to check whenever you think a system is disconnected from the network (Figure 5-60).

Figure 5-60
Mmmm, pretty lights!

A link light tells you that the NIC is connected to a switch. Switches also have link lights, enabling you to check the connectivity at both ends of the cable. If a PC can't access a network and is acting disconnected, always check the link lights first. Multispeed devices usually have a link light that tells you the speed of the connection. In Figure 5-61, the light for port 2 in the top photo is orange, signifying that the other end of the cable is plugged into either a 10BaseT or 100BaseT NIC. The same port connected to a Gigabit NIC—that's the lower picture—displays a green LED.

Figure 5-61
Multispeed lights

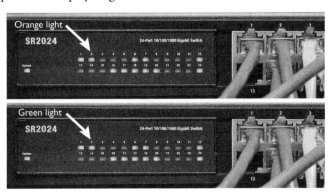

A properly functioning link light is on and steady when the NIC is connected to another device. No flickering, no on and off, just on. A link light that is off or flickering indicates a connection problem.

Another light is the *activity light*. This little guy turns on when the card detects network traffic, so it intermittently flickers when operating properly. The activity light is a lifesaver for detecting problems, because in the real world, the connection light will sometimes lie to you. If the connection light says the connection is good, the next step is to try to copy a file or do something else to create network traffic. If the activity light does not flicker, there's a problem.

You might run into yet another light on some much older NICs, called a collision light. As you might suspect from the name, the *collision light* flickers when it detects collisions on the network. Modern NICs don't have these, but you might run into this phrase on the CompTIA Network+ certification exam.

Keep in mind that the device on the other end of the NIC's connection has link lights, too! Figure 5-62 shows the link lights on a modern switch. Most switches have a single LED per port to display connectivity and activity.

Figure 5-62
Link lights on
a switch

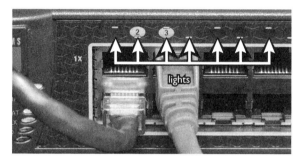

No standard governs how NIC manufacturers use their lights, and, as a result, they come in an amazing array of colors and layouts. When you encounter a NIC with a number of LEDs, take a moment to try to figure out what each one means. Although different NICs have various ways of arranging and using their LEDs, the functions are always the same: link, activity, and speed.

Many fiber-optic NICs don't have lights, making diagnosis of problems a bit more challenging. Nevertheless, most physical connection issues for fiber can be traced to the connection on the NIC itself. Fiber-optic cabling is incredibly delicate; the connectors that go into NICs are among the few places that anyone can touch fiber optics, so the connectors are the first thing to check when problems arise. Those who work with fiber always keep around a handy optical tester to enable them to inspect the quality of the connections. Only a trained eye can use such a device to judge a good fiber connection from a bad one—but once you learn how to use it, this kind of tester is extremely handy (Figure 5-63).

Figure 5-63
Optical
connection tester

Diagnostics and Repair of Physical Cabling

"The network's down!" is easily the most terrifying phrase a network tech will ever hear. Networks fail for many reasons, and the first thing to know is that good-quality, professionally installed cabling rarely goes bad. Chapter 20, "Network Monitoring," covers principles of network diagnostics and support that apply to all networking scenarios, but let's take a moment now to discuss what to do when faced with a scenario that points to a problem with your physical network.

Diagnosing Physical Problems

Look for errors that point to physical disconnection. A key clue that you may have a physical problem is that a user gets a "No server is found" error, or tries to use the operating system's network explorer utility (like Network in Windows) and doesn't see any systems besides his or her own. First, try to eliminate software errors: if one particular application fails, try another. If the user can't browse the Internet, but can get e-mail, odds are good that the problem is with software, not hardware—unless someone unplugged the e-mail server!

Multiple systems failing to access the network often points to hardware problems. This is where knowledge of your network cabling helps. If all the systems connected to one switch suddenly no longer see the network, but all the other systems in your network still function, you not only have a probable hardware problem but also a suspect—the switch.

Check Your Lights

If you suspect a hardware problem, first check the link lights on the NIC and switch. If they're not lit, you know the cable isn't connected somewhere. If you're not physically at the system in question (if you're on a tech call, for example), you can have the user check his or her connection status through the link lights or through software. Every operating system has some way to tell you on the screen if it detects the NIC is disconnected. The network status icon in the Notification Area in Windows 7, for example, will display a little red × when a NIC is disconnected (Figure 5-64). A user who's unfamiliar with link lights (or who may not want to crawl under his or her desk) will have no problem telling you if the icon says "Not connected."

Figure 5-64
Disconnected
NIC in Windows

If your problem system is clearly not connecting, eliminate the possibility of a failed switch or other larger problem by checking to make sure other people can access the network, and that other systems can access the shared resource (server) that the problem system can't see. Make a quick visual inspection of the cable running from the back of the PC to the outlet.

Finally, if you can, plug the system into a known-good outlet and see if it works. A good network tech always keeps a long patch cable for just this purpose. If you get connectivity with the second outlet, you should begin to suspect bad wiring in structured cable running from the first outlet to the switch. Or, it could be a bad connector. Assuming the cable is installed properly and has been working correctly before this event, a simple continuity test will confirm your suspicion in most cases.

Check the NIC

Be warned that a bad NIC can also generate this "can't see the network" problem. Use the utility provided by your OS to verify that the NIC works. If you've got a NIC with diagnostic software, run it—this software will check the NIC's circuitry. The NIC's female connector is a common failure point, so NICs that come with diagnostic software often include a special test called a *loopback test*. A loopback test sends data out of the NIC and checks to see if it comes back. Some NICs perform only an internal loopback, which tests the circuitry that sends and receives, but not the actual connecting pins. A true external loopback requires a *loopback adapter*, also known as a *loopback plug*, inserted into the NIC's port (Figure 5-65). If a NIC is bad or has a *bad port*, replace it—preferably with an identical NIC so you don't have to reinstall drivers!

Figure 5-65
Loopback plug

 NOTE Onboard NICs on laptops are especially notorious for breaking due to constant plugging and unplugging. On some laptops, the NICs are easy to replace; others require a motherboard replacement.

Cable Testing

The vast majority of network disconnect problems occur at the work area. If you've tested those connections, though, and the work area seems fine, it's time to consider deeper issues.

With the right equipment, diagnosing a bad horizontal cabling run is easy. Anyone with a network should own a midrange tester with TDR such as the Fluke MicroScanner.

With a little practice, you can easily determine not only whether a cable is disconnected but also where the disconnection takes place. Sometimes patience is required, especially if you've failed to label your cable runs, but you will find the problem.

When you're testing a cable run, always include the patch cables as you test. This means unplugging the patch cable from the PC, attaching a tester, and then going to the telecommunications room. Here you'll want to unplug the patch cable from the switch and plug the tester into that patch cable, making a complete test, as shown in Figure 5-66.

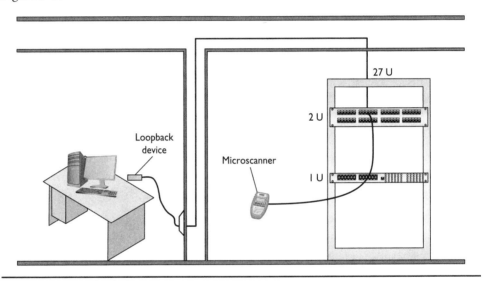

Figure 5-66   Loopback plug in action

Testing in this manner gives you a complete test from the switch to the system. In general, a broken cable must be replaced. Fixing a bad patch cable is easy, but what happens if the horizontal cable is to blame? In these cases, I get on the phone and call my local installer. If a cable's bad in one spot, the risk of it being bad in another is simply too great to try anything other than total replacement.

Finally, check the coupler if one is used to extend a cable run. *Couplers* are small devices with two female ports that enable you to connect two pieces of cable together to overcome *distance limitations*. UTP couplers are most common, but you can find couplers for every type of network: fiber couplers, even coaxial or BNC couplers. The plastic UTP couplers are relatively easily broken if exposed to humans.

Problems in the Telecommunications Room

Even a well-organized telecommunications room is a complex maze of equipment racks, switches, and patch panels. The most important issue to remember as you work is to keep your diagnostic process organized and documented. For example, if you're testing a series of cable runs along a patch panel, start at one end and don't skip connections. Place a sticker as you work to keep track of where you are on the panel.

Your biggest concerns in the telecommunications room are power and environmental issues.

All those boxes in the rack need good-quality power. Even the smallest rack should run off of a good *uninterruptible power supply (UPS)*, a battery backup that plugs into the wall. Make sure you get one that can handle the amount of wattage used by all the equipment in the rack.

A UPS provides several benefits. First, it acts as an inverter. It stores power as direct current in its battery, then inverts that power to alternating current as the servers and other boxes in the rack system require. A good UPS acts as a *power monitoring tool* so it can report problems when there's any fluctuation in the electrical supply. All UPS boxes can provide security from power spikes and sags.

A UPS enables you to shut down in an orderly fashion. It does *not* provide enough power for you to continue working. The device that handles the latter service is called a *generator*.

NOTE You can purchase two different types of UPSs—online and standby. An online UPS continuously charges a battery that, in turn, powers the computer components. If the telecommunications room loses power, the computers stay powered up without missing a beat, at least until the battery runs out.

A standby power supply (SPS) also has a big battery but doesn't power the computer unless the power goes out. Circuitry detects the power outage and immediately kicks on the battery.

Pay attention to how often your UPS kicks in. Don't assume the power coming from your physical plant (or power company) is okay. If your UPS comes on too often, it might be time to install a voltage event recorder (Figure 5-67). As its name implies, a *voltage event recorder* plugs into your power outlet and tracks the voltage over time. These devices often reveal interesting issues. For example, a small network was having trouble sending an overnight report to a main branch—the uploading servers reported that they were not able to connect to the Internet. Yet in the morning the report could be run manually with no problems. After placing a voltage event recorder in the telecommunications room, we discovered that the building management was turning off the power as a power-saving measure. This would have been hard to determine without the proper tool.

The temperature in the telecommunications room should be maintained and monitored properly. If you lose the air conditioning, for example, and leave systems running, the equipment will overheat and shut down—sometimes with serious damage. To prevent this, all serious telecommunications rooms should have *temperature monitors* as part of their *rack monitoring system*.

Likewise, you need to control the level of humidity in a telecommunications room. You can install *environmental monitors* that keep a constant watch on humidity, temperature, and more, for just a few hundred dollars. The devices cost little in comparison to the equipment in the telecommunications room that you're protecting.

Figure 5-67
An excellent
voltage event
recorder (photo
courtesy of Fluke
Networks)

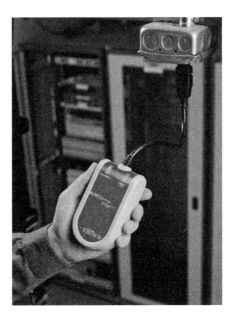

 NOTE Using a high-quality UPS and installing temperature and environmental monitors enable business continuity and disaster recovery, part of "managing risk." Managing risk is a big topic, so I've devoted all of Chapter 18 to it.

Toners

It would be nice to say that all cable installations are perfect and that over the years they won't tend to grow into horrific piles of spaghetti-like, unlabeled cables. In the real world, though, you might eventually find yourself having to locate or *trace* cables. Even in the best-planned networks, labels fall off ports and outlets, mystery cables appear behind walls, new cable runs are added, and mistakes are made counting rows and columns on patch panels. Sooner or later, most network techs will have to be able to pick out one particular cable or port from a stack.

When the time comes to trace cables, network techs turn to a device called a toner for help. *Toner* is the generic term for two separate devices that are used together: a tone generator and a tone probe. The *tone generator* connects to the cable using alligator clips, tiny hooks, or a network jack, and it sends an electrical signal along the wire at a certain frequency. The *tone probe* emits a sound when it is placed near a cable connected to the tone generator (Figure 5-68). These two devices are often referred to by the brand-name Fox and Hound, a popular model of toner made by the Triplett Corporation.

 EXAM TIP You'll see a tone probe referred to on the CompTIA Network+ exam as a toner probe.

Figure 5-68
Fox and Hound

To trace a cable, connect the tone generator to the known end of the cable in question, and then position the tone probe next to the other end of each of the cables that might be the right one. The tone probe makes a sound when it's placed next to the right cable. Some toners have one tone probe that works with multiple tone generators. Each generator emits a separate frequency, and the probe sounds a different tone for each one. Even good toners are relatively inexpensive ($75); although inexpensive toners can cost less than $25, they don't tend to work well, so spending a little more is worthwhile. Just keep in mind that if you have to support a network, you'd do best to own a decent toner.

More advanced toners include phone jacks, enabling the person manipulating the tone generator to communicate with the person manipulating the tone probe: "Jim, move the tone generator to the next port!" These either come with their own headset or work with a *butt set*, the classic tool used by telephone repair technicians for years (Figure 5-69).

Figure 5-69
Technician with
a butt set

A good, medium-priced cable tester and a good toner are the most important tools for folks who must support, but not install, networks. A final tip: be sure to bring along a few extra batteries—there's nothing worse than sitting on the top of a ladder holding a cable tester or toner that has just run out of juice!

Chapter Review

Questions

1. Which of the following cables should never be used in a structured cabling installation?

   A. UTP

   B. STP

   C. Fiber-optic

   D. Coax

2. Which of the following enables you to use multiple NICs in a computer to achieve a much faster network speed?

   A. Bonding

   B. Linking

   C. SLI

   D. Xing

3. How many pairs of wires are in a Cat 5e-rated cable?

   A. 2

   B. 4

   C. 8

   D. It doesn't specify.

4. A(n) _____ organizes and protects the horizontal cabling in the telecommunications room.

   A. rack

   B. patch panel

   C. outlet

   D. 110 jack

5. Which of the following would never be seen in an equipment rack?

   A. Patch panel

   B. UPS

   C. PC

   D. All of the above may be seen in an equipment rack.

6. What are patch cables used for? (Select two.)

   A. To connect different telecommunications rooms.

   B. To connect the patch panel to the switch.

   C. They are used as crossover cables.

   D. To connect PCs to outlet boxes.

7. Which of the following network technologies use UTP cabling in a star topology?

   A. Crosstalk

   B. Fiber optics

   C. 100BaseFX

   D. 100BaseT

8. Jane needs to increase network throughput on a 10BaseT network that consists of 1 hub and 30 users. Which of the following hardware solutions would achieve this most inexpensively?

   A. Add a fiber backbone.

   B. Upgrade the network to 100BaseT.

   C. Replace the hub with a switch.

   D. Add a router.

9. What two devices together enable you to pick a single cable out of a stack of cables? (Select two.)

   A. Tone aggregator

   B. Tone binder

   C. Tone generator

   D. Tone probe

10. Rack-mounted equipment has a height measured in what units?

   A. Mbps

   B. MBps

   C. Inches

   D. U

Answers

1. **D.** Coax cable should not be used in structured cabling networks.

2. **A.** Bonding, or link aggregation, is the process of using multiple NICs as a single connection, thus increasing speed.

3. **B.** The Cat 5e rating requires four pairs of wires.

4. **B.** A patch panel organizes and protects the horizontal cabling in the telecommunications room.

5. **D.** All these devices may be found in equipment racks.

6. **B** and **D.** Patch cables are used to connect the patch panel to the switch and the PCs to the outlet boxes.

7. **D.** 100BaseT uses UTP cabling in a star topology.

8. **C.** Upgrading to 100BaseT will work, but replacing the hub with a switch is much less expensive.

9. **C** and **D.** A tone generator and tone probe work together to enable you to pick a single cable out of a stack of cables.

10. **D.** Rack-mounted equipment uses a height measurement known as a unit (U).

TCP/IP Basics

The CompTIA Network+ certification exam expects you to know how to

- 1.1 Explain the purposes and uses of ports and protocols
- 1.3 Explain the concepts and characteristics of routing and switching
- 1.4 Given a scenario, configure the appropriate IP addressing components
- 1.8 Explain the functions of network services
- 5.5 Given a scenario, troubleshoot common network service issues

To achieve these goals, you must be able to

- Describe how the TCP/IP protocol suite works
- Explain CIDR and subnetting
- Describe the functions of static and dynamic IP addresses

The mythical MHTechEd network (remember that from Chapter 1?) provided an overview of how networks work. At the bottom of every network, at OSI Layers 1 and 2, resides the network hardware: the wires, network cards, switches, and more that enable data to move physically from one computer to another. Above the Physical and Data Link layers, the "higher" layers of the model—such as Network and Transport—work with the hardware to make the network magic happen.

Chapters 2 through 5 provided details of the hardware at the Physical and Data Link layers of the OSI model. You learned about the network protocols, such as Ethernet, that create uniformity within networks, so that the data frame created by one NIC can be read properly by another NIC.

This chapter begins a fun journey into the software side of networking. You'll learn the details about the IP addressing scheme that enables computers on one network to communicate with each other and computers on other networks. You'll get the full story on how TCP/IP networks divide into smaller units—subnets—to make management of a large TCP/IP network easier. And you won't just get it from a conceptual standpoint. This chapter provides the details you've undoubtedly been craving—it teaches you how to set up a network properly. The chapter finishes with an in-depth discussion on implementing IP addresses.

Historical/Conceptual

The early days of networking, roughly the 1980s, exposed a problem in the way the software used to make networks run was being developed. Unlike the hardware organizations that worked together to make solid standards, the different organizations developing network software worked separately, secretly, and competitively. The four major players—Microsoft, Apple, Novell, and UNIX developers such as AT&T—created network software solutions that not only were all but incompatible, but also exposed very separate answers to the question: "What do we share on a network?"

Microsoft, Apple, and Novell created networking software that for the most part did nothing more than share different computers' folders and printers (and they all did this sharing differently). AT&T and the universities developing the UNIX operating system saw networks as a way to share terminals, send e-mail messages, and transfer files. As a result, everyone's software had its own set of Rules of What a Network Should Do and How to Do It. These sets of rules—and the software written to follow these rules—were broken down into individual rules or languages called *protocols*. No one protocol could do everything a network needed to do, so companies lumped together all their necessary protocols under the term *protocol suite*. Novell called its protocol suite IPX/SPX; Microsoft's was called NetBIOS/NetBEUI; Apple called its AppleTalk; and the UNIX folks used this wacky protocol suite called TCP/IP.

It took about 20 very confusing years, but eventually TCP/IP replaced every other protocol suite in all but the most rare and unique situations. To get ahead today, to get on the Internet, and to pass the CompTIA Network+ exam, you only need to worry about TCP/IP. Microsoft, Apple, and Linux developers no longer actively support anything but TCP/IP. You live in a one-protocol-suite world, the old stuff is forgotten, and you kids don't know how good you've got it!

Test Specific

The TCP/IP Protocol Suite

A great way to explore the TCP/IP protocol suite is to refer back to the TCP/IP model covered in Chapter 1. Let's take a second look, and this time examine some of the more critical protocols that reside at each layer. I'll also explore and develop the IP packet in more detail to show you how it organizes these protocols. Remember, part of the power of TCP/IP comes from the fact that IP packets may exist in almost any type of network technology. The Link layer, therefore, counts on technologies outside the TCP/IP protocol suite (like Ethernet, cable modem, or DSL) to get the IP packets from one system to the next (Figure 6-1).

Figure 6-1
The Link layer is important, but it's not part of the TCP/IP protocol suite.

When discussing the software layers of the TCP/IP protocol suite, let's focus on only the three top layers in the TCP/IP model: Internet, Transport, and Application (Figure 6-2). I'll revisit each of these layers and add representative protocols from the protocol suite so you gain a better understanding of "who's who" in TCP/IP.

Figure 6-2
The TCP/IP protocol suite redux

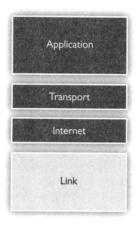

NOTE The TCP/IP protocol suite consists of thousands of different protocols doing thousands of different things. For the most part, the rest of this book discusses TCP/IP protocols. Right now, my goal is to give you an idea of which protocols go where in the TCP/IP protocol suite.

If you look at an IP packet, certain parts of that packet fit perfectly into layers of the TCP/IP model. The parts, conceptualized in Figure 6-3, consist of a series of nested headers with data. The header for a higher layer is part of the data for a lower layer. The packet's payload, for example, can be a TCP segment that consists of data from layers above and a sequence number. The higher you go up the model, more headers are stripped away until all you have left is the data delivered to the application that needs it.

Figure 6-3
IP packet
showing headers

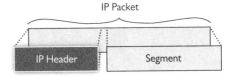

Internet Layer Protocols

The *Internet Protocol (IP)* works at the Internet layer, taking data chunks from the Transport layer, adding addressing, and creating the final IP packet. IP then hands the IP packet to Layer 2 for encapsulation into a frame. Let's look at the addressing in more depth.

I think it's safe to assume that most folks have seen IP addresses before. Here's a typical example:

192.168.1.115

This type of address—four values ranging from 0 to 255, separated by three periods—is known officially as an *Internet Protocol version 4 (IPv4)* address.

This chapter introduces you to IPv4 addresses. You should understand the correct name for this older type of address because the world is moving to a newer, longer type of IP address called IPv6. Here's an example of an IPv6 address:

2001:0:4137:9e76:43e:2599:3f57:fe9a

IPv4 and IPv6 addresses aren't the only protocols that work at the Internet layer. Several applications test basic issues at this layer, asking questions such as: "Is there a computer with the IP address of 192.168.1.15?" These applications use the *Internet Control Message Protocol (ICMP)*. TCP/IP users rarely start a program that uses ICMP. For the most part, ICMP features are called automatically by applications as needed without direct user action. There are very useful programs that run under ICMP, however, such as the ping utility.

When thinking about the Internet layer, remember the following three protocols:

- IPv4 (normally referred to as simply "IP")
- IPv6
- ICMP

 NOTE The TCP/IP model's Internet layer corresponds roughly to the OSI model's Network layer.

Figure 6-4 shows a highly simplified IP header.

Figure 6-4
Simplified IP
header

The full IP packet header has 14 different fields. As you would expect, the destination and source IP addresses are part of the Internet layer. Other fields include version, header length, and more. Dissecting the entire set of fields isn't important this early in the discussion, but here are a few descriptions just to whet your appetite:

- **Version**   The version (Ver) field defines the IP address type: 4 for IPv4, 6 for IPv6.

- **Header length**   The total size of the IP portion of the packet in words (32 bits) is displayed in the header length field.

- **Differentiated services code point (DSCP)**   The DSCP field contains data used by bandwidth-sensitive applications like Voice over IP. (Network techs with long memories will note that this field used to be called the *type of service* field.)

- **Time to live (TTL)**   Implementations of routers on the Internet are not perfect and engineers sometimes create loops. The TTL field prevents an IP packet from indefinitely spinning through the Internet by using a counter that decrements by one every time a packet goes through a router. This number cannot start higher than 255; many applications start at 128.

- **Protocol**   In the vast majority of cases, the protocol field is either TCP or UDP and identifies what's encapsulated inside the packet. See the next section for more information.

Transport Layer Protocols

When moving data from one system to another, the TCP/IP protocol suite needs to know if the communication is connection-oriented or connectionless. When you want to be positive that the data moving between two systems gets there in good order, use a connection-oriented application. If it's not a big deal for data to miss a bit or two, then connectionless is the way to go. The connection-oriented protocol used with TCP/IP is called the *Transmission Control Protocol (TCP)*. The connectionless one is called the *User Datagram Protocol (UDP)*.

Let me be clear: you don't *choose* TCP or UDP. The people who developed the applications decide which protocol to use. When you fire up your Web browser, for example, you're using TCP because Web browsers use a protocol called Hypertext Transfer Protocol (HTTP) and the developers of HTTP decided to build HTTP using TCP.

TCP

Most TCP/IP applications use TCP—that's why we call the protocol suite "TCP/IP" and not "UDP/IP." TCP gets an application's data from one machine to another reliably and completely. As a result, TCP comes with communication rules that require both the sending and receiving machines to acknowledge the other's presence and readiness to send and receive data. We call this process the TCP three-way handshake of SYN, SYN-ACK, and ACK (Figure 6-5). TCP also chops up data into *segments*, gives the segments a sequence number, and then verifies that all sent segments were received. If a segment goes missing, the receiving system must request the missing segments.

Figure 6-5

TCP three-way handshake in action

Client   Server

Figure 6-6 shows a simplified TCP header. Notice the source port and the destination port. Port numbers are values ranging from 1 to 65,535 and are used by systems to determine what application needs the received data. Each application is assigned a specific port number on which to listen/send. Web servers use port 80 (HTTP) or 443 (HTTPS), for example, whereas port 143 is used to receive e-mail messages from e-mail servers (IMAP4).

Figure 6-6 TCP header

The client uses the source port number to remember which client application requested the data. The rest of this book dives much deeper into ports. For now, know that the TCP or UDP headers of an IP packet store these values.

Ports aren't the only items of interest in the TCP header. The header also contains these fields:

- **Sequence and ACK numbers**   These numbers enable the sending and receiving computers to keep track of the various pieces of data flowing back and forth.

- **Flags**   These individual bits give both sides detailed information about the state of the connection.

- **Checksum**   The checksum checks the TCP header for errors.

UDP

UDP is the "fire and forget" missile of the TCP/IP protocol suite. As you can see in Figure 6-7, a UDP *datagram* doesn't possess any of the extras you see in TCP to make sure the data is received intact. UDP works best when you have a lot of data that doesn't need to be perfect or when the systems are so close to each other that the chances of a problem occurring are too small to bother worrying about. A few dropped frames on a Voice over IP call, for example, won't make much difference in the communication between two people. So, there's a good reason to use UDP: it's smoking fast compared to TCP. Two of the most important networking protocols, Domain Name System (DNS) and Dynamic Host Configuration Protocol (DHCP), use UDP.

Figure 6-7

UDP header

NOTE You saw this back in Chapter 1, but I'll mention it again here. Data gets chopped up into chunks at the Transport layer when using TCP. The chunks are called *segments* with TCP. UDP *datagrams* don't get chopped up at the Transport layer; they just get a header.

Application Layer Protocols

TCP/IP applications use TCP/IP protocols to move data back and forth between servers and clients. Because every application has different needs, I can't show you a generic application header. Instead, we'll look at one sample header from one function of possibly the most popular application protocol of all: HTTP.

As mentioned previously, Web servers and Web browsers use HTTP to communicate. Figure 6-8 shows a sample header for HTTP. Specifically, this header is a response segment from the Web server telling the remote system that the last set of data transfers is complete. This header begins with the value "HTTP/1.1" and the number "200" followed by "OK\r\n," which means "OK, go to the next line." The data (the contents of the Web page) begins below the header.

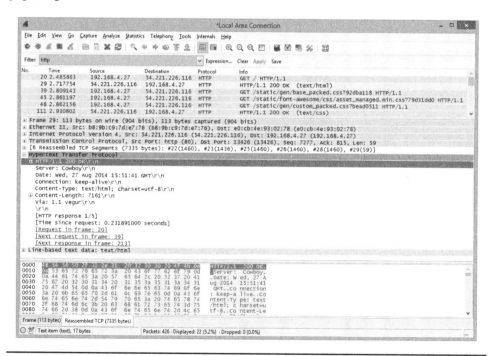

Figure 6-8 HTTP header

NOTE I'm simplifying the call and response interaction between a Web server and a Web client. The explanation here is only the first part of the process in accessing a Web page.

Super! Now that you're comfortable with how the TCP/IP protocols fit into clear points on the TCP/IP model, let's head back to the Internet layer and explore IP addressing.

IP and Ethernet

TCP/IP supports simple networks and complex networks. You can use the protocol suite to connect a handful of computers to a switch and create a local area network (LAN). TCP/IP also enables you to interconnect multiple LANs into a wide area network (WAN). Let's start by understanding how *IP addressing* works in a simple network, a LAN.

At the LAN level, every host runs TCP/IP software over Ethernet hardware, creating a situation where every host has two addresses: an IP address and an Ethernet MAC address (Figure 6-9). While at first this seems redundant, it's the power behind TCP/IP's ability to support both LANs and WANs. But again, we're only talking about LANs at this point.

Figure 6-9
Two addresses

IP address: 192.168.32.2

MAC address: 04-00-3F-12-B6-45

Imagine a situation where one computer, Computer A, wants to send an IP packet to another computer, Computer B, on the LAN. To send an IP packet to another computer, the sending computer (Computer A) must insert the IP packet into an Ethernet frame as shown in Figure 6-10.

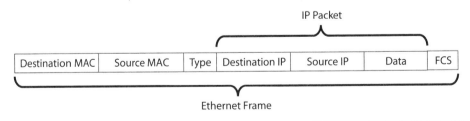

Figure 6-10 Encapsulation

Note that the IP packet is completely encapsulated inside the Ethernet frame. Also note that the Ethernet frame has both a destination MAC address and a source MAC address, while the IP packet encapsulated in the Ethernet frame has both a source IP address and a destination IP address. This encapsulation idea works great, but there's a problem: Computer A knows Computer B's IP address, but how does Computer A know the MAC address of Computer B? (See Figure 6-11.)

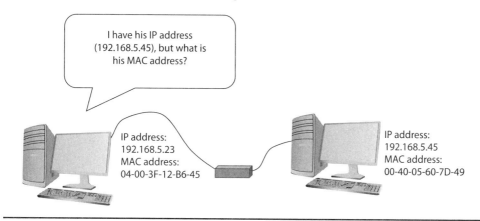

Figure 6-11   What is his MAC address?

To get Computer B's MAC address, Computer A sends a very special command called an Address Resolution Protocol (ARP) request to MAC address FF-FF-FF-FF-FF-FF, the universal MAC address for broadcast (Figure 6-12).

Figure 6-12
Sending an ARP
request

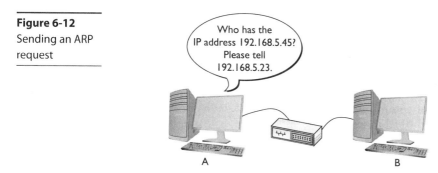

Computer B responds to the ARP request by sending Computer A an ARP reply (Figure 6-13). Once Computer A has Computer B's MAC address, it starts sending unicast Ethernet frames directly to Computer B.

Figure 6-13
Computer B
responds.

Try This!

ARP in Windows

To show Windows' current ARP cache, open a command line and type

```
arp -a
```

You should see results like this:

```
Interface: 192.168.4.71 --- 0x4

Internet Address Physical Address Type
192.168.4.76   00-1d-e0-78-9c-d5   dynamic
192.168.4.81   00-1b-77-3f-85-b4   dynamic
```

Now delete one of the entries in the ARP table with this command:

```
arp -d [ip address from the previous results]
```

Run the **arp -a** command again. The line for the address you specified should be gone. Now ping the address you deleted and check the ARP table again. Did the deleted address return?

IP addresses provide several benefits that MAC addresses alone cannot offer. First, every machine on a TCP/IP network—small or large—gets a unique IP address that identifies the machine on that network. Second, IP addresses group together sets of computers into logical networks, so you can, for example, distinguish one LAN from another. Finally, because TCP/IP network equipment understands the IP addressing scheme, computers can communicate with each other *between* LANs, in a WAN. Let's go into more detail on IP addresses.

IP Addresses

The most common type of IP address (officially called IPv4, but usually simplified to just "IP") consists of a 32-bit value. Here's an example of an IP address:

11000000101010000000010000000010

Whoa! IP addresses are just strings of 32 binary digits? Yes, they are, but to make IP addresses easier for humans to use, the 32-bit binary value is broken down into four groups of eight, separated by periods, or *dots*, like this:

11000000.10101000.00000100.00000010

Each of these 8-bit values is, in turn, converted into a decimal number between 0 and 255. If you took every possible combination of eight binary values and placed them in a spreadsheet, it would look something like the list in the left column. The right column shows the same list with a decimal value assigned to each.

00000000	00000000 = 0
00000001	00000001 = 1
00000010	00000010 = 2
00000011	00000011 = 3
00000100	00000100 = 4
00000101	00000101 = 5
00000110	00000110 = 6
00000111	00000111 = 7
00001000	00001000 = 8
(skip a bunch in the middle)	*(skip a bunch in the middle)*
11111000	11111000 = 248
11111001	11111001 = 249
11111010	11111010 = 250
11111011	11111011 = 251
11111100	11111100 = 252
11111101	11111101 = 253
11111110	11111110 = 254
11111111	11111111 = 255

Converted, the original value of 11000000.10101000.00000100.00000010 is displayed as 192.168.4.2 in IPv4's *dotted decimal notation* (also referred to as the *dotted octet numbering system*). Note that dotted decimal is simply a shorthand way for people to discuss and configure the binary IP addresses computers use.

People who work on TCP/IP networks must know how to convert dotted decimal to binary and back. You can convert easily using any operating system's calculator. Every OS has a calculator (UNIX/Linux systems have about 100 different ones to choose from) that has a scientific or programmer mode like the ones shown in Figure 6-14.

Figure 6-14
Windows (left) and macOS (right) Calculators in Programmer mode

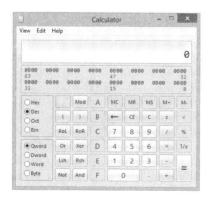

SIM Check out the two excellent Chapter 6 "Binary Calculator" sims over at **http://totalsem.com/007**. View the Show!, then practice on the Click!

To convert from decimal to binary, just go to decimal view, type in the value, and then switch to binary view to get the result. To convert to decimal, just go into binary view, enter the binary value, and switch to decimal view to get the result. Figure 6-15 shows the result of Windows 10 Calculator converting the decimal value 47 into binary. Notice the result is 101111—the leading two zeroes do not appear. When you work with IP addresses, you must always have eight digits, so just add two more to the left to get 00101111.

Figure 6-15

Converting decimal to binary with Windows 10 Calculator

NOTE Using a calculator utility to convert to and from binary/decimal is a critical skill for a network tech. Later on you'll do this again, but by hand!

Just as every MAC address must be unique on a network, every IP address must be unique as well. For logical addressing to work, no two computers on the same network may have the same IP address. In a small TCP/IP network, every computer has both an IP address and a MAC address (Figure 6-16), as you saw earlier in the chapter.

Every operating system comes with utilities to display a system's IP address and MAC address. Figure 6-17 shows a macOS system's Network utility with TCP/IP information displayed. Note the IP address (192.168.4.42). Figure 6-18 shows the Hardware information in the same utility, which shows the MAC address.

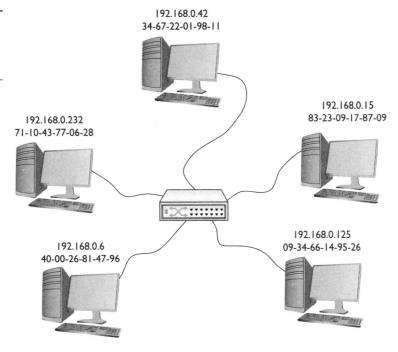

Figure 6-16
A small network
with both IP and
MAC addresses

192.168.0.42
34-67-22-01-98-11

192.168.0.15
83-23-09-17-87-09

192.168.0.232
71-10-43-77-06-28

192.168.0.6
40-00-26-81-47-96

192.168.0.125
09-34-66-14-95-26

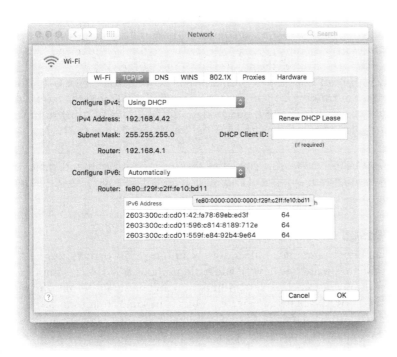

Figure 6-17 macOS Network utility

Figure 6-18
macOS Network
utility displaying
a MAC address

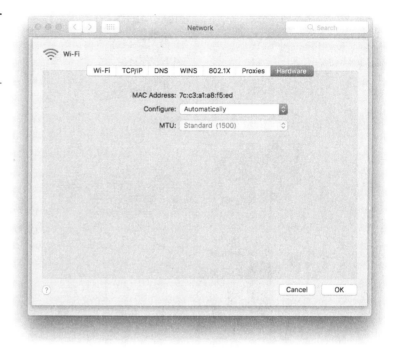

Every operating system also has a command-line utility that gives you this information. In Windows, for example, you can use *ipconfig* to display the IP and MAC addresses. Run `ipconfig /all` to see the results shown in Figure 6-19.

In macOS, you can run the very similar *ifconfig* command. Figure 6-20, for example, shows the result of running `ifconfig` ("eth0" is the NIC) from the terminal.

Linux systems can use ifconfig, but modern distributions (distros) run `ip a` from a terminal to display a system's IP and MAC addresses. See Figure 6-21.

EXAM TIP   Make sure you know that ipconfig, ifconfig, and ip provide a tremendous amount of information regarding a system's TCP/IP settings.

IP Addresses in Action

Now that you understand that an IP address is nothing more than a string of 32 ones and zeroes, it's time to (finally) see how IP addressing supports WANs. It's important to keep in mind that the IP numbering system must support both WANs and the many LANs connected by the WANs. This can create problems in some circumstances, such as when a computer needs to send data both to computers in its own network and to computers in other networks at the same time.

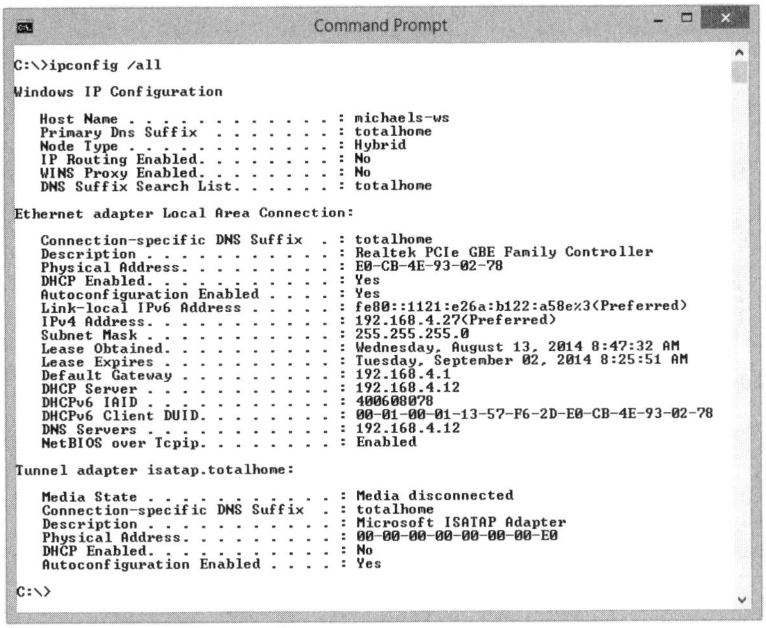

```
 ██                        Command Prompt                     — □  ×
C:\>ipconfig /all

Windows IP Configuration

    Host Name . . . . . . . . . . . . : michaels-ws
    Primary Dns Suffix  . . . . . . . : totalhome
    Node Type . . . . . . . . . . . . : Hybrid
    IP Routing Enabled. . . . . . . . : No
    WINS Proxy Enabled. . . . . . . . : No
    DNS Suffix Search List. . . . . . : totalhome

Ethernet adapter Local Area Connection:

    Connection-specific DNS Suffix  . : totalhome
    Description . . . . . . . . . . . : Realtek PCIe GBE Family Controller
    Physical Address. . . . . . . . . : E0-CB-4E-93-02-78
    DHCP Enabled. . . . . . . . . . . : Yes
    Autoconfiguration Enabled . . . . : Yes
    Link-local IPv6 Address . . . . . : fe80::1121:e26a:b122:a58e%3(Preferred)
    IPv4 Address. . . . . . . . . . . : 192.168.4.27(Preferred)
    Subnet Mask . . . . . . . . . . . : 255.255.255.0
    Lease Obtained. . . . . . . . . . : Wednesday, August 13, 2014 8:47:32 AM
    Lease Expires . . . . . . . . . . : Tuesday, September 02, 2014 8:25:51 AM
    Default Gateway . . . . . . . . . : 192.168.4.1
    DHCP Server . . . . . . . . . . . : 192.168.4.12
    DHCPv6 IAID . . . . . . . . . . . : 400608078
    DHCPv6 Client DUID. . . . . . . . : 00-01-00-01-13-57-F6-2D-E0-CB-4E-93-02-78
    DNS Servers . . . . . . . . . . . : 192.168.4.12
    NetBIOS over Tcpip. . . . . . . . : Enabled

Tunnel adapter isatap.totalhome:

    Media State . . . . . . . . . . . : Media disconnected
    Connection-specific DNS Suffix  . : totalhome
    Description . . . . . . . . . . . : Microsoft ISATAP Adapter
    Physical Address. . . . . . . . . : 00-00-00-00-00-00-00-E0
    DHCP Enabled. . . . . . . . . . . : No
    Autoconfiguration Enabled . . . . : Yes

C:\>
```

Figure 6-19 `ipconfig /all` results

```
 ● ● ●                  ⌂ ivanalmanza — -bash — 107×39
Last login: Tue Nov 28 09:08:07 on console
mediamac-2:~ ivanalmanza$ ifconfig
lo0: flags=8049<UP,LOOPBACK,RUNNING,MULTICAST> mtu 16384
        options=1203<RXCSUM,TXCSUM,TXSTATUS,SW_TIMESTAMP>
        inet 127.0.0.1 netmask 0xff000000
        inet6 ::1 prefixlen 128
        inet6 fe80::1%lo0 prefixlen 64 scopeid 0x1
        nd6 options=201<PERFORMNUD,DAD>
gif0: flags=8010<POINTOPOINT,MULTICAST> mtu 1280
stf0: flags=0<> mtu 1280
en0: flags=8863<UP,BROADCAST,SMART,RUNNING,SIMPLEX,MULTICAST> mtu 1500
        options=10b<RXCSUM,TXCSUM,VLAN_HWTAGGING,AV>
        ether 3c:07:54:7a:d4:d8
        inet6 fe80::1839:d11d:5a0f:46a9%en0 prefixlen 64 secured scopeid 0x4
        inet6 2603:300c:d:cd01:1c48:fd01:ac72:aa52 prefixlen 64 autoconf secured
        inet6 2603:300c:d:cd01:e846:afc4:4ef5:1815 prefixlen 64 deprecated autoconf temporary
        inet 192.168.4.29 netmask 0xffffff00 broadcast 192.168.4.255
        inet6 2603:300c:d:cd01:84d4:c0a5:a3cf:c494 prefixlen 64 autoconf temporary
        nd6 options=201<PERFORMNUD,DAD>
        media: autoselect (1000baseT <full-duplex,flow-control>)
        status: active
en1: flags=8863<UP,BROADCAST,SMART,RUNNING,SIMPLEX,MULTICAST> mtu 1500
        ether 7c:c3:a1:a8:f5:ed
        inet6 fe80::3f:f777:7287:696b%en1 prefixlen 64 secured scopeid 0x5
        inet 192.168.4.42 netmask 0xffffff00 broadcast 192.168.4.255
        inet6 2603:300c:d:cd01:42:fa78:69eb:ed3f prefixlen 64 autoconf secured
        inet6 2603:300c:d:cd01:596:c814:8189:712e prefixlen 64 deprecated autoconf temporary
        inet6 2603:300c:d:cd01:559f:e84:92b4:9e64 prefixlen 64 autoconf temporary
        nd6 options=201<PERFORMNUD,DAD>
        media: autoselect
        status: active
fw0: flags=8863<UP,BROADCAST,SMART,RUNNING,SIMPLEX,MULTICAST> mtu 4078
        lladdr 3c:07:54:ff:fe:bd:d2:8c
        nd6 options=201<PERFORMNUD,DAD>
        media: autoselect <full-duplex>
        status: inactive
en2: flags=963<UP,BROADCAST,SMART,RUNNING,PROMISC,SIMPLEX> mtu 1500
        options=60<TSO4,TSO6>
        ether d2:00:1b:dd:28:c0
```

Figure 6-20 Results from running `ifconfig` in macOS

```
                ubadmin@ubadmin-VirtualBox: ~
ubadmin@ubadmin-VirtualBox:~$ ip a
1: lo: <LOOPBACK,UP,LOWER_UP> mtu 65536 qdisc noqueue state UNKNOWN group defaul
t qlen 1
    link/loopback 00:00:00:00:00:00 brd 00:00:00:00:00:00
    inet 127.0.0.1/8 scope host lo
       valid_lft forever preferred_lft forever
    inet6 ::1/128 scope host
       valid_lft forever preferred_lft forever
2: enp0s3: <BROADCAST,MULTICAST,UP,LOWER_UP> mtu 1500 qdisc pfifo_fast state UP
group default qlen 1000
    link/ether 08:00:27:ec:7c:8d brd ff:ff:ff:ff:ff:ff
    inet 192.168.4.68/24 brd 192.168.4.255 scope global dynamic enp0s3
       valid_lft 518321sec preferred_lft 518321sec
    inet6 2603:300c:d:cd01:1401:e139:a8c6:727d/64 scope global temporary dynamic

       valid_lft 86323sec preferred_lft 14323sec
    inet6 2603:300c:d:cd01:3b1c:5944:e7d1:419e/64 scope global mngtmpaddr nopref
ixroute dynamic
       valid_lft 86323sec preferred_lft 14323sec
    inet6 fe80::6a10:44d0:be6:ab8d/64 scope link
       valid_lft forever preferred_lft forever
ubadmin@ubadmin-VirtualBox:~$ []
```

Figure 6-21   Results from running `ip a` in Ubuntu

To make all this work, the IP numbering system must do three things:

- Create network IDs, a way to use IP addresses so that each LAN has its own identification.

- Interconnect the LANs using routers and give those routers some way to use the network identification to send packets to the right network.

- Use a subnet mask to give each computer on the network a way to recognize if a packet is for the LAN or for a computer on the WAN, so it knows how to handle the packet.

Network IDs

A WAN is nothing more than a group of two or more interconnected LANs. For a WAN to work, each LAN needs some form of unique identifier called a network ID.

To differentiate LANs from one another, each computer on a single LAN must share a very similar, but not identical, IP address. Some parts of the IP address will match all the others on the LAN. Figure 6-22 shows a LAN where all the computers share the first three numbers of the IP address, with only the last number being unique on each system.

In this example, every computer has an IP address of 202.120.10.*x*, where the *x* value is unique for every host, but every host's IP address starts with 202.120.10. That means the *network ID* is 202.120.10.0. The *x* part of the IP address is the *host ID*. Combine the network ID (after dropping the ending 0) with the host ID to get an individual system's IP address. No individual computer can have an IP address that ends with 0 because that is reserved for network IDs.

Figure 6-22
IP addresses for
a LAN

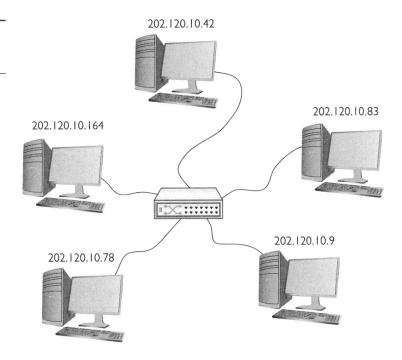

202.120.10.42

202.120.10.83

202.120.10.164

202.120.10.9

202.120.10.78

NOTE   Two things to note here. First, the network ID and the host ID are combined to make a system's IP address. Second, a host ID *can* end in 0— although this is uncommon—but we have to discuss subnetting before any of this will make sense. Read on!

Interconnecting LANs

To organize all those individual LANs into a larger network, every TCP/IP LAN that wants to connect to another TCP/IP LAN must have a router connection. There is no exception to this critical rule. A router, therefore, needs an IP address on every LAN that it interconnects (Figure 6-23), so it can correctly send (route) the packets to the correct LAN.

The router interface that connects a single LAN to the router is known as the *default gateway*. In a typical scenario configuring a client to access the network beyond the router, you use the IP address of the default gateway. The default gateway is in the same network ID as the host. The person who sets up the router must make sure that they configure the router's LAN interface to have an address in the LAN's network ID. By convention, most network administrators give the LAN-side NIC on the default gateway the lowest host address in the network, usually the host ID of 1. Therefore, if a network ID is 22.33.4.*x*, the router is configured to use the address 22.33.4.1.

Figure 6-23
LAN with router

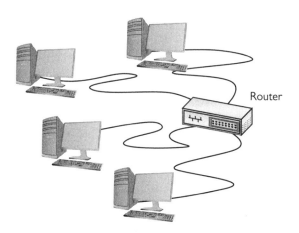

Routers use network IDs to determine network traffic. Figure 6-24 shows a diagram for a small, two-NIC router similar to the ones you see in many homes. Note that one port (202.120.10.1) connects to the LAN and the other port connects to the Internet service provider's network (14.23.54.223). Built into this router is a *routing table*, the actual instructions that tell the router what to do with incoming packets and where to send them.

Figure 6-24
Router diagram

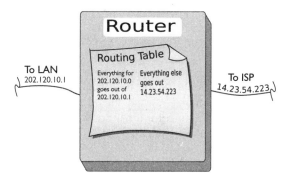

Now let's add in the LAN and the Internet (Figure 6-25). When discussing networks in terms of network IDs, by the way, especially with illustrations in books, the common practice is to draw circles around stylized networks. Here, you should concentrate on the IDs—not the specifics of the networks.

 NOTE Routing tables are covered in more detail in Chapter 7.

Network IDs are very flexible, as long as no two interconnected networks share the same network ID. If you wished, you could change the network ID of the 202.120.10.0 network to 202.155.5.0, or 202.21.8.0, just as long as you can guarantee no other LAN

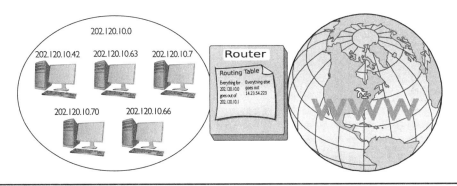

Figure 6-25   LAN, router, and the Internet

on the WAN shares the same network ID. On the Internet, powerful governing bodies carefully allocate network IDs to ensure no two LANs share the same network ID. I'll talk more about how this works later in the chapter.

So far, you've only seen examples of network IDs where the last value is zero. This is common for small networks, but it creates a limitation. With a network ID of 202.120.10.0, for example, a network is limited to IP addresses from 202.120.10.1 to 202.120.10.254. (202.120.10.255 is a broadcast address used to talk to every computer on the LAN.) This provides only 254 IP addresses: enough for a small network, but many organizations need many more IP addresses. No worries! You can simply use a network ID with more zeroes, such as 170.45.0.0 (for a total of 65,534 hosts) or even 12.0.0.0 (for around 16.7 million hosts).

Network IDs enable you to connect multiple LANs into a WAN. Routers then connect everything together, using routing tables to keep track of which packets go where. So that takes care of the second task: interconnecting the LANs using routers and giving those routers a way to send packets to the right network.

Now that you know how IP addressing works with LANs and WANs, let's turn to how IP enables each computer on a network to recognize if a packet is going to a computer on the LAN or to a computer on the WAN. The secret to this is something called the subnet mask.

Subnet Mask

Picture this scenario. Three friends sit at their computers—Computers A, B, and C—and want to communicate with each other. Figure 6-26 illustrates the situation. You can tell from the drawing that Computers A and B are in the same LAN, whereas Computer C is on a completely different LAN. The IP addressing scheme can handle this communication, so let's see how it works.

The process to get a packet to a local computer is very different from the process to get a packet to a faraway computer. If one computer wants to send a packet to a local computer, it must send a broadcast to get the other computer's MAC address. (It's easy to forget about the MAC address, but remember that the network uses Ethernet and

Figure 6-26
The three amigos, separated by walls or miles

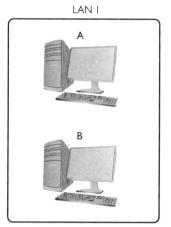

LAN I

LAN 2

must have the MAC address to get the packet to the other computer.) If the packet is for some computer on a faraway network, the sending computer must send the packet to the default gateway (Figure 6-27).

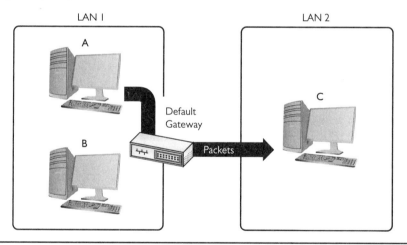

Figure 6-27 Sending a packet remotely

In the scenario illustrated in Figure 6-26, Computer A wants to send a packet to Computer B. Computer B is on the same LAN as Computer A, but that begs a question: How does Computer A know this? Every TCP/IP computer needs a tool to tell the sending computer whether the destination IP address is local or long distance. This tool is the subnet mask.

A *subnet mask* is nothing more than a string of ones followed by some number of zeroes, always totaling exactly 32 bits, typed into every TCP/IP host. Here's an example of a typical subnet mask:

11111111111111111111111100000000

For the courtesy of the humans reading this (if any computers are reading this book, please call me—I'd love to meet you!), let's convert this to dotted decimal. First, add some periods:

11111111.11111111.11111111.00000000

Then convert each octet into decimal (use a calculator):

255.255.255.0

When you line up an IP address with a corresponding subnet mask in binary, the portion of the IP address that aligns with the ones of the subnet mask is the network ID portion of the IP address. The portion that aligns with the zeroes is the host ID. With simple IP addresses, you can see this with dotted decimal, but you'll want to see this in binary for a true understanding of how the computers work.

 EXAM TIP At this point, you should memorize that 0 = 00000000 and 255 = 11111111. You'll find knowing this very helpful throughout the rest of the book.

The IP address 192.168.5.23 has a subnet mask of 255.255.255.0. Convert both numbers to binary and then compare the full IP address to the ones and zeroes of the subnet mask:

	Dotted Decimal	Binary
IP address	192.168.5.23	11000000.10101000.00000101.00010111
Subnet mask	255.255.255.0	11111111.11111111.11111111.00000000
Network ID	192.168.5.0	11000000.10101000.00000101.*x*
Host ID	*x.x.x*.23	*x.x.x*.00010111

Before a computer sends out any data, it first compares the destination IP address to its own IP address using the subnet mask. If the destination IP address matches the computer's IP address wherever there's a 1 in the subnet mask, then the sending computer knows the destination is local. The network IDs match. If even one bit of the destination IP address where the 1s are on the subnet mask is different, then the sending computer knows it's a long-distance call. The network IDs do not match.

 NOTE The explanation about comparing an IP address to a subnet mask simplifies the process, leaving out how the computer uses its routing table to accomplish the goal. We'll get to routing and routing tables in Chapter 7. For now, stick with the concept of the node using the subnet mask to determine the network ID.

Let's head over to Computer A and see how the subnet mask works. Computer A's IP address is 192.168.5.23. Convert that into binary:

11000000.10101000.00000101.00010111

Now drop the periods because they mean nothing to the computer:

11000000101010000000010100010111

Let's say Computer A wants to send a packet to Computer B. Computer A's subnet mask is 255.255.255.0. Computer B's IP address is 192.168.5.45. Convert this address to binary:

11000000101010000000010100101101

Computer A compares its IP address to Computer B's IP address using the subnet mask, as shown in Figure 6-28. For clarity, I've added a line to show you where the ones end and the zeroes begin in the subnet mask. Computers certainly don't need the pretty (red) line!

Figure 6-28

Comparing
addresses

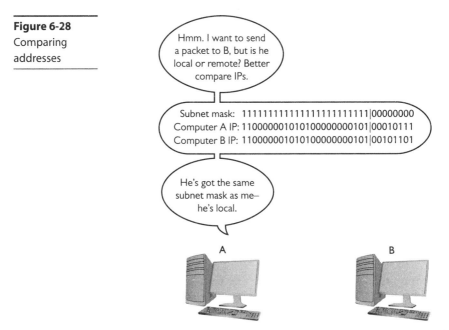

A-ha! Computer A's and Computer B's network IDs match! It's a local call. Knowing this, Computer A can now send out an ARP request, which is a broadcast, as shown in Figure 6-29, to determine Computer B's MAC address. *Address Resolution Protocol (ARP)* is how a TCP/IP network figures out the MAC address based on the destination IP address, as you'll recall from earlier in the chapter.

But what happens when Computer A wants to send a packet to Computer C? First, Computer A compares Computer C's IP address to its own using the subnet mask (Figure 6-29). It sees that the IP addresses do not match in the 1s part of the subnet mask—meaning the network IDs don't match; therefore, this is a long-distance call.

Whenever a computer wants to send to an IP address on another LAN, it knows to send the packet to the default gateway. It still sends out an ARP request, but this time it's to learn the MAC address for the default gateway (Figure 6-30). Once Computer A gets the default gateway's MAC address, it then begins to send packets.

Figure 6-29
Comparing
addresses again

Subnet masks are represented in dotted decimal like IP addresses—just remember that both are really 32-bit binary numbers. All the following (shown in both binary and dotted decimal formats) can be subnet masks:

11111111111111111111111100000000 = 255.255.255.0
11111111111111110000000000000000 = 255.255.0.0
11111111000000000000000000000000 = 255.0.0.0

Most network folks represent subnet masks using special shorthand: a / character followed by a number equal to the number of ones in the subnet mask. Here are a few examples:

11111111111111111111111100000000 = /24 (24 ones)
11111111111111110000000000000000 = /16 (16 ones)
11111111000000000000000000000000 = /8 (8 ones)

Figure 6-30
Sending an ARP
request to the
gateway

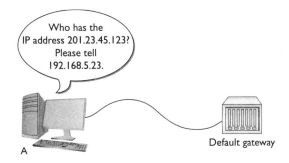

An IP address followed by the / and number tells you the IP address and the subnet mask in one statement. For example, 201.23.45.123/24 is an IP address of 201.23.45.123 with a subnet mask of 255.255.255.0. Similarly, 184.222.4.36/16 is an IP address of 184.222.4.36 with a subnet mask of 255.255.0.0.

Fortunately, computers do subnet filtering automatically. Network administrators need only to enter the correct IP address and subnet mask when they first set up their systems, and the rest happens without any human intervention.

 NOTE By definition, all computers on the same network have the same subnet mask and network ID.

If you want a computer to work in a routed internetwork (like the Internet), you absolutely must have an IP address that's part of its network ID, a subnet mask, and a default gateway. No exceptions!

Class IDs

The Internet is by far the biggest and the most complex TCP/IP internetwork. Numbering over half a billion computers already a decade ago, it has grown so quickly that now it's nearly impossible to find an accurate number. One challenge for the Internet is to make sure no two devices share the same public IP address. To support the dispersion of IP addresses, an organization called the *Internet Assigned Numbers Authority (IANA)* was formed to track and disperse IP addresses to those who need them. Initially handled by a single person (the famous Jon Postel) until 1998, IANA has grown dramatically and now oversees five Regional Internet Registries (RIRs) that parcel out IP addresses to large ISPs and major corporations. The RIR for North America is called the *American Registry for Internet Numbers (ARIN)*. All end users get their IP addresses from their respective ISPs. IANA passes out IP addresses in contiguous chunks called *network blocks* (or just *blocks*), which are outlined in the following table:

	First Decimal Value	Addresses	Hosts per Network ID
Class A	1–126	1.0.0.0–126.255.255.255	16,277,214
Class B	128–191	128.0.0.0–191.255.255.255	65,534
Class C	192–223	192.0.0.0–223.255.255.255	254
Class D	224–239	224.0.0.0–239.255.255.255	Multicast
Class E	240–254	240.0.0.0–254.255.255.255	Experimental

A typical Class A network block, for example, has a network ID that starts between 1 and 126; hosts on that network have only the first octet in common, with any numbers for the other three octets. Having three octets to use for hosts means you have an enormous number of possible hosts, over 16 million different number combinations. The subnet mask for Class A network blocks is 255.0.0.0, which means you have 24 bits for host IDs.

EXAM TIP   CompTIA and many techs use the term *classful* to describe the traditional class blocks. Thus you'll see *classful A, B, C, D, and E addressing* on the exam. Keep reading and this will make sense.

Do you remember binary math? 2^{24} = 16,277,216. Because the host can't use all zeroes or all ones (those are reserved for the network ID and broadcast IP, respectively), you subtract two from the final number to get the available host IDs.

A Class B network block, with a subnet mask of 255.255.0.0, uses the first two octets to define the network ID. This leaves two octets to define host IDs, which means each Class B network ID can have up to 65,534 different hosts.

A Class C network block uses the first three octets to define only the network ID. All hosts in network 192.168.35.0, for example, would have all three first numbers in common. Only the last octet defines the host IDs, which leaves only 254 possible unique addresses. The subnet mask for a Class C block is 255.255.255.0.

Multicast class blocks are used for one-to-many communication, such as in streaming video conferencing. There are three types of ways to send a packet: a *broadcast*, which is where every computer on the LAN hears the message; a *unicast*, where one computer sends a message directly to another user; and a *multicast*, where a single computer sends a packet to a group of interested computers. Multicast is often used when routers talk to each other.

Experimental addresses are reserved and never used except for occasional experimental reasons. These were originally called Reserved addresses.

EXAM TIP   Make sure you memorize the IP class blocks! You should be able to look at any IP address and know its class block. Here's a trick to help: The first binary octet of a Class A address always begins with a 0 (0*xxxxxxx*); for Class B, it begins with a 10 (10*xxxxxx*); for Class C, with 110 (110*xxxxx*); for Class D, with 1110 (1110*xxxx*); and for Class E, it begins with 1111 (1111*xxxx*).

IP class blocks worked well for the first few years of the Internet but quickly ran into trouble because they didn't quite fit for everyone. Early on, IANA gave away IP network blocks rather generously, perhaps too generously. Over time, unallocated IP addresses became scarce. Additionally, the IP class block concept didn't scale well. If an organization needed 2,000 IP addresses, for example, it either had to take a single Class B network block (wasting 63,000 addresses) or eight Class C blocks. As a result, a new method of generating blocks of IP addresses, called *Classless Inter-Domain Routing (CIDR)*, was developed.

EXAM TIP   Note the loopback and reserved addresses for the exam. Reserved are Experimental.

CIDR and Subnetting

CIDR is based on a concept called *subnetting*: taking a single class of IP addresses and chopping it up into multiple smaller groups. CIDR and subnetting are virtually the same thing. Subnetting is done by an organization—it is given a block of addresses and then breaks the single block of addresses into multiple subnets. CIDR is done by an ISP—it is given a block of addresses, subnets the block into multiple subnets, and then passes out the smaller individual subnets to customers. Subnetting and CIDR have been around for quite a long time now and are a critical part of all but the smallest TCP/IP networks. Let's first discuss subnetting and then visit CIDR.

Subnetting

Subnetting enables a much more efficient use of IP addresses compared to class blocks. It also enables you to separate a network for security (separating a bank of public access computers from your more private computers) and for bandwidth control (separating a heavily used LAN from one that's not so heavily used).

 EXAM TIP You need to know how to subnet to pass the CompTIA Network+ exam.

The cornerstone to subnetting lies in the subnet mask. You take an existing /8, /16, or /24 subnet and extend the subnet mask by adding more ones (and taking away the corresponding number of zeroes). For example, let's say you have an Internet café with about 50 computers, 40 of which are for public use and 10 of which are used in the back office for accounting and such (Figure 6-31). Your network ID is 192.168.4.0/24. You want to prevent people who are using the public systems from accessing your private machines, so you decide to create subnets. You also have wireless Internet and want to separate wireless clients (never more than 10) on their own subnet.

You need to keep two things in mind about subnetting. First, start with the given subnet mask and move it to the right until you have the number of subnets you need. Second, forget the dots. They no longer define the subnets.

Never try to subnet without first converting to binary. Too many techs are what I call "victims of the dots." They are so used to working only with class blocks that they forget there's more to subnets than just /8, /16, and /24 networks. There is no reason network IDs must end on the dots. The computers, at least, think it's perfectly fine to have subnets that end at points between the periods, such as /26, /27, or even /22. The trick here is to stop thinking about network IDs and subnet masks just in their dotted decimal format and instead return to thinking of them as binary numbers.

 NOTE Classful subnets are always /8, /16, or /24. When we stop using that convention and start using classless subnet masks, we are using a *custom subnet mask*.

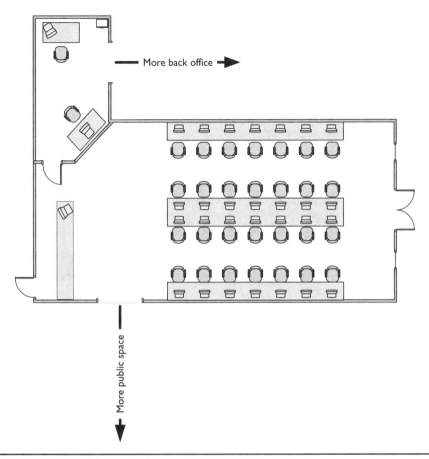

Figure 6-31 Layout of the network

Let's begin subnetting the café's network of 192.168.4.0/24. Start by changing a zero to a one on the subnet mask so the /24 becomes a /25 subnet:

```
11111111111111111111111110000000
```

Calculating Hosts

Before going even one step further, you need to answer this question: On a /24 network, how many hosts can you have? If you used dotted decimal notation you might say the following:

192.168.4.1 to 192.168.4.254 = 254 hosts

But do this from the binary instead. In a /24 network, you have eight zeroes that can be the host ID:

00000001 to 11111110 = 254

There's a simple piece of math here: $2^x - 2$, where x represents the number of zeroes in the subnet mask.

$$2^8 - 2 = 254$$

If you remember this simple formula, you can always determine the number of hosts for a given subnet. This is critical! Memorize this!

If you have a /16 subnet mask on your network, what is the maximum number of hosts you can have on that network?

1. Because a subnet mask always has 32 digits, a /16 subnet means you have 16 zeroes left after the 16 ones.

2. $2^{16} - 2 = 65,534$ total hosts.

If you have a /26 subnet mask on your network, what is the maximum number of hosts you can have on that network?

1. Because a subnet mask always has 32 digits, a /26 subnet means you have 6 zeroes left after the 26 ones.

2. $2^6 - 2 = 62$ total hosts.

Excellent! Knowing how to determine the number of hosts for a subnet mask will help you tremendously, as you'll see in a moment.

Making a Subnet

Let's now make a subnet. All subnetting begins with a single network ID. In this scenario, you need to convert the 192.168.4.0/24 network ID for the café into three network IDs: one for the public computers, one for the private computers, and one for the wireless clients.

 NOTE You cannot subnet without using binary!

The primary tool for subnetting is the existing subnet mask. Write it out in binary. Place a line at the end of the ones, as shown in Figure 6-32.

Figure 6-32
Step 1 in
subnetting

Subnet mask   11111111111111111111111111|00000000

Now draw a second line one digit to the right, as shown in Figure 6-33. You've now separated the subnet mask into three areas that I call (from left to right) the default subnet mask (DSM), the network ID extension (NE), and the hosts (H). These are not industry terms, so you won't see them on the CompTIA Network+ exam, but they're a handy Mike Trick that makes the process of subnetting a lot easier.

Figure 6-33
Organizing the
subnet mask

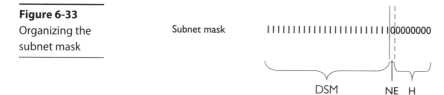

You now have a /25 subnet mask. At this point, most people first learning how to subnet start to freak out. They're challenged by the idea that a subnet mask of /25 isn't going to fit into one of the three pretty subnets of 255.0.0.0, 255.255.0.0, or 255.255.255.0. They think, "That can't be right! Subnet masks are made of only 255s and 0s." That's not correct. A subnet mask is a string of ones followed by a string of zeroes. People only convert it into dotted decimal to enter things into computers. So, convert /25 into dotted decimal. First write out 25 ones, followed by 7 zeroes. (Remember, subnet masks are *always* 32 binary digits long.)

```
1111111111111111111111110000000
```

Insert the periods in between every eight digits:

```
11111111.11111111.11111111.10000000
```

Then convert them to dotted decimal:

```
255.255.255.128
```

Get used to the idea of subnet masks that use more than 255s and 0s. Here are some examples of perfectly legitimate subnet masks. Try converting these to binary to see for yourself.

```
255.255.255.224
255.255.128.0
255.248.0.0
```

Calculating Subnets

When you subnet a network ID, you need to follow the rules and conventions dictated by the good folks who developed TCP/IP to ensure that your new subnets can interact properly with each other and with larger networks. All you need to remember for subnetting is this: start with a beginning subnet mask and extend the subnet extension until you have the number of subnets you need. The formula for determining how many subnets you create is 2^y, where y is the number of bits you add to the subnet mask.

Let's practice this a few times. Figure 6-34 shows a starting subnet of 255.255.255.0. If you move the network ID extension over one, it's only a single digit, 2^1.

That single digit is only a zero or a one, which gives you two subnets. You have only one problem—the café needs three subnets, not just two! So, let's take /24 and

Figure 6-34

Initial subnetting

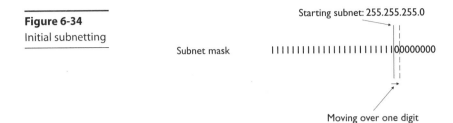

subnet it down to /26. Extending the network ID by two digits creates four new network IDs, $2^2 = 4$. To see each of these network IDs, first convert the original network ID—192.168.4.0—into binary. Then add the four different network ID extensions to the end, as shown in Figure 6-35.

Figure 6-35

Creating the new network IDs

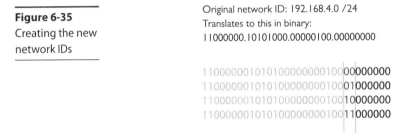

Figure 6-36 shows all the IP addresses for each of the four new network IDs.

Figure 6-36

New network ID address ranges

```
11000000101010000000010000000001
11000000101010000000010000000010
11000000101010000000010000000011
11000000101010000000010000000100

11000000101010000000010001000001
11000000101010000000010001000010
11000000101010000000010001000011
11000000101010000000010001000100

11000000101010000000010010000001
11000000101010000000010010000010
11000000101010000000010010000011
11000000101010000000010010000100

11000000101010000000010011000001
11000000101010000000010011000010
11000000101010000000010011000011
11000000101010000000010011000100
```

Now convert these four network IDs back to dotted decimal:

Network ID	Host Range	Broadcast Address
192.168.4.0/26	(192.168.4.1–192.168.4.62)	192.168.4.63
192.168.4.64/26	(192.168.4.65–192.168.4.126)	192.168.4.127
192.168.4.128/26	(192.168.4.129–192.168.4.190)	192.168.4.191
192.168.4.192/26	(192.168.4.193–192.168.4.254)	192.168.4.255

Congratulations! You've just taken a single network ID, 192.168.4.0/24, and subnetted it into four new network IDs! Figure 6-37 shows how you can use these new network IDs in a network.

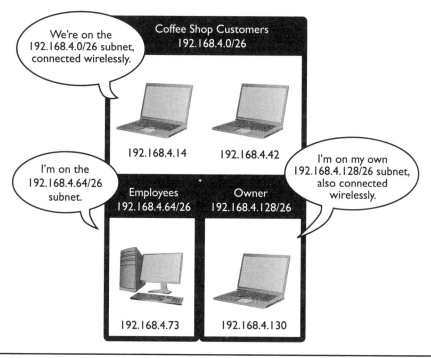

Figure 6-37   Three networks using the new network IDs

You may notice that the café only needs three subnets, but you created four—you're wasting one. Because subnets are created by powers of two, you will often create more subnets than you need—welcome to subnetting.

NOTE   If wasting subnets seems contrary to the goal of efficient use, keep in mind that subnetting has two goals: efficiency and making multiple network IDs from a single network ID. This example is geared more toward the latter goal.

For a little more subnetting practice, let's create eight subnets on a /27 network. First, move the NE over three digits (Figure 6-38).

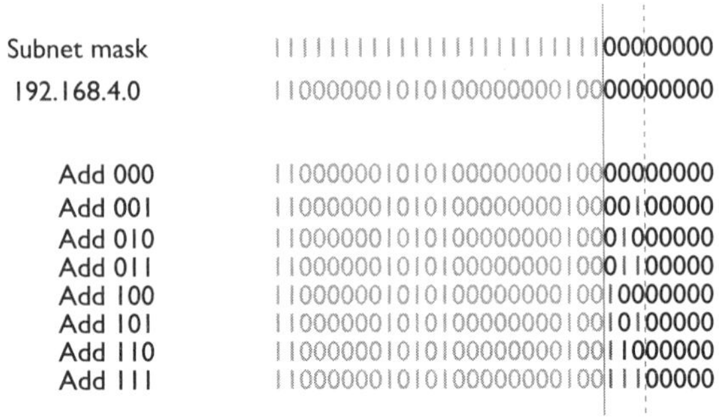

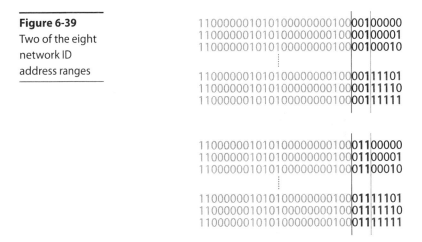

Figure 6-38
Moving the network ID extension three digits

To help you visualize the address range, I'll calculate the first two subnets—using 000 and 001 (Figure 6-39). Please do the other six for practice.

Figure 6-39
Two of the eight network ID address ranges

Note that in this case you only get $2^5 - 2 = 30$ hosts per network ID! These better be small networks!

Converting these to dotted decimal, you get:

192.168.4.0/27 (192.168.4.1–192.168.4.30)
192.168.4.32/27 (192.168.4.33–192.168.4.62)
192.168.4.64/27 (192.168.4.65–192.168.4.94)
192.168.4.96/27 (192.168.4.97–192.168.4.126)
192.168.4.128/27 (192.168.4.129–192.168.4.158)
192.168.4.160/27 (192.168.4.161–192.168.4.190)
192.168.4.192/27 (192.168.4.193–192.168.4.222)
192.168.4.224/27 (192.168.4.225–192.168.4.254)

These two examples began with a Class C address. However, you can begin with any starting network ID. Nothing changes about the process you just learned.

 EXAM TIP CompTIA and many techs refer to a CIDR address as a *classless address*, meaning the subnet used does not conform to the big three on the classful side: A, B, or C. When you see that term on the exam, you'll know you should look for subnetting.

The examples used in this introduction to subnetting took a single network ID and chopped it into identically sized subnets. The simplest subnetting example, in other words, created four /26 subnets from one /24 network ID. You can vary the size of the subnets created, however, with *variable length subnet masking (VLSM)*. ISPs might do this to accommodate different customer needs, taking a single network ID and handing out custom subnets. John's tiny company might get a /30 subnet; Jennie's larger company might get a /26 subnet to accommodate many more users.

 EXAM TIP Expect to see a question or two on the CompTIA Network+ exam that asks you to compare CIDR notation (IPv4 vs. IPv6). The former should be familiar, with four octets and a /# for the subnet mask. See Chapter 12 for IPv6.

Manual Dotted Decimal to Binary Conversion

The best way to convert from dotted decimal to binary and back is to use a calculator. It's easy, fast, and accurate. There's always a chance, however, that you may find yourself in a situation where you need to convert without a calculator. Fortunately, manual conversion, although a bit tedious, is also easy. You just have to remember a single number: 128.

Take a piece of paper and write the number **128** in the top-left corner. Now, what is half of 128? That's right, 64. Write **64** next to 128. Now keep dividing the previous number in half until you get to the number 1. The result will look like this:

```
128   64   32   16   8   4   2   1
```

Notice that you have eight numbers. Each of these numbers corresponds to a position of one of the eight binary digits. To convert an 8-bit value to dotted decimal, just take the binary value and put the numbers under the corresponding eight digits. Wherever there's a 1, add that decimal value.

Let's take the binary value 10010110 into decimal. Write down the numbers as shown, and then write the binary values underneath each corresponding decimal number:

```
128   64   32   16   8   4   2   1
  1    0    0    1   0   1   1   0
```

Add the decimal values that have a 1 underneath:

128+16+4+2 = 150

Converting from decimal to binary is a bit more of a challenge. You still start with a line of decimal numbers starting with 128, but this time, you place the decimal value above. If the number you're trying to convert is greater than or equal to the number underneath, subtract it and place a 1 underneath that value. If not, then place a 0 under it and move the number to the next position to the right. Let's give this a try by converting 221 to binary. Begin by placing 221 over the 128:

```
221
128   64   32   16   8   4   2   1
93
1
```

Now place the remainder, 93, over the 64:

```
      93
128   64   32   16   8   4   2   1
      29
1      1
```

Place the remainder, 29, over the 32. The number 29 is less than 32, so place a 0 underneath the 32 and move to 16:

```
               29
128   64   32   16   8   4   2   1
               13
  1    1    0    1
```

Then move to the 8:

```
                    13
128   64   32   16    8   4   2   1
                     5
  1    1    0    1    1
```

Then the 4:

```
                         5
128   64   32   16   8    4   2   1
                         1
  1    1    0    1   1    1
```

Then the 2. The number 1 is less than 2, so drop a 0 underneath and move to 1:

```
                              1
128   64   32   16   8   4    2   1
  1    1    0    1   1   1    0   1
```

Finally, the 1; 1 is equal to 1, so put a 1 underneath and you're done. The number 221 in decimal is equal to 11011101 in binary.

EXAM TIP   Make sure you can manually convert decimal to binary and binary to decimal.

CIDR: Subnetting in the Real World

I need to let you in on a secret—there's a better than average chance that you'll never have to do subnetting in the real world. That's not to say that subnetting isn't important. It's a critical part of the Internet's structure. Subnetting most commonly takes place in two situations: ISPs that receive network blocks from an RIR and then subnet those blocks for customers, and very large customers that take subnets (sometimes already subnetted class blocks from ISPs) and make their own subnets. Even if you'll never make a working subnet in the real world, there are several reasons to learn subnetting.

First and most obvious, the CompTIA Network+ exam expects you to know subnetting. For the exam, you need to be able to take any existing network ID and break it down into a given number of subnets. You need to know how many hosts the resulting network IDs possess. You need to be able to calculate the IP addresses and the new subnet masks for each of the new network IDs.

Second, even if you never do your own subnetting, you will most likely get CIDR addresses from an ISP. You can't think about subnet masks in terms of dotted decimal. You need to think of subnets in terms of CIDR values like /10, /22, /26, and so on.

Third, there's a better than average chance you'll look to obtain more advanced IT certifications. Most Cisco, many Microsoft, and many other certifications assume you understand subnetting. Subnetting is a competency standard that everyone who's serious about networking understands in detail—it's a clear separation between those who know networks and those who do not.

You've done well, my little Padawan. Subnetting takes a little getting used to. Go take a break. Take a walk. Play some World of Warcraft. Or fire up your Steam client and see if I'm playing Counter-Strike or Left 4 Dead (player name "desweds"). After a good mental break, dive back into subnetting and *practice*. Take any old network ID and practice making multiple subnets—lots of subnets!

IP Address Assignment

Whew! After all that subnetting, you've reached the point where it's time to start using some IP addresses. That is, after all, the goal of going through all that pain. There are two ways to give a host an IP address, subnet mask, and default gateway: either by typing in all the information (called *static addressing*) or by having a server program running on a system that automatically passes out all the IP information to systems as they boot up on or connect to a network (called *dynamic addressing*). Additionally, you must learn about several specialty IP addresses that have unique meanings in the IP world to make this all work.

 EXAM TIP The CompTIA Network+ exam objectives use the term *address assignments* to describe methods for setting device IP addresses. Note that that term applies to both the static and dynamic methods discussed here.

Static IP Addressing

Static addressing means typing all the IP information into each of your hosts. But before you type in anything, you must answer two questions: What are you typing in and where do you type it? Let's visualize a four-node network like the one shown in Figure 6-40.

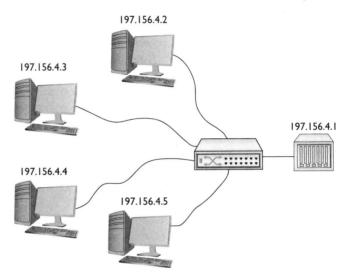

Figure 6-40
A small network

197.156.4.2

197.156.4.3

197.156.4.1

197.156.4.4

197.156.4.5

To make this network function, each computer must have an IP address, a subnet mask, and a default gateway. First, decide what network ID to use. In the old days, your ISP gave you a block of IP addresses to use. Assume that's still the method and you've been allocated a Class C network block for 197.156.4.0/24. The first rule of Internet addressing is ... no one talks about Internet addressing. Actually, we can maul the *Fight Club* reference and instead say, "The first rule of Internet addressing is that you can do whatever you want with your own network ID." There are no rules other than to make sure every computer gets a legit IP address and subnet mask for your network ID and make sure every IP address is unique. You don't have to use the numbers in order, you don't have to give the default gateway the 192.156.4.1 address—you can do it any way you want. That said, most networks follow a common set of principles:

1. Give the default gateway the first IP address in the network ID.

2. Try to use the IP addresses in sequential order.

3. Try to separate servers from clients. For example, servers could have the IP addresses 197.156.4.10 to 197.156.4.19, whereas the clients range from 197.156.4.200 to 197.156.4.254.

4. Document whatever you choose to do so the person who comes after you understands.

These principles have become unofficial standards for network techs, and following them will make you very popular with whoever has to manage your network in the future.

Now you can give each of the computers an IP address, subnet mask, and default gateway.

Every operating system has some method for you to enter in the static IP information. In Windows, you use the Internet Protocol Version 4 (TCP/IPv4) Properties dialog, as shown in Figure 6-41.

Figure 6-41

Entering static IP information in Windows Internet Protocol Version 4 (TCP/IPv4) Properties dialog

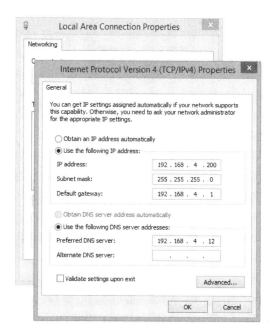

In macOS, run the Network utility in System Preferences to enter in the IP information (Figure 6-42).

The universal tool for entering IP information on UNIX/Linux systems is the command-line `ip` command:

```
# ip addr add 192.168.4.10 dev eth1
```

 EXAM TIP You might get a question about setting a static IP address in Linux where ip *isn't* one of the choices. Go with the deprecated ifconfig command in that case.

A warning about setting static IP addresses with `ip`: any address entered will not be permanent and will be lost on reboot. To make the new IP address permanent, you need to find and edit your network configuration files. Fortunately, modern distros make your life a bit easier. Almost every flavor of UNIX/Linux comes with some handy graphical program, such as Network Configuration in the popular Ubuntu Linux distro (Figure 6-43).

Figure 6-42

Entering static IP information in the macOS Network utility

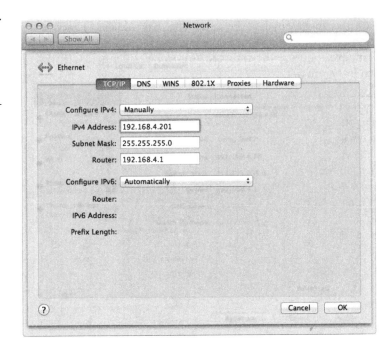

 SIM Check out the excellent "Static IP in Linux" Show! over at http://totalsem.com/007. It'll take you through the process of setting up a static IP in a typical Linux distro.

Once you've added the IP information for at least two systems, you should always verify using the ping command, as shown in Figure 6-44.

Figure 6-43

Ubuntu's Network Configuration utility

Figure 6-44

Two pings
(successful
ping on top,
unsuccessful
ping on bottom)

```
                        Command Prompt                    ─  □   ×
C:\>ping 192.168.4.8

Pinging 192.168.4.8 with 32 bytes of data:
Reply from 192.168.4.8: bytes=32 time<1ms TTL=128
Reply from 192.168.4.8: bytes=32 time<1ms TTL=128
Reply from 192.168.4.8: bytes=32 time<1ms TTL=128
Reply from 192.168.4.8: bytes=32 time<1ms TTL=128

Ping statistics for 192.168.4.8:
    Packets: Sent = 4, Received = 4, Lost = 0 (0% loss),
Approximate round trip times in milli-seconds:
    Minimum = 0ms, Maximum = 0ms, Average = 0ms

C:\>ping 192.168.4.8

Pinging 192.168.4.8 with 32 bytes of data:
Request timed out.
Request timed out.
Request timed out.
Reply from 192.168.5.200: Destination host unreachable.

Ping statistics for 192.168.4.8:
    Packets: Sent = 4, Received = 1, Lost = 3 (75% loss),

C:\>
```

CAUTION Always verify with ping—it's too easy to make a typo when entering static IP addresses.

If you've entered an IP address and your ping is not successful, first check your IP settings. Odds are good you made a typo. Otherwise, check your connections, driver, and so forth. Static addressing has been around for a long time and is still heavily used for more critical systems on your network. Static addressing poses one big problem, however: making any changes to the network is a serious pain. Most systems today use a far easier and more flexible method to get their IP information: dynamic IP addressing.

Dynamic IP Addressing

Dynamic IP addressing, better known as *Dynamic Host Configuration Protocol (DHCP)*, automatically assigns an IP address whenever a computer connects to the network. DHCP works very simply. Any network using DHCP consists of a DHCP server and lots of DHCP clients. Clients request IP information from DHCP servers. DHCP servers in turn pass out IP information to the clients (Figure 6-45). In most networks, most

Figure 6-45

DHCP server and
clients

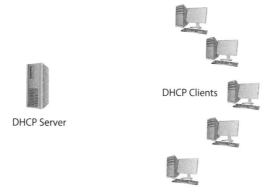

DHCP Clients

DHCP Server

hosts—desktops, laptops, and mobile devices—are DHCP clients. Most networks have a single DHCP server that often is built into a router for small office/home office (SOHO) networks or runs on a server in enterprise networks.

 EXAM TIP   A very early protocol called *Bootstrap Protocol (BOOTP)* preceded DHCP in providing dynamic IP addressing. It's been dead for many decades, but has been known to appear, zombie like, on CompTIA exams. If you see BOOTP or *BootP*, substitute DHCP and you'll see the right answer.

How DHCP Works

When a DHCP client boots up, it automatically sends out a special *DHCP Discover* message using the broadcast address. This DHCP Discover message asks, "Are there any DHCP servers out there?" (See Figure 6-46.)

Figure 6-46
Computer
sending out a
DHCP Discover
message

The DHCP server hears the request and then sends the DHCP client a *DHCP Offer* message (Figure 6-47). This message includes an IP address, subnet mask and gateway (as well as other information not yet covered in this book).

Figure 6-47
DHCP server
sending a DHCP
Offer message

DHCP Offer

Figure 6-48
DHCP Request
and DHCP
Acknowledgment

The DHCP client sends out a *DHCP Request*—a poor name choice as it is really accepting the offer—verifying that the offer is still valid. The DHCP Request is very important as it tells the network that this client is accepting IP information from this and only this DHCP server.

The DHCP server then sends a *DHCP Acknowledgment* and lists the MAC address as well as the IP information given to the DHCP client in a database (Figure 6-48).

At the end of this four-step DHCP dance (called the *DHCP four-way handshake*, or *DORA*, for Discover, Offer, Request, and Acknowledgment), the DHCP client gets a *DHCP lease*. A DHCP lease is set for a fixed amount of time, often one to eight days. Near the end of the lease time, the DHCP client sends another DHCP Request message.

The DHCP server looks at the MAC address information and always gives the DHCP client the same IP information, including the same IP address.

 NOTE   Using the acronym DORA—for Discover, Offer, Request, and Acknowledgment—will help you remember the DHCP four-way handshake.

Configuring DHCP

A properly functioning DHCP network requires properly configured DHCP clients and DHCP servers. Let's look at the configuration of both a client and a server.

Configuring a DHCP client is simple and, in most cases, every host is preconfigured as a DHCP client by default. Every OS has some method to tell the computer to use DHCP, as in the Windows example shown in Figure 6-49.

 EXAM TIP   DHCP uses *UDP* ports 67 and 68. And yes, memorize the numbers.

 SIM   Check out the excellent Chapter 6 "DHCP Client Setup" Click! over at **http://totalsem.com/007**. It walks you through the process of setting up DHCP in Windows.

Figure 6-49
Setting up for
DHCP

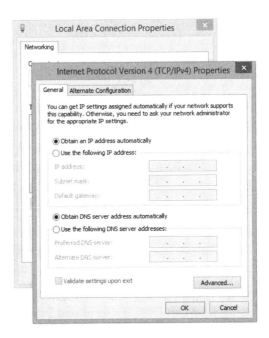

DHCP servers, on the other hand, require some hands-on configuration. Consider what a DHCP server requires:

- It needs a pool of legitimate IP addresses that it can pass out to clients.
- It needs to know the subnet mask for the network.
- It needs to know the IP address for the default gateway for the network.

When a technician installs a range (or *pool*) of IP addresses, this is called a *DHCP scope*. Figure 6-50 shows a typical home router's DHCP settings. Note that it is passing out a DHCP scope of 192.168.1.100 to 192.168.1.150. You can also see the place to enter the subnet mask. It also passes out other information, known as *scope options*, that cover many choices, such as the default gateway, DNS server, Network Time server, and so on.

So where is the default gateway setting? This home router assumes that it is the default gateway (a fairly safe guess), so it automatically passes out its own IP address (configured on a different screen).

Note the settings of Enable, Disable, and DHCP Relay in Figure 6-50. Since in all but the rarest cases there should only be one DHCP server on a small LAN, it's handy to give an option to disable the DHCP server on this router. DHCP relay is a bit more complex, so let's take some time to understand this powerful feature.

DHCP Relay　DHCP relies on broadcasting to work. DORA initially consists of three broadcasts as the DHCP client tries to find the DHCP server and the DHCP server provides IP information. Only the fourth step—Acknowledge—is unicast. (On a DHCP renew, everything's unicast because the client already has a valid IP address and knows the

Figure 6-50
DHCP server
main screen

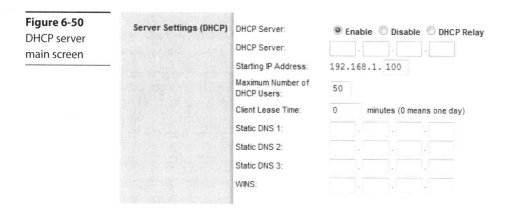

Server Settings (DHCP)	DHCP Server:	● Enable ○ Disable ○ DHCP Relay
	DHCP Server:	☐ . ☐ . ☐ . ☐
	Starting IP Address:	192.168.1. 100
	Maximum Number of DHCP Users:	50
	Client Lease Time:	0 minutes (0 means one day)
	Static DNS 1:	☐ . ☐ . ☐ . ☐
	Static DNS 2:	☐ . ☐ . ☐ . ☐
	Static DNS 3:	☐ . ☐ . ☐ . ☐
	WINS:	☐ . ☐ . ☐ . ☐

DHCP server's IP address.) Using broadcasting works well within a broadcast domain. But all routers block broadcast traffic (if they didn't, the entire Internet would consist of nothing but broadcasts). See Figure 6-51.

Figure 6-51
Routers block
DHCP broadcasts.

There are situations, however, where it's difficult or impractical to place a DHCP server in the same LAN as the DHCP clients. A single organization with many individual LANs would also need many individual DHCP servers, an administrative nightmare. These cases require the use of a *DHCP relay* (or DHCP relay agent). A DHCP relay, built into most routers, accepts DHCP broadcasts from clients and then sends them via unicast addresses directly to the DHCP server (Figure 6-52).

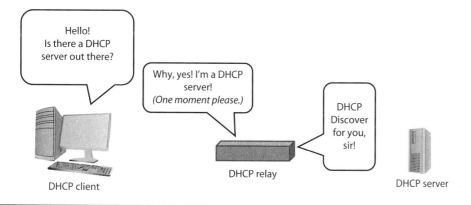

Figure 6-52   DHCP relays enable DHCP traffic to cross routers.

To make a DHCP relay-capable device work, you must give the relay the IP address of the real DHCP server, also known as the *IP helper* address. Refer to Figure 6-50 to see where the IP helper address is added just below the DHCP Server radio buttons.

NOTE The CompTIA objectives list DHCP TTL (Time to Live?) as something of interest. As a 25-year user of DHCP, I've never had this issue. After much research, there are some DHCP clients that need a TTL setting to determine how many routers (hops) a DHCP relay can be from the IP helper. I say "Nuts" to CompTIA.

DHCP Reservation The DHCP servers that come with SOHO routers are more than sufficient for small networks, but use only a small part of the power of DHCP, in particular DHCP IP reservations. An enterprise network often contains hosts that use only static IP addresses. File servers, printers, cameras, multipurpose devices, and many other hosts should never use DHCP; users need a permanent, fixed, statically assigned IP address to locate these devices easier (Figure 6-53).

Figure 6-53
Many devices do not need DHCP.

We want static IP addresses!

Printers

Cameras

Servers

In most cases it's a good idea to set aside IP addresses for certain types of devices. Here is one example, using the network ID 192.168.4.0:

- Routers and switches get .1 to .10 in the last octet.
- Servers get .11 to .30 in the last octet.
- Wired DHCP clients get .31 to .99 in the last octet.
- Printers, cameras, and wireless access points get .100 to .149 in the last octet.
- Wireless DHCP clients get .150 to .254 in the last octet.

In some cases, however, there might be an address or two inside a DHCP pool that is already configured for static that you do not want the DHCP server to issue to a DHCP client. In such a scenario an *IP exclusion* is used. Figure 6-54 shows the configuration screen for setting an IP exclusion in the built-in DHCP tool that comes with Windows Server.

MAC Reservations Another interesting though rarely used option for DHCP is the MAC reservation. For some networks, it's more convenient to assign a server a

Figure 6-54
DHCP Server configuration screen showing IP exclusion

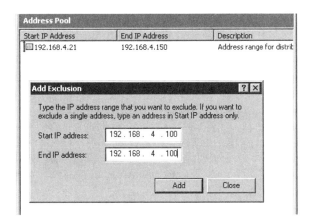

DHCP-assigned address than to set it up statically. To do this, set up the DHCP server to use a *MAC reservation*. A MAC reservation assigns a specific IP address to a specific MAC address. Always. From now on, anytime the system with that MAC address makes a DHCP Request, the DHCP reservation guarantees that that system will get the same IP address. Figure 6-55 shows Windows DHCP Server configuring a MAC reservation.

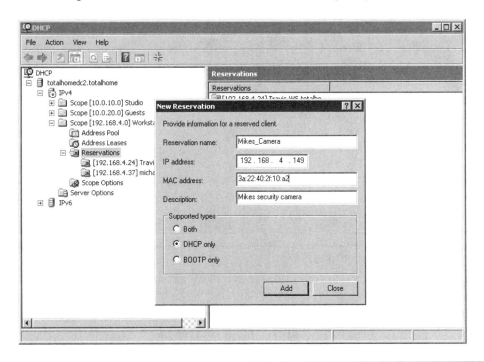

Figure 6-55 DHCP Server configuration screen showing MAC reservation

Speaking of Windows DHCP, Figure 6-56 shows the configuration screen from the popular DHCP Server that comes with Windows Server. Note the single scope. Figure 6-57 shows the same DHCP Server tool, in this case detailing the options screen. At this point, you're probably not sure what any of these options are for. Don't worry. I'll return to these topics in later chapters.

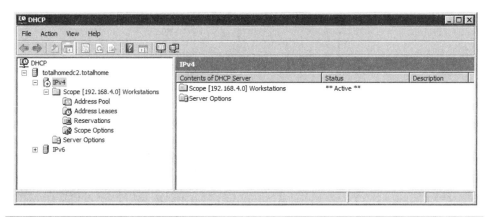

Figure 6-56   DHCP Server configuration screen

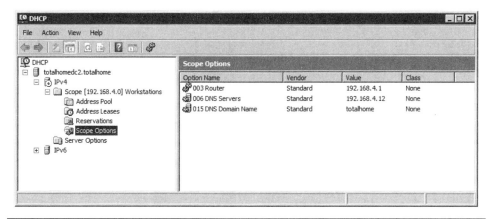

Figure 6-57   DHCP Server options screen

Living with DHCP

DHCP is very convenient and, as such, very popular. It's also completely transparent to users. They just turn on their desktops, laptops, and mobile devices and DHCP works. This transparency comes at a cost in that when DHCP breaks, users don't get IP information and they don't get on the network, making something very transparent very apparent—in a spectacular way! Taking the time to understand a few basic problems that come up with DHCP makes these spectacular incidents a lot less spectacular.

Figure 6-58
DHCP error in
Windows 7

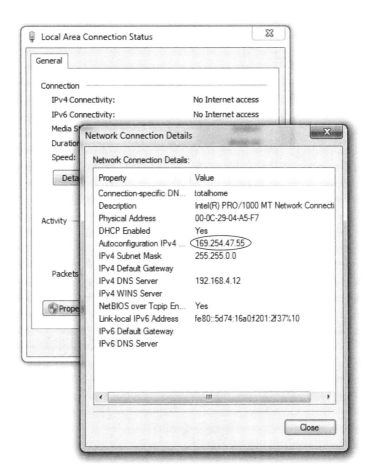

No DHCP Server The single biggest issue is when a DHCP client tries to get a DHCP address and fails. You'll know when this happens because the operating system will post some form of error telling you there's a problem (Figure 6-58) and the DHCP client will have a rather strange address in the 169.254.0.0/16 network ID.

This special IP address is generated by a version of *zero-configuration networking (zeroconf)*. Microsoft's implementation is called *Automatic Private IP Addressing (APIPA)*. (That's the one you'll see on the exam.)

All DHCP clients are designed to generate an APIPA address automatically if they do not receive a response to a DHCP Discover message. The client only generates the last two octets of an APIPA address. This at least allows the dynamic clients on a single network to continue to communicate with each other because they are on the same network ID.

Unfortunately, APIPA cannot issue a default gateway, so you'll never get on the Internet using APIPA. That provides a huge clue to a DHCP problem scenario: you can communicate with other computers on your network that came up *after* the DHCP server went down, but you can't get to the Internet or access computers that retain a DHCP-given address.

 EXAM TIP Systems that use static IP addressing can never have DHCP problems.

If you can't get to the Internet, use whatever tool your OS provides to check your IP address. If it's an APIPA address, you know instantly that you have a DHCP problem. First, try to reestablish the lease manually. Every OS has some way to do this. In Windows, you can type the following command:

```
ipconfig /renew
```

With macOS, go to System Preferences and use the Network utility (Figure 6-59).

Figure 6-59
Network utility
in System
Preferences

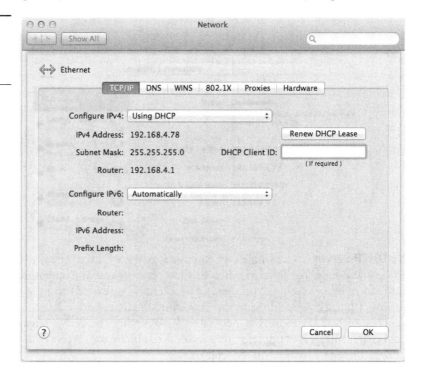

 EXAM TIP CompTIA loves TCP and UDP port numbers, so make sure you know that DHCP servers use UDP port 67 and clients use port 68.

Sometimes you might find yourself in a situation where your computer gets confused and won't grab an IP address no matter what you try. In these cases, you should first force the computer to release its lease. In Windows, get to a command prompt and type these two commands; follow each by pressing ENTER:

```
ipconfig /release
ipconfig /renew
```

In macOS, use the `ifconfig` command to release and renew a DHCP address. Here's the syntax to release:

```
sudo ifconfig eth0 down
```

And here's the syntax to renew:

```
sudo ifconfig eth0 up
```

Linux can use the deprecated ifconfig command with the same syntax as above, but a better tool is dhclient. Here's the syntax to release, followed by the syntax to renew:

```
sudo dhclient -r
sudo dhclient
```

 EXAM TIP Make sure you know how to configure your computers to use static IP addressing and know that you use ping to ensure they can communicate. For dynamic IP addressing, make sure you know DHCP. Understand that each client must have some way to "turn on" DHCP. Also understand the concept of a DHCP client and a DHCP server. Be comfortable with APIPA and releasing and renewing a lease on a client.

Multiple DHCP Servers A single DHCP server provides a single point of failure for a network. If this server dies, at best no one can get on the Internet; at worst, no one can do anything at all. To avoid this problem, bigger networks—think enterprise, here—run more than one DHCP server. You can do this in a couple ways. That way it doesn't matter which DHCP server answers. Assume you have a network ID of 172.13.14.0. You could configure the two DHCP servers as such:

> DHCP Server 1: Scope 172.13.14.200–172.13.14.225
> DHCP Server 2: Scope 172.13.14.226–172.13.14.250

Each DHCP server would still use the same subnet mask, default gateway, etc.

Two independent DHCP servers add double the administrative load, so a far more elegant solution is called DHCP failover. In DHCP failover, two—and only two—DHCP servers work together to provide DHCP for the network. First widely implemented in Windows Server 2012, a DHCP failover pair consists of a primary DHCP server and a secondary DHCP server. As opposed to two independent DHCP servers, the DHCP failover pair shares a single scope. If either fails, the other picks up the load and the end users never notice a thing. DHCP failover is quite common in large networks.

Rogue DHCP Server   A DHCP client will accept IP information from the first DHCP it hears, creating a bit of a problem. It's too easy to add another DHCP server to a network, passing out incorrect IP information to clients. This is called a *rogue DHCP server*. Rogues happen in one of two ways: someone in the organization brings in a home router and accidently plugs it into the network or someone evil is trying to attack your network. In either case a rogue server is bad.

An unintentional rogue server is usually easy to detect. Consider this scenario. A legitimate user in your network plugs a home router into a wall outlet in your location with the desire to provide a wireless network for their little corner of the world. Sadly, the router also has a DHCP server running by default. This DHCP server is invariably running a default IP address range such as 192.168.1/24, and hopefully your network ID is anything BUT this default. As new DHCP clients request leases, the rogue DHCP server might respond before the legitimate DHCP server. Then the client can't get on the Internet or access local network resources. Anytime a network administrator notices that some users can access resources and some cannot, it's time to check for a rogue DHCP server. Usually a quick `ipconfig` will show DHCP clients with incorrect network IDs.

Let's assume that your network ID is 10.11.12/24. A user complains that they can't get on the Internet. You go to the user's machine, run the `ipconfig` command, and see the following:

```
Ethernet LAN adapter #1:
   Connection-specific DNS Suffix  . : mikemeyers.net
   IPv4 Address. . . . . . . . . . : 172.18.13.110
   Subnet Mask . . . . . . . . . . : 255.255.255.0
   Default Gateway . . . . . . . . : 172.18.13.1
```

A good network administrator would quickly see that this system is gathering incorrect DHCP information from … somewhere. That somewhere is a rogue DHCP server.

A properly configured rogue DHCP server with malicious intent can cause serious problems. Plus rogue DHCP servers are tough to detect because they give IP addresses in the same scope as the legitimate DHCP server, but change the default gateway. This enables the rogue server to intercept or capture incoming and outgoing traffic. What it does with this information depends on the nature of the attack. See Chapter 19 for the scoop on bad people doing bad things to good networks.

 NOTE   Good network admins always know their network IDs!

Special IP Addresses

The folks who invented TCP/IP created several special IP addresses you need to know about. The first special address is 127.0.0.1—the *loopback address*. When you tell a device to send data to 127.0.0.1, you're telling that device to send the packets to itself. The loopback address has several uses. One of the most common is to use it with the ping command. I use the command **ping 127.0.0.1** to test a computer's network stack.

EXAM TIP Even though, by convention, you use 127.0.0.1 as the loopback address, the entire 127.0.0.0/8 subnet is reserved for loopback addresses! You can use any address in the 127.0.0.0/8 subnet as a loopback address.

Lots of folks use TCP/IP in networks that either aren't connected to the Internet or include computers they want to hide from the rest of Internet. Certain groups of IP addresses, known as *private IP addresses*, are available to help in these situations. All routers block private IP addresses. Those addresses can never be used on the Internet, making them a handy way to hide systems. Anyone can use these private IP addresses, but they're useless for systems that need to access the Internet—unless you use the mysterious and powerful NAT, which I'll discuss in the next chapter. (Bet you're dying to learn about NAT now!) For the moment, however, let's just look at the ranges of addresses that are designated as private IP addresses:

- 10.0.0.0 through 10.255.255.255 (1 Class A network block)
- 172.16.0.0 through 172.31.255.255 (16 Class B network blocks)
- 192.168.0.0 through 192.168.255.255 (256 Class C network blocks)

All other IP addresses are public IP addresses.

 EXAM TIP Make sure you can quickly tell the difference between a private IP address and a public IP address for the CompTIA Network+ exam. The objectives mention the distinction as *private vs. public*.

Chapter Review

Questions

1. How many bits does an IPv4 address consist of?

    A. 16

    B. 32

    C. 64

    D. 128

2. Identify the network ID section of the following IP address and subnet mask: 10.14.12.43–255.255.255.0.

    A. 10.14

    B. 43

    C. 10.14.12

    D. 14.12.43

3. Which of the following is a proper subnet mask?

A. 11111111111111111111111100000000

B. 00000000000000000000000011111111

C. 10101010101010101010101011111111

D. 01010101010101010101010100000000

4. What does ARP stand for?

A. Address Reconciliation Process

B. Automated Ranking Protocol

C. Address Resolution Protocol

D. Advanced Resolution Protocol

5. Identify the class of the following IP address: 146.203.143.101.

A. Class A

B. Class B

C. Class C

D. Class D

6. What does IANA stand for?

A. International Association Numbers Authority

B. International Association Numbering Authority

C. Internet Assigned Numbering Authority

D. Internet Assigned Numbers Authority

7. What is the maximum number of hosts in a /19 subnet?

A. 254

B. 8192

C. 16,382

D. 8190

8. What is the number 138 in binary?

A. 10001010

B. 10101010

C. 10000111

D. 11001010

9. When DHCP Discover fails, what process will the client use to generate an address for itself?

   A. ATAPI (Automatic Temporary Address Program Initiator)

   B. APIPA (Automatic Private IP Addressing)

   C. ATIPA (Automatic Temporary IP Address)

   D. APFBA (Automatic Programmable Fall Back Address)

10. Which of the following is a valid loopback address?

    A. 128.0.0.1

    B. 127.0.0.0

    C. 128.0.0.255

    D. 127.24.0.1

Answers

1. **B.** An IPv4 address consists of 32 bits.

2. **C.** The network ID is the first three octets when using the specified subnet.

3. **A.** A subnet is all ones followed by zeroes.

4. **C.** ARP is the Address Resolution Protocol, which is how a TCP/IP network figures out the MAC address based on the destination IP address.

5. **B.** The address is Class B.

6. **D.** The correct choice for IANA is Internet Assigned Numbers Authority.

7. **D.** The total number of hosts is 8190 ($2^{13} - 2$).

8. **A.** 10001010 is the number 138 in binary.

9. **B.** A client uses APIPA (Automatic Private IP Addressing) to generate an address when DHCP Discover fails.

10. **D.** 127.24.0.1. Any address in the 127.0.0.0/8 subnet will work as a loopback.

Routing

The CompTIA Network+ certification exam expects you to know how to

- 1.3 Explain the concepts and characteristics of routing and switching

To achieve these goals, you must be able to

- Explain how routers work
- Describe dynamic routing technologies
- Install and configure a router successfully

The true beauty and amazing power of TCP/IP lies in one word: routing. Routing enables us to interconnect individual LANs into WANs. Routers, the magic boxes that act as the interconnection points, have all the built-in smarts to inspect incoming packets and forward them toward their eventual LAN destination. Routers are, for the most part, automatic. They require very little in terms of maintenance once their initial configuration is complete because they can talk to each other to determine the best way to send IP packets. The goal of this chapter is to take you into the world of routers and show you how they do this.

The chapter discusses how routers work, including an in-depth look at different types of Network Address Translation (NAT), and then dives into an examination of various dynamic routing protocols. You'll learn about vector protocols, including Routing Information Protocol (RIP) and Border Gateway Protocol (BGP), among others. The chapter finishes with the nitty-gritty details of installing and configuring a router successfully. Not only will you understand how routers work, you should be able to set up a basic home router and diagnose common router issues by the end of this chapter.

Historical/Conceptual

How Routers Work

A *router* is any piece of hardware or software that forwards packets based on their destination IP address. Routers work, therefore, at the Network layer of the OSI model and at the Internet layer of the TCP/IP model.

Classically, routers are dedicated boxes that contain at least two connections, although many routers contain many more connections. In a business setting, for example, you might see a Cisco 2600 Series device, one of the most popular routers ever made. These routers are a bit on the older side, but Cisco builds their routers to last. With occasional software upgrades, a typical router will last for many years. The 2611 router shown in Figure 7-1 has two connections (the other connections are used for maintenance and configuration). The two "working" connections are circled. One port leads to one network; the other leads to another network. The router reads the IP addresses of the packets to determine where to send the packets. (I'll elaborate on how that works in a moment.)

Figure 7-1
Cisco 2611 router

Most techs today get their first exposure to routers with the ubiquitous home routers that enable PCs to connect to a cable or fiber modem (Figure 7-2). The typical home router, however, serves multiple functions, often combining a router, a switch, and other features like a firewall (for protecting your network from intruders), a DHCP server, and much more into a single box.

Figure 7-2
Business end of
a typical home
router

 NOTE See Chapter 19, "Protecting Your Network," for an in-depth look at firewalls and other security options.

Figure 7-3 shows the electronic diagram for a two-port Cisco router, whereas Figure 7-4 shows the diagram for a home router.

Figure 7-3
Cisco router
diagram

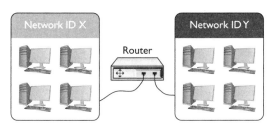

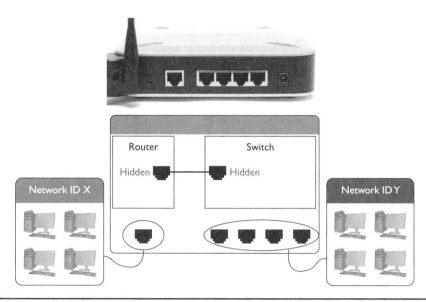

Figure 7-4 Linksys home router diagram

Note that both boxes connect two networks. The big difference is that one side of the Linksys home router connects directly to a built-in switch. That's convenient! You don't have to buy a separate switch to connect multiple computers to the home router.

All routers—big and small, plain or bundled with a switch—examine packets and then send the packets to the proper destination. Let's look at that process in more detail now.

 EXAM TIP A switch that works at more than one layer of the OSI model is called a multilayer switch (MLS). An MLS that handles routing is often called a *Layer 3 switch* because it handles IP traffic.

Test Specific

Routing Tables

Routing begins as packets come into the router for handling (Figure 7-5). The router immediately strips off any of the Layer 2 information and drops the resulting IP packet into a queue (Figure 7-6). The important point to make here is that the router doesn't care where the packet originated. Everything is dropped into the same queue based on the time it arrived.

The router inspects each packet's destination IP address and then sends the IP packet out the correct port. To perform this inspection, every router comes with a *routing table* that tells the router exactly where to send the packets. This table is the key to understanding and controlling the process of forwarding packets to their proper destination. Figure 7-7 shows a very simple routing table for a typical home router. Each row in this

Figure 7-5
Incoming
packets

Figure 7-6 All incoming packets stripped of Layer 2 data and dropped into a common queue

routing table defines a single route. Each column identifies one of two specific criteria. Some columns define which packets are for the route and other columns define which port to send them out. (We'll break these down shortly.)

Figure 7-7
Routing table from a home router

Routing Table Entry List   Refresh

Destination LAN IP	Subnet Mask	Gateway	Interface
10.12.14.0	255.255.255.0	0.0.0.0	LAN
76.30.4.0	255.255.254.0	0.0.0.0	WAN
0.0.0.0	0.0.0.0	76.30.4.1	WAN

Close

The router in this example has only two ports internally: one port that connects to an Internet service provider, labeled as WAN in the Interface column of the table, and another port that connects to the router's built-in switch, labeled LAN in the table. Due to the small number of ports, this little router table has only four routes. Wait a minute: four routes and only two ports? No worries, there is *not* a one-to-one correlation of routes to ports, as you will soon see. Let's inspect this routing table.

Reading Figure 7-7 from left to right shows the following:

- **Destination LAN IP**   A defined network ID. Every network ID directly connected to one of the router's ports is always listed here.

- **Subnet Mask**   To define a network ID, you need a subnet mask (described in Chapter 6).

The router uses the combination of the destination LAN IP and subnet mask to see if a packet matches that route. For example, if you had a packet with the destination 10.12.14.26 coming into the router, the router would check the network ID and subnet mask. It would quickly determine that the packet matches the first route shown in Figure 7-8.

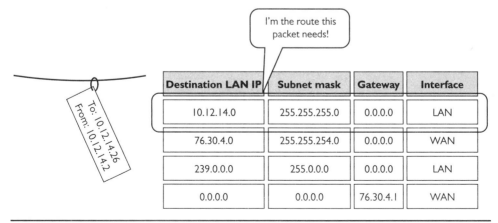

Figure 7-8   Routing table showing the route for a packet

The other two columns in the routing table tell the router what to do with the packet:

- **Gateway** The IP address for the *next hop* router; in other words, where the packet should go. If the outgoing packet is for a network ID that's not directly connected to the router, the Gateway column tells the router the IP address of a router to which to send this packet. That router then handles the packet, and your router is done. (Well-configured routers ensure a packet will get to where it needs to go.) If the network ID is directly connected to the router, then you don't need a gateway. If there is no gateway needed, most routing tables put either 0.0.0.0 or *On-link* in this column.

- **Interface** Tells the router which of its ports to use. On this router, it uses the terms "LAN" and "WAN." Other routing tables use the port's IP address or some other description. Some routers, for example, use gig0/0 or Gig0/1, and so on.

A routing table looks like a table, so there's an assumption that the router will start at the top of the table and march down until it finds the correct route. That's not accurate. The router compares the destination IP address on a packet to every route listed in the routing table and only then sends the packet out. If a packet works for more than one route, the router will use the better route (we'll discuss this more in a moment).

The most important trick to reading a routing table is to remember that a zero (0) means "anything." For example, in Figure 7-7, the first route's destination LAN IP is 10.12.14.0. You can compare that to the subnet mask (255.255.255.0) to confirm that this is a /24 network. This tells you that any value (between 1 and 254) is acceptable for the last value in the 10.12.14/24 network ID.

A properly configured router must have a route for any packet it might encounter. Routing tables tell you a lot about the network connections. From just this single routing table, for example, the diagram in Figure 7-9 can be drawn.

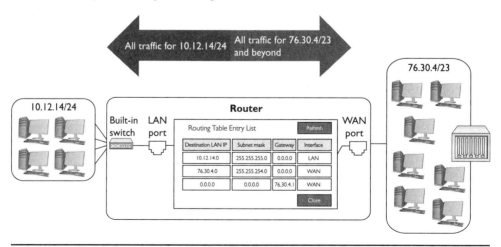

Figure 7-9 The network based on the routing table in Figure 7-7

Take another look at Figure 7-8. Notice the last route. How do I know the 76.30.4.1 port connects to another network? The third line of the routing table shows the default route for this router, and every router has one. (See the note below on the two exceptions to this rule.) This line says

(Any destination address) (with any subnet mask) (forward it to 76.30.4.1) (using my WAN port)

```
Destination LAN IP    Subnet Mask        Gateway         Interface
        0.0.0.0         0.0.0.0         76.30.4.1             WAN
```

The *default route* is very important because this tells the router exactly what to do with every incoming packet *unless* another line in the routing table gives another route. Excellent! Interpret the other two lines of the routing table in Figure 7-7 in the same fashion:

(Any packet for the 10.12.14.0) (/24 network ID) (don't use a gateway) (just ARP on the LAN interface to get the MAC address and send it directly to the recipient)

```
Destination LAN IP      Subnet Mask      Gateway      Interface
     10.12.14.0      255.255.255.0      0.0.0.0           LAN
```

(Any packet for the 76.30.4.0) (/23 network ID) (don't use a gateway) (just ARP on the WAN interface to get the MAC address and send it directly to the recipient)

```
Destination LAN IP      Subnet Mask      Gateway      Interface
      76.30.4.0      255.255.254.0      0.0.0.0           WAN
```

 NOTE There are two places where you'll find routers that do not have default routes: isolated (as in not on the Internet) internetworks, where every router knows about every single network, and the monstrous "Tier One" backbone, where you'll find the routers that make the main connections of the Internet.

I'll let you in on a little secret. Routers aren't the only devices that use routing tables. In fact, every node (computer, printer, TCP/IP-capable soda dispenser, whatever) on the network also has a routing table.

At first, this may seem silly—doesn't every computer only have a single Ethernet connection and, therefore, all data traffic has to go out that port? Every packet sent out of your computer uses the routing table to figure out where the packet should go, whether directly to a node on your network or to your gateway. Here's an example of a routing table in Windows. This machine connects to the home router described earlier, so you'll recognize the IP addresses it uses.

Warning! The results screen of the route print command is very long, even on a basic system, so I've deleted a few parts of the output for the sake of brevity.

```
C:\>route print
===========================================================================
Interface List
13 ..00 11 d8 30 16 c0. .....NVIDIA nForce Networking Controller
 1........................Software Loopback Interface 1
57...00 00 00 00 00 00 00 e0 Microsoft ISATAP Adapter #15
56...00 00 00 00 00 00 00 e0 Teredo Tunneling Pseudo-Interface
===========================================================================
IPv4 Route Table
===========================================================================
Active Routes:
Network Destination        Netmask          Gateway       Interface  Metric
          0.0.0.0          0.0.0.0      10.12.14.1    10.12.14.201     25
        127.0.0.0        255.0.0.0         On-link       127.0.0.1    306
        127.0.0.1  255.255.255.255         On-link       127.0.0.1    306
  127.255.255.255  255.255.255.255         On-link       127.0.0.1    306
       10.12.14.0    255.255.255.0         On-link    10.12.14.201    281
     10.12.14.201  255.255.255.255         On-link    10.12.14.201    281
     10.12.14.255  255.255.255.255         On-link    10.12.14.201    281
        224.0.0.0        240.0.0.0         On-link       127.0.0.1    306
        224.0.0.0        240.0.0.0         On-link    10.12.14.201    281
  255.255.255.255  255.255.255.255         On-link       127.0.0.1    306
  255.255.255.255  255.255.255.255         On-link    10.12.14.201    281
===========================================================================
Persistent Routes:
None
```

Unlike the routing table for the typical home router you saw in Figure 7-7, this one seems a bit more complicated. My PC has only a single NIC, though, so it's not quite as complicated as it might seem at first glance. Take a look at the details. First note that my computer has an IP address of 10.12.14.201/24 and 10.12.14.1 as the default gateway.

NOTE Every modern operating system gives you tools to view a computer's routing table. Most techs use the command line or terminal window interface—often called simply terminal—because it's fast. To see your routing table in Linux or in macOS, for example, type this command at a terminal:

```
netstat -r
```

The netstat -r command works in Windows too, plus you can use route print as an alternative.

You should note two differences in the columns from what you saw in the previous routing table. First, the interface has an actual IP address—10.12.14.201, plus the loopback of 127.0.0.1—instead of the word "LAN." Second—and this is part of the magic of routing—is something called the metric.

A *metric* is a relative value that defines the "cost" of using this route. The power of routing is that a packet can take more than one route to get to the same place. If a route were to suddenly cut off, then you would have an alternative. Figure 7-10 shows a networked router with two routes to the same place. The router has a route to Network B with a metric of 1 using Route 1, and a second route to Network B using Route 2 with a metric of 10.

Figure 7-10
Two routes to the same network

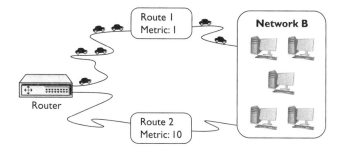

NOTE When a router has more than one route to the same network, it's up to the person in charge of that router to assign a different metric for each route. With dynamic routing protocols (discussed in detail later in the chapter in "Dynamic Routing"), the routers determine the proper metric for each route.

Lowest routes always win. In this case, the router will always use the route with the metric of 1, unless that route suddenly stopped working. In that case, the router would automatically switch to the route with the 10 metric (Figure 7-11). This is the cornerstone of how the Internet works! The entire Internet is nothing more than a whole bunch of big, powerful routers connected to lots of other big, powerful routers. Connections go up and down all the time, and routers (with multiple routes) constantly talk to each other, detecting when a connection goes down and automatically switching to alternate routes.

Figure 7-11
When a route no longer works, the router automatically switches.

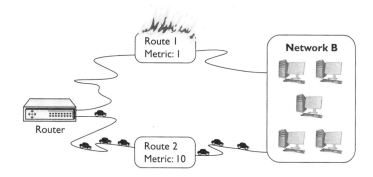

I'll go through this routing table one line at a time. Remember, every address is compared to every line in the routing table before it goes out, so it's no big deal if the default route is at the beginning or the end.

The top line defines the default route: (*Any destination address*) (*with any subnet mask*) (*forward it to my default gateway*) (*using my NIC*) (*Metric of* 25 *to use this route*). Anything that's not local goes to the router and from there out to the destination (with the help of other routers).

```
Network Destination    Netmask        Gateway      Interface    Metric
        0.0.0.0        0.0.0.0      10.12.14.1   10.12.14.201     25
```

The next three lines tell your system how to handle the loopback address. The second line is straightforward, but examine the first and third lines carefully. Earlier you learned that only 127.0.0.1 is the loopback, but according to the first route, any 127.0.0.0/8 address is the loopback. The third line is a little weird and is placed in the routing table to satisfy a loopback addressing requirement. Bottom line: no matter how you use a loopback address, as long as you start the address with 127, it will always go to 127.0.0.1.

```
Network Destination             Netmask       Gateway     Interface    Metric
        127.0.0.0           255.0.0.0      On-link     127.0.0.1      306
        127.0.0.1     255.255.255.255      On-link     127.0.0.1      306
  127.255.255.255     255.255.255.255      On-link     127.0.0.1      306
```

The next line defines the local connection: (*Any packet for the* 10.12.14.0) (*/24 network ID*) (*don't use a gateway*) (*just ARP on the LAN interface to get the MAC address and send it directly to the recipient*) (*Cost of* 1 *to use this route*).

```
Network Destination             Netmask       Gateway      Interface    Metric
        10.12.14.0      255.255.255.0        On-link    10.12.14.201       1
```

Okay, on to the next line. This one's easy. Anything addressed to this machine should go right back to it through the loopback (127.0.0.1).

```
Network Destination             Netmask       Gateway     Interface    Metric
      10.12.14.201     255.255.255.255      On-link     127.0.0.1       1
```

The next line is for broadcasting to the other computers on the same network ID. In rare cases, you could have more than one network ID on the same network. This line targets only the nodes with the same network ID.

```
Network Destination             Netmask       Gateway      Interface    Metric
      10.12.14.255     255.255.255.255      On-link    10.12.14.201       1
```

The next two lines are for the multicast address range. Most operating systems put these lines in automatically.

```
Network Destination     Netmask       Gateway      Interface    Metric
        224.0.0.0     240.0.0.0     On-link      127.0.0.1      306
        224.0.0.0     240.0.0.0     On-link    10.12.14.201     281
```

The bottom lines define the default IP broadcast. If you send out an IP broadcast (255.255.255.255), your NIC knows to send it out to the local network. This will reach every node on the network, even nodes with varying network IDs.

```
Network Destination             Netmask       Gateway      Interface    Metric
   255.255.255.255     255.255.255.255      On-link      127.0.0.1      306
   255.255.255.255     255.255.255.255      On-link    10.12.14.201     281
```

Try This!

Getting Looped

Try pinging any 127.0.0.0/8 address to see if it loops back like 127.0.0.1. What happens?

Just for fun, let's add one more routing table; this time from my old Cisco 2811, which is still connecting me to the Internet after all these years! I access the Cisco router remotely from my Windows system using a tool called PuTTY (you'll see more of PuTTY throughout this book), log in, and then run this command:

```
show ip route
```

Don't let all the text confuse you. The first part, labeled Codes, is just a legend to let you know what the letters at the beginning of each row mean:

```
Gateway# show ip route

Codes: C - connected, S - static, R - RIP, M - mobile, B - BGP
       D - EIGRP, EX - EIGRP external, O - OSPF, IA - OSPF inter area
       N1 - OSPF NSSA external type 1, N2 - OSPF NSSA external type 2
       E1 - OSPF external type 1, E2 - OSPF external type 2
       i - IS-IS, su - IS-IS summary, L1 - IS-IS level-1, L2 - IS-IS level-2
       ia - IS-IS inter area, * - candidate default, U - per-user static route
       o - ODR, P - periodic downloaded static route

Gateway of last resort is 208.190.121.38 to network 0.0.0.0

C    208.190.121.0/24 is directly connected, GigabitEthernet0/1
C    192.168.4.0/24 is directly connected, GigabitEthernet0/0
S*   0.0.0.0/0 [1/0] via 208.190.121.38
```

These last three lines are the routing table. The router has two Ethernet interfaces called FastEthernet0/1 and FastEthernet0/0. This is how Cisco names router interfaces.

Reading from the top, you see that FastEthernet0/1 is directly connected (the C at the beginning of the line) to the network 208.190.121.0/24. Any packets that match 208.190.121.0/24 go out on FastEthernet0/1. Equally, any packets for the connected 192.168.4.0/24 network go out on FastEthernet0/0. The last route gets an S for static because I entered it in manually. The asterisk (*) shows that this is the default route.

In this section, you've seen three different types of routing tables from three different types of devices. Even though these routing tables have different ways to list the routes and different ways to show the categories, they all perform the same job: moving IP packets to the correct interface to ensure they get to where they need to go.

Freedom from Layer 2

Routers enable you to connect different types of network technologies. You now know that routers strip off all of the Layer 2 data from the incoming packets, but thus far you've only seen routers that connect to different Ethernet networks—and that's just fine with routers. But routers can connect to almost anything that stores IP packets. Not to take away from some very exciting upcoming chapters, but Ethernet is not the only networking technology out there. Once you want to start making long-distance connections, Ethernet disappears, and technologies with names like Data-Over-Cable Service Interface Specification (DOCSIS) (for cable modems), Frame Relay, and Asynchronous Transfer Mode (ATM) take over. These technologies are not Ethernet, and they all work very differently than Ethernet. The only common feature of these technologies is they all carry IP packets inside their Layer 2 encapsulations.

NOTE Frame Relay and ATM are ancient technologies that you won't see in the real world. You'll see them on the CompTIA Network+ exam, though, so I'll discuss them in historical context in this book.

Most industry (that is, not home) routers enable you to add interfaces. You buy the router and then snap in different types of interfaces depending on your needs. Note the Cisco router in Figure 7-12. Like most Cisco routers, it comes with removable modules. If you're connecting Ethernet to a DOCSIS (cable modem) network, you buy an Ethernet module and a DOCSIS module.

Figure 7-12
Modular Cisco
router

Network Address Translation

Many regions of the world have depleted their available IPv4 addresses already and the end for everywhere else is in sight. Although you can still get an IP address from an Internet service provider (ISP), the days of easy availability are over. Routers running some form of *Network Address Translation (NAT)* hide the IP addresses of computers on the LAN but still enable those computers to communicate with the broader Internet. NAT extended the useful life of IPv4 addressing on the Internet for many years. NAT is extremely common and heavily in use, so learning how it works is important. Note that many routers offer NAT as a feature *in addition to* the core capability of routing. NAT is not routing, but a separate technology. With that said, you are ready to dive into how NAT works to protect computers connected by router technology and conserve IP addresses as well.

The Setup

Here's the situation. You have a LAN with five computers that need access to the Internet. With classic TCP/IP and routing, several things have to happen. First, you need to get a block of legitimate, unique, expensive IP addresses from an ISP. You could call up an ISP and purchase a network ID, say 1.2.3.136/29. Second, you assign an IP address to each computer and to the LAN connection on the router. Third, you assign the IP address for the ISP's router to the WAN connection on the local router, such as 1.2.4.1. After everything is configured, the network looks like Figure 7-13. All of the clients on the network have the same default gateway (1.2.3.137). This router, called a *gateway router* (or simply a *gateway*), acts as the default gateway for a number of client computers.

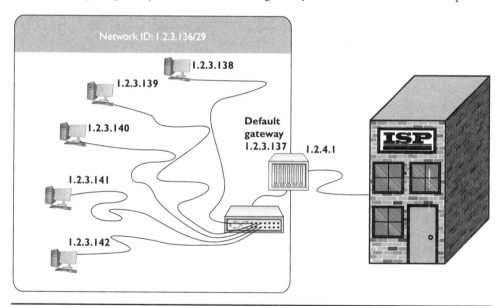

Figure 7-13 Network setup

This style of network mirrors how computers in LANs throughout the world connected to the Internet for the first 20+ years, but the major problem of a finite number of IP addresses worsened as more and more computers connected.

 EXAM TIP NAT replaces the source IP address of a computer with the source IP address from the outside router interface on outgoing packets. NAT is performed by NAT-capable routers.

Port Address Translation

Most internal networks today don't have one machine, of course. Instead, they use a block of private IP addresses for the hosts inside the network. They connect to the Internet through one or more public IP addresses.

The most common form of NAT that handles this one-to-many connection—called *Port Address Translation (PAT)*—uses port numbers to map traffic from specific machines in the network. Let's use a simple example to make the process clear. John has a network at his office that uses the private IP addressing space of 192.168.1.0/24. All the computers in the private network connect to the Internet through a single router using PAT with the global IP address of 208.190.121.12/24. See Figure 7-14.

Figure 7-14
John's network
setup

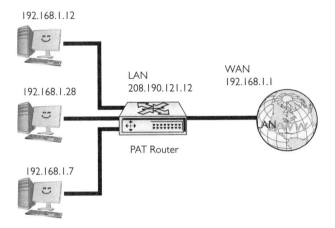

When an internal machine initiates a session with an external machine, such as a Web browser accessing a Web site, the source and destination IP addresses and port numbers for the TCP segment or UDP datagram are recorded in the NAT table, and the private IP address is swapped for the public IP address on each packet. Plus, the port number used by the internal computer for the session is also translated into a unique port number and the router records this as well. See Figure 7-15.

Table 7-1 shows a sample of the translation table inside the PAT router. Note that more than one computer translation has been recorded.

Source	Translated Source	Destination
192.168.1.12:52331	208.190.121.12:55030	
192.168.1.24:61324	208.190.121.12:65321	17.5.85.11:80

Table 7-1 Sample NAT Translation Table

When the receiving system sends the packet back, it reverses the IP addresses and ports. The router compares the incoming destination port and source IP address to the entry in the *NAT translation table* to determine which IP address to put back on the packet. It then sends the packet to the correct computer on the network.

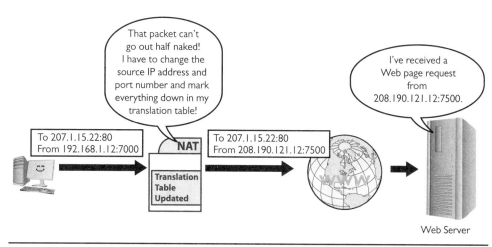

Figure 7-15 PAT in action—changing the source IP address and port number to something usable on the Internet

This mapping of internal IP address and port number to a translated IP address and port number enables perfect tracking of packets out and in. PAT can handle many internal computers with a single public IP address because the TCP/IP port number space is big, as you'll recall from previous chapters, with values ranging from 1 to 65535. Some of those port numbers are used for common protocols, but many tens of thousands are available for PAT to work its magic.

NOTE Chapter 8, "TCP/IP Applications," goes into port numbers in great detail.

PAT takes care of all of the problems facing a network exposed to the Internet. You don't have to use legitimate Internet IP addresses on the LAN, and the IP addresses of the computers behind the routers are invisible and protected from the outside world.

Since the router is revising the packets and recording the IP address and port information already, why not enable it to handle ports more aggressively? Enter port forwarding, stage left.

Port Forwarding

The obvious drawback to relying exclusively on PAT for network address translation is that it only works for outgoing communication, not incoming communication. For traffic originating *outside* the network to access an *internal* machine, such as a Web server hosted inside your network, you need to use other technologies.

Static NAT (SNAT) maps a single routable (that is, not private) IP address to a single machine, enabling you to access that machine from outside the network. The NAT keeps track of the IP address or addresses and applies them permanently on a one-to-one basis with computers on the network.

With *port forwarding*, you can designate a specific local address for various network services. Computers outside the network can request a service using the public IP address of the router and the port number of the desired service. The port-forwarding router would examine the packet, look at the list of services mapped to local addresses, and then send that packet along to the proper recipient.

You can use port forwarding to hide a service hosted inside your network by changing the default port number for that service. To hide an internal Web server, for example, you could change the request port number to something other than port 80, the default for HTTP traffic. The router in Figure 7-16, for example, is configured to forward all port 8080 packets to the internal Web server at port 80.

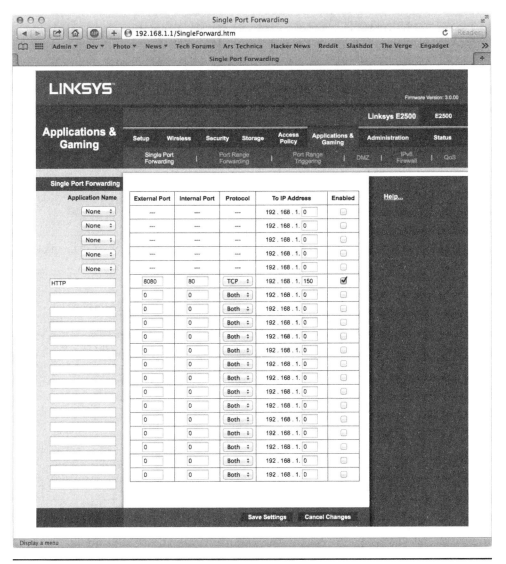

Figure 7-16   Setting up port forwarding on a home router

To access that internal Web site from outside your local network, you would have to change the URL in the Web browser by specifying the port request number. Figure 7-17 shows a browser that has :8080 appended to the URL, which tells the browser to make the HTTP request to port 8080 rather than port 80.

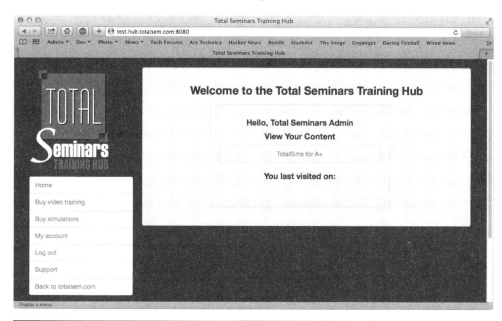

Figure 7-17 Changing the URL to access a Web site using a nondefault port number

NOTE Most browsers require you to write out the full URL, including HTTP://, when using a nondefault port number.

Dynamic NAT

With *dynamic NAT (DNAT)*, many computers can share a pool of routable IP addresses that number fewer than the computers. The NAT might have 10 routable IP addresses, for example, to serve 40 computers on the LAN. LAN traffic uses the internal, private IP addresses. When a computer requests information beyond the network, the NAT doles out a routable IP address from its pool for that communication. Dynamic NAT is also called pooled NAT. This works well enough—unless you're the unlucky 11th person to try to access the Internet from behind the company NAT—but has the obvious limitation of still needing many true, expensive, routable IP addresses.

Configuring NAT

Configuring NAT on home routers is a no-brainer as these boxes invariably have NAT turned on automatically. Figure 7-18 shows the screen on my home router for NAT. Note the radio buttons that say Gateway and Router.

Figure 7-18

NAT setup on home router

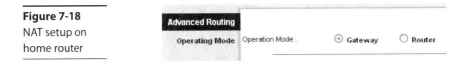

By default, the router is set to Gateway, which is Linksys-speak for "NAT is turned on." If I wanted to turn off NAT, I would set the radio button to Router.

Figure 7-19 shows a router configuration screen on a Cisco router. Commercial routers enable you to do a lot more with NAT.

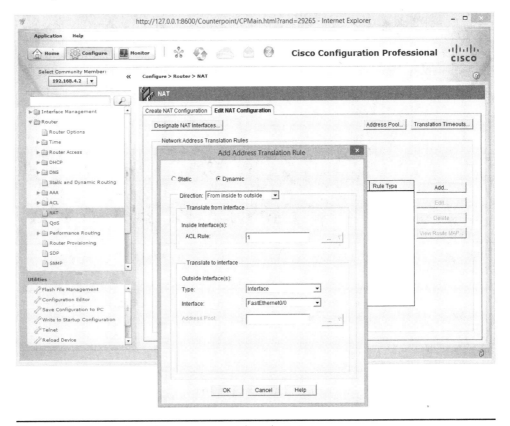

Figure 7-19 Configuring NAT on a commercial-grade router

Dynamic Routing

Based on what you've read up to this point, it would seem that routes in your routing tables come from two sources: either they are manually entered or they are detected at setup by the router. In either case, a route seems to be a static beast, just sitting there and never changing. And based on what you've seen so far, that is absolutely true. Routers have *static routes*. But most routers also have the capability to update their routes *dynamically*, with *dynamic routing protocols* (both IPv4 and IPv6).

If you've been reading carefully, you might be tempted at this point to say, "Why do I need this dynamic routing stuff? Don't routers use metrics so I can add two or more routes to another network ID in case I lose one of my routes?" Yes, but metrics really only help when you have direct connections to other network IDs. What if your routers look like Figure 7-20?

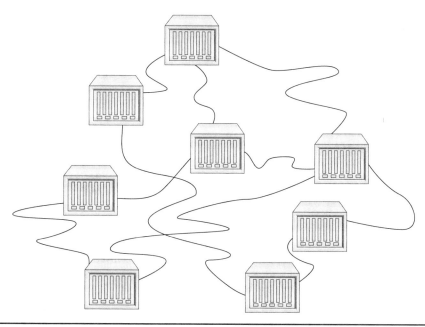

Figure 7-20 Lots of routers

Do you really want to try to set up all these routes statically? What happens when something changes? Can you imagine the administrative nightmare? Why not just give routers the brainpower to talk to each other so they know what's happening not only to the other directly connected routers but also to routers two or more routers away? A *hop* is defined as each time a packet goes through a router. Let's talk about hops for a moment. Figure 7-21 shows a series of routers. If you're on a computer in Network ID X and you ping a computer in Network ID Y, you go one hop. If you ping a computer in Network ID Z, you go two hops.

Routing protocols have been around for a long time, and, like any technology, there have been a number of different choices and variants over those years. CompTIA Network+ competencies break these many types of routing protocols into three distinct groups: distance vector, link state, and hybrid. CompTIA obsesses over these different types of routing protocols, so this chapter does too!

Routing Metrics

Earlier in the chapter, you learned that routing tables contain a factor called a *metric*. A metric is a relative value that routers use when they have more than one route to get to

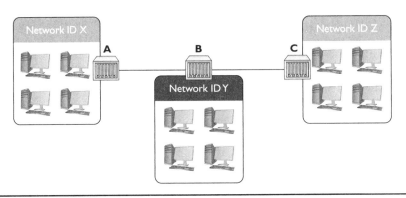

Figure 7-21   Hopping through a WAN

another network. Unlike the gateway routers in our homes, a more serious router will often have multiple connections to get to a particular network. This is the beauty of routers combined with dynamic protocols. If a router suddenly loses a connection, it has alternative routes to the same network. It's the role of the metric setting for the router to decide which route to use.

NOTE   If a routing table has two or more valid routes for a particular IP address destination, it always chooses the route with the lowest metric.

There is no single rule to set the metric value in a routing table. The various types of dynamic protocols use different criteria. Here are the most common criteria for determining a metric.

- **Hop count**   The *hop count* is a fundamental metric value for the number of routers a packet will pass through on the way to its destination network. For example, if router A needs to go through three intermediate routers to reach a network connected to router C, the hop count is 4. The hop occurs when the packet is handed off to each subsequent router. (I'll go a lot more into hops and hop count in "Distance Vector and Path Vector," next.)

- **Bandwidth**   Some connections handle more data than others. An old dial-up connection theoretically tops out at 64 Kbps. A cable modem easily handles many millions of bits per second.

- **Delay**   Say you have a race car that has a top speed of 200 miles per hour, but it takes 25 minutes to start the car. If you press the gas pedal, it takes 15 seconds to start accelerating. If the engine runs for more than 20 minutes, the car won't go faster than 50 miles per hour. These issues prevent the car from doing what it should be able to do: go 200 miles per hour. *Delay* is like that. Hundreds of issues occur that slow down network connections between routers. These issues are known collectively as *latency*. A great example is a satellite connection. The distance between the satellite and the antenna causes a delay that has nothing to do with the speed of the connection.

- **Cost** Some routing protocols use *cost* as a metric for the desirability of that particular route. A route through a low-bandwidth connection, for example, would have a higher cost value than a route through a high-bandwidth connection. A network administrator can also manually add cost to routes to change the route selection.

Different dynamic routing protocols use one or more of these routing metrics to calculate their own routing metric. As you learn about these protocols, you will see how each of these calculates its own metrics differently.

EXAM TIP The CompTIA Network+ objectives list MTU as a switching or routing metric, and it definitely falls into the former category. The *maximum transmission unit (MTU)* determines the largest frame a particular technology can handle. Ethernet uses 1500-byte frames. Other technologies use smaller or larger frames.

 If an IP packet is too big for a particular technology, that packet is broken into pieces to fit into the network protocol in what is called fragmentation. Fragmentation is bad because it slows down the movement of IP packets. By setting the optimal MTU size before IP packets are sent, you avoid or at least reduce fragmentation.

Distance Vector and Path Vector

Distance vector routing protocols were the first to appear in the TCP/IP routing world. The cornerstone of all distance vector routing protocols is some form of total cost. The simplest total cost sums the hops (the hop count) between a router and a network, so if you had a router one hop away from a network, the cost for that route would be 1; if it were two hops away, the cost would be 2.

All network connections are not equal. A router might have two one-hop routes to a network—one using a fast connection and the other using a slow connection. Administrators set the metric of the routes in the routing table to reflect the speed. The slow single-hop route, for example, might be given the metric of 10 rather than the default of 1 to reflect the fact that it's slow. The total cost for this one-hop route is 10, even though it's only one hop. Don't assume a one-hop route always has a cost of 1.

Distance vector routing protocols calculate the total cost to get to a particular network ID and compare that cost to the total cost of all the other routes to get to that same network ID. The router then chooses the route with the lowest cost.

For this to work, routers using a distance vector routing protocol transfer their entire routing table to other routers in the WAN. Each distance vector routing protocol has a maximum number of hops that a router will send its routing table to keep traffic down.

Assume you have four routers connected as shown in Figure 7-22. All of the routers have routes set up between each other with the metrics shown. You add two new networks, one that connects to Router A and the other to Router D. For simplicity, call them Network ID X and Network ID Y. A computer on one network wants to send packets to a computer on the other network, but the routers in between Routers A and D don't yet know the two new network IDs. That's when distance vector routing protocols work their magic.

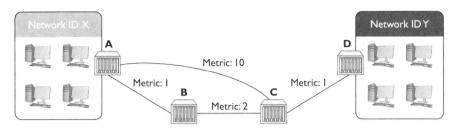

Figure 7-22   Getting a packet from Network ID X to Network ID Y? No clue!

Because all of the routers use a distance vector routing protocol, the problem gets solved quickly. At a certain defined time interval (usually 30 seconds or less), the routers begin sending each other their routing tables (the routers each send their entire routing table, but for simplicity just concentrate on the two network IDs in question). On the first iteration, Router A sends its route to Network ID X to Routers B and C. Router D sends its route to Network ID Y to Router C (Figure 7-23).

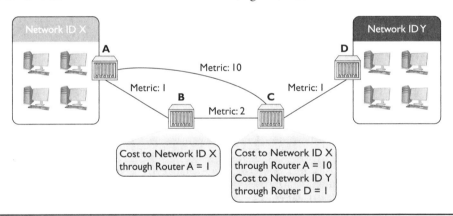

Figure 7-23   Routes updated

This is great—Routers B and C now know how to get to Network ID X, and Router C can get to Network ID Y. There's still no complete path, however, between Network ID X and Network ID Y. That's going to take another interval. After another set amount of time, the routers again send their now updated routing tables to each other, as shown in Figure 7-24.

Router A knows a path now to Network ID Y, and Router D knows a path to Network ID X. As a side effect, Router B and Router C have two routes to Network ID X. Router B can get to Network ID X through Router A and through Router C. Similarly, Router C can get to Network ID X through Router A and through Router B. What to do? In cases where the router discovers multiple routes to the same network ID, the distance vector routing protocol deletes all but the route with the lowest total cost (Figure 7-25).

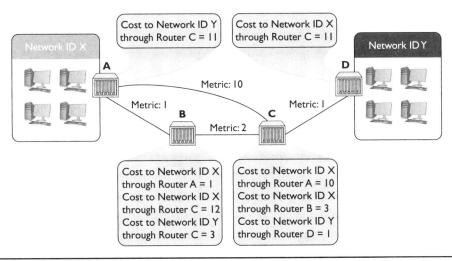

Figure 7-24   Updated routing tables

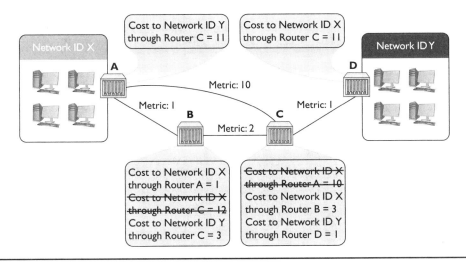

Figure 7-25   Deleting higher-cost routes

On the next iteration, Routers A and D get updated information about the lower total-cost hops to connect to Network IDs X and Y (Figure 7-26).

Just as Routers B and C only kept the routes with the lowest costs, Routers A and D keep only the lowest-cost routes to the networks (Figure 7-27).

Now Routers A and D have a lower-cost route to Network IDs X and Y. They've removed the higher-cost routes and begin sending data.

At this point, if routers were human they'd realize that each router has all the information about the network and stop sending each other routing tables. Routers using distance

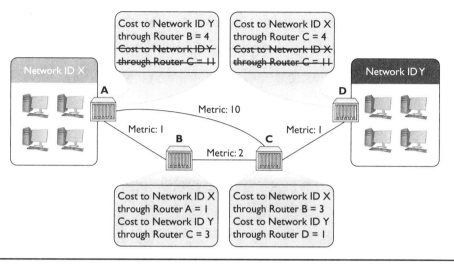

Figure 7-26 Argh! Multiple routes!

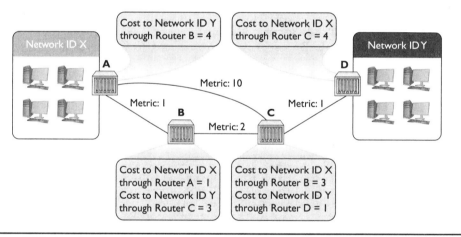

Figure 7-27 Last iteration

vector routing protocols, however, aren't that smart. The routers continue to send their complete routing tables to each other, but because the information is the same, the routing tables don't change.

At this point, the routers are in *convergence* (also called *steady state*), meaning the updating of the routing tables for all the routers has completed. Assuming nothing changes in terms of connections, the routing tables will not change. In this example, it takes three iterations to reach convergence.

So what happens if the route between Routers B and C breaks? The routers have deleted the higher-cost routes, only keeping the lower-cost route that goes between Routers B and C. Does this mean Router A can no longer connect to Network ID Y and Router D can no longer connect to Network ID X? Yikes! Yes, it does. At least for a while.

Routers that use distance vector routing protocols continue to send to each other their entire routing table at regular intervals. After a few iterations, Routers A and D will once again know how to reach each other, although they will connect through the once-rejected slower connection.

Distance vector routing protocols work fine in a scenario such as the previous one that has only four routers. Even if you lose a router, a few minutes later the network returns to convergence. But imagine if you had tens of thousands of routers (the Internet). Convergence could take a very long time indeed. As a result, a pure distance vector routing protocol works fine for a network with a few (less than ten) routers, but it isn't good for large networks.

Routers can use one of two distance vector routing protocols: RIPv1 or RIPv2. Plus there's an option to use a path vector routing protocol, BGP.

RIPv1

The granddaddy of all distance vector routing protocols is the *Routing Information Protocol (RIP)*. The first version of RIP—called *RIPv1*—dates from the 1980s, although its predecessors go back all the way to the beginnings of the Internet in the 1960s. RIP (either version) has a maximum hop count of 15, so your router will not talk to another router more than 15 routers away. This plagues RIP because a routing table request can literally loop all the way around back to the initial router.

RIPv1 sent out an update every 30 seconds. This also turned into a big problem because every router on the network would send its routing table at the same time, causing huge network overloads.

As if these issues weren't bad enough, RIPv1 didn't know how to use *variable-length subnet masking (VLSM)*, where networks connected through the router use different subnet masks. Plus RIPv1 routers had no authentication, leaving them open to hackers sending false routing table information. RIP needed an update.

RIPv2

RIPv2, adopted in 1994, is the current version of RIP. It works the same way as RIPv1, but fixes many of the problems. VLSM has been added, and authentication is built into the protocol.

Most routers still support RIPv2, but RIP's many problems, especially the time to convergence for large WANs, makes it obsolete for all but small, private WANs that consist of a few routers. The growth of the Internet demanded a far more robust dynamic routing protocol. That doesn't mean RIP rests in peace! RIP is both easy to use and simple for manufacturers to implement in their routers, so most routers, even home routers, have the ability to use RIP (Figure 7-28). If your network consists of only two, three, or four routers, RIP's easy configuration often makes it worth putting up with slower convergence.

Figure 7-28

Setting RIP in a home router

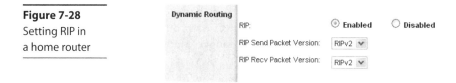

BGP

The explosive growth of the Internet in the 1980s required a fundamental reorganization in the structure of the Internet itself, and one big part of this reorganization was the call to make the "big" routers use a standardized dynamic routing protocol. Implementing this was much harder than you might think because the entities that govern how the Internet works do so in a highly decentralized fashion. Even the organized groups, such as the Internet Society (ISOC), the Internet Assigned Numbers Authority (IANA), and the Internet Engineering Task Force (IETF), are made up of many individuals, companies, and government organizations from across the globe. This decentralization made the reorganization process take time and many meetings.

What came out of the reorganization eventually was a multitiered structure. At the top of the structure sits many Autonomous Systems. An *Autonomous System (AS)* is one or more networks that are governed by a single dynamic routing protocol within that AS. Figure 7-29 illustrates the decentralized structure of the Internet.

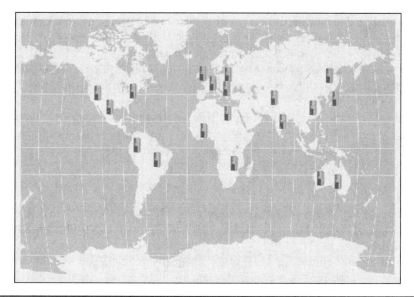

Figure 7-29   The Internet

Autonomous Systems do not deliver data between each other using IP addresses, but rather use a special globally unique Autonomous System Number (ASN) assigned by IANA. Originally a 16-bit number, the current ASNs are 32 bits, displayed as two 16-bit numbers separated by a dot. So, 1.33457 would be a typical ASN. Just as you would assign an IP address to a router, you would configure the router to use or be the ASN assigned by IANA. See Figure 7-30.

Figure 7-30

Configuring a
Cisco router to
use an ASN

```
Router2811(config)#router bgp ?
  <1-65535>   Autonomous system number

Router2811(config)#router bgp 1902
```

Autonomous Systems communicate with each other using a protocol, called generically an *Exterior Gateway Protocol (EGP)*. The network or networks within an AS communicate with protocols as well; these are called generically *Interior Gateway Protocols (IGPs)*.

Let me repeat this to make sure you understand the difference between EGP and IGP. Neither EGP nor IGP is a dynamic routing protocol; rather these are terms used by the large Internet service providers to separate their interconnected routers using ASNs from other interconnected networks that are not part of this special group of companies. The easy way to keep these terms separate is to appreciate that although many protocols are used *within* Autonomous Systems, such as RIP, the Internet has settled on one protocol for communication between each AS: the *Border Gateway Protocol (BGP)*. BGP is the glue of the Internet, connecting all of the Autonomous Systems. Other dynamic routing protocols such as RIP are, by definition, IGP. The current version of BGP is BGP-4.

> ### Try This!
>
> **Discovering the Autonomous System Numbers**
> You can see the AS for most Web sites by using this handy little Firefox add-on:
>
> > https://addons.mozilla.org/en-US/firefox/addon/asnumber/
>
> It doesn't work for every Web site, but it's still interesting.

The CompTIA Network+ exam objectives list BGP as a *hybrid routing protocol,* but it's more technically a *path vector* routing protocol. BGP doesn't have the same type of routing table as you've seen so far. BGP routers advertise information passed to them from different Autonomous Systems' *edge routers*—that's what the AS-to-AS routers are called. BGP forwards these advertisements that include the ASN and other very non-IP items.

 EXAM TIP The CompTIA Network+ objectives list BGP as a hybrid routing protocol. Read the question carefully and if BGP is your only answer as hybrid, take it.

BGP also knows how to handle a number of situations unique to the Internet. If a router advertises a new route that isn't reliable, most BGP routers will ignore it. BGP also supports policies for limiting which and how other routers may access an ISP.

BGP implements and supports *route aggregation*, a way to simplify routing tables into manageable levels. Rather than trying to keep track of every other router on the Internet, the backbone routers track the location of routers that connect to subsets of locations.

Route aggregation is complicated, but an analogy should make its function clear. A computer in Prague in the Czech Republic sends a packet intended to go to a computer in Chicago, Illinois. When the packet hits one of the BGP routers, the router doesn't have to know the precise location of the recipient. It knows the router for the United States and sends the packet there. The U.S. router knows the Illinois router, which knows the Chicago router, and so on.

BGP is an amazing and powerful dynamic routing protocol, but unless you're working deep in the router room of an AS, odds are good you'll never see it in action. Those who need to connect a few routers together usually turn to a family of dynamic routing protocols that work very differently from distance vector routing protocols.

Link State

The limitations of RIP motivated the demand for a faster protocol that took up less bandwidth on a WAN. The basic idea was to come up with a dynamic routing protocol that was more efficient than routers that simply sent out their entire routing table at regular intervals. Why not instead simply announce and forward individual route changes as they appeared? That is the basic idea of a *link state* dynamic routing protocol. There are only two link state dynamic routing protocols: OSPF and IS-IS.

OSPF

Open Shortest Path First (OSPF) is the most commonly used IGP in the world. Most large enterprises use OSPF on their internal networks. Even an AS, while still using BGP on its edge routers, will use OSPF internally because OSPF was designed from the ground up to work within a single AS. OSPF converges dramatically faster and is much more efficient than RIP. Odds are good that if you are using dynamic routing protocols, you're using OSPF.

OSPF offers a number of improvements over RIP. When you first launch OSPF-capable routers, they send out *Hello packets,* looking for other OSPF routers (see Figure 7-31). After two adjacent routers form a *neighborship* through the Hello packets, they exchange information about routers and networks through *link state advertisement (LSA)* packets. LSAs are sourced by each router and are flooded from router to router through each OSPF area.

Once all the routers communicate, they individually decide their own optimal routes, and convergence happens almost immediately. If a route goes down, OSPF routers quickly recompute a new route with stored LSAs.

OSPF's metric is *cost*, which is a function of bandwidth. All possible ways to get to a destination network are computed based on cost, which is proportional to bandwidth, which is in turn proportional to the interface type (Gigabit Ethernet, 10-Gigabit Ethernet, and so on). The routers choose the lowest total cost route to a destination network.

In other words, a packet could go through more routers (hops) to get to a destination when OSPF is used instead of RIP. However, more hops doesn't necessarily mean slower.

Chapter 7: Routing

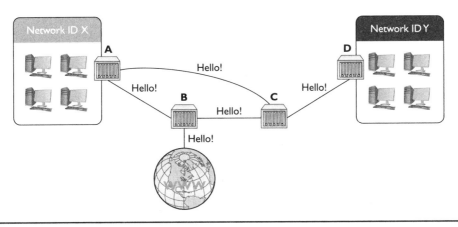

Figure 7-31 Hello!

If a packet goes through three hops where the routers are connected by fiber, for example, as opposed to a slow 56-Kbps link, the packet would get to its destination quicker. We make these decisions everyday as humans, too. I'd rather drive more miles on the highway to get somewhere quicker, than fewer miles on local streets where the speed limit is much lower. (Red lights and stop signs introduce driving latency as well!)

OSPF isn't popular by accident. It scales to large networks quite well and is supported by all but the most basic routers. By the way, did I forget to mention that OSPF also supports authentication and that the shortest-path-first method, by definition, prevents loops?

Why would anyone use anything else? Well, OSPF had one problem that wasn't repaired until fairly recently: support for something called IPv6 (see Chapter 12 for details on IPv6). Not to preempt Chapter 12, but IPv6 is a new addressing system for IP that dumps the old 32-bit address, replacing it with a 128-bit address. IPv6 is quickly gaining popularity and will one day replace 32-bit IP addressing. Just for the record, I've been predicting the end of 32-bit IP addressing for so long I'm now afraid to predict anymore when it's going to happen—but it will eventually.

 EXAM TIP OSPF corrects link failures and creates convergence almost immediately, making it the routing protocol of choice in most large enterprise networks. OSPF Version 2 is used for IPv4 networks, and OSPF Version 3 includes updates to support IPv6.

IS-IS

If you want to use a link state dynamic routing protocol and you don't want to use OSPF, your only other option is *Intermediate System to Intermediate System (IS-IS)*. IS-IS is extremely similar to OSPF. It uses the concept of areas and send-only updates to routing tables. IS-IS was developed at roughly the same time as OSPF and had the one major advantage of working with IPv6 from the start. IS-IS is the *de facto* standard for ISPs. Make sure you know that IS-IS is a link state dynamic routing protocol, and if you ever see two routers using it, call me as I've never seen IS-IS in action.

EIGRP

There is exactly one protocol that doesn't really fit into either the distance vector or link state camp: Cisco's proprietary *Enhanced Interior Gateway Routing Protocol (EIGRP)*. Back in the days when RIP was dominant, there was a huge outcry for an improved RIP, but OSPF wasn't yet out. Cisco, being the dominant router company in the world (a crown it still wears to this day), came out with the Interior Gateway Routing Protocol (IGRP), which was quickly replaced with EIGRP.

EIGRP has aspects of both distance vector and link state protocols, placing it uniquely into its own "hybrid" category. Cisco calls EIGRP an *advanced distance vector protocol*.

 EXAM TIP   The CompTIA Network+ objectives list EIGRP as a distance vector protocol, right along with RIP. Read questions carefully and if EIGRP is the only right answer as a distance vector protocol, take it.

Dynamic Routing Makes the Internet

Without dynamic routing, the complex, self-healing Internet we all enjoy today couldn't exist. So many routes come and go so often that manually updating static routes would be impossible. Review Table 7-2 to familiarize yourself with the differences among the different types of dynamic routing protocols.

Protocol	Type	IGP or BGP?	Notes
RIPv1	Distance vector	IGP	Old; only used variable subnets within an AS
RIPv2	Distance vector	IGP	Supports VLSM and discontiguous subnets
BGP	Path vector	BGP	Used on the Internet, connects Autonomous Systems
OSPF	Link state	IGP	Fast, popular, uses Area IDs (Area 0/backbone)
IS-IS	Link state	IGP	Alternative to OSPF
EIGRP	Hybrid	IGP	Cisco proprietary

Table 7-2   Dynamic Routing Protocols

Route Redistribution

Wow, there sure are many routing protocols out there. It's too bad they can't talk to each other … or can they?

The routers cannot use different routing protocols to communicate with each other, but many routers can speak multiple routing protocols simultaneously. When a router takes routes it has learned by one method, say RIP or a statically set route, and announces those routes over another protocol such as OSPF, this is called *route redistribution*.

This feature can come in handy when you have a mix of equipment and protocols in your network, such as occurs when you switch vendors or merge with another organization.

Working with Routers

Understanding the different ways routers work is one thing. Actually walking up to a router and making it work is a different animal altogether. This section examines practical router installation. Physical installation isn't very complicated. With a home router, you give it power and then plug in connections. With a business-class router, you insert it into a rack, give it power, and plug in connections.

The complex part of installation comes with the specialized equipment and steps to connect to the router and configure it for your network needs. This section, therefore, focuses on the many methods and procedures used to access and configure a router.

The single biggest item to keep in mind here is that although there are many different methods for connecting, hundreds of interfaces, and probably millions of different configurations for different routers, the functions are still the same. Whether you're using an inexpensive home router or a hyper-powerful Internet backbone router, you are always working to do one main job: connect different networks.

Also keep in mind that routers, especially gateway routers, often have a large number of other features that have nothing to do with routing. Because gateway routers act as a separator between the computers and "The Big Scary Rest of the Network," they are a convenient place for all kinds of handy features like DHCP, protecting the network from intrusion (better known as firewalls), and NAT.

Connecting to Routers

When you take a new router out of the box, it's not good for very much. You need to somehow plug into that shiny new router and start telling it what you want to do. There are a number of different methods, but one of the oldest (yet still very common) methods is to use a special serial connection. This type of connection is almost completely unique to Cisco-brand routers, but Cisco's massive market share makes understanding this type of connection a requirement for anyone who wants to know how to configure routers. Figure 7-32 shows the classic Cisco console cable, more commonly called a *rollover* or *Yost cable*.

Figure 7-32
Cisco console cable

NOTE The term *Yost cable* comes from its creator's name, Dave Yost. For more information visit http://yost.com/computers/RJ45-serial.

At this time, I need to make an important point: switches as well as routers often have some form of configuration interface. Granted, you have nothing to configure on a basic switch, but in later chapters, you'll discover a number of network features that you'll want to configure more advanced switches to use. Both routers and these advanced switches are called *managed devices*. In this section, I use the term *router*, but it's important for you to appreciate that all routers and many better switches are all managed devices. The techniques shown here work for both!

When you first unwrap a new Cisco router, you plug the rollover cable into the console port on the router (Figure 7-33) and a serial port on a PC. If you don't have a serial port, then buy a USB-to-serial adapter.

Figure 7-33
Console port

Once you've made this connection, you need to use a terminal emulation program to talk to the router. The two most popular programs are PuTTY (www.chiark.greenend .org.uk/~sgtatham/putty) and HyperTerminal (www.hilgraeve.com/hyperterminal). Using these programs requires that you to know a little about serial ports, but these basic settings should get you connected:

- 9600 baud
- 8 data bits
- 1 stop bit
- No parity

Every terminal emulator has some way for you to configure these settings. Figure 7-34 shows these settings using PuTTY.

Figure 7-34
Configuring
PuTTY

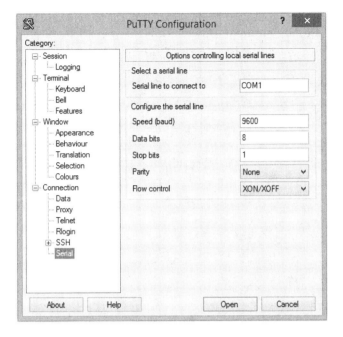

NOTE Much initial router configuration harkens back to the methods used in the early days of networking when massive mainframe computers were the computing platform available. Researchers used dumb terminals— machines that were little more than a keyboard, monitor, and network connection—to connect to the mainframe and interact. You connect to and configure many modern routers using software that enables your PC to pretend to be a dumb terminal. These programs are called terminal emulators; the screen you type into is called a console.

Now it's time to connect. Most Cisco products run *Cisco IOS*, Cisco's proprietary operating system. If you want to configure Cisco routers, you must learn IOS. Learning IOS in detail is a massive job and outside the scope of this book. No worries, because Cisco provides a series of certifications to support those who wish to become "Cisco People." Although the CompTIA Network+ exam won't challenge you in terms of IOS, it's important to get a taste of how this amazing operating system works.

NOTE IOS used to stand for *Internetwork Operating System*, but it's just IOS now with a little trademark symbol.

Once you've connected to the router and started a terminal emulator, you should see the initial router prompt, as shown in Figure 7-35. (If you plugged in and then started the router, you could actually watch the router boot up first.)

```
COM3 - PuTTY                                                              —  □  ×
*Mar  1 00:00:02.076: % Error opening nvram:/ifIndex-table No such file or directory
*Mar  1 00:00:15.021: %VPN_HW-6-INFO_LOC: Crypto engine: onboard 0  State changed to: Initialized
*Mar  1 00:00:15.025: %VPN_HW-6-INFO_LOC: Crypto engine: onboard 0  State changed to: Enabled
*Mar  1 00:00:16.986: %LINK-3-UPDOWN: Interface FastEthernet0, changed state to up
*Mar  1 00:00:16.986: %LINK-3-UPDOWN: Interface FastEthernet4, changed state to up
*Mar  1 00:00:17.994: %LINEPROTO-5-UPDOWN: Line protocol on
R4> Interface FastEthernet0, changed state to up
*Mar  1 00:00:17.994: %LINEPROTO-5-UPDOWN: Line protocol on Interface FastEthernet4, changed state to up
*Mar  1 00:00:25.991: %LINEPROTO-5-UPDOWN: Line protocol on Interface FastEthernet4, changed state to down
*Mar  1 00:00:45.341: %SYS-5-CONFIG_I: Configured from memory by console
*Mar  4 12:14:25.112: %LINEPROTO-5-UPDOWN: Line protocol on Interface Vlan1, changed state to down
*Mar  4 12:14:25.608: %SYS-5-RESTART: System restarted --
Cisco IOS Software, SR520 Software (SR520-ADVIPSERVICESK9-M), Version 12.4(24)T7, RELEASE SOFTWARE (fc2)
Technical Support: http://www.cisco.com/techsupport
Copyright (c) 1986-2012 by Cisco Systems, Inc.
Compiled Tue 28-Feb-12 14:20 by prod_rel_team
*Mar  4 12:14:25.612: %SNMP-5-COLDSTART: SNMP agent on host R4 is undergoing a cold start
*Mar  4 12:14:25.648: %SSH-5-ENABLED: SSH 1.99 has been enabled
*Mar  4 12:14:25.692: %CRYPTO-6-ISAKMP_ON_OFF: ISAKMP is OFF
*Mar  4 12:14:26.696: %LINK-5-CHANGED: Interface FastEthernet4, changed state to administratively down
*Mar  4 12:14:26.984: %LINK-3-UPDOWN: Interface FastEthernet3, changed state to up
*Mar  4 12:14:26.984: %LINK-3-UPDOWN: Interface FastEthernet2, changed state to up
*Mar  4 12:14:26.996: %LINK-3-UPDOWN: Interface FastEthernet1, changed state to up
*Mar  4 12:14:26.996: %LINK-3-UPDOWN: Interface FastEthernet0, changed state to up
*Mar  4 12:14:27.984: %LINEPROTO-5-UPDOWN: Line protocol on Interface FastEthernet3, changed state to down
*Mar  4 12:14:27.984: %LINEPROTO-5-UPDOWN: Line protocol on Interface FastEthernet2, changed state to down
*Mar  4 12:14:27.996: %LINEPROTO-5-UPDOWN: Line protocol on Interface FastEthernet1, changed state to down
*Mar  4 12:14:27.996: %LINEPROTO-5-UPDOWN: Line protocol on Interface FastEthernet0, changed state to down
R4>
```

Figure 7-35   Initial router prompt

This is the IOS user mode prompt—you can't do too much here. To get to the fun, you need to enter privileged EXEC mode. Type **enable**, press ENTER, and the prompt changes to

```
Router#
```

NOTE   A new Cisco router often won't have a password, but all good admins know to add one.

From here, IOS gets very complex. For example, the commands to set the IP address for one of the router's ports look like this:

```
Router# configure terminal
Router(config)# interface GigabitEthernet 0/0
Router(config-if)# ip address 192.168.4.10 255.255.255.0
Router(config-if)# ^Z
Router# copy run start
```

Cisco has long appreciated that initial setup is a bit of a challenge, so a brand-new router will show you the following prompt:

```
Would you like to enter the initial configuration dialog?
[yes/no]?
```

Simply follow the prompts, and the most basic setup is handled for you.

You will run into Cisco equipment as a network tech, and you will need to know how to use the console from time to time. For the most part, though, you'll access a router—especially one that's already configured—through Web access or network management software.

Web Access

Most routers come with a built-in Web interface that enables you to do everything you need on your router and is much easier to use than Cisco's command-line IOS. For a Web interface to work, however, the router must have a built-in IP address from the factory, or you have to enable the Web interface after you've given the router an IP address. Bottom line? If you want to use a Web interface, you have to know the router's IP address. If a router has a default IP address, you will find it in the documentation, as shown in Figure 7-36.

Figure 7-36
Default IP
address

How to open the browser-based utility

For **ALL**

To access some advanced settings, you need to open the browser-based utility.

> **CAUTION**
> If you change settings in the browser-based utility, you might not be able to run Cisco Connect later.

To open the browser-based utility:

1. Run Cisco Connect, click **Change** under *Router settings*, click **Advanced settings**, then click **OK**.

   – or –

   Open a web browser on a computer connected to your network, then go to **192.168.1.1**. If your router is version 2 (look for **V2** on router's bottom label), you can go to **myrouter.local** instead.

   The router prompts you for a user name and password.

Never plug a new router into an existing network! There's no telling what that router might start doing. Does it have DHCP? You might now have a rogue DHCP server. Are there routes on that router that match up to your network addresses? Then you see packets disappearing into the great bit bucket in the sky. Always fully configure your router before you place it online.

Most router people use a laptop and a crossover cable to connect to the new router. To get to the Web interface, first set a static address for your computer that will place your PC on the same network ID as the router. If, for example, the router is set to 192.168.1.1/24 from the factory, set your computer's IP address to 192.168.1.2/24.

Then connect to the router (some routers tell you exactly where to connect, so read the documentation first), and check the link lights to verify you're properly connected. Open up your Web browser and type in the IP address, as shown in Figure 7-37.

Figure 7-37
Entering the
IP address

> ✎ **NOTE** Many routers are also DHCP servers, making the initial connection much easier. Check the documentation to see if you can just plug in without setting an IP address on your PC.

Assuming you've done everything correctly, you almost always need to enter a default user name and password, as shown in Figure 7-38.

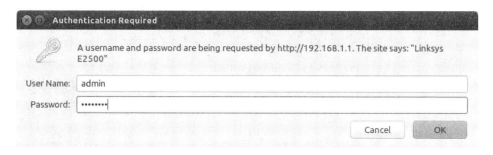

Figure 7-38   User name and password

The default user name and password come with the router's documentation. If you don't have that information, plenty of Web sites list this data. Do a Web search on **"default user name password"** to find one.

Once you've accessed the Web interface, you're on your own to poke around to find the settings you need. There's no standard interface—even between different versions of the same router make and model. When you encounter a new interface, take some time and inspect every tab and menu to learn about the router's capabilities. You'll almost always find some really cool features!

Network Management Software

The idea of a "Web-server-in-a-router" works well for single routers, but as a network grows into lots of routers, administrators need more advanced tools that describe, visualize, and configure their entire network. These tools, known as *Network Management*

Software (NMS), know how to talk to your routers, switches, and even your computers to give you an overall view of your network. In most cases, NMS manifests as a Web site where administrators may inspect the status of the network and make adjustments as needed.

I divide NMS into two camps: proprietary tools made by the folks who make managed devices (OEM) and third-party tools. OEM tools are generally very powerful and easy to use, but only work on that OEM's devices. Figure 7-39 shows an example of Cisco Network Assistant, one of Cisco's NMS applications. Others include the Cisco Configuration Professional and Cisco Prime Infrastructure, an enterprise-level tool.

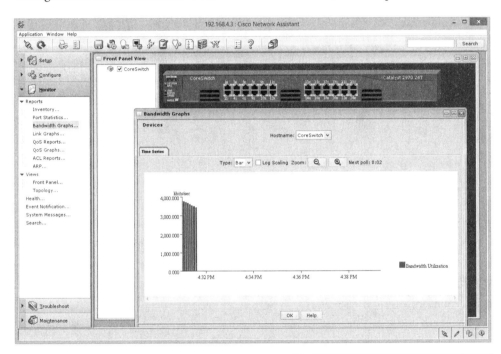

Figure 7-39 Cisco Network Assistant

A number of third-party NMS tools are out there as well; you can even find some pretty good freeware NMS options. These tools are invariably harder to configure and must constantly be updated to try to work with as many devices as possible.

They usually lack the amount of detail you see with OEM NMS and lack interactive graphical user interfaces. For example, various Cisco products enable you to change the IP address of a port, whereas third-party tools will only let you see the current IP settings for that port. Figure 7-40 shows OpenNMS, a popular open source NMS.

Unfortunately, no single NMS tool works perfectly. Network administrators are constantly playing with this or that NMS tool in an attempt to give themselves some kind of overall picture of their networks.

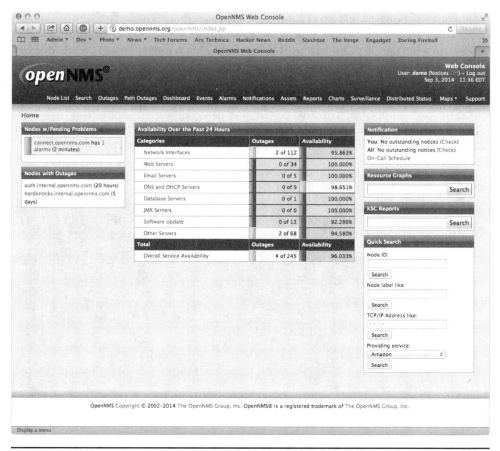

Figure 7-40   OpenNMS

Other Connection Methods

Be aware that most routers have even more ways to connect. Many home routers come with USB ports and configuration software. More powerful routers may enable you to connect using the ancient Telnet protocol or its newer and safer equivalent Secure Shell (SSH). These are terminal emulation protocols that look exactly like the terminal emulators seen earlier in this chapter but use the network instead of a serial cable to connect (see Chapter 8 for details on these protocols).

NOTE   The PuTTY utility works with the old-style terminal emulation as well as Telnet and SSH.

Basic Router Configuration

A router, by definition, must have at least two connections. When you set up a router, you must configure every port on the router properly to talk to its connected network IDs, and you must make sure the routing table sends packets to where you want them to go. As a demonstration, Figure 7-41 uses an incredibly common setup: a single gateway router used in a home or small office that's connected to an ISP.

Figure 7-41
The setup

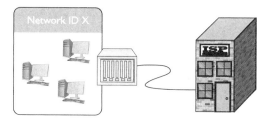

Step 1: Set Up the WAN Side

To start, you need to know the network IDs for each side of your router. The WAN side invariably connects to an ISP, so you need to know what the ISP wants you to do. If you bought a static IP address, type it in now. However—brace yourself for a crazy fact—most home Internet connections use DHCP! That's right, DHCP isn't just for your PC. You can set up your router's WAN connection to use it too. DHCP is by far the most common connection to use for home routers. Access your router and locate the WAN connection setup. Figure 7-42 shows the setup for my home router set to DHCP.

Figure 7-42
WAN router
setup

NOTE I'm ignoring a number of other settings here for the moment. I'll revisit most of these in later chapters.

But what if I called my ISP and bought a single static IP address? This is rarely done anymore, but virtually every ISP will gladly sell you one (although you will pay three to four times as much for the connection). If you use a static IP, your ISP will tell you what to enter, usually in the form of an e-mail message like the following:

```
Dear Mr. Meyers,
Thank you for requesting a static IP address from
totalsem.com!
Here's your new static IP information:
IP address: 1.151.35.55
Default Gateway: 1.151.32.132
Subnet Mask: 255.255.128.0
```

```
Installation instructions can be found at:
http://totalsem.com/setup/
Support is available at:
http://helpdesk.totalsem.com or by calling (281)922-4166.
```

In such a case, I would need to change the router setting to Static IP (Figure 7-43). Note how changing the drop-down menu to Static IP enables me to enter the information needed.

Figure 7-43
Entering a
static IP

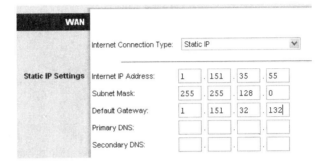

Once you've set up the WAN side, it's time to head over to set up the LAN side of the router.

Step 2: Set Up the LAN

Unlike the WAN side, you usually have total control on the LAN side of the router. You need to choose a network ID, almost always some arbitrarily chosen private range unless you do not want to use NAT. This is why so many home networks have network IDs of 192.168.1/24, 192.168.0/24, and so forth. Once you decide on your LAN-side network ID, you need to assign the correct IP information to the LAN-side NIC. Figure 7-44 shows the configuration for a LAN NIC on my home router.

Figure 7-44
Setting up an IP
address for the
LAN side

Step 3: Establish Routes

Most routers are pretty smart and use the information you provided for the two interfaces to build a routing table automatically. If you need to add more routes, every router provides some method to add routes. The following shows the command entered on a Cisco router to add a route to one of its Ethernet interfaces. The term "gig0/0" is how Cisco describes Ethernet NICs in its device software. It is short for GigabitEthernet, which you may remember as being the common name (when you add a space) for 1000BaseT.

```
ip route 192.168.100.0 255.255.255.0 gig0/0 192.168.1.10
```

Step 4 (Optional): Configure a Dynamic Protocol

The rules for using any dynamic routing protocol are fairly straightforward. First, dynamic routing protocols are tied to individual NICs, not the entire router. Second, when you connect two routers together, make sure those two NICs are configured to use the same dynamic routing protocol. Third, unless you're in charge of two or more routers, you're probably not going to use any dynamic routing protocol.

The amazing part of a dynamic routing protocol is how easy it is to set up. In most cases you just figure out how to turn it on and that's about it. It just starts working.

Step 5: Document and Back Up

Once you've configured your routes, take some time to document what you've done. A good router works for years without interaction, so by that time in the future when it goes down, odds are good you will have forgotten why you added the routes. Last, take some time to back up the configuration. If a router goes down, it will most likely forget everything and you'll need to set it up all over again. Every router has some method to back up the configuration, however, so you can restore it later.

Router Problems

The CompTIA Network+ exam will challenge you on some basic router problems. All of these questions should be straightforward for you as long as you do the following:

- Consider other issues first because routers don't fail very often.
- Keep in mind what your router is supposed to do.
- Know how to use a few basic tools that can help you check the router.

Any router problem starts with someone not connecting to someone else. Even a small network has a number of NICs, computers, switches, and routers between you and whatever it is you're not connecting to. Compared to most of these, a router is a pretty robust device and shouldn't be considered as the problem until you've checked out just about everything else first.

In their most basic forms, routers route traffic. Yet you've seen in this chapter that routers can do more than just plain routing—for example, NAT. As this book progresses, you'll find that the typical router often handles a large number of duties beyond just routing. Know what your router is doing and appreciate that you may find yourself checking a router for problems that don't really have anything to do with routing at all.

Be aware that routers have some serious but rare potential problems. One place to watch is your routing table. For the most part, today's routers automatically generate directly connected routes, and dynamic routing takes care of itself, leaving one type of route as a possible suspect: the static routes. This is the place to look when packets aren't getting to the places you expect them to go. Look at the following sample static route:

```
Net Destination         Netmask         Gateway         Interface       Metric
    22.46.132.0     255.255.255.255   22.46.132.1      22.46.132.11         1
```

No incoming packets for network ID are getting out on interface 22.46.132.11. Can you see why? Yup, the Netmask is set to 255.255.255.255, and there are no computers that have exactly the address 22.46.132.0. Entering the wrong network destination, subnet mask, gateway, and so on, is very easy. If a new static route isn't getting the packets moved, first assume you made a typo.

Make sure to watch out for missing routes. These usually take place either because you've forgotten to add them (if you're entering static routes) or, more commonly, there is a convergence problem in the dynamic routing protocols. For the CompTIA Network+ exam, be ready to inspect a routing table to recognize these problems.

When it comes to tools, networking comes with so many utilities and magic devices that it staggers the imagination. You've already seen some, like good old ping and route, but let's add two more tools: traceroute and mtr.

The *traceroute* tool, as its name implies, records the route between any two hosts on a network. On the surface, traceroute is something like ping in that it sends a single packet to another host, but as it progresses, it returns information about every router between them.

Every operating system comes with traceroute, but the actual command varies among them. In Windows, the command is tracert and looks like this (I'm running a traceroute to the router connected to my router—a short trip):

```
C:\>tracert 96.165.24.1

Tracing route to 96.165.24.1 over a maximum of 30 hops:

    1    1 ms     1 ms     1 ms     10.12.14.1
    2   10 ms    10 ms     8 ms     96.165.24.1
Trace complete.
```

The macOS/UNIX/Linux command is traceroute and looks like this:

```
michaelm@ubuntu:~$ traceroute 96.165.24.1
traceroute to 96.165.24.1 (96.165.24.1), 30 hops max, 40 byte
packets
1    10.12.14.1 (10.12.14.1)  0.763 ms 0.432 ms  0.233 ms
2    96.165.24.1 (96.165.24.1) 12.233 ms 11.255 ms 14.112 ms
michaelm@ubuntu:~$
```

The traceroute tool is handy, not so much for what it tells you when everything's working well, but for what it tells you when things are not working. Look at the following:

```
:\>tracert 96.165.24.1

Tracing route to 96.165.24.1 over a maximum of 30 hops
    1    1 ms     1 ms     1 ms   10.12.14.1
    2    *        *         *        Request timed out
    3  96.165.24.1  reports: Destination host unreachable.
```

If this traceroute worked in the past but now no longer works, you know that something is wrong between your router and the next router upstream. You don't know what's wrong exactly. The connection may be down; the router may not be working; but at least traceroute gives you an idea where to look for the problem and where not to look.

My traceroute (mtr) is very similar to traceroute, but it's dynamic, continually updating the route that you've selected (Figure 7-45). You won't find mtr in Windows; mtr is a Linux tool. Instead, Windows users can use pathping. This utility will ping each node on the route just like mtr, but instead of showing the results of each ping in real time, the pathping utility computes the performance over a set time and then shows you the summary after it has finished.

```
         ● ○ ○                mtr totalsem.com — mtr — ssh — 99×28
                              My traceroute  [v0.85]
michaels-moble (0.0.0.0)                                    Tue Sep  2 16:26:16 2014
Keys:  Help   Display mode   Restart statistics   Order of fields   quit
                                                     Packets            Pings
 Host                                               Loss%  Snt   Last   Avg  Best  Wrst StDev
  1. Router.totalhome                               0.0%   19     0.9   0.9   0.7   1.2   0.0
  2. ???
  3. xe-4-0-0-32767-sur02.airport.tx.houston.comcast.net  0.0%   19     9.2  13.7   7.5  50.6  11.0
  4. ae-4-0-ar01.bearcreek.tx.houston.comcast.net  0.0%   19    15.6  12.2   9.9  15.6   1.5
  5. 68.86.166.229                                  0.0%   19    25.6  19.5  15.6  25.6   2.4
  6. pos-0-1-0-0-pe01.1950stemmons.tx.ibone.comcast.net  0.0%   19    21.2  21.8  16.5  62.0  10.0
  7. ae10.bbr01.eq01.dal03.networklayer.com         0.0%   19    19.4  17.1  15.0  26.3   2.3
  8. ae0.bbr01.sr02.hou02.networklayer.com          0.0%   19    22.2  22.5  20.0  31.8   3.1
  9. po31.dsr01.hstntx2.networklayer.com            0.0%   19    21.8  27.7  20.3 117.3  21.8
 10. po1.car02.hstntx2.networklayer.com             0.0%   18    23.7  24.3  20.3  37.5   4.6
 11. totalsem.com                                   0.0%   18    22.0  22.8  20.1  31.2   2.3
```

Figure 7-45   mtr in action

Chapter Review

Questions

1. What is a router?

    A. A piece of hardware that forwards packets based on IP address

    B. A device that separates your computers from the Internet

    C. A piece of hardware that distributes a single Internet connection to multiple computers

    D. A synonym for a firewall

2. Routers must use the same type of connection for all routes, such as Ethernet to Ethernet or ATM to ATM.

    A. True

    B. False

3. What technology allows you to share a single public IP address with many computers?

   A. Static Address Translation

   B. Natural Address Translation

   C. Computed Public Address Translation

   D. Port Address Translation

4. Given the following routing table:

```
Destination LAN IP      Subnet Mask        Gateway          Interface
      10.11.12.0      255.255.255.0        0.0.0.0                LAN
      64.165.5.0      255.255.255.0        0.0.0.0                WAN
         0.0.0.0            0.0.0.0     64.165.5.1                WAN
```

where would a packet with the address 64.165.5.34 be sent?

   A. To the default gateway on interface WAN.

   B. To the 10.11.12.0/24 network on interface LAN.

   C. To the 64.165.5.0/24 network on interface WAN.

   D. Nowhere; the routing table does not have a route for that address.

5. Distance vector routing protocols such as RIP rely on what metric to determine the best route?

   A. Hop count.

   B. Link speed.

   C. Ping time.

   D. Routes are chosen at random.

6. What are two big advantages to using OSPF over RIP? (Select two.)

   A. OSPF is a modern protocol that does not have legacy problems.

   B. OSPF chooses routes based on link speed, not hop count.

   C. OSPF runs on all routers, big and small.

   D. OSPF sends only routing table changes, reducing network traffic.

7. What is Area 0 called in OSPF?

   A. Local Area

   B. Primary Zone

   C. Trunk

   D. Backbone

8. What is the name of the cable that you use to connect to the console port on Cisco routers?

   A. Router console cable

   B. Yost cable

   C. That funny blue Cisco cable

   D. Null modem cable

9. When you are first setting up a new router, you should never plug it into an existing network.

   A. True

   B. False

10. The traceroute utility is useful for?

    A. Configuring routers remotely

    B. Showing the physical location of the route between you and the destination

    C. Discovering information about the routers between you and the destination address

    D. Fixing the computer's local routing table

Answers

1. **A.** A router is a piece of hardware that forwards packets based on IP address.

2. **B.** False; a router can interconnect different Layer 2 technologies.

3. **D.** Port Address Translation, commonly known as PAT, enables you to share a single public IP address with many computers.

4. **C.** It would be sent to the 64.165.5.0/24 network on interface WAN.

5. **A.** Distance vector routing protocols use hop count to determine the best route.

6. **B** and **D.** OSPF bases routes on speed and sends only route changes to minimize traffic.

7. **D.** Area 0 is called the backbone area.

8. **B.** You use Yost cable, which was invented to standardize the serial console interface, to connect to the console port on Cisco routers.

9. **A.** True; never plug a new router into an existing network.

10. **C.** The traceroute utility is useful for discovering information about the routers between you and the destination address.

TCP/IP Applications

The CompTIA Network+ certification exam expects you to know how to

- 1.1 Explain the purposes and uses of ports and protocols
- 1.8 Explain the functions of network services
- 3.4 Given a scenario, use remote access methods

To achieve these goals, you must be able to

- Describe common Transport and Network layer protocols
- Explain the power of port numbers
- Define common TCP/IP applications such as HTTP, HTTPS, Telnet, SSH, e-mail (SMTP, POP3, and IMAP4), and FTP

We network to get work done. Okay, sometimes that "work" involves a mad gaming session in which I lay some smack down on my editors, but you know what I mean. Thus far in the book, everything you've read about networking involves connecting computers together. This chapter moves further up the OSI seven-layer model and the TCP/IP model to look at applications such as Web browsers, e-mail messaging, and more.

To understand the applications that use TCP/IP networks, a tech needs to know the structures below those applications. Have you ever opened multiple Web pages on a single computer? Have you ever run multiple Internet apps, such as a Web browser, an e-mail client, and a remote connectivity app, all at the same time? Clearly, a lot of data is moving back and forth between your computer and many other computers. With packets coming in from two, three, or more computers, there has to be a mechanism or process that knows where to send and receive that data.

In this chapter, you'll discover the process used by TCP/IP networks to ensure the right data gets to the right applications on your computer. This process uses very important Transport and Network layer protocols—TCP, UDP, and ICMP—and port numbering. When used together, TCP and UDP along with port numbers enable you to get work done on a network.

Historical/Conceptual

Transport Layer and Network Layer Protocols

I hate to tell you this, but you've been lied to. Not by me. Even though I've gone along with this Big Lie, I need to tell you the truth.

There is no such thing as TCP/IP. *TCP over IP* is really many other things, such as *HTTP*, *DHCP*, *POP*, and about 500 more terms over *TCP*, plus *UDP* and *ICMP* over *IP*. Given that this overly complex but much more correct term is too hard to use, the people who invented this network protocol stack decided to call it *TCP/IP*, even though that term is way too simplistic to cover all the functionality involved. A common way to refer all the aspects and protocols that make up TCP/IP is to call it the *TCP/IP suite*.

NOTE There is a strong movement toward using the term *Internet Protocol* instead of the term *TCP/IP*. This movement has not yet reached the CompTIA Network+ certification.

This chapter explores many of the protocols used in TCP/IP networks and shows how they help make applications work. This section looks at the big three—TCP, UDP, and ICMP, plus IGMP for fun. (Subsequent sections of this chapter explore many more TCP/IP protocols.) Let's start the process with an analogy, by considering how human beings communicate. You'll see some very interesting commonalities between computers and people.

How People Communicate

Imagine you walk into a school cafeteria to get some lunch. You first walk up to the guy making custom deli sandwiches (this is a great cafeteria!) and say, "Hello!" He says, "How may I help you?" You say, "I'd like a sandwich please." He says, "What kind of sandwich would you like?" and you order your sandwich. After you get your sandwich you say, "Thanks!" and he says, "You're welcome." What a nice guy! In the networking world, we would call this a *connection-oriented* communication. Both you and the lunch guy first acknowledge each other. You then conduct your communication; finally, you close the communication.

While you're in line, you see your friend Janet sitting at your usual table. The line is moving fast so you yell out, "Janet, save me a seat!" before you rush along in the line. In this case, you're not waiting for her to answer; you just yell to her and hope she hears you. We call this a *connectionless* communication. There is no acknowledgment or any closing.

In networking, any single communication between a computer and another computer is called a *session*. When you open a Web page, you make a session. When you call your buddy (using the Internet, not the cellular networks), you create a session. All sessions must begin and eventually end.

Test Specific

TCP

The *Transmission Control Protocol (TCP)* enables connection-oriented communication in networks that use the TCP/IP protocol suite. TCP is by far the most common type of session on a typical TCP/IP network. Figure 8-1 shows two computers. One computer (Server) runs a Web server and the other (Client) runs a Web browser. When you enter a computer's address in the browser running on Client, it sends a single SYN (synchronize) segment to the Web server. If Server gets that segment, it returns a single SYN, ACK (synchronize, acknowledge) segment. Client then sends Server a single ACK (acknowledge) segment and immediately requests that Server begin sending the Web page. This process is called the *TCP three-way handshake*.

Figure 8-1

A connection-oriented session starting

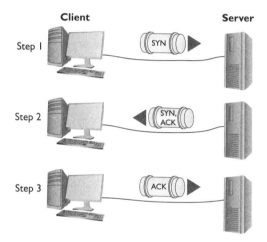

Once Server finishes sending the Web page, it sends a FIN (final) segment. Client responds with an ACK segment and then sends its own FIN segment. The server then responds with an ACK; now both parties consider the session closed (Figure 8-2).

Most TCP/IP applications use TCP because connection-oriented sessions are designed to check for errors. If a receiving computer detects a missing segment, it just asks for a repeat as needed.

UDP

User Datagram Protocol (UDP) runs a distant second place to TCP in terms of the number of applications that use it, but that doesn't mean UDP is not important. UDP is perfect for the types of sessions that don't require the overhead of all that connection-oriented stuff.

Figure 8-2
A connection-oriented session ending

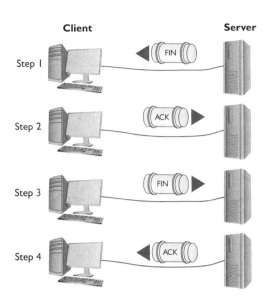

 NOTE Domain Name System (DNS) protocol traffic uses UDP. That's the protocol that enables (among other things) people to use names rather than IP addresses to access resources on TCP/IP networks like the Internet. DNS is so important that most of Chapter 9, "Network Naming," is devoted to how it works and what network techs need to know to support it.

DHCP

Dynamic Host Configuration Protocol (DHCP) uses UDP and provides a good example of connectionless communication. DHCP can't assume another computer is ready on either side of the session, so each step of a DHCP session just sends the information for that step without any confirmation (Figure 8-3). Sending a connectionless packet also makes sense because the client won't have an IP address to begin the three-way hand-shake. Plus, if the server doesn't respond, the client can simply ask again.

As you learned in Chapter 6, "TCP/IP Basics," DHCP uses two port numbers. DHCP clients use port 67 for sending data to and receiving data from the DHCP server, and DHCP servers use port 68 for sending and receiving data to and from DHCP clients.

NTP/SNTP

Two popular applications that use UDP are Network Time Protocol (NTP) and his lightweight little brother, Simple Network Time Protocol (SNTP). These protocols synchronize the clocks of devices on a network. Computers need to use the same time so things like Kerberos authentication work properly. If a device requires NTP/SNTP, you will be able to enter the IP address for an NTP/SNTP server. NTP/SNTP uses port 123.

Figure 8-3
DHCP steps

TFTP

You might also be tempted to think that UDP wouldn't work for any situation in which a critical data transfer takes place—untrue! *Trivial File Transfer Protocol (TFTP)* enables you to transfer files from one machine to another. TFTP, using UDP, doesn't have any data protection, so you would never use TFTP between computers across the Internet. The typical scenario for using TFTP is moving files between computers on the same LAN, where the chances of losing packets is very small. TFTP uses port 69.

 EXAM TIP Expect to get a question that compares *connection-oriented vs. connectionless* communication in general, or the protocols commonly used in each.

ICMP

While TCP and UDP differ dramatically—the former connection-oriented and the latter connectionless—both manage and modify packets in the classic sense with a destination IP address, source IP address, destination port numbers, and source port numbers. A single session might be one packet or a series of packets.

On the other hand, sometimes applications are so simple that they're always connectionless and never need more than a single packet. The *Internet Control Message Protocol (ICMP)* works at Layer 3 to deliver connectionless packets. ICMP handles mundane issues such as host unreachable messages.

Ping is one place where you'll see ICMP in action. Ping is an ICMP application that works by sending a single ICMP packet called an *echo request* to an IP address you specify. All computers running TCP/IP (assuming no firewall is involved) respond to echo requests with an *echo reply*, as shown in Figure 8-4.

Figure 8-4

Ping in action

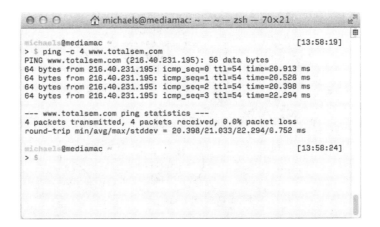

NOTE A *firewall* is a device or software that filters all the packets between two computers (or groups of computers) and acts like a club bouncer deciding who gets in and who gets blocked. Firewalls are vital for securing modern networks and will be discussed in Chapter 11, "Advanced Network Devices."

Ping provides a couple of responses that indicate problems locating the remote computer. If your computer has no route to the address listed, ping will display *destination host unreachable*. You might get the same message from a router upstream if that router can't go forward. If you ping a device and no echo reply comes back before the default time, ping will respond with *request timed out*. (The default time varies by platform, but within a few seconds.) This can be caused by a slow network, excess traffic, a downed router, and more. Ping responses could be disabled on the target computer.

EXAM TIP CompTIA has used the term *unreachable default gateway* as an ICMP-related issue. If you ping the default gateway and get a *destination host unreachable* response, you could infer that the default gateway is unreachable.

Many years ago, ping had a bug that allowed malicious users to send malformed ping packets to a destination. This *ping of death* would cause the recipient computer to crash. Ping was long ago fixed and you'll only hear this term from ancient techs—and perhaps see it on the CompTIA Network+ exam.

IGMP

Do you remember the idea of IP multicast addresses, described in Chapter 6? The challenge to multicasting is determining who wants to receive the multicast and who does not. The *Internet Group Management Protocol (IGMP)* enables routers to communicate with hosts to determine a "group" membership. As you might remember from Chapter 6, multicast is in the Class D range (224.0.0.0–239.255.255.255). Multicast addresses only use a subset of the Class D range. Multicast also doesn't assign IP addresses to individual hosts in the same manner as you've seen thus far. Instead, a particular multicast (called an *IGMP group*) is assigned to an address in the Class D range, and those who wish to receive this multicast must tell their upstream router or switch (which must be configured to handle multicasts) that they wish to receive it. To do so, they join the IGMP group (Figure 8-5).

Figure 8-5   IGMP in action

The Power of Port Numbers

If you want to understand the power of TCP/IP, you have to get seriously into port numbers. If you want to pass the CompTIA Network+ exam, you need to know how TCP/IP uses port numbers and you have to memorize a substantial number of common port numbers. As you saw in the previous chapter, port numbers make NAT work. As you progress through this book, you'll see a number of places where knowledge of port numbers is critical to protect your network, make routers work better, and address a zillion other issues. There is no such thing as a network administrator who isn't deeply into the magic of port numbers and who cannot manipulate them for his or her network's needs.

 EXAM TIP   TCP/IP port numbers between 0 and 1023 are the well-known port numbers. You'll find them at every party.

Let's review and expand on what you learned about port numbers in Chapters 1 and 7. Thus far, you know that every TCP/IP application requires a server and a client. Clearly defined port numbers exist for every popular or *well-known* TCP/IP application. A port number is a 16-bit value between 0 and 65535. Web servers, for example, use port number 80. Port numbers from 0 to 1023 are called *well-known port numbers* and are reserved for specific TCP/IP applications.

When a Web client (let's say your computer running Firefox) sends an HTTP ACK to a Web server to request the Web page, your computer's IP packet looks like Figure 8-6.

Figure 8-6

HTTP ACK packet

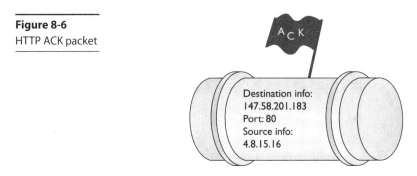

Destination info:
147.58.201.183
Port: 80
Source info:
4.8.15.16

As you can see, the destination port number is 80. The computer running the Web server reads the destination port number, telling it to send the incoming segment to the Web server program (Figure 8-7).

Figure 8-7

Dealing with the incoming packet

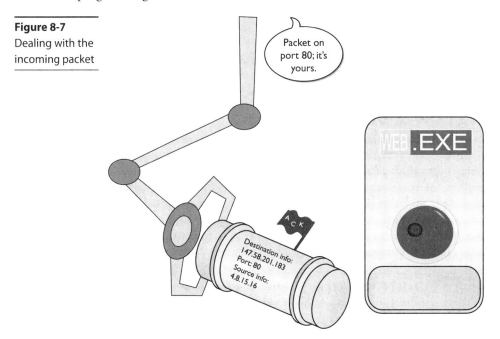

Packet on port 80; it's yours.

Destination info:
147.58.201.183
Port: 80
Source info:
4.8.15.16

WEB.EXE

The Web client's source port number is generated pseudo-randomly by the Web client computer. This value has varied by operating system over the decades, but generally falling within the values 1024–5000 (the port numbers classically assigned as *ephemeral port numbers*) and 49152–65535 (the *dynamic port numbers* or *private port numbers*).

In the early days of the Internet, only ports 1024–5000 were used, but modern computers can use up all of those. More port numbers were added later.

The Internet Assigned Numbers Authority (IANA) today recommends using only ports 49152–65535 as ephemeral port numbers. That's what current versions of Windows use as well. Let's redraw Figure 8-6 to show the more complete packet (Figure 8-8).

Figure 8-8
A more complete
IP packet

When the serving system responds to the Web client, it uses the ephemeral port number as the destination port to get the information back to the Web client running on the client computer (Figure 8-9).

Figure 8-9
Returning the
packet

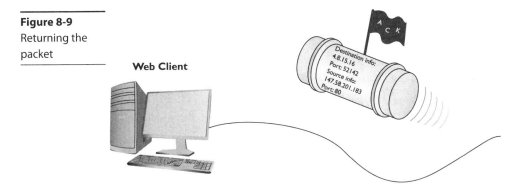

Registered Ports

The port numbers from 1024 to 49151 are called *registered ports*. Less-common TCP/IP applications can register their ports with the IANA. Unlike well-known ports, anyone can use these port numbers for their servers or for ephemeral numbers on clients. Most operating systems steer away (or are in the process of steering away) from using these port numbers for ephemeral ports, opting instead for the dynamic/private port numbers. Here's the full list of ports:

0–1023	Well-known port numbers
1024–49151	Registered ports
49152–65535	Dynamic or private ports

Each computer on each side of a session must keep track of the status of the communication. In TCP/IP, the session information (a combination of the IP address and port number) stored in RAM is called a *socket* or *endpoint*. When discussing the data each computer stores about the connection between two computers' TCP/IP applications, the term to use is *socket pairs* or *endpoints*. A *session* or *connection* refers to the connection in general, rather than anything specific to TCP/IP. Many people still use the term *session*, however. Here's a summary of the terms used:

- Terms for the session information (IP address and port number) stored on a single computer—*socket* or *endpoint*

- Terms for the connection data stored on two computers about the same connection—*socket pairs* or *endpoints*

- Terms for the whole interconnection—*connection* or *session*

As two computers begin to communicate, they store the information about the session—the endpoints—so they know where to send and receive data. At any given point in time, your computer probably has a large number of communications going on. If you want to know who your computer is communicating with, you need to see this list of endpoints. As you'll recall from Chapter 7, "Routing," Windows, Linux, and macOS come with *netstat*, the universal "show me the endpoint" utility. Netstat works at the command line, so open one up and type **netstat -n** to see something like this:

```
C:\>netstat -n
Active Connections
   Proto  Local Address          Foreign Address        State
   TCP    192.168.4.27:57913     216.40.231.195:80      ESTABLISHED
   TCP    192.168.4.27:61707     192.168.4.8:445        ESTABLISHED
C:\>
```

When you run `netstat -n` on a typical computer, you'll see many more than just two connections! The preceding example is simplified for purposes of discussing the details. It shows two connections: My computer's IP address is 192.168.4.27. The top connection is an open Web page (port 80) to a server at http://216.40.231.195. The second connection is an open Windows Network browser (port 445) to my file server (192.168.4.8). Looking on my Windows Desktop, you would certainly see at least these two windows open (Figure 8-10).

 NOTE Even though almost all operating systems use netstat, there are subtle differences in options and output among the different versions.

Don't think that a single open application always means a single connection. The following example shows what `netstat -n` looks like when I open the well-known www.microsoft.com Web site (I removed lines unrelated to the Web browser's connections to www.microsoft.com):

```
C:\>netstat -n
Active Connections
   Proto  Local Address          Foreign Address        State
   TCP    192.168.4.27:50015     80.12.192.40:80        ESTABLISHED
   TCP    192.168.4.27:50016     80.12.192.40:80        ESTABLISHED
   TCP    192.168.4.27:50017     80.12.192.40:80        ESTABLISHED
```

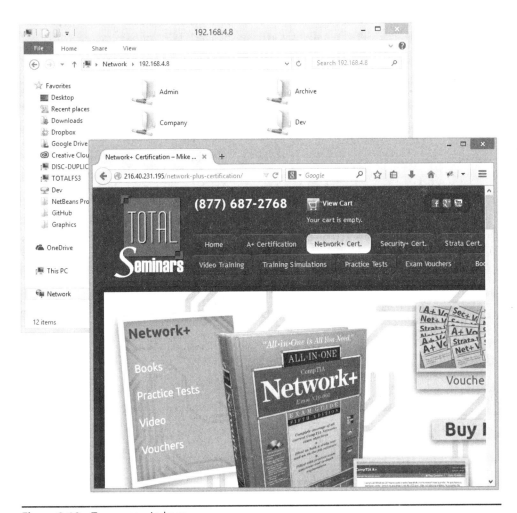

Figure 8-10 Two open windows

```
TCP    192.168.4.27:50018    80.12.192.40:80    ESTABLISHED
TCP    192.168.4.27:50019    80.12.192.40:80    ESTABLISHED
TCP    192.168.4.27:50020    80.12.192.51:80    ESTABLISHED
TCP    192.168.4.27:50021    80.12.192.40:80    ESTABLISHED
TCP    192.168.4.27:50022    80.12.192.40:80    ESTABLISHED
TCP    192.168.4.27:50023    80.12.192.40:80    ESTABLISHED
TCP    192.168.4.27:50024    80.12.192.40:80    ESTABLISHED
TCP    192.168.4.27:50025    80.12.192.51:80    ESTABLISHED
TCP    192.168.4.27:50027    80.12.192.40:80    ESTABLISHED
TCP    192.168.4.27:50028    80.12.192.40:80    ESTABLISHED
TCP    192.168.4.27:50036    80.12.192.75:80    ESTABLISHED
```

A single simple Web page needs only a single connection, but this Web page is very complex. Different elements in the Web page, such as advertisements, each have their own connection.

EXAM TIP Netstat enables you to see active TCP/IP connections at a glance.

Netstat is a powerful tool, and you will see it used throughout this book. The CompTIA Network+ exam also tests your netstat skills. On the other hand, connections come and go constantly on your computer, and netstat, being a command-line utility, can't update to reflect changes automatically. All of the cool, hip, network techs use graphical endpoint tools. Take a moment right now and download the popular, powerful, and completely free TCPView, written by Mark Russinovich, the Guru of Windows utilities. Just type **TCPView** into your search engine to find it or try going here:

https://docs.microsoft.com/en-us/sysinternals/

Click the **Networking Utilities** icon to get the latest copy. Figure 8-11 shows TCPView in action. The bars are colored, though you can't tell from this screen shot: red is for closing connections and green shows new connections as they appear.

Process	PID	Protocol	Local Address	Local Port	Remote Address	Remote Port	State
svchost.exe	1876	UDPV6	[fe80:0:0:0:1121:e...	57015	x	x	
svchost.exe	1876	UDPV6	[0:0:0:0:0:0:0:1]	57016	x	x	
svchost.exe	96	UDPV6	michaels-ws.totalh...	59830	x	x	
svchost.exe	900	UDPV6	[fe80:0:0:0:1121:e...	546	x	x	
synergyd.exe	2348	TCP	michaels-ws	24801	michaels-ws	0	LISTENING
System	4	TCP	michaels-ws.totalh...	netbios-ssn	michaels-ws	0	LISTENING
System	4	TCP	michaels-ws.totalh...	1272	totalfs3.totalhome	microsoft-ds	ESTABLISHED
System	4	TCP	michaels-ws	http	michaels-ws	0	LISTENING
System	4	TCP	michaels-ws	microsoft-ds	michaels-ws	0	LISTENING
System	4	TCP	michaels-ws	wsd	michaels-ws	0	LISTENING
System	4	UDP	michaels-ws.totalh...	netbios-ns	x	x	
System	4	UDP	michaels-ws.totalh...	netbios-dgm	x	x	
System	4	TCPV6	michaels-ws.totalh...	http	michaels-ws.totalh...	0	LISTENING
System	4	TCPV6	michaels-ws.totalh...	microsoft-ds	michaels-ws.totalh...	0	LISTENING
System	4	TCPV6	michaels-ws.totalh...	wsd	michaels-ws.totalh...	0	LISTENING
System	4	TCP	michaels-ws.totalh...	1785	192.168.4.12	microsoft-ds	ESTABLISHED
thunderbird.exe	464	TCP	michaels-ws	1773	localhost	1774	ESTABLISHED
thunderbird.exe	464	TCP	michaels-ws	1774	localhost	1773	ESTABLISHED
thunderbird.exe	464	TCP	michaels-ws.totalh...	1775	dfw06s32-in-f17.1...	https	ESTABLISHED
thunderbird.exe	464	TCP	michaels-ws.totalh...	1776	dfw06s32-in-f6.1e...	http	ESTABLISHED
thunderbird.exe	464	TCP	michaels-ws.totalh...	1777	mail1.megamailse...	pop3s	ESTABLISHED
thunderbird.exe	464	TCP	michaels-ws.totalh...	1779	bedrock-prod.zlb.p...	https	ESTABLISHED
thunderbird.exe	464	TCP	michaels-ws.totalh...	1781	72.21.91.29	http	ESTABLISHED
thunderbird.exe	464	TCP	michaels-ws.totalh...	1783	ocsp.ams1.verisig...	http	ESTABLISHED
thunderbird.exe	464	TCP	michaels-ws.totalh...	1786	mail1.megamailse...	pop3s	ESTABLISHED
vmware-authd...	2804	TCP	michaels-ws	902	michaels-ws	0	LISTENING
vmware-authd...	2804	TCP	michaels-ws	912	michaels-ws	0	LISTENING
vmware-conv...	2452	TCP	michaels-ws	9089	michaels-ws	0	LISTENING
vmware-conv...	2452	TCPV6	michaels-ws.totalh...	9089	michaels-ws.totalh...	0	LISTENING
vmware-conv...	2588	TCP	michaels-ws	54321	michaels-ws	0	LISTENING
vmware-conv...	2588	TCP	michaels-ws	56789	michaels-ws	0	LISTENING
vmware-conv...	2588	TCPV6	michaels-ws.totalh...	54321	michaels-ws.totalh...	0	LISTENING
vmware-conv...	2588	TCPV6	michaels-ws.totalh...	56789	michaels-ws.totalh...	0	LISTENING
vmware-hostd...	3404	TCP	michaels-ws	https	michaels-ws	0	LISTENING
vmware-hostd...	3404	TCP	michaels-ws	8307	michaels-ws	0	LISTENING
vmware-hostd...	3404	TCPV6	michaels-ws.totalh...	https	michaels-ws.totalh...	0	LISTENING
vmware-hostd...	3404	TCPV6	[0:0:0:0:0:0:0:1]	8307	michaels-ws.totalh...	0	LISTENING

Endpoints: 145   Established: 31   Listening: 53   Time Wait: 3   Close Wait: 0

Figure 8-11 TCPView in action

TCPView won't work on anything but Windows, but other operating systems have equivalent programs. Linux folks often use the popular Net Activity Viewer (Figure 8-12), available here: http://netactview.sourceforge.net.

Protocol ▲	Local Port	State	Remote Address	Remote Port	Remote Host	Pid	Program
tcp	139 netbios-ssn	LISTEN	*	*	.		
tcp	53 domain	LISTEN	*	*	.		
tcp	22 ssh	LISTEN	*	*	.		
tcp	631 ipp	LISTEN	*	*	.		
tcp	17500 db-lsp	LISTEN	*	*	.	2287	dropbox
tcp	445 microsoft-ds	LISTEN	*	*	.		
tcp	56495	ESTABLISHED	108.160.167.174	80 http	sjd-rd12-7b.sjc.dropbox.com	2287	dropbox
tcp	41870	CLOSE_WAIT	91.189.89.144	80 http	mistletoe.canonical.com	490	ubuntu-geoip-provider
tcp6	139 netbios-ssn	LISTEN	*	*	.		
tcp6	22 ssh	LISTEN	*	*	.		
tcp6	631 ipp	LISTEN	*	*	.		
tcp6	445 microsoft-ds	LISTEN	*	*	.		
tcp6	34537	CLOSE_WAIT	::1	631 ipp	ip6-localhost		
udp	2492		*	*	.		
udp	631 ipp		*	*	.		
udp	45857		*	*	.		
udp	17500		*	*	.	2287	dropbox
udp	5353 mdns		*	*	.		
udp	53 domain		*	*	.		
udp	68 bootpc		*	*	.		
udp	137 netbios-ns		*	*	.		
udp	137 netbios-ns		*	*	.		
udp	137 netbios-ns		*	*	.		

Established: 1/29   Sent: 9.5 KB +0 B/s   Received: 25 KB +32 B/s

Figure 8-12   Net Activity Viewer in action

Connection Status

Connection states change continually, and it's helpful when using tools such as netstat or TCPView to understand the status of a connection at any given moment. Let's look at the various connection statuses so you understand what each means—this information is useful for determining what's happening on networked computers.

NOTE   The −a switch tells netstat to show all used ports, including "listening" ports not engaged in active communications. The −n switch instructs netstat to show raw port numbers and IP addresses.

A socket that is prepared to respond to any IP packets destined for that socket's port number is called an *open port* or *listening port*. Every serving application has an open port. If you're running a Web server on a computer, for example, it will have an open port 80. That's easy enough to appreciate, but you'll be amazed at the number of open ports on just about *any* computer. Fire up a copy of netstat and type

netstat -an to see all of your listening ports. Running netstat -an gives a lot of information, so let's just look at a small amount:

```
C:\>netstat -an
Active Connections
   Proto  Local Address              Foreign Address          State
   TCP    0.0.0.0:7                  0.0.0.0:0                LISTENING
   TCP    0.0.0.0:135                0.0.0.0:0                LISTENING
   TCP    0.0.0.0:445                0.0.0.0:0                LISTENING
   TCP    0.0.0.0:912                0.0.0.0:0                LISTENING
   TCP    0.0.0.0:990                0.0.0.0:0                LISTENING
   TCP    127.0.0.1:27015            0.0.0.0:0                LISTENING
   TCP    127.0.0.1:52144            127.0.0.1:52145          ESTABLISHED
   TCP    127.0.0.1:52145            127.0.0.1:52144          ESTABLISHED
   TCP    127.0.0.1:52146            127.0.0.1:52147          ESTABLISHED
   TCP    127.0.0.1:52147            127.0.0.1:52146          ESTABLISHED
   TCP    192.168.4.27:139           0.0.0.0:0                LISTENING
   TCP    192.168.4.27:52312         74.125.47.108:80         TIME_WAIT
   TCP    192.168.4.27:57913         63.246.140.18:80         CLOSE_WAIT
   TCP    192.168.4.27:61707         192.168.4.10:445         ESTABLISHED
```

First look at this line:

```
TCP    0.0.0.0:445                0.0.0.0:0                LISTENING
```

This line shows a listening port ready for incoming packets that have a destination port number of 445. Notice the local address is 0.0.0.0. This is how Windows tells you that the open port works on all NICs on this PC. In this case, my PC has only one NIC (192.168.4.27), but even if you have only one NIC, netstat still shows it this way. This computer is sharing some folders on the network. At this moment, no one is connected, so netstat shows the Foreign Address as 0.0.0.0. Incoming requests use port number 445 to connect to those shared folders. If another computer on my network (192.168.4.83) was accessing the shared folders, this line would look like

```
TCP    192.168.4.27:445           192.168.4.83:1073        ESTABLISHED
```

Established ports are active, working endpoint pairs. Over time all connections eventually close like this one:

```
TCP    192.168.4.27:57913         63.246.140.18:80         CLOSE_WAIT
```

This line shows a Web browser making a graceful closure, meaning each side of the conversation sees the session closing normally.

If data's going to move back and forth between computers, some program must always be doing the sending and/or receiving. Take a look at this line from netstat -an:

```
TCP    192.168.4.27:52312         74.125.47.108:80         ESTABLISHED
```

You see the 80 and might assume the connection is going out to a Web server. But what program on the computer is sending it? Enter the command **netstat -ano** (the -o switch tells netstat to show the process ID). Although you'll see many lines, the one for this connection looks like this:

```
   Proto  Local Address       Foreign Address       State        PID
   TCP    192.168.4.27:52312  74.125.47.108:80      ESTABLISHED  112092
```

Every running program on your computer gets a process ID (PID), a number used by the operating system to track all the running programs. Numbers aren't very helpful to you, though, because you want to know the name of the running program. In most operating systems, finding this out is fairly easy to do. In Windows, type **netstat -b**:

```
Proto          Local Address      Foreign Address          State
TCP            127.0.0.1:43543    Sabertooth:43544         ESTABLISHED
[firefox.exe]
```

In Linux, you can use the `ps` command:

```
michaelm@ubuntu:~$ ps
PID TTY        TIME CMD
3225 pts/1    00:00:00 bash
3227 pts/1    00:00:00 ps
```

If you want to find out the PID of a process, you can use the trusty Task Manager. The PIDs are hidden, by default, in versions of Windows prior to 8, but they are easy to enable. Simply fire up Task Manager, select the **Processes** tab, select the **View** menu, and click the **Select Columns...** option. The first option in the list will be PID (Process Identifier). Check the box and then click **OK**. Task Manager will now show you the PID for all running programs. In Windows 8 or later, open Task Manager and select **More Details** (if you haven't already), then jump over to the **Details** tab to see the PIDs.

Another great tool for discovering a PID (and a whole lot more) is Mark Russinovich's Process Explorer; it is a perfect tool for this. Figure 8-13 shows Process Explorer scrolled down to the bottom so you can see the program using PID 456—good old Firefox!

 NOTE   To get Process Explorer, enter **"Process Explorer"** in your search engine to find it or try going here:

https://docs.microsoft.com/en-us/sysinternals/

Click the **Process Utilities** icon to get the latest copy.

You might be tempted to say "Big whoop, Mike—what else would use port 80?" Then consider the possibility that you run netstat and see a line like the one just shown, but *you don't have a browser open!* You determine the PID and discover the name of the process is "Evil_Overlord.exe." Something is running on your computer that should not be there.

Understanding how TCP/IP uses ports is a base skill for any network tech. To pass the CompTIA Network+ exam, you need to memorize a number of different well-known ports and even a few of the more popular registered ports. You must appreciate how the ports fit into the process of TCP/IP communications and know how to use netstat and other tools to see what's going on inside your computer.

The biggest challenge is learning what's supposed to be running and what's not. No one on Earth can run a netstat command and instantly recognize every connection and why it's running, but a good network tech should know most of them. For those connections that a tech doesn't recognize, he or she should know how to research them to determine what they are.

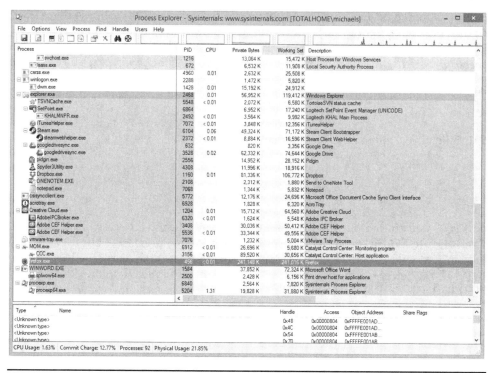

Figure 8-13 Process Explorer

Rules for Determining Good vs. Bad Communications

Here is the general list of rules I follow for determining good versus bad communications (as far as networking goes, at least!):

1. Memorize a bunch of known ports for common TCP/IP applications. The next section in this chapter will get you started.

2. Learn how to use netstat to see what's happening on your computer. Learn to use switches such as –a, –n, –o, and –b to help you define what you're looking for.

3. Take the time to learn the ports that normally run on your operating system. When you see a connection using ports you don't recognize, figure out the process running the connection using a utility such as Linux's ps or Process Explorer for Windows.

4. Take the time to learn the processes that normally run on your operating system. Most operating systems have their own internal programs (such as Windows' svchost.exe) that are normal and important processes.

5. When you see a process you don't recognize, just enter the filename of the process in a Web search. Hundreds of Web sites are dedicated to researching mystery processes that will tell you what the process does.

6. Get rid of bad processes.

Common TCP/IP Applications

Finally! You now know enough about the Transport layer, port numbering, and sockets to get into some of the gritty details of common TCP/IP applications. There's no pretty way to do this, so let's start with the big daddy of them all, the Web. The rest of this section tackles Telnet and SSH, e-mail protocols, and FTP.

The World Wide Web

Where would we be without the World Wide Web? If you go up to a non-nerd and say "Get on the Internet," most of them will automatically open a Web browser, because to them the Web *is* the Internet. The Internet is the infrastructure that enables the Web to function, but it's certainly more than just the Web. I think it's safe to assume you've used the Web, firing up your Web browser to surf to one cool site after another, learning new things, clicking links, often ending up somewhere completely unexpected . . . it's all fun! This section looks at the Web and the tools that make it function, specifically the protocols that enable communication over the Internet.

The Web is composed of servers that store specially formatted documents using languages such as Hypertext Markup Language (HTML). Figure 8-14 shows the Web interface built into my wireless access point.

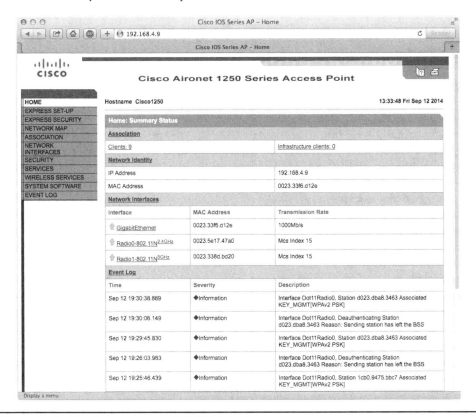

Figure 8-14   My wireless access point's Web interface

HTML has been around for a long time and, as a result, has gone through many versions. Today many developers use the latest HTML version called HTML5. See Figure 8-15.

Figure 8-15 HTML5 source code

 EXAM TIP HTML is the most well-known markup language, but many others roam the Web today, adding to HTML's capabilities. Expect to see the *Extensible Markup Language (XML)* on the exam. XML provides the basic format or markup language for everything from RSS feeds to Microsoft Office documents.

Web browsers are designed to request HTML pages from Web servers and then open them. To access a Web page, you enter **http://** plus the IP address of the Web server. When you type the address of a Web server, such as **http://192.168.4.1**, you tell the browser to go to 192.168.4.1 and ask for a Web page. All Web servers have a default Web page that they open unless you enter something more complex like **http://192.168.4.1/ status**.

 NOTE Some Web browsers are pretty forgiving. If you only type in **192.168.4.1**, forgetting the "http://" part, they just add it for you.

Granted, most people don't enter IP addresses into browsers, but rather enter text like www.totalsem.com or www.google.com. Memorizing text addresses is much easier than memorizing IP addresses. Web site text addresses use a naming protocol called Domain Name System (DNS), which you will learn about in the next chapter. For now, just enter the IP address as shown.

HTTP

The *Hypertext Transfer Protocol (HTTP)* is the underlying protocol used by the Web, and it runs, by default, on TCP port 80. When you enter **http://** at the beginning of a Web server's IP address, you are identifying how messages are formatted and transmitted, requesting and responding to the transfer of HTML-formatted files. HTTP defines what actions Web servers and browsers should take in response to various commands.

HTTP has a general weakness in its handling of Web pages: it relays commands executed by users without reference to any commands previously executed. The problem with this is that Web designers continue to design more complex and truly interactive Web pages. HTTP is pretty dumb when it comes to remembering what people have done on a Web site. Luckily for Web designers everywhere, other technologies exist to help HTTP relay commands and thus support more-interactive, intelligent Web sites. These technologies include JavaScript/AJAX, server-side scripting, and cookies.

EXAM TIP Before connections to the Web became fast, many people used a completely different Internet service for swapping information, ideas, and files. *USENET* enjoyed great popularity for some years, though it barely survives today. Clients used the *Network News Transfer Protocol (NNTP)* to access USENET over TCP port 119. It might show up as an incorrect answer choice on the exam.

Publishing a Web Site

In the simplest sense, a Web site consists of a Web page hosted by a Web server. To share an HTML document—a Web page—with the rest of the world, find a Web server that will "host" the page. You most certainly can install a Web server on a computer, acquire a public IP address for that computer, and host the Web site yourself. Self-hosting is a time-consuming and challenging project, though, so most people use other methods.

NOTE Many Web site developers today use premade customizable templates and some sort of Web technology, such as WordPress. These Web technologies enable powerful and dynamic Web site experiences for your visitors. The questions you'll see on the CompTIA Network+ exam focus on the concepts, rather than modern implementations, of Web sites.

Most Internet service providers (ISPs) provide Web servers of their own, or you can find relatively inexpensive Web hosting service companies. The price of Web hosting usually depends on the services and drive space offered. Web hosts typically charge around US$10 a month for simple Web sites.

One option that has been available for a while is free Web hosting. Usually the services are not too bad, but free Web hosts have limitations. Nearly all free Web hosts insist on the right to place ads on your Web page. Third-party ads are not as much of an issue if you are posting a basic blog or fan Web page, but if you do any sort of business with your Web site, ads can be most annoying to your customers. The worst sort of free Web host services place pop-up ads *over* your Web page. Beyond annoying!

Once you have uploaded HTML pages to a Web host, the Web server takes over. What's a Web server? I'm glad you asked!

Web Servers and Web Clients

A Web server is a computer that delivers (or *serves up*) Web pages. Web servers listen on port 80, fetching requested HTML pages and sending them to browsers. You can turn any computer into a Web server by installing server software and connecting the machine to the Internet, but you need to consider the operating system and Web server program you'll use to serve your Web site. Microsoft's server is *Internet Information Services (IIS)*, shown in Figure 8-16.

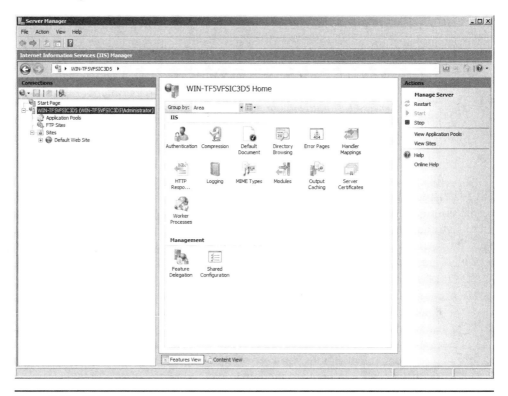

Figure 8-16   IIS in action

IIS enables you to set a maximum connection limit on your Web server based on available bandwidth and memory. This enables you to protect your network against an overwhelming number of requests due to a particularly popular page or a type of malicious attack called a denial of service (DoS) attack (more on DoS attacks in Chapter 19, "Protecting Your Network").

Microsoft builds an artificial 20-connection limit into Windows client versions, so you should only run IIS on Server versions of Windows (unless you don't expect too many people to visit your Web site at one time).

A majority of UNIX/Linux-based operating systems run *Apache HTTP Server*. As of this writing, Apache serves ~44 percent of the *active Web sites* on the Internet. Apache is incredibly popular, runs on multiple operating systems (including Windows), and, best of all, is *free!* In comparison, even with the weight of Microsoft behind it, IIS only commands about 7 percent market share of active Web sites. [The other big players are nginx (free and open source with ~21 percent active sites) and Google (used for Google's online services with ~9 percent active sites)].

NOTE An *active site* is a Web site that's functioning by serving Web pages. The percent of market share mentioned here changes a lot when you add in *parked sites*, domain names that have been registered but don't really do anything, like Web or e-mail servers.

Apache is nothing more than an executable program and a bunch of text files, so it isn't much to look at. To ease configuration, many Web administrators use add-on graphical user interfaces (GUIs) such as Webmin that make administering Apache a breeze. Figure 8-17 illustrates the wonderful simplicity that is Webmin.

Other common Web servers on the Internet include nginx, which is ranked second for active sites, and Google Web Server (GWS), which is in fourth place. GWS, used only by Google's servers, has about 8 percent of the total active Web server market! There are literally hundreds of other Web servers, but you'll rarely see them outside of small personal Web sites.

Web clients are the programs used to surf the Web. A client program (a Web browser) reads Web pages supplied by the Web server. To access a server, type either an IP address or, more commonly, the complete name of the Web server in the address bar. The complete name is often referred to as the *uniform resource locator (URL)*.

The most popular Web browsers are Microsoft Edge, Mozilla Firefox, Apple Safari, and Google Chrome. (You might also see mention of Microsoft's old and discontinued browser, Internet Explorer (IE), on the CompTIA Network+ exam. Microsoft recommends *not* using IE in real Web surfing today.)

SSL/TLS and HTTPS

Any nosy person who can plug into a network can see and read the HTTP packets moving between a Web server and a Web client. Less than nice people can easily create a fake Web site to trick people into thinking it's a legitimate Web site and then steal their user names and passwords.

EXAM TIP HTTP is a perfect example of a common network vulnerability and threat, an *unsecure protocol*. Other vulnerabilities include open ports, like we discussed earlier, and other unsecure protocols that we'll hit next. For more in-depth coverage of vulnerabilities, see Chapter 19.

Figure 8-17 Webmin Apache module

For an Internet application to be secure, it must have the following:

- **Authentication**   User names and passwords
- **Encryption**   Stirring up the data so others can't read it
- **Nonrepudiation**   Source is not able to deny a sent message

While all of Chapter 10, "Securing TCP/IP," is dedicated to these concepts, I can't mention HTTP without at least touching on its secure counterpart, HTTPS. The Web has blossomed into a major economic player, requiring serious security for those who wish to do online transactions (e-commerce). In the early days of e-commerce, people feared that a simple credit card transaction on a less-than-secure Web site could transform their dreams of easy online buying into a nightmare of being robbed blind and ending up living in a refrigerator box. I can safely say that it was *never* as bad as all that.

Nowadays, many tools can protect your purchases *and* your anonymity. One early safeguard was called *Secure Sockets Layer (SSL)*, a protocol developed by Netscape for transmitting private documents securely over the Internet. *Transport Layer Security (TLS)* is the latest version of SSL, although techs use the terms interchangeably. SSL/TLS uses encryption to set up a secure private connection. All the popular Web browsers and Web servers support SSL/TLS, and many Web sites use the protocol to obtain confidential user information, such as credit card numbers. One way to tell if a site is using SSL/TLS is by looking at the Web page address. By convention, Web pages that use an SSL/TLS connection start with *https* instead of *http*. Read Chapter 10 for more details on SSL and TLS.

EXAM TIP HTTP enables you to access the Web, but HTTPS gets you there securely. HTTPS uses TLS to provide the security.

HTTPS stands for *Hypertext Transfer Protocol over SSL*. HTTPS uses TCP port 443. You can also look for a small lock icon in the address bar of your browser. Figure 8-18 shows a typical secure Web page. The *https:* in the address and the lock icon are circled.

Figure 8-18 Secure Web page

EXAM TIP Many techs refer to HTTPS as Hypertext Transfer Protocol *Secure*, probably because it's easier to explain to non-techs that way. Don't be surprised to see it listed this way on the CompTIA Network+ exam.

Telnet and SSH

Roughly one billion years ago, there was no such thing as the Internet or even networks.... Well, maybe it was only about 40 years ago, but as far as nerds like me are concerned, a world before the Internet was filled with brontosauruses and palm fronds. The only computers were huge monsters called mainframes and to access them required a dumb terminal like the one shown in Figure 8-19.

Figure 8-19
WANG dumb
terminal

 NOTE A dumb terminal is a local system—generally a monitor, keyboard, and mouse—that enables you to access a distant system that has all the computing power. The dumb terminal can't do any work on its own, even though it might look like a personal computer.

Operating systems didn't have windows and pretty icons. The interface to the mainframe was a command line, but it worked just fine for the time. Then the cavemen who first lifted their heads up from the computer ooze known as mainframes said to themselves, "Wouldn't it be great if we could access each other's computers from the comfort of our own caves?" That was what started the entire concept of a network. Back then the idea of sharing folders or printers or Web pages hadn't been considered yet. The entire motivation for networking was so people could sit at their dumb terminals and, instead of accessing only their local mainframes, access totally different mainframes. The protocol to do this was called the *Telnet Protocol* or simply *Telnet*.

Modern PCs can (but shouldn't) use Telnet to connect remotely to another computer via the command line (Figure 8-20). Telnet runs on TCP port 23, enabling you to connect to a Telnet server and run commands on that server as if you were sitting right in front of it.

Figure 8-20   Telnet client

Telnet enables you to remotely administer a server and communicate with other servers on your network. As you can imagine, this is sort of risky. If you can remotely control a computer, what is to stop others from doing the same? Thankfully, Telnet does not allow just *anyone* to log on and wreak havoc with your network. You must enter a user name and password to access a Telnet server.

Unfortunately, Telnet does not have any form of encryption. If someone intercepted the conversation between a Telnet client and Telnet server, he or she would see all of the commands you type as well as the results from the Telnet server. As a result, in no scenario should you use Telnet on the Internet. Instead, use *Secure Shell (SSH)*, a terminal emulation program that looks exactly like Telnet but encrypts the data and the authentication.

NOTE   Telnet only enables command-line remote access; it does not enable GUI access. If you want to access another computer's desktop remotely, you need another type of program.

Telnet/SSH Servers and Clients

The oldest Telnet server, found on UNIX and Linux systems, is telnetd. Like most UNIX/Linux servers, telnetd isn't much to look at, so let's move over to Windows. Since the halcyon days of Windows NT, Windows has come with a basic Telnet server. It is disabled, by default, in modern Windows systems, because Telnet is a gaping security hole. The built-in server is very limited and Microsoft discourages its use. I prefer to use a great little third-party server called freeSSHd (Figure 8-21). Note the name—freeSSHd, not "freeTelnet." As Telnet fades away and SSH becomes more dominant, finding a Telnet-only server these days is hard. All of the popular Telnet servers are also SSH servers.

Figure 8-21

FreeSSHd

A Telnet or SSH client is the computer from which you log into the remote server. Most operating systems have a built-in Telnet client that you run from a command prompt. Figure 8-22 shows the Telnet client built into macOS. Just open a terminal window and type **telnet** and the IP address of the Telnet server.

Command-prompt clients lack a number of handy features. They can't, for example, remember the IP addresses, user names, or passwords for Telnet or SSH servers, so every time you use Telnet or SSH, you have to enter all that information again. Third-party Telnet/SSH clients, such as the very popular PuTTY, which you saw in Chapter 7, store all this information and much more (Figure 8-23).

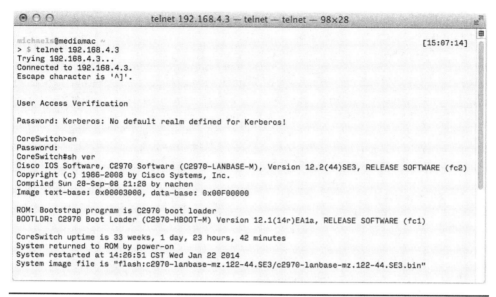

Figure 8-22 macOS Telnet

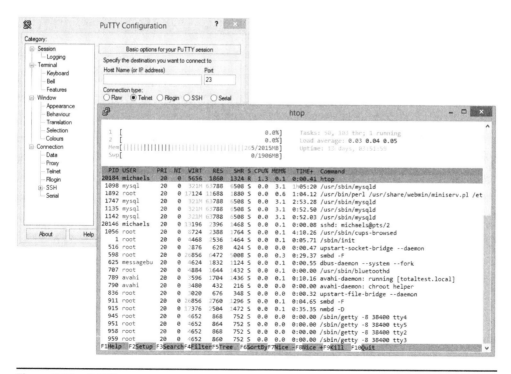

Figure 8-23 PuTTY

Configuring a Telnet/SSH Client

When you configure a Telnet or SSH client, you must provide the host name, a valid login name, and the password. As I mentioned previously, you must have permission to access the server to use Telnet or SSH. A *host name* is the name or IP address of the computer to which you want to connect. For instance, you might connect to a Web server with the host name websrv.mhteched.com. The user *login name* you give Telnet or SSH should be the same login name you'd use if you logged into the server at its location.

Some computers, usually university libraries with online catalogs, have open systems that enable you to log in with Telnet. These sites either display a banner before the login prompt that tells you what login name to use, or they require no login name at all. As with the login name, you use the same password for a Telnet login that you'd use to log into the server directly. It's that simple. Computers with open access either tell you what password to use when they tell you what login name to use, or they require no login name/password at all.

EXAM TIP   Telnet and SSH enable you to control a remote computer from a local computer over a network.

SSH and the Death of Telnet

From the earliest days of the Internet, Telnet has seen long and heavy use in the TCP world, but it suffers from lack of any security. Telnet passwords as well as data are transmitted in cleartext and are thus easily hacked. To that end, SSH has now replaced Telnet for every serious terminal emulation. In terms of what it does, SSH is extremely similar to Telnet in that it creates a terminal connection to a remote host. Every aspect of SSH, however, including both login and data transmittal, is encrypted. To get the full SSH understanding, we need to talk about encryption standards, which we'll get to in Chapter 10. SSH uses TCP port 22 instead of Telnet's port 23.

EXAM TIP   SSH enables you to control a remote computer from a local computer over a network, just like Telnet. Unlike Telnet, SSH enables you to do it securely!

E-mail

Electronic mail (e-mail) has been a major part of the Internet revolution, and not just because it has streamlined the junk mail industry. E-mail provides an extremely quick way for people to communicate with one another, letting them send messages and attachments (like documents and pictures) over the Internet. It's normally offered as a free service by ISPs. Most e-mail client programs provide a rudimentary text editor for composing messages, but many can be configured to let you edit your messages using more sophisticated editors.

E-mail consists of e-mail clients and e-mail servers. When a message is sent to your e-mail address, it is normally stored in an electronic mailbox on your e-mail server until you tell the e-mail client to download the message. Most e-mail client programs can be configured to signal you in some way when a new message has arrived or to download e-mails automatically as they come to you. Once you read an e-mail message, you can archive it, forward it, print it, or delete it. Most e-mail programs are configured to delete messages from the e-mail server automatically when you download them to your local machine, but you can usually change this configuration option to suit your circumstances.

E-mail programs use a number of application-level protocols to send and receive information. Specifically, the e-mail you find on the Internet uses SMTP to send e-mail, and either POP3 or IMAP4 to receive e-mail.

SMTP, POP3, and IMAP4, Oh My!

The following is a list of the different protocols that the Internet uses to transfer and receive mail:

SMTP The *Simple Mail Transfer Protocol (SMTP)* is used to send e-mail. SMTP travels over TCP port 25 and is used by clients to send messages.

POP3 *Post Office Protocol version 3 (POP3)* is one of the two protocols that receive e-mail from SMTP servers. POP3 uses TCP port 110. POP3 is on its way out today, though you'll see it on the exam.

IMAP4 *Internet Message Access Protocol version 4 (IMAP4)* is a preferred alternative to POP3. Like POP3, IMAP4 retrieves e-mail from an e-mail server. IMAP4 uses TCP port 143 and supports some features that are not supported in POP3. For example, IMAP4 enables synchronization of mail among many devices, meaning you can access e-mail messages at your Windows desktop, your macOS portable, and your Android smartphone. (It works for any combination; I used those three as an example.) IMAP4 also supports the concept of folders that you can place on the IMAP4 server to organize your e-mail. Some POP3 e-mail clients have folders, but that's not a part of POP3, just a nice feature added to the client.

 NOTE A zillion smartphone users access e-mail through *Exchange ActiveSync*, a proprietary Microsoft protocol. Like IMAP4, ActiveSync enables synchronization of e-mail among devices, so you can access mail via a desktop Microsoft Outlook client and on your smartphone with an e-mail app. Although it's *not* on the CompTIA Network+ exam, we'll explore Exchange ActiveSync in more detail in Chapter 16 because it's in widespread use today.

Alternatives to SMTP, POP3, and IMAP4

Although SMTP, POP3, and IMAP4 are the traditional tools for sending and receiving e-mail, two other options are widely popular: Web-based e-mail and proprietary solutions. (Plus, as I mentioned earlier, Exchange ActiveSync is widely used with mobile devices.)

Web-based mail, as the name implies, requires a Web interface. From a Web browser, you simply surf to the Web-mail server, log in, and access your e-mail. The cool part is that you can do it from anywhere in the world where you find a Web browser and an

Internet hookup! You get the benefit of e-mail without even needing to own a computer. Some of the more popular Web-based services are Google's Gmail (Figure 8-24), Microsoft's Outlook.com/Outlook Mail, and Yahoo!'s Yahoo! Mail.

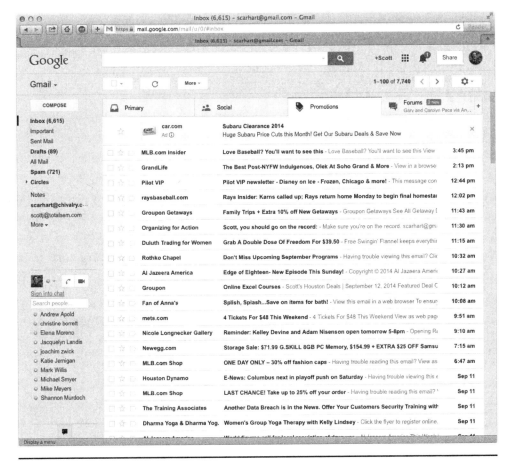

Figure 8-24   Gmail in action

 EXAM TIP   The CompTIA Network+ exam has viewed Web-based e-mail as one of many *Web services*. Web services also include applications that you access on the Internet, like Google Docs and Google Sheets, online word processing and spreadsheet programs, respectively. You might run into a question that uses this phrase, though most likely you'll see *Cloud-based services*. See Chapter 15 for more on the Cloud.

The major contrast between Web services and local services involves access. Web services offer access from any machine, as long as that machine is connected to the Internet. Local applications (usually) require local access, but don't need any other connectivity.

The key benefits of Web-based e-mail services are as follows:

- You can access your e-mail from anywhere.
- They're free.
- They're handy for throw-away accounts (like when you're required to give an e-mail address to download something, but you know you're going to get spammed if you do).

E-mail Servers

Two mail server types dominate the once-fragmented e-mail server space: Exim and Postfix. With well over 50 percent market share, Exim runs on just about everything, from Unix/Linux to Windows. It even runs on the tiny Raspberry Pi! Exim, at heart, is a configuration file that you can manage by hand or through a graphical tool like cPanel (Figure 8-25).

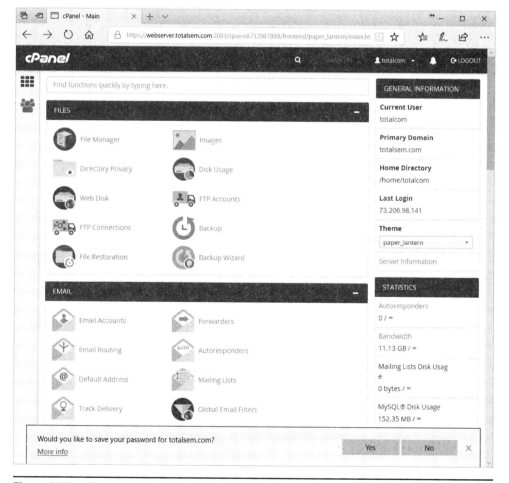

Figure 8-25 cPanel used to manage Exim mail server

Microsoft, of course, has its own e-mail server, Microsoft Exchange Server, and like IIS, it only runs on Windows. Figure 8-26 shows the Exchange admin center for Office 365. Exchange Server is both an SMTP and a POP3/IMAP4/Exchange ActiveSync/ MAPI/etc. server in one package.

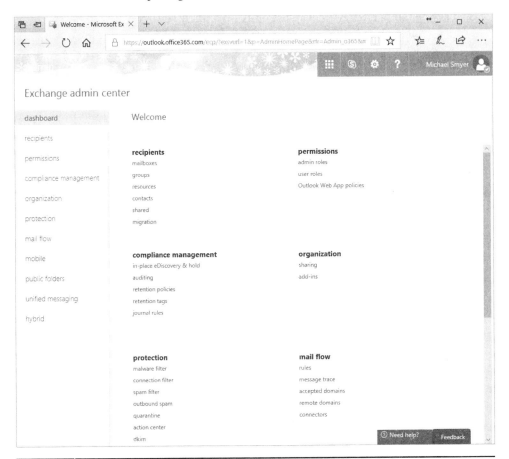

Figure 8-26   Microsoft Exchange Server

E-mail servers accept incoming mail and sort out the mail for recipients into individual storage area mailboxes. These *mailboxes* are special separate holding areas for each user's e-mail. An e-mail server works much like a post office, sorting and arranging incoming messages, and kicking back those messages that have no known recipient.

E-mail servers are difficult to manage. E-mail servers store user lists, user rights, and messages, and are constantly involved in Internet traffic and resources. Setting up and administering an e-mail server takes a lot of planning, although it's getting easier. Most e-mail server software runs in a GUI, but even the command-line-based interface of e-mail servers is becoming more intuitive.

E-mail Client

An *e-mail client* is a program that runs on a computer and enables you to send, receive, and organize e-mail. The e-mail client program communicates with the SMTP e-mail server to send mail and communicates with the IMAP4 or POP3 e-mail server to download the messages from the e-mail server to the client computer. There are hundreds of e-mail programs, two of the most popular of which are Microsoft Outlook (Figure 8-27) and Mozilla Thunderbird.

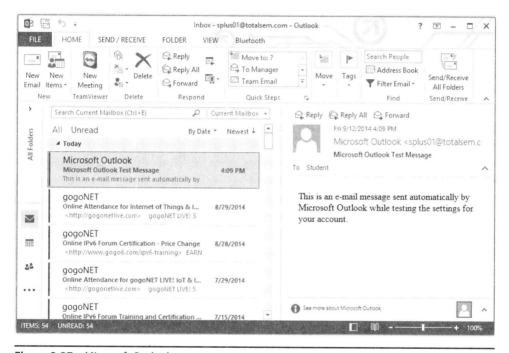

Figure 8-27   Microsoft Outlook

Configuring an E-mail Client   Configuring a client is an easy matter. Your mail administrator will give you the server's domain name and your mailbox's user name and password. You need to enter the POP3 or IMAP4 server's domain name and the SMTP server's domain name to the e-mail client (Figure 8-28). Every e-mail client has a different way to add the server domain names or IP addresses, so you may have to poke around, but you'll find the option there somewhere! In many cases, this may be the same name or address for both the incoming and outgoing servers—the folks administering the mail servers will tell you. Besides the e-mail server domain names or addresses, you must also enter the user name and password of the e-mail account the client will be managing.

FTP

File Transfer Protocol (FTP) is the original protocol used on the Internet for transferring files. The old active FTP used TCP ports 21 and 20 by default, although passive

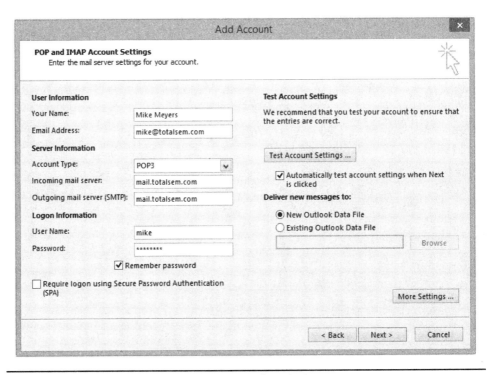

Figure 8-28 Entering server information in Microsoft Outlook

FTP only uses port 21 for a default. See the discussion on active versus passive FTP later in this chapter.

FTP sites are either anonymous sites, meaning that anyone can log on, or secured sites, meaning that you must have a user name and password to access the site and transfer files. A single FTP site can offer both anonymous access and protected access, but you'll see different resources depending on which way you log in.

FTP Servers and FTP Clients

The FTP server does all the real work of storing the files, accepting incoming connections and verifying user names and passwords, and transferring the files. The client logs onto the FTP server (either from a Web site, a command line, or a special FTP application) and downloads the requested files onto the local hard drive.

FTP Servers We don't set up servers for Internet applications nearly as often as we set up clients. I've set up only a few Web servers over the years, whereas I've set up thousands of Web browsers. FTP servers are the one exception, as we nerds like to exchange files. If you have a file you wish to share with a lot of people (but not the entire Internet), a reliable, old-school method is to put up a quick FTP server. Most versions of Linux/UNIX have built-in FTP servers, but many third-party applications offer better solutions. One of the simpler ones for Windows, especially for those "let me put up an FTP server so you guys can get a copy" type of scenarios, is the open source FileZilla Server (Figure 8-29).

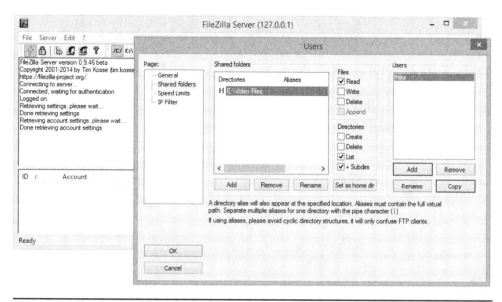

Figure 8-29   FileZilla Server

NOTE   Most Web servers are also FTP servers. These bundled versions of FTP servers are robust but do not provide all the options one might want.

FTP is not very secure because data transfers are not encrypted by default, so you don't want to use straight FTP for sensitive data. But you can add user names and passwords to prevent all but the most serious hackers from accessing your FTP server. I avoid using the anonymous login because unscrupulous people could use the server for exchanging illegal software.

Another thing to check when deciding on an FTP server setup is the number of clients you want to support. Most anonymous FTP sites limit the number of users who may download at any one time to around 500. This protects you from a sudden influx of users flooding your server and eating up all your Internet bandwidth.

Try This!

Doing FTP

Never done FTP? Do a Web search for **"Public FTP servers"** and try accessing a few from your Web browser. Then download a dedicated FTP client and try again! There are thousands of public FTP servers out there.

FTP Clients FTP clients, as noted before, can access an FTP server through a Web site, a command line, or a special FTP application. Usually special FTP applications offer the most choices for accessing and using an FTP site.

 NOTE Every operating system has a command-line FTP client. I avoid using them unless I have no other choice, because they lack important features like the ability to save FTP connections to use again later.

You have many choices when it comes to FTP clients. For starters, some Web browsers handle FTP as well as HTTP, although they lack a few features. For example, Firefox only supports an anonymous login. To use your Web browser as an FTP client, type **ftp://** followed by the IP address or domain name of the FTP server (Figure 8-30).

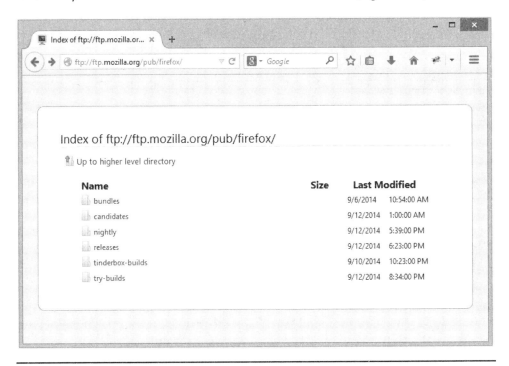

Figure 8-30 FTP in a Web browser

The best way to use FTP is to use a dedicated FTP client. So many good ones are available that I find myself using a different one all the time. FileZilla comes in a client version, for example, but these days, I'm using CyberDuck (Figure 8-31).

Active vs. Passive FTP

FTP has two ways to transfer data: *active* and *passive* FTP. Traditionally, FTP used the active process—let's see how this works. Remember that FTP uses TCP ports 20 and 21? Well, when your client sends an FTP request, it goes out on port 21. When your FTP

Figure 8-31   CyberDuck dedicated FTP client

server responds, however, it sends the data back using an ephemeral destination port and port 20 as a source port.

Active FTP works great unless your client uses NAT. Since your client didn't initiate the incoming port 20, your NAT router has no idea where to send this incoming packet. Additionally, any good firewall sees this incoming connection as something evil because it doesn't have anything inside the network that started the link on port 20. No problem! Good FTP clients all support passive FTP. With passive FTP, the server doesn't use port 20. Instead, the client sends an FTP request on port 21, just like active FTP. But then the server sends back a random port number, telling the client which port it's listening on for data requests. The client, in turn, sends data to the port specified by the FTP server. Because the client initiates all conversations, the NAT router knows where to send the packet.

The only trick to passive FTP is that the client needs to expect this other incoming data. When you configure an FTP client for passive, you're telling it to expect these packets.

NOTE   Trivial File Transfer Protocol (TFTP) is used for transferring files and has a similar-sounding name to FTP, but beyond that it is very different. TFTP uses UDP port 69 and does not use user names and passwords, although you can usually set some restrictions based on the client's IP address. TFTP is not at all secure, so never use it on any network that's less than trustworthy.

Internet Applications

Use Table 8-1 as a review tool to help you remember each Internet application.

Application	TCP/UDP	Port	Notes
HTTP	TCP	80	The Web
HTTPS	TCP	443	The Web, securely
Telnet	TCP	23	Terminal emulation
SSH	TCP	22	Secure terminal emulation
SMTP	TCP	25	Sending e-mail
POP3	TCP	110	E-mail delivery
IMAP4	TCP	143	E-mail delivery
FTP	TCP	20/21 (active)21 (passive)	File transfer
TFTP	UDP	69	File transfer

Table 8-1   Internet Application Ports and Protocols

   SIM   Check out the excellent Chapter 8 "Ports and Protocols" Challenge! over at **http://totalsem.com/007**. It'll help greatly in memorizing the port numbers that each protocol uses.

Chapter Review

Questions

1. The protocol developed by Netscape for transmitting private documents over the Internet is known as

   A. SSS

   B. SSA

   C. SSL

   D. NSSL

2. Which of the following are key benefits of Web-based mail? (Select two.)

   A. You can use a third-party application, like Microsoft Outlook, to download your e-mail.

   B. You can access your e-mail from anywhere in the world using a Web browser and an Internet connection.

   C. It is completely spam-free.

   D. It is great for creating throw-away accounts.

3. An SSL/TLS URL connection starts with which prefix?

   A. http

   B. www

   C. ftp

   D. https

4. Which statements about SSH and Telnet are true? (Select two.)

   A. Windows comes with preinstalled SSH and Telnet clients.

   B. SSH is more secure than Telnet because it encrypts data.

   C. Telnet is a command-line tool, whereas SSH is a GUI tool.

   D. SSH uses port 22, and Telnet uses port 23.

5. Why might you use the netstat utility?

   A. To see the route an IP packet takes across multiple routers

   B. To see your IP address and configuration details

   C. To see the endpoints of your sessions

   D. To issue commands to a remote server

6. Why might you use a Telnet client?

   A. To see the route an IP packet takes across multiple routers

   B. To see your IP address and configuration details

   C. To see the endpoints of your sessions

   D. To issue commands to a remote server

7. Port 110 (POP) is what kind of port?

   A. Well-known

   B. Registered

   C. Ephemeral

   D. Reserved

8. What ports does FTP use traditionally? (Select two.)

   A. 20

   B. 21

   C. 23

   D. 25

9. Which of the following protocols are used to receive e-mail from servers? (Select two.)

   A. IMAP

   B. ICMP

   C. IGMP

   D. POP

10. Which statements about netstat switches (in Windows) are true? (Select three.)

   A. -a shows all used ports.

   B. -n shows raw port numbers and IP addresses.

   C. -o shows the process ID.

   D. -s shows the application name.

Answers

1. **C.** Secure Sockets Layer (SSL) is a protocol that was developed by Netscape for transmitting private documents over the Internet securely.

2. **B** and **D.** You can access a Web-based e-mail account from any browser on any machine connected to the Internet. These accounts are great for creating throwaway e-mail addresses.

3. **D.** URLs that use an SSL/TLS connection start with https instead of http.

4. **B** and **D.** SSH encrypts data and is more secure than Telnet. Also, SSH uses port 22, whereas Telnet uses port 23.

5. **C.** Use netstat to see the endpoints of your sessions.

6. **D.** Telnet is used to issue commands to a remote server. Aside from the CompTIA Network+ exam, though, use SSH instead.

7. **A.** Ports 0–1023 are well-known ports.

8. **A** and **B.** Active FTP used ports 20 and 21. Passive FTP only uses port 21 and a random port.

9. **A** and **D.** IMAP and POP are used to receive e-mail.

10. **A, B,** and **C.** -a shows all used ports; -n shows raw port numbers and IP addresses; and -o shows the process ID.

Network Naming

The CompTIA Network+ certification exam expects you to know how to

- 1.1 Explain the purposes and uses of ports and protocols
- 1.8 Explain the functions of network services

To achieve these goals, you must be able to

- Analyze and configure early name resolution solutions
- Describe the function and capabilities of DNS
- Use common TCP/IP utilities to diagnose problems with DNS

Every host on the Internet has a unique IP address. Then why do we use *names* such as www.totalsem.com to access hosts, such as a Web server, instead of an IP address?

Although computers use IP addresses to communicate with each other over a TCP/IP network, people need easy-to-remember names. To resolve this conflict, long ago, even before TCP/IP and the Internet took over, network developers created a process called *name resolution* that automatically converts computer names to logical addresses or physical addresses (MAC addresses) to make it easier for people to communicate with computers (Figure 9-1).

Like any process that's been around for a long time, name resolution has evolved over the years. Ancient networking protocols would resolve a computer name such as Mike's Laptop to a MAC address. As TCP/IP gained dominance, name resolution concentrated on resolving names to IP addresses. Even within TCP/IP, there have been many changes in name resolution. Entire TCP/IP applications have been written, only to be supplanted (but never totally abandoned) by newer name resolution protocols.

All TCP/IP networks, including the Internet, use a name resolution protocol called *Domain Name System (DNS)*. DNS is a powerful, extensible, flexible system that supports name resolution on tiny in-house networks, as well as the entire Internet. Most of this chapter covers DNS, but be warned: your brand-new system, running the latest version of whatever operating system, still fully supports a few older name resolution protocols that predate DNS. This makes name resolution in contemporary networks akin to a well-run house that's also full of ghosts; ghosts that can do very strange things if you don't understand how those ghosts think.

Figure 9-1

Turning names
into numbers

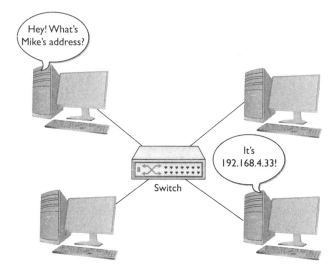

In this chapter, you'll take an in-depth tour of name resolution, starting with a discussion of two ghostly precursors to DNS: Microsoft's ancient NetBIOS protocol and the hosts file. The chapter then turns to DNS, explaining how it works, and how DNS servers and clients are used today.

Odds are good you have a system connected—or that at least can connect—to the Internet. If I were you, I'd fire up that system and use it while you read this chapter. The vast majority of the programs you're going to learn about here come free with every operating system.

Test Specific

Before DNS

Early name resolution solutions offered simple but effective network naming. While most of these are long dead, there are two name resolution solutions that continue to work in modern systems: Microsoft's NetBIOS names and hosts files.

NetBIOS

Even though TCP/IP was available back in the 1980s, Microsoft developed and popularized a light and efficient networking protocol called *NetBIOS/NetBEUI*. It had a very simple naming convention (the NetBIOS part) that used broadcasts for name resolution. When a computer booted up, it broadcast its name (Figure 9-2) along with its MAC address. Every other NetBIOS/NetBEUI system heard the message and stored the information in a cache. Any time a system was missing a NetBIOS name, the broadcasting started all over again.

Figure 9-2
NetBIOS
broadcast

 NOTE Microsoft didn't lump NetBIOS and NetBEUI into a single protocol, but they were used often enough together that I'm lumping them for convenience of discussion. You *won't* see NetBEUI on the CompTIA Network+ exam.

NetBIOS was suitable only for small networks for two reasons. First, it provided no logical addressing like IP addresses; each system had to remember the NetBIOS name and the MAC address. Without a logical address, there was no way to support routing. Second, all of the broadcasting made it unacceptable for large networks.

Microsoft's networking was designed for small, unrouted networks of no more than around 40 hosts. There was no such thing as Telnet, e-mail, Minecraft, or the Web with NetBIOS, but it worked well for what it did at the time.

By the mid-1990s, Microsoft realized the world was going with TCP/IP and DNS, and it needed to switch too. The problem was that there was a massive installed base of Windows networks that needed NetBIOS/NetBEUI.

Microsoft designed a new TCP/IP protocol that enabled it to keep using the NetBIOS names but dump the NetBEUI protocol. The new protocol, *NetBIOS over TCP/IP (NetBT)*, runs NetBIOS on top of TCP/IP. In essence, Microsoft created its own name resolution protocol that had nothing to do with DNS.

 EXAM TIP Getting NetBIOS to play nicely with TCP/IP requires proper protocols. NetBIOS over TCP/IP uses TCP ports 137 and 139, and UDP ports 137 and 138.

NetBT made things weird on Windows systems. Windows systems used NetBT names for local network jobs such as accessing shared printers or folders, but they also used DNS for everything else. It basically meant that every Windows computer had one name used on the local network—like MIKES-PC—and a DNS name for use on the Internet.

To be more accurate, NetBIOS only handled host names, it didn't actually do any of the resource sharing. Microsoft used another protocol called *Server Message Block (SMB)* that ran on top of NetBT to support sharing folders and files. SMB used NetBIOS names to support the sharing and access process. SMB isn't dependent on NetBIOS and today runs by itself using TCP port 445.

Try This!

Checking Out NetBIOS

Grab a handy Windows or Linux system and try running `netstat -a -n` from a command line. Can you find open or listening ports on port numbers 137, 138, 139, and 445? If you have a Windows system, you will see these. Systems listening on those ports show NetBT and SMB running just fine.

---

hosts

When the Internet was very young and populated with only a few hundred computers, name resolution was pretty simple. The original TCP/IP specification implemented name resolution using a special text file called hosts. A copy of this file was stored on every computer system on the Internet. The *hosts file* contained a list of IP addresses for every computer on the Internet, matched to the corresponding system names. Part of an old hosts file might look something like this:

```
192.168.2.1        fred
201.32.16.4        school2
23.54.122.103      bobs computer and feed store
123.21.44.16       server
```

If your system wanted to access the system called fred, it looked up the name fred in its hosts file and then used the corresponding IP address to contact fred. Every hosts file on every system on the Internet was updated every morning at 2 A.M.

Not only was the Internet a lot smaller then, but also there weren't yet rules about how to compose Internet names, such as that they must end in .com or .org, or start with www or ftp. People could name computers pretty much anything they wanted (there were a few restrictions on length and allowable characters) as long as nobody else had snagged the name first.

This hosts file naming system worked fine when the Internet was still the province of a few university geeks and some military guys, but when the Internet grew to about 5000 systems, it became impractical to make every system use and update a hosts file. This created the motivation for a more scalable name resolution process, but the hosts file did not go away.

Believe it or not, the hosts file is still alive and well in every computer. You can find the hosts file in \Windows\System32\Drivers\Etc in Windows 10. On macOS and Linux systems, you usually find hosts in the /etc folder.

The hosts file is just a text file that you can open with any text editor. Here are a few lines from the default hosts file that comes with Windows:

```
# Additionally, comments (such as these) may be inserted on individual
# lines or following the machine name denoted by a '#' symbol.
#
# For example:
```

```
#
#              102.54.94.97    rhino.acme.com    # source server
#               38.25.63.10    x.acme.com    #    x client host
# localhost name resolution is handled within DNS itself.
#     127.0.0.1          localhost
#     ::1                localhost
```

See the # signs? Those are remark symbols that designate lines as comments (for humans to read) rather than code. Windows ignores any line that begins with #. Remove the # and Windows will read the line and try to act on it. Although all operating systems continue to support the hosts file, few users will actively modify and employ it in the day-to-day workings of most TCP/IP systems.

Try This!

Editing the hosts File

Every Windows computer has a hosts file that you can edit, so try this!

1. Log into the computer as a local administrator

2. Go to a command prompt and type **ping www.totalsem.com**. You may or may not be successful with the ping utility, but you will get the IP address for my Web site. (You may get a different IP address from the one shown in this example.)

   ```
   C:\>ping www.totalsem.com
   Pinging www.totalsem.com [75.126.29.106] with 32 bytes of data:
   Reply from 75.126.29.106: bytes=32 time=60ms TTL=51
   Reply from 75.126.29.106: bytes=32 time=60ms TTL=51
   Reply from 75.126.29.106: bytes=32 time=60ms TTL=51
   Reply from 75.126.29.106: bytes=32 time=60ms TTL=51
   Ping statistics for 75.126.29.106:
       Packets: Sent = 4, Received = 4, Lost = 0 (0% loss),
   Approximate round trip times in milli-seconds:
       Minimum = 60ms, Maximum = 60ms, Average = 60ms
   ```

3. Open your hosts file using any text editor and add this line (keep in mind you may have a different IP address from the one shown in this example). Just press the SPACEBAR a few times to separate the IP address from the word "timmy."

   ```
   75.126.29.106  timmy
   ```

4. Save the hosts file and close the text editor.

5. Reboot the computer.

6. Open a Web browser and type **timmy**. You can also type **http://timmy** if you'd like. What happens?

The Internet stopped using hosts files and replaced them with the vastly more powerful DNS. The hosts file still has a place today. Some folks place shortcut names in a hosts file to avoid typing long names in certain TCP/IP applications. It's also used by some of the nerdier types as a tool to block adware/malware. There are a number of people who make hosts files you can copy and place into your own hosts file. Do a Google search for **"hosts file replacement"** and try a few.

NOTE A lot of anti-malware software solutions use a custom hosts file to block known malicious or pesky sites. Check out this site for perhaps the best custom hosts file available: http://someonewhocares.org/hosts/.

DNS

When the Internet folks decided to dump the hosts file for name resolution and replace it with something better, they needed a flexible naming system that worked across cultures, time zones, and different sizes of networks. They needed something that was responsive to thousands, millions, even billions of requests. They implemented the Domain Name System (DNS) to solve these problems. This section looks at how DNS works, then examines the servers that make the magic happen. DNS wraps up with troubleshooting scenarios.

EXAM TIP The CompTIA Network+ objectives list *DNS service* as a network service type. This is technically true, but DNS is most commonly referred to as simply DNS. Be prepared for any of these terms on the exam.

How DNS Works

DNS relies on that time-tested bureaucratic solution: delegation! The top-dog DNS system would delegate parts of the job to subsidiary DNS systems that, in turn, would delegate part of their work to other systems, and so on, potentially without end. These systems run a special DNS server program and are called, amazingly enough, *DNS servers*.

EXAM TIP DNS servers primarily use UDP port 53 (and sometimes TCP port 53, although not for queries or responses).

NOTE The DNS root for the entire Internet consists of 13 powerful DNS server clusters scattered all over the world. Go to www.root-servers.org to see exactly where all the root servers are located.

This is all peachy, but it raises another issue: the DNS servers needed some way to decide how to divvy up the work. Toward this end, the Internet folks created a naming system designed to facilitate delegation. The top-dog DNS server is actually a bunch of powerful computers dispersed around the world. They work as a team and are known collectively as the *DNS root servers* (or simply as the *DNS root*). The Internet name of this computer team is "."—that's right, just "dot." Sure, it's weird, but it's quick to type, and they had to start somewhere.

 EXAM TIP The original top-level domain names were .com, .org, .net, .edu, .gov, .mil, and .int.

The DNS root servers have only one job: to delegate name resolution to other DNS servers. Just below the DNS root in the hierarchy is a set of DNS servers—called the *top-level domain servers*—that handle what are known as the *top-level domain (TLD) names*. These are the .com, .org, .net, .edu, .gov, .mil, and .int names, as well as international country codes such as .us, .eu, etc. The top-level DNS servers delegate to hundreds of thousands (maybe millions by now?) of second-level DNS servers; these servers handle the millions of names like totalsem.com and whitehouse.gov that have been created within each of the top-level domains. Second-level DNS servers support individual computers. For example, stored on the DNS server controlling the totalsem.com domain is a listing that looks like this:

```
www   209.29.33.25
```

 NOTE The *Internet Corporation for Assigned Names and Numbers (ICANN)* has the authority to create new TLDs. Since 2001, they've added many TLDs, such as .biz for businesses, .info for informational sites, and .pro for accountants, engineers, lawyers, and physicians in several Western countries.

This means the totalsem.com domain has a computer called *www* with the IP address of 209.29.33.25. Only the DNS server controlling the totalsem.com domain stores the actual IP address for *www*.totalsem.com. The DNS servers above this one have a hierarchical system that enables any other computer to find the DNS server that controls the totalsem.com domain.

 NOTE The Internet DNS names are usually consistent with this three-tier system, but if you want to add your own DNS server(s), you can add more levels, allowing you to name a computer www.houston.totalsem .com if you wish. The only limit is that a DNS name can have a maximum of 255 characters.

Name Spaces

The DNS *hierarchical name space* is an imaginary tree structure of all possible names that could be used within a single system. By contrast, a hosts file uses a *flat name space*—basically just one big undivided list containing all names, with no grouping whatsoever. In a flat name space, all names must be absolutely unique—no two machines can ever share the same name under any circumstances. A flat name space works fine on a small, isolated network, but not so well for a large organization with many interconnected networks.

To avoid naming conflicts, all its administrators would need to keep track of all the names used throughout the entire corporate network.

A hierarchical name space offers a better solution, permitting a great deal more flexibility by enabling administrators to give networked systems longer, more fully descriptive names. The personal names people use every day are an example of a hierarchical name space. Most people address our town postman, Ron Samuels, simply as Ron. When his name comes up in conversation, people usually refer to him as Ron. The town troublemaker, Ron Falwell, and Mayor Jones's son, Ron, who went off to Toledo, obviously share first names with the postman.

In some conversations, people need to distinguish between the good Ron, the bad Ron, and the Ron in Toledo (who may or may not be the ugly Ron). They could use a medieval style of address and refer to the Rons as Ron the Postman, Ron the Blackguard, and Ron of Toledo, or they could use the modern Western style of address and add their surnames: "That Ron Samuels—he is such a card!" "That Ron Falwell is one bad apple." "That Ron Jones was the homeliest child I ever saw." You might visualize this as the People name space, illustrated in Figure 9-3. Adding the surname creates what you might fancifully call a *Fully Qualified Person Name*—enough information to prevent confusion among the various people named Ron.

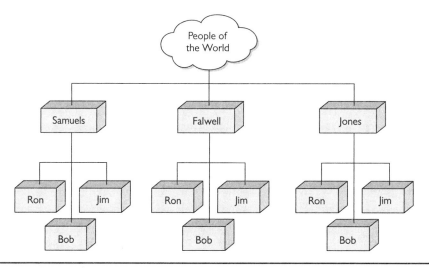

Figure 9-3   Our People name space

A name space most of you are already familiar with is the hierarchical file name space used by hard drive volumes. Hard drives formatted using one of the popular file formats, like Windows' NTFS or Linux's ext4, use a hierarchical name space; you can create as many files named data.txt as you want, as long as you store them in different parts of the file tree.

In the example shown in Figure 9-4, two different files named data.txt can exist simultaneously on the same system, but only if they are placed in different directories, such as C:\Program1\Current\data.txt and C:\Program1\Backup\data.txt. Although both files

have the same basic filename—data.txt—their fully qualified names are different: C:\
Program1\Current\data.txt and C:\Program1\Backup\data.txt. Additionally, multiple
subfolders can use the same name. Having two subfolders that use the name data is no
problem, as long as they reside in different folders. Any Windows file system will happily let you create both C:\Program1\Data and C:\Program2\Data folders. Folks like this
because they often want to give the same name to multiple folders doing the same job
for different applications.

Figure 9-4

Two data.txt
files in different
directories on the
same system

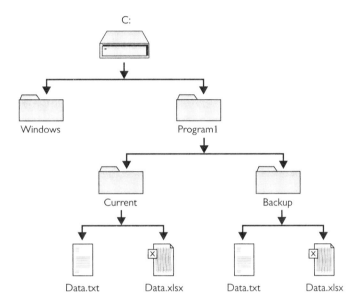

In contrast, imagine what would happen if your computer's file system didn't support
folders/directories. Windows would have to store all the files on your hard drive in the
root directory! This is a classic example of a flat name space. Because all your files would
be living together in one directory, each one would have to have a unique name. Naming
files would be a nightmare! Software vendors would have to avoid sensible descriptive
names like *readme.txt* because they would almost certainly have been used already. You'd
probably have to do what the Internet does for IP addresses: An organization of some
sort would assign names out of the limited pool of possible filenames. With a hierarchical name space, on the other hand, which is what all file systems use (thank goodness!),
naming is much simpler. Lots of programs can have files called readme.txt because each
program can have its own folder and subfolders.

NOTE As hard as this may be to believe, some early file systems used a flat
name space. Back in the late 1970s and early 1980s, operating systems such
as CP/M and the early versions of DOS did not have the capability to use
directories, creating a flat name space where all files resided on a single
drive.

The DNS name space works in a manner extremely similar to how your computer's file system works. The DNS name space is a hierarchy of *DNS domains* and individual computer names organized into a tree-like structure that is called, rather appropriately, a *DNS tree*. Each domain is like a folder—a domain is not a single computer, but rather a holding space into which you can add computer names.

At the top of a DNS tree is the root. The *root* is the holding area to which all domains connect, just as the root directory in your file system is the holding area for all your folders. Individual computer names—more commonly called *host names* in the DNS naming convention—fit into domains. In the PC, you can place files directly into the root directory. DNS also enables us to add computer names to the root, but with the exception of a few special computers (described in a moment), this is rarely done.

Each domain can have subdomains, just as the folders on your PC's file system can have subfolders. You separate each domain from its subdomains with a period. Characters for DNS domain names and host names are limited to letters (A–Z, a–z), numbers (0–9), and the hyphen (-). No other characters may be used.

NOTE Even though you may use uppercase or lowercase letters, DNS does not differentiate between them.

Don't think DNS is only for computers on the Internet. If you want to make your own little TCP/IP network using DNS, that's fine, although you will have to set up at least one DNS server as the root for your little private *intranet*. Every DNS server program can be configured as a root; just don't connect that DNS server to the Internet because it won't work outside your little network. Figure 9-5 shows a sample DNS tree for a small TCP/IP network that is not attached to the Internet. In this case, there is only one domain: ABCDEF. Each computer on the network has a host name, as shown in the figure.

Figure 9-5
Private DNS
network

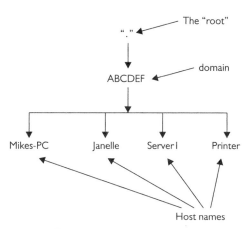

When you write out the complete path to a file stored on your PC, the naming convention starts with the root directory on the left, followed by the first folder, then any subfolders (in order), and finally the name of the file—for example, C:\Sounds\Thunder\mynewcobra.wav.

The DNS naming convention is *exactly the opposite*. A complete DNS name, including the host name and all of its domains (in order), is called a *fully qualified domain name (FQDN)*, and it's written with the root on the far right, followed by the names of the domains (in order) added to the left of the root, and the host name on the far left. Figure 9-5 shows the FQDNs for two systems in the ABCDEF domain. Note the period for the root is on the far *right* of each FQDN!

Mikes-PC.ABCDEF.
Janelle.ABCDEF.

Given that every FQDN will always have a period on the end to signify the root, it is commonplace to drop the final period when writing out FQDNs. To make the two example FQDNs fit into common parlance, therefore, you'd skip the last period:

Mikes-PC.ABCDEF Janelle.ABCDEF

If you're used to seeing DNS names on the Internet, you're probably wondering about the lack of ".com," ".net," or other common DNS domain names. Those conventions are needed for computers that are visible on the Internet, such as Web servers, but they're not required for DNS names on a private TCP/IP network. If you make a point never to make these computers visible on the Internet, you can skip the Internet top-level domains.

NOTE Don't get locked into thinking FQDNs always end with names like ".com" or ".net." True, DNS names on the Internet must always end with them, but private TCP/IP networks can (and often do) ignore this and use whatever naming scheme they want with their DNS names.

Let's look at another DNS name space example, but make it a bit more complex. This network is not on the Internet, so I can use any domain I want. The network has two domains, Houston and Dallas, as shown in Figure 9-6. Note that each domain has a computer called Server1.

Figure 9-6
Two DNS
domains

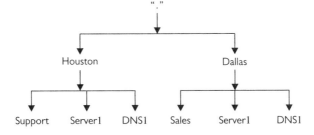

Because the network has two different domains, it can have two systems (one on each domain) with the same host name, just as you can have two files with the same name in different folders on your PC. Now, let's add some subdomains to the DNS tree, so that it looks like Figure 9-7.

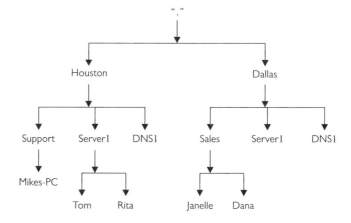

Figure 9-7
Subdomains
added

 EXAM TIP The DNS naming convention allows for DNS names up to 255 characters, including the separating periods.

You write out the FQDN from left to right, starting with the host name and moving up to the top of the DNS tree, adding all domains until you get to the top of the DNS tree:

Mikes-PC.Support.Houston
Tom.Server1.Houston
Janelle.Sales.Dallas
Server1.Dallas

Name Servers

So where does this naming convention reside and how does it work? The power of DNS comes from its incredible flexibility. DNS works as well on a small, private network as it does on the biggest network of all time—the Internet. Let's start with three key players:

- **DNS server**   A *DNS server* is a computer running DNS server software.

- **Zone**   A *zone* is a container for a single domain that gets filled with records.

- **Record**   A *record* is a line in the zone data that maps an FQDN to an IP address.

Systems running DNS server software store the DNS information. When a system needs to know the IP address for a specific FQDN, it queries the DNS server listed in its TCP/IP configuration. Assuming the DNS server stores the zone for that particular FQDN, it replies with the computer's IP address.

A simple network usually has one DNS server for the entire domain. This DNS server has a single zone that lists all the host names on the domain and their corresponding IP addresses. It's known as the *authoritative name server* for the domain.

If you've got a powerful computer, you can put lots of zones on a single DNS server and let that server support them all without a problem. A single DNS server, therefore, can act as the authoritative name server for one domain or many domains (Figure 9-8).

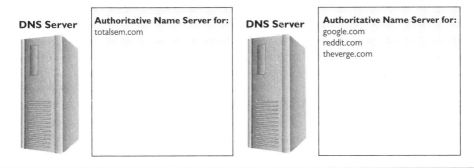

Figure 9-8   A single authoritative name server can support one or more domains.

On the opposite end of the spectrum, a single domain can use more than one DNS server. Imagine how busy the google.com domain is—it needs lots of DNS servers to support all the incoming DNS queries.

A larger-scale domain starts with a *primary (master) DNS server* and one or more *secondary (slave) DNS servers*. The secondary servers are subordinate to the primary server, but all support the same domain (Figure 9-9).

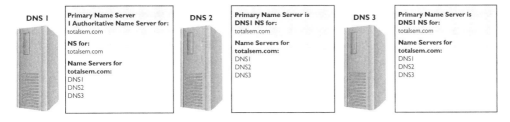

Figure 9-9   DNS flexibility

If you have a lot of DNS servers all supporting the same domain, they need to be able to talk to each other frequently. If one DNS server gets a new record, that record must propagate to all the name servers on the domain. To support this, every DNS server in the domain knows the name and address of the primary name server(s) as well as the name and address of every secondary name server in the domain. The primary name server's job is to make sure that all the other name servers are updated for changes.

Let's say you add to the totalsem.com domain a new computer called ftp.totalsem .com with the IP address 192.168.4.22. As an administrator, you typically add this data to the primary name server. The primary name server then automatically distributes this information to the other name servers in the domain (Figure 9-10).

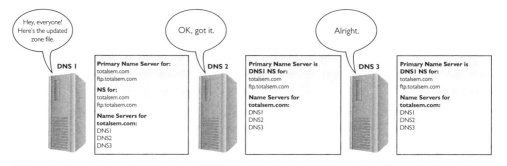

Figure 9-10   New information passed out

Now let's see how root servers work in DNS. What if Mikes-PC.Support.Dallas needs the IP address of Server1.Houston? Refer to Figure 9-11 for the answer. The image shows two DNS servers: DNS1.Dallas and DNS1.Houston. DNS1.Dallas is the primary DNS server for the Dallas domain and DNS1.Houston is in charge of the Houston domain.

Figure 9-11

Root server in action

NOTE   In the early days of DNS, you had to enter manually into your DNS server the host name and IP address of every system on the network. See "Dynamic DNS," later in this chapter, for the way it's done today.

As a root server, the Dallas server has a listing for the primary name server in the Houston domain. This does *not* mean it knows the IP address for every system in the Houston network. As a root server, it only knows that if any system asks for an IP address from the Houston side, it will tell that system the IP address of the Houston server. The requesting system will then ask the Houston DNS server (DNS1.Houston) for the IP address of the system it needs. That's the beauty of DNS root servers—they don't know the IP addresses for all of the computers, but they know where to send the requests!

 EXAM TIP Just because most Web servers are named www doesn't mean they must be named www! Naming a Web server www is etiquette, not a requirement.

The hierarchical aspect of DNS has a number of benefits. For example, the vast majority of Web servers are called www. If DNS used a flat name space, only the first organization that created a server with the name www could use it. Because DNS naming appends domain names to the server names, however, the servers www.totalsem.com and www.microsoft.com can both exist simultaneously. DNS names like www.microsoft.com must fit within a worldwide hierarchical name space, meaning that no two machines should ever have the same FQDN.

Figure 9-12 shows the host named accounting with an FQDN of accounting.texas .totalsem.com.

Figure 9-12
DNS domain

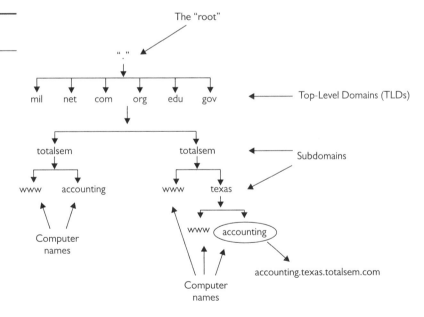

 NOTE Technically, the texas.totalsem.com domain shown in Figure 9-12 is a *child domain* of totalsem.com (the *parent domain*).

These domain names must be registered for Internet use with ICANN (www.icann .org). They are arranged in the familiar *second level.top level* domain name format, where the *top level* is .com, .org, .net, and so on, and the *second level* is the name of the individual entity registering the domain name.

Name Resolution

In the early years of the Internet, DNS worked interchangeably with IP addressing. You could surf to a Web site, in other words, by typing in the FQDN or the IP address of the Web server. Figure 9-13 shows a browser accessing the awesome tech site AnandTech by IP address rather than by typing www.anandtech.com.

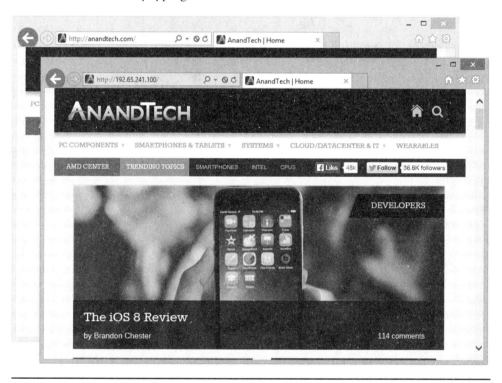

Figure 9-13   Accessing a Web site via IP address rather than name

Modern Web sites don't really function well without DNS. A Web server that houses a company's domain name, for example, might host a dozen or more domain names. If you try to access the Web site by IP address, the Web server won't know which domain is being requested!

You'll still find this 1:1 correlation of DNS name to IP address with simpler devices like IP security cameras. These are cameras with an Ethernet connection, a public IP address, and a built-in interface for viewing and control.

Once you get into how computers communicate on the Web, name resolution becomes an integral part of the process. When you type in a Web address, your browser must resolve that name to the Web server's IP address to make a connection to that Web server. In the early days, it could resolve the name by broadcasting or by consulting the locally stored hosts text file. Today, the browser consults the host's DNS resolver cache (more on this in a moment) or queries a DNS server.

To *broadcast* for name resolution, the host sent a message to all the machines on the network, saying something like, "Hey! If your name is JOESCOMPUTER, please respond with your IP address." All the networked hosts received that packet, but only JOESCOM-PUTER responded with an IP address. Broadcasting worked fine for small networks, but was limited because it could not provide name resolution across routers. Routers do not forward broadcast messages to other networks, as illustrated in Figure 9-14.

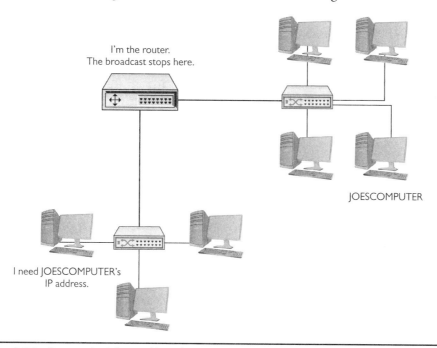

Figure 9-14   Routers don't forward broadcasts!

As discussed earlier, a hosts file functions like a little black book, listing the names and addresses of machines on a network, just like a little black book lists the names and phone numbers of people. Clients in early TCP/IP networks consulted the hosts file for name resolution.

Modern hosts automatically map the hosts file to the host's *DNS resolver cache*, a memory area that also includes any recently resolved addresses. When a host looks for an IP address that corresponds to a Web site name, it first checks the DNS resolver cache. Getting the address locally is obviously much more efficient than going out to a DNS server. Which leads us to . . . .

The final way to resolve a name to an IP address is to use DNS. Let's say you type **www.microsoft.com** in your Web browser. To resolve the name www.microsoft.com, the host contacts its DNS server and requests the IP address, as shown in Figure 9-15.

Figure 9-15
A host contacts
its local DNS
server.

Client

Client's DNS server

1. The client asks its
DNS server for the
www.microsoft.com
IP address.

2. The DNS server doesn't
know the IP address, so
it asks the root DNS server.

To request the IP address of www.microsoft.com, your PC needs the IP address of its DNS server. You must enter DNS information into your system. DNS server data is part of the critical basic IP information such as your IP address, subnet mask, and default gateway, so you usually enter it at the same time as the other IP information. You configure DNS in Windows using the Internet Protocol Version 4 (TCP/IPv4) Properties dialog box. Figure 9-16 shows the DNS settings for my system. Note that I have more than one DNS server setting; the second one is a backup in case the first one isn't working. Two DNS settings is not a rule, however, so don't worry if your system shows only one DNS server setting.

Figure 9-16
DNS information
in Windows

Every operating system has a way for you to enter DNS server information. Just about every version of Linux has some form of graphical editor, for example, to make this an easy process. Figure 9-17 shows Ubuntu's Network Configuration utility.

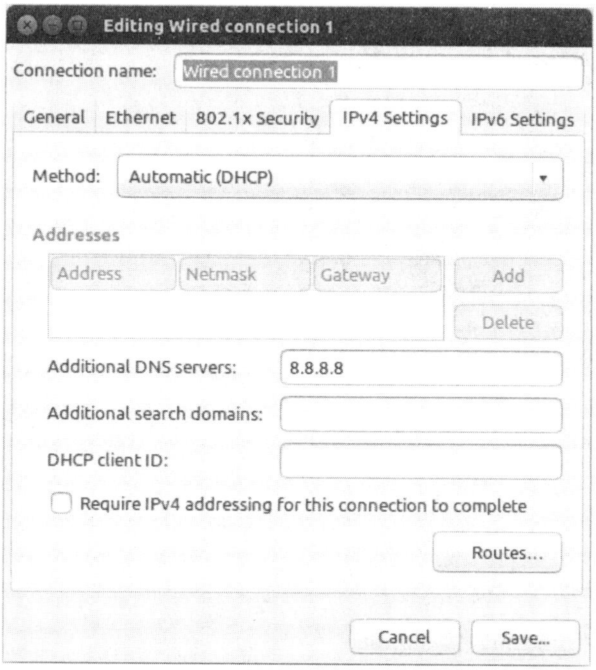

Figure 9-17
Entering DNS
information in
Ubuntu

Every operating system also comes with a utility you can use to verify the DNS server settings. The tool in Windows, for example, is called *ipconfig*. You can see your current DNS server settings in Windows by typing `ipconfig /all` at the command prompt (Figure 9-18). In UNIX/Linux, type the following: `cat /etc/resolv.conf`.

Now that you understand how your system knows the DNS server's IP address, let's return to the DNS process.

The DNS server receives the request for the IP address of www.microsoft.com from your client computer. At this point, your DNS server checks its resolver cache of previously resolved FQDNs to see if www.microsoft.com is there (Figure 9-19). In this case, www.microsoft.com is not in the server's DNS resolver cache.

Now your DNS server needs to get to work. The local DNS server may not know the address for www.microsoft.com, but it does know the addresses of the DNS root servers. The 13 root servers (composed of hundreds of machines), maintained by 12 root name server operators, know all the addresses of the top-level domain DNS servers. The root servers don't know the address of www.microsoft.com, but they do know the address of the DNS servers in charge of all .com addresses. The root servers send your DNS server an IP address for a .com server (Figure 9-20).

The .com DNS server also doesn't know the address of www.microsoft.com, but it knows the IP address of the microsoft.com DNS server. It sends that IP address to your DNS server (Figure 9-21).

The microsoft.com DNS server does know the IP address of www.microsoft.com and can send that information back to the local DNS server. Figure 9-22 shows the process of resolving an FQDN into an IP address.

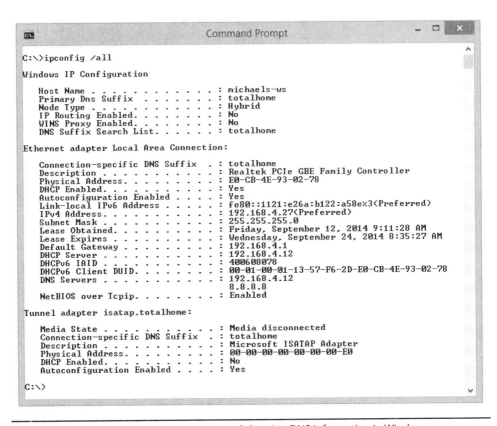

Figure 9-18 The `ipconfig /all` command showing DNS information in Windows

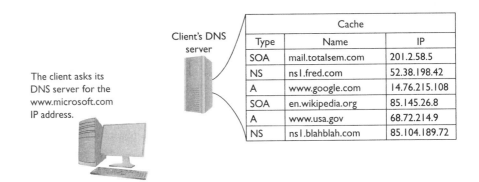

Figure 9-19 Checking the DNS resolver cache

Figure 9-20
Talking to a root
server

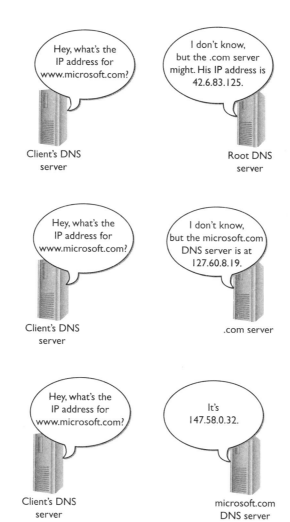

Figure 9-21
Talking to the
.com server

Figure 9-22
Talking to the
microsoft.com
DNS server

Now that your DNS server has the IP address for www.microsoft.com, it stores a copy in its cache and sends the IP information to your PC. Your Web browser then begins the HTTP request to get the Web page.

 NOTE   A local DNS server, like the one connected to a LAN, is not authoritative, but rather is used just for internal queries from internal clients, and caching.

Your computer also keeps a cache of recently resolved FQDNs, plus all entries from the hosts file. In Windows, for example, open a command prompt and type `ipconfig /displaydns` to see them. Here's a small part of the results of typing `ipconfig /displaydns`:

```
www.theverge.com

----------------------------------------
Record Name . . . . . : www.theverge.com
Record Type . . . . . : 1
Time To Live  . . . . : 259
Data Length . . . . . : 4
Section . . . . . . . : Answer
A (Host) Record . . . : 192.5.151.3
ftp.totalsem.com
_____

Record Name . . . . . : ftp.totalsem.com
Record Type . . . . . : 1
Time To Live  . . . . : 83733
Data Length . . . . . : 4
Section . . . . . . . : Answer
A (Host) Record . . . : 209.29.33.25
C:\>
```

DNS Servers

I've been talking about DNS servers for so long, I feel I'd be untrue to my vision of a Mike Meyers' book unless I gave you at least a quick peek at a DNS server in action. Lots of operating systems come with built-in DNS server software, including Windows Server and just about every version of UNIX/Linux. A number of third-party DNS server programs are also available for virtually any operating system. I'm going to use the DNS server program that comes with Microsoft Windows Server, primarily because (1) it takes the prettiest screen snapshots and (2) it's the one I use here at the office. You access the Windows DNS server by selecting **Start | Administrative Tools | DNS**. When you first open the DNS server, you won't see much other than the name of the server itself. In this case, Figure 9-23 shows a server, imaginatively named TOTALHOMEDC2.

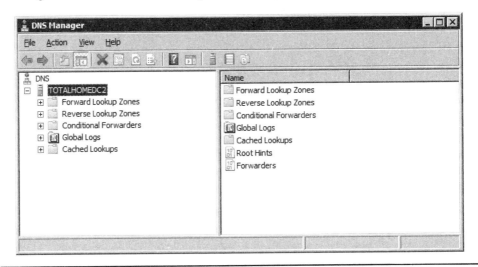

Figure 9-23   DNS server main screen

EXAM TIP The most popular DNS server used in UNIX/Linux systems is called BIND.

The DNS server has (at least) three folder icons visible: Forward Lookup Zones, Reverse Lookup Zones, and Cached Lookups. Depending on the version of Windows Server you're running and the level of customization, your server might have more than three folder icons. Let's look at the three that are important for this discussion, starting with the Cached Lookups.

Every DNS server keeps a list of *cached lookups*—that is, all the IP addresses it has already resolved—so it won't have to re-resolve an FQDN it has already checked. The cache has a size limit, of course, and you can also set a limit on how long the DNS server holds cache entries. Windows does a nice job of separating these cached addresses by placing all cached lookups in little folders that share the first name of the top-level domain with subfolders that use the second-level domain (Figure 9-24). This sure makes it easy to see where folks have been Web browsing!

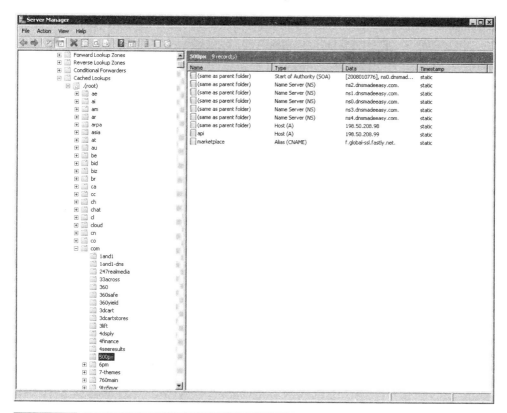

Figure 9-24 Inspecting the DNS cache

Now let's watch an actual DNS server at work. Basically, you choose to configure a DNS server to work in one of two ways: as an authoritative DNS server or as a cache-only DNS server. *Authoritative DNS servers* store IP addresses and FQDNs of systems for a particular domain or domains. *Cache-only DNS servers* are never the authoritative server for a domain. They are only used to talk to other DNS servers to resolve IP addresses for DNS clients. Then they cache the FQDN to speed up future lookups (Figure 9-25).

Figure 9-25
Authoritative vs.
cache-only DNS
server

Cache		
Type	Name	IP
SOA	mail.totalsem.com	201.2.58.5
NS	ns1.fred.com	52.38.198.42
A	www.google.com	14.76.215.108
SOA	en.wikipedia.org	85.145.26.8
A	www.usa.gov	68.72.214.9
NS	ns1.blahblah.com	85.104.189.72

Authoritative   Cache-only

 NOTE Microsoft DNS servers use a folder analogy to show lookup zones even though they are not true folders.

The IP addresses and FQDNs for the computers in a domain are stored in special storage areas called *forward lookup zones*. Forward lookup zones are the most important part of any DNS server. Figure 9-26 shows the DNS server for my small corporate network. My domain is called "totalhome." I can get away with a domain name that's not Internet

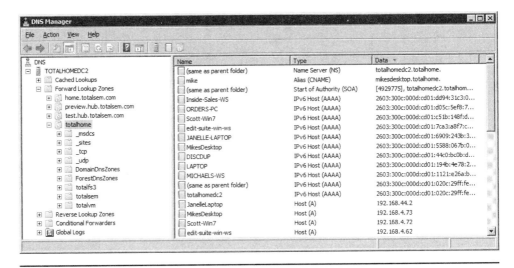

Figure 9-26   Forward lookup zone totalhome

legal because none of these computers are visible on the Internet. The totalhome domain only works on my local network for local computers to find each other. I have created a forward lookup zone called totalhome.

Let's look at the contents of the totalhome domain. First, notice a number of folders: _msdcs, _sites, _tcp, and _udp. These folders are unique to Microsoft DNS servers, and you'll see what they do in a moment. For now, ignore them and concentrate on the individual rows of data. Each row defines a forward lookup zone record. Each record consists of Name, Type, and Data. While Name and Data (showing IPv6 and IPv4 addresses, for the most part) are obvious, the DNS record type—Type—needs a bit of discussion.

DNS Record Types

Part of the power and flexibility of DNS comes from the use of record types. Each record type helps different aspects of DNS do their job. Let's take a moment and review all the DNS record types you'll see on the CompTIA Network+ exam.

Individual hosts each get their own unique *A record*. A records are the workhorse records in any forward lookup zone. There are some common conventions here. A Web server on a forward lookup zone, for example, usually gets an A record called www, if for no other reason than users expect a Web site URL to start with www.

While A records are the most common, every forward lookup zone contains other very important record types. These are, in no specific order: SOA, NS, CNAME, AAAA, MX, SRV, and TXT. Let's go through each one of these.

SOA   Every forward lookup zone requires a *Start of Authority (SOA) record* that defines the primary name server in charge of the forward lookup zone. The SOA record in the folder totalhome in Figure 9-26, for example, indicates that my server is the primary DNS server for a domain called totalhome. The primary and any secondary name servers are authoritative.

NS   The *NS record* in Figure 9-26 shows the primary name server for totalhome. My network could (and does) have a second name server to provide redundancy. These secondary name servers are also authoritative for the totalhome domain. Having two DNS servers ensures that if one fails, the totalhome domain will continue to have a DNS server.

Every DNS forward lookup zone will have one SOA and at least one NS record. In the vast majority of cases, a forward lookup zone will have some number of A records. You will also see other records in a standard DNS server. Figure 9-27 shows additional types of DNS records: CNAME and AAAA. You'll also see MX records in domains that have a mail server.

CNAME   A *canonical name (CNAME) record* acts like an alias. My computer's name is mikesdesktop.totalhome, but you can also now use mike.totalhome to reference that computer. A ping of mike.totalhome returns the following:

```
C:\>ping mike.totalhome
Pinging mikesdesktop.totalhome [192.168.4.73] with 32 bytes of data:
Reply from 192.168.4.73: bytes=32 time=2ms TTL=128
Reply from 192.168.4.73: bytes=32 time<1ms TTL=128

(rest of ping results deleted)
```

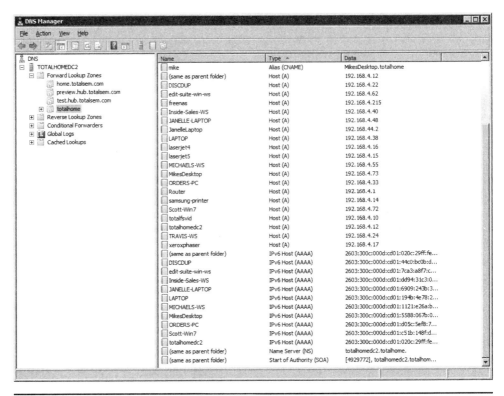

Figure 9-27 Additional DNS record types

If your computer is a member of a domain and you are trying to access another computer in that domain, you can even skip the domain name, because your PC will simply add it back:

```
C:\>ping mike
Pinging mikesdesktop.totalhome [192.168.4.73] with 32 bytes of data:
Reply from 192.168.4.73: bytes=32 time=2ms TTL=128
Reply from 192.168.4.73: bytes=32 time<1ms TTL=128

(rest of ping results deleted)
```

A different tool, dig, shows the process more clearly. (I cover dig more completely in the "Troubleshooting DNS" section, later in this chapter.) Figure 9-28 shows the text output of a dig query. Querying the CNAME (mike.totalhome) returns the host (mikesdesktop.totalhome), which is recognized as an A record. The query finishes with the IP address for the host.

AAAA *AAAA records* are the equivalent of A records, but reserved for a newer type of IP addressing called IPv6. You'll learn a lot more about IPv6 in Chapter 12, "IPv6."

```
dig CNAME query.txt - Notepad                              ↔    —   □   ×
File  Edit  Format  View  Help
$ dig mike.totalhome

; <<>> DiG 9.8.3-P1 <<>> mike.totalhome
;; global options: +cmd
;; Got answer:
;; ->>HEADER<<- opcode: QUERY, status: NOERROR, id: 50875
;; flags: qr aa rd ra; QUERY: 1, ANSWER: 2, AUTHORITY: 0, ADDITIONAL: 0

;; QUESTION SECTION:
;mike.totalhome.                     IN      A

;; ANSWER SECTION:
mike.totalhome.         3600    IN    CNAME   mikesdesktop.totalhome.
mikesdesktop.totalhome. 1200    IN    A       192.168.4.73

;; Query time: 20 msec
;; SERVER: 192.168.4.12#53(192.168.4.12)
;; WHEN: Fri Jan  5 13:49:23 2018
;; MSG SIZE  rcvd: 75
```

Figure 9-28   Results of running `dig` on a CNAME

MX   *MX records* are used exclusively by SMTP servers to determine where to send mail. I have an in-house SMTP server on a computer I cleverly called mail. If other SMTP servers wanted to send mail to mail.totalhome (although they can't because the SMTP server isn't connected to the Internet and lacks a legal FQDN), they would use DNS to locate the mail server.

NOTE   MX stands for Mail eXchanger.

SRV   The idea of creating MX records to directly support e-mail motivated the Elders of the Internet to develop a generic DNS record that supports any type of server, the *SRV record*. SRV records have a different look than most other DNS records. The basic format of an SRV record is as follows:

`_service._proto.name. TTL IN SRV priority weight port target.`

- *service*   Name of the service supported by this record
- *proto*   TCP or UDP

- *name*   The domain name for this server (ends with a period)
- *TTL*   Time to live in seconds
- *priority*   The priority of the target host; this is used when multiple servers are present (value is 0 when only one server)
- *weight*   An arbitrary value to give certain services priority over others
- *port*   The TCP or UDP port on which the service is to be found
- *target*   The FQDN of the machine providing the service, ending in a dot

Here is an example of an SRV record for a Session Initiation Protocol (SIP) service:

```
_sip._tcp.testserve.com. 86400 IN SRV 0 5 5060 sipserver.mikemeyers.com.
```

Several common services use SRV records. These include Kerberos servers, LDAP, SIP, and, surprisingly, the popular game Minecraft!

TXT   A *TXT record* is a freeform type of record that can be used for … anything. TXT records allow any text to be added to a forward lookup zone. One use of TXT records is documentation. A TXT record might look like this:

```
TXT Mike Meyers set up the AAAA records on 6/6/19
```

TXT records can support protocols designed to deter e-mail spoofing. Solutions such as DomainKeys Identified Mail (DKIM) and Sender Policy Framework (SPF) use special TXT records that enable domains to verify that e-mail being received by a third-party e-mail server is sent by a legitimate server within the domain. The following is an example of SPF information stored in a TXT record:

```
v=spf1 include:spf.protection.outlook.com ip4:99.16.129.16 -all
```

Primary and Secondary Zones

There are two common types of forward lookup zones: a primary zone and a secondary zone. *Primary zones* are created on the DNS server that will act as the primary name server for that zone. *Secondary zones* are created on other DNS servers to act as backups to the primary zone. It's standard practice to have at least two DNS servers for any forward lookup zone: one primary and one secondary, both of which are authoritative. Even in my small network, I have two DNS servers: TOTALDNS1, which runs the primary zone, and TOTALDNS2, which runs a secondary zone (Figure 9-29). Any time a change is placed on TOTALDNS1, TOTALDNS2 is quickly updated.

 NOTE   If you're looking at a Windows server and adding a new forward lookup zone, you'll see a third type called an Active Directory–integrated forward lookup zone. I'll cover that in just a moment.

Figure 9-29
Two DNS servers
with updating
taking place

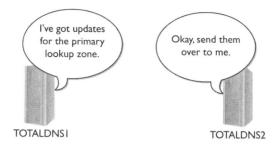

TOTALDNS1   TOTALDNS2

A *reverse lookup zone* (Figure 9-30) enables a system to determine an FQDN by know-ing the IP address; that is, it does the exact reverse of what DNS normally does! Reverse lookup zones take a network ID, reverse it, and add a unique domain called "in-addr .arpa" to create the zone. The record created is called a *pointer record (PTR)*.

Figure 9-30
Reverse lookup
zone

Reverse lookup zone

A few low-level functions (like mail) and some security programs use reverse lookup zones, so DNS servers provide them. In most cases, the DNS server asks you if you want to make a reverse lookup zone when you make a new forward lookup zone. When in doubt, make one. If you don't need it, it won't cause any trouble.

Microsoft added some wrinkles to DNS servers with the introduction of Windows 2000 Server, and each subsequent version of Windows Server retains the wrinkles. Win-dows Server can do cached lookups, primary and secondary forward lookup zones, and reverse lookup zones, just like UNIX/Linux DNS servers. But Windows Server also has a Windows-only type of forward lookup zone called an Active Directory–integrated zone.

 EXAM TIP Make sure you know the difference between forward vs. reverse zones. Forward enables a system to determine an IP address by knowing the FQDN; reverse enables a system to determine an FQDN by knowing the IP address.

Enter Windows

DNS works beautifully for any TCP/IP application that needs an IP address for another computer, but based on what you've learned so far, it has one glaring weakness: you need to add A records to the DNS server manually. Adding these can be a problem, especially in a world where you have many DHCP clients whose IP addresses may change from time to time. Interestingly, it was a throwback to the old Microsoft Windows NetBIOS protocol that fixed this and a few other problems all at the same time.

The solution was simple. Microsoft managed to crowbar the NetBIOS naming system into DNS by making the NetBIOS name the DNS name and by making the SMB protocol (which you learned about at the beginning of this chapter) run directly on TCP/IP without using NetBT.

 EXAM TIP SMB running atop NetBIOS over TCP uses the same ports UDP 137 and 138, TCP 137 and 139. Without NetBIOS, SMB uses TCP port 445.

Microsoft has used DNS names with the SMB protocol to provide folder and printer sharing in small TCP/IP networks. SMB is so popular that other operating systems have adopted support for SMB. UNIX/Linux systems come with the very popular Samba, the most popular tool for making non-Windows systems act like Windows computers (Figure 9-31).

Figure 9-31
Samba on Ubuntu (it's so common that the OS doesn't even use the term in the dialog)

Living with SMB SMB makes most small networks live in a two-world name resolution system. When your computer wants to access another computer's folders or files, it uses a simple SMB broadcast to get the name. If that same computer wants to do anything "Internety," it uses its DNS server. Both SMB and DNS live together perfectly well and, although many alternatives are available for this dual name resolution scheme, the vast majority of us are happy with this relationship.

Well, except for one little item we're almost happy: Windows continues to support an old organization of your computers into *groups*. There are three types of groups: workgroup, Windows domain, and Active Directory. A *workgroup* is just a name that organizes a group of computers. A computer running Windows (or another operating system running Samba) joins a workgroup, as shown in Figure 9-32. When a computer joins a workgroup, all the computers in the Network folder are organized, as shown in Figure 9-33.

Figure 9-32
Joining a
workgroup

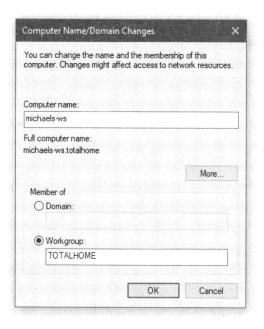

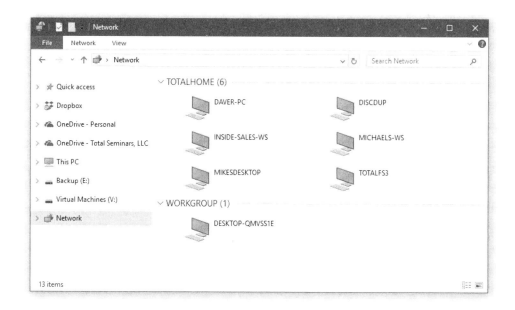

Figure 9-33   Network folder with a single workgroup

A *Windows domain* is a group of computers controlled by a computer running Windows Server. This Windows Server computer is configured as a domain controller. You then have your computers join the domain.

All the computers within a domain authenticate to the domain controller when they log in. Windows gives you this very powerful control over who can access what on your network (Figure 9-34).

Figure 9-34
Logging into the domain

Primary domain controller

Note that a Windows domain is not the same as a DNS domain. In the early days, a Windows domain didn't even have a naming structure that resembled the DNS hierarchically organized structure. Microsoft eventually revamped its domain controllers to work as part of DNS, however, and Windows domains now use DNS for their names. A Windows domain must have a true DNS name. DNS domains that are not on the Internet should use the top-level name .local (although you can cheat, as I do on my totalhome network, and not use it).

On a bigger scale, a Windows network can get complicated, with multiple domains connecting over long distances. To help organize this, Windows uses a type of super domain called Active Directory. An *Active Directory* domain is an organization of related computers that shares one or more Windows domains. Windows domain controllers are also DNS servers.

The beauty of Active Directory is that it has no single domain controller: all the domain controllers are equal partners, and any domain controller can take over if one domain controller fails (Figure 9-35).

Figure 9-35
If one domain controller goes down, another automatically takes over.

Primary domain controller   Primary domain controller

Active Directory–Integrated Zones   Now that you have an understanding of Windows domains and Active Directory, let's return to forward lookup zones and DNS. A standard primary zone stores the DNS information in text files on the DNS server. You then use secondary zones on other DNS servers to back up that server. If the primary DNS server goes down, the secondary servers can resolve FQDNs, but you can't add any new records. Nothing can be updated until the primary DNS server comes back up.

In an Active Directory–integrated zone, all of the domain controllers (which are all also DNS servers) are equal and the whole DNS system is not reliant on a single DNS server. The DNS servers store their DNS information in the Active Directory. The Active Directory is stored across the servers in the domain. All Active Directory–enabled DNS servers automatically send DNS information to each other, updating every machine's DNS information to match the others. This eliminates zone transfers.

Placing DNS Servers

Every host that connects to the Internet needs access to a DNS server. Additionally, if an internal network uses a DNS server, then every host needs access to that DNS server just to find other computers on the local network. So, the question is: where do we place DNS servers to do the job they need to do? There are many options and best practices to follow here depending on what's required for a DNS server, as well as options for offloading DNS server administration.

NOTE   DNS is incredibly flexible, making server placement a challenge. In many cases there's more than one good option and it's little more than a matter of preference.

The biggest first question that must be asked when deciding on server placement is whether the individual hosts need DNS to resolve hosts on the local network. Most homes and small offices use SMB for local resolution and do not need a DNS server. Organizations that use DNS to enable individual local computers to resolve names need an internal DNS server. For example, any organization using Windows domains must have a local DNS server (Figure 9-36). Let's call this *local DNS*.

The second question is usually easy: do the individual hosts need DNS to resolve Internet names? No matter how small or how large the network, if hosts need the Internet, the answer is always *yes*. Let's call this *Internet DNS* (Figure 9-37).

Local DNS   The traditional method to provide DNS resolution for a local network is an *internal* DNS server. An internal DNS server is an on-premises DNS server owned and administered by in-house personnel. An internal DNS server contains a forward lookup zone for the in-house domain (like totalhome.local), providing DNS name resolution for all hosts on the network (Figure 9-38). It is standard procedure to have both a primary and a secondary internal DNS server.

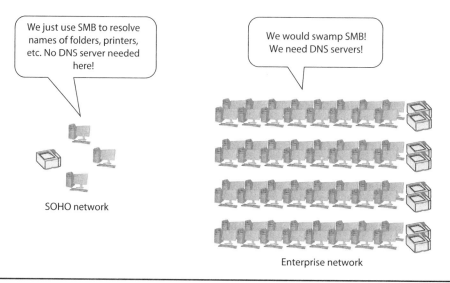

Figure 9-36 Small networks rarely need DNS servers to resolve local resources. Large ones usually do.

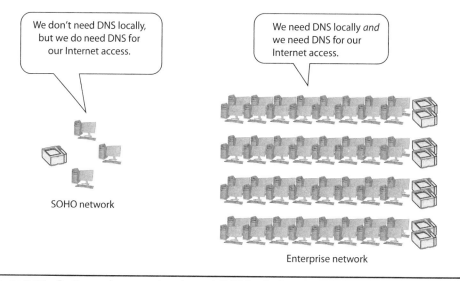

Figure 9-37 Pretty much every network needs DNS for the Internet.

A local DNS server can also handle Internet naming needs. To do this, a DNS server may be configured to forward any DNS request for which the DNS server is not authoritative. This is called *DNS forwarding*. As Figure 9-39 shows, a DNS request for the local domain is handled by the local DNS server, while all other DNS requests are forwarded to another DNS server.

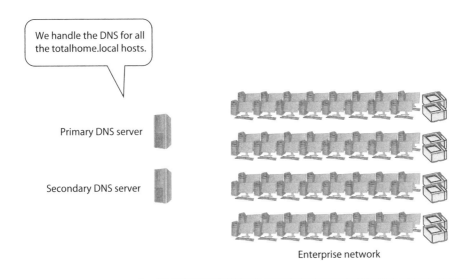

Figure 9-38 Internal DNS servers

Figure 9-39 DNS forwarding in action

In small networks that don't require a DNS server for local resolution, it's very common to use a gateway router that contains a rudimentary DNS server that only performs DNS forwarding and caching. Any DNS server that has no forward lookup zones and contains no root hints is called a cache-only (or caching-only) DNS server.

Private vs. Public DNS   A DNS server will be either private or public. Internal DNS servers that provide DNS to domains like totalhome.local are private. The computers of totalhome.local are invisible to the Internet. Therefore, the DNS server itself is also behind a firewall and in many cases resolving computers with private IP addresses. Public DNS servers are exposed to the Internet and resolve legitimate, registered, fully qualified domain names. These public servers are never behind a firewall and must have public IP addresses.

Every DNS server that resolves legitimate, registered Internet domains is public, but there is also a type of public DNS server that's designed to handle all requests for any FQDN equally, known as *public DNS servers*. These public DNS servers often offer faster

DNS resolution, are all but guaranteed to never go down, and many times avoid DNS redirections that some ISPs do to their customers. Here's a small sampling of the more famous public DNS servers:

Provider	Primary DNS	Secondary DNS
Level3	209.244.0.3	209.244.0.4
Cloudflare	1.1.1.1	1.0.0.1
Google	8.8.8.8	8.8.4.4
Quad9	9.9.9.9	149.112.112.112
DNS WATCH	84.200.69.80	84.200.70.40
OpenDNS	208.67.222.222	208.67.220.220
SafeDNS	195.46.39.39	195.46.39.40

External DNS Servers   Any DNS server that is not internal to an organization is an external DNS server. External DNS servers are an integral part of the DNS structure if for no other reason than every DNS server except for root DNS servers must connect to other DNS servers that are always external to their organization.

There are, however, certain forms of external DNS servers that can take on jobs often handled by internal DNS servers. These servers can handle private or public domains, and other functions. There are two places we see these servers. First are third-party DNS server companies. These companies provide public and private DNS servers. They may also provide other products such as Web hosting, e-mail, etc. One example is Name-cheap.com, one I use a lot (Figure 9-40).

Another type of DNS server is exclusively cloud-based. Third-party cloud services such as Amazon AWS and Microsoft Azure provide cloud-hosted DNS servers to support your own cloud servers and, in some cases, even support private domains.

Dynamic DNS

In the early days of TCP/IP networks, DNS servers required manual updates of their records. This was not a big deal until the numbers of computers using TCP/IP exploded in the 1990s. Then every office had a network and every network had a DNS server to update. DHCP helped to some extent. You could add a special option to the DHCP server, which is generally called the *DNS suffix*. This way the DHCP clients would know the name of the DNS domain to which they belonged. It didn't help the manual updating of DNS records, but clients don't need records. No one accesses the clients! The DNS suffix helps the clients access network resources more efficiently.

 NOTE   All DHCP servers provide an option called *DNS server* that tells clients the IP address of the DNS server or servers.

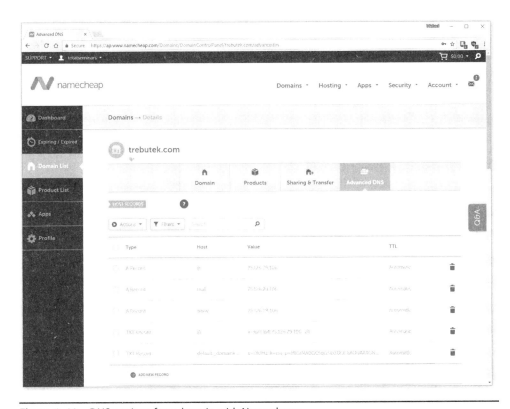

Figure 9-40 DNS settings for a domain with Namecheap

Today, manual updating of DNS records is still the norm for most Internet-serving systems like Web servers and e-mail servers. DNS has moved beyond Internet servers; even the smallest Windows networks that run Active Directory use it. Whereas a popular Web server might have a phalanx of techs to adjust DNS settings, small networks in which most of the computers run DHCP need an alternative to old-school DNS. Luckily, the solution was worked out over a decade ago.

The TCP/IP folks came up with a new protocol called *Dynamic DNS (DDNS)* in 1997 that enabled DNS servers to get automatic updates of IP addresses of computers in their forward lookup zones, mainly by talking to the local DHCP server. All modern DNS servers support DDNS, and all but the most primitive DHCP servers support DDNS as well.

Windows leans heavily on DDNS. Windows networks use DDNS for the DHCP server to talk to the DNS server. When a DHCP server updates its records for a DHCP client, it reports to the DNS server. The DNS server then updates its A records accordingly. DDNS simplifies setting up and maintaining a LAN tremendously. If you need to force a DNS server to update its records, use the `ipconfig /registerdns` command from the command prompt.

DNS Security Extensions

If you think about what DNS does, you can appreciate that it can be a big security issue. Simply querying a DNS server gives you a list of every computer name and IP address that it serves. This isn't the kind of information we want bad guys to have. The big fix is called *DNS Security Extensions (DNSSEC)*. DNSSEC is an authorization and integrity protocol designed to prevent bad guys from impersonating legitimate DNS servers. It's implemented through *extension mechanisms for DNS (EDNS)*, a specification that expanded several parameter sizes but maintained backward compatibility with earlier DNS servers.

Dynamic DNS on the Internet

I'd like to apologize on behalf of the Network industry. There's another kind of Dynamic DNS that has nothing to do with Microsoft's DDNS and it's called Dynamic DNS. To make it worse, Internet-based DDNS is also very popular, so it's important for you to recognize the difference between the two. Let's look at Dynamic DNS on the Internet.

The proliferation of dedicated high-speed Internet connections to homes and businesses has led many people to use those connections for more than surfing the Web from inside the local network. Why not have a Web server in your network, for example, that you can access from anywhere on the Web? You could use Windows Remote Desktop to take control of your home machine. (See Chapter 14 for more details on Remote Desktop.)

The typical high-speed Internet connection presents a problem in making this work. Most folks have a cable or DSL modem connected to a router. The router has a DHCP server inside, and that's what dishes out private IP addresses to computers on the LAN. The router also has an external IP address that it gets from the ISP, usually via DHCP. That external address can change unless you pay extra for a static IP address. Most people don't.

IPAM

Running DNS and DHCP at the same time creates some syncing challenges. To work together, the DHCP server must work closely with the DNS server, letting the DNS server know every time a host is given a DHCP lease so that the DNS server can then update the host's DNS record with the correct A or AAAA records.

To deal with the issue, a number of companies provide software, known as *IP Address Management (IPAM)*, that includes at a minimum a DHCP server and a DNS server that are specially designed to work together to administer IP addresses for a network. Windows Server deploys IPAM, for example. You'll find it used to support SQL databases, from MySQL to Oracle to Microsoft SQL Server.

Troubleshooting DNS

As I mentioned earlier, most DNS problems result from a problem with the client systems. This is because DNS servers rarely go down, and if they do, most clients have a secondary DNS server setting that enables them to continue to resolve DNS names. DNS servers have been known to fail, however, so knowing when the problem is the client system, and when you can complain to the person in charge of your DNS server, is important. All of the tools you're about to see come with every operating system that supports TCP/IP, with the exception of the `ipconfig` commands, which I'll mention when I get to them.

So how do you know when to suspect DNS is causing the problem on your network? Well, just about everything you do on an IP network depends on DNS to find the right system to talk to for whatever job the application does. E-mail clients use DNS to find their e-mail servers; FTP clients use DNS for their servers; Web browsers use DNS to find Web servers; and so on. The first clue something is wrong is generally when a user calls, saying he's getting a "server not found" error. Server not found errors look different depending on the application, but you can count on something being there that says in effect "server not found." Figure 9-41 shows how this error appears in an FTP client.

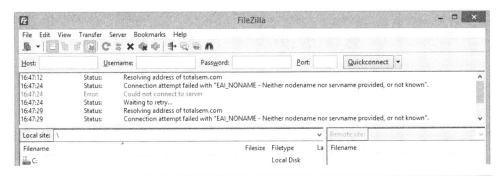

Figure 9-41   DNS error

Before you start testing, you need to eliminate any DNS caches on the local system. If you're running Windows, run the **ipconfig /flushdns** command now.

Your best friend when testing DNS is *ping*. Run ping from a command prompt, followed by the name of a well-known Web site, such as `ping www.microsoft.com`. Watch the output carefully to see if you get an IP address. You may get a "request timed out" message, but that's fine; you just want to see if DNS is resolving FQDNs into IP addresses (Figure 9-42).

 EXAM TIP   When troubleshooting, ping is your friend. If you can ping an IP address but not the name associated with that address, check DNS.

If you get a "server not found" error, you need to ping again using just an IP address. If ping works with the IP address but not with the Web site name, you know you have a DNS problem.

Once you've determined that DNS is the problem, check to make sure your system has the correct DNS server entry. Again, this information is something you should keep around. I can tell you the DNS server IP address for every Internet link I own—two in the office, one at the house, plus two dial-ups I use on the road. You don't have to memorize the IP addresses, but you should have all the critical IP information written down. If that isn't the problem, run `ipconfig /all` to see if those DNS settings are the same as the ones in the server; if they aren't, you may need to refresh your DHCP settings. I'll show you how to do that next.

```
C:\>ipconfig /flushdns

Windows IP Configuration

Successfully flushed the DNS Resolver Cache.

C:\>ping www.totalsem.com

Pinging www.totalsem.com [216.40.231.195] with 32 bytes of data:
Reply from 216.40.231.195: bytes=32 time=24ms TTL=54
Reply from 216.40.231.195: bytes=32 time=20ms TTL=54
Reply from 216.40.231.195: bytes=32 time=20ms TTL=54
Reply from 216.40.231.195: bytes=32 time=24ms TTL=54

Ping statistics for 216.40.231.195:
    Packets: Sent = 4, Received = 4, Lost = 0 (0% loss),
Approximate round trip times in milli-seconds:
    Minimum = 20ms, Maximum = 24ms, Average = 22ms

C:\>
```

Figure 9-42   Using ping to check DNS

If you have the correct DNS settings for your DNS server and the DNS settings in `ipconfig /all` match those settings, you can assume the problem is with the DNS server itself. The *nslookup* (name server lookup) tool enables DNS server queries. All operating systems have a version of nslookup.

EXAM TIP   Make sure you know how to use nslookup to determine if a DNS server is active!

You run `nslookup` from a command prompt. With nslookup, you can (assuming you have the permission) query all types of information from a DNS server and change how your system uses DNS. Although most of these commands are far outside the scope of the CompTIA Network+ exam, you should definitely know nslookup. For instance, just running `nslookup` alone from a command prompt shows you some output similar to the following:

```
C:\>nslookup
Default Server:  totalhomedc2.totalhome
Address:  192.168.4.155
>
```

Running `nslookup` gives me the IP address and the name of my default DNS server. If I got an error at this point, perhaps a "server not found" error, I would know that either my primary DNS server is down or I might not have the correct DNS server information in my DNS settings. I can attach to any DNS server by typing **server**, followed by the IP address or the domain name of the DNS server:

```
> server totalhomedc1
Default Server:  totalhomedc1.totalhome
Addresses:  192.168.4.157, 192.168.4.156
```

This new server has two IP addresses; it has two multihomed NICs to ensure there's a backup in case one NIC fails. If I get an error on one DNS server, I use `nslookup` to check for another DNS server. I can then switch to that server in my TCP/IP settings as a temporary fix until my DNS server is working again.

Those using UNIX/Linux have an extra DNS tool called *domain information groper (dig)*. The dig tool is very similar to nslookup, but it runs noninteractively. In nslookup, you're in the command until you type **exit**; nslookup even has its own prompt. The dig tool, on the other hand, is not interactive—you ask it a question, it answers the question, and it puts you back at a regular command prompt. When you run `dig`, you tend to get a large amount of information. The following is a sample of a `dig` command run from a Linux prompt:

```
[mike@localhost]$dig -x 13.65.14.4
; <<>> DiG 8.2 <<>> -x
;; res options: init recurs defnam dnsrch
;; got answer:
;; ->>HEADER<<- opcode: QUERY, status: NOERROR, id: 4
;; flags: qr aa rd ra; QUERY: 1, ANSWER: 1, AUTHORITY: 2,
ADDITIONAL: 2
;; QUERY SECTION:
;;      4.14.65.13.in-addr.arpa, type = ANY, class = IN
;; ANSWER SECTION:
4.14.65.13.in-addr.arpa.   4H IN PTR
server3.houston.totalsem.com.
;; AUTHORITY SECTION:
65.14.4.in-addr.arpa.   4H IN NS   kernel.risc.uni-linz.ac.at.
65.14.4.in-addr.arpa.   4H IN NS   kludge.risc.uni-linz.ac.at.
;; ADDITIONAL SECTION:
kernel.risc.uni-linz.ac.at.   4H IN A   193.170.37.225
kludge.risc.uni-linz.ac.at.   4H IN A   193.170.37.224
;; Total query time: 1 msec
;; FROM: kernel to SERVER: default - 127.0.0.1
;; WHEN: Thu Feb 10 18:03:41 2000
;; MSG SIZE  sent: 44  rcvd: 180
[mike@localhost]$
```

SIM   Check out the excellent Chapter 9 "Name Resolution" Type! over at **http://totalsem.com/007**. Working with the command line is cool!

Diagnosing TCP/IP Networks

I've dedicated all of Chapter 21, "Network Troubleshooting," to network diagnostic procedures, but TCP/IP has a few little extras that I want to talk about here. TCP/IP is a pretty robust protocol, and in good networks, it runs like a top for years without problems. Most of the TCP/IP problems you'll see come from improper configuration, so I'm going to assume you've run into problems with a new TCP/IP install, and I'll show you some classic screw-ups common in this situation. I want to concentrate on making sure you can ping anyone you want to ping.

I've done thousands of IP installations over the years, and I'm proud to say that, in most cases, they worked right the first time. My users jumped on the newly configured systems, fired up their My Network Places/Network, e-mail software, and Web browsers, and were last seen typing away, smiling from ear to ear. But I'd be a liar if I didn't also admit that plenty of setups didn't work so well. Let's start with the hypothetical case of a user who can't see something on the network. You get a call: "Help!" he cries. The first troubleshooting point to remember here: it doesn't matter *what* he can't see. It doesn't matter if he can't see other systems in his network or can't see the home page on his browser—you go through the same steps in any event.

Remember to use common sense wherever possible. If the problem system can't ping by DNS name, but all the other systems can, is the DNS server down? Of course not! If something—*anything*—doesn't work on one system, *always* try it on another one to determine whether the problem is specific to one system or affects the entire network.

One thing I always do is check the network connections and protocols. I'm going to cover those topics in greater detail later in the book, so, for now, assume the problem systems are properly connected and have good protocols installed. Here are some steps to take:

1. *Diagnose the NIC.* If you're lucky enough to own a higher-end NIC that has its own Control Panel applet, use the diagnostic tool to see if the NIC is working.

2. *Check your NIC's driver.* Replace if necessary.

3. *Diagnose locally.* If the NIC's okay, diagnose locally by pinging a few neighboring systems by both IP address and DNS name. If you're using NetBIOS, use the net view command to see if the other local systems are visible (Figure 9-43). If you can't ping by DNS, check your DNS settings. If you can't see the network using net view, you may have a problem with your NetBIOS settings.

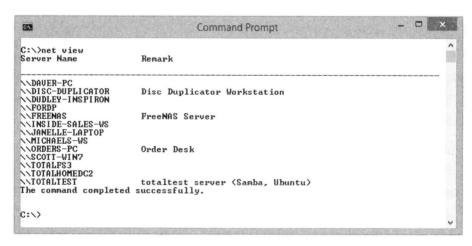

Figure 9-43 The net view command in action

4. *Check IP address and subnet mask.* If you're having a problem pinging locally, make sure you have the right IP address and subnet mask. Oh, if I had a nickel for every time I entered those incorrectly! If you're on DHCP, try renewing the lease—sometimes that does the trick. If DHCP fails, call the person in charge of the server.

5. *Run netstat.* At this point, another little handy program comes into play called *netstat*. The netstat program offers a number of options. The two handiest ways to run `netstat` are with no options at all and with the `-s` option. Running netstat with no options shows you all the current connections to your system. Look for a connection here that isn't working with an application— that's often a clue to an application problem, such as a broken application or a sneaky application running in the background. Figure 9-44 shows a `netstat` command running.

```
Select Command Prompt
C:\>netstat

Active Connections

  Proto  Local Address          Foreign Address        State
  TCP    127.0.0.1:1046         michaels-ws:5354       ESTABLISHED
  TCP    127.0.0.1:1047         michaels-ws:5354       ESTABLISHED
  TCP    127.0.0.1:5354         michaels-ws:1046       ESTABLISHED
  TCP    127.0.0.1:5354         michaels-ws:1047       ESTABLISHED
  TCP    127.0.0.1:7526         michaels-ws:27015      ESTABLISHED
  TCP    127.0.0.1:7537         michaels-ws:7538       ESTABLISHED
  TCP    127.0.0.1:7538         michaels-ws:7537       ESTABLISHED
  TCP    127.0.0.1:7688         michaels-ws:7689       ESTABLISHED
  TCP    127.0.0.1:7689         michaels-ws:7688       ESTABLISHED
  TCP    127.0.0.1:11308        michaels-ws:19872      ESTABLISHED
  TCP    127.0.0.1:19872        michaels-ws:11308      ESTABLISHED
  TCP    127.0.0.1:27015        michaels-ws:7526       ESTABLISHED
  TCP    192.168.4.27:7517      sinwns2012211:https    ESTABLISHED
  TCP    192.168.4.27:7539      74.125.198.125:5222    ESTABLISHED
  TCP    192.168.4.27:7546      74.125.198.125:5222    ESTABLISHED
  TCP    192.168.4.27:7547      xmpp-shv-04-frc3:5222  ESTABLISHED
  TCP    192.168.4.27:7550      bos-m003c-rdr2:https   ESTABLISHED
```

Figure 9-44 The `netstat` command in action

6. *Run netstat –s.* Running `netstat` with the `-s` option displays several statistics that can help you diagnose problems. For example, if the display shows you are sending but not receiving, you almost certainly have a bad cable with a broken receive wire.

 NOTE `netstat` can display the executable the connection goes to using the `-b` option. This requires elevated privileges, but is better than `-s`.

7. *Diagnose to the gateway.* If you can't get on the Internet, check to see if you can ping the router. Remember, the router has two interfaces, so try both: first the local interface (the one on your subnet) and then the one to the Internet. You *do* have both of those IP addresses memorized, don't you? You should! If not, run `ipconfig` to display the LAN interface address.

8. If you can't ping the router, either it's down or you're not connected to it. If you can only ping the near side, something in the router itself is messed up, like the routing table.

9. *Diagnose to the Internet.* If you can ping the router, try to ping something on the Internet. If you can't ping one address, try another—it's always possible that the first place you try to ping is down. If you still can't get through, you can try to locate the problem using the *traceroute* (trace route)utility. Run `tracert` to mark out the entire route the ping packet traveled between you and whatever you were trying to ping. It may even tell you where the problem lies (see Figure 9-45).

```
                                          Command Prompt                           – □ ×

C:\>tracert 216.40.231.195

Tracing route to totalsem.com [216.40.231.195]
over a maximum of 30 hops:

  1    <1 ms    <1 ms    <1 ms  Router.totalhome [192.168.4.1]
  2    11 ms     8 ms    10 ms  96.120.17.193
  3    66 ms     7 ms     8 ms  68.85.249.209
  4    10 ms     9 ms    10 ms  ae-4-0-ar01.bearcreek.tx.houston.comcast.net [68.85.87.145]
  5    20 ms    15 ms    15 ms  68.86.166.229
  6    17 ms    20 ms    18 ms  pos-0-1-0-0-pe01.1950stemmons.tx.ibone.comcast.net [68.86.86.94]

  7    20 ms    16 ms    17 ms  ae10.bbr01.eq01.dal03.networklayer.com [75.149.228.34]
  8    20 ms    19 ms    20 ms  ae0.bbr01.sr02.hou02.networklayer.com [173.192.18.219]
  9    22 ms    24 ms    19 ms  po31.dsr01.hstntx2.networklayer.com [173.192.18.233]
 10    21 ms    24 ms    20 ms  po1.car02.hstntx2.networklayer.com [74.55.252.70]
 11    20 ms    19 ms    19 ms  totalsem.com [216.40.231.195]

Trace complete.

C:\>
```

Figure 9-45   Using `tracert`

Chapter Review

Questions

1. NetBIOS uses what type of name space?

   A. Hierarchical name space

   B. People name space

   C. DNS name space

   D. Flat name space

2. The DNS root directory is represented by what symbol?

   A. . (dot)

   B. / (forward slash)

   C. \ (back slash)

   D. $ (dollar sign)

3. What command do you run to see the DNS cache on a Windows system?

    A. `ping /showdns`

    B. `ipconfig /showdns`

    C. `ipconfig /displaydns`

    D. `ping /displaydns`

4. The users on your network haven't been able to connect to the server for 30 minutes. You check and reboot the server, but you're unable to ping either its own loopback address or any of your client systems. What should you do?

    A. Restart the DHCP server.

    B. Restart the DNS server.

    C. Replace the NIC on the server because it has failed.

    D. Have your users ping the server.

5. A user calls to say she can't see the other systems on the network when she looks in My Network Places. You are not using NetBIOS. What are your first two troubleshooting steps? (Select two.)

    A. Ping the address of a known Web site.

    B. Ping the loopback address to test her NIC.

    C. Ping several neighboring systems using both DNS names and IP addresses.

    D. Ping the IP addresses of the router.

6. What is checked first when trying to resolve an FQDN to an IP address?

    A. hosts file

    B. LMHOSTS file

    C. DNS server

    D. WINS server

7. Which type of DNS record is used by mail servers to determine where to send e-mail?

    A. A record

    B. CNAME record

    C. MX record

    D. SMTP record

8. Running which command enables you to reset the DNS cache?

    A. `ipconfig`

    B. `ipconfig /all`

    C. `ipconfig /dns`

    D. `ipconfig /flushdns`

9. Running which command enables you to query the functions of a DNS server?

   A. `ipconfig`

   B. `nslookup`

   C. `ping`

   D. `xdns`

10. Where does a DNS server store the IP addresses and FQDNs for the computers within a domain?

   A. Forward lookup zone

   B. Canonical zone

   C. MX record

   D. SMTP record

Answers

1. **D.** NetBIOS uses a flat name space whereas DNS servers use a hierarchical name space.

2. **A.** The DNS root directory is represented by a dot (.).

3. **C.** To see the DNS cache on a Windows system, run the command `ipconfig /displaydns` at a command prompt.

4. **C.** You should replace the server's NIC because it's bad. It doesn't need either DNS or DHCP to ping its loopback address. Having the users ping the server is also pointless, as you already know they can't connect to it.

5. **B** and **C.** Your first two troubleshooting steps are to ping the loopback address to check the client's NIC, and then to ping neighboring systems. If the NIC and the local network check out, then you might try pinging the router and a Web site, but those are later steps.

6. **A.** The hosts file is checked first when trying to resolve an FQDN to an IP address.

7. **C.** The MX record is used by mail servers to determine where to send e-mail.

8. **D.** Running the command `ipconfig /flushdns` resets the DNS cache.

9. **B.** The tool to use for querying DNS server functions is nslookup.

10. **A.** A DNS server stores the IP addresses and FQDNs for the computers within a domain in the forward lookup zone.

## CHAPTER 10

Securing TCP/IP

The CompTIA Network+ certification exam expects you to know how to

- 1.1 Explain the purposes and uses of ports and protocols
- 2.3 Explain the purposes and use cases for advanced networking devices
- 3.4 Given a scenario, use remote access methods
- 4.2 Explain authentication and access controls
- 4.5 Given a scenario, implement network device hardening

To achieve these goals, you must be able to

- Discuss the standard methods for securing TCP/IP networks
- Compare TCP/IP security standards
- Implement secure TCP/IP applications

If you want to enter the minds of the folks who invented TCP/IP, Vint Cerf and Bob Kahn, look at TCP/IP from a security perspective. TCP/IP wasn't designed with any real security in mind. Oh sure, you can put user names and passwords on FTP, Telnet, and other TCP/IP applications, but everything else is basically wide open. Perhaps Cerf and Kahn thought the intent of the Internet was openness?

Sadly, today's world reveals a totally different perspective. Every device with a public IP address on the Internet is constantly bombarded with malicious packets trying to gain some level of access to our precious data. Even data moving between two hosts is relatively easily intercepted and read. Bad guys make millions by stealing our data in any of hundreds of thousands of different ways, and TCP/IP in its original form is all but powerless to stop them. Luckily for us, Cerf and Kahn gave TCP/IP a tremendous amount of flexibility, which over time has enabled developers to add substantial security to pretty much anything you want to send in an IP packet.

This chapter takes you on a tour of the many ways smart people have improved TCP/IP to protect our data from those who wish to do evil things to or with it. It's an interesting story of good intentions, knee-jerk reactions, dead ends, and failed attempts that luckily ends with a promise of easy-to-use protocols that protect our data.

This chapter examines the ways to make TCP/IP data and networks secure. I'll first give you a look at security concepts and then turn to specific standards and protocols used to implement security. The chapter wraps with a discussion on secure TCP/IP applications and their methods.

Test Specific

Making TCP/IP Secure

I break down TCP/IP security into five areas: encryption, integrity, nonrepudiation, authentication, and authorization.

Encryption means to scramble, mix up, or change data in such a way that bad guys can't read it. Of course, this scrambled-up data must also be easily descrambled by the person receiving the data.

Integrity is the process that guarantees that the data received is the same as originally sent. Integrity is designed to cover situations in which someone intercepts your data on-the-fly and makes changes.

Nonrepudiation means that a person cannot deny he or she took a specific action. Mike sends a message; that message can be traced back specifically to Mike.

Authentication means to verify that whoever is trying to access the data is the person you want accessing that data. The most classic form of authentication is the user name and password combination, but there are plenty more ways to authenticate.

Authorization defines what an authenticated person can do with that data. Different operating systems and applications provide different schemes for authorization, but the classic scheme for Windows is to assign permissions to a user account. An administrator, for example, can do a lot more after being authenticated than a limited user can do.

Encryption, integrity, nonrepudiation, authentication, and authorization may be separate issues, but they overlap a lot in TCP/IP security practices. If you send a user name and password over the Internet, wouldn't it be a good idea to encrypt the user name and password so others can't read it? Similarly, if you send someone a "secret decoder ring" over the Internet so she can unscramble the encryption, wouldn't it be a good idea for the recipient to know that the decoder ring actually came from you? In TCP/IP security, you have protocols that combine encryption, integrity, nonrepudiation (sometimes), authentication, and authorization to create complete security solutions for one TCP/IP application or another.

Encryption

All data on your network is nothing more than ones and zeroes. Identifying what type of data the strings of ones and zeroes in a packet represent usually is easy. A packet of data on the Internet often comes with a port number, for example, so a bad guy quickly knows what type of data he's reading.

All data starts as *plaintext*, a somewhat misleading term that simply means the data is in an easily read or viewed industry-wide standard format. Plaintext, often also referred to as *cleartext*, implies that all data starts off as text—untrue! Data often is text, but it also might be a binary file such as a photograph or an executable program. Regardless of the type of data, it all starts as plaintext. I'll use the image in Figure 10-1 as a universal figure for a piece of plaintext.

Figure 10-1
Plaintext

If you want to take some data and make figuring out what it means difficult for other people, you need a cipher. A *cipher* is a general term for a way to encrypt data. An *algorithm* is the mathematical formula that underlies the cipher.

Substitution

One of the earliest forms of cryptography we know about uses *substitution*, swapping letters of the alphabet for other letters of the alphabet. How early? Julius Caesar used substitution to secure communication during his military campaigns, thus this kind of encryption is often called a *Caesar cipher*. Here's how it works.

See if you can crack the following code:

```
WKH TXLFN EURZQ IRA MXPSV RYHU WKH ODCB GRJ
```

This is a classic example of the Caesar cipher. You just take the letters of the alphabet and transpose them:

```
Real Letter: ABCDEFGHIJKLMNOPQRSTUVWXYZ
Code letter: DEFGHIJKLMNOPQRSTUVWXYZABC
```

Caesar ciphers are very easy to crack by using word patterns, frequency analysis, or brute force. The code "WKH" shows up twice, which means it's the same word (*word patterns*). The letters *W* and *H* show up fairly often too. Certain letters of the alphabet are used more than others, so a code-breaker can use that to help decrypt the code (*frequency analysis*). Assuming that you know this is a Caesar cipher, a computer can quickly go through every different code possibility and determine the answer (*brute force*). Incredibly, even though it's not as obvious, binary code also suffers from the same problem.

So let's solve the code:

W=T; K=H; H=E; first word: The
T=Q; X=U; L=I; F=C; N=K; second word: quick
E=B; U=R; R=O; Z=W; Q=N; third word: brown

Get it yet? The full text is "The quick brown fox jumps over the lazy dog." Use this simple Caesar cipher to amaze your friends and family, and baffle your instructors!

Substitution is used in modern computing encryption, although in a much more sophisticated way than in a Caesar cipher. Let's go on.

XOR

Let's say you have a string of ones and zeroes that looks like this:

```
01001101010010010100101101000101
```

This string may not mean much to you, but if it was part of an HTTP segment, your Web browser would instantly know that this is Unicode—that is, numbers representing letters and other characters—and convert it into text:

```
01001101 01001001 01001011 01000101
M        I        K        E
```

So let's create a cipher to encrypt this cleartext. All binary encryption requires some interesting binary math. You could do something really simple such as add 1 to every value (and ignore carrying the 1):

```
0 + 1 = 1 and 1 + 1 = 0 10110010101101101011010010111010
```

No big deal; that just reversed the values. Any decent hacker would see the pattern and break this code in about three seconds. Let's try something harder to break by bringing in a second value (a key) of any eight binary numbers (let's use 10101010 for this example) and doing some math to every eight binary values using this algorithm:

If cleartext is...	And key value is...	Then the result is...
0	0	0
0	1	1
1	0	1
1	1	0

This is known as a binary *XOR (eXclusive OR)*. Line up the key against the first eight values in the cleartext:

```
10101010
01001101010010010100101101000101
11100111
```

Then do the next eight binary values:

```
1010101010101010
01001101010010010100101101000101
1110011111100011
```

Then the next eight:

```
101010101010101010101010
01001101010010010100101101000101
111001111110001111100001
```

Then the final eight:

```
1010101010101010101010101010101010
0100110101001001010010110_1000101_
1110011111100011111000011_11101111_
```

If you want to decrypt the data, you need to know the algorithm and the key. This is a very simple example of how to encrypt binary data. At first glance, you might say this is good encryption, but the math is simple, and a simple XOR is easy for someone to decrypt. An XOR works with letters as well as numbers.

In computing, you need to make a cipher hard for anyone to break, yet make it accessible to the people you want to read the data. Luckily, computers do more complex algorithms very quickly (it's just math), and you can use longer keys to make the code much harder to crack.

Okay, let's take the information above and generate some more symbols to show this process. When you run cleartext through a cipher algorithm using a key, you get what's called *ciphertext* (Figure 10-2).

Figure 10-2
Encryption
process

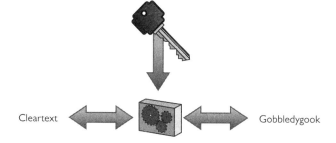

Cleartext ⬌ Gobbledygook

Over the years, computing people have developed hundreds of different complete algorithms for use in encrypting binary data. Of these, only a few were or still are commonly used in TCP/IP networks. The math behind all of these complete algorithms is incredibly complex and way beyond the scope of the CompTIA Network+ exam, but all of them have two items in common: a complex algorithm underlying the cipher and a key or keys used to encrypt and decrypt the text.

Any encryption that uses the same key for both encryption and decryption is called symmetric-key encryption or a *symmetric-key algorithm*. If you want someone to decrypt what you encrypt, you have to make sure they have some tool that can handle the algorithm and you have to give them the key. Any encryption that uses different keys for encryption and decryption is called asymmetric-key encryption or an *asymmetric-key algorithm*. Let's look at symmetric-key encryption first, and then turn to asymmetric-key encryption.

Symmetric-Key Encryption

There is one difference among symmetric-key algorithms. Most algorithms are called *block ciphers* because they encrypt data in single "chunks" of a certain length at a time. Let's say you have a 100,000-byte Microsoft Word document you want to encrypt. One type of encryption will take 128-bit chunks and encrypt each one separately (Figure 10-3).

Block ciphers work well when data comes in clearly discrete chunks. Data crossing wired networks comes in IP packets, for example, so block ciphers are very popular with these sorts of packets.

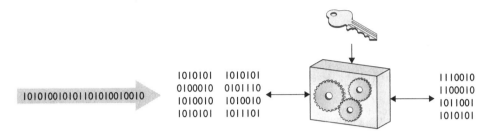

Figure 10-3 Block cipher

The granddaddy of all TCP/IP symmetric-key algorithms is the *Data Encryption Standard (DES)*. DES used a 64-bit block and a 56-bit key. Over time, the 56-bit key made DES susceptible to brute-force attacks. The computing industry came up with a number of derivatives of DES to try to address this issue, with names such as 3DES, International Data Encryption Algorithm (IDEA), and Blowfish.

The alternative to a block cipher is the much quicker *stream cipher*, which takes a single bit at a time and encrypts on-the-fly (Figure 10-4). Stream ciphers were very popular whenever data came in long streams (such as with older wireless networks or cell phones).

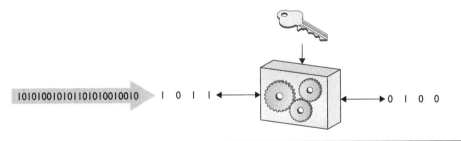

Figure 10-4 Stream cipher

Rivest Cipher 4 (RC4) was (and still is) pretty amazing: lightning fast, easy to use, and, most importantly, free. Created by Ron Rivest, RC4 quickly became the dominant stream cipher, used in wireless, Web pages, remote desktops … the list goes on and on. Unfortunately, starting around 2001 and continuing to 2013, a number of weaknesses were discovered in RC4, making the security industry lose trust in RC4 and creating a move to block ciphers that continues to this day. So even though some encryptions (wireless, HTTP, RDP) still support RC4, it's quickly being looked at as a legacy cipher. As a result, almost all TCP/IP applications have moved to *Advanced Encryption Standard (AES)* for symmetric cryptography.

NOTE RC4 found a home in wireless communication, which you'll see in Chapter 14, "Wireless Networking."

AES is a block cipher that uses a 128-bit block size and 128-, 192-, or 256-bit key size. AES is incredibly secure, practically uncrackable (for now at least), and so fast even applications that traditionally used stream ciphers are switching to AES.

Not at all limited to TCP/IP, you'll find AES used for many applications, from file encryption to wireless networking to Web sites that support newer versions of TLS. Many TCP/IP applications are still in the process of moving toward adoption.

EXAM TIP When in doubt on a question about symmetric encryption algorithms, always pick AES. You'll be right most of the time.

Asymmetric-Key Cryptography

Symmetric-key encryption has one serious weakness: anyone who gets a hold of the key can encrypt or decrypt data with it. The nature of symmetric-key encryption forces us to send the key to the other person in one way or another, making it a challenge to use symmetric-key encryption safely by itself. As a result, folks have been strongly motivated to create a methodology that allows the encrypter to send a symmetric key to the decrypter without fear of interception (Figure 10-5).

Figure 10-5
How do we safely deliver the key?

Sending...

The answer to the problem of key sharing came in the form of using two different keys—one to encrypt and one to decrypt, thus, an asymmetric-key algorithm.

Here's how *public-key cryptography*—the primary asymmetric implementation—works. Imagine two people, Mike and Melissa, who wish to establish an encrypted connection (Figure 10-6).

Before Melissa can send encrypted communication to Mike, Mike first generates *two* keys. One of these keys is kept on his computer (the *private* key), and the other key is sent to anyone from whom he wants to receive encrypted e-mail (the *public* key). These two

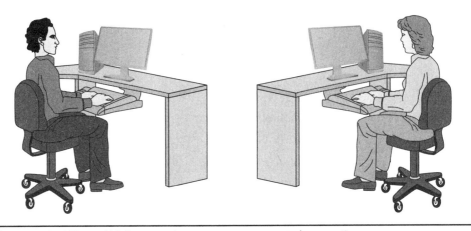

Figure 10-6　Mike and Melissa, wanting to create an encrypted connection

keys—called a *key pair*—are generated at the same time and are designed to work together. Data encrypted with the public key, for example, requires the private key for decryption, and vice versa.

Mike sends a copy of the public key to Melissa (Figure 10-7).

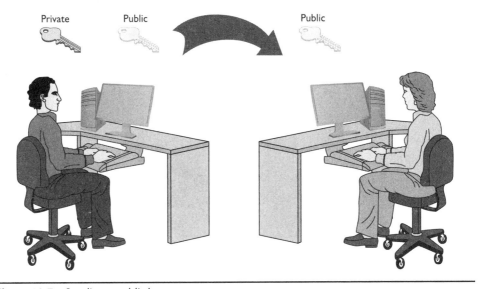

Figure 10-7　Sending a public key

Public-key cryptography today works by encrypting a symmetric key with a public key and then decrypting the symmetric key with a private key. The connection, once made, exchanges encrypted data using symmetric encryption.

NOTE   Most asymmetric cryptographic implementations today use *RSA* (for its creators—*Rivest, Shamir, and Adleman*). Other systems are out there, but RSA is the most common.

Encryption and the OSI Model

The process of encryption varies dramatically depending on what you want to encrypt. To make life a bit easier, let's look at how you encrypt using the OSI seven-layer model:

- **Layer 1**   No common encryption is done at this layer, until you get to some of the bigger WAN technologies, like SONET. We'll cover those in Chapter 14.

- **Layer 2**   No common encryption is done at this layer.

- **Layer 3**   Only one common protocol encrypts at Layer 3: IPsec. IPsec is typically implemented via software that encrypts the IP packet. A new outer packet completely encapsulates and encrypts the inner packet.

- **Layer 4**   Neither TCP nor UDP offers any encryption methods, so nothing happens security-wise at Layer 4.

- **Layers 5, 6, and 7**   Important encryption standards (such as SSL and TLS used in e-commerce) happen within these layers, but don't fit cleanly into the OSI model.

Integrity

It's important to us that we receive the same data that was sent. It's not too terribly hard for bad luck and bad players to maul our data, however, so we need tools to ensure our data has the integrity we need. There are a number of tools to do this, but the one of greatest interest for the CompTIA Network+ exam is the hash function.

Hash

In computer security, a *hash* (or more accurately, a *cryptographic hash function*) is a mathematical function that you run on a string of binary digits of any length that results in a value of some fixed length (often called a *checksum* or a *message digest*). No matter how long or how short the input, the hash's message digest will always be the same length (usually around 100 to 500 bits long, depending on the type of hash you use).

A cryptographic hash function is a one-way function. One-way means the hash is irreversible in that you cannot re-create the original data from the hash, even if you know the hashing algorithm and the checksum. A cryptographic hash function should also have a unique message digest for any two different input streams (Figure 10-8).

Figure 10-8
A hash at work

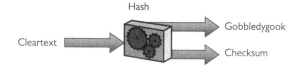

Cryptographic hash functions have a huge number of uses, but a common one is for verifying file integrity. If I'm downloading a file from a reputable source, there are two main threats to its integrity: accidental damage caused by networking/storage issues, and tampering by an attack that has compromised the site or my connection.

When the download provider hashes the contents of the file—called *file hashing*—and publishes the resulting message digest, I can hash the copy I downloaded and compare the digests to verify the file on my system is most-likely identical. This provides the best protection from accidental damage; an attacker capable of altering the file I download might also be able to alter the message digest published on the site. I can increase my confidence in its integrity by verifying the digest with more than one reputable source.

Operating systems and applications use hashes to store passwords on mass storage. It's not a good idea to store plaintext passwords, and encrypting a password always leaves a chance that a bad actor could crack them. So why not use a hash? When a user creates a password, the operating system hashes the password and only stores the hash. From then on, when anyone provides a password, the operating system just hashes the value entered and compares the hash to the stored hash. If they match, the password is correct.

There have been quite a few different hashing algorithms over the years. The first commonly used hash algorithm was called *Message-Digest Algorithm version 5*—best known as *MD5*. MD5 was introduced in 1991, creating a 128-bit message digest (Figure 10-9).

Figure 10-9
Using MD5

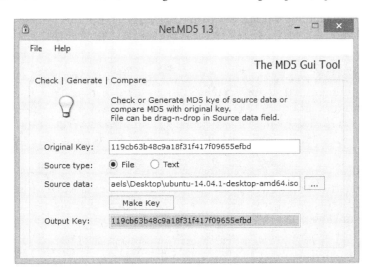

These days, *Secure Hash Algorithm (SHA)* is the primary family of cryptographic hash functions. It includes SHA-1, SHA-2, and SHA-3. SHA-1 produces a 160-bit message digest. SHA-2 has four variants (confusingly dropping the -2 in the name), all producing different-sized message digests:

- **SHA-224**   SHA-2 with a 224-bit message digest
- **SHA-256**   SHA-2 with a 256-bit message digest
- **SHA-384**   SHA-2 with a 384-bit message digest
- **SHA-512**   SHA-2 with a 512-bit message digest

One thing to keep in mind about cryptographic functions is that we err on the side of caution. Once someone demonstrates a practical attack against an algorithm, recommendations shift quickly to newer functions with improved security. Still, existing uses of the old functions can linger for a long time.

As the result of a number of attacks, MD5 and SHA-1 have both ended up on this list of hash functions that are no longer recommended as safe. Because of their popularity, you're likely to run into these in the wild or see them on the CompTIA Network+ exam, but don't use them in the real world.

Right now SHA-2 is the most popular hash algorithm used and SHA-2 continues to resist any attacks. Yet it's never a bad idea to keep making hashes more robust. To that end, the US National Institute of Standards (NIST) adopted a new family of hash algorithms called SHA-3. Like SHA-2, SHA-3 comes in a few variants, each with a different message digest length (and adding a "3" to make it less confusing). The most common SHA-3 variants are SHA3-224, SHA3-256, SHA3-384 and SHA3-512.

Try This!

Is This the File I Think It Is?

Let's download a common program—the latest version of Mozilla's Firefox browser—and use the trustworthy hash functions that come with our operating system to confirm our copy matches the hashes Mozilla has published. We'll use the SHA-512 algorithm for this exercise.

1. Download a copy of the latest Firefox (for Windows 32-bit, English language) from https://download.mozilla.org/?product=firefox-latest&os=win&lang=en-US, but don't install it when the download completes.

2. Make sure to note the version you have downloaded.

3. Navigate to https://download-origin.cdn.mozilla.net/pub/firefox/releases/<version you downloaded> and look for the files ending with "SUMS". Each of these contains a long list of hashes computed using a given algorithm for all of the files in the directory. The part of the file name before "SUMS" specifies the algorithm used.

4. Click the SHA512SUMS file. The left-hand column contains hashes, and the right-hand column contains relative file paths.

5. The way we actually calculate the hash varies a bit from platform to platform. Pick your platform below and type the appropriate command, replacing `<filename>` with the name or path of the file downloaded in step 1.

(Continued)

Linux and macOS:

a. Open a terminal window and navigate to the directory you downloaded the file to.

b. At the prompt, type this command:

```
shasum -a 512 "<filename>"
```

c. This command will output a single line in the same format as the SHA512SUMS file. Select and copy the hash.

Windows 8 or newer:

a. Open Windows PowerShell—not to be confused with the regular Windows command line—and navigate to the directory you downloaded the file to.

b. At the PowerShell prompt, type this sequence of commands:

```
(Get-FileHash -Algorithm SHA512 '<filename>').hash | clip
```

c. This command generates and copies the hash directly to your clipboard.

6. Switch back to your browser and use **Find** to search the SHA512SUMS document for the hash you copied in step 4. If your file downloaded properly, you'll usually get a single match. Since there are unique installer files for different platforms and languages, the file path on the matched line should specify your platform, language, and the name of the file you downloaded in step 1 and hashed in step 4.

Many encryption and authentication schemes also use hashes. Granted, you won't actually see the hashes as they're used, but trust me: hashes are everywhere. For example, some SMTP servers use a special form of MD5, called *Challenge-Response Authentication Mechanism-Message Digest 5 (CRAM-MD5)*, as a tool for server authentication. (See the discussion of CHAP later in the "User Authentication Standards" section for details on how challenge-response works.) Now that you understand hashes, let's return to public-key cryptography and see how digital signatures provide nonrepudiation and make public-key cryptography even more secure.

 EXAM TIP Look for CRAM-MD5 to show up on the CompTIA Network+ exam as a tool for server authentication.

Nonrepudiation

Nonrepudiation, as mentioned earlier, simply means that a person cannot deny that he or she took a specific action. A big part of making TCP/IP secure is to provide methods that enable nonrepudiation. Several methods combine encryption and hashing to accomplish this goal. Probably the best example of nonrepudiation is a digital signature.

Digital Signatures

As mentioned earlier, public-key cryptography suffers from the risk that you might be getting a public key from someone who isn't who they say they are. To avoid this problem, you add a digital signature. A *digital signature* is a hash of the public key encrypted by the private key. The person with the matching public key decrypts the digital signature using the public key, generates their own hash, and compares it to the decrypted hash to verify it came from the intended sender. Digital signatures are very popular with e-mail users. Figure 10-10 shows an e-mail message being both encrypted and digitally signed in Mozilla Thunderbird.

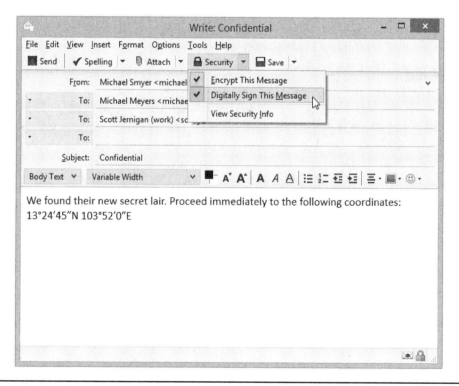

Figure 10-10 Digitally signed

PKI

Digital signatures are great, but what happens when you want to do business with some-one you do not know? Before you enter a credit card number to buy that new USB 3.0 Blu-ray Disc player, wouldn't you like to know that the Web site you are doing business with truly is eBay? To address that need the industry came up with the idea of certificates. A *certificate* is a standardized type of file that includes a public key with a digital signature, and the digital signature of a trusted third party—a person or a company that guaran-tees that who is passing out this certificate truly is who they say they are. As you might imagine, certificates are incredibly common with secure Web pages. When you go to eBay to sign in, your browser redirects to a secure Web page. These are easy to identify by the lock icon at the bottom of the screen or in the address bar (Figure 10-11) or the https:// used (instead of http://) in the address bar.

Figure 10-11   Secure Web page

EXAM TIP If you see https:// or a small lock icon, you are most likely on a secure Web site.

In the background, several actions take place (all before the secure Web page loads). First, the Web server automatically sends a copy of its certificate. Built into that certificate is the Web server's public key and a signature from the third party that guarantees this is really eBay. Go to your national version of eBay (I'm in the United States, so I'll use eBay.com) and click **Sign In** (you don't even need an eBay account to do this). Now look at the certificate for the current session. Depending on the Web browser you use, you'll see it in different ways. Try clicking the little lock icon in the address bar as this usually works. Figure 10-12 shows the certificate for this session.

Figure 10-12
eBay sign-in
certificate

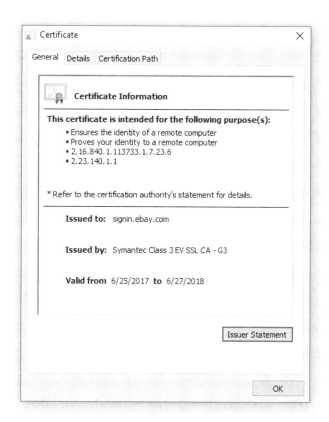

So a company called Symantec issued this certificate. That's great, but how does your computer check all this? Symantec is a certificate authority (CA). Every Web browser keeps a list of certificate authority certificates that it checks against when it receives a digital certificate. Figure 10-13 shows the certificate authority certificates stored on my system.

Figure 10-13
Certificate
authority
certificates on
a system

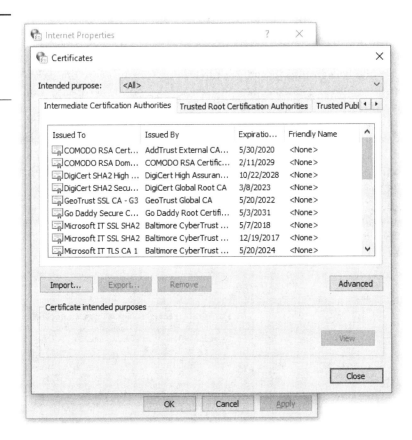

 NOTE Becoming a root certificate authority with enough respect to have
Web browsers install your certificate is very difficult!

When someone wants to create a secure Web site, he or she buys a certificate signed by
a certificate authority, such as Comodo (the biggest player in the market and the one I'll
use for this example). Comodo acts as the root, and the new Web site's certificate contains
Comodo's signature. For more advanced situations, Comodo includes an intermediate
certificate authority between Comodo's root certificate authority and the user's certificate. This creates a tree of certificate authorization, with the root authorities at the top
and issued certificates at the bottom.

You can also have intermediate authorities, although these are not as heavily used.
Together, this organization is called a *public-key infrastructure (PKI)* (Figure 10-14).

You don't have to use PKI to use certificates. First, you can create your own unsigned
certificates. These are perfectly fine for lower-security situations (e-mail among friends,

Figure 10-14

Comodo's PKI
tree

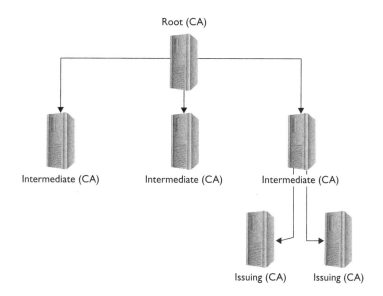

personal Web page, and so forth), but don't expect anyone to buy products on a Web site or send highly sensitive e-mail without a signed certificate from a well-known certificate authority like Comodo, Symantec, or GoDaddy. Digital certificates and asymmetric cryptography are closely linked because digital certificates verify the ownership of public keys.

NOTE   Almost all e-mail clients support encryption—you just need to get a certificate. If you want to start playing with e-mail encryption and signing, grab a free personal e-mail certificate from any of a number of different providers. Check out Comodo at www.instantssl.com/ssl-certificate-products/free-email-certificate.html. Instructions for certificate generation and installation are on the respective Web sites.

Authentication

As mentioned at the beginning of this chapter, authentication is the process of positively identifying users trying to access data. The first exposure to authentication for most users is *local authentication*, coming across a login screen prompting you to enter a user name and password, to log into a Windows or macOS computer. But there are many other ways to authenticate, especially when networking is added into the mix. A network technician should understand not only how different authentication methods control user names and passwords, but also some of the authentication standards used in today's TCP/IP networks.

Passwords offer significant security challenges. What happens after you type in a user name and password? How is this data transferred? Who or what reads this? What is the data compared to? A series of TCP/IP security standards that use combinations of user names, passwords, and sometimes certificates, all handled in a usually secure manner, address these issues, as described in the upcoming section "TCP/IP Security Standards."

But you can't stop with user names and passwords. What if someone gets a hold of your user name and password? To defeat those types of bad guys, some systems require a second form of authentication. These second forms of authentication include items you carry, like a smart card. They might also be something that uniquely identifies you, such as your retinal patterns or fingerprints. We call these *biometrics*. Whatever the case, when you use passwords and one or more other forms of authentication, we call this *multifactor authentication* (or sometimes *two-factor authentication*).

Multifactor authentication means using two or more distinctly different methods for authentication. Generally, these methods fall into one of six categories, the first five of which you need to remember for the CompTIA Network+ exam:

- Something you know
- Something you have
- Something you are
- Somewhere you are
- Something you do
- Some when you are

Something you know is a user name, a password, a passphrase, or a personal identification number (PIN). Something you have, like a key fob you scan to get into your gym at night. Something you are indicates some distinguishing, unique characteristic, like the biometrics just mentioned.

Somewhere you are—the location factor—requires you to be in a space to authenticate. You might have to be at the computer in a specific office, for example.

Something you do is a little vague. Using a pattern to log into a smartphone, for example, is an action. (It's also something you know, so I'm not sure if that's what CompTIA wants on the exam.) A better example is writing your signature.

Some when you are, a temporal factor, isn't on the exam but factors into various authentication criteria. You could restrict access to a certain time of day, for example.

Authorization

A large part of the entire networking process involves one computer requesting something from another computer. A Web client might ask for a Web page, for example, or a Common Internet File System (CIFS) client might ask a file server for access to a folder. A computer far away might ask another computer for access to a private network. Whatever the case, you should carefully assign levels of access to your resources. This is authorization. To help define how to assign levels of access, you use an access control list.

EXAM TIP *Network access control (NAC)* defines a newer series of protection applications that combine the features of what traditionally was done by separate applications. There is no perfect single definition for NAC. There are, however, certain functions that a NAC often does. A NAC usually prevents computers lacking anti-malware and patches from accessing the network. NACs also create policies (their own policies, not Windows policies) that define what individual systems can do on the network, including network access, segregation of portions of the network, etc.

An *access control list (ACL)* is nothing more than a clearly defined list of permissions that specifies what an authenticated user may perform on a shared resource. Over the years the way to assign access to resources has changed dramatically. To help you to understand these changes, the security industry likes to use the idea of *ACL access models.* There are three types of ACL access models: mandatory, discretionary, and role based.

In a *mandatory access control (MAC)* security model, every resource is assigned a label that defines its security level. If the user lacks that security level, he or she does not get access. MAC is used in many operating systems to define what privileges programs have to other programs stored in RAM. The MAC security model is the oldest and least common of the three.

Discretionary access control (DAC) is based on the idea that a resource has an owner who may at his or her discretion assign access to that resource. DAC is considered much more flexible than MAC.

Role-based access control (RBAC) is the most popular model used in file sharing. RBAC defines a user's access to a resource based on the roles the user plays in the network environment. This leads to the idea of creating groups. A group in most networks is nothing more than a name that has clearly defined accesses to different resources. User accounts are placed into various groups. A network might have a group called "Sales" on a Web server that gives any user account that is a member of the Sales group access to a special Web page that no other groups can see.

Keep in mind that these three types of access control are models. Every TCP/IP application and operating system has its own set of rules that sometimes follows one of these models, but in many cases does not. But do make sure you understand these three models for the CompTIA Network+ exam!

TCP/IP Security Standards

Now that you have a conceptual understanding of encryption, integrity, nonrepudiation, authentication, and authorization, it's time to see how the TCP/IP folks have put it all together to create standards so you can secure just about anything in TCP/IP networks.

TCP/IP security standards are a rather strange mess. Some are authentication standards, some are encryption standards, and some are so unique to a single application that I'm not even going to talk about them in this section and instead will wait until the "Secure TCP/IP Applications" discussion at the end of this chapter. There's a reason for all this confusion: TCP/IP was never really designed for security. As you read through this section, you'll discover that almost all of these standards either predate the whole Internet, are slapped-together standards that have some serious issues, or, in the case of the most recent standards, are designed to combine a bunch of old, confusing standards. So hang tight—it's going to be a bumpy ride!

User Authentication Standards

Authentication standards are some of the oldest standards used in TCP/IP. Many are so old they predate the Internet itself. Once upon a time, nobody had fiber-optic, cable, or DSL connections to their ISPs. For the most part, if you wanted to connect to the Internet you had a choice: go to the computer center or use dial-up.

Dial-up, using telephone lines for the most part, predates the Internet, but the nerds of their day didn't want just anybody dialing into their computers. To prevent unauthorized access, they developed some excellent authentication methods that TCP/IP adopted for itself. A number of authentication methods were used back in these early days, but, for the most part, TCP/IP authentication started with something called the Point-to-Point Protocol.

PPP

Point-to-Point Protocol (PPP) enables two point-to-point devices to connect, authenticate with a user name and password, and negotiate the network protocol the two devices will use (Figure 10-15). Today that network protocol is almost always TCP/IP.

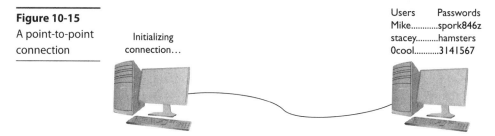

Figure 10-15
A point-to-point connection

Initializing connection...

Users   Passwords
Mike............spork846z
stacey..........hamsters
0cool...........3141567

PPP came with two methods of *user authentication*, the process of authenticating a user name and password. The original way—called *Password Authentication Protocol (PAP)*—simply transmits the user name and password over the connection in plaintext. Unfortunately, that means anyone who can tap the connection can learn the user name and password (Figure 10-16).

Figure 10-16
PAP in action

Initializing connection...

User: mike
Password: spork846z

Users   Passwords
Mike............spork846z
stacey..........hamsters
0cool...........3141567

Fortunately, PPP also includes the safer *Challenge Handshake Authentication Protocol (CHAP)* to provide a more secure authentication routine. CHAP relies on hashes based on a shared secret, usually a password that both ends of the connection know. When the initiator of the connection makes the initial connection request, the authenticator creates some form of challenge message. The initiator then makes a hash using the password and sends that to the authenticator. The authenticator, in turn, compares that value to its own hash calculation based on the password. If they match, the initiator is authenticated (Figure 10-17).

Figure 10-17
CHAP in action

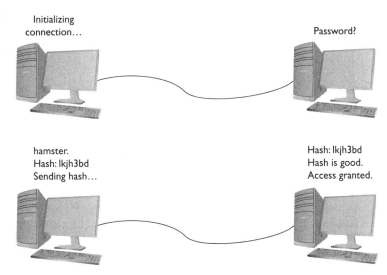

Initializing connection...

Password?

hamster.
Hash: lkjh3bd
Sending hash...

Hash: lkjh3bd
Hash is good.
Access granted.

Once the connection is up and running, CHAP keeps working by periodically repeating the entire authentication process. This prevents man-in-the-middle attacks, where a third party inserts an independent connection, intercepts traffic, reads or alters it, and then forwards it on without either the sender or recipient being aware of the intrusion.

CHAP works nicely because it never sends the actual password over the link. The CHAP standard leaves a number of issues undefined, however, like "If the hash doesn't match, what do I do?" The boom in dial-up connections to the Internet in the 1990s led Microsoft to invent a more detailed version of CHAP called *MS-CHAP*. The current version of MS-CHAP is called MS-CHAPv2. MS-CHAPv2 is still the most common authentication method for the few of us using dial-up connections. Believe it or not, dial-up is still being used, and even the latest operating systems support it. Figure 10-18 shows the dial-up connection options for Windows 10.

 EXAM TIP If you get a question on PAP, CHAP, and MS-CHAP on the CompTIA Network+ exam, remember that MS-CHAP offers the most security.

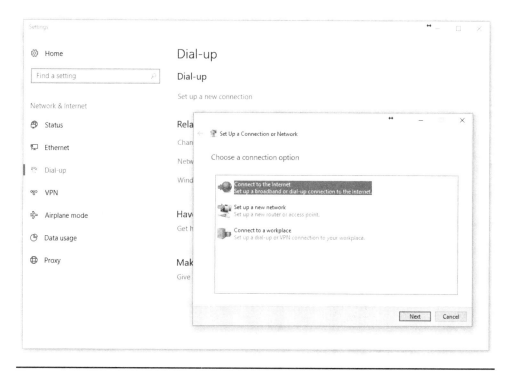

Figure 10-18   MS-CHAP is alive and well.

AAA

PPP does a great job of handling authentication for point-to-point connections, but it has some limitations. The biggest problem is that, in many cases, a network might have more than one point for an initiator to enter. PPP assumes that the authenticator at the endpoint has all the user name and password information, but that's not necessarily true. In traditional modem communication, for example, an ISP has a large bank of modems to support any number of users. When a user dials in, the modem bank provides the first available connection, but that means that any modem in the bank has to support any of the users. You can't put the database containing all user names and passwords on every modem (Figure 10-19).

In this use case, you need a central database of user names and passwords. That's simple enough, but it creates another problem—anyone accessing the network can see the passwords unless the data is somehow protected and encrypted (Figure 10-20). PPP is good at the endpoints, but once the data gets on the network, it's unencrypted.

Thus, the folks overseeing central databases full of user names and passwords needed to come up with standards to follow to protect that data. They first agreed upon a philosophy called *Authentication, Authorization, and Accounting (AAA)*. AAA is designed for

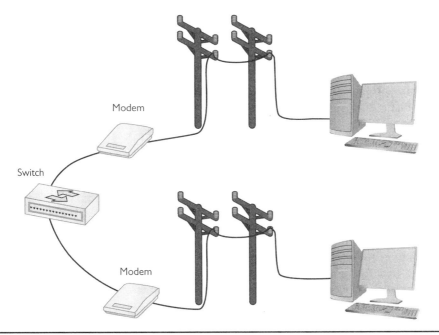

Figure 10-19 Where do you put the user names and passwords?

the idea of port authentication—the concept of allowing remote users authentication to a particular point of entry (a port) to another network.

- **Authentication** A computer that is trying to connect to the network must present some form of credential for access to the network. This credential most commonly starts with identification via a user name and password, which is then checked against a credentials database. If the credentials match up, the user is authenticated. User name and password are common for identification, but it might also be a security token such as a smart card, retinal scan, or digital certificate. It might even be a combination of some of these. The authentication gives the computer the right to access the network.

Figure 10-20
Central servers
are vulnerable to
attack.

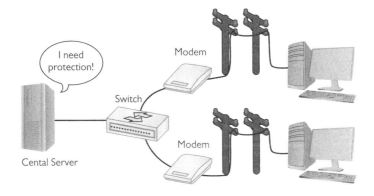

- **Authorization** Once authenticated, the computer determines what it can or cannot do on the network. It might only be allowed to use a certain amount of bandwidth. It might be limited to working only certain times of day or might be limited to using only a certain set of applications.

- **Accounting** The authenticating server should do some form of *auditing*, such as logging data traffic, session action, user bandwidth usage, and so on.

Once the idea of AAA took shape, those smart Internet folks developed two standards: RADIUS and TACACS+. Both standards offer authentication, authorization, and accounting.

RADIUS *Remote Authentication Dial-In User Service (RADIUS)* is the better known of the two AAA standards and, as its name implies, was created to support ISPs with hundreds if not thousands of modems in hundreds of computers to connect to a single central database. While originally designed for dial-up connections, RADIUS still works hard in a huge number of different types of networks, both wired and wireless, and I'm sure there are a few ancient dial-up networks still working somewhere as well. RADIUS consists of three devices: the RADIUS server that has access to a database of user names and passwords, a number of *network access servers (NASs)* that control the modems, and a group of systems that in some way connect to the network (Figure 10-21).

Figure 10-21
RADIUS setup

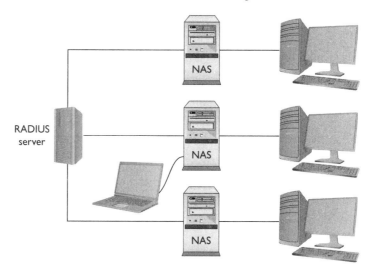

RADIUS server

NAS

NAS

NAS

 EXAM TIP NAS stands for either *network access server* or *network attached storage*. The latter is a type of dedicated file server used in many networks. Make sure you read the question to see which NAS it's looking for!

To use RADIUS, you need a RADIUS server. The most popular choice for Microsoft environments is *Internet Authentication Service (IAS)*. IAS comes built in with most versions of Microsoft Windows Server operating systems. For the UNIX/Linux crowd, the popular (yet, in my opinion, hard to set up) *FreeRADIUS* is the best choice. If you prefer a more prepackaged server, you might look at Pulse Secure's Steel-Belted RADIUS powerful and somewhat easy-to-set-up servers that many people feel are well worth the price tag.

A single RADIUS server can support multiple NASs and provide a complete PPP connection from the requesting system, through the NAS, all the way to the RADIUS server. Like any PPP connection, the RADIUS server supports PAP, CHAP, and MS-CHAP. Even if you use PAP, RADIUS hashes the password so at no time is the user name/password exposed. Newer versions of RADIUS support even more authentication methods, as you will soon see. RADIUS performs this authentication on either UDP ports 1812 and 1813 or UDP ports 1645 and 1646.

 EXAM TIP You might see the term *AAA/RADIUS server* on the CompTIA Network+ exam. It's more common to refer to RADIUS servers without the AAA, but as an implementation of AAA, putting the two together makes sense.

TACACS+ Routers and switches need administration. In a simple network, you can access the administration screen for each router and switch by entering a user name and password for each device. When a network becomes complex, with many routers and switches, logging into each device separately starts to become administratively messy. The answer is to make a single server store the ACL for all the devices in the network. To make this secure, you need to follow the AAA principles.

Terminal Access Controller Access Control System Plus (TACACS+) is a protocol developed by Cisco to support AAA in a network with many routers and switches. TACACS+ is very similar to RADIUS in function, but uses TCP port 49 by default and separates authorization, authentication, and accounting into different parts. TACACS+ uses PAP, CHAP, and MD5 hashes, but can also use something called Kerberos as part of the authentication scheme.

Kerberos

Up to this point almost all the authentication schemes I've discussed either are based on PPP or at least take the idea of PPP and expand upon it. Of course, every rule needs an exception and Kerberos is the exception here.

Kerberos is an authentication protocol that has no connection to PPP. Twenty years ago, some Internet folks began to appreciate that TCP/IP was not secure and thus designed Kerberos. Kerberos is an authentication protocol for TCP/IP networks with many clients all connected to a single authenticating server—no point-to-point here! Kerberos works nicely in a network, so nicely that Microsoft adopted it as the authentication protocol for all Windows networks using a domain controller.

Kerberos is the cornerstone of the all-powerful Microsoft Windows domain. Be careful here—the use of domains I'm about to describe has nothing to do with DNS. A Windows domain is a group of computers that defers all authentication to a *domain controller*, a special computer running some version of Windows Server (with the appropriate role installed).

The Windows domain controller stores a list of all user names and passwords. When you log on at a computer that is a member of a Windows domain, your user name and password go directly to the domain controller, which uses Kerberos for authentication.

 NOTE Kerberos uses UDP or TCP port 88 by default.

The cornerstone of Kerberos is the *Key Distribution Center (KDC)*, which has two processes: the *Authentication Server (AS)* and the Ticket-Granting Service (TGS). In Windows server environments, the KDC is installed on the domain controller (Figure 10-22).

Figure 10-22
Windows
Kerberos setup

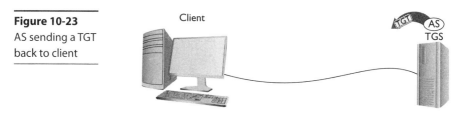

When your client logs onto the domain, it sends a request that includes a hash of the user name and password to the AS. The AS compares the results of that hash to its own hash (as it also stores the user name and password) and, if they match, sends a *Ticket-Granting Ticket (TGT)* and a timestamp (Figure 10-23). The ticket has a default lifespan in Windows of ten hours. The client is now authenticated but not yet authorized.

Figure 10-23
AS sending a TGT
back to client

 NOTE The TGT is sometimes referred to as *Ticket to Get Ticket*.

The client then sends the timestamped TGT to the TGS for authorization. The TGS sends a timestamped service ticket (also called a *token* or *access token*) back to the client (Figure 10-24).

This token is the key that the client uses to access any single resource on the entire domain. The access token contains the *security identifier (SID)* for the user's account, plus SIDs for the groups of which the user is a member. This is where authorization takes place.

Figure 10-24
TGS sending
token to client

Client

AS
(TGS)

The token authorizes the user to access resources without reauthenticating. Any time the client attempts to access a folder, printer, or service anywhere in the domain, the server sharing that resource uses the token to see exactly what access the client may have to that resource. If you try to access some other feature under Windows, such as retrieve your e-mail via Microsoft Exchange Server, you won't need to log in again. The ability to log in only one time and use the same token to access any resource (that you're allowed to access) on an entire network is called *single sign-on*.

Timestamping is important for Kerberos because it forces the client to request a new token every eight hours. This prevents third parties from intercepting the tokens and attempting to crack them. Kerberos tokens can be cracked, but it's doubtful this can be done in under eight hours.

Kerberos is very popular, but has some serious weaknesses. First, if the KDC goes down, no one has access. That's why Microsoft and other operating systems that use Kerberos always stress the importance of maintaining a backup KDC. In Windows, it is standard practice to have at least two domain controllers. Second, timestamping requires that all the clients and servers synchronize their clocks. This is fairly easy to do in a wired network (such as a Windows domain or even a bunch of connected switches or routers using TACACS+), but it adds an extra level of challenge in dispersed networks (such as those connected across the country).

NOTE Wireless networks use authentication protocols that differ from those of wired networks. Chapter 14 will explore the varieties of the Extensible Authentication Protocol (EAP) and the 802.1X standard.

I'm not done explaining authentication and authorization, but at least you now understand the basics of the popular authentication and authorization protocols and standards. You have more protocols to learn, but all of them are rather specialized for specific uses and thus are covered at various places throughout the book.

Encryption Standards

The Internet had authentication long before it had encryption. As a result, almost all encryption came out as a knee-jerk reaction to somebody realizing that his or her TCP/IP application wasn't secure. For years, there were new secure versions of just about every protocol in existence. New versions of all the classics started to appear, almost all starting with the word "Secure": Secure FTP, Secure SMTP, and even Secure POP were developed.

They worked, but there were still hundreds of not-yet-secured protocols and the specter of redoing all of them was daunting. Fortunately, some new, all-purpose encryption protocols were developed that enabled a client to connect to a server in a secure way while still using their older, unsecure protocols—and it all started because of Telnet.

SSH

The broad adoption of the Internet by the early 1990s motivated programmers to start securing their applications. Telnet had a big problem. It was incredibly useful and popular, but it was a completely unsecure protocol. Telnet credentials were (and are) sent in cleartext, an obvious vulnerability.

 NOTE SSH servers listen on TCP port 22.

Telnet needed to be fixed. As the story goes, Tatu Ylonen of the Helsinki University of Technology, reacting to an attack that intercepted Telnet user names and passwords on his network, invented a new *secure protocol* replacement for Telnet called *Secure Shell (SSH)*. You've already seen SSH in action (in Chapter 8, "TCP/IP Applications") as a secure version of Telnet, but now that you know more about security, let's look at scenario where you implement network device hardening via SSH.

SSH servers use PKI in the form of an RSA key. The first time a client tries to log into an SSH server, the server sends its public key to the client (Figure 10-25).

Figure 10-25
PuTTY getting an
RSA key

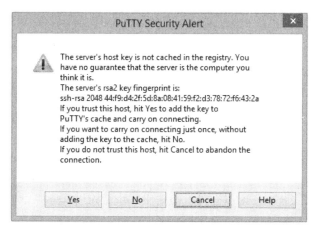

After the client receives this key, it creates a session ID, encrypts it using the public key, and sends it back to the server. The server decrypts this session ID and uses it in all data transfers going forward. Only the client and the server know this session ID. Next, the client and server negotiate the type of encryption to use for the session, generally AES. The negotiation for the cipher is automatic and invisible to the user.

Using RSA and a cipher makes a very safe connection, but the combination doesn't tell the server who is using the client. All SSH servers, therefore, add user names and passwords to authenticate the client (Figure 10-26). Once a user logs in with a user name and password, he or she has access to the system.

Figure 10-26

Users on an SSH server

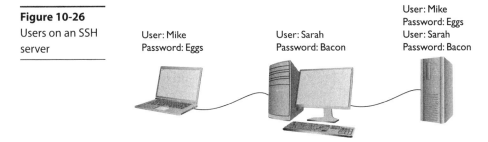

User: Mike
Password: Eggs

User: Sarah
Password: Bacon

User: Mike
Password: Eggs
User: Sarah
Password: Bacon

In addition to using a password for authentication, SSH also can use public keys to identify clients. This opens up some interesting possibilities such as noninteractive logins. You can also turn off password login altogether, hardening your server even further. To use public/private keys for authentication, you must first generate a pair of RSA or Digital Signature Algorithm (DSA) keys with a tool such as PuTTYgen (Figure 10-27). The public key is then copied to the server, and the private key is kept safe on the client.

Figure 10-27

Generated keys in PuTTYgen

When you connect to the server, your client generates a signature using its private key and sends it to the server. The server then checks the signature with its copy of the public key, and if everything checks out, you will be authenticated with the server.

If SSH stopped here as a secure replacement for Telnet, that would be fantastic, but SSH has another trick up its sleeve: the capability to act as a *tunnel* for *any* TCP/IP application. Let's see what tunnels are and how they work.

Tunneling

Simply, a *tunnel* is an encrypted link between two programs on two separate computers. Let's look at an SSH link between a server and a client. Once established, anything you enter into the client application is encrypted, sent to the server, decrypted, and then acted upon (Figure 10-28).

Figure 10-28
SSH in action

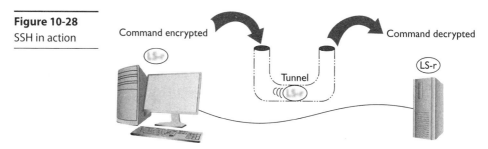

Command encrypted   Command decrypted

Tunnel

The nature of SSH is such that it took very little to extend the idea of SSH to accept input from any source, even another program (Figure 10-29). As long as the program can redirect to the SSH client and then the SSH server can redirect to the server application, anything can go through an SSH connection encrypted. This is an SSH tunnel.

Figure 10-29
Encrypting a Web client

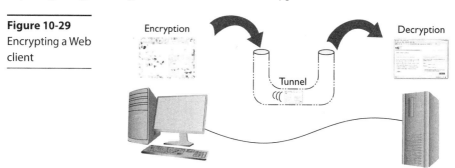

Encryption   Decryption

Tunnel

SSH tunnels are wildly popular and fairly easy to set up. Equally, all of the popular SSH clients and servers are designed to go into tunnel mode, usually with no more than a simple click of a check box (Figure 10-30).

Many tunneling protocols and standards are used in TCP/IP. SSH is one of the simplest types of tunnels so it's a great first exposure to tunneling. As the book progresses, you'll see more tunneling protocols, and you'll get the basics of tunneling. For now, make sure you understand that a tunnel is an encrypted connection between two endpoints.

Figure 10-30
Turning on tunneling in freeSSHd server

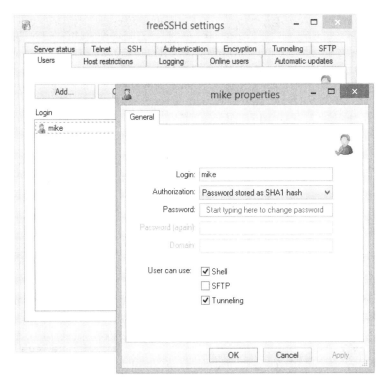

Any packet that enters the encrypted tunnel, including a packet with unencrypted data, is automatically encrypted, goes through the tunnel, and is decrypted on the other endpoint.

SSH may be popular, but it's not the only option for encryption. All of the other encryption standards are built into combined authentication/encryption standards, as covered in the next section.

Combining Authentication and Encryption

The rest of the popular authentication and encryption standards are combined to include both authentication and encryption in a single standard. Lumping together authentication and encryption into the same standard does not make it weaker than the standards already discussed. These are some of the most popular standards on the Internet today, because they offer excellent security.

SSL/TLS

The introduction and rapid growth of e-commerce on the World Wide Web in the mid-1990s made it painfully obvious that some form of authentication and encryption was needed. Netscape Corporation took the first shot at a new standard. At the time, the dominant Web browser was Netscape Navigator. Netscape created a standard called *Secure Sockets Layer (SSL)*. SSL requires a server with a certificate. When a client requests access to an SSL-secured server, the server sends to the client a copy of the certificate. The SSL client checks this certificate (all Web browsers come with an exhaustive list of CA root certificates preloaded), and if the certificate checks out, the server is authenticated and the client negotiates a symmetric-key cipher for use in the session (Figure 10-31). The session is now in a very secure encrypted tunnel between the SSL server and the SSL client.

Figure 10-31
SSL at work

The *Transport Layer Security (TLS)* protocol was designed as an upgrade to SSL. TLS is very similar to SSL, working in almost the same way. TLS is more robust and flexible and works with just about any TCP application. SSL is limited to HTML, FTP, SMTP, and a few older TCP applications. TLS has no such restrictions and is used in securing Voice over IP (VoIP) and virtual private networks (VPNs), but it is still most heavily used in securing Web pages. Every Web browser today uses TLS for HTTPS-secured Web sites, and EAP-TLS (discussed in Chapter 14) is common for more-secure wireless networks.

 NOTE SSL/TLS also supports mutual authentication, but this is relatively rare.

IPsec

Every authentication and encryption protocol and standard you've learned about so far works *above* the Network layer of the OSI seven-layer model. *Internet Protocol Security (IPsec)* is an authentication and encryption protocol suite that works at the Internet/ Network layer and should become the dominant authentication and encryption protocol suite as IPv6 continues to roll out and replace IPv4. (See Chapter 12 for details on IPv6.)

 NOTE The *Internet Engineering Task Force (IETF)* specifies the IPsec protocol suite, managing updates and revisions. One of those specifications regards the acronym for the protocol suite, calling it *IPsec* with a lowercase "s" rather than IPS or IPSec. Go figure.

IPsec works in two different modes: Transport mode and Tunnel mode. In Transport mode, only the actual payload of the IP packet is encrypted: the destination and source IP addresses and other IP header information are still readable. In Tunnel mode, the entire IP packet is encrypted and then placed into an IPsec endpoint where it is encapsulated inside another IP packet. The mode you use depends on the application (Figure 10-32). IPv6 will use the IPsec Transport mode by default.

Figure 10-32
IPsec's two
modes

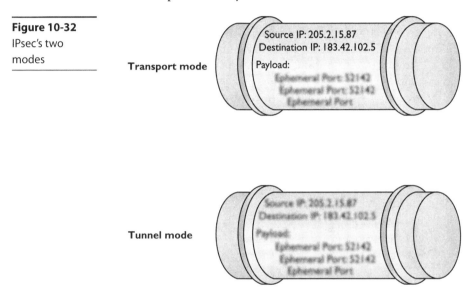

The IPsec protocol suite uses many open source protocols to provide both tight authentication and robust encryption. You do not need to know how each of the protocols works for the CompTIA Network+ exam. (And you'll see the term as *IPSec* rather than IPsec on the exam.)

IPsec is an incredibly powerful authentication/encryption protocol suite, but until IPv6 is widely implemented, its only common current use is creating secure tunnels between two computers: a job it performs very well. (See the discussion of virtual private networks—VPNs—in Chapter 11, "Advanced Networking Devices," for the scoop.)

Keep an eye out for IPsec!

Secure TCP/IP Applications

I've covered quite a few TCP/IP security standards and protocols thus far in the chapter, but I really haven't put anything to work yet. Now is the time to talk about actual applications that use these tools to make secure connections. As mentioned earlier, this is in no way a complete list, as there are thousands of secure TCP applications; I'll stick to ones you will see on the CompTIA Network+ exam. Even within that group, I've saved discussion of some of the applications for other chapters that deal more directly with certain security aspects (such as remote connections).

HTTPS

You've already seen HTTPS back in Chapter 8, so let's do a quick review and then take the coverage a bit deeper. You know that HTTPS pages traditionally start with https:// and that most browsers also show a small lock icon in the lower-right corner or in the address bar. You also know that HTTPS uses SSL/TLS for the actual authentication and encryption process. In most cases, all of this works very well, but what do you do when HTTPS has trouble?

Since you won't get an HTTPS connection without a good certificate exchange, the most common problems are caused by bad certificates. When a certificate comes in from an HTTPS Web site, your computer checks the expiration date to verify the certificate is still valid and checks the Web site's URL to make sure it's the same as the site you are on. If either of these is not correct, you get an error such as the one shown in Figure 10-33.

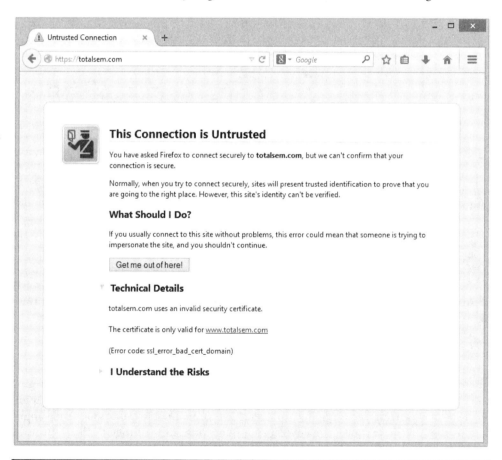

Figure 10-33 Certificate problem

If you get one of these errors, you need to decide what to do. Good certificates do go bad (this even happened on my own Web site once) and sometimes the URLs on the certificates are not exactly the same as the site using them. When in doubt, stop. On the other hand, if the risk is low (for example, you're not entering a credit card number or other sensitive information) and you know and trust the site, proceeding is safe in most cases. A courtesy e-mail or phone call to the Web site administrator notifying him or her about the invalid certificate is usually greatly appreciated.

Invalid certificates aren't the only potential problems. After this basic check, the browser checks to see if the certificate has been revoked. Root authorities, like Comodo, generate Certificate Revocation Lists (CRLs) that a Web browser can check against. Certificates are revoked for a number of reasons, but most of the time the reasons are serious, such as a compromised private key.

If you get a revoked certificate error, it's better to stay away from the site until they fix the problem.

SCP

One of the first SSH-enabled programs to appear after the introduction of SSH was the *Secure Copy Protocol (SCP)*. SCP was one of the first protocols used to transfer data securely between two hosts and thus might have replaced FTP. SCP works well but lacks features such as a directory listing. SCP still exists, especially with the well-known UNIX scp command-line utility, but it has, for the most part, been replaced by the more powerful SFTP.

SFTP

SSH File Transfer Protocol (SFTP) was designed as a replacement for FTP after many of the inadequacies of SCP (such as the inability to see the files on the other computer) were discovered. Although SFTP and FTP have similar names and perform the same job of transferring files, the way in which they do that job differs greatly.

 EXAM TIP   You'll hear some techs refer to SSH FTP as *Secure FTP*. That's not technically correct, but it's common. If you see Secure FTP on the CompTIA Network+ exam, think SSH FTP and you'll be fine.

SFTP is a unique protocol—that is, not FTP over SSH or anything to do with FTP—designed to run over an SSH session. It offers secure file transfers, resumption of interrupted file transfers, deletion of files on the server, and more. SFTP uses TCP port 23.

 NOTE   SFTP is often incorrectly equated with FTPS, which is FTP using SSL/TLS to add security. They're very different animals! SFTP is technologically superior to FTPS, though you'll find both running out there in the wild.

SNMP

The *Simple Network Management Protocol (SNMP)* is a very popular method for querying the state of SNMP-capable devices. SNMP can tell you a number of settings like CPU usage, network utilization, and detailed firewall hits. SNMP uses *agents* (special client programs) to collect network information from a *Management Information Base (MIB)*, SNMP's version of a server. To use SNMP, you need SNMP-capable devices and some tool to query them. One tool is Cacti (www.cacti.net), shown in Figure 10-34. Cacti, like most good SNMP tools, enables you to query an SNMP-capable device for hundreds of different types of information.

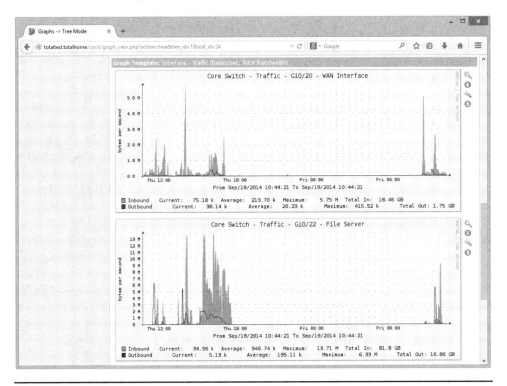

Figure 10-34   Cacti at work

SNMP is a useful tool for network administrators, but the first version, SNMPv1, sent all data, including the passwords, unencrypted over the network. SNMPv2c still lacked encryption and was rather challenging to use. SNMPv3 is the standard version used today and combines solid, fairly easy-to-use authentication and encryption.

 NOTE   SNMP runs on UDP ports 161 and 162.

LDAP

The *Lightweight Directory Access Protocol (LDAP)* is the tool that programs use to query and change a database used by the network. The networks today employ many different databases that are used in many different ways. I'm not talking about databases used by normal people to enter sales calls or to inventory trucks! These are databases used to track who is logged into the network, how many DHCP clients are currently active, or the location of all the printers in the local network.

One of the most complex and also most used databases is Windows Active Directory. Active Directory is the power behind single sign-on and network information (where's the closest printer to me?). Every Windows domain controller stores a copy of the Active Directory database.

If a domain controller fails, another domain controller can and must instantly take over. To do this, every domain controller must have an identical copy of the Active Directory database. That means if a single domain controller makes a change to the Active Directory database, it must quickly send that change to other domain controllers.

Enter LDAP. LDAP is the tool used in virtually every situation where one computer needs to access another computer's database for information or to make an update. Specifically, LDAP can talk to Active Directory and other directory service providers to query and modify items. You will probably never use LDAP manually. Your domain controllers will use it automatically and transparently in the background to keep your databases in good order. LDAP uses TCP and UDP ports 389 by default.

The now-deprecated secure version of LDAP, *LDAPS*, used TCP port 636. You'll see it on the CompTIA Network+ exam, but LDAP version 2 made it obsolete.

NTP

The *Network Time Protocol (NTP)* does one thing: it gives you the current time. NTP is an old protocol and isn't in and of itself much of a security risk unless you're using some timestamping protocol like Kerberos. Windows is by far the most common Kerberos user, so just make sure all of your computers have access to an NTP server so users don't run into problems when logging in. NTP uses UDP port 123.

Chapter Review

Questions

1. Any encryption that uses the same key for encryption and decryption is called?

   A. Encoded key

   B. Symmetric key

   C. Single key

   D. Synthetic key

2. RC4 is a(n) _____ cipher.

   A. block

   B. forwarding

   C. stream

   D. asymmetric

3. In a PKI encryption method, which key encrypts the data?

   A. Public

   B. Private

   C. Both

   D. Depends on who sends the data

4. The process of verifying with a high degree of confidence that the sender is who the receiver thinks he or she should be is called _____.

   A. PKI

   B. authentication

   C. locking

   D. nonrepudiation

5. A hash function is by definition a _____.

   A. complex function

   B. PKI function

   C. one-way function

   D. systematic function

6. Which of the following is a common hash function?

   A. SHA-3

   B. RC4

   C. AES

   D. BMX

7. In order to have a PKI you must have a(n) _____.

   A. Web server

   B. Web of trust

   C. root authority

   D. unsigned certificate

8. Which type of access control requires a label to define its sensitivity?

    A. MAC

    B. DAC

    C. RBAC

    D. VAC

9. If you saw some traffic running on UDP ports 1812 and 1813, what AAA standard would you know was running?

    A. PPP

    B. RADIUS

    C. MS-CHAP

    D. TACACS+

10. Which authentication standard is highly time sensitive?

    A. PAP

    B. RADIUS

    C. 802.1X

    D. Kerberos

Answers

    1. B. Symmetric-key encryption uses the same key.

    2. C. RC4 is a stream cipher.

    3. A. You send someone a public key that he or she, in turn, uses to encrypt the data. The private key can decrypt data encrypted with the public key.

    4. D. This is the definition of nonrepudiation.

    5. C. Hash functions must be one-way. They should be complex, but complexity is not a requirement.

    6. A. Of the choices listed, only SHA-3 is a hash function.

    7. C. A PKI must have a root authority.

    8. A. Mandatory access control must use a label to define sensitivity.

    9. B. RADIUS uses UDP ports 1812 and 1813.

    10. D. All Kerberos tickets are timestamped.

Advanced Networking Devices

The CompTIA Network+ certification exam expects you to know how to

- 1.3 Explain the concepts and characteristics of routing and switching
- 1.8 Explain the functions of network services
- 2.2 Given a scenario, determine the appropriate placement of networking devices on a network and install/configure them
- 2.3 Explain the purposes and use cases for advanced networking devices
- 2.5 Compare and contrast WAN technologies
- 3.4 Given a scenario, use remote access methods
- 4.2 Explain authentication and access controls
- 4.6 Explain common mitigation techniques and their purposes

To achieve these goals, you must be able to

- Describe the features and functions of VPNs
- Define the capabilities and management of managed switches
- Configure and deploy VLANs
- Implement advanced switch features

So far in this book we've looked at networks in a rather simplistic way. First, we explored network topologies. Second, we've seen a number of devices with very clear distinctions about their functions according to the OSI model. From cabling humming along at Layer 1, switches at Layer 2, and routers at Layer 3, each performs specific services without overlap. This is a great way to begin learning about networking, but it's not a complete view of how many networks function. It's time to go into more depth.

This chapter starts with virtual private networks: technology for connecting remote users to local resources. The chapter then turns to managing devices that handle switching, security, and more. The third portion examines VLANs: technology built into better switches that segments a single network into multiple virtual networks. The chapter finishes with a discussion about multilayer switches—boxes that do pretty much everything from Layer 1 all the way to Layer 7.

Test Specific

Virtual Private Networks

Remote connections have been around for a long time, even before the Internet existed. The biggest drawback to remote connections was the cost to connect. If you were on one side of the continent and had to connect to your LAN on the other side of the continent, the only connection option was a telephone. Or, if you needed to connect two LANs across the continent, you ended up paying outrageous monthly charges for a private connection. The introduction of the Internet gave people wishing to connect to their home or work networks a very inexpensive connection option, but there was one problem—the whole Internet was (and is) open to the public. People wanted to stop using dial-up and expensive private connections and use the Internet instead, but they wanted to be able to do it securely.

If you read the previous chapter, you might think you could use some of the tools for securing TCP/IP to help, and you would be correct. Several standards use encrypted tunnels between a computer or a remote network and a private network through the Internet (Figure 11-1), resulting in what is called a *virtual private network (VPN)*.

Figure 11-1
VPN connecting computers across the United States

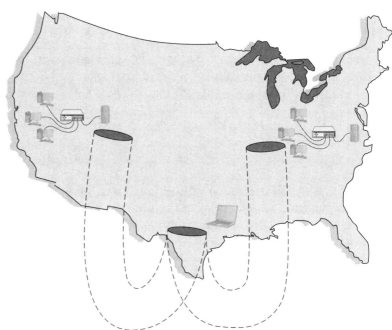

An encrypted tunnel requires *endpoints*—the ends of the tunnel where the data is encrypted and decrypted. In the tunnels you've seen thus far, the client for the application sits on one end and the server sits on the other. VPNs do the same thing. Either some software running on a computer or, in some cases, a dedicated box must act as an end-point for a VPN (Figure 11-2).

Figure 11-2
Typical tunnel

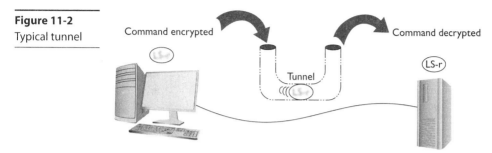

The key with the VPN is that the computers should be on the same network—and that means they must all have the same network ID. You would want the laptop that you use in the Denver airport lounge, for example, to have the same network ID as the computers in the LAN back at the office. But there's no simple way to do this. If it's a single client trying to access a network, that client is going to take on the IP address from its local DHCP server. In the case of your laptop in the airport, your network ID and IP address come from the DHCP server in the airport, not the DHCP server back at the office.

To make the VPN work, you need VPN software installed on your local machine—the laptop at the Denver airport—and VPN software or hardware at your office. You connect your laptop first to the Internet using the airport DHCP and all that; it's just a normal Internet connection. Second, the VPN software creates a virtual NIC on your laptop (endpoint 1), makes a connection with the VPN server at the office (endpoint 2), and then, in essence, creates a virtual direct cable from the virtual NIC to the office (Figure 11-3). That "virtual cable" is called a *VPN tunnel*. The laptop now has two IPv4 addresses. One is local from the airport DHCP server. The other is "local," but works with the office network. That second IP address goes with the virtual NIC.

Figure 11-3
Endpoints must have their own IP addresses.

Clever network engineers have come up with many ways to make this work, and those implementations function at different layers of the OSI model. PPTP and L2TP, for example, work at the Data Link layer. Many VPNs use IPsec at the Network layer to handle encryption needs. SSL and TLS VPNs don't really fit into the OSI model well at all, with some features in the Session layer and others in the Presentation layer.

PPTP VPNs

So how do you make IP addresses appear out of thin air? What tunneling protocol have you learned about that has the smarts to query for an IP address? That's right, Point-to-Point Protocol (PPP) can make the connection.

Microsoft got the ball rolling with the *Point-to-Point Tunneling Protocol (PPTP)*, an advanced version of PPP that handles the connection right out of the box. Microsoft places the PPTP endpoints on the client and the server. The server endpoint is a special remote access server program on a Windows server, called *Routing and Remote Access Service (RRAS)*. Figure 11-4 shows Remote Access in Windows Server 2016.

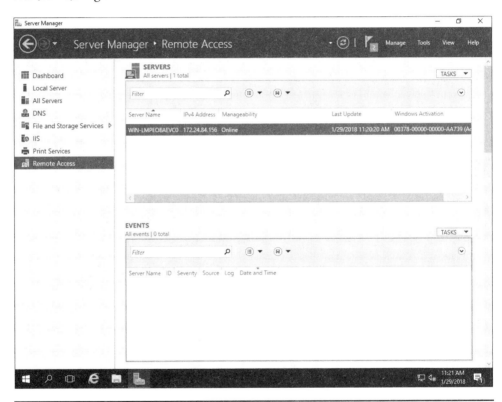

Figure 11-4   RRAS in action

On the Windows client side, you run **Add a VPN connection** in Settings in the Control Panel. (With older versions of Windows, you'd run the **Create a new connection** option in the Network and Sharing Center applet.) This creates a virtual NIC that, like any other NIC, does a DHCP query and gets an IP address from the DHCP server on the private network (Figure 11-5).

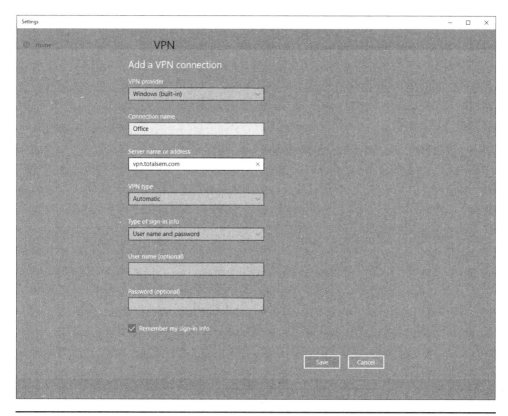

Figure 11-5 Setting up a VPN connection in Windows 10

 EXAM TIP A system connected to a VPN looks as though it's on the local network but performs much slower than if the system was connected directly back at the office because it's not local at all.

When your computer connects to the RRAS server on the private network, PPTP creates a secure tunnel through the Internet to the private LAN. Your client takes on an IP address of that network, as if your computer is directly connected to the LAN at the office, even down to the default gateway. In the early days of VPNs, if you opened a Web browser, your client would go across the Internet to the local LAN and then use the LAN's default gateway to get to the Internet! Using a Web browser would be much slower when you were on a VPN. Nowadays, using a Web browser on a VPN-connected machine will use the faster local Internet connectivity, so this is not an issue.

Every operating system comes with some type of built-in VPN client that supports PPTP (among others). Figure 11-6 shows Network, the macOS VPN connection tool.

This type of VPN connection, where a single computer logs into a remote network and becomes, for all intents and purposes, a member of that network, is commonly called a *host-to-site* connection.

Figure 11-6   VPN on a macOS system

L2TP VPNs

The VPN protocol called *Layer 2 Tunneling Protocol (L2TP)* took all the good features of PPTP and a Cisco protocol called *Layer 2 Forwarding (L2F)* and added support to run on almost any type of connection possible, from telephones to Ethernet to ultra-high-speed optical connections. The endpoint on the local LAN went from a server program to a VPN-capable router, called a *VPN concentrator*.

Cisco provides free client software to connect a single faraway PC to a Cisco VPN. This creates a typical host-to-site or *client-to-site* connection. Network people often directly connect two Cisco VPN concentrators to connect two separate LANs permanently. It's slow, but inexpensive, compared to a dedicated high-speed connection between two faraway LANs. This kind of connection enables two LANs to function as a single network, sharing files and services as if in the same building. This is called a *site-to-site* VPN connection.

EXAM TIP   Aside from client-to-site and site-to-site VPNs, you'll sometimes see *host-to-host* connections discussed. A *host-to-host* VPN deals with a specific single connection between two machines using VPN software or hardware.

L2TP differs from PPTP in that it has no authentication or encryption. L2TP generally uses IPsec for all security needs. Technically, you should call an L2TP VPN an "L2TP/IPsec" VPN. L2TP works perfectly well in the single-client-connecting-to-a-LAN scenario, too. Every operating system's VPN client fully supports L2TP/IPsec VPNs.

SSL VPNs

Cisco makes VPN hardware that enables *SSL VPNs*. These types of VPN offer an advantage over Data Link– or Network-based VPNs because they don't require any special client software. Clients connect to the VPN server using a standard Web browser, with the traffic secured using Transport Layer Security (TLS). (TLS replaced Secure Sockets Layer, or SSL, many years ago, but the SSL VPN moniker stuck.) The two most common types of SSL VPNs are SSL portal VPNs and SSL tunnel VPNs.

 NOTE Many VPN connections use the terms *client* and *server* to denote the functions of the devices that make the connection. You'll also see the terms *host* and *gateway* to refer to the connections, such as a *host-to-gateway tunnel*.

With SSL portal VPNs, a client accesses the VPN and is presented with a secure Web page. The client gains access to anything linked on that page, be it e-mail, data, links to other pages, and so on.

With tunnel VPNs, in contrast, the client Web browser runs some kind of active control, such as Java, and gains much greater access to the VPN-connected network. SSL tunnel VPNs create a more typical host-to-site connection than SSL portal VPNs, but the user must have sufficient permissions to run the active browser controls.

DTLS VPNs

Datagram TLS (DTLS) VPNs optimize connections for delay-sensitive applications, such as voice and video over a VPN. After establishing a traditional TLS tunnel, DTLS VPNs use UDP datagrams rather than TCP segments for communication. This enhances certain types of VPN traffic. Cisco AnyConnect DTLS VPN is the prototypical example of this sort of VPN implementation.

DMVPN

Extending VPN access across a company with multiple locations can create some logistical problems. The Bayland Widgets corporation has a main office in Houston and two satellite offices for manufacturing, one in El Paso and the other in Laredo. A traditional VPN located at the center location would become a bottleneck for traffic. Site-to-site traffic follows a familiar pattern, with the El Paso to Houston and Laredo to Houston connections going to the central VPN. But what about connections between El Paso and Laredo? With a traditional VPN, all that traffic would route through the main VPN in Houston. That seems inefficient!

A *dynamic multipoint VPN (DMVPN)* fixes this problem by enabling direct VPN connections between multiple locations directly. With a DMVPN solution, traffic between El Paso and Laredo happens directly, with no need to travel through the main Houston VPN. The typical DMVPN solution, such as a Cisco DMVPN, employs standard security (IPsec) to make all the connections secure from unwanted prying.

Alternative VPNs

There are other popular VPN options beyond PPTP, L2TP, and SSL/TLS, such as OpenVPN and SSH. The most common VPN today offers pure (no L2TP) IPsec solutions. These *IPsec VPN* technologies use IPsec tunneling for VPNs, such as Cisco IOS Easy VPN.

Another alternative is the *Generic Routing Encapsulation (GRE)* protocol paired with IPsec for encryption. You can use GRE to make a point-to-point tunnel connection that carries all sorts of traffic over Layer 3, including multicast and IPv6 traffic.

Switch Management

Managed switches have programming and logic to handle switching, security, and many other functions, taking the concept of a switch well beyond the simple switches discussed so far in this book.

 NOTE   These methods of switch management work for any type of managed device (such as routers).

A managed switch, by definition, requires some configuration. You can connect to a managed switch to tell it what you want it to do. Exactly how you do this varies from switch to switch, but generally there are three ways:

- Directly plug into a serial interface and use a virtual terminal program to connect to a command-line interface.
- Get the switch on the network and then use a virtual terminal over SSH to connect to the same command-line interface.
- Get the switch on the network and use the switch's built-in Web interface.

Let's look at the steps involved in each method.

First, many managed switches have a special serial port called a *console port*. Plug a laptop into the console port on the back of the switch (Figure 11-7). Then, run a terminal program like PuTTY to access the command-line interface on the switch. As long as you speak the language of the switch's command prompt, you're good to go. It's very common to use a console port for initial configuration of a new managed switch.

The second and third methods require the managed switch to be connected to the network and have an accessible IP address. Connect to the switch over the network and run some sort of software—either PuTTY or a Web browser—to manage the switch.

Figure 11-7
Plugging into
a managed
switch's console
port using a
serial cable

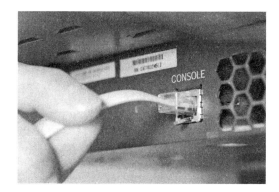

Wait! It's a switch. Switches that we've discussed in the book so far operate at Layer 2 of the OSI model. IP addresses don't show up until Layer 3. Here's the scoop in a nutshell. A managed switch needs an IP address to enable configuration on Layer 3.

This means a new, out-of-the-box managed switch has all the same configuration issues a new router would have. It's going to have a default IP address (but you should assign an IP address that's applicable to your network). It'll have a default user name and password (but you should change those!). And it'll have a bunch of other default settings that you'll probably want to change once you know what they mean.

 NOTE A managed switch enables you to configure every port on the switch in a lot of different ways, depending on the purpose and complexity of the switch. For example, it's easy to set the *speed and duplexing* of a port to match the client.

Like any IP device, a managed switch needs good, basic maintenance. One example would be updating the firmware. Managed switches support firmware updates over the Internet. That's a nice idea, but it means your switch needs a default gateway, a DNS server, and so forth to be able to access content over the Internet.

 EXAM TIP You configure a default gateway on a switch by telling the switch the IP address of the router. For most implementations, type in the IP address of your Internet connection box, such as a fiber-optic or cable modem.

Armed with the IP address, configure your client or client software to connect to the managed switch. And now let's get serious.

As you might imagine, it would be scary to let unauthorized people have access to your switch management configuration interface. In the preceding examples, where you configure the switch over the network (*in-band management*), anyone who knows the IP addresses of the managed devices will be able to access them if they can get past the user name and password. To reduce exposure, it's common to dedicate one port on every managed device as a *management port*. You can do *interface configuration* only by directly connecting to that port.

Then, plug all those dedicated ports into a switch that's totally separate from the rest of the network, which will prevent unauthorized access to those ports. This is one example of *out-of-band management*.

In many cases a switch might be in a far-flung location, making it important to provide some method of remote management. Switches with Web management interfaces often provide a well-protected *HTTPS/management URL* that administrators can use to log into the switch via the Internet (another example of in-band management). An older but more common method is to skip the Internet completely and use an out-of-band technique such as a common telephone *modem,* connected to a classic phone line on one side and to the *console port* on the switch on the other.

 EXAM TIP You'll find out-of-band management options—management URL, modem connection, console port—on switches and on routers. CompTIA uses the term *console router* to describe a router with out-of-band management capabilities.

Let's turn now to a technology that managed switches make possible: VLANs.

Virtual LANs

Today's LANs are complex places. It's rare to see any serious network that doesn't have remote incoming connections, public Web or e-mail servers, wireless networks, and a string of connected switches. Leaving all of these different features on a single broadcast domain creates a tremendous amount of broadcast traffic and creates security challenges. What if you could segment the network using the switches you already own? A *virtual local area network (VLAN)* enables you to segment a physical network into multiple discreet networks without having to add additional hardware.

To create a VLAN, you take a single physical broadcast domain made up of one or more switches and chop it up into multiple broadcast domains. This is most simply done by assigning each port to a specific VLAN. VLANs require switches with specific programming to create the virtual networks.

Imagine a single switch with a number of computers connected to it. Up to this point, a single switch creates a single broadcast domain, but that's about to change. You've decided to take this single switch and turn it into two VLANs. VLANs typically get the name "VLAN" plus a number, like VLAN1 or VLAN275. The devices usually start at 1, although there's no law or rules on the numbering. In this example, I'll configure the ports on a single switch to be in one of two VLANs: VLAN1 or VLAN2 (Figure 11-8). I promise to show you how to configure ports for different VLANs shortly, but I've got a couple of other concepts to hit first.

Figure 11-9 shows a switch configured to assign individual ports to VLANs. Managed switches can handle any number of VLANs. Every port starts with the default VLAN, VLAN1, so even if you don't specify multiple VLANs, you get one by default.

Figure 11-8
Switch with two
VLANs

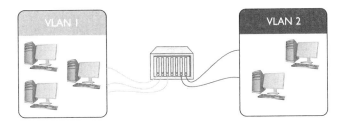

Figure 11-9
Every port
is VLAN1 by
default.

To set up a VLAN switch, create one or more VLANs, then assign ports to those VLANs. Any traffic sent from a host plugged into a port for VLAN1, therefore, becomes part of the broadcast domain VLAN1.

A single switch configured into two VLANs is the simplest form of VLAN possible. More serious networks usually have more than one switch. Let's say you added a switch to a simple network. You'd like to keep VLAN1 and VLAN2 but use both switches. You can configure the new switch to use VLAN1 and VLAN2, but you've got to enable data to flow between the two switches, regardless of VLAN. That's where trunking comes into play.

Trunking

Trunking is the process of transferring VLAN traffic between two or more switches. Imagine two switches, each configured with a VLAN1 and a VLAN2, as shown in Figure 11-10.

Figure 11-10
Two switches,
each with a
VLAN1 and a
VLAN2

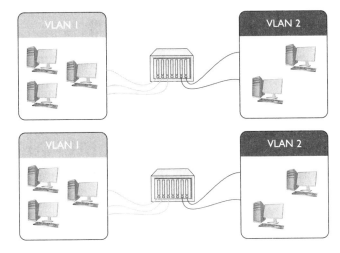

You want the computers connected to VLAN1 on one switch to talk to all of the computers connected to VLAN1 on the other switch. Of course, you want to do this with VLAN2 also. To do this, configure a port on each switch as a *trunk port*, a port on a switch configured to carry all traffic, regardless of VLAN number, between all switches in a LAN (Figure 11-11). The VLAN designation for a trunk port is its *native VLAN*. This becomes important when we discuss how data flows within a VLAN network. (See "Tagging" a bit later in the chapter.)

Figure 11-11
Trunk ports

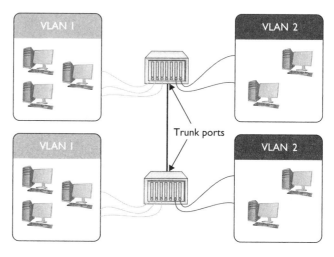

Every Ethernet switch uses the IEEE 802.1Q trunk standard that enables you to connect switches from different manufacturers.

  SIM   Check out the excellent Chapter 11 Challenge! Sim, "Trunking," to test your understanding of trunking. You'll find it here: http://totalsem.com/007.

Configuring a VLAN-Capable Switch

If you want to configure a VLAN-capable switch, you need a method to perform that configuration. One method uses a console port like the one described in Chapter 7, "Routing." The most common method is to log into the switch using SSH—not Telnet, because you need security—and use the command-line interface. The command line is going to be fast and precise. Alternatively, you can access the switch with a Web browser interface, like the one shown in Figure 11-12.

Every switch manufacturer has its own interface for configuring VLANs, but the interface shown in Figure 11-13 is a classic example. This is Cisco Network Assistant, a GUI tool that enables you to configure multiple Cisco devices through the same interface. Note that you first must define your VLANs.

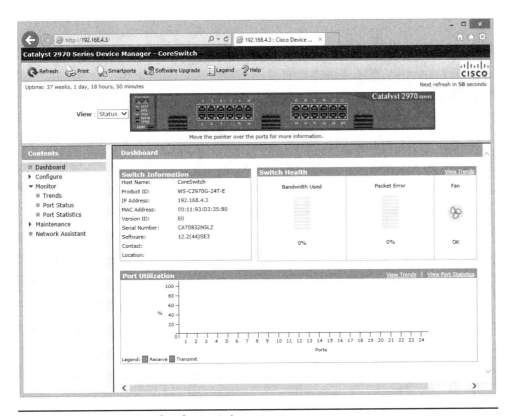

Figure 11-12   Browser interface for a switch

EXAM TIP   Expect a question or two on *segmentation and interface properties* of VLANs and 802.1Q. These will ask you about what each accomplishes and perhaps how a configuration screen should function.

After you create the VLANs, you assign ports to VLANs. This process is called *VLAN assignment*. Assigning each port to a VLAN means that whatever computer plugs into that port, its traffic will get tagged with that port's VLAN. (See the following section, "Tagging.") Figure 11-14 shows a port being assigned to a particular VLAN.

NOTE   VLANs based on ports are the most common type of VLAN and are commonly known as *static VLANs*. VLANs based on MAC addresses are called *dynamic VLANs*. The latter method is never used these days.

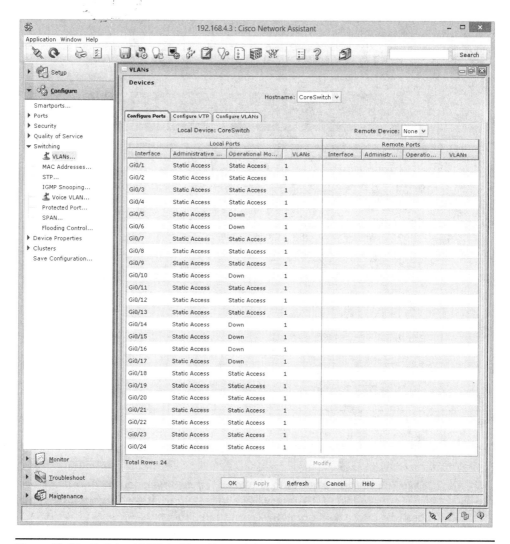

Figure 11-13   Defining VLANs in Cisco Network Assistant

Tagging

When you have a busy network with multiple switches and multiple VLANs, how does a frame from a workstation in VLAN100 make it to a destination workstation in the same VLAN? What if the workstations are several switches apart? The key tool that makes this happen is *tagging*.

Workstations plug into *access ports*—regular ports that have been configured as part of a VLAN—that do the work of tagging traffic with the appropriate VLAN when frames enter the switch. Note that access ports are ports, just like trunk ports, but configured

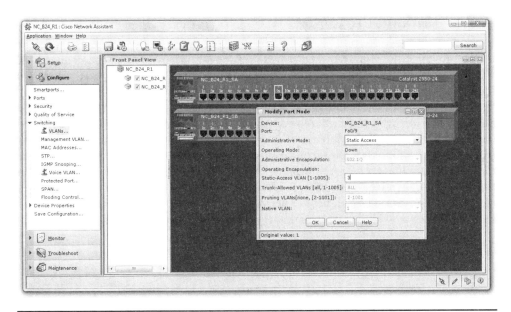

Figure 11-14   Assigning a port to a VLAN

for the opposite purpose. Access ports connect to workstations; trunk ports connect to other trunk ports.

When the data enters the access port, the switch tags the frames with the appropriate VLAN ID. If the destination workstation is connected to the same switch, the frames flow to that workstation's access port. The tag is stripped off each frame and traffic flows as you would expect. If the destination workstation connects to a different switch, the initial switch sends the frames out its trunk port. What happens next is determined by how the trunk port is configured.

If the trunk port has a native VLAN that differs from the tag placed on the frame as it entered the access port, the switch leaves the tag on the frame and sends the tagged frame along to the next switch or switches. If the trunk port's native VLAN is the same as the access port's VLAN, then the switch drops the tag and sends the untagged frame out the trunk port.

 EXAM TIP   Expect a question or two on the CompTIA Network+ exam that checks your knowledge of *tagging and untagging ports* on VLAN switches. Also, you'll get a question on why you would want to *change a native VLAN* (to mitigate against double-tagging attacks).

Native VLANs exist to provide compatibility with older or simpler non-VLAN tagging switches, but there is a catch. The native VLAN opens your network to a nasty vulnerability called a *double-tagging attack* that lets the attacker access VLANs they should not be able to access. For this reason, in modern networks the native VLAN is set to an unused VLAN and the trunk port is configured to tag its native VLAN traffic as well.

VLAN Trunking Protocol

A busy network with many VLAN switches can require periods of intensive work to update. Imagine the work required to redo all the VLAN switches if you changed the VLAN configuration by adding or removing a VLAN. You'd have to access every switch individually, changing the port configuration to alter the VLAN assignment, and so on. The potential for errors is staggering. What if you missed updating one switch? Joe in Sales might wrongly have access to a sensitive accounting server or Phyllis in accounting might not be able to get her job done on time.

Cisco uses a proprietary protocol called *VLAN Trunking Protocol (VTP)* to automate the updating of multiple VLAN switches. With VTP, you put each switch into one of three states: server, client, or transparent. When you make changes to the VLAN configuration of the server switch, all the connected client switches update their configurations within minutes. The big job of changing every switch manually just went away.

 NOTE VTP offers *VTP pruning*, a tool for minimizing broadcast traffic. This can be a very useful tool on larger-scale networks.

When you set a VLAN switch to transparent, you tell it not to update but to hold onto its manual settings. You would use a transparent mode VLAN switch in circumstances where the overall VLAN configuration assignments did not apply.

 NOTE Clients can update servers the same way servers update clients. The difference is that VLAN information can only be changed on servers.

InterVLAN Routing

Once you've configured a switch to support multiple VLANs, each VLAN is its own broadcast domain, just as if the two VLANs were on two completely separate switches and networks. There is no way for data to get from one VLAN to another unless you use a router or a multilayer switch. (See "Multilayer Switches" later in the chapter for the scoop on these devices.)

The process of making a router work between two VLANs is called *interVLAN routing*. In the early days of interVLAN routing, you commonly used a router with multiple ports as a backbone for the network. Figure 11-15 shows one possible way to connect two VLANs with a single router. Note that the router has one port connected to VLAN100 and another connected to VLAN200. Devices on VLAN100 may now communicate with devices on VLAN200.

More commonly, you'd see a *router-on-a-stick* configuration, which used a single router interface to connect to multiple VLANs on a switch. The router interface had to be set up as a trunk port.

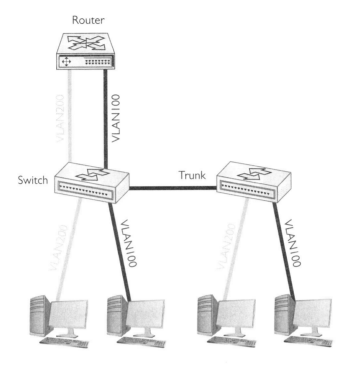

Figure 11-15
One router
connecting
multiple VLANs

Adding a physical router isn't a very elegant way to connect VLANs. This forces almost all traffic to go through the router, and it's not a very flexible solution if you want to add more VLANs in the future. As a result, many VLAN-capable switches also do routing. Figure 11-16 shows an older interVLAN routing–capable switch, the Cisco Catalyst 3550.

Figure 11-16 Cisco 3550

From the outside, the Cisco 3550 looks like any other switch. On the inside, it's a flexible device that not only supports VLANs, but also provides routing to interconnect these VLANs. Figure 11-17 shows a GUI configuration screen for the 3550's interVLAN routing between two VLANs.

If the Cisco 3550 is a switch and a router, on what layer of the OSI seven-layer model does it operate? If it's a switch, then it works at Layer 2. But routers work at Layer 3. This isn't an ordinary switch. The Cisco 3550 works at both Layers 2 and 3 at the same time.

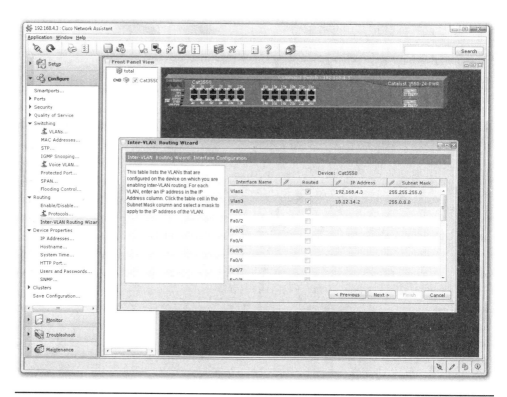

Figure 11-17   Setting up interVLAN routing

DHCP and VLANs

DHCP is an awesome tool to automate, track, and manage *IP address assignments*, as you know from previous chapters. Unfortunately, its native functions are limited to a single subnet. By default, DHCP requests can't pass through a router. So, if you have a set of VLANs in a network, connected via routers, you need some method for getting IP addresses and other TCP/IP information to hosts.

When a *relay agent* (CompTIA calls this *DHCP relay*) is enabled and configured within a router, the router will pass DHCP messages across the router interfaces. So now we can use a single DHCP server to serve addresses to multiple networks or subnetworks.

Cisco implements DHCP relay through a configuration command called *IP helper* (the command is technically `ip helper-address`). IP helper enables DHCP relay support (ports 67 and 68). It also enables relaying for TFTP (port 69), Network Time Protocol (port 123), TACACS+ (port 49), DNS (port 53), NetBIOS (port 137), and NetBIOS Datagram (port 138).

Troubleshooting VLANs

At this level, troubleshooting a new VLAN is mostly about port assignment. If you give an incorrect VLAN assignment to a device, either you won't be able to see it or that device won't have access to resources it needs. The fix is the obvious one: change the VLAN assignment.

Multilayer Switches

The Cisco 3550 is an amazing box in that it seems to defy the entire concept of a switch because of its support for interVLAN routing. Up to this point, I've said a switch works at Layer 2 of the OSI model, but now you've just seen a switch that clearly also works at Layer 3. The Cisco 3550 is one example of a *multilayer switch*.

At this point you must stop thinking that a "switch" always works at Layer 2. A *Layer 2 switch* forwards traffic based on MAC addresses, whereas a *Layer 3 switch* forwards traffic based on IP addresses. A Layer 3 switch is a router that does what a traditional router does in software … in hardware. A Layer 3 switch, by definition, is a multilayer switch. From here on out, I will carefully address at what layer of the OSI seven-layer model a switch operates.

The challenge to multilayer switches comes with the ports. On a classic Layer 2 switch, individual ports don't have IP addresses. They don't need them. On a router, however, every port must have an IP address because the routing table uses the IP address to determine where to send packets.

A multilayer switch needs some option or feature for configuring ports to work at Layer 2 or Layer 3. Cisco uses the terms *switchport* and *router port* to differentiate between the two types of port. You can configure any port on a multilayer switch to act as a switchport or a router port, depending on your needs. Multilayer switches are incredibly common and support a number of interesting features, clearly making them part of what I call *advanced networking devices*.

I'm going to show you four areas where multilayer switches are very helpful: load balancing, quality of service, port bonding, and network protection. (Each term is defined in its respective section.) These four areas aren't the only places where multiplayer switches solve problems, but they are the most popular and the ones that the CompTIA Network+ exam covers. Each section covers common-use cases, in CompTIA speak, for these devices. In other words, I'll explain when and where to use each function.

 NOTE Any device that works at multiple layers of the OSI seven-layer model, providing more than a single service, is called a *multifunction network device*.

Load Balancing

Popular Internet servers are exactly that—popular. So popular that a single system cannot possibly support the thousands, if not millions, of requests per day that bombard them. But from what you've learned thus far about servers, you know that a single server has a

single IP address. Put this to the test. Go to a command prompt and type **ping www**
.google.com and press ENTER.

```
C:\>ping www.google.com

Pinging www.1.google.com [74.125.95.147] with 32 bytes of data:
Reply from 74.125.95.147: bytes=32 time=71ms TTL=242
Reply from 74.125.95.147: bytes=32 time=71ms TTL=242
Reply from 74.125.95.147: bytes=32 time=70ms TTL=242
Reply from 74.125.95.147: bytes=32 time=70ms TTL=242
```

A seriously epic site like google.com will handle trillions of search requests per year.
Let's throw hypothetical math into the mix. Imagine 2 trillion requests; the average
would be well over 5 billion search requests a day and 60,000 per second. Each of
those 60,000 requests might require the Web server to deliver thousands of HTTP segments. A single, powerful, dedicated Web server simply can't handle that load. A busy
Web site often needs more than one Web server to handle all the requests. Let's say a
Web site needs three servers to handle the traffic. How does that one Web site, using
three different servers, use a single IP address? The answer is found in something called
load balancing.

 NOTE Coming to a consensus on statistics like the number of requests/day
or how many requests a single server can handle is difficult. Just concentrate
on the concept. If some nerdy type says your numbers are way off, nicely
agree and walk away. Just don't invite them to any parties.

Load balancing means making a bunch of servers look like a single server, creating
a *server cluster*. Not only do you need to make them look like one server, you need to
make sure that requests to these servers are distributed evenly so no one server is bogged
down while another is idle. There are a few ways to do this, as you are about to see.
Be warned, not all of these methods require an advanced network device called a *load
balancer*, but it's common to use one. Employing a device designed to do one thing
really well is always much faster than using a general-purpose computer and slapping
on software.

DNS Load Balancing

Using DNS for load balancing is one of the oldest and still very common ways to support multiple Web servers. In this case, each Web server gets its own (usually) public IP
address. Each DNS server for the domain has multiple "A" DNS records, each with the
same fully qualified domain name (FQDN). The DNS server then cycles around these
records, so the same domain name resolves to different IP addresses. Figure 11-18 shows
a DNS server with multiple A records for the same FQDN.

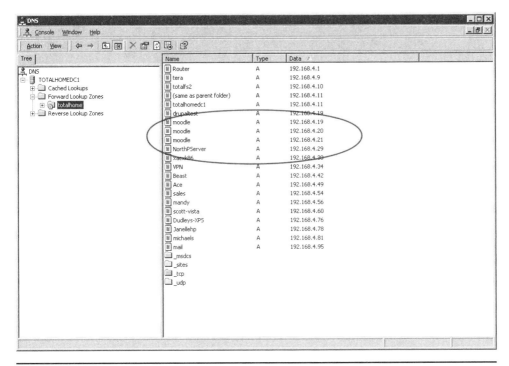

Figure 11-18　Multiple IP addresses, same name

Now that the A records have been added, you need to tell the DNS server to cycle around these names. It should be fairly obvious where to do this. In a Windows DNS Server, for example, you'll select a checkbox to do this, as shown in Figure 11-19.

When a computer comes to the DNS server for resolution, the server cycles through the DNS A records, giving out first one and then the next in a cyclic (round robin) fashion.

The popular BIND DNS server has a very similar process but adds even more power and features such as weighting one or more servers more than others or randomizing the DNS response.

Content Switch

Many multilayer switches handle load balancing by functioning at multiple layers. An alternative is a *content switch*. Content switches always work at Layer 7 (Application layer). Content switches designed to work with Web servers, for example, can read incoming HTTP and HTTPS requests. With this, you can perform very advanced actions, such as handling SSL certificates and cookies, on the content switch, removing the workload from the Web servers. Not only can these devices load balance in the ways previously

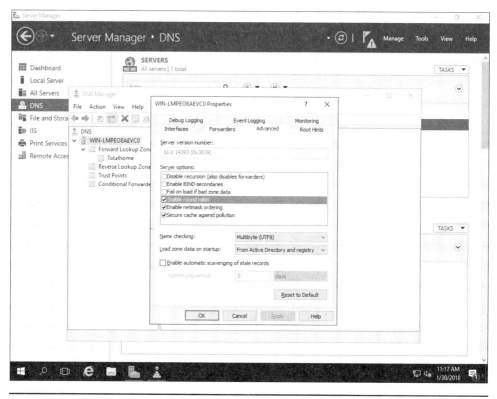

Figure 11-19   Enabling round robin

described, but their HTTP savvy can actually pass a cookie to HTTP requesters—Web browsers—so the next time that client returns, it is sent to the same server.

EXAM TIP   The CompTIA Network+ exam refers to a content switch as a *content filter* network appliance.

QoS and Traffic Shaping

Just about any router you buy today has the capability to block packets based on port number or IP address, but these are simple mechanisms mainly designed to protect an internal network. What if you need to control how much of your bandwidth is used for certain devices or applications? In that case, you need *quality of service (QoS)* policies to prioritize traffic based on certain rules. These rules control how much bandwidth a protocol, PC, user, VLAN, or IP address may use (Figure 11-20).

On many advanced routers and switches, you can implement QoS through bandwidth management, such as *traffic shaping* where you control the flow of packets into or out of the network according to the type of packet or other rules.

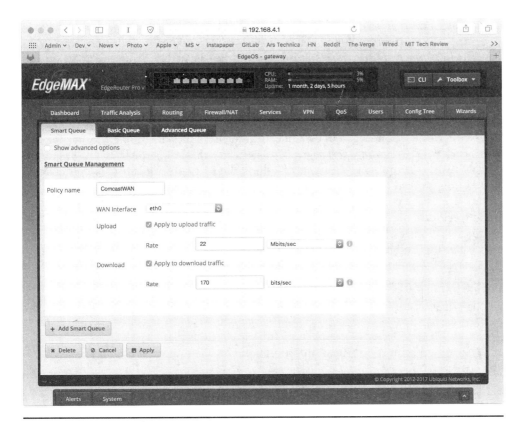

Figure 11-20   QoS configuration on a router

EXAM TIP   The term *bandwidth shaping* is synonymous with *traffic shaping*. The routers and switches that can implement traffic shaping are commonly referred to as *shapers*.

Traffic shaping is very important when you must guarantee a device or application a certain amount of bandwidth and/or latency, such as with VoIP or video. Traffic shaping is also very popular in places such as schools, where IT professionals need to control user activities, such as limiting HTTP usage or blocking certain risky applications such as peer-to-peer file sharing.

Port Bonding

There are times when the data capacity of a connection between a switch and another device isn't enough to meet demand. Situations like these are encountered regularly in large data centers where tremendous amounts of data must be moved between racks of storage devices to vast numbers of users. Sometimes the solution is simple, like changing from a low-capacity standard like 100-megabit Ethernet to Gigabit Ethernet.

But there are other ways to achieve high-speed links between devices without having to upgrade the infrastructure. One of those ways is to join two or more connections' ports logically in a switch so that the resulting bandwidth is treated as a single connection and the throughput is multiplied by the number of linked connectors. All of the cables from the joined ports must go to the same device—another switch, a storage area network (SAN), a station, or whatever. That device must also support the logical joining of all of the involved ports. This is called *port bonding*.

Elsewhere, port bonding goes by a pile of different names, including *link aggregation, NIC bonding, NIC teaming, port aggregation*—the last two terms you'll see on the Comp-TIA Network+ exam—and a bunch of others. The Cisco protocol for accomplishing aggregation is called *Port Aggregation Protocol (PAgP)*. You may also run across it in a very common implementation called *Link Aggregation Control Protocol (LACP)*, which is an IEEE specification. As it stands now, LACP is designated as IEEE 802.1AX-2014. LACP specifies a number of features and options to automate the negotiation, management, load balancing, and failure modes of aggregated ports.

Network Protection

The last area where you're likely to encounter advanced networking devices is network protection. *Network protection* is my term to describe four different areas:

- Intrusion protection/intrusion prevention
- Port mirroring
- Proxy serving
- AAA

Intrusion Detection/Intrusion Prevention

Intrusion detection and intrusion prevention detect that something has intruded into a network and then do something about it. Odds are good you've heard the term *firewall*. Firewalls are hardware or software tools that filter traffic based on various criteria, such as port number, IP address, or protocol. A firewall works at the border of your network, between the outside and the inside. (A *host-based firewall*, one installed on a single computer, similarly works on the border of that system.)

An *intrusion detection system (IDS)* is an application (often running on a dedicated IDS box) that inspects packets, looking for active intrusions. An IDS functions inside the network. A good IDS knows how to find attacks that a firewall might miss, such as viruses, illegal logon attempts, and other well-known attacks. Plus, because it inspects traffic inside the network, a good IDS can discover internal threats, like the activity of a vulnerability scanner smuggled in on a flash drive by a disgruntled worker planning an attack on an internal database server.

An IDS in promiscuous mode inspects a *copy* of every packet on a network. This placement outside the direct flow of traffic has three effects. First, there's a slight delay between something malicious hitting the network and the detection occurring. Second, there's no impact on network traffic flow. Third, if the IDS goes down, traffic keeps flowing normally.

An IDS always has some way to let the network administrators know if an attack is taking place: at the very least the attack is logged, but some IDSs offer a pop-up message, an e-mail, or even a text message to your phone.

An IDS can also respond to detected intrusions with action. The IDS can't stop the attack directly, but can request assistance from other devices—like a firewall—that can.

Modern IDS tools come in two flavors: network-based or host-based. A *network-based IDS (NIDS)* consists of multiple sensors placed around the network, often on one or both sides of the gateway router. These sensors report to a central application that, in turn, reads a signature file to detect anything out of the ordinary (Figure 11-21).

Figure 11-21
Diagram of network-based IDS

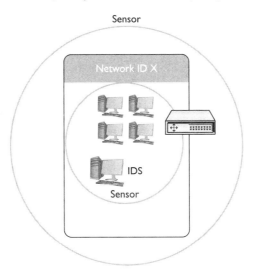

Different types of network traffic have detectable patterns, called *signatures*. Anti-malicious software (anti-malware) developers create *definition files*—collections of these signatures—for known malware. We'll see a lot more of this in Chapter 19, but for now note that many advanced networking devices can detect and filter traffic based on signatures.

 EXAM TIP Several companies enable *signature management* in the cloud, to help monitor and protect network traffic from malicious code, picking out known and suspect malware signatures with continuously updating definition files. Check out www.threatconnect.com for a prototypical example. And look for a signature management question on the CompTIA Network+ exam.

A *host-based IDS (HIDS)* is software running on individual systems that monitors for events such as system file modification or registry changes (Figure 11-22). More expensive IDSs do all this and can provide a single reporting source—very handy when one person is in charge of anything that goes on throughout a network.

Figure 11-22   OSSEC HIDS

 EXAM TIP   The CompTIA Network+ exam can refer to an IDS system by either its location on the network—thus NIDS or HIDS—or by what the IDS system does in each location. The network-based IDS scans using signature files, thus it is a *signature-based IDS*. A host-based IDS watches for suspicious behavior on systems, thus it is a *behavior-based IDS*.

An *intrusion prevention system (IPS)* is very similar to an IDS, but an IPS sits directly in the flow of network traffic. This active monitoring has a trio of consequences. First, an IPS can stop an attack while it is happening. No need to request help from any other devices. Second, the network bandwidth and latency take a hit. Third, if the IPS goes down, the link might go down too.

Depending on what IPS product you choose, an IPS can block incoming packets on-the-fly based on IP address, port number, or application type. An IPS might go even further, literally fixing certain packets on-the-fly. A *host-based intrusion prevention system (HIPS)* is located on a host. As you might suspect, you can roll out an IPS on a network and it gets a new name: a *network intrusion prevention system (NIPS)*.

 EXAM TIP Expect a question on the appropriate placement of a multilayer switch such as an IPS or IDS within a network. This tackles the differences among HIDS, NIDS, HIPS, and NIPS. Some of these devices might have *routing* functions as well as *switching* functions, so be prepared for either word to be used in the description.

Port Mirroring

Many managed switches have the capability to copy data from any or all physical ports on a switch to a single physical port. This is called *port mirroring*. It's as though you make a customized, fully configurable promiscuous port. Port mirroring is incredibly useful for any type of situation where an administrator needs to inspect packets coming to or from certain computers.

There are two forms of port mirroring: local and remote. Local port mirroring copies data from one or more ports on a single switch to a specific port on that switch. To monitor this data, you have to plug directly into the switch with ports being monitored. Remote port mirroring enables you to access data copied from one or more specific ports on a switch without plugging directly into that switch.

Proxy Serving

A *proxy server* sits in between clients and external servers, essentially pocketing the requests from the clients for server resources and making those requests itself. The client computers never touch the outside servers and thus stay protected from any unwanted activity. A proxy server usually *does something* to those requests as well. Let's see how proxy servers work using HTTP, one of the oldest uses of proxy servers.

Since proxy serving works by redirecting client requests to a proxy server, you first must tell the Web client not to use the usual DNS resolution to determine the Web server and instead to use a proxy. Every Web client comes with a program that enables you to set the IP address of the proxy server, as shown in the example in Figure 11-23.

Once the proxy server is configured, HTTP requests move from the client directly to the proxy server. Built into every HTTP request is the URL of the target Web server, so the Web proxy knows where to get the requested data once it gets the request. In the simplest format, the proxy server simply forwards the requests using its own IP address and then forwards the returning packets to the client (Figure 11-24).

This simple version of using a proxy server prevents the Web server from knowing where the client is located—a handy trick for those who wish to keep people from knowing where they are coming from, assuming you can find a public proxy server that accepts your HTTP requests (there are plenty!). There are many other good reasons to use a proxy server. One big benefit is caching. A proxy server keeps a copy of the served resource, giving clients a much faster response.

Figure 11-23
Setting a proxy
server in Mozilla
Firefox

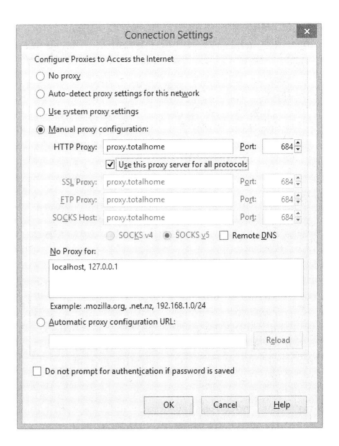

Figure 11-24
Web proxy at
work

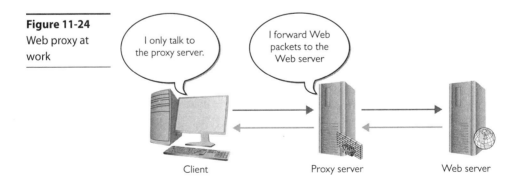

A *forward proxy server* acts on behalf of clients, getting information from various sources and handing that information to the clients. The sources (servers) don't know about the clients, only the proxy server.

NOTE If a proxy server caches a Web page, how does it know if the cache accurately reflects the real page? What if the real Web page was updated? In this case, a good proxy server uses querying tools to check the real Web page to update the cache.

A *reverse proxy server*, in contrast, acts on behalf of its servers. Clients contact the reverse proxy server, which gathers information from its associated server(s) and hands that information to the clients. The clients don't know about the servers behind the scenes. The reverse proxy server is the only machine with which they interact.

A proxy server might inspect the contents of the resource, looking for inappropriate content, viruses/malware, or just about anything else the creators of the proxy might desire it to identify.

HTTP proxy servers are the most common type of proxy server, but any TCP application can take advantage of proxy servers. Numerous proxy serving programs are available, such as Squid, shown in Figure 11-25. Proxy serving takes some substantial processing, so many vendors sell proxy servers in a box, such as the Symantec ProxySG.

Figure 11-25 Squid Proxy Server software

AAA

Authentication, authorization, and accounting (AAA), as you'll recall from Chapter 10, are vitally important for security on switches to support *port authentication*. Port authentication gives us a way to protect our network from unwanted people trying to access the network. Let's say that someone wants to bypass network security by bringing in a laptop and plugging the Ethernet connection straight into a switch port, or using that same laptop to connect wirelessly into one of the network WAPs. To prevent these types of intrusions, we use intelligent switches that support AAA.

When someone attempts a connection, he or she must have something at the point of connection to authenticate, and that's where advanced networking devices come into play. Many switches, and almost every wireless access point, come with feature sets to support port authentication. My routers support RADIUS and 802.1X port authentication.

Configuring a switch for AAA is arguably one of the most complex configuration jobs a network tech may ever face. Before you get anywhere near the switch, you'll need to make a number of decisions, such as the version of AAA you want to use (RADIUS or TACACS+), the type of 802.1X authentication methods you will use (passwords, certificates, retina scanners), deciding on and setting up the authentication database system, and opening up security polices to make sure it all works. This list is long, to say the least.

Once your AAA infrastructure is set up, you then configure a AAA-capable switch to support one or more methods of authentication. This is complicated too! There are ten flavors and "subflavors" of authentication supported by Cisco, for example, ranging from simple passwords to a local database to a RADIUS server and a TACACS+ server.

Configuring a switch for AAA—especially the first time—almost guarantees that you'll run into plenty of *TACACS+/RADIUS misconfiguration* issues. While it's impossible to name every possible misconfiguration issue, here's a list of some of the more common ones:

- *Failing to point the switch to the correct RADIUS/TACACS+ server.* You need to give the switch the right IP address. It's a simple issue, but one that often happens.

- *Improperly configuring the correct authentication method for the switch.* If you configure the switch for EAP-PEAP and the server is expecting EAP-TLS, it won't work properly. If you want to use a certificate-based authentication, you'll need a valid certificate that the server can use.

- *Failing to give the switch proper security policies on the server.* The switch won't be allowed to do its job.

Again, the list of misconfiguration issues setting up AAA is vast. The secret to dealing with these problems is locating and reading errors that come up on the switch and the AAA server. If a switch can get to the AAA server, then all the errors you need to know will be neatly listed for you on the server itself. How these errors manifest varies by the brand of AAA server you use. Microsoft's RADIUS server (called Network Policy Server, or NPS), for example, places all authentication errors in the Event Viewer. It's going to take some research and practice on your part, but once you have your misconfiguration issues handled, most AAA systems tend to run invisibly for years.

One of the really cool things about switch- and router-level authentication is the ability to fall back or failover to a "next method" of authentication. You can configure as many fallback methods as you like, as long as the method is supported by the switch you configure. The system attempts to authenticate using the first method in a list. If that first method isn't available (for instance, if the RADIUS server is down), it reverts to the second method in the list, and so forth.

Try This!

Exploring Switch Capabilities

If you have access to a managed switch of any kind, now would be a great time to explore its capabilities. Use a Web browser of choice and navigate to the switch. What can you configure? Do you see any options for proxy serving, load balancing, or other fancy capability? How could you optimize your network by using some of these more advanced capabilities?

Chapter Review

Questions

1. Which VPN technology enables direct connections between satellite locations?

    A. PPTP VPN

    B. IPsec VPN

    C. SSL VPN

    D. DMVPN

2. Which of the following is a protocol popular with today's VPNs?

    A. PPTP

    B. L2TP

    C. IPsec

    D. PPPoE

3. A static VLAN assigns VLANs to _____.

    A. IP addresses

    B. MAC addresses

    C. ports

    D. trunks

4. Which of the following is the trunking protocol used in today's VLANs?

   A. 802.1Q

   B. 802.1X

   C. 802.1t

   D. 802.1z

5. A content switch always works at least at which layer of the OSI model?

   A. 2

   B. 3

   C. 4

   D. 7

6. When the network is very busy, VoIP calls start to sound badly clipped. What solution might improve the quality of the VoIP calls?

   A. 802.1z

   B. Traffic shaping

   C. DNS

   D. Content switching

7. What are the benefits of caching on a Web proxy? (Select two.)

   A. Response time

   B. Virus detection

   C. Tracking

   D. Authentication

8. 802.1X is a great example of _____.

   A. encryption

   B. content switching

   C. port authentication

   D. VLAN trunking

9. What's the most common method used to configure a VLAN-capable switch?

   A. Log into the switch using SSH and use the command-line interface.

   B. Plug into the switch with a console cable and use the command-line interface.

   C. Log into the switch via a Web browser and use the GUI.

   D. Plug into the switch with a VLAN cable and use the command-line interface.

10. Which of the following statements best applies to an IDS?

   A. An IDS inspects a copy of all traffic in a network and can respond to detected intrusions with actions.

   B. An IDS inspects all traffic as it enters a network and can respond to detected intrusions with actions.

   C. An IDS inspects a copy of all traffic in a network and reports intrusions to a configured user account.

   D. An IDS inspects all traffic as it enters a network and reports intrusions to a configured user account.

Answers

1. **D.** A dynamic multipoint VPN (DMVPN) enables direct VPN connections between multiple locations.

2. **C.** Most VPNs use native IPsec today.

3. **C.** Static VLANs assign VLANs to physical ports.

4. **A.** The 802.1Q standard is almost universal for VLAN trunking.

5. **D.** Content switches usually work at Layers 4 through 7, but they must work at least at Layer 7.

6. **B.** Traffic shaping will provide extra bandwidth to the VoIP applications, improving sound quality.

7. **A** and **B.** Cached Web pages can be sent to clients quickly. The contents can also be checked for viruses.

8. **C.** 802.1X is port authentication.

9. **A.** The most common method used to configure a VLAN-capable switch is to log into the switch using SSH and then use the command-line interface.

10. **A.** An IDS inspects a copy of all traffic in a network and can respond to detected intrusions with actions.

IPv6

The CompTIA Network+ certification exam expects you to know how to

- 1.3 Explain the concepts and characteristics of routing and switching
- 1.4 Given a scenario, configure the appropriate IP addressing components

To achieve these goals, you must be able to

- Discuss the fundamental concepts of IPv6
- Describe IPv6 practices
- Implement IPv6 in a TCP/IP network

The Internet developers wanted to make a networking protocol that had serious longevity, so they had to define a large enough IP address space to last well beyond the foreseeable future. They had to determine how many computers might exist in the future and then make the IP address space even bigger. But how many computers would exist in the future? Keep in mind that TCP/IP development took place in the early 1970s. There were fewer than 1000 computers in the entire world at the time, but that didn't keep the IP developers from thinking big! They decided to go absolutely crazy (as many people considered at the time) and around 1979 created the *Internet Protocol version 4 (IPv4)* 32-bit IP address space, creating about four billion IP addresses. That should have held us for the foreseeable future.

It didn't. First, the TCP/IP folks wasted huge chunks of IP addresses due to classful addressing and a generally easygoing, wasteful method of parceling out IP addresses. Second, the Internet reached a level of popularity way beyond the original developers' imaginations. By the late-1980s the rate of consumption for IP addresses started to worry the Internet people and the writing was on the wall for IPv4's 32-bit addressing.

As a result, the Internet Engineering Task Force (IETF) developed the *Internet Protocol version 6 (IPv6)* addressing system. IPv6 extended the 32-bit IP address space to 128 bits, allowing up to 2^{128} (that's close to 3.4×10^{38}) addresses. Take all the grains of sand on earth and that will give you an idea of how big a number that is.

 NOTE If you really want to know how many IP addresses IPv6 provides, here's your number: 340,282,366,920,938,463,463,374,607,431,768,211,456.

But IPv6 wasn't just about expanding the IP address space. IPv6 also improves security by making the Internet Protocol Security (IPsec) protocol support a standard part of every IPv6 stack. That doesn't mean you actually have to use IPsec, just that manufacturers must support it. If you use IPsec, every packet sent from your system is encrypted.

IPv6 also provides a more efficient routing scheme. Taking advantage of aggregation (see the section "Aggregation," later in this chapter), routing tables in IPv6 offer a much smaller footprint than routing tables in IPv4, enabling faster routing.

IPv6 has been the future of TCP/IP network addressing since I was a wee network technician. Someday, we knew, we'd flip the switch from IPv4 to IPv6 and transform the Internet and TCP/IP networking forever. That switch started flipping rapidly in 2017. All the major ISPs in Japan, for example, deployed IPv6 in 2017. Mobile device networks and the Internet of Things (IoT) are all IPv6. The rollout and changes are happening throughout the globe as I type these words. And it's not just the ISPs flipping to IPv6.

As you read through this exam guide, more and more companies are making the switch from IPv4 to IPv6. This is very much cost driven, because you have to pay for addresses separately. Why roll out IPv4 today, when IPv6 is ready to roll now and for the foreseeable future?

If you're reading this later in the cycle of the N10-007 certification, IPv6 has surpassed IPv4 in the marketplace. Change the slightly future-tense emphasis of this chapter to present tense and you'll be ready for a job as a network tech today. This chapter breaks the exploration of IPv6 into three parts. First, you need the basic concepts, such as how the numbers work. Second, you need to learn how to enable or apply IPv6 in a variety of technologies, such as DHCP. Finally, you need answers on how to deploy IPv6 today.

Test Specific

IPv6 Basics

Although they achieve the same function—enabling computers on IP networks to send packets to each other—IPv6 and IPv4 differ a lot when it comes to implementation. The addressing numbers work differently, for example, and don't look alike. IPv6 *always* uses link-local addressing for communicating on a local network. (The IPv4 version of an automatically generated local address, APIPA/zeroconf—169.254.0.0/16—always means something's wrong!) Subnetting works differently as well. You also need to understand the concepts of multicast, global addresses, and aggregation. Let's look at all these topics.

IPv6 Address Notation

The 32-bit IPv4 addresses are written as 197.169.94.82, using four octets. IPv6 has 128 bits, so octets are gone. IPv6 addresses are written like this:

```
2001:0000:0000:3210:0800:200c:00cf:1234
```

IPv6 uses a colon as a separator, instead of the period used in IPv4's dotted decimal format. Each group—called a *quartet* or *hextet*—is a hexadecimal number between 0000 and ffff.

EXAM TIP You'll see the hexadecimal letters in IPv6 written in both uppercase and lowercase. It doesn't matter to the computer, but the people behind IPv6 insist (per RFC 5952) that notation should be lowercase. That's the convention used here. You might see the letters uppercase on the CompTIA Network+ exam. It's all the same, so don't get thrown off!

An IPv6 address generally splits into two 64-bit sections: the *network prefix* is the first 64 bits and is used for routing. The second 64 bits is the user address, called the *interface ID*. The network prefix further gets broken into a *global routing prefix* and a *subnet ID* (Figure 12-1). I've added space between the sections for emphasis.

Figure 12-1
Typical IPv6 address components

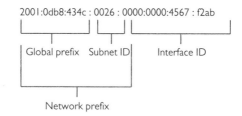

NOTE For those who don't play with hex regularly, one hexadecimal character (for example, *f*) represents 4 bits, so four hexadecimal characters make a 16-bit group.

A complete IPv6 address always has eight groups of four hexadecimal characters. If this sounds like you're going to type in really long IP addresses, don't worry, IPv6 offers a number of shortcuts.

First, leading zeroes can be dropped from any group, so 00cf becomes cf and 0000 becomes 0. Let's rewrite that IPv6 address using this shortcut:

```
2001:0:0:3210:800:200c:cf:1234
```

To write IPv6 addresses containing strings of zeroes, you can use a pair of colons (::) to represent a string of consecutive groups with a value of zero. For example, using the :: rule, you can write the IPv6 address

```
2001:0:0:3210:800:200c:cf:1234
```

as

```
2001::3210:800:200c:cf:1234
```

Double colons are very handy, but you have to be careful when you use them. Take a look at this IPv6 address:

```
fe80:0000:0000:0000:00cf:0000:ba98:1234
```

If I convert it to

```
fe80::cf:0:ba98:1234
```

I may not use a second :: to represent the third-to-last group of four zeroes—only one :: is allowed per address! There's a good reason for this rule. If more than one :: was used, how could you tell how many sets of zeroes were in each group? Answer: you couldn't.

IPv6 uses the "*/x*" *prefix length* naming convention, similar to the Classless Inter-Domain Routing (CIDR) naming convention in IPv4. Here's how to write an IP address and prefix length for a typical IPv6 host:

```
fe80::cf:0:ba98:1234/64
```

The /64 tells the reader that the network prefix is 64 bits. The address starts with fe80 followed by some number of hextets of all zeroes: 0000. With the /64, you know to make the prefix thus:

```
fe80:0000:0000:0000
```

Here's an example of a very special IPv6 address that takes full advantage of the double colon, the IPv6 loopback address:

```
::1
```

Without using the double-colon notation, this IPv6 address would look like this:

```
0000:0000:0000:0000:0000:0000:0000:0001
```

NOTE   The unspecified address (all zeroes) can never be used, and neither can an address that contains all ones (all *f*s in IPv6 notation).

Link-Local Address

The folks who created IPv6 worked hard to make it powerful and easy to use, but you pretty much have to forget all the rules you learned about IPv4 addressing. The biggest item to wrap your mind around is that a host no longer has a single IP address unless the network isn't connected to a router. When a computer running IPv6 first boots up, it gives itself a *link-local address*. Think of a link-local address as IPv6's equivalent to IPv4's APIPA/zeroconf address. The first 64 bits of a link-local address are always fe80::/10, followed by 54 zero bits. That means every link-local address always begins with fe80:0000:0000:0000.

NOTE Although only the fe80::/10 denotes the link-local address, according to the Request for Comments that defined link-local addressing (RFC 4291), the next 54 bits have to be zeroes. That means in implementation, a link-local address will start with fe80::/64.

The second 64 bits of a link-local address, the interface ID, are generated in two ways. Every current operating system generates a 64-bit random number (Figure 12-2). Very old operating systems, such as Windows XP and Windows Server 2003, used the device's MAC address to create a 64-bit number called an *Extended Unique Identifier, 64-bit (EUI-64)*. (You only need to know the EUI-64 trivia for the CompTIA Network+ exam. There's no scenario for this usage today.)

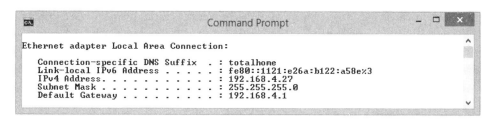

Figure 12-2   Link-local address in Windows

The link-local address does all the hard work in IPv6, and, as long as you don't need an Internet connection, it's all you need. The old concepts of static and DHCP addressing don't really make much sense in IPv6 unless you have dedicated servers (even in IPv6, servers generally still have static IP addresses). Link-local addressing takes care of all your local network needs!

IPv6 Prefix Lengths

Systems use IPv6 *prefix lengths* to determine whether to send packets to a local MAC address or to the default gateway to send the packets out to the Internet. But you need to focus on two rules:

- The last 64 bits of an IPv6 address are generated by the NIC, leaving a maximum of 64 bits for the prefix. Therefore, no prefix is ever longer than /64.
- The five Regional Internet Registries (RIRs) pass out /48 prefixes to big ISPs and end users who need large allotments. ISPs and others will borrow another 16 bits for subnetting and then pass out /64 interface IDs to end users. Link-local addressing uses a prefix length of /64.

Other types of IPv6 addresses get the subnet information automatically from their routers (described next).

The End of Broadcast

A system's IPv6 link-local address is a *unicast address*, a unique address that is exclusive to that system. IPv4 also relies on unicast addresses. But IPv6 completely drops the idea of broadcast addresses, replacing it with the idea of *multicast*.

Multicast isn't some new idea introduced with IPv6. Multicast addressing has been around for a long time and works well in IPv4 as well as in IPv6. A *multicast address* is a set of reserved addresses designed to go only to certain systems. As you've learned in previous chapters, any IPv4 address that starts with 224.0.0.0/4 (the old Class D network addresses) is reserved for multicast. Within that reserved range, individual addresses are assigned to specific applications that wish to use multicast. For example, if a system is configured to use the *Network Time Protocol (NTP)*, it will listen on multicast address 224.0.1.1 for time information.

IPv6 multicast functions similarly to IPv4 multicast, though with IPv6 addressing (NTP uses ff0*x*::101, for example, where *x* represents a variable scope). IPv6 multicast also adds additional functions not found in IPv4 multicast. If an IPv6 system sends out a multicast to the address ff02::2, for example, only routers read the message while everyone else ignores it (Figure 12-3).

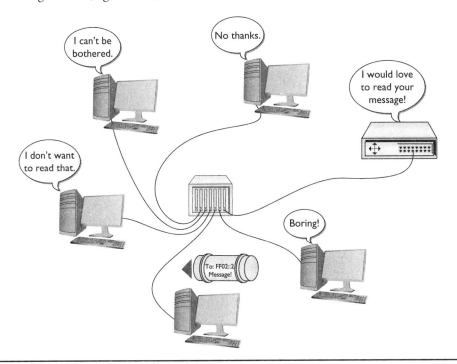

Figure 12-3   Multicast to routers

Multicast packets are encapsulated into Ethernet frames just like any other packet. Ethernet reserves the address 01-00-5e-*xx-xx-xx* for IPv4 multicast frame destination addresses. The Ethernet address 33-33-*xx-xx-xx-xx* is used on Ethernet frames that encapsulate IPv6 multicast packets.

NOTE Here's a bit of geeky trivia for you. Why 33-33? That's the address of Xerox PARC (Palo Alto Research Center), the birthplace of Ethernet and many other networking technologies used today.

Every computer sees the multicast frame, but only the computers specifically set up to process the frame process it. The rest drop the frame at Layer 2. Table 12-1 shows a few of the more useful IPv6 multicast addresses. You've just seen ff02::2; I'll explain the rest later in this chapter.

Table 12-1	Address	Function
A Few IPv6 Multicast Addresses	ff02::1	All Nodes Address
	ff02::2	All Routers Address
	ff02::1:ff*xx:xxxx*	Solicited-Node Address

Looking at the first listing, ff02::1, you might ask: "How is that different from a broadcast?" The answer lies more in the definition of multicast than in what really takes place. A computer must be configured as a member of a particular group to read a particular multicast. In this case, if a computer is a member of "All Nodes," then it reads the message.

NOTE All-Nodes multicasts are pretty much just used by routers, not typical traffic.

Beyond unicast and multicast, IPv6 uses a third type of addressing called *anycast*. An anycast address is a bit of a strange animal, so it's helpful to know why you need an anycast address before you try to understand what one is. The best place to learn how anycast works and why it is needed is the one place where its use is very common: DNS.

You learned in Chapter 9, "Network Naming," that the top of the DNS root structure consists of a number of root DNS servers. Every DNS server on the Internet keeps the IP addresses of the root servers in a file called *root hints*. Here's one part of the root hints file from my DNS server:

```
                             NS    F.ROOT-SERVERS.NET.
F.ROOT-SERVERS.NET.          A     192.5.5.241
F.ROOT-SERVERS.NET.          AAAA  2001:500:2f::f
```

At first glance, you might think that this root server is a single physical box because it only has a single IPv4 address and a single IPv6 address. It's not. It is a whole bunch of server clusters strategically placed all over the world. In Chapter 11, "Advanced Networking Devices," you saw how DNS can make a cluster of computers act as a single server, but none of those solutions can make a bunch of clusters all over the world act as a single server in an efficient way to make sure the DNS queries are answered as quickly as possible. To do this, we need anycasting.

Anycasting starts by giving a number of computers (or clusters of computers) the same IP address. Then routers (in the case of DNS, only the biggest Tier 1 Internet routers) use Border Gateway Protocol (BGP) to determine which computer in the cluster is closest. When that router gets a packet addressed to that IP address, it sends it only to the closest root DNS server, even though it may know where others are located. That is an anycast address.

An anycast address is a unicast address, and, in most cases, the computer sending the packet doesn't know or care to know that the address is anycast. The only device that knows (and cares) is the top-tier router that has the smarts to send the packet only to the closest root DNS server.

Global Unicast Address

To get on the Internet, your system needs a second IPv6 address called a *global unicast address*, often referred to as a "global address." The most common way to get a global unicast address is from your default gateway, which must be configured to pass out global IPv6 addresses. When your computer boots up, it sends out a router solicitation message on multicast address ff02::2 looking for a router. Your router hears this message and tells your computer the prefix. See Figure 12-4.

Figure 12-4
Getting a global
unicast address

With prefix in hand, the computer generates the rest of the global unicast address, the last 64 bits, just as it creates the last 64 bits of a link-local address. Your computer now has a global unicast address as well as a link-local address. Figure 12-5 shows the IPv6 information on an Apple computer running macOS.

A global unicast address is a true Internet address. If another computer is running IPv6 and also has a global address, it can access your system unless you have some form of firewall running.

Figure 12-5 IPv6 information on macOS

As routers make the transition from IPv4 to IPv6, one important feature to enable to allow router solicitation to work is called *prefix delegation* (Figure 12-6). Enabling it simply tells the router to go upstream to the ISP and get a prefix to hand out to clients.

EXAM TIP Computers using IPv6 need a global unicast address to access the Internet.

Aggregation

Routers need to know where to send every packet they encounter. Most routers have a default path on which they send packets that aren't specifically defined to go on any other route. As you get to the top of the Internet, the Tier 1 routers that connect to the other Tier 1 routers can't have any default route (Figure 12-7). We call these the *no-default routers*.

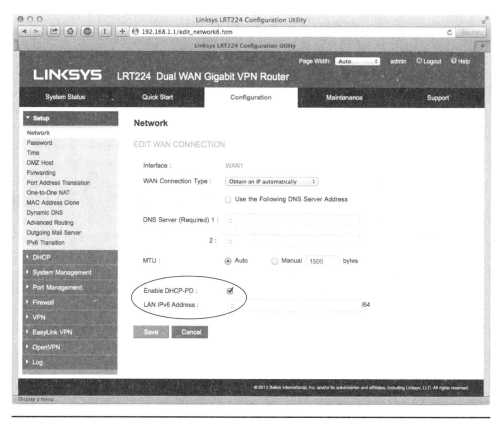

Figure 12-6   Enabling prefix delegation on a SOHO router (called DHCP-PD on this router)

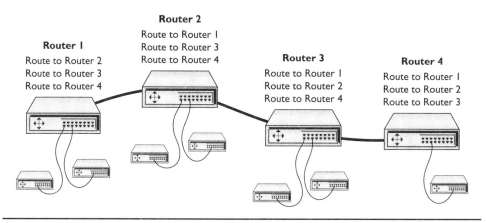

Figure 12-7   No-default routers

The current state of the Internet's upper tiers is rather messy. A typical no-default router has somewhere around 750,000 routes in its routing table, requiring a router with massive firepower. But what would happen if the Internet was organized as shown in Figure 12-8? Note how every router underneath one router always uses a subset of that router's existing routes. This is called *aggregation*.

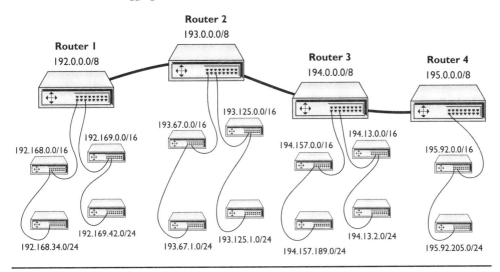

Figure 12-8 Aggregation

Aggregation would drastically reduce the size and complexity of routing tables and make the Internet faster. Aggregation would also give a more detailed, geographic picture of how the Internet is organized—you could get a good idea of where a person is physically located just by looking at the IP address.

It's way too late for IPv4 to use aggregation. Many organizations that received class licenses 20 to 30 years ago simply will not relinquish them. Toward the end of the IPv4 address allocation, the RIRs handed them out in a geographical way. The amount of effort necessary to make aggregation work throughout IPv4 would require a level of synchronization that would bring the entire Internet to its knees.

But aggregation is part and parcel with IPv6. Remember, your computer gets the 64-bit interface ID from your default gateway. The router, in turn, gets a (usually) 48-bit prefix from its upstream router and adds a 16-bit subnet ID.

 NOTE Keep this formula in mind: A 48-bit prefix from upstream router + 16-bit subnet ID from default gateway + 64-bit interface ID = 128-bit IPv6 address.

This method enables the entire IPv6 network to change IP addresses on-the-fly to keep aggregation working. Imagine you have a default gateway connected to an upstream router from your ISP, as shown in Figure 12-9.

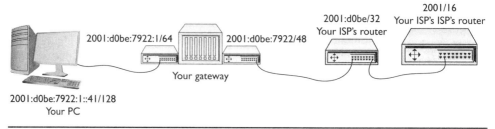

Figure 12-9   An IPv6 group of routers

Your PC's IPv6 address is 2001:d0be:7922:1:fc2d:aeb2:99d2:e2b4. Let's cut out the last 64 bits and look at the prefix and see where this comes from:

Your network's prefix: 2001:d0be:7922:1/64

IPv6 addresses begin at the very top of the Internet with the no-default routers. We'll assume your *ISP's* ISP is one of those routers. Your ISP gets (usually) a 32-bit prefix from an RIR or from its ISP if it is small.

In this case, the prefix is 2001:d0be/32. This prefix comes from the upstream router, and your ISP has no control over it. The person setting up the ISP's router, however, will add a 16-bit subnet ID to the prefix, as shown in Figure 12-10.

Figure 12-10

Adding the first prefix

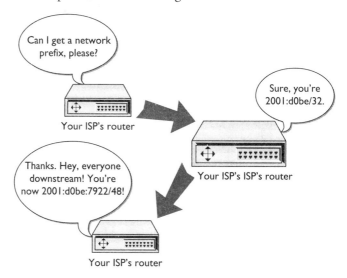

Your router receives a 48-bit prefix (in this case, 2001:d0be:7922/48) from your ISP's router. Your router has no control over that prefix. The person setting up your gateway, however, adds a 16-bit subnet ID (in this case, :0001 or :1) to the 48-bit prefix to make the 64-bit prefix for your network (Figure 12-11).

What makes all this particularly interesting is that any router upstream of anyone else may change the prefix it sends downstream, keeping aggregation intact. To see this in action, let's watch what happens if your ISP decides to change to another upstream ISP (Figure 12-12). In this case, your ISP moves from the old ISP (ISP1) to a new ISP (ISP2). When your ISP makes the new connection, the new ISP passes out a different 32-bit prefix

Figure 12-11
Adding the
second prefix

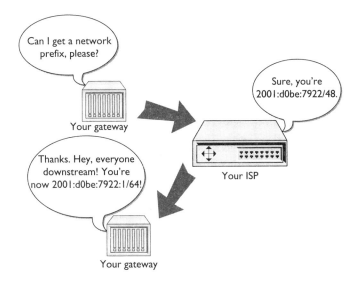

(in this example, 2ab0:3c05/32). As quickly as this change takes place, all of the down-stream routers make an "all nodes" multicast and all clients get new IP addresses.

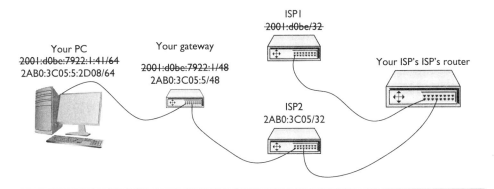

Figure 12-12   New IP address updated downstream

Aggregation is an intrinsic but for the most part completely transparent part of IPv6. Know that your IPv6 Internet addresses may suddenly change from time to time and that the address changes are a fairly rare but normal aspect of using IPv6.

Regional Internet Registries

IANA doesn't pass out IPv6 prefixes. This job is delegated to the five Regional Internet Registries (RIRs):

- American Registry for Internet Numbers (ARIN) supports North America and many Caribbean and North Atlantic islands.

- RIPE Network Coordination Centre (RIPE NCC) supports Europe, the Middle East, and Central Asia.

- Asia-Pacific Network Information Centre (APNIC) supports Asia and the Pacific region.

- Latin American and Caribbean Internet Addresses Registry (LACNIC) supports Central and South America and parts of the Caribbean.

- African Network Information Centre (AfriNIC) supports Africa.

Using IPv6

Once IPv6 replaces IPv4 for typical user traffic, we will find ourselves in a very different world from the one we left in terms of configuration. In this section, you will see what it takes to turn on IPv6 for your network. This section also assumes you've turned off IPv4—which isn't a realistic option right now because IPv4 is still prevalent, but it makes understanding some aspects of using IPv6 much easier. You'll also learn how IPv6 works (or doesn't work, as the case may be) with NAT, DHCP, and DNS. We'll cover the idea of running IPv6 and IPv4 at the same time in the next section.

It Just Works

IPv6 works, with almost no interference or interaction from you or any other network technician. Assuming your ISP has implemented IPv6 and you're running a modern operating system, IPv6 will be set up and functioning. You rarely need static IP addresses, and DHCP—so common and necessary in IPv4—is almost nonexistent in IPv6.

The *Neighbor Discovery Protocol (NDP)* makes the IPv6 automation magic work. NDP has five packet types:

- Neighbor solicitation
- Neighbor advertisement
- Router solicitation
- Router advertisement
- Redirect (don't worry about this one)

 EXAM TIP You'll see the term *neighbor discovery* in documentation about uses of the Neighbor Discovery Protocol. You'll also see the term on the CompTIA Network+ exam.

Neighbor Solicitation/Advertisement

When an IPv6 computer joins a network, it sends out multicast *neighbor solicitation* packets searching for other computers on its broadcast domain. Because these packets all begin with ff02, only IPv6-capable machines on the broadcast domain will hear the multicast packet. Any IPv6 host that hears the multicast solicitation will respond with a *neighbor advertisement* packet, essentially saying, "I hear you and this is who I am." This is the functional equivalent to IPv4 ARP.

Router Solicitation/Advertisement

For IPv6 networks to function, they need unique network IDs. Router advertisements make this happen. Let's go through the most common example of all, a small network connected to an ISP via a single router. Just like IPv4, the network behind the router must have a unique network ID. With IPv4, we often use NAT and give the internal network a private network ID.

IPv6 changes the paradigm. Instead of NAT and private network IDs, IPv6 relies on *router advertisements*. First, the router needs a WAN address, so it listens for a router advertisement from its upstream router. The upstream router tells the local router its WAN IP address, its prefix length, its default gateway and DNS server, and so on.

So how does the router get its LAN ID? That's the trick and it relies on router advertisements as well. The router receives both the global prefix (usually 48 bits) and a unique subnet ID for the LAN (usually 16 bits), creating a unique 64-bit network ID for the LAN.

The router sends that information to all the LAN hosts via a router advertisement. A *router solicitation* only comes into play if a computer hasn't heard from the router recently and demands a router advertisement.

Is IPv6 Working?

The fastest way to verify if your system runs IPv6 is to check the IP status for your OS. In Windows, go to a command prompt and type `ipconfig` and press ENTER (Figure 12-13). In Linux or macOS, go to a terminal and type `ip addr` (Linux), or `ifconfig` (macOS) and press ENTER (Figure 12-14).

DHCPv6

You'd think with router advertisements that we wouldn't need DHCP any more. In some situations, unfortunately, we can't count on router advertisement information to enable a local network to run properly. For example, what if you want all your users to run on a local DNS server rather than one from your ISP? In this scenario, *DHCPv6* gives you better control over the LAN.

DHCPv6 works like traditional DHCP in that you have to configure a DHCPv6 server. A DHCPv6 server works in one of two modes: stateful or stateless. A *stateful* DHCPv6 server works very similarly to an IPv4 DHCP server, passing out complete IPv6 information: addresses and default gateways, as well as items like DNS server addresses. Figure 12-15 shows the DHCPv6 server on Windows Server. A *stateless* DHCPv6 server relies on router advertisements to give some information to individual hosts, making small changes to what the router advertisements would normally show, such as the address of the DNS server.

 NOTE   IPv6 DHCP servers use DHCPv6. This is not the sixth version of DHCP, mind you, just the name of DHCP for IPv6.

```
Command Prompt                                                              —  □  ×

Microsoft Windows [Version 10.0.16299.371]
(c) 2017 Microsoft Corporation. All rights reserved.

[15:17:49.68] C:\Users\michaels
>ipconfig

Windows IP Configuration


Ethernet adapter Local Area Connection:

   Connection-specific DNS Suffix  . : totalhome
   IPv6 Address. . . . . . . . . . . : 2603:300c:d:cd01:1121:e26a:b122:a58e
   Temporary IPv6 Address. . . . . . : 2603:300c:d:cd01:64c2:ccc1:d3b:e636
   Link-local IPv6 Address . . . . . : fe80::1121:e26a:b122:a58e%6
   IPv4 Address. . . . . . . . . . . : 192.168.4.55
   Subnet Mask . . . . . . . . . . . : 255.255.255.0
   Default Gateway . . . . . . . . . : fe80::f29f:c2ff:fe10:bd11%6
                                       192.168.4.1

Ethernet adapter Ethernet:

   Connection-specific DNS Suffix  . :
   Link-local IPv6 Address . . . . . : fe80::8de8:d540:fb4c:fe38%12
   IPv4 Address. . . . . . . . . . . : 192.168.231.1
   Subnet Mask . . . . . . . . . . . : 255.255.255.0
   Default Gateway . . . . . . . . . :

Ethernet adapter Ethernet 2:

   Connection-specific DNS Suffix  . :
   Link-local IPv6 Address . . . . . : fe80::b103:f8f4:e53d:ec25%14
   IPv4 Address. . . . . . . . . . . : 192.168.5.1
   Subnet Mask . . . . . . . . . . . : 255.255.255.0
   Default Gateway . . . . . . . . . :

[15:17:58.42] C:\Users\michaels
>
```

Figure 12-13   IPv6 enabled in Windows

```
                                fish /home/michaels

 File  Edit  View  Search  Terminal  Help
michaels@ubuntu-mbl ~> ip addr
1: lo: <LOOPBACK,UP,LOWER_UP> mtu 65536 qdisc noqueue state UNKNOWN group default qlen 1000
    link/loopback 00:00:00:00:00:00 brd 00:00:00:00:00:00
    inet 127.0.0.1/8 scope host lo
       valid_lft forever preferred_lft forever
    inet6 ::1/128 scope host
       valid_lft forever preferred_lft forever
2: enp9s0: <NO-CARRIER,BROADCAST,MULTICAST,UP> mtu 1500 qdisc mq state DOWN group default qlen 1000
    link/ether 00:25:64:5b:8a:0c brd ff:ff:ff:ff:ff:ff
3: wlp12s0: <BROADCAST,MULTICAST,UP,LOWER_UP> mtu 1500 qdisc fq_codel state UP group default qlen 1000
    link/ether 0c:60:76:34:f7:4f brd ff:ff:ff:ff:ff:ff
    inet 192.168.4.88/24 brd 192.168.4.255 scope global dynamic noprefixroute wlp12s0
       valid_lft 490857sec preferred_lft 490857sec
    inet6 2603:300c:d:cd01:19c0:51dc:20cd:1929/64 scope global temporary dynamic
       valid_lft 86332sec preferred_lft 14332sec
    inet6 2603:300c:d:cd01:a0e4:da31:bdaa:aa90/64 scope global dynamic mngtmpaddr noprefixroute
       valid_lft 86332sec preferred_lft 14332sec
    inet6 fe80::caee:68da:e374:dfeb/64 scope link noprefixroute
       valid_lft forever preferred_lft forever
4: docker0: <NO-CARRIER,BROADCAST,MULTICAST,UP> mtu 1500 qdisc noqueue state DOWN group default
    link/ether 02:42:dd:6f:cc:34 brd ff:ff:ff:ff:ff:ff
    inet 172.17.0.1/16 scope global docker0
       valid_lft forever preferred_lft forever
michaels@ubuntu-mbl ~> █
```

Figure 12-14   IPv6 enabled in Ubuntu

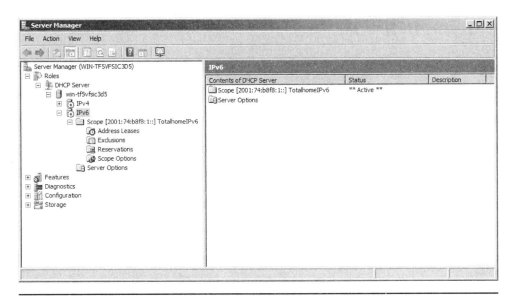

Figure 12-15   DHCPv6 server in action

DNS in IPv6

Just about every DNS server today supports IPv6 addresses. So setting up DNS requires little from network administrators. All IPv6 addresses have a record type of AAAA (chosen because it's 4× the length of IPv4 addresses). Figure 12-16 shows some IPv6 addresses in Windows Server.

 SIM   Check out the excellent pair of Sims for Chapter 12 at **http://hub .totalsem.com/007**. You'll find both a Show! and a Click! called "IPv6 Configuration" that walk you through the process of configuring IPv6 in Windows.

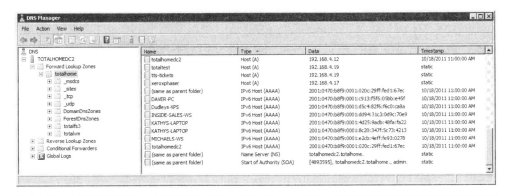

Figure 12-16   IPv6 addresses on DNS server

Moving to IPv6

There's no reason for you *not* to try running IPv6 today—like right now! At the very least, a whole world of IPv6-only Web sites are out there for you to explore. At the most, you may very well become the IPv6 expert in your organization. You almost certainly have an operating system ready to do IPv6; the only trick is to get you connected to the rest of us fun-loving IPv6-capable folks.

IPv4 and IPv6

The first and most important point to make right now is that you can run both IPv4 and IPv6 on your computers and routers at the same time, just as my computer does, as shown in Figure 12-17. This ability is a critical part of the process enabling the world to migrate slowly from IPv4 to IPv6.

```
Command Prompt                                                    —    □    ×
Ethernet adapter vEthernet (Default Switch):

   Connection-specific DNS Suffix  . :
   Link-local IPv6 Address . . . . . : fe80::f511:950f:fd10:f359%7
   IPv4 Address. . . . . . . . . . . : 172.24.84.145
   Subnet Mask . . . . . . . . . . . : 255.255.255.240
   Default Gateway . . . . . . . . . :

Ethernet adapter VirtualBox Host-Only Network:

   Connection-specific DNS Suffix  . :
   Link-local IPv6 Address . . . . . : fe80::a445:1a55:3f3c:564d%10
   IPv4 Address. . . . . . . . . . . : 192.168.56.1
   Subnet Mask . . . . . . . . . . . : 255.255.255.0
   Default Gateway . . . . . . . . . :

Ethernet adapter Ethernet:

   Connection-specific DNS Suffix  . : hsd1.tx.comcast.net.
   Link-local IPv6 Address . . . . . : fe80::7857:8f1a:6e4f:41dc%17
   IPv4 Address. . . . . . . . . . . : 192.168.0.173
   Subnet Mask . . . . . . . . . . . : 255.255.255.0
   Default Gateway . . . . . . . . . : 192.168.0.1

Ethernet adapter Ethernet 2:

   Media State . . . . . . . . . . . : Media disconnected
   Connection-specific DNS Suffix  . :

C:\Users\scott>
```

Figure 12-17   IPv4 and IPv6 on one computer

All modern operating systems support IPv6, and almost all routers support IPv6. Not all routers on the Internet have IPv6 support turned on.

Eventually, every router and every computer on the Internet will support IPv6, but the Internet is not yet there. Two critical parts of the Internet are ready, however:

- All the root DNS servers support IPv6 resolution.

- Almost all the Tier 1 ISP routers properly forward IPv6 packets.

The problem is that the routers and DNS servers between your IPv6-capable computer and the other IPv6-capable computers to which you would like to connect are not yet IPv6-ready. How do you get past this IPv6 gap (Figure 12-18)?

Figure 12-18
The IPv6 gap

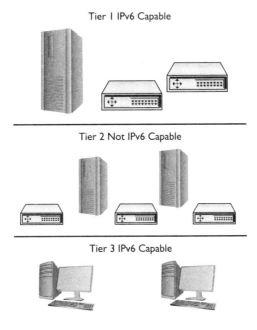

Tier 1 IPv6 Capable

Tier 2 Not IPv6 Capable

Tier 3 IPv6 Capable

 NOTE Depending on when you're reading this chapter, you may not need a tunnel for typical Internet traffic because the gap won't exist. Read through this next section specifically for items you'll find on the N10-007 exam.

Transition Mechanisms

To get on the IPv6 network, you need to leap over this gap, to implement an IPv4-to-IPv6 transition mechanism. The folks who developed IPv6 have several ways for you to do this using one of many IPv4-to-IPv6 *tunneling standards*, such as the one you'll see on the exam, *4to6*.

4to6

An IPv4-to-IPv6 tunnel works like any other tunnel, encapsulating one type of data into another. In this case, you encapsulate IPv4 traffic into an IPv6 tunnel to get to an IPv6-capable router, as shown in Figure 12-19.

To make this tunnel, you would download a tunneling client and install it on your computer. You would then fire up the client and make the tunnel connection—it's very easy to do.

 EXAM TIP You might see a now-deprecated tunneling protocol called 6to4 on the CompTIA Network+ exam. In theory, this protocol enabled IPv6 traffic over the IPv4 Internet. In practice, it proved unsuitable for widespread deployment. (See RFC 7526 for more information if you're curious.)

Figure 12-19

The IPv4-to-IPv6 tunnel

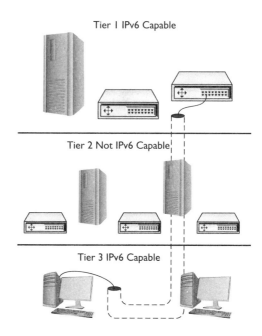

6in4

6in4 (also called IPv6-in-IPv4) is one of the most popular IPv6 tunneling standards. 6in4 is one of only two IPv6 tunneling protocols that can go through IPv4 NAT (called *NAT traversal*).

Teredo and Miredo

Teredo is the second NAT-traversal IPv6 tunneling protocol. Teredo is built into Microsoft Windows and, as a result, sees some adoption. Teredo addresses start with 2001:0000:/32. Most people prefer to skip Windows built-in support and instead get a third-party tool that supports 6to4 or 6in4.

Miredo is an open source implementation of Teredo for Linux and some other UNIX-based systems.

ISATAP

Intra-Site Automatic Tunnel Addressing Protocol (ISATAP) is designed to work within an IPv4 network by adding the IPv4 address to an IPv6 prefix to create a rather interesting but nonstandard address for the endpoints. One example of an ISATAP address is 2001:db8::98ca:200:131.107.28.9. ISATAP has a strong following, but other tunneling standards are gaining ground because they use a more common IPv6 addressing structure.

 NOTE You rarely have a choice of tunneling protocol. The tunneling protocol you use is the one your tunnel broker provides and is usually invisible to you.

Tunnel Brokers

Setting up an IPv6 tunnel can be a chore. You have to find someone willing to act as the far endpoint; you have to connect to them somehow; and then you have to know the tunneling standard they use. To make life easier, those who provide the endpoints have created the idea of the *tunnel broker*. Tunnel brokers create the actual tunnel and (usually) offer a custom-made endpoint client for you to use, although more advanced users can often make a manual connection.

Many tunnel brokers take advantage of one of two automatic configuration protocols, called *Tunnel Setup Protocol (TSP)* and *Tunnel Information and Control (TIC) protocol*. These protocols set up the tunnel and handle configuration as well as login. If it wasn't for TSP and TIC, there would be no such thing as automatic third-party tunnel endpoint clients for you to use.

 NOTE The biggest tunnel broker player is *Hurricane Electric*, based in Fremont, California. They have a huge IPv6 global transit network, offer IPv6 certifications, and more. Check them out at www.he.net.

Overlay Tunnels

An *overlay tunnel* enables two IPv6 networks to connect over an existing IPv4 infrastructure, such as the Internet. In more precise terms, the routers that connect the IPv6 networks to the IPv4 infrastructure run *dual stack*—both IPv4 and IPv6—and can encapsulate the traffic from the local network into IPv4 packets. Those IPv4 packets travel over the IPv4 infrastructure and the router at the other end of the tunnel strips the IPv4 stuff off the packet and sends the remaining IPv6 packet on its merry way.

Routers can use the same protocols used to connect an IPv4 client to an IPv6 network—4to6, ISATAP, and such (previously discussed)—or can be configured manually. A *manual tunnel* creates a simple point-to-point connection between the two IPv6 networks. Manual tunnels are good for regular, secure (via IPsec) communication between two networks.

NAT64

IPv6 has no need or use for classic network address translation (NAT), as implemented in IPv4 to offset the problem of address exhaustion. In the structure of IPv6, with its massive address space, old NAT is irrelevant.

NAT64 is a transition mechanism that embeds IPv4 packets into IPv6 packets for network traversal. Typically, you'll have a NAT64 gateway that handles the traffic between the IPv4 and IPv6 segments, doing the address translation on-the-fly and keeping track of who's who on either end.

Chapter Review

Questions

1. Which of the following is a valid IPv6 address?

    A. 2001:bead:beef::1

    B. 2001:30f5::3d62::04ffe

    C. 192.168.1.4:ff45:129g:48fd:1

    D. 2001.0470.b33e.23f4.27de.d34a.aed2.1827

2. DHCP is required to receive an IPv6 address automatically.

    A. True

    B. False

3. What kind of DNS records do IPv6 addresses use?

    A. A

    B. SIX

    C. AAAA

    D. NSSIX

4. Is NAT needed with IPv6?

    A. No, because NAT has been replaced with a new version called NAT6.

    B. No, the address space is so large that rationing routable addresses is unnecessary.

    C. Yes, because it is the only way to protect against hackers.

    D. Yes, because of the limited nature of IPv6 addressing.

5. What does a client need to access IPv6 content on the Internet?

    A. A link-local address.

    B. A multicast address.

    C. A global unicast address.

    D. The IPv6 Internet is currently unreachable.

6. What is the /16 prefix for all 6to4 address?

    A. 2001

    B. 2003

    C. 2002

    D. 2021

7. Which of the following operating systems have Teredo built in? (Select two).

    A. Windows 7

    B. macOS

    C. Windows 10

    D. Linux

8. What service do tunnel brokers provide?

    A. A way for users to jump the gap between their computers and the IPv6 Internet routers.

    B. They provide no useful service.

    C. Access to IPv6 DNS records.

    D. A second connection for multihoming.

9. What is the /48 prefix of the address 2001:0480:b6f3:0001::0001?

    A. 2001:480:b6f3:1

    B. 2001:480:b6f3

    C. 2001:480:b6f3:1:0000::1

    D. 2001:480:b6f3:1:0000:0000:0000:1

10. Which of the following is the valid reduced version of the address 2001:0489:000f:0000:0000:1f00:0000:000d?

    A. 2001:489:f::1f:0:d

    B. 2001:489:f::1f00::d

    C. 2001:0489:000f::1f00:0000:000d

    D. 2001:489:f::1f00:0:d

Answers

1. **A.** B has two sets of double colons. C is using IPv4 numbers. D is using periods instead of colons.

2. **B.** Router advertisements allow clients to receive a valid IPv6 address without a DHCP server.

3. **C.** The DNS system uses AAAA for IPv6 records.

4. **B.** NAT is no longer needed because of the massive size of the IPv6 address space.

5. **C.** A client needs a global unicast address to access the IPv6 Internet.

6. **C.** The /16 prefix designated by IANA for all 6to4 addresses is 2002.

7. **A** and **C.** Teredo is built into Windows.

8. **A.** Tunnel brokers provide a way to jump the gap between users' computers and the IPv6 Internet.

9. **B.** The /48 prefix consists of only the first three groups of the address.

10. **D.** Leading zeroes can be dropped and only one group of contiguous zeroes can be represented by a double colon.

Remote Connectivity

The CompTIA Network+ certification exam expects you to know how to

- 1.1 Explain the purposes and uses of ports and protocols
- 1.3 Explain the concepts and characteristics of routing and switching
- 1.4 Given a scenario, configure the appropriate IP addressing components
- 1.5 Compare and contrast the characteristics of network topologies, types and technologies
- 2.1 Given a scenario, deploy the appropriate cabling solution
- 2.2 Given a scenario, determine the appropriate placement of networking devices on a network and install/configure them
- 2.5 Compare and contrast WAN technologies
- 3.4 Given a scenario, use remote access methods

To achieve these goals, you must be able to

- Describe WAN telephony technologies, such as SONET, T1, and T3
- Compare last-mile connections for connecting homes and businesses to the Internet
- Discuss and implement various remote access connection methods
- Troubleshoot various WAN scenarios

Computers connect to other computers locally in a *local area network (LAN)*—you've read about LAN connections throughout this book—and remotely through a number of different methods. Interconnecting computers over distances, especially when the connections cross borders or jurisdictions, creates a *wide area network (WAN)*, though the term is pretty flexible. This chapter takes both an historical and a modern look at ways to interconnect a local computer or network with distant computers, what's called *remote connectivity*.

Historical/Conceptual

Remote connections have been around for a long time. Before the Internet, network users and developers created ways to take a single system or network and connect it to another faraway system or network. This wasn't the Internet! These were private interconnections of private networks. These connections were very expensive and, compared to today's options, pretty slow.

As the Internet developed, most of the same technologies used to make the earlier private remote connections became the way the Internet itself interconnects. Before the Internet was popular, many organizations used dedicated lines, called *T1 lines* (discussed in more detail later in this chapter), to connect far-flung offices. T1 is a dying technology and rarely used today.

This chapter shows you all the ways you can make remote connections. You'll see every type of remote connection currently in popular use, from good-old telephone lines to advanced fiber-optic carriers, and even satellites. There are so many ways to make remote connections that this chapter is broken into four parts. The first part, "Telephony and Beyond," gives you a tour of the technologies that originally existed for long-distance voice connections that now also support data. The next part, "The Last Mile," goes into how we as individual users connect to those long-distance technologies and demonstrates how wireless technologies come into play in remote connectivity. Third, "Using Remote Access" shows you the many different ways to use these connections to connect to another, faraway computer. The chapter finishes with a section on trouble-shooting various WAN scenarios. Let's get started!

Telephony and Beyond

We've already discussed the Tier 1 ISPs of the Internet, but let's look at them once again in a different way. Describing the Tier 1 Internet is always an interesting topic. Those of us in the instruction business invariably start this description by drawing a picture of the United States and then adding lines connecting big cities, as shown in Figure 13-1.

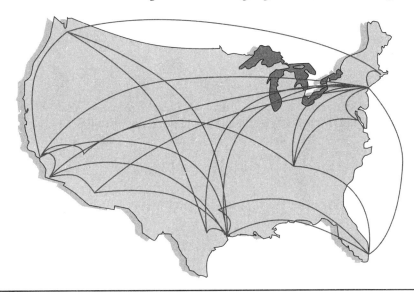

Figure 13-1　The Tier 1 Internet

But what are these lines and where did they come from? If the Internet is just a big TCP/IP network, wouldn't these lines be Ethernet connections? Maybe copper, maybe fiber, but surely they're Ethernet? Well, traditionally they're not. The vast majority of the long-distance connections that make up the Internet use a unique type of signal called SONET. SONET was originally designed to handle special heavy-duty circuits with names like T1. Never heard of SONET or T1? Don't worry—you're about to learn quite a bit.

NOTE Even as you read this, more and more of the Internet interconnections are moving toward Gigabit and 10-Gigabit Ethernet. Telephone technologies, however, continue to dominate.

Most of the connections that make up the high-speed backbone of the Internet use technologies designed at least 20 years ago to support telephone calls. We're not talking about your cool, cell phone–type calls here, but rather the old-school, wire-runs-up-to-the-house, telephone-connected-to-a-phone-jack connections. (See "Public Switched Telephone Network" later in this chapter for more on this subject.) If you want to understand how the Internet connects, you have to go way back to the 1970s and 1980s, before the Internet really took off, and learn how the U.S. telephone system developed to support networks.

The Dawn of Long Distance

Have you ever watched one of those old-time movies in which someone makes a phone call by picking up the phone and saying, "Operator, get me Mohawk 4, 3-8-2-5!" Suddenly, the scene changes to some person sitting at a switchboard like the one shown in Figure 13-2.

Figure 13-2
Old-time telephone operator (photo courtesy of the Richardson Historical and Genealogical Society)

This was the telephone operator. The telephone operator made a physical link between your phone and the other phone, making your connection. The switchboard acted as a *circuit switch*, where plugging in the two wires created a physical circuit between the two phones. This worked pretty well in the first few years of telephones, but it quickly became a problem as more and more phone lines began to fill the skies overhead (Figure 13-3).

Figure 13-3
Now that's a lot of telephone lines!

These first generations of long-distance telephone systems (think 1930s here) used analog signals, because that was how your telephone worked—the higher and lower the pitch of your voice, the lower or greater the voltage. If you graphed out a voice signal, it looked something like Figure 13-4. This type of transmission had issues, however, because analog signals over long distances, even if you amplified them, lost sound quality very quickly.

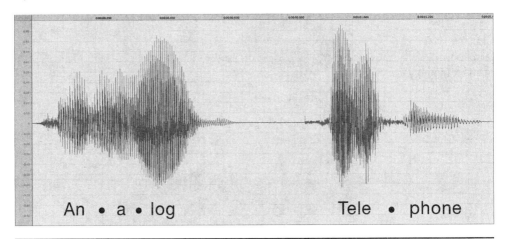

Figure 13-4   Another problem of early long-distance telephone systems

The first problem to take care of was the number of telephone wires. Individual wires were slowly replaced with special boxes called multiplexers. A *multiplexer* took a circuit and combined it with a few hundred other circuits into a single complex circuit on one wire. A *demultiplexer* (devices were both multiplexers and demultiplexers) on the other end of the connection split the individual connections back out (Figure 13-5).

 EXAM TIP The various multiplexing and demultiplexing technologies and protocols, both analog and digital, are collectively referred to as *modulation techniques*, a term you might see on the CompTIA network+ exam. Modulation more technically means converting a digital signal to analog or pushing an analog signal to a higher frequency. Pay attention to the wording of any exam questions on modulation.

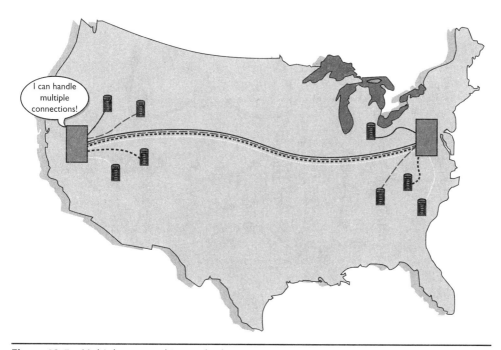

Figure 13-5 Multiplexers combine multiple circuits.

Over time, the entire United States was divided into hundreds, eventually thousands, of local exchanges. *Local exchanges* were a defined grouping of individual phone circuits served by a single multiplexer (calls within the exchange were handled first by human operators who were replaced, eventually, with dial tones and special switches that interpreted your pulses or tones for a number). One or more exchanges were (and still are) housed in a physical building called a *central office* (Figure 13-6) where individual voice circuits all came together. Local calls were still manually connected (although automatic exchanges began to appear in earnest by the 1950s, after which many operators lost their jobs), but any connection between exchanges was carried over these special multiplexed trunk lines. Figure 13-7 shows a very stylized example of how this worked.

Figure 13-6
A central office
building

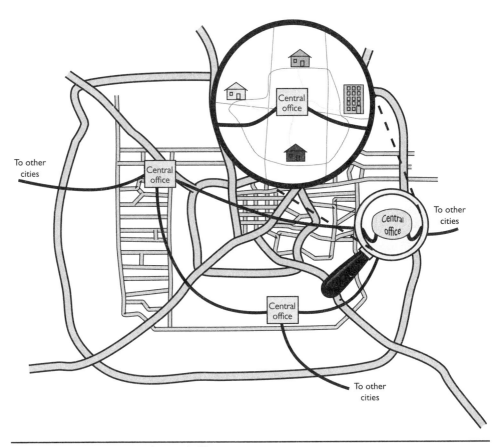

Figure 13-7   Interconnected central offices

These old-style trunk lines were fascinating technology. How did they put a bunch of voice calls on a single piece of cable, yet still somehow keep them separate? To understand the trick, you need to appreciate a little bit about frequency. A typical telephone only detects a fairly limited frequency range—from around 350 Hz to around 4000 Hz. This range covers enough of the human speech range to make a decent phone call. As the individual calls came into the multiplexer, it added a certain frequency multiplier to each call, keeping every separate call in its own unique frequency range (Figure 13-8). This process is called *frequency division multiplexing (FDM)*.

Figure 13-8
Multiplexed FDM

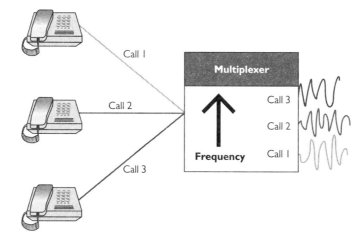

This analog network still required a physical connection from one phone to the other, even if those phones were on opposite sides of the country. Long distance used a series of trunk lines, and at each intersection of those lines an operator had to connect the calls. When you physically connect two phones together on one circuit, you are using something called *circuit switching*. As you might imagine, circuit switching isn't that great for long distance, but it's your only option when you use analog.

NOTE The long-distance lines used for voice calls are the same ones that carry our Internet data. There is no difference as far as the carriers are concerned.

This analog system worked pretty well through the 1930s to the 1950s, but telephones became so common and demand so heavy that the United States needed a new system to handle the load. The folks developing this new system realized that they had to dump analog and replace it with a digital system—sowing the seeds for the remote connections that eventually became the Internet.

Digital data transmits much easier over long distances than analog data because you can use repeaters. (You cannot use repeaters on analog signals.) A repeater is not an amplifier. An amplifier just increases the voltage and includes all the pops and hisses created by all kinds of interferences. A *repeater* takes the entire digital signal and re-creates it out the other end (Figure 13-9).

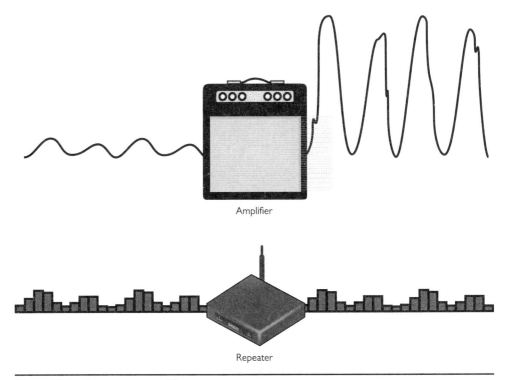

Amplifier

Repeater

Figure 13-9   Repeater vs. amplifier

The downside to adopting a digital system was that the entire telephone system was analog: every telephone, every switch, every multiplexer. The task of converting the entire analog voice system to digital was a massive undertaking. Luckily, virtually the entire U.S. phone system at that time was a monopoly run by a company called AT&T. A single company could make all of its own decisions and its own standards—one of the few times in history where a monopoly was probably a good thing. The AT&T folks had a choice here: completely revamp the entire U.S. phone system, including replacing every single telephone in the United States, or just make the trunk lines digital and let the central offices convert from analog to digital. They chose the latter.

Even today, a classic telephone line in your home or small office uses analog signals—the rest of the entire telephone system is digital. The telecommunications industry calls the connection from a central office to individual users the *last mile*. The telephone company's decision to keep the last mile analog has had serious repercussions that still challenge us even in the 21st century (Figure 13-10).

 NOTE   Attempts were made to convert the entire telephone system, including your telephones, to digital, but these technologies never took off (except in a few niches). See "ISDN" later in this chapter.

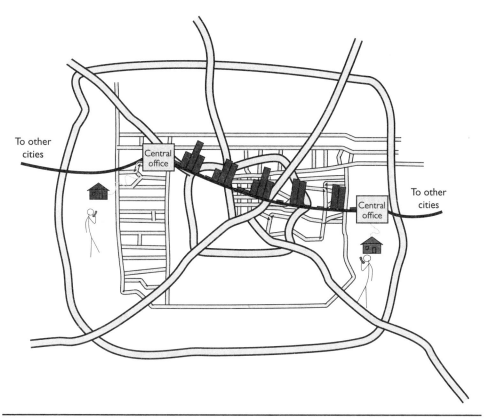

Figure 13-10 Analog and digital

Test Specific

Digital Telephony

You'll find digital telephony easy to understand, because most of the aspects you've already learned about computer networking work roughly the same way in a telephone network. In fact, most of the concepts that created computer networking came from the telephone industry. For example, the telephone industry was the first technology to adopt heavily the idea of digital packets. It was the first to do what is now called switching. Heck, the telephone industry even made the first working topologies! Let's take advantage of what you already know about how networks work to learn about how the telephone industry invented the idea of digital networks.

When you learned about networks in the first few chapters of this book, you learned about cabling, frame types, speeds, switching, and so on. All of these are important for computer networks. Well, let's do it again (in a much simpler format) to see the cabling, frame types, speed, and switching used in telephone systems. Don't worry—unlike computer networks, in which a certain type of cable might run different types of frames at different speeds, most of the remote connections used in the telephony world tend to have one type of cable that only runs one type of frame at one speed.

Let's begin with the most basic data chunk you get in the telephone world: DS0.

It All Starts with DS0

When AT&T decided to go digital, it knew all phone calls had to be broken into a digital sample. AT&T determined that if it took an analog signal of a human voice and converted it into 8-bit chunks 8000 times a second, it would be good enough to re-create the sound later. Figure 13-11 shows an example of the analog human voice seen earlier being converted into a digital sample.

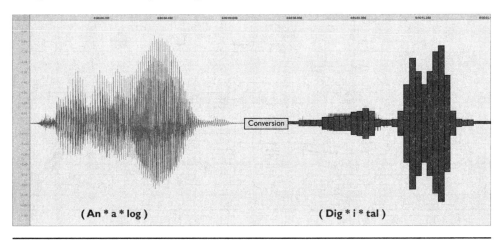

(An * a * log)   (Dig * i * tal)

Figure 13-11   Analog to digital

NOTE   A modulator takes a digital signal and converts it into an analog signal. A demodulator takes an analog signal and converts it into a digital signal. You call a device that does both a *modulator-demodulator*, better known as a *modem*. Because many people refer to modern DSL and cable boxes as "modems," you'll hear the term analog modem to describe the old-style analog-to-digital devices. See "The Last Mile" later in this chapter for the scoop on all the ways to connect today.

Converting analog sound into 8-bit chunks 8000 times a second creates a data stream (called a *digital signal*) of 8 × 8000 = 64 kilobits per second (Kbps). This digital signal rate, known as *DS0*, makes up the simplest data stream (and the slowest rate) of the digital part of the telephone system. Each analog voice call gets converted into a DS0 signal at the telephone company's central office. From there they are multiplexed into larger circuits.

Now that we have our voice calls converted to digital data, we need to get them to the right telephone. First, we need network technologies to handle the cabling, frames, and speed. Second, we need to come up with a method to switch the digital voice calls across a network. To handle the former, we need to define the types of interconnections, with names like T1 and OC-3. To handle the latter, we no longer connect via multiplexed circuit switching, as we did back with analog, but rather are now switching packets. I'll show you what I mean as I discuss the digital lines in use today.

Copper Carriers: T1 and T3

The first (and still popular) digital trunk carriers used by the telephone industry are called *T-carriers*. There are a number of different versions of T-carriers and the CompTIA Network+ exam expects you to know something about them. Let's begin with the most common and most basic, the venerable T-carrier level 1 (T1).

 NOTE What does the "T" stand for in T1? The most common explanation is "trunk-level," because T1 and later T-carriers functioned as trunk lines. The more definitive explanation is "terrestrial," so named in the early 1960s to differentiate between ground-based and space-based communications when the first satellites went into orbit.

T1 has several meanings. First, it refers to a digital networking technology called a *T1 connection*. Second, the term *T1 line* refers to the specific, shielded, two-pair cabling that connects the two ends of a T1 connection (Figure 13-12). Two wires are for sending data and two wires are for receiving data. The cable ends with a modular jack, called an *RJ-48C*, that looks a lot like the RJ-45 connector you're used to seeing with Ethernet cables.

Figure 13-12
T1 line

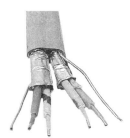

At either *termination* of a T1 line, you'll find an unassuming box called a *Channel Service Unit/Digital Service Unit (CSU/DSU)*. The CSU/DSU has a second connection that goes from the phone company (where the boxes reside) to a customer's equipment (usually a router). A T1 connection is point-to-point—you cannot have more than two CSU/DSUs on a single T1 line.

EXAM TIP   You can connect two CSU/DSU boxes together directly by using a *T1 crossover cable*. Like the UTP crossover cables you've seen previously in the book, the T1 crossover cable simply reverses the send/receive pairs on one end of the cable. You'll only see this in use to connect older routers together. The CSU/DSU connections provide convenient link points.

T1 uses a special signaling method called a *digital signal 1 (DS1)*.

DS1 uses a relatively primitive frame—the frame doesn't need to be complex because with point-to-point no addressing is necessary. Each DS1 frame has 25 pieces: a framing bit and 24 channels. Each DS1 channel holds a single 8-bit DS0 data sample. The framing bit and data channels combine to make 193 bits per DS1 frame. These frames are transmitted 8000 times/sec, making a total throughput of 1.544 Mbps (Figure 13-13). DS1 defines, therefore, a data transfer speed of 1.544 Mbps, split into 24 64-Kbps DS0 channels. The process of having frames that carry a portion of every channel in every frame sent on a regular interval is called *time division multiplexing (TDM)*.

 NOTE   Each 64-Kbps channel in a DS1 signal is a DS0.

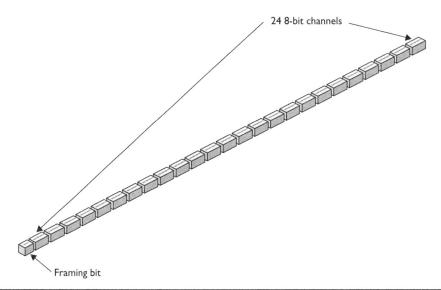

Figure 13-13   DS1 frame

When discussing T1 technology in class, I like to use an analogy of a conveyor belt in a milk-bottling factory. At regular intervals, big crates with 24 bottles come rolling down the belt. When they reach the filling machine, the bottles get filled with milk, and the crate keeps rolling down to the other end where two machines take over: the labeling and sorting machines. The labeling machine plucks out the bottles and applies a label to each, appropriate to the contents. The sorting machine sorts the bottles into cases of each type.

This is pretty simple if the filling machine uses only one type of milk. All 24 bottles fill with whole milk; all are labeled as whole milk; and all go into the case marked "Whole Milk." Once enough full bottles of milk arrive, the case gets completed, and you have a product.

That's pretty much how an Ethernet frame works, right? The whole frame encapsulates a single set of data, such as an IP packet that, in turn, encapsulates a single type of TCP segment, UDP datagram, or ICMP packet. It generally takes multiple frames to get the data to the recipient, where the frames are removed, the IP packet is removed, and the segment or datagram gets put together to make the data transfer complete.

The cool thing about the DS1 frame, though, is that you don't have to use the whole frame for a single set of data. With the right CSU/DSU at either end, you can specify which channels go with a specific thread of data. Sloshing back into the analogy, the milk company produces four types of milk: whole milk, low-fat milk, chocolate milk, and strawberry milk. The strawberry milk is seasonal; the whole milk sells the most, followed by chocolate, and then low fat.

To accommodate the different products, the factory master might designate channels 1–10 for whole milk, 11–18 for chocolate milk, 19–22 for low-fat milk, and 23–24 for strawberry. Now the labeling and sorting machines are going to have to work for a living! When a crate reaches the filling machine, the bottles get filled with the various types of milk, and then the crate trundles on down the belt. The labeling machine knows the numbering system, so it labels bottles 1–10 as whole milk, 11–18 as chocolate, and so on. The sorting machine also knows the system and has four cases at hand, one for each product. As the bottles arrive, it places them into the appropriate cases. Note that the cases will fill at different rates of speed. The strawberry milk case will take longer to fill, especially compared to the whole milk case, because only two channels in each crate carry strawberry.

What happens if the cows temporarily stop producing chocolate milk? Will the whole factory need to be reordered so the filling machine's eight chocolate dispensers can dispense some other kind of milk? Not in this factory. The crates continue to roll down the conveyor belt at regular intervals. The filling machine fills the bottles in channels 1–10 with whole milk, leaves the bottles in channels 11–18 empty, and puts low fat and strawberry in channels 19–22 and 23–24, respectively.

DS1/T1 work the same way. The frame just keeps jetting down the line, even if some of the channels contain no data. The CSU/DSU at the other end collects the data streams and keeps them separate. To paraphrase the immortal words of Professor Egon, "Never cross the streams." (You have seen *Ghostbusters*, right?) Otherwise you'd lose data.

 NOTE People rarely use the term "DS1." Because T1 lines only carry DS1 signals, you usually just say T1 when describing the signal, even though the term DS1 is more accurate.

To bring the milk bottling–factory analogy completely into the realm of networking and T1 connections, keep in mind that two conveyor belts are running in opposite directions. Milk flows in; milk flows out. You can both send and receive on T1 connections.

A T1 line is a dedicated phone connection that you lease, usually on a monthly basis, from the telephone company. It has no telephone number, and it's always connected. An entire T1 bundle is expensive (and obsolete), so some telephone companies let you buy just some of these individual channels, a practice known as *fractional T1 access*.

A *T3 line* supports a data rate of about 45 Mbps on a dedicated telephone connection. It consists of 672 individual DS0 channels. T3 lines (sometimes referred to as *DS3 lines*) are mainly used by regional telephone companies and ISPs connecting to the Internet.

Similar to the North American T1 line, E-carrier level 1 (*E1*) is the European format for digital transmission. An E1 line carries signals at 2.048 Mbps (32 channels at 64 Kbps), compared to the T1's 1.544 Mbps (24 channels at 64 Kbps). E1 and T1 lines can interconnect for international use. There are also *E3* lines, which carry 16 E1 lines, with a bandwidth of about 34 Mbps.

EXAM TIP E1 and SONET use a derivative of the *High-Level Data Link Control (HDLC)* protocol as the control channel.

A CSU/DSU, as mentioned earlier, connects a leased T1 or T3 line from the telephone company to a customer's equipment. A CSU/DSU has (at least) two connectors, one that goes to the T1/T3 line running out of your demarc and another connection that goes to your router. It performs line encoding and conditioning functions and often has a loopback function for testing. Many newer routers have CSU/DSUs built into them.

The CSU part of a CSU/DSU protects the T1 or T3 line and the user equipment from lightning strikes and other types of electrical interference. It also stores statistics and has capabilities for loopback testing. The DSU part supplies timing to each user port, taking the incoming user's data signals and converting the input signal into the specified line code and then framing the format for transmission over the provided line.

Make sure you know the four T-carriers shown in Table 13-1!

Table 13-1 T-carriers	Carrier	Channels	Speed
	T1	24	1.544 Mbps
	T3	672	44.736 Mbps
	E1	32	2.048 Mbps
	E3	512	34.368 Mbps

Fiber Carriers: SONET/SDH and OC

T-carriers were a great start into the digital world, but in the early 1980s, fiber-optic cabling became the primary tool for long-distance communication all over the world. By now, AT&T as a monopoly was gone, replaced by a number of competing carriers (including a smaller AT&T). Competition was strong and everyone was making their own fiber transmission standards. In an incredible moment of corporate cooperation, in 1987, all of the primary fiber-optic carriers decided to drop their own standards and move to a new international standard called *Synchronous Optical Network (SONET)* in the United States and *Synchronous Digital Hierarchy (SDH)* in Europe.

NOTE Students often wonder why two separate names exist for the same technology. In reality, SONET and SDH vary a little in their signaling and frame type, but routers and other magic boxes on the Internet handle the interoperability between the standards. The American National Standards Institute (ANSI) publishes the standard as SONET; the International Telecommunication Union (ITU) publishes the standard as SDH, but includes SONET signaling. For simplicity's sake, and because SONET is the more common term in the United States, this book uses SONET as the term for this technology.

All of these carriers adopting the same standard created a world of simple interconnections between competing voice and data carriers. This adoption defined the moment that truly made the Internet a universal network. Before SONET, interconnections happened, but they were outlandishly expensive, preventing the Internet from reaching many areas of the world.

SONET remains the primary standard for long-distance, high-speed, fiber-optic transmission systems. SONET defines interface standards at the Physical and Data Link layers of the OSI seven-layer model. The physical aspect of SONET is partially covered by the Optical Carrier standards, but it also defines a ring-based topology that most SONET adopters now use. SONET does not require a ring, but a SONET ring has fault tolerance in case of line loss. As a result, most of the big long-distance optical pipes for the world's telecommunications networks are SONET rings.

EXAM TIP SONET is one of the most important standards for making all WAN interconnections—and it's also the standard you're least likely to see because it's hidden away from all but the biggest networks.

The real beauty of SONET lies in its multiplexing capabilities. A single SONET ring can combine multiple DS1, DS3, even European E1 signals, and package them into single, huge SONET frames for transmission. Clearly, SONET needs high-capacity fiber optics to handle such large data rates. That's where the Optical Carrier standards come into play!

The *Optical Carrier (OC)* standards denote the optical data-carrying capacity (in bps) of fiber-optic cables in networks conforming to the SONET standard. The OC standard describes an escalating series of speeds, designed to meet the needs of medium-to-large corporations. SONET establishes OC speeds from 51.8 Mbps (OC-1) to 39.8 Gbps (OC-768).

Still want more throughput? Many fiber devices use a very clever feature called *wavelength division multiplexing (WDM)* or its newer and more popular version, *dense wavelength division multiplexing (DWDM)*. DWDM enables an individual single-mode fiber to carry multiple signals by giving each signal a different wavelength (using different colors of laser light). The result varies, but a single DWDM fiber can support ~150 signals, enabling, for example, a 51.8-Mbps OC-1 line run at 51.8 Mbps × 150 signals = 7.6 *gigabits per second!* DWDM has become very popular for long-distance lines as it's usually less expensive to replace older SONET/OC-*x* equipment with DWDM than it is to add more fiber lines.

 NOTE DWDM isn't just upgrading SONET lines; DWDM works just as well on long-distance fiber Ethernet.

A related technology, *coarse wavelength division multiplexing (CWDM)*, also relies on multiple wavelengths of light to carry a fast signal over long distances. It's simpler than DWDM, which limits its practical distances to a mere 60 km. You'll see it used in higher-end LANs with 10GBase-LX4 networks, for example, where its lower cost (compared to direct competitors) offers benefits.

SONET uses the *Synchronous Transport Signal (STS)* signal method. The STS consists of two parts: the *STS payload* (which carries data) and the *STS overhead* (which carries the signaling and protocol information). When folks talk about STS, they add a number to the end of "STS" to designate the speed of the signal. For example, STS-1 runs a 51.85-Mbps signal on an OC-1 line. STS-3 runs at 155.52 Mbps on OC-3 lines, and so on. Table 13-2 describes the most common optical carriers.

Table 13-2 Common Optical Carriers	SONET Optical Level	Line Speed	Signal Method
	OC-1	51.85 Mbps	STS-1
	OC-3	155.52 Mbps	STS-3
	OC-12	622.08 Mbps	STS-12
	OC-24	1.244 Gbps	STS-24
	OC-48	2.488 Gbps	STS-48
	OC-192	9.955 Gbps	STS-192
	OC-256	13.22 Gbps	STS-256
	OC-768	39.82 Gbps	STS-768

Packet Switching

All of these impressive connections that start with *T*s and *O*s are powerful, but they are not in and of themselves a complete WAN solution. These WAN connections with their unique packets (DS0, STS, and so on) make up the entire mesh of long-range connections called the Internet, carrying both packetized voice data and TCP/IP data packets. All of these connections are point-to-point, so you need to add another level of devices to enable you to connect multiple T1s, T3s, or OC connections together to make that mesh. That's where packet switching comes into play.

 NOTE The first generation of packet-switching technology was called *X.25* or the *CCITT Packet Switching Protocol*. It enabled remote devices to communicate with each other across high-speed digital links without the expense of individual leased lines.

Packets, as you know, need some form of addressing scheme to get from one location to another. The telephone industry came up with its own types of packets that run on T-carrier and OC lines to get data from one central office to another. These packet-switching protocols are functionally identical to routable network protocols like TCP/IP. WAN connections traditionally used two different forms of packet switching: Frame Relay and ATM. Both are dying or dead today, respectively, but they're on the CompTIA Network+ exam, so here goes.

 EXAM TIP Machines that forward and store packets using any type of packet-switching protocol are called *packet switches*.

Frame Relay

Frame Relay is an extremely efficient packet-switching standard, designed for and used primarily with T-carrier lines. It works especially well for the off-again/on-again traffic typical of most LAN applications.

 NOTE Frame Relay works at both Layer 1 and Layer 2 of the OSI model, using frames rather than packets.

Frame Relay switches frames quickly, but without any guarantee of data integrity at all. You can't even count on it to deliver all the frames, because it will discard frames whenever there is network congestion. At first this might sound problematic—what happens if you have a data problem? In practice, however, a Frame Relay network delivers data quite reliably because T-carrier digital lines that use Frame Relay have very low error rates. It's up to the higher-level protocols to error-check as needed. Frame Relay was extremely popular in its day, but newer technologies such as MPLS have replaced it.

ATM

Don't think automatic teller machine here! *Asynchronous Transfer Mode (ATM)* was a network technology originally designed for high-speed LANs in the early 1990s. ATM only saw limited success in the LAN world but became extremely popular in the WAN world. In fact, until the advent of MPLS (see "MPLS" next), most of the SONET rings that moved voice and data all over the world used ATM for packet switching. ATM integrated voice, video, and data on one connection, using short and fixed-length frames called *cells* to transfer information. Every cell sent with the same source and destination traveled over the same route.

ATM existed because data and audio/video transmissions have different transfer requirements. Data tolerates a delay in transfer, but not signal loss (if it takes a moment for a Web page to appear, you don't care). Audio and video transmissions, on the other hand, tolerate signal loss but not delay (delay makes phone calls sound choppy and clipped). Because ATM transferred information in fixed-length cells (53 bytes long), it handled both types of transfers well. ATM transfer speeds ranged from 155.52 to 622.08 Mbps and beyond. If your location was big enough to order an OC line from your ISP, odds were good that OC line connected to an ATM switch.

MPLS

Frame Relay and ATM were both fantastic packet-switching technologies, but they were designed to support any type of traffic that might come over the network. Today, TCP/IP, the predominant data technology, has a number of issues that neither Frame Relay nor ATM address. For example, ATM uses a very small frame, only 53 bytes, which adds quite a bit of overhead to 1500-byte Ethernet frames. To address this and other issues, many ISPs (and large ISP clients) use an improved technology called *Multiprotocol Label Switching (MPLS)* as a replacement for Frame Relay and ATM switching.

MPLS adds an MPLS label that sits between the Layer 2 header and the Layer 3 information. Layer 3 is always IP, so MPLS labels sit between Layer 2 and the IP headers. Figure 13-14 shows the structure of an MPLS header.

Figure 13-14
MPLS header

The MPLS header consists of four parts:

- **Label**   A unique identifier, used by MPLS-capable routers to determine how to move data.

- **Experimental Bits (Exp)**   A relative value used to determine the importance of the labeled packet to be able to prioritize some packets over others.

- **Bottom of Label Stack (S)**   In certain situations, a single packet may have multiple MPLS labels. This single bit value is set to 1 for the initial label.

- **Time to Live (TTL)**   A value that determines the number of hops the label can make before it's eliminated

Figure 13-15 shows the location of the MPLS header.

The original idea for MPLS was to give individual ISPs a way to move traffic through their morass of different interconnections and switches more quickly and efficiently by providing network-wide quality of service. MPLS-capable routers avoid running

Figure 13-15   MPLS header inserted in a frame

IP packets through their full routing tables and instead use the header information to route packets quickly. Where "regular" routers use QoS on an individual basis, MPLS routers use their existing dynamic routing protocols to send each other messages about their overhead, enabling QoS to span an entire group of routers (Figure 13-16).

Figure 13-16
MPLS routers talk to each other about their overhead.

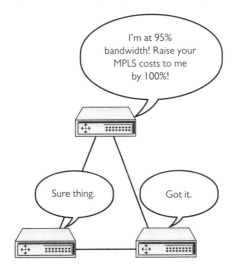

Let's see how the MPLS-labeled packets, combined with MPLS-capable routers, create improved throughput. To see this happen, I need to introduce a few MPLS terms:

- **Forwarding Equivalence Class (FEC)**   FEC is a set of packets that can be sent to the same place, such as a single broadcast domain of computers connected to a router.

- **Label switching router (LSR)**   An LSR looks for and forwards packets based on their MPLS label. These are the "MPLS routers" mentioned previously.

- **Label edge router (LER)**   An LER is an MPLS router that has the job of adding MPLS labels to incoming packets that do not yet have a label; and stripping labels off outgoing packets.

- **Label Distribution Protocol (LDP)**   LSRs and LERs use LDP to communicate dynamic information about their state.

Figure 13-17 shows a highly simplified MPLS network. Note the position of the LERs and LSRs.

Figure 13-17
Sample MPLS
network

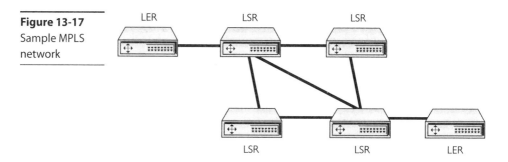

When an MPLS network comes online, administrators will configure initial routing information, primarily setting metrics to routes (Figure 13-18).

Figure 13-18
MPLS initial
routes added

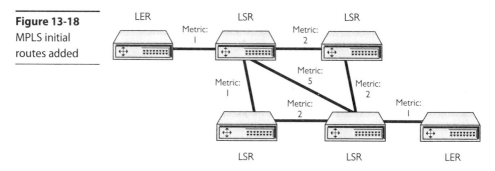

LERs have the real power in determining routes. Because LERs are the entrances and exits for an MPLS network, they talk to each other to determine the best possible routes. As data moves from one FEC, the LERs add an MPLS label to every packet. LSRs strip away incoming labels and add their own. This progresses until the packets exit out the opposing LER (Figure 13-19).

Figure 13-19
Data routing
through an MPLS
network

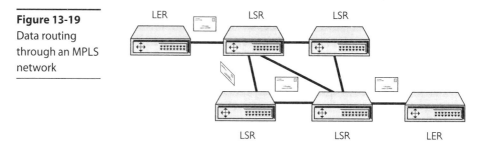

Although MPLS was originally used just to move data quickly between LERs, MPLS's label-stacking ability makes it a perfect candidate for end-user VPNs. Instead of having to set up your own VPN, an ISP using MPLS can set up and lease you a fully functional connection to your network. The ISP makes the VPN for you; you just insert an RJ-45 plug into the switch in your office and it works. This feature of MPLS is called a *permanent virtual circuit (PVC)* and is a popular product sold by ISPs to connect two customer locations.

 EXAM TIP Look for a question or two comparing packet-switched versus circuit-switched network technologies. Current networks use packet switching; ancient networks used circuit switching.

Real-World WAN

There are two reasons to use a telephony WAN connection: to get your LAN on the Internet or to make a private connection between two or more of your private LANs. How you go about getting one of these lines changes a bit depending on which you want to do. Let's start with connecting to the Internet.

Traditionally, getting a WAN Internet connection was a two-step process: you talked to the telephone company to get the copper line physically installed and then talked to an ISP to provide you with Internet access. Today, almost every telephone company is also an ISP, so this process is usually simple. Just go online and do a Web search of ISPs in your area and give them a call. You'll get a price quote, and, if you sign up, the ISP will do the installation.

You can use a few tricks to reduce the price, however. If you're in an office building, odds are good that an ISP is already serving people in your building. Talk to the building supervisor. If there isn't a T1 or better line, you have to pay for a new line. If an interconnect is nearby, this option might be inexpensive. If you want the telephone company to run an OC line to your house, however, brace for a quote of thousands of dollars just to get the line.

The telephone company runs your T-carrier (or better) line to a *demarcation point* for termination. This demarc is important because this is where the phone company's responsibility ends. Everything on "your" side of the demarc is your responsibility. From there, you or your ISP installs a CSU/DSU (for T-carriers) and that device connects to your router.

Depending on who does this for you, you may encounter a tremendous amount of variance here. The classic example (sticking with T-carrier) consists of a demarc, CSU/DSU, and router setup, as shown in Figure 13-20.

Figure 13-20
Old-school
T-carrier setup

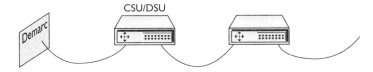

T-carriers have been around so long that many of these parts are combined. You'll often see a single box that combines the CSU/DSU and the router in one handy device.

WAN telephony carriers are incredibly dependable—far more dependable than inexpensive alternatives (like cable modems)—and that's one of the main reasons people still use them. But you should definitely know how to test your end of the connection if you ever suspect a problem. The single most important test is called the *Bit Error Rate*

Test (BERT). A BERT test verifies the T-carrier connection from end to end. Every CSU/DSU has a different way to perform a BERT test. Just make sure you know how to perform the test on yours!

Alternative to Telephony WAN

Telephony WANs were the first big connections. They're still the core of what makes up most of the Internet backbone and private connections, but they've given way to more advanced technologies. The biggest newer technology for WAN connectivity is Ethernet.

Over the last decade or more, ISPs have replaced their T1, T3, and OC-*x* equipment with good-old Ethernet. Well, not "good-old" Ethernet—rather, superfast 10-Gbps Ethernet, 40-Gbps Ethernet, or 100-Gbps Ethernet running on single-mode fiber and connected to DWDM-capable switches. As a result, in many areas—especially metropolitan areas—you can get *metro Ethernet*—Ethernet throughout a city—right to your office. Anyone want a 10-, 40-, or 100-Gbps connection to their router? If you've got the money and you're in a lucky city, you can get it now.

 EXAM TIP The CompTIA Network+ objectives call a city-wide network, like the metro Ethernet described here, a *Metropolitan Area Network (MAN)*.

These Ethernet connections also work great for dedicated connections. A good friend of mine leases a dedicated 10-Gbps Ethernet connection from his company's data center in Houston, Texas, to his office in London, England. It works great!

The Last Mile

Speed is the key to the Internet, but historically there's always been one big challenge: getting data from central offices to individual users. Although this wasn't a problem for larger companies that could afford their own WAN connections, what about individuals and small companies that couldn't or wouldn't pay hundreds of dollars a month for a T1? This area, the infamous last mile, was a serious challenge early on for both Internet connections and private connections because the only common medium was standard telephone lines. A number of last-mile solutions have appeared over the years, and the CompTIA Network+ exam tests you on the most popular—and a few obscure ones as well. Here's the list:

- Dial-up
- DSL
- Broadband cable
- Satellite
- Fiber

NOTE Cellular networking technology most definitely should be considered when discussing the last mile for many modern networks. Cellular gets its own section in Chapter 16, "Mobile Networking."

Dial-Up

Many different types of telephone lines are available, but all the choices break down into two groups: dedicated and dial-up. *Dedicated lines* are always off the hook (that is, they never hang up on each other).

A dedicated line (like a T1) does not have a phone number. In essence, the telephone company creates a permanent, hard-wired connection between the two locations, rendering a phone number superfluous. *Dial-up lines*, by contrast, have phone numbers; they must dial each other up to make a connection. When they're finished communicating, they hang up. Two technologies make up the overwhelming majority of dial-up connections: PSTN and ISDN.

Public Switched Telephone Network

The oldest and slowest original phone connection is the *public switched telephone network (PSTN)*. See Figure 13-21. PSTN is also known as *plain old telephone service (POTS)*. PSTN is just a regular phone line, the same line that used to run to everybody's home telephone jacks from the central office of your *Local Exchange Carrier (LEC)*. The LEC is the telephone company (telco) that provides local connections and usually the one that owns your local central office.

 EXAM TIP A company that provides local telephone service to individual customers is called a *Local Exchange Carrier (LEC)*. A company that provides long-distance service is called an *Interexchange Carrier (IXC)*. Classically, LECs owned the central offices and IXCs owned the lines and equipment that interconnected them. Over time, the line between LECs and IXCs has become very blurred.

Figure 13-21
Ancient telephone switchboard, just because

Because the PSTN was designed long before computers were common, it was designed to work with only one type of data: sound. Here's how it works. The telephone's microphone takes the sound of your voice and translates it into an electrical analog waveform. The telephone then sends that signal through the PSTN line to the phone on the other end of the connection. That phone translates the signal into sound on the other end using its speaker. Note the word *analog*. The telephone microphone converts the sounds into electrical waveforms that cycle 2400 times a second. An individual cycle is known as a *baud*. The number of bauds per second is called the *baud rate*. Pretty much all phone companies' PSTN lines have a baud rate of 2400. PSTN connections use a connector called RJ-11. It's the classic connector you see on all telephones (Figure 13-22).

Figure 13-22
RJ-11 connectors
(top and side
views)

When you connect your modem to a phone jack, the line then runs to either your *network interface unit (NIU)* or the demarc. The term "network interface unit" usually describes the small box on the side of a home that accepts the incoming lines from the telephone company and then splits them to the different wall outlets. "Demarc" more commonly describes large connections used in businesses. The terms always describe the interface between the lines the telephone company is responsible for and the lines for which you are responsible (Figure 13-23).

Computers, as you know, don't speak analog—only digital/binary (0 or 1) will do. In addition, the people who invented the way PCs communicate decided to divide any digital signal going in and out of your computer into 8 bits at a time. To connect over phone lines, PCs need two devices: one that converts this 8-bit-wide (parallel) digital signal from the computer into serial (1-bit-wide) digital data and then another device to convert (modulate) the data into analog waveforms that can travel across PSTN lines.

You already know that the device that converts the digital data to analog and back is called a modem. A modem also contains a device called a *Universal Asynchronous Receiver/Transmitter (UART)*. The UART takes the 8-bit-wide digital data and converts it into 1-bit-wide digital data and hands it to the modem for conversion to analog. The process is reversed for incoming data. Even though internal modems are actually both a UART and a modem, we just say the word "modem" (Figure 13-24).

 NOTE Modems and dial-up might seem 20th century to a lot of folks, but as of this writing, some 10 million Americans still use dial-up.

Figure 13-23
Typical home
demarc

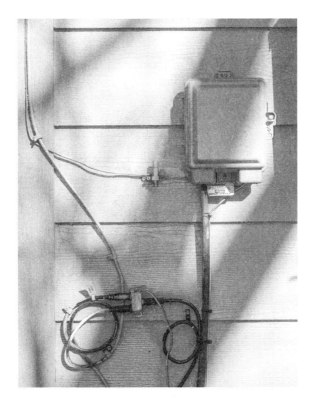

Bit Rates vs. Baud Rate

Modems use phone lines to transmit data at various speeds. These speeds cause a world of confusion and problems for computer people. This is where a little bit of knowledge becomes dangerous. Standard modems you can buy for your home computer normally transmit data at speeds up to 56 Kbps. That's 56 kilobits per second, *not* 56 kilobaud! Many people confuse the terms *baud* and *bits per second*. This confusion arises because the baud rate and the bit rate are the same for modems until the data transfer rate surpasses 2400 bps.

A PSTN phone line takes analog samples of sound 2400 times a second. This standard *sampling size* was determined a long time ago as an acceptable rate for sending voice traffic over phone lines. Although 2400-baud analog signals are fine for voice communication, they are a big problem for computers trying to send data because computers only work with digital signals. The job of the modem is to take the digital signals it receives from the computer and send them out over the phone line in an analog form, using the baud cycles from the phone system. A 2400-bps modem—often erroneously called a 2400-baud modem—uses 1 analog baud to send 1 bit of data.

As technology progressed, modems became faster and faster. To get past the 2400-baud limit, modems modulated the 2400-baud signal multiple times in each cycle. A 4800-bps modem modulated 2 bits per baud, thereby transmitting 4800 bps. All PSTN

Figure 13-24
Internal modem

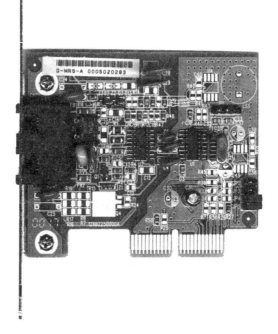

modem speeds are a multiple of 2400, with the latest (and last) generation of modems achieving 2400 × 24 = 57,600 bps (56 Kbps).

V Standards

For two modems to communicate with each other at their fastest rate, they must modulate signals in the same fashion. The two modems must also negotiate with, or *query*, each other to determine the fastest speed they share. The modem manufacturers themselves originally standardized these processes as a set of proprietary protocols. The downside to these protocols was that unless you had two modems from the same manufacturer, modems often would not work together. In response, the International Telegraph and Telephone Consultative Committee (CCITT), a European standards body, established standards for modems. These standards, known generically as the *V standards*, define the speeds at which modems can modulate. The most common of these speed standards are as follows:

- **V.22** 1200 bps
- **V.22bis** 2400 bps
- **V.32** 9600 bps

- **V.32bis**   14,400 bps
- **V.34**   28,000 bps
- **V.90**   57,600 bps
- **V.92**   57,600 bps

The current modem standard now on the market is the *V.92 standard*. V.92 has the same download speed as the V.90, but upstream rates increase to as much as 48 Kbps. If your modem is having trouble getting 56-Kbps rates with V.90 in your area, you will not notice an improvement. V.92 also offers a Quick Connect feature that implements faster handshaking to cut connection delays. Finally, the V.92 standard offers a Modem On Hold feature that enables the modem to stay connected while you take an incoming call or even initiate an outgoing voice call. This feature only works if the V.92 server modem is configured to enable it.

In addition to speed standards, the CCITT, now known simply as the International Telecommunication Union (ITU), has established standards controlling how modems compress data and perform error checking when they communicate. These standards are as follows:

- **V.42**   Error checking
- **V.42bis**   Data compression
- **V.44**   Data compression
- **MNP5**   Both error checking and data compression

 EXAM TIP   Do not memorize these V standards—just know what they do.

The beauty of these standards is that you don't need to do anything special to enjoy their benefits. If you want the theoretical 56-Kbps data transfers, for example, you simply need to ensure that the modems in the local system and the remote system both support the V.90 standard.

ISDN

PSTN lines traditionally just aren't that good. While the digital equipment that connects to a PSTN supports a full 64-Kbps DS0 channel, the combination of the lines themselves and the conversion from analog to digital means that most PSTN lines rarely go faster than 33 Kbps—and, yes, that includes the 56-Kbps connections.

A PSTN telephone connection has many pieces. First, there's the modem in your computer that converts the digital information to analog. Then there's the phone line that runs from your phone out to your NIU and into the central office. The central office stores the modems that convert the analog signal back to digital and the telephone switches that interconnect multiple individual local connections into the larger telephone network. A central office switch connects to long-distance carriers via high-capacity *trunk lines* (at least a T1) and also connects to other nearby central offices. The analog last mile was an awful way to send data, but it had one huge advantage: most everyone owned a telephone line.

During this upgrade period, customers continued to demand higher throughput from their phone lines. The phone companies were motivated to come up with a way to generate higher capacities. Their answer was fairly straightforward: make the last mile digital. Since everything but the last mile was already digital, by adding special equipment at the central office and the user's location, phone companies felt they could achieve a true, steady, dependable throughput of 64 Kbps per line over the same copper wires already used by PSTN lines. This process of sending telephone transmission across fully digital lines end-to-end is called *Integrated Services Digital Network (ISDN)* service.

NOTE ISDN also supports voice but requires special ISDN telephones.

ISDN service consists of two types of channels: *Bearer channels (B channels)* carry data and voice information using standard DS0 channels (64 Kbps), whereas *Delta channels (D channels)* carry setup and configuration information at 16 Kbps. Most ISDN providers let the user choose either one or two B channels. The more common setup is two B/one D, called a *Basic Rate Interface (BRI)* setup. A BRI setup uses only one physical line, but each B channel sends 64 Kbps, doubling the throughput total to 128 Kbps.

Another type of ISDN is called *Primary Rate Interface (PRI)*. ISDN PRI is actually just a full T1 line, carrying 23 B channels.

The physical connections for ISDN bear some similarity to PSTN modems. An ISDN wall socket is usually something that looks like a standard RJ-45 network jack. This line runs to your demarc. In home installations, many telephone companies install a second demarc separate from your PSTN demarc. The most common interface for your computer is a device called a *terminal adapter (TA)*. TAs look like regular modems and, like modems, come in external and internal variants. You can even get TAs that also function as hubs, enabling your system to support a direct LAN connection (Figure 13-25).

Figure 13-25
A TeleWell ISDN
terminal adapter

EXAM TIP   Remember, a B channel is a DS0 channel.

You generally need to be within approximately 18,000 feet of a central office to use ISDN. When you install an ISDN TA, you must configure the other ISDN telephone number you want to call, as well as a special number called the *Service Profile ID (SPID)*. Your ISP provides the telephone number, and the telephone company gives you the SPID. (In many cases, the telephone company is also the ISP.) Figure 13-26 shows a typical installation screen for an internal ISDN TA in an old version of Windows. Note that each channel has a phone number in this case.

Figure 13-26
ISDN settings in
an old version of
Windows

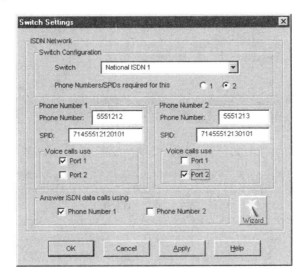

DSL

Many telephone companies offer a *digital subscriber line (DSL)* connection, a fully digital, dedicated (no phone number) connection. DSL represented the next great leap forward past ISDN for telephone lines. A physical DSL connection manifests as just another PSTN connection, using the same telephone lines and RJ-11 jacks as any regular phone line. DSL comes in a number of versions, but the two most important to know for the CompTIA Network+ exam are *symmetric DSL (SDSL)* and *asymmetric DSL (ADSL)*.

SDSL

SDSL provides equal upload and download speeds and, in theory, provides speeds up to 15 Mbps, although the vast majority of ISPs provide packages ranging from 192 Kbps to 9 Mbps.

ADSL

ADSL uses different upload and download speeds. ADSL download speeds are much faster than the upload speeds. Most small office and home office (SOHO) users are primarily concerned with fast *downloads* for things like Web pages and can tolerate slower upload speeds. ADSL provides theoretical maximum download speeds up to 15 Mbps and upload speeds up to 1 Mbps. Real-world ADSL download speeds vary from 384 Kbps to 15 Mbps, and upload speeds go from as low as 128 Kbps to around 768 Kbps. ADSL is less expensive than SDSL.

NOTE AT&T (along with other telecoms) uses a very fast DSL version in some of its Internet offerings called very-high-bit-rate DSL (VDSL). The current version, VDSL2, can provide simultaneous upload and download speeds in excess of 100 Mbps, though only at short distances (~300 meters). Typical speeds using this technology are a lot slower, in the range of 8 to 16 Mbps down and 1 to 2 Mbps up.

Try This!

Comparing Options in Your Neighborhood

So what do your local providers offer in terms of higher-speed service, if any? Try this! Call your local phone company or shop them on the Web (https:// broadbandnow.com is an excellent reference). Does the company offer DSL? What speed options do you have? If you want to compare with other parts of the United States, check one of the national *speed test sites*, such as MegaPath's Speakeasy Speed Test (www.speakeasy.net/speedtest/).

DSL Features

One nice aspect of DSL is that you don't have to run new phone lines. The same DSL lines you use for data can simultaneously transmit your voice calls.

All versions of DSL have the same central office–to–end user distance restrictions as ISDN—around 18,000 feet from your demarc to the central office. At the central office, your DSL provider has a device called a *DSL Access Multiplexer (DSLAM)* that connects multiple customers to the Internet.

As you'll recall from Chapter 5, the DSL modem in your house is considered a termination point, a demarc. Any DSL modem today is a *smart jack*, a NIU that enables loopback testing so the ISP can remotely check your line and box.

Installing DSL

DSL operates using your preexisting telephone lines (assuming they are up to specification). This is wonderful but also presents a technical challenge. For DSL and your run-of-the-mill POTS line to coexist, you need to filter out the DSL signal on the POTS line. A DSL line has three information channels: a high-speed downstream channel, a medium-speed duplex channel, and a POTS channel.

Segregating the two DSL channels from the POTS channel guarantees that your POTS line will continue to operate even if the DSL fails. You accomplish this by inserting a filter on each POTS line, or a splitter mechanism that allows all three channels to flow to the DSL modem but sends only the POTS channel down the POTS line. The DSL company should provide you with a few POTS filters for your telephones. If you need more, most computer/electronics stores stock DSL POTS filters.

NOTE   If you install a telephone onto a line in your home with DSL and you forget to add a filter, don't panic. You won't destroy anything, although you won't get a dial tone either! Just insert a DSL POTS filter and the telephone will work.

A common early DSL installation consisted of a *DSL modem* connected to a telephone wall jack and to a standard network interface card (NIC) in your computer (Figure 13-27). The DSL line ran into a DSL modem via a standard phone line with RJ-11 connectors. Today you'd add a router in between the DSL modem and the wall jack.

Figure 13-27
A DSL modem
connection
between a PC
and telco

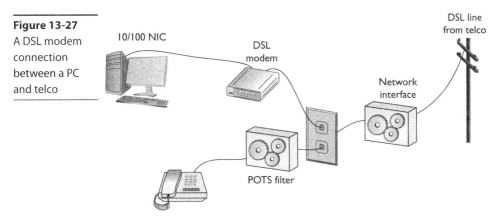

The DSL modem connects to the gateway router with a Cat 5/6 patch cable, which, in turn, connects to the company's switch. Figure 13-28 shows an ADSL modem and a router.

The first generation of DSL providers used a *bridged connection*; once the DSL line was running, it was as if you had snapped an Ethernet cable into your NIC. You were on the network. Those were good days for DSL. You just plugged your DSL modem into your NIC and, assuming your IP settings were whatever the DSL folks told you to use, you were running.

The DSL providers didn't like that too much. There was no control—no way to monitor who was using the DSL modem. As a result, the DSL folks started to use *Point-to-Point Protocol over Ethernet (PPPoE)*, a protocol that was originally designed to encapsulate PPP frames into Ethernet frames. The DSL people adopted it to make stronger controls over

Figure 13-28
DSL connection

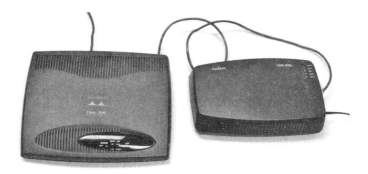

your DSL connection. In particular, you could no longer simply connect; you now had to log on with an account and a password to make the DSL connection. PPPoE is now predominant on DSL. If you get a DSL line, your operating system has software to enable you to log onto your DSL network. Most SOHO routers come with built-in PPPoE support, enabling you to enter your user name and password into the router itself (Figure 13-29).

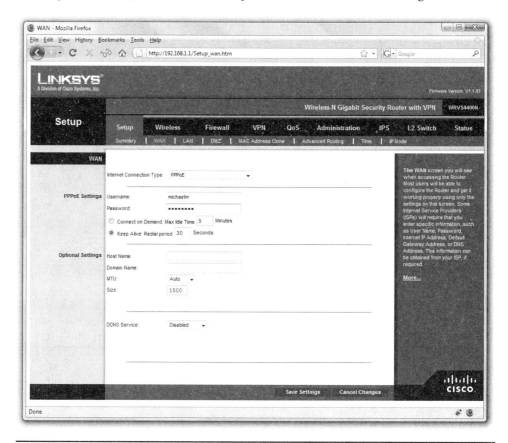

Figure 13-29 PPPoE settings in SOHO router

Broadband Cable

The first big competition for ADSL came from the cable companies. A majority of houses in America have a coax cable for cable TV. In a moment of genius, the cable industry realized that if it could put the Home Shopping Network and the History Channel into every home, why not provide Internet access? The entire infrastructure of the cabling industry had to undergo some major changes to deal with issues like bidirectional communication, but cable modem service quickly became common in the United States. Cable modems are now as common as cable TV boxes.

Cable modems have the impressive benefit of phenomenal top speeds. These speeds vary from cable company to cable company, but most advertise speeds in the 5 to 200 Mbps range. Many cable modems provide a throughput speed of 30 to 200 Mbps for downloading and 5 Mbps to 10 Mbps for uploading—there is tremendous variance among different providers.

In a cable modem installation, the cable modem connects to an outlet via a coaxial cable. It's separate from the one that goes to the television. It's the same cable line, just split from the main line as if you were adding a second cable outlet for another television. A cable modem connects to a router, which in turn connects to a PC using a standard NIC and UTP cabling (Figure 13-30).

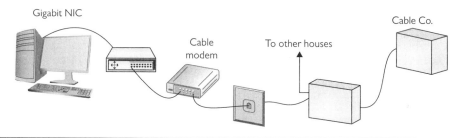

Figure 13-30   Cable modem

Cable modems connect using coax cable to a head end, similar to a telephone company's central office. Head ends, in turn, connect to the cable company's network. This network uses a unique protocol called *Data Over Cable Service Interface Specification (DOCSIS)*. The current specification is DOCSIS 3.1.

You'll have a hard time telling a cable modem from a DSL modem. The only difference, other than the fact that one will have "cable modem" printed on it whereas the other will say "DSL modem," is that the cable modem has a coax F-connector and an RJ-45 connector; the DSL modem has an RJ-11 connector and an RJ-45 connector.

Cable companies aggressively market high-speed packages to business customers, making cable a viable option for businesses.

Satellite

Living in the countryside may have its charms, but you'll have a hard time getting high-speed Internet out on the farm. For those too far away to get anything else, satellite may be your only option. Satellite access comes in two types: one-way and two-way. *One-way* means that you download via satellite, but you must use a PSTN/dial-up modem connection for uploads. *Two-way* means the satellite service handles both the uploading and downloading.

NOTE Companies that design satellite communications equipment haven't given up on their technology. At the time of this writing, at least one company, HughesNet, offered download speeds up to 25 Mbps. You can surf with that kind of speed!

Satellite requires a small satellite antenna, identical to the ones used for satellite television. This antenna connects to a satellite modem, which, in turn, connects to your PC or your network (Figure 13-31).

EXAM TIP Neither cable modems nor satellites use PPP, PPPoE, or anything else that begins with three Ps.

Figure 13-31
Satellite
connection

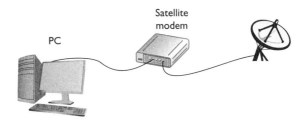

Fiber

DSL was the first popular last-mile WAN option, but over the years cable modems have taken the lead. In an attempt to regain market share, telephone providers rolled out fiber-to-the-home/fiber-to-the-premises options that are giving the cable companies a scare. In the United States, two companies, AT&T and Verizon (Fios), offer Internet connectivity, television, and phone services at super speeds. Some markets also have Internet-only fiber offerings, such as Google Fiber, where users connect at 1 Gbps.

To make rollouts affordable, most fiber-to-the-home technologies employ a version of *passive optical network (PON)* architecture that uses a single fiber to the neighborhood switch and then individual fiber runs to each final destination. PON uses WDM to enable multiple signals to travel on the same fiber and then passively splits the signal at the switch to send traffic to its proper recipient.

NOTE Most municipalities in the United States have very tight deals in place with telephone and cable companies, allowing little room for any other high-speed Internet service. A few cities have bucked the regional monopolies and done pretty well, such as Chattanooga, Tennessee. Their publicly owned electric utility—EPB—rolled out fiber to every home and business by 2011 and currently offers Internet speeds up to 10 Gbps.

Which Connection?

With so many connection options for homes and small offices, making a decision is often a challenge. Your first question is availability: Which services are available in your area? The second question is, how much bandwidth do you need? The latter is a question of great debate. Most services are more than happy to increase service levels if you find that a certain level is too slow. I usually advise clients to start with a relatively slow level and then increase if necessary. After all, once you've tasted the higher speeds, going slower is hard, but the transition to faster is relatively painless!

Try This!

Going Connection Shopping

You've already checked the availability of DSL in your neighborhood, but now you have more choices! Try this! Do you have cable or satellite available? A great Web site to start your search is www.dslreports.com. It has a handy search feature that helps you determine the types of service and the costs for DSL, cable, and other services. Which one makes sense for you?

Using Remote Access

Because most businesses are no longer limited to a simple little shop like you would find in a Dickens novel, many people need to be able to access files and resources over a great distance. Enter remote access. *Remote access* uses WAN and LAN connections to enable a computer user to log onto a network from the other side of a city, a state, or even the globe. As people travel, information has to remain accessible. Remote access enables users to connect a server at the business location and log into the network as if they were in the same building as the company. The only problem with remote access is that there are so many ways to do it! I've listed the six most common forms of remote access here:

- **Dial-up to the Internet** Using a dial-up connection to connect to your ISP
- **Private dial-up** Using a dial-up connection to connect to your private network
- **Virtual private network (VPN)** Using an Internet connection to connect to a private network
- **Dedicated connection** Using a non-dial-up connection to another private network or the Internet
- **Remote terminal** Using a terminal emulation program to connect to another computer
- **VoIP** Voice over IP

In this section, I discuss the issues related to configuring these six types of connections. After seeing how to configure these types of remote connections, I move into observing some security issues common to every type of remote connection.

 NOTE You'll see the term *extranet* more in books than in the day-to-day workings of networks and network techs. So what is an extranet? Whenever you allow authorized remote users to access some part of your private network, you have created an extranet.

Dial-Up to the Internet

Dialing up to the Internet is the oldest and least expensive method to connect to the Internet, but it is rare today. Even with broadband and wireless so prevalent, every self-respecting network tech (or maybe just old network techs like me) keeps a dial-up account as a backup. You buy a dial-up account from an ISP (many wireless and broadband ISPs give free dial-up—just ask). All operating systems come with dial-up support programs, but you'll need to provide:

- A modem (most operating systems check for a modem before setting up a dial-up connection)
- The telephone number to dial (provided to you by the ISP)
- User name and password (provided to you by the ISP)
- Type of connection (dial-up always uses PPP)
- IP information (provided to you by the ISP—usually just DHCP)

Every operating system comes with the software to help you set up a dial-up connection. In Windows, you go to the **Set up a dial-up connection** option in the Network and Sharing Center (Figure 13-32). Whatever the name, this tool is what you use to create dial-up connections.

Private Dial-Up

A private dial-up connection connects a remote system to a private network via a dial-up connection. Private dial-up does not use the Internet! Private dial-up requires two systems. One system acts as a *remote access server (RAS)*. The other system, the client, runs a connection tool (usually the same tool you just read about in the previous section).

In Windows, a RAS is a server running the Routing and Remote Access Service (RRAS), dedicated to handling users who are not directly connected to a LAN but who need to access file and print services on the LAN from a remote location. For example, when a user dials into a network from home using an analog modem connection, she is dialing into a RAS. See Figure 13-33. Once the user authenticates, she can access shared drives and printers as if her computer were physically connected to the office LAN.

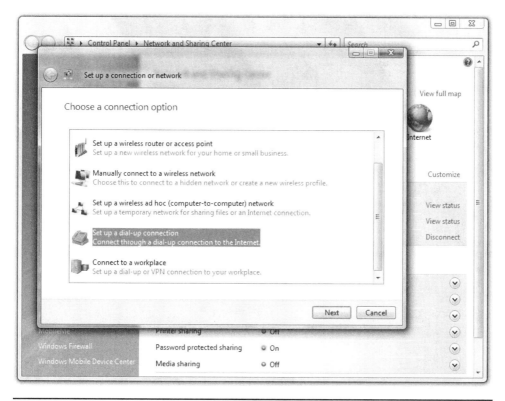

Figure 13-32 Dial-up in Windows

NOTE When you run Microsoft's Routing and Remote Access Service on a server, you turn that server into a remote access server.

You must set up a server in your LAN as a RAS server. That RAS server, which must have at least one modem, accepts incoming calls and handles password authentication. RAS servers use all the standard authentication methods (PAP, CHAP, EAP, 802.1X, and so on) and have separate sets of permissions for dial-in users and local users. You must also configure the RAS server to set the rights and permissions for all of the dial-in users. Configuring a RAS server is outside the scope of this book, however, because each one is different.

NOTE Remote access server refers to the hardware component (servers built to handle the unique stresses of a large number of clients calling in), but it can also refer to the software service component of a remote access solution. You might call it a catchall phrase. Most techs call RAS "razz," rather than using the initials, "R-A-S." This creates a seemingly redundant phrase used to describe a system running RAS: "RAS server." This helps distinguish servers from clients and makes geeks happier.

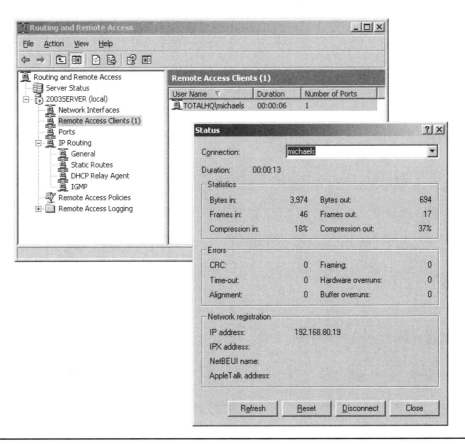

Figure 13-33 Windows RRAS in action

Creating the client side of a private dial-up connection is identical to setting up a dial-up connection to the Internet. The only difference is that instead of having an ISP tell you what IP settings, account name, and password to use, the person who sets up the RAS server tells you this information (Figure 13-34).

VPNs
A VPN enables you to connect through a tunnel from a local computer to a remote network securely, as you'll recall from the in-depth discussion in Chapter 11. Refer to that chapter for the details.

Dedicated Connection

Dedicated connections are remote connections that are never disconnected. Dedicated connections can be broken into two groups: dedicated private connections between

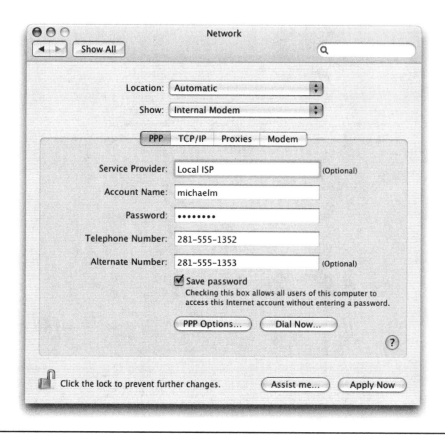

Figure 13-34 Dial-up on macOS

two locations and dedicated connections to the Internet. Dedicated private connections manifest themselves as two locations interconnected by a connection such as a T1 line (Figure 13-35).

Each end of the T1 line goes into a router (after going through a CSU/DSU, of course). Note that this connection does not use the Internet in any way—it is not a VPN connection. Private dedicated connections of this type are expensive and are only used by organizations that need the high bandwidth and high security these connections provide. These connections are invisible to the individual computers on each network. There is no special remote connection configuration of the individual systems, although you may have to configure DHCP and DNS servers to ensure that the network runs optimally.

DSL and Cable

Dedicated connections to the Internet are common today. Cable modems and DSL have made dedicated connections to the Internet inexpensive and very popular.

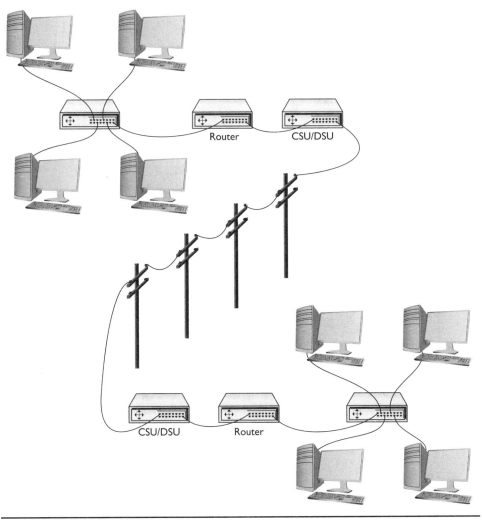

Figure 13-35 Dedicated private connection

In most cases, you don't have to configure anything in these dedicated connections. Figure 13-36 shows the DSL wizard built into Windows 7. This program enables you to connect by entering your PPPoE information for your ADSL connection. Once started, these programs usually stay running in the system tray until your next reboot.

Cable Issues

Dedicated cable connections provide the only exception to the "plug them in and they work" rule because most cable networks bring television and often voice communication into the same line. This complicates things in one simple way: *splitters.*

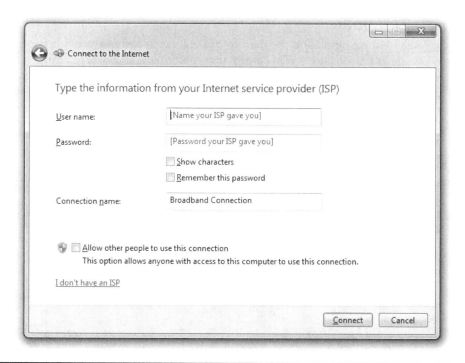

Figure 13-36 PPPoE connection

If you have a cable connection coming to your house and you have a television set in two rooms, how do you get cable in both rooms? Easy, right? Just grab a two-way splitter from an electronics store and run an extra pair of cables, one to each room. The problem comes from the fact that every time you split a cable signal, the signal degrades by half. This is called, logically, a *split cable* problem.

The quality of a signal can be measured in *decibels (dB)*, a unit that describes a ratio between an ideal point—a reference point—and the current state of the signal. When discussing signal strength, a solid signal is 0 dB. When that signal degrades, it's described as a *dB loss* and a negative number. An increase in signal is *gain* and gets a positive number. Decibels are logarithmic units. This means the scale is in simple numbers, but each additional unit reflects a large percentage change. Adding 10 dB to a signal makes it 1000 percent stronger.

For example, when you split a cable signal into two, you get half the signal strength into each new cable. That's described as a –3 dB signal. Split it again and you've got a –6 dB signal. Although 6 isn't a big number in standard units, it's horribly huge in networking. You might have a 20-Mbps cable connection into your house, but split it twice and you're left with a 5-Mbps connection. Ouch!

The standard procedure with cable connections is to split them once: one cable goes to the cable modem and the other to the television. You can then split the television cable into as many connections as you need or can tolerate as far as reception quality.

Remote Terminal

You can use a terminal emulation program to create a *remote terminal*, a connection on a faraway computer that enables you to control that computer as if you were sitting in front of it, logged in. Terminal emulation has been a part of TCP/IP from its earliest days, in the form of good-old Telnet. Because it dates from pre-GUI days, Telnet is a text-based utility; most modern operating systems are graphical, so there was a strong desire to come up with graphical remote terminal tools. Citrix Corporation made the first popular terminal emulation products—the *WinFrame/MetaFrame* products (Figure 13-37). (Their current product is called XenApp.)

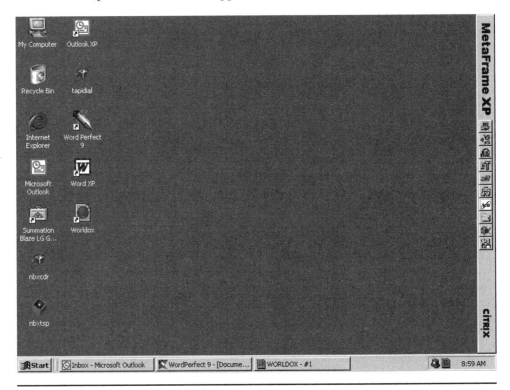

Figure 13-37   Citrix MetaFrame

Remote terminal programs all require a server and a client. The server is the computer to be controlled. The client is the computer from which you do the controlling. Citrix created a standard called *Independent Computing Architecture (ICA)* that defined how terminal information was passed between the server and the client. Citrix made a breakthrough product—so powerful that Microsoft licensed the Citrix code and created its own product called Windows Terminal Services. Not wanting to pay Citrix any more money, Microsoft then created its own standard called *Remote Desktop Protocol (RDP)* and unveiled a new remote terminal called *Remote Desktop Connection (RDC)* starting with Windows XP (so it's been around a long time). Figure 13-38 shows Windows Remote Desktop Connection running on a Windows 10 system, connecting to a Windows Server.

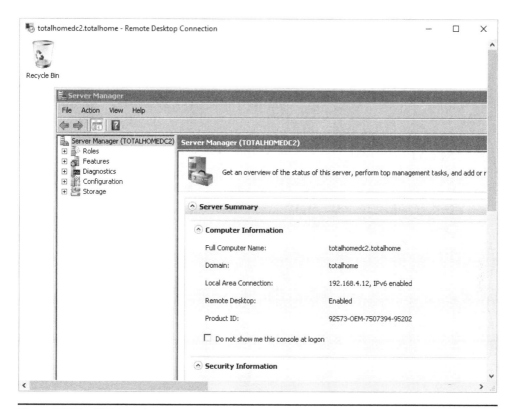

Figure 13-38   RDC in action

NOTE   All RDP applications run on port 3389 by default.

A number of third parties make absolutely amazing terminal emulation programs that run on any operating system. The best of these, *VNC* (VNC stands for Virtual Network Computing), doesn't let you share folders or printers because it is only a terminal emulator (Figure 13-39), but it runs on every operating system, is solid as a rock, and even runs from a Web browser. It works nicely in Secure Shell (SSH) tunnels for great security, plus it comes, by default, with every copy of macOS and almost every Linux distro. Why bother sharing if you can literally be at the screen? Oh, and did I mention that VNC is completely free?

VoIP

Voice over IP (VoIP) uses an IP network to transfer voice calls. VoIP works so well because it uses an existing network you're already paying for (your Internet connection) to replace another network you're also paying for (PSTN lines). The technology needed for VoIP

Figure 13-39   VNC in action

isn't very challenging, but making a VoIP system that's standardized so everyone can use it (and still contact those who choose to use PSTN) requires international standards, making it quite a bit harder. VoIP is still a very fractured world, but it's getting closer to universally adopted standards—one day everyone will be able to contact everyone else, no matter what brand of VoIP they use. To do this, you need to know three important standards: RTP, SIP, and H.323.

RTP

The *Real-time Transport Protocol (RTP)*, the heavily adopted bedrock of VoIP standards, defines the type of packets used on the Internet to move voice or data from a server to clients. The vast majority of VoIP solutions available today use RTP.

SIP and H.323

Session Initiation Protocol (SIP) and *H.323* handle the initiation, setup, and delivery of VoIP sessions. SIP and H.323 both run on top of RTP. Most VoIP solutions are either SIP/RTP or H.323/RTP. SIP uses TCP ports 5060 and 5061. H.323 uses port 1720. SIP and H.323 both have methods for handling multicasting.

Skype

Almost every VoIP solution available today uses SIP or H.323 running on top of RTP, with one huge exception: the very famous and incredibly popular Skype. Skype was unveiled in 2003 by Niklas Zennström, a Swedish computer guy famous for inventing the Kazaa peer-to-peer file-sharing system. Skype is completely different from and completely incompatible with any other type of VoIP solution: Skype doesn't use servers, but instead uses a peer-to-peer topology that is identical to the old Kazaa network. Skype calls are also encrypted using a proprietary encryption method. No one has a standard method for VoIP encryption at this time, although many smart people are working hard on the issue.

Streaming Media with RTSP

VoIP isn't the only thing that takes advantage of protocols such as RTP. Streaming video is now mainstream and many streaming video severs (Windows Media Player, QuickTime, and many others) use a popular protocol called Real-Time Streaming Protocol (RTSP). Like SIP and H.323, RTSP runs on top of RTP. RTSP has a number of features that are perfect for video streaming such as the ability to run, pause, and stop videos. RTSP runs on TCP port 554.

In-Band Management

VNC and SSH enable *in-band management* of resources, meaning software installed on both the client and the remote system enables direct control over resources. The interaction uses the primary network connection for both devices, thus it's in-band and sharing resources (and traffic) with the regular network.

This is fast and inexpensive, but has a couple of drawbacks in a busy network. First, the remote system must be booted up with its operating system fully loaded for this to work. Second, putting management of a remote system on the main network doesn't provide as much security or control as a dedicated, alternative connection would provide.

Many servers employ *lights-out-management (LOM)* capabilities that enable *out-of-band management* to address these issues. We'll see a lot more of these technologies when we discuss network monitoring and management in Chapter 20.

WAN Troubleshooting Scenarios

Competent network techs can recognize and deal with typical remote connectivity issues in a WAN setting. Sometimes the problem lies well beyond the job description, but that's when the tech knows to escalate the problem. This section looks at four very important CompTIA Network+ problem areas: loss of Internet connectivity, interface errors, DNS issues, and interference.

Loss of Internet Connectivity

Given that the core reason to use all these forms of remote connectivity is to get to the Internet in the first place, I don't look at loss of Internet connectivity as a problem. It's more a symptom. Be sure to watch for WAN scenarios on the CompTIA Network+ exam that really aren't always WAN scenarios.

If you want to connect a computer to the Internet, that computer needs a legitimate IP address, subnet mask, default gateway, and DNS address. These needs don't change whether you connect through a Gigabit Ethernet wired network or through a cable modem. Use the utilities already covered in the book in such a scenario, such as ping, ipconfig, netstat, nslookup, and so forth, to verify that the device has a solid IP connection.

Interface Errors

CompTIA loves to use the term *interface errors* as a catchall term to describe the many connections between your computer and the remote connection that enables you to get to the Internet. In a WAN scenario you'll have at least one more interface than in a native Ethernet world. Think about a typical office environment.

Local Ethernet Interface/LAN Interfaces

When you use DSL or cable or any other form of remote connection, it's very easy to forget all of the LAN connections that make connectivity possible. It's plausible, if you're anything like me, that you'll call an ISP like Comcast or AT&T and complain, only to find that you don't have a patch cable plugged into the right connection on the back of the computer. (Not that I've ever done this. Twice.)

Before you blame Comcast or AT&T for losing your connection, make sure to verify that everything on your end is in order. Is the computer properly connected to the LAN? If you are using a router, is it providing good IP information? Can you access the router and see if it is reporting that it has a proper upstream connection? Before you blame the WAN interface, always first confirm everything on the LAN.

Modem Interface

It doesn't really matter what type of remote connection you use. There's always a modem. Be careful here: "modem" is the term I use for any box that sits in your location and connects your LAN to the WAN, even if your ISP calls it something loftier like: cable modem, router, or customer premises equipment (CPE). Everything said here that references "modem" works for whatever CPE device your ISP provides.

The modem's job is to connect your LAN to the WAN, so by definition it's going to have at least two interfaces: one to the LAN and one to the WAN. First of all, familiarize yourself with the lights on your modem, preferably before you have problems. Any modem is going to have a power LED, link LEDs to both the LAN and the WAN, and some form of activity LED. Study them first when you're looking for interface issues. In almost every case of a bad interface, you'll verify connections and reset the modem.

DNS Issues

There is one specific DNS issue that comes up in WANs: choosing what DNS server to use. Every ISP has their own DNS server(s) and, in almost every case, your modem is going to propagate those DNS settings down to every device in your LAN. In most cases there isn't any problem with this, but there are two cases where you might want to consider manually adding DNS to your local devices or your local router. First, an ISP's DNS servers can fail.

Second, some ISPs notoriously use *DNS helpers*, DNS servers that redirect your browser to advertising when you type in an incorrect URL.

In either of these cases, the rules you learned back in Chapter 6, "TCP/IP Basics," still apply. Get yourself a fast public DNS IP address—I love the Google 8.8.8.8 and 8.8.4.4 addresses—and at the very least load one of those as a secondary DNS server.

NOTE In 2017, the Global Cyber Alliance (a group dedicated to reducing cyber crime) and IBM and other players launched Quad9, a free public DNS server that blocks the bad domains and whitelists the good domains. Phishing and scammer domains are blocked; Google and Amazon, for example, are not. Check it out by changing your DNS server to 9.9.9.9. The computer you save might be your own!

Interference

Interference at the WAN level—that CompTIA Network+ techs can fix—generally implies the connection between the LAN and the WAN. The point at which the ISP's responsibility ends and the customer's begins is the demarc. Let's look at both sides of the demarc for interference.

On the customer side, the CPE can create problems. In a busy office building, for example, new installations or connections can add electromagnetic interference (EMI) and create disturbances. New things added to old environments, in other words, can create interference in existing networks.

When my company changed locations, for example, the building we moved into had several offices, connected to Internet and corporate WANs with several dedicated T1 lines (Figure 13-40). With the local cable company offering 100-Mbps connections, we opted to have cable installed in the building for us (T1 at 1.5 Mbps, not so much).

If the cable company had not been careful or used properly shielded boxes and cables, this could have wreaked havoc on the other folks in the building.

Figure 13-40
Demarc at my office building

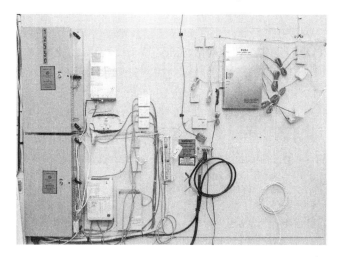

In a consumer space, the CPE doesn't run into interference that would block connectivity at the demarc, unless you overly broaden the term "interference" to include "failure." Then you can point to the "modem" as the only major failure culprit.

Once you go to the ISP side of the demarc, there's not much interference involved, especially with existing, previously well-functioning networks. Again, WAN interference only happens if you extend the definition to include failure. Then storms, downed power lines, extraterrestrial activity, and so on can cause problems.

In a home network, there are only two times you should worry about interference in a WAN outside the demarc: during installation and when changing the connection in any way. Every form of remote connection has very clear interference tolerances, and you should have the installation tech verify this. Cable and DSL self-installations are a big issue here as most people don't have access to the tools necessary to confirm their PSTN or coax cabling. If I'm installing a new DSL or cable modem, I refuse the self-install option and gladly pay the extra money to verify my cabling can handle the connection.

It's incredibly easy to introduce interference into an otherwise perfectly functioning wired WAN connection by adding splitters, noisy devices, splices, and so on. This is especially true for tech folks (like your humble author) who have learned this the hard way. In general, be conservative when disturbing your WAN connection and be ready to call support if needed.

Chapter Review

Questions

1. What is the signal rate for DS0?

    A. 1.544 Mbps

    B. 64 Kbps

    C. 2.048 Mbps

    D. 128 Kbps

2. Which of the following provides the fastest throughput?

    A. PSTN

    B. ISDN BRI

    C. ADSL

    D. POTS

3. What is the popular Microsoft remote access server program called?

    A. RRAS

    B. Dial-Up Networking

    C. Dial-Up Server

    D. Microsoft Client for Networks

4. What device do you use to connect to a T1 line?

  A. Router

  B. CSU/DSU

  C. Modem

  D. WIC-2T

5. BRI ISDN uses _____.

  A. 1 B channel and 24 D channels

  B. 24 B channels and 1 D channel

  C. 1 B channel and 2 D channels

  D. 2 B channels and 1 D channel

6. The V.90 standard defines a modem speed of _____.

  A. 56 Kbps

  B. 33.6 K baud

  C. 28.8 Kbps

  D. 2400 baud

7. You have just had DSL installed at your house. Although the Internet connection is fast, your phones no longer work. What is the problem?

  A. The installer failed to install the POTS filters on the phones.

  B. Nothing; the phones can't function at the same time as the Internet.

  C. The house phone lines can't handle the bandwidth of both the phone and DSL.

  D. The DSL modem is missing the filter and is causing line interference.

8. What protocol do cable modems use?

  A. ACMSIS

  B. CMAS

  C. DOCSIS

  D. CCSIP

9. What is SONET used for?

  A. Short-distance, high-speed, fiber-optic transmission

  B. Long-distance, high-speed, fiber-optic transmission

  C. Long-distance, low-speed, copper cable transmission

  D. Short-distance, low-speed, copper cable transmission

10. What does SIP stand for?

    A. Standard Initiation Protocol

    B. System Internetworking Protocol

    C. Session Initiation Protocol

    D. Sector Information Protocol

Answers

1. B. DS0 operates at a constant rate of 64 Kbps.

2. C. ADSL can run up to 15 Mbps.

3. A. The popular Microsoft remote access server is called Routing and Remote Access Service, or RRAS.

4. B. A CSU/DSU is required to connect to a T1 line.

5. D. BRI ISDN uses two B channels and one D channel.

6. A. The V.90 standard defines a 56-Kbps modem speed.

7. A. The problem is that the installer did not install POTS filters on the jacks with phones attached.

8. C. Cable modems use DOCSIS (Data Over Cable Service Interface Specification).

9. B. SONET is used for long-distance, high-speed, fiber-optic transmission.

10. C. Session Initiation Protocol; SIP is one of the main protocols for VoIP.

## CHAPTER 14

Wireless Networking

The CompTIA Network+ certification exam expects you to know how to

- 1.3 Explain the concepts and characteristics of routing and switching
- 1.5 Compare and contrast the characteristics of network topologies, types and technologies
- 1.6 Given a scenario, implement the appropriate wireless technologies and configurations
- 2.2 Given a scenario, determine the appropriate placement of networking devices on a network and install/configure them
- 2.3 Explain the purposes and use cases for advanced networking devices
- 4.2 Explain authentication and access controls
- 4.3 Given a scenario, secure a basic wireless network
- 4.4 Summarize common networking attacks
- 5.2 Given a scenario, use the appropriate tool
- 5.4 Given a scenario, troubleshoot common wireless connectivity and performance issues
- 5.5 Given a scenario, troubleshoot common network service issues

To achieve these goals, you must be able to

- Explain wireless networking standards
- Describe the process for implementing Wi-Fi networks
- Describe troubleshooting techniques for wireless networks

Every type of network covered thus far in the book assumes that your PCs connect to your network with some kind of physical cabling. Now it's time to cut the cord and look at the many technologies that collectively changed the way we use the Internet: wireless networking.

Historical/Conceptual

You need to be careful when talking about wireless networking. Wireless is everywhere. It's in our phones and our homes. It's at work and in our schools. Wireless is so transparent and handy we tend to forget that wireless isn't a single technology. There are a number of technologies that collectively make up wireless networking.

Let's start with the basics. Instead of a physical set of wires running among networked PCs, servers, printers, or what-have-you, a *wireless network* uses radio frequency (RF) waves to enable these devices to communicate with each other. Wireless technologies disconnected us from the wires that started the networking revolution and have given us incredible flexibility and mobility.

NOTE   Because the networking signal is freed from wires, you'll sometimes hear the term *unbounded media* to describe wireless networking.

For all their disconnected goodness, wireless networks share more similarities than differences with wired networks. With the exception of the first two OSI layers, wireless networks use the same protocols as wired networks. The thing that differs is the type of media—radio waves instead of cables—and the protocols for transmitting and accessing data. Different wireless networking solutions have come and gone in the past, but the wireless networking market these days is dominated by the most common implementation of the IEEE 802.11 wireless standard, *Wi-Fi*.

This chapter looks first at the standards for modern wireless networks and then turns to implementing those networks. The chapter finishes with a discussion on troubleshooting Wi-Fi.

Test Specific

Wi-Fi Standards

Wi-Fi is by far the most widely adopted wireless networking type today, especially for accessing the Internet. You'd be hard pressed to find a location, work or home, that doesn't have Wi-Fi. Millions of private businesses and homes have wireless networks, and most public places, such as coffee shops and libraries, offer Internet access through wireless networks.

NOTE   Wi-Fi originally stood for *wireless fidelity* to make it cutely equated with *high fidelity (Hi-Fi)*, but it doesn't really stand for anything anymore.

Wi-Fi technologies have been around since the late 1990s, supported and standardized under the umbrella IEEE 802.11 standard. So in reality, Wi-Fi is really 802.11. The 802.11 standard has been updated continuously since then, manifested by a large number of amendments to the standard. These amendments have names such as 802.11g and 802.11ac. It's important for you to understand all of these 802.11 amendments in detail, as well as the original version, 802.11.

802.11

The *802.11* standard defines both how wireless devices communicate and how to secure that communication. The original 802.11 standard, now often referred to as *802.11-1997*, is no longer used, but it established the baseline features common to all subsequent Wi-Fi standards.

The 802.11-1997 standard defined certain features, such as a wireless network cards, special configuration software, and the capability to run in multiple styles of networks. In addition, 802.11-1997 defined how transmissions work, so we'll look at frequencies of radio signals, transmission methods, and collision avoidance.

Hardware

Wireless networking hardware serves the same function as hardware used on wired PCs. Wireless Ethernet NICs take data passed down from the upper OSI layers, encapsulate it into frames, send the frames out on the network media in streams of ones and zeroes, and receive frames sent from other computing devices. The only difference is that instead of charging up a network cable with electrical current or firing off pulses of light, these devices transmit and receive radio waves.

NOTE It's the same concept, but 802.11 frames are not addressed and encapsulated the same way as 802.3 Ethernet frames.

Wireless networking capabilities of one form or another are built into many modern computing devices. Almost all portable devices have built-in wireless capabilities. Desktop computers can easily go wireless by adding an expansion card. Figure 14-1 shows a wireless PCI Express (PCIe) Ethernet card.

You can also add wireless network capabilities using USB wireless network adapters, as shown in Figure 14-2. The USB NICs have the added benefit of being *placeable*—that is, you can move them around to catch the wireless signal as strongly as possible, akin to moving the rabbit ears on old pre-cable television sets.

Is the wireless network adapter in all your devices the only hardware you need to create a wireless network? Well, if your needs are simple—for example, if you're connecting a few laptops on a long train ride so you and your buddies can play a game together—then the answer is yes. If, however, you need to extend the capabilities of a wireless network— say, connecting a wireless network segment to a wired network—you need additional equipment. This typically means a wireless access point.

Figure 14-1
Wireless PCIe NIC

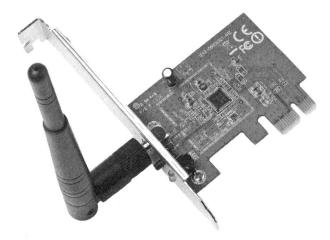

Figure 14-2
External USB
wireless NIC

A *wireless access point (WAP)* is a device designed to interconnect wireless network nodes with wired networks. A basic WAP operates like a hub and works at OSI Layer 1. Many WAP manufacturers combine multiple devices into one box, however, to create a WAP with a built-in switch and/or router, all rolled into one and working at several OSI layers. The Linksys device shown in Figure 14-3 is an example of this type of combo device.

NOTE Many manufacturers drop the word "wireless" from wireless access points and simply call them *access points*. Furthermore, many sources abbreviate both forms, so you'll see the former written as *WAP* and the latter as *AP*.

Figure 14-3
Linksys device
that acts as
wireless access
point, switch,
and DSL router

Software

Every wireless network adapter needs two pieces of software to function with an operating system: a device driver to talk to the wireless NIC and a configuration utility.
Installing drivers for wireless networking devices is usually automatic these days, but you
should always consult your vendor's instructions before popping that card into a slot.

You also need a utility for configuring how the wireless hardware connects to other
wireless devices. Every operating system has built-in wireless clients for configuring these
settings, but these clients may lack advanced features for more complex wireless networks, requiring wireless clients provided by the wireless network adapter vendor or a
third party. Figure 14-4 shows a typical wireless network adapter's client configuration
utility. Using this utility, you can determine important things like the *link state* (whether
your wireless device is connected) and the *signal strength* (a measurement of how well
your wireless device is connecting to other devices). You can also configure items such as
your wireless networking *mode*, security encryption, power-saving options, and so on. I'll
cover each of these topics in detail later in this chapter.

You typically configure WAPs through browser-based setup utilities. The section
"Implementing Wi-Fi" covers this process a bit later in this chapter. For now, let's look at
the different modes that wireless networks use.

Wireless Network Modes

802.11 networks operate in one of two modes. In the uncommon *ad hoc* mode, two or
more devices communicate directly without any other intermediary hardware. The much
more common *infrastructure* mode uses a WAP that, in essence, acts as a hub for all wireless clients. A WAP also bridges wireless network segments to wired network segments.

Ad Hoc Mode   *Ad hoc mode* is sometimes called *peer-to-peer mode*, with each wireless
node in direct contact with each other node in a decentralized free-for-all, as shown in
Figure 14-5. Ad hoc mode does not use a WAP and instead uses a *mesh* topology, as discussed in Chapter 2, "Cabling and Topology."

Two or more wireless nodes communicating in ad hoc mode form an *Independent
Basic Service Set (IBSS)*. This is a basic unit of organization in wireless networks. If you
think of an IBSS as a wireless workgroup, you won't be far off the mark.

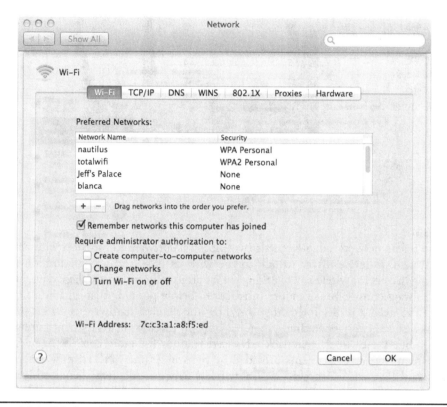

Figure 14-4   Wireless client configuration utility

Figure 14-5
Wireless ad hoc
mode network

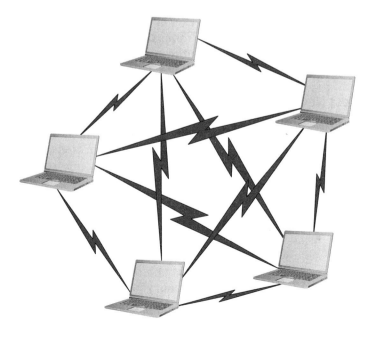

Ad hoc mode networks work well for small groups of computers (fewer than a dozen or so) that need to transfer files or share printers. Ad hoc networks are also good for temporary networks, such as study groups or business meetings.

Hardly anyone uses ad hoc networks for day-to-day work, however, simply because you can't use an ad hoc network to connect to other networks (unless one of the machines is running Internet Connection Sharing [ICS] or some equivalent).

Infrastructure Mode   Wireless networks running in *infrastructure mode* use one or more WAPs to connect the wireless network nodes centrally, as shown in Figure 14-6. This configuration is similar to the physical *star* topology of a wired network. This creates a *wireless local area network (WLAN)*. You also use infrastructure mode to connect wireless network segments to wired segments. If you plan to set up a wireless network for a large number of computing devices, or you need to have centralized control over the wireless network, use infrastructure mode.

Figure 14-6
Wireless
infrastructure
mode network

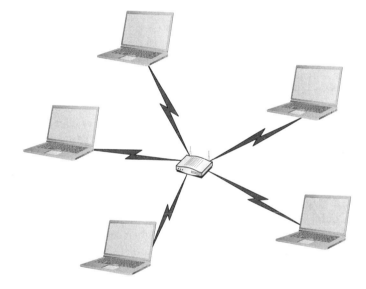

A single WAP servicing a given area is called a *Basic Service Set (BSS)*. This service area can be extended by adding more access points. This is called, appropriately, an *Extended Service Set (ESS)*.

NOTE   Many techs have dropped the word "basic" from the Extended Basic Service Set, the early name for an infrastructure-mode wireless network with more than one WAP. Accordingly, you'll see the initials for the Extended Basic Service Set as ESS. Using either EBSS or ESS is correct.

Wireless networks running in infrastructure mode require a little more planning—such as where you place the WAPs to provide adequate coverage—than ad hoc mode networks, and they provide a stable environment for permanent wireless network installations. Infrastructure mode is better suited to business networks or networks that need to share dedicated resources such as Internet connections and centralized databases. (See "Implementing Wi-Fi" later in this chapter.)

Range

Wireless networking range is hard to define. You'll see most descriptions listed with qualifiers such as "*around* 150 feet" and "*about* 300 feet." Wireless range is greatly affected by environmental factors. Interference from other wireless devices and solid objects affects range.

The maximum ranges listed in the sections that follow are those presented by wireless manufacturers as the *theoretical* maximum ranges. In the real world, you'll achieve these ranges only under the most ideal circumstances. Cutting the manufacturer's listed range in half is often a better estimate of the true effective range.

BSSID, SSID, and ESSID

Wireless devices connected together into a network, whether ad hoc or infrastructure, require some way to identify that network. Frames bound for computers within the network need to go where they're supposed to go, even when you have overlapping Wi-Fi networks. The jargon gets a little crazy here, especially because marketing has come into the mix. Stay with me.

The *Basic Service Set Identifier (BSSID)* defines the most basic infrastructure mode network—a BSS of one WAP and one or more wireless clients. With such a simple network, the Wi-Fi folks didn't see any reason to create some new numbering or naming scheme, so they made the BSSID the same as the MAC address for the WAP. Simple! Ah, but what do you do about ad hoc networks that don't have a WAP? The nodes that connect in an IBSS randomly generate a 48-bit string of numbers that looks and functions just like a MAC address, and that BSSID goes in every frame.

You could, if required, discover the MAC address for the WAP in a BSS and manually type that into the network name field when setting up a wireless computer. But that causes two problems. First, people don't want to remember strings of 48 binary digits, even if translated out as six hexadecimal octets, like A9–45–F2–3E–CA–12. People want names. Second, how do you connect two or more computers together into an IBSS when the BSSID has to be randomly generated?

The Wi-Fi folks created another level of naming called a *Service Set Identifier (SSID)*, a standard name applied to the BSS or IBSS to help the connection happen. The SSID— sometimes called a *network name*—is a 32-bit identification string that's inserted into the header of each frame processed by a WAP. Every Wi-Fi device must share the same SSID to communicate in a single network. By default, a WAP advertises its existence by sending out a continuous *SSID broadcast*. It's the SSID broadcast that lets you see the wireless networks that are available on your wireless devices.

To really see the power of 802.11 in action, let's take it one step further into a Wi-Fi network that has multiple WAPs: an ESS. How do you determine the network name at this level? You just use the SSID, only you apply it to the ESS as an *Extended Service Set Identifier (ESSID)*. In an ESS, every WAP connects to a central switch or switches to become part of a single broadcast domain.

With multiple WAPs in an ESS, clients will connect to whichever WAP has the strongest signal. As clients move through the space covered by the broadcast area, they will change WAP connections seamlessly, a process called *roaming*.

Most Wi-Fi manufacturers just use the term *SSID*, by the way, and not *ESSID*. When you configure a wireless device to connect to an ESS, you're technically using the ESSID rather than just the SSID, but the manufacturer often tries to make it simple for you by using only the term *SSID*.

Broadcasting Frequency

One of the biggest issues with wireless communication is the potential for interference from other wireless devices. To solve this, different wireless devices must operate in specific broadcasting frequencies. Knowing these wireless frequency ranges will assist you in troubleshooting interference issues from other devices operating in the same wireless band. The original 802.11 standards use either 2.4-GHz or 5.0-GHz radio frequencies.

Broadcasting Methods

The original IEEE 802.11 wireless Ethernet standard defined methods by which devices may communicate using *spread-spectrum* radio waves. Spread-spectrum broadcasts data in small, discrete chunks over the different frequencies available within a certain frequency range.

The 802.11 standard defines three different spread-spectrum broadcasting methods: *direct-sequence spread-spectrum (DSSS)*, *frequency-hopping spread-spectrum (FHSS)*, and *orthogonal frequency-division multiplexing (OFDM)*. DSSS sends data out on different frequencies at the same time, whereas FHSS sends data on one frequency at a time, constantly shifting (or *hopping*) frequencies. DSSS uses considerably more bandwidth than FHSS—around 22 MHz as opposed to 1 MHz. DSSS is capable of greater data throughput, but it's also more prone to interference than FHSS. OFDM is the latest of these three methods, better at dealing with interference, and is used on all but the earliest 802.11 networks.

Channels

Every Wi-Fi network communicates on a *channel*, a portion of the spectrum available. For the 2.4-GHz band, the 802.11 standard defines 14 channels of 20-MHz each (that's the *channel bandwidth*), but different countries limit exactly which channels may be used. In the United States, for example, a WAP using the 2.4-GHz band may only use channels 1 through 11. These channels have some overlap, so two nearby WAPs should not use close channels like 6 and 7. WAPs use channels 1, 6, or 11 by default because these are the only non-overlapping channels. You can fine-tune a network by changing the channels on WAPs to avoid overlap with other nearby WAPs. This capability is especially important in environments with many wireless networks sharing the same physical space. See the section "Configuring the Access Point" later in this chapter for more details on channel utilization.

The 5.0-GHz band offers many more channels than the 2.4-GHz band. In general there are around 40 different channels in the spectrum, and different countries have wildly different rules for which channels may or may not be used. The versions of 802.11

that use the 5.0-GHz band use automatic channel switching, so from a setup standpoint we don't worry about channels when we talk about 5.0-GHz 802.11 standards.

CSMA/CA

Because only a single device can use any network at a time in a physical bus topology, network nodes must have a way to access the network media without stepping on each other's frames. Wired Ethernet networks use *carrier sense multiple access with collision detection (CSMA/CD)*, as you'll recall from previous chapters, but Wi-Fi networks use *carrier sense multiple access with collision avoidance (CSMA/CA)*. Let's compare both methods.

 EXAM TIP Wired Ethernet networks use CSMA/CD. Wi-Fi networks use CSMA/CA.

How do multiple devices share network media, such as a cable? Sharing is fairly simple: Each device listens in on the network media by measuring the level of voltage currently on the wire. If the level is below the threshold, the device knows that it's clear to send data. If the voltage level rises above a preset threshold, the device knows that the line is busy and it must wait before sending data. Typically, the waiting period is the length of the current frame plus a short, predefined silence period called an *interframe gap (IFG)*. So far, so good—but what happens when two devices both detect that the wire is free and try to send data simultaneously? As you probably guessed, frames transmitted on the network from two different devices at the same time will corrupt each other's signals. This is called a *collision*. Collisions are a fact of networking life. So how do network nodes deal with collisions? They both react to collisions after they happen, and take steps to avoid collisions in the first place.

Modern wired networks use switches running in full-duplex mode, so they don't have to worry about collisions. You'll recall that from back in Chapter 1. CSMA/CD is disabled with full-duplex. Wireless networks don't have this luxury.

With CSMA/CD, each sending node detects the collision and responds by generating a random timeout period for itself, during which it doesn't try to send any more data on the network—this is called a *backoff*. Once the backoff period expires (remember that I'm talking about only milliseconds here), the node goes through the whole process again. This approach may not be very elegant, but it gets the job done.

CSMA/CD won't work for wireless networking because wireless devices simply can't detect collisions, for two reasons. First, radio is a half-duplex transmission method. Wireless devices cannot listen and send at the same time. Second, wireless node A wanting to communicate with wireless node B can't hear the third, hidden node (Wi-Fi C) that's also trying to communicate with B. A collision might occur in that circumstance.

Wireless networks need another way to deal with potential collisions. The CSMA/CA access method, as the name implies, proactively takes steps to avoid collisions, as does CSMA/CD. The difference comes in the collision avoidance.

The 802.11 standard defines two methods for collision avoidance: *Distributed Coordination Function (DCF)* and *Point Coordination Function (PCF)*. Currently, only DCF is implemented. DCF specifies rules for sending data onto the network media. For instance, if a wireless network node detects that the network is busy, DCF defines a backoff period on top of the normal IFG wait period before a node can try to access the network again. DCF also requires that receiving nodes send an acknowledgment (ACK) for every frame that they process. The ACK also includes a value that tells other wireless nodes to wait a certain duration before trying to access the network media. This period is calculated to be the time that the data frame takes to reach its destination based on the frame's length and data rate. If the sending node doesn't receive an ACK, it retransmits the same data frame until it gets a confirmation that the packet reached its destination.

 EXAM TIP   Current CSMA/CA devices use the Distributed Coordination Function (DCF) method for collision avoidance. Optionally, they can use Ready to Send/Clear to Send (RTS/CTS) to avoid collisions.

The 802.11-1997 standard was the very oldest wireless standard (see Table 14-1). Over time, more detailed additions to 802.11 came along that improved speeds and took advantage of other frequency bands.

 EXAM TIP   As you read about the many speeds listed for 802.11, you need to appreciate that wireless networking has a tremendous amount of overhead and latency. WAPs send out almost continuous streams of packets that do nothing more than advertise their existence or maintain connections. Wireless devices may sometimes stall due to processing or timeouts.

The end result is that only a percentage of the total throughput speed is actually achieved in real data bits getting to the applications that need them. The *actual* number of useful bits per second is called the *goodput* of the wireless network.

Standard	Frequency	Spectrum	Speed	Range	Compatibility
802.11-1997	2.4 GHz	DSSS	2 Mbps	~300'	802.11

Table 14-1   802.11 Summary

802.11b

The first widely adopted Wi-Fi standard—*802.11b*—supported data throughput of up to 11 Mbps and a range of up to 300 feet under ideal conditions. The main downside to using 802.11b was its frequency. The 2.4-GHz frequency is a crowded place, so you were more likely to run into interference from other wireless devices. Table 14-2 gives you the 802.11b summary.

Standard	Frequency	Spectrum	Speed	Range	Backward Compatibility
802.11b	2.4 GHz	DSSS	11 Mbps	~300'	n/a

Table 14-2   802.11b Summary

802.11a

The *802.11a* standard differed from the other 802.11-based standards in significant ways. Foremost was that it operated in a different frequency range, 5.0 GHz. The 5.0-GHz range is much less crowded than the 2.4-GHz range, reducing the chance of interference from devices such as telephones and microwave ovens. Too much signal interference can increase *latency*, making the network sluggish and slow to respond. Running in the 5.0-GHz range greatly reduces this problem.

 NOTE Despite the *a* designation for this extension to the 802.11 standard, 802.11a was available on the market *after* 802.11b.

The 802.11a standard also offered considerably greater throughput than 802.11b, with speeds up to 54 Mbps. Range, however, suffered somewhat and topped out at about 150 feet. Despite the superior speed of 802.11a, it never enjoyed the popularity of 802.11b.

Table 14-3 gives you the 802.11a summary.

Standard	Frequency	Spectrum	Speed	Range	Backward Compatibility
802.11a	5.0 GHz	OFDM	54 Mbps	~150'	n/a

Table 14-3 802.11a Summary

802.11g

The *802.11g* standard offered data transfer speeds equivalent to 802.11a—up to 54 Mbps—and the wider 300-foot range of 802.11b. More importantly, 802.11g was backward-compatible with 802.11b, so the same 802.11g WAP could service both 802.11b and 802.11g wireless nodes.

If an 802.11g network only had 802.11g devices connected, the network ran in *native mode*—at up to 54 Mbps—whereas when 802.11b devices connected, the network dropped down to *mixed mode*—all communication ran up to only 11 Mbps. Table 14-4 gives you the 802.11g summary.

Standard	Frequency	Spectrum	Speed	Range	Backward Compatibility
802.11g	2.4 GHz	OFDM	54 Mbps	~300'	802.11b

Table 14-4 802.11g Summary

Later 802.11g manufacturers incorporated *channel bonding* into their devices, enabling the devices to use two channels for transmission. Channel bonding is not part of the 802.11g standard, but rather proprietary technology pushed by various companies to increase the throughput of their wireless networks. Both the NIC and WAP, therefore, had to be from the same company for channel bonding to work.

802.11n

The *802.11n* standard brings several improvements to Wi-Fi networking, including faster speeds and new antenna technology implementations.

The 802.11n specification requires all but handheld devices to use multiple antennas to implement a feature called *multiple in/multiple out (MIMO)*, which enables the devices to make multiple simultaneous connections called streams. With up to four antennas, 802.11n devices can achieve amazing speeds. They also can implement channel bonding to increase throughput even more. (The official standard supports throughput of up to 600 Mbps, although practical implementation drops that down substantially.)

Many 802.11n WAPs employ *transmit beamforming*, a multiple-antenna technology that helps get rid of dead spots—places where the radio signal just does not penetrate at all—or at least make them not so bad. The antennas adjust the signal once the WAP discovers a client to optimize the radio signal.

Like 802.11g, 802.11n WAPs can support earlier, slower 802.11b/g devices. The problem with supporting these older types of 802.11 is that 802.11n WAPs need to encapsulate 802.11n frames into 802.11b or 802.11g frames. This adds some overhead to the process. Worse, if any 802.11b devices join the network, traffic drops to 802.11b speeds. (802.11g devices don't cause this behavior on 802.11n networks.)

To handle these issues, 802.11 WAPs can transmit in three different modes: legacy, mixed, and greenfield. These modes are also sometimes known as connection types.

Legacy mode means the 802.11n WAP sends out separate packets just for legacy devices. This is a terrible way to utilize 802.11n, but it's been added as a stopgap measure if the other modes don't work. In *mixed mode*, also often called *high-throughput* or *802.11a-ht/802.11g-ht*, the WAP sends special packets that support the older standards yet also can improve the speed of those standards via 802.11n's wider bandwidth. *Greenfield mode* is exclusively for 802.11n-only wireless networks. The WAP will only process 802.11n frames. Dropping support for older devices gives greenfield mode the best goodput.

 EXAM TIP If an 802.11g device shows a connection type of 802.11g-ht, this means it is connecting to an 802.11n WAP running in mixed mode.

Table 14-5 gives you the 802.11n summary.

Standard	Frequency	Spectrum	Speed	Range	Backward Compatibility
802.11n	2.4 GHz[1]	OFDM (QAM)	100+ Mbps	~300'	802.11b/g/[2]

[1] Dual-band 802.11n devices can function simultaneously at both 2.4- and 5.0-GHz bands.
[2] Many dual-band 802.11n WAPs support 802.11a devices as well as 802.11b/g/n devices. This is not part of the standard, but something manufacturers have implemented.

Table 14-5 802.11n Summary

802.11ac

802.11ac is a natural expansion of the 802.11n standard, incorporating even more streams, wider bandwidth, and higher speed. To avoid *device density* issues in the 2.4-GHz band, 802.11ac only uses the 5.0-GHz band. (See "What Wireless Is Already There?" later in this chapter for more on device density and how to deal with it.) Table 14-6 gives you the 802.11ac summary.

Standard	Frequency	Spectrum	Speed	Range	Backward Compatibility
802.11ac	5 GHz	OFDM (QAM)	Up to 1 Gbps	~300'	802.11a

Table 14-6 802.11ac Summary

The latest versions of 802.11ac include a new version of MIMO called *Multiuser MIMO (MU-MIMO)*. MU-MIMO gives a WAP the ability to broadcast to multiple users simultaneously.

 NOTE For a broadcasting method, the 802.11n and 802.11ac devices use a special version of OFDM called *quadruple-amplitude modulated (QAM)*.

WPS

By around 2006, 802.11 was everywhere and it was starting to get popular for non-PC devices such as printers, scanners, and speakers. The challenge with these devices was that they lacked any kind of interface to make it easy to configure the wireless settings.

To make configuration easier, the wireless industry created a special standard called *Wi-Fi Protected Setup (WPS)*. WPS works in two modes: push button method or PIN method. (There were other modes, but they never were popular). With the push button method, you press a button on one device (all WPS-compatible devices have a physical or virtual push button) and then press the WPS button on the other device. That's it. The two devices automatically configure themselves on an encrypted connection.

The PIN method was for connecting a PC to a WPS device (usually a WAP). You press the button on the WAP, locate the SSID on your device, and then enter an eight-digit PIN number as the WPA personal shared key (more on WPA shortly). All WPS WAPs have the PIN printed on the device.

WPS is very easy to use but is susceptible to different forms of *WPS attacks*. By design, the WPS PIN numbers are short. WPS attacks, therefore, concentrate on hacking the PIN number. By hacking the PIN, a bad actor can easily take control of the WAP, giving him or her access to the entire infrastructure. Use caution if you use WPS.

Wi-Fi Security

One of the biggest problems with wireless networking devices is that right out of the box they provide *no* security. Vendors go out of their way to make setting up their devices easy, so usually the only thing that you have to do to join a wireless network is turn your wireless devices on and let them find each other. Setting up an *open* Wi-Fi network is relatively simple. Once you decide to add security, on the other hand, you need to decide how you plan to share access with others.

EXAM TIP Expect a question about wireless authentication and authorization, comparing techniques and technologies between a *shared or open* network. The latter, of course, doesn't have any authentication or authorization by default!

We need to use a number of techniques to make a wireless network secure, to *harden* it from malicious things and people. Wireless security is network hardening. (For details about network hardening techniques that apply to all kinds of networks, see Chapter 19, "Protecting Your Network.")

NOTE All the methods used in wireless network security—authentication, encryption, MAC address filtering—can be considered network hardening techniques.

You also need to consider that your network's data frames float through the air on radio waves instead of zipping safely along wrapped up inside network cabling. What's to stop an unscrupulous network tech with the right equipment from grabbing those frames out of the air and reading that data?

To address these issues, 802.11 networks use three methods: MAC address filtering, authentication, and data encryption. The first two methods secure access to the network itself—*access control*—and the third secures the data that's moving around the network. All three of these methods require you to configure the WAPs and wireless devices. Let's take a look.

MAC Address Filtering

Most WAPs support *MAC address filtering*, a method that enables you to limit access to your network based on the physical addresses of wireless NICs. MAC address filtering creates a type of "accepted users" list—an *access control list (ACL)*—to restrict access to your wireless network. This is a *common mitigation technique* for undesired access to a network. A table stored in the WAP lists the MAC addresses that are permitted to participate in the wireless network, called a *whitelist*. Any network frames that don't contain the MAC address of a node listed in the table are rejected.

EXAM TIP WAPs use an *access control list (ACL)* to enable or deny specific MAC addresses. Note that a WAP's ACL has *nothing* to do with ACL in NTFS; it's just the same term used for two different things.

Many WAPs also enable you to deny specific MAC addresses from logging onto the network, creating a *blacklist*. This works great in close quarters, such as apartments or office buildings, where your wireless network signal goes beyond your perimeter. You can check the WAP and see the MAC addresses of every node that connects to your network. Check that list against the list of your computers, and you can readily spot any unwanted interloper. Putting an offending MAC address in the "deny" column effectively blocks that system from piggybacking onto your wireless connection.

 EXAM TIP MAC filtering with a whitelist means you allow only specific computers to join the network. When you deny specific computers, you create a blacklist. Whitelisting and blacklisting are labor-intensive processes, with whitelisting requiring far more work.

Although address filtering works, a hacker can very easily *spoof* a MAC address—make the NIC report a legitimate address rather than its own—and access the network. Worse, a hacker doesn't have to connect to your network to grab your network traffic out of thin air!

If you have data so important that a hacker would want to get at it, you should seriously consider using a wired network or separating the sensitive data from your wireless network in some fashion.

Wireless Authentication

Implementing authentication enables you to secure a network so only users with the proper credentials can access network resources. Authentication in a wired network, as you'll recall from Chapter 10, "Securing TCP/IP," generally takes the form of a centralized security database that contains user names, passwords, and permissions, like the Active Directory in a Windows Server environment. Wireless network clients can use the same security database as wired clients, but getting the wireless user authenticated takes a couple of extra steps.

The first real 802.11 security standard was known as 802.11i. 802.11i addressed both authentication and encryption, but for right now let's just discuss authentication under 802.11i. (Encryption under 802.11i is discussed a bit later in the "Data Encryption Using WPA" section.)

802.11i uses the IEEE *802.1X* standard to enable you to set up a network with some seriously secure authentication using a RADIUS server and passwords encrypted with *Extensible Authentication Protocol (EAP)*. Let's look at the components and the process.

A *RADIUS server* stores user names and passwords, enabling you to set a user's rights once in the network. A RADIUS server functions like a typical server, but the remote aspect of it requires you to learn new jargon. The terms "client" and "server" are *so* Active Directory, after all.

 NOTE RADIUS stands for *Remote Authentication Dial-In User Service*. Say that five times.

Here's how it works. The client wireless computer, called a *supplicant*, contacts the WAP, called a *Network Access Server (NAS)*, and requests permission to access the network. The NAS collects the supplicant's user name and password and then contacts the RADIUS server to see if the supplicant appears in the RADIUS server's security database. If the supplicant appears and the user name and password are correct, the RADIUS server sends a packet back to the supplicant, through the WAP, with an Access-Accept code and an Authenticator section that proves the packet actually came from the RADIUS server. Then the remote user gets access to the network resources. That's some serious security! See Figure 14-7.

Figure 14-7
Authenticating using RADIUS

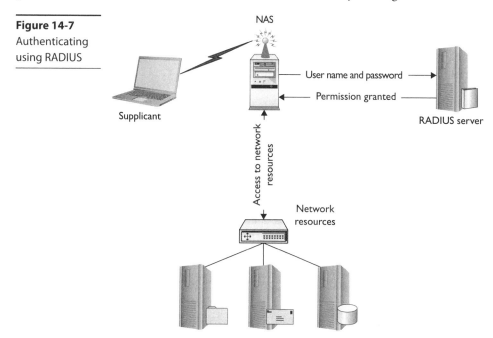

But here's where it gets tricky. What are the points of potential security failure here? All over the place, right? The connection between each of these devices must be secure; several protocols make certain of that security. PPP, for example, provides a secure connection between the supplicant and the NAS. IPsec often provides the security between the NAS and the RADIUS server. We then need some form of authentication standard that encrypts all this authentication process. That's where 802.11i calls for the Extensible Authentication Protocol (EAP). See Figure 14-8.

Figure 14-8
Authentication using RADIUS with protocols in place

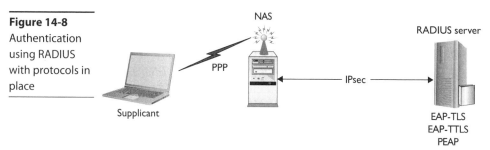

EAP

One of the great challenges to authentication is getting the two ends of the authentication process to handle the many different types of authentication options. Even though PPP pretty much owned the user name/password authentication business, proprietary forms of authentication using smartcards/tokens, certificates, and so on, began to show up on the market, threatening to drop practical authentication into a huge mess of competing standards.

EAP was developed to create a single standard to allow two devices to authenticate. Despite the name, EAP is not a protocol in the classic sense, but rather it is a PPP wrapper that EAP-compliant applications can use to accept one of many types of authentication. Although EAP is a general-purpose authentication wrapper, its only substantial use is in wireless networks. EAP comes in various types, but currently only seven types are in common use:

- **EAP-PSK**   Easily the most popular form of authentication used in wireless networks today, EAP-PSK (Pre-shared key) is nothing more than a shared secret code that's stored on both the wireless access point and the wireless client, encrypted using the powerful AES encryption. (See the *Encryption type* field in Figure 14-9.) Note that CompTIA loses the hyphen, so *preshared key*.

- **EAP-TLS**   EAP with Transport Layer Security (TLS) defines the use of a RADIUS server as well as mutual authentication, requiring certificates on both the server and every client. On the client side, a smart card may be used in lieu of a certificate. EAP-TLS is very robust, but the client-side certificate requirement is an administrative challenge. Even though it's a challenge, the most secure wireless networks all use EAP-TLS. EAP-TLS is only used on wireless networks, but TLS is used heavily on secure Web sites.

- **EAP-TTLS**   EAP-TTLS (Tunneled TLS) is similar to EAP-TLS but only uses a single server-side certificate. EAP-TTLS is very common for more secure wireless networks.

- **EAP-MS-CHAPv2**   More commonly known as Protected EAP (PEAP), EAP-MS-CHAPv2 uses a password function based on MS-CHAPv2 with the addition of an encrypted TLS tunnel similar to EAP-TLS. This is the most common implementation of EAP.

- **EAP-MD5**   This is a very simple version of EAP that uses only MD5 hashes for transfer of authentication credentials. EAP-MD5 is weak and the least used of all the versions of EAP described.

- **LEAP**   Lightweight EAP (LEAP) is a proprietary EAP authentication used almost exclusively by Cisco wireless products. LEAP is an interesting combination of MS-CHAP authentication between a wireless client and a RADIUS server.

- **EAP-FAST**   *EAP Flexible Authentication via Secure Tunneling* is Cisco's replacement for LEAP. All current operating systems support EAP-FAST (assuming the right software is installed).

Figure 14-9
Setting EAP
authentication
scheme

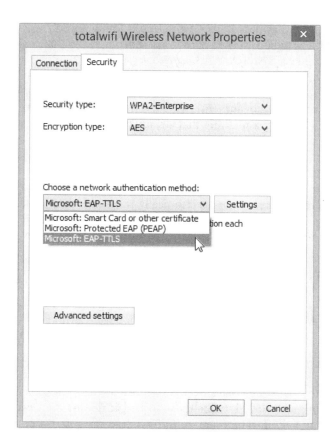

802.1X

EAP was a huge success and almost overnight gave those who needed point-to-point authentication a one-stop-shop methodology to do so. EAP was so successful that there was a cry to develop an EAP solution for Ethernet networks. This solution is called 802.1X. Whereas traditional EAP is nothing more than an authentication method wrapped in PPP, 802.1X gets rid of the PPP (Ethernet is not a point-to-point protocol!) and instead puts the EAP information inside an Ethernet frame.

802.1X is a port-based authentication network access control mechanism for networks. In other words, it's a complete authentication standard designed to force devices to go through a full AAA process to get anywhere past the interface on a gateway system. Before 802.1X, a system on a wired network could always access another system's port. Granted, an attacker wouldn't be able to do much until he gave a user name/password or certificate, but he could still send packets to any computer on the network. This wasn't good because it enabled attackers to get to the systems to try to do evil things. 802.1X prevented them from even getting in the door until they were authenticated and authorized.

The interesting part is that you already know about most of the parts of 802.1X because the standard worked hard to use existing technologies. From a distance, 802.1X looks a lot like a RADIUS AAA setup.

802.1X combines the RADIUS-style AAA with EAP versions to make a complete authentication solution. The folks who developed 802.1X saw it as a total replacement for every other form of authentication (even Kerberos), but the reality is that most people don't like changing something that already works. To that end, only wireless networking broadly adopted 802.1X.

Data Encryption

The main way we secure a wireless network is by encrypting the data packets that are floating around. *Encryption* electronically scrambles data packets and locks them with an encryption key before transmitting them onto the wireless network. The receiving network device has to possess the decryption key to unscramble the packet and process the data. Thus, a hacker who grabs any data frames out of the air can't read those frames unless he or she has the decryption key. Enabling wireless encryption through WPA2 provides a good level of security to data packets in transit.

 NOTE The encryption/decryption works with both symmetric encryption, where both parties have the same key, and asymmetric encryption, where parties use public and private keys.

Over the years there have been a number of encryption methods for wireless. There was the original 802.11 (which was so bad it doesn't even warrant discussion), WEP, WPA, and WPA2. There are additional features that tie encryption standards with authentication, such as WPA-PSK and WPA-Enterprise. Let's cover all of these.

 NOTE By the time you read this, WPA3 will have debuted (it was announced during this writing). WPA3 solves the problem with open Wi-Fi networks (think neighborhood café), creating individual security channels. Once you connect with your portable device, in other words, nothing can snoop on your communication.

Data Encryption Using WEP   The granddaddy of wireless security, *Wired Equivalent Privacy (WEP)*, uses a 64- or 128-bit encryption algorithm to scramble data frames. But even with the strongest encryption enabled, WEP isn't a particularly robust security solution. In fact, WEP can be cracked in under a minute with just a regular laptop and open source software.

WEP is subject to many types of *WEP attacks*. Hackers can easily crack WEP, for two reasons: the size of the encryption key and the way the key is updated. First, the WEP keys were never really 64- and 128-bit. WEP uses an encryption cipher called *RC4*. There's nothing inherently wrong with RC4, but RC4 is a stream cipher and needs a little code to start the encryption process, just like a water pump needs some water in the pump before it works. This extra code is stored in the key in the form of what's called an *initialization vector (IV)*. The IV with WEP is 24 bits, which means the encryption part of a WEP key is only 40-bit or 104-bit.

The second problem with WEP is that the encryption key is both static (never changes from session to session) and shared (the same key is used by all network nodes). This means it's not that hard to crack assuming you can capture enough WEP-encrypted packets to figure out the code. WEP is simply a disaster.

WEP also fails to provide a mechanism for performing user authentication. That is, network nodes that use WEP encryption are identified by their MAC address, and no other credentials are offered or required. With just a laptop and some open source software, MAC addresses are very easy to sniff out and duplicate, thus opening you up to a possible spoofing attack. (See Chapter 19, "Protecting Your Network," for the scoop on spoofing and other common attacks.)

The key thing (pun intended) to remember about WEP is that it is outdated and should never be used. The only security WEP provides today is to prevent casual people from connecting to your WAP. Its encryption is so easily cracked that you might as well be transmitting plaintext. WEP is like a No Trespassing sign on a post, but without the fence. Modern WAPs don't offer WEP as an option.

Data Encryption Using WPA　The 802.11i standard was designed to address the problems with WEP and to provide proper authentication. The full standard took a while to complete, so the wireless industry implemented an intermediate fix. They invented a sales term called *Wi-Fi Protected Access (WPA)* that adopted most (not all) of the 802.11i standard, fixing some of the weaknesses of WEP. WPA offers security enhancements such as dynamic encryption key generation (keys are issued on a per-user and per-session basis) and an encryption key integrity-checking feature.

WPA works by using an extra layer of security, called the *Temporal Key Integrity Protocol (TKIP)*, around the WEP encryption scheme. It's not, therefore, a complete replacement protocol for WEP and still uses RC4 for cipher initialization—hence the name *TKIP-RC4*. TKIP added a 128-bit encryption key that seemed unbreakable when first introduced. Within four years of introduction, however, researchers showed methods by which hackers could waltz through WPA security almost as quickly as through WEP security. Another solution had to be found.

Data Encryption Using WPA2　The IEEE *802.11i* standard amended the 802.11 standard to add much-needed security features. I already discussed the 802.1X authentication measure using EAP to provide secure access to Wi-Fi networks. 802.11i also replaced TKIP-RC4 with the much more robust *CCMP-AES*, a 128-bit block cipher that's much tougher to crack.

 NOTE　CCMP stands for *Counter Mode Cipher Block Chaining Message Authentication Code Protocol*. Whew! That's why we commonly just use the initials, CCMP. AES stands for *Advanced Encryption Standard*.

Implementing the full 802.11i standard took time because most of the installed Wi-Fi hardware couldn't be updated to handle AES encryption. WPA held the title of "most secure wireless" for a number of years.

Eventually, enough devices were made that could support AES that the full 802.11i standard was implemented under the sales term *Wi-Fi Protected Access 2 (WPA2)*. A "WPA2-compliant device" is really just a marketing term for a device that fully supports the 802.11i standard. WPA2 is the current top security standard used on 802.11 networks. WPA2 is not hack-proof, but it definitely offers a much tougher encryption standard that stops the casual hacker cold.

The most common way to set up WPA or WPA2 encryption is to use a simple version called WPA (or WPA2) Pre-shared key (PSK). Basically, with these PSK versions, you create a secret key that must be added to any device that is going to be on that SSID. There is no authentication with WPA-PSK or WPA2-PSK.

WPA attacks and WPA2 attacks can happen, especially with wireless networks using WPA-Personal or WPA2-Personal passphrases. The attacks take place by using sophisticated methods that make a number of assumptions about the passphrase, and the fact that certain passphrases are used quite often. The most important thing to do to prevent these attacks from succeeding is to use long passphrases (16 or more characters), thus making the network hard to crack. Otherwise, you need authentication. If you want authentication you move into what most wireless folks will call an enterprise setup. For example, when you use a RADIUS server for authentication with WPA2 to create an amazingly secure wireless network, it gets a fancy name: *WPA2-Enterprise*. Let's talk about enterprise wireless a bit more.

Enterprise Wireless

A simple BSSID or ESSID is incredibly easy to set up. You can take a few cheap WAPs from your local electronics store, connect them to a switch, use a Web interface to configure each WAP, and start connecting clients. Inexpensive SOHO WAPs and wireless routers have been around so long—almost as long as 802.11 itself—that for many of us this is what we think a "wireless network" means.

But as wireless networks become more important, complex, and busy, the cheap SOHO boxes just aren't going to work anymore. When you want dependable, robust, secure, administrable wireless networks, you need enterprise-class wireless equipment. In general, an enterprise wireless device differs from a SOHO device in five areas: robust device construction, centralized management, VLAN pooling, Power over Ethernet, and bringing personal wireless devices into the enterprise environment.

Robust Device Construction

If you compare a typical SOHO WAP to an enterprise WAP, you'll notice immediately that the enterprise WAP is made of better materials (often metal instead of plastic). Enterprise WAPs for the most part will also be more configurable. Most enterprise WAPs enable you to swap out antennas and radios, so you can keep WAPs while upgrading them to the latest technologies. Figure 14-10 shows an enterprise WAP.

Figure 14-10
Cisco Enterprise
WAP

Enterprise Wireless Administration

An enterprise wireless infrastructure is almost certainly going to consist of a large number of WAPs. It's impossible to administer a large number of WAPs when you have to access each WAP individually. Imagine something as simple as changing the password on a WPA2-encrypted ESSID on a wireless network with 50+ WAPs (Figure 14-11). The job would take forever!

Figure 14-11
Configuring
WAPs

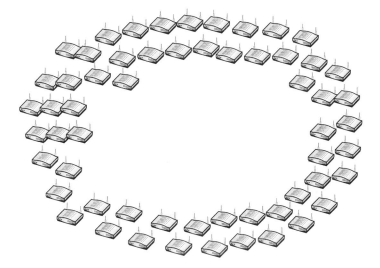

The wireless industry long ago appreciated the complexity of enterprise-level wireless networks and created tools to make administration easier. The important point to any wireless network is that all of the WAPs, at least on a single SSID, connect to a single switch or group of switches. What if we offload the job of configuration to a switch that's designed to handle a number of WAPs simultaneously? We call these switches *wireless controllers* (Figure 14-12).

Figure 14-12
Wireless
controller

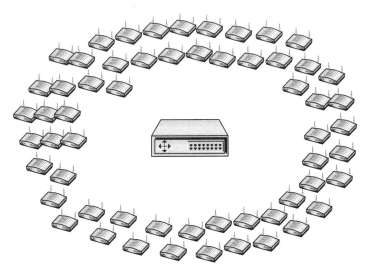

 NOTE Wireless controllers have a number of other names, such as wireless switch, wireless LAN switch, and so forth.

Any WAP that you can access directly and configure singularly via its own interface is called a *thick client*. A WAP that can only be configured by a wireless controller is called a *thin client*. For years, these centralized configuration methods were proprietary for each wireless manufacturer, making for little or no cross-brand interoperability. This incompatibility in thin and thick clients was a common wireless issue back in the day. Today, most manufacturers use the *Lightweight Access Point Protocol (LWAPP)* to ensure interoperability. Given LWAPP's broad acceptance, most WAPs will accept commands from any wireless controller.

VLAN Pooling

One of the big challenges to larger enterprise networks is the large number of clients that might be on a single SSID at any given moment. As the number of devices grows, you get a huge amount of broadcasts on the network. The traditional method to reduce this is to divide the WLAN into multiple broadcast domains and use routers to interconnect the domains. In many cases, though, the needs of the wireless network require a single domain; instead we create a pool of VLANs for a single SSID and randomly assign wireless clients to one of the VLANs. This is called *VLAN pooling*.

Power over Ethernet

Wireless access points need electrical power, but they're invariably placed in strange locations (like ceilings or high up on walls) where providing electrical power is not convenient. No worries! Better WAPs support an IEEE standard (802.3af) called *Power over Ethernet (PoE)*, which enables them to receive their power from the same Ethernet cables that transfer their data. The switch that connects the WAPs must support PoE, but as long as both the WAP and the switches to which they connect support PoE, you don't have to do anything other than just plug in Ethernet cables. PoE works automatically. As you might imagine, it costs extra to get WAPs and switches that support PoE, but the convenience of PoE for wireless networks makes it a popular option.

The original PoE standard came out in 2003 with great response from the industry. Its popularity revealed a big problem: the original 802.3af standard only supported a maximum of 14.4 watts of DC power and many devices needed more. In 2009, 802.3af was revised to output as much as 25.5 watts. This new PoE amendment to 802.3 is called 802.3at, PoE plus, or PoE+.

Implementing Wi-Fi

Installing and configuring a Wi-Fi network requires a number of discrete steps. You should start with a site survey to determine any obstacles (existing wireless, interference, and so on) you need to overcome and to determine the best location for your access points. You'll need to install one or more access points, and then configure both the access point(s) and wireless clients. Finally, you should put the network to the test, verifying that it works as you intended.

Performing a Site Survey

As mentioned, the first step of installing a wireless network is the site survey. A *site survey* will reveal any obstacles to creating the wireless network and will help determine the best possible location for your access points. The main components for creating a site survey are a floor plan of the area you wish to provide with wireless and a site survey tool such as NETSCOUT's AirMagnet Survey Pro (Figure 14-13). *Wireless survey tools* help you discover any other wireless networks in the area and will integrate a drawing of your floor plan with interference sources clearly marked. This enables you to get the right kind of hardware you need and makes it possible to get the proper network coverage.

What Wireless Is Already There?

Discovering any wireless network signals other than your own in your space enables you to set both the SSID and channel to avoid networks that overlap. One part of any good site survey is a wireless analyzer. A *wireless analyzer* or *Wi-Fi analyzer* is any device that looks for and documents all existing wireless networks in the area. Wireless analyzers are handy tools that are useful for diagnosing wireless network issues and conducting site surveys. You can get dedicated, hand-held wireless analyzer tools or you can run site survey software on a laptop or mobile wireless device. Wireless survey tools like AirMagnet Survey Pro always include an analyzer as well. Figure 14-14 shows a screenshot of Acrylic WiFi, a free and popular wireless analyzer.

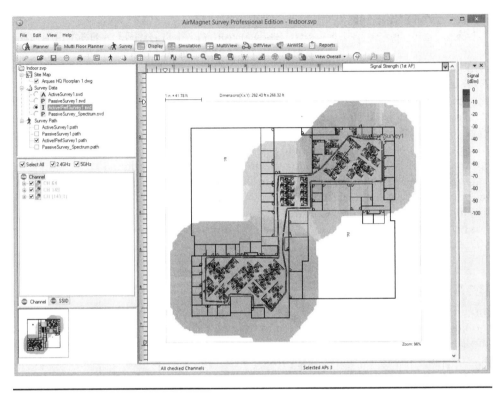

Figure 14-13 AirMagnet Survey Pro

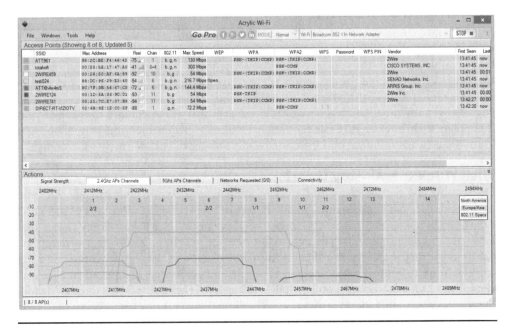

Figure 14-14 Acrylic WiFi

SIM Check out the excellent Chapter 14 Show! Sim about third-party wireless utilities at **http://totalsem.com/007**. It's a cool sim about non-Microsoft implementations.

Wireless networks send out radio signals on the 2.4- or 5.0-GHz spectrum using one of a number of discrete channels. In early wireless networks, a big part of the setup was to determine the channels used nearby in order to avoid them. In more modern wireless networks, we rarely adjust channels manually anymore. Instead we rely on powerful algorithms built into WAPs to locate the least congested channels automatically. The bigger challenge today is the preexistence of many Wi-Fi networks with lots of clients, creating *high device density environments*. You need a wireless solution that handles many users running on the few wireless frequencies available.

There are plenty of tools like AirMagnet Survey Pro to support a wireless survey. All good survey utilities share some common ways to report their findings. One of the most powerful reports that they generate is called a heat map. A *heat map* is nothing more than a graphical representation of the RF sources on your site, using different colors to represent the intensity of the signal. Figure 14-15 shows a sample heat map.

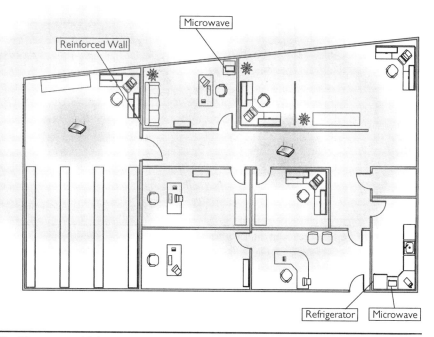

Figure 14-15   Site survey with heat map

Interference Sources

It might seem like overkill in a small network, but any network beyond a simple one should have a sketched-out site survey with any potential interference sources clearly marked (Figure 14-16). Refrigerators, reinforced walls, metal plumbing, microwave ovens; all of these can create horrible dead spots where your network radio wave can't easily penetrate. With a difficult or high-interference area, you might need to move up to 802.11n or 802.11ac equipment with three or four antennas just to get the kind of coverage you want. Or you might need to plan a multiple WAP network to wipe out the dead zones. A proper site survey gives you the first tool for implementing a network that works.

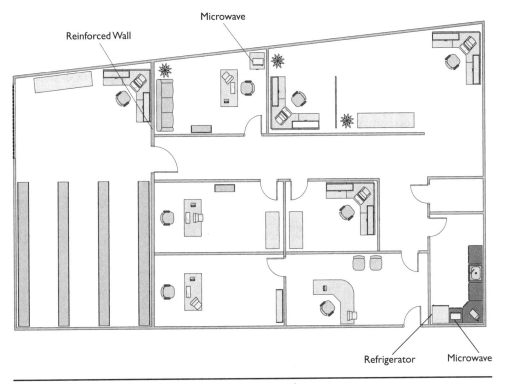

Figure 14-16   Site survey with interference sources noted

Installing the Client

Because every Wi-Fi network needs clients (otherwise, what's the point?), you need to install Wi-Fi client hardware and software. Pretty much every type of mobile device (smartphones, laptops, tablets, and so forth) comes with a built-in client, usually part of the operating system.

Desktop systems are a different story. Most desktops don't have built-in wireless, so you'll need to install a wireless NIC. You have a choice between installing a PCIe card or a USB device. With a PCIe NIC, power down the PC, disconnect from the AC source, and open the case. Following good CompTIA A+ technician procedures, locate a free slot on the motherboard, remove the slot cover, remove the NIC from its anti-static bag, install the NIC, and affix the retaining screw. See Figure 14-17. Often you'll need to attach the antenna. Button everything up, plug it in, and start the computer. If prompted, put in the disc that came from the manufacturer and install drivers and any other software necessary.

Figure 14-17
Wi-Fi NIC
installed

With a USB NIC, you should install the drivers and software before you connect the NIC to the computer. This is standard operating procedure for any USB device, as you most likely recall from your CompTIA A+ certification training (or from personal experience).

Setting Up an Ad Hoc Network

Although ad hoc networks are rare, they are on the CompTIA Network+ exam. Plus, you might need to set one up in the real world, so let's look at the process.

Configuring NICs for ad hoc mode networking requires you to address four things: SSID, IP addresses, channel, and sharing. (Plus, of course, you have to set the NICs to function in ad hoc mode!) Each wireless node must be configured to use the same network name (SSID). It's common for one system to set up an ad hoc node and then have other nodes attach to that node. Of course, no two nodes can use the same IP address, although this is unlikely because all operating systems use Automatic Private IP Addressing (APIPA). Finally, ensure that the File and Printer Sharing service is running on all nodes. Figure 14-18 shows a wireless network configuration utility with ad hoc mode selected.

Figure 14-18
Selecting ad
hoc mode
in a wireless
configuration
utility

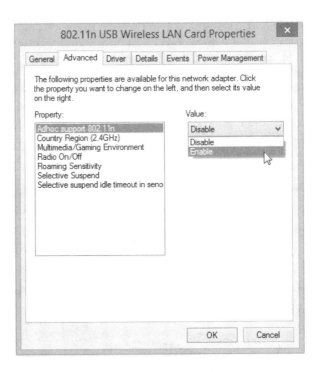

Try This!

Ad Hoc-ing

If you have access to a Wi-Fi-enabled device and a friend or classmate has one as well, try this! Set up your Wi-Fi for ad hoc using the configuration utility, and then try to connect with your partner's device. Use default settings. Once you connect with the defaults, you can start playing with your ad hoc network! Select Home for your network and set up a HomeGroup. Copy the sample images from one machine to another. Throw a big file into a Public folder and try copying that one, too. Then do it again, but with variations of distance and channels. How far can you separate your devices and still communicate? What happens if you change channels in the configuration utility, such as moving both devices from channel 6 to channel 4?

Setting Up an Infrastructure Network

Site survey in hand and Wi-Fi technology selected, you're ready to set up a wireless network in infrastructure mode. You need to determine the optimal location for your WAP, configure the WAP, and then configure any clients to access that WAP. Seems pretty straightforward, but the devil, they say, is in the details.

Placing the Access Points/Antennas

All wireless access points have antennas that radiate the 802.11 signal to the clients, so the optimal location for a WAP depends on the area you want to cover and whether you care if the signal bleeds out beyond the borders. You also need to use antennas that provide enough signal and push that signal in the proper direction. There are some interesting options here and you should know them both for modern networking and for the CompTIA Network+ exam.

Antenna placement on the WAPs is also very important. WAP antennas come in many shapes and sizes. In the early days it was common to see WAPs with two antennas (Figure 14-19). Some WAPs have only one antenna and some (802.11n and 802.11ac) have more than two, like the one you saw in Figure 14-3. Even a WAP that doesn't seem to have antennas is simply hiding them inside the case.

Figure 14-19
WRT54G showing
two antennas

There are three basic types of antennas common in 802.11 networks: omnidirectional, unidirectional, and patch. Each offers different solutions for coverage of specific wireless network setups. Let's look at all three.

Omnidirectional   In general, an *omnidirectional antenna* radiates the signal outward from the WAP in all directions. For a typical network, you want blanket coverage and would place a WAP with an omnidirectional antenna in the center of the area (Figure 14-20). This has the advantage of ease of use—anything within the signal radius can potentially access the network. The standard straight-wire antennas that provide the most omnidirectional function are called *dipole antennas*.

The famous little black antennas seen on older WAPs are all dipoles. A dipole antenna has two radiating elements that point in opposite directions. But if you look at a WAP antenna, it looks like it only points in one direction (Figure 14-21). If you open up one of these antennas, however, you'll see that it has two opposing radiating elements (Figure 14-22).

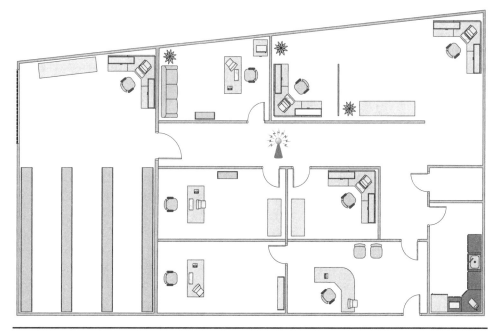

Figure 14-20   Office layout with WAP in the center

Figure 14-21   Typical WAP dipole antenna—where are the two elements?

Figure 14-22   Same antenna from Figure 14-21 opened, showing the two elements

A dipole antenna doesn't radiate in a perfect ball. It actually is more of a doughnut shape, as shown in Figure 14-23. Note that this shape is great for outdoors or a single floor, but it doesn't send much signal above or below the WAP.

The omnidirectional and centered approach does not work for every network, for three reasons. First, if the signal exceeds the size of the network space, that signal bleeds out. The signal can bleed out a lot in some cases, particularly if your specific space doesn't allow you to put the WAP in the center, but rather off-center. This presents a security risk as well, because someone outside your network space could lurk, pick up the signal, and do unpleasant things to your network. Second, if your network space exceeds the signal of your WAP, you'll need to get some sort of signal booster. Third, any obstacles will produce glaring dead spots in network coverage. Too many dead spots make a less-than-ideal solution. To address these issues, you might need to turn to other solutions.

An antenna strengthens and focuses the RF output from a WAP. The ratio of increase—what's called *gain*—is measured in decibels (dB). The gain from a typical WAP is 2 dB, enough to cover a reasonable area, but not a very large room. Increasing the

Figure 14-23
Dipole radiation
pattern

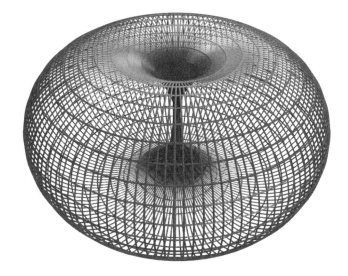

signal requires a bigger device antenna. Many WAPs have removable device antennas. To increase the signal in an omnidirectional and centered setup, simply replace the factory device antennas with one or more bigger device antennas (Figure 14-24). Get a big enough antenna and you can crank it all the way up to 11!

Figure 14-24
Replacement
antenna on a
WAP

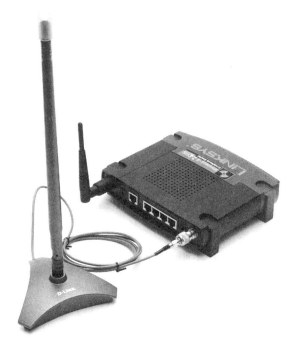

Unidirectional   When you don't necessarily want to broadcast to the world, you can use one or more *directional antennas* to create a nicely focused network. A *unidirectional antenna*, as the name implies, focuses a radio wave into a beam of sorts. Unidirectional antennas come in a variety of flavors, such as parabolic, dish, and Yagi, to name a just a few. A *parabolic antenna* looks like a satellite dish. A *Yagi antenna* (named for one of its Japanese inventors) is often called a *beam antenna* and can enable a focused radio wave to travel a long way, even miles (Figure 14-25)! If you need to connect in a narrow beam (down a hallway or from one faraway point to another), unidirectional antennas are the way to go.

Figure 14-25
Yagi antenna

Patch Antennas   *Patch antennas* are flat, plate-shaped antennas that generate a half-sphere beam. Patch antennas are always placed on walls. The half-sphere is perfect for indoor offices where you want to fill the room with a strong signal but not broadcast to the room behind the patch (Figure 14-26).

Figure 14-26
Patch antenna

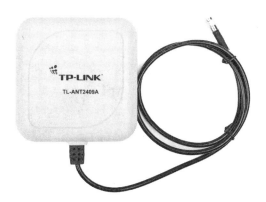

Optimal Antenna Placement   Optimal antenna placement varies according to the space to fill and security concerns. You can use the site survey and the same wireless analyzer tools to find dead spots, odd corners, and so on. Use the right kind of antenna on each WAP to fill in the space.

Configuring the Access Point

Wireless access points have a browser-based setup utility. Typically, you fire up the Web browser on one of your network client workstations and enter the access point's default IP address, such as 192.168.1.1, to bring up the configuration page. You need to supply an administrative password, included with your access point's documentation, to log in (Figure 14-27).

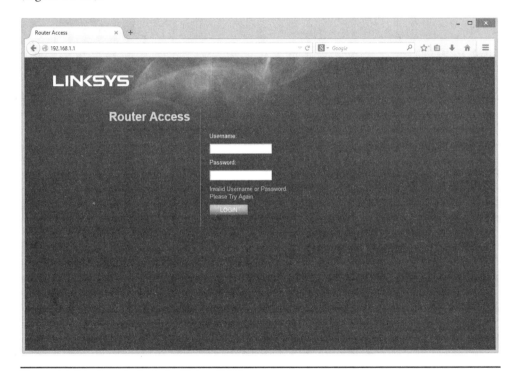

Figure 14-27   Security login for Linksys WAP

Once you've logged in, you'll see configuration screens for changing your basic setup, access point password, security, and so on. Different access points offer different configuration options. Figure 14-28 shows the initial setup screen for a popular Linksys WAP/router.

Configuring the SSID and Beacon   The SSID option is usually located somewhere obvious on the configuration utility. On the Linksys model shown in Figure 14-28, this option is on the Setup tab. Configure your SSID to something unique.

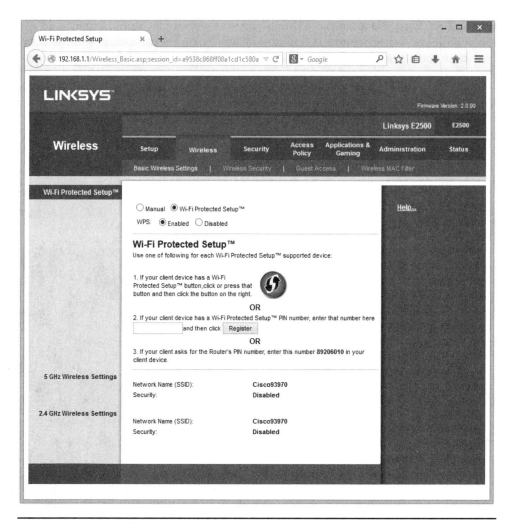

Figure 14-28   Linksys WAP setup screen

The primary way we locate wireless networks is by using our clients to scan for SSIDs. All wireless networks have a function to turn off the SSID broadcast. You can choose not to broadcast the SSID, but this only stops casual users—sophisticated wireless intruders have tools to detect networks that do not broadcast their SSIDs. Turning off SSID broadcast forces users to configure the connection to a particular SSID manually.

Aside from the SSID, broadcast traffic includes the *beacon*, essentially a timing frame sent from the WAP at regular intervals. The beacon frame enables Wi-Fi networks to function, so this is fairly important. Beacon traffic also makes up a major percentage of network traffic because most WAPs have beacons set to go off every 100 ms! You can adjust the rate of the beacon traffic down and improve your network traffic speeds, but you lower the speed at which devices can negotiate to get on the network, among other things. Figure 14-29 shows the Beacon Interval setting on a Linksys router.

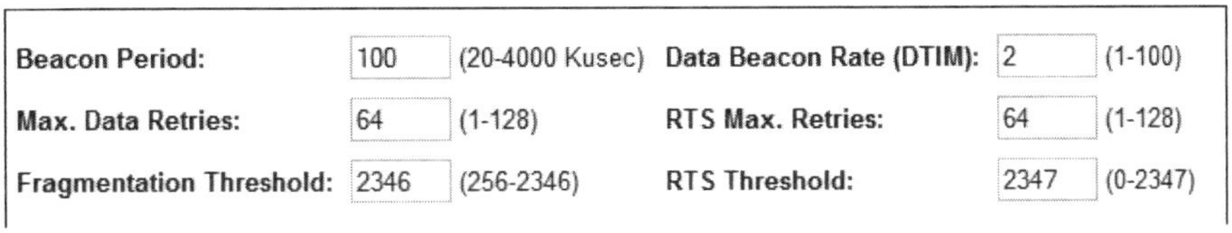

Beacon Period:	100	(20-4000 Kusec)	**Data Beacon Rate (DTIM):**	2	(1-100)
Max. Data Retries:	64	(1-128)	**RTS Max. Retries:**	64	(1-128)
Fragmentation Threshold:	2346	(256-2346)	**RTS Threshold:**	2347	(0-2347)

Figure 14-29 Setting the beacon interval

Configuring MAC Address Filtering   Increase security even further by using MAC address filtering to build a list of wireless network clients that are permitted or denied access to your wireless network based on their unique MAC addresses. Figure 14-30 shows the MAC address filtering configuration screen on a Linksys WAP. Simply enter the MAC address of a wireless node that you want to allow or deny access to your wireless network.

Configuring Encryption   Enabling encryption ensures that data frames are secured against unauthorized access. To set up encryption, you turn on encryption at the WAP and generate a unique security key. Then you configure all connected wireless nodes on the network with the same key information. Figure 14-31 shows the WPA2 key configuration screen for a Linksys WAP.

You can generate a set of encryption keys either automatically or manually. You can save yourself a certain amount of effort by using the automatic method. Select an encryption level—the usual choices are either 64-bit or 128-bit—and then enter a unique *passphrase* and click the **Generate** button (or whatever the equivalent button is called in your WAP's software). Then select a default key and save the settings.

The encryption level, key, and passphrase must match on the wireless client node or communication fails. Many access points have the capability to export the encryption key data onto removable media for easy importing onto a client workstation, or you can configure encryption manually using the vendor-supplied configuration utility, as shown in Figure 14-32.

If you have the option, choose WPA2 encryption for both the WAP and the NICs in your network. You configure WPA2 the same way you would WPA. Note that the settings such as WPA2 for the Enterprise assume you'll enable authentication using a RADIUS server (Figure 14-33). Always use the strongest encryption you can. If you have WPA2, use it. If not, use WPA. WEP is always a terrible choice.

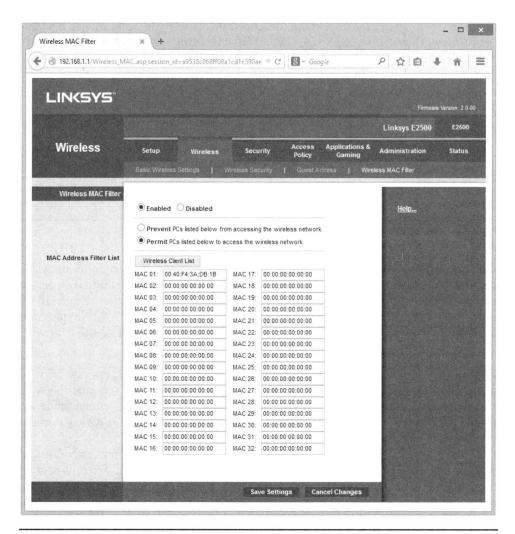

Figure 14-30 MAC address filtering configuration screen for a Linksys WAP

Configuring Channel and Frequency With most home networks, you can simply leave the channel and frequency of the WAP at the factory defaults, but in an environment with overlapping Wi-Fi signals, you'll want to adjust one or both features. Using a wireless analyzer, see current channel utilization and then change your channel to something that doesn't conflict. To adjust the channel, find the option in the WAP configuration screens and simply change it. Figure 14-34 shows the channel option in a Linksys WAP.

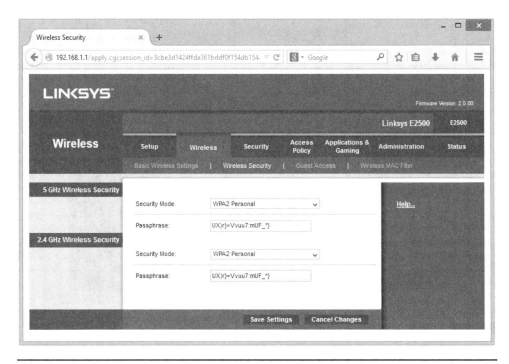

Figure 14-31   Encryption key configuration screen on Linksys WAP

Figure 14-32
Encryption
screen on
client wireless
network adapter
configuration
utility

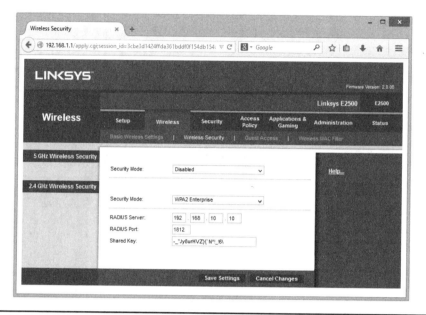

Figure 14-33 Encryption screen with RADIUS option

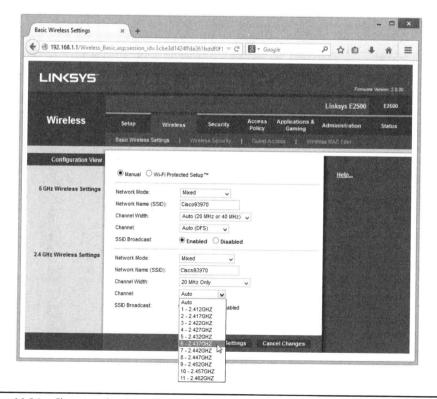

Figure 14-34 Changing the channel

With dual-band 802.11n WAPs, you can choose which band to put 802.11n traffic on, either 2.4 GHz or 5.0 GHz. In an area with overlapping signals, most of the traffic will be on the 2.4-GHz frequency because most devices are either 802.11b or 802.11g. You can avoid any kind of conflict with your 802.11n devices by using the 5.0-GHz frequency band instead. Figure 14-35 shows the configuration screen for a dual-band 802.11n WAP.

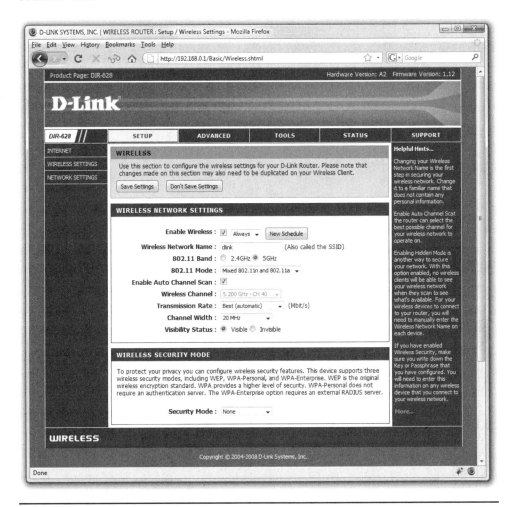

Figure 14-35 Selecting frequency

Configuring the Client

As with ad hoc mode wireless networks, infrastructure mode networks require that the same SSID be configured on all nodes and access points. Normally, the client would pick up a broadcast SSID and all you need to do is type in the security passphrase or encryption key. With nonbroadcasting networks, on the other hand, you need to type in a valid SSID as well as the security information (Figure 14-36).

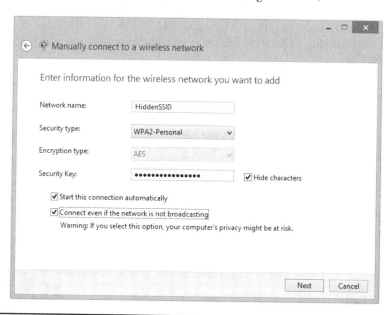

Figure 14-36   Typing in an SSID manually

The important thing to remember is that once you successfully connect to a wireless network, your client will store the settings for that client in a profile. From now on, whenever the client sees a particular SSID, your device will automatically try to connect to that SSID using the encryption and key stored in the profile. Of course, if the wireless network changes in any way—for example, if the encryption password is changed—you won't be able to access the network unless you delete the profile and reacquire the wireless network.

Extending the Network

Creating a Basic Service Set network with a single WAP and multiple clients works in a relatively small area, but you can extend a Wi-Fi network in a few ways if you have difficult spaces—with lots of obstructions, for example—or a need to communicate beyond the ~300-foot range of the typical wireless network. Most commonly, you'd add one or more WAPs to create an Extended Service Set. You can also install a wireless bridge to connect two or more wired networks.

Many companies make *wireless range extenders,* devices that pick up your Wi-Fi signal and rebroadcast it. Some look like a WAP; other models plug directly into an electrical outlet. Current wireless range extenders require very little setup and can extend your network between floors and into dead spots.

Adding a WAP

To add a WAP to a Wi-Fi network, you'll need to run a cable from a switch on the network to where you want to install it. Configuration is pretty straightforward. Both WAPs require the same ESSID, and if the WAPs are near each other, use separate channels.

Wireless Bridges

Dedicated *wireless bridges* are used to connect two wired networks together, or to join wireless and wired networks together in the same way that wired switches do.

Wireless bridges come in two different flavors: point-to-point and point-to-multipoint. Point-to-point bridges can only communicate with a single other bridge and are used to connect two wired network segments. Point-to-multipoint bridges can talk to more than one other bridge at a time and can connect multiple network segments. Figure 14-37 shows a wireless bridge.

Figure 14-37
Linksys wireless bridge device

Verifying the Installation

Once you've completed the initial installation of a Wi-Fi network, test it. Move some traffic from one computer to another using the wireless connection. Never leave a job site without verifying the installation.

Troubleshooting Wi-Fi

Wireless networks are pretty magical when they work right, but the nature of no wires often makes them vexing things to troubleshoot when they don't.

As with any troubleshooting scenario, your first step in troubleshooting a wireless network is to break down your tasks into logical steps. First, figure out the scope of the wireless networking problem. I like to break wireless problems into three symptom types:

- You can't get on the wireless network. Your client (or clients) may or may not think it's connected, but you can't access shared resources (Web pages, remote folders, and so on).

- Your wireless connections are way too slow. Your clients are accessing shared resources.

- Your wireless connection is doing weird things.

CompTIA Network+ objective 5.4 says "Given a scenario, troubleshoot common wireless connectivity and performance issues" and then lists a large number of issues. You can bet good money that CompTIA will give you one or more scenario questions that mention one or more of these issues. Every one of these issues will fit into the three symptoms I just listed. So let's use these symptoms as a tool to organize how you will address these scenarios on the exam (and in the real world as well).

No Connection

Wi-Fi networks want to connect. You rarely if ever get an error on a device that says "You may not speak to WAP55 that is supporting SSID X." Instead, you get more subtle errors such as repeated prompts for passwords, APIPA addresses, and such.

 EXAM TIP Be prepared for scenario questions that quiz you about the limits of the wireless standards. This includes throughput speeds (11-, 54-, 100+-Mbps), frequencies, distances, and channel usage. See the standards discussion earlier in the chapter for the limitations of each standard.

Channel Problems

If you're working with one of the older 802.11 versions using the 2.4-GHz channel, you may have problems with channels. One issue is *channel overlap*, where 2.4-GHz channels overlap with their nearest channel neighbors. For example, channel 3 overlaps with channels 1, 2, 4, and 5. Some folks make the mistake of configuring an SSID and setting each WAP only one channel apart. This will lead to connection problems, so always try to stick to using channels 1, 6, and 11 only. *Frequency mismatch*, where you set the SSID information correctly but a device is using a different channel than the WAP, may still take place. However, automatic channel selection is now the norm and mismatched channels are extremely rare. If you suspect this is a problem, set your wireless device to auto channel selection.

 EXAM TIP You can use wireless scanning tools to check for *wireless channel utilization*. These are software tools that give you metrics and reports about nearby devices and which one is connected to which WAP. These tools enable you to discover overworked WAPs, saturated areas, and so on, so you can deploy WAPs to optimize your network.

Security Type Mismatch

The CompTIA objectives use the term *security type mismatch* to define one of two things: either you've connected manually to a wireless network and have set up the incorrect encryption type, or you've automatically accessed a particular SSID and entered the *wrong passphrase*. Entering the wrong encryption type is rare, only happening when you set up a wireless connection manually. However, entering the wrong passphrase is the classic no-errors-but-won't-work issue. In older operating systems, you often would only get one chance to enter a key and if you failed your only clue was that your client got an APIPA/zeroconf address. More modern operating systems say something clearer, such as a message like *wrong passphrase*. Pretty much every wireless NIC is set to DHCP and if you don't have the right password your client won't get past the WAP to talk to anything on the network, including the DHCP server.

- Symptoms: not on network, continual prompting for password, APIPA/zeroconf address
- Solution: Enter the correct password

Signal/Power Levels

802.11 is a low-power radio and has a limited range. If the WAP doesn't have enough power, you'll have signal attenuation and your device won't be able to access the wireless network. All of the 802.11 standards have *distance limitations;* exceeding those limitations will reduce performance. Certainly a quick answer is to move closer to the WAP, but there are a number of issues that cause *power levels* to drop too low to connect beyond the obvious "you're too far away" from the WAP.

NOTE   Interference can also cause signal loss, but I choose to treat this as a separate issue later in this section. For now, we are talking about simple signal loss due to insufficient power.

If your WAP lacks enough signal power you have five choices: get closer to the WAP, avoid physical issues, turn up the power, use a better antenna, or upgrade to a newer 802.11 version (like 802.11ac) with features that enable them to use the power they have more efficiently. I'm going to skip moving closer to the WAP as that's a bit obvious, but let's cover the other four.

A physical issue is what it sounds like, something physical in the way keeps the signal from reaching its destination. When installing a network, you must watch out for concrete walls, metal (especially metal studs), and the use of special RF-blocking window film. The solution is more careful planning of WAP placement and realizing that even in the best-planned environment it is not at all uncommon to move WAPs based on the need to clear dead spots. We'll cover more about physical issues later in this chapter.

Increasing the power is not that hard to do, depending on the wireless device. Most WAP manufacturers set their radio power levels relatively low out of the box. A few manufacturers—a great example is Cisco on their high-end WAPs—enable you to increase or to decrease the power (Figure 14-38). Sadly, very few low-end/SOHO devices have a method to increase radio power using the OEM interface. If you're willing to gamble, however, you should be able to find a third-party firmware such as OpenWrt which, on certain devices, gives you this capability.

Figure 14-38 Increasing power on a Cisco WAP

Too many 802.11 installations ignore the antennas, dropping in WAPs using their default antennas. In most cases the omnidirectional antennas that come with WAPs are very good—which is why they are so often the default antennas—but in many cases they are simply the *incorrect antenna type* and need to be replaced. If you're losing signal, don't forget to consider if the antenna is wrong for the wireless setup. Watch for scenarios on the CompTIA Network+ exam where replacing an omnidirectional antenna with one or more unidirectional antennas makes an easy fix. Also, look for *incorrect antenna placement*, where moving a few inches away from an obstacle can make big changes in performance.

The last power/signal issue is the fact that the MIMO features in 802.11n and 802.11ac are absolutely amazing in their ability to overcome dead spots and similar issues that on earlier versions of 802.11 can only be fixed with aggressive tweaking of WAP locations and antenna types. While MIMO and MU-MIMO aren't only to increase signal distance, it's almost certain you'll see a scenario where simply updating WAPs to 802.11n or 802.11ac will automatically fix otherwise tricky problems.

Slow Connection

Slow wireless connections are far more difficult to troubleshoot than no connection at all. Unlike a disconnection, where you have obvious and clear clues, a slowdown is just… slow. In these situations, you are clearly connected to an SSID, you have a good IP address, and the client itself runs well; but data transfer is slow: Web pages load slowly, applications time out, and you sense a general, hard-to-measure, irritating slowness.

NOTE There are plenty of reasons for a device to run slowly that have nothing to do with wireless. Don't forget issues such as insufficient RAM, malware, and so forth.

In general you can trace the cause of this slowness to one of three issues: either you have too many devices overworking your WAPs; there are physical problems with signals going between your WAP and your clients; or there is too much RFI on the network. Let's look at these three issues.

Overworked WAPs

An individual WAP has a very specific amount of bandwidth that depends on the version of 802.11 and the way it is configured. Once you hit the maximum bandwidth, you're going to have network slowdowns as the overworked WAP tries to handle all of the incoming wireless connections.

We overwork WAPs in many different ways, but one of the most common is by attaching too many devices to a single SSID over time, what's called *device saturation*. This creates *overcapacity* issues, such as slow speeds and inability to connect to the network. Avoid device saturation by adding more capacity. Careful placement of extra WAPs in high-demand areas is a huge step in the right direction. Usually the best, but most expensive, method is to upgrade your hardware: leaping from the 802.11g to the 802.11ac standard alone makes a massive difference in eliminating device saturation.

Jitter is the loss of packets due to an overworked WAP. Jitter shows up as choppy conversations over a video call, strange jumps in the middle of an online game—pretty much anything that feels like the network has missed some data. *Latency* is when data stops moving for a moment due to a WAP unable to do the work. This manifests as a Word document that stops loading, for example, or an online file that stops downloading.

Speaking of 802.11ac, the biggest single issue causing device saturation is the imbalance of many devices using the 2.4-GHz band versus few devices using the 5.0-GHz band. In almost every midsized or larger wireless network, the 2.4-GHz band is filled to capacity, even with careful use of multiple channels. We call this *bandwidth saturation* and it's a huge issue with 802.11 networks. There is no answer other than to move to the 5.0-GHz band using primarily 802.11ac.

Physical Issues

Any physical item placed on or near the straight-line path between a WAP and a wireless client can cause problems with a wireless signal. The problem depends on what is in the way and how it affects the radio signals as they encounter the physical item. Let's take a moment to discuss physical issues.

Absorption   Non-metallic building materials such as brick, sheetrock and wood absorb radio signals, greatly reducing or in some case eliminating a Wi-Fi signal completely. This phenomenon is called *absorption*.

Reflection   Metallic materials like pipes, radiators, metal doors and windows frames will reflect (or bounce) radio waves, sending them in unsuspected directions and keeping them from getting to their target device. This phenomenon is called *reflection*.

Refraction   Glass is notorious for bending radio waves as the waves pass through them. What may look like a straight line between a WAP and client suddenly may run into problems if a glass door is placed between them. This phenomenon is called *refraction*.

The result of all these physical problems is *attenuation,* the progressive loss of radio signal strength as the radio wave passes through different mediums (even things like air and rain reduce signal strength).

Be careful here! Different materials may cause more than one of these effects. A concrete wall may both absorb and reflect radio whereas a metal framed door with glass inserts may both reflect and refract a radio wave.

Dealing with Physical Issues

Physical effects prevent clear, strong radio signals from reaching their target devices. These attenuation effects are different in every case and therefore tricky to predict during a site survey, requiring serious troubleshooting after the installation of a wireless network. A solid concrete wall is easy to predict as a problem (and a workaround created). A room full of thick-walled, metal-framed room dividers might not be as easy to identify during a survey and won't come to light as a physical problem until the users start complaining about slow connections.

When a tech suspects a physical problem, the first step is another site survey. Find physical barriers that prevent hosts at specific locations that need good access. Often a quick look-around is all that's needed to identify and move a physical barrier or to move or add WAPs or antennas as needed. Secondly, the tech can install WAPs with multiple antennas, creating *multipath*.

Captive Portal

Many public facilities like airports employ a *captive portal* to control access to their public Wi-Fi networks. An attempt to connect to the network opens a Web browser that insists you follow the terms of service (*acceptable use policy*) and that sort of thing. Because it's an extra step in Internet connectivity, that captive portal can result in a seemingly slow connection. Higher security standards in your Web browser can also block this content and thus your access to the network.

Interference

Radio frequency interference (RFI) is an equally big problem when it comes to wireless network slowdowns. The 802.11 standard is pretty impressive in its ability to deal with noisy RF environments, but there's a point where any environment gets too noisy for 802.11. Interference comes from a number of sources, but basically we can break them down into two categories: RFI from non-Wi-Fi sources and RFI from Wi-Fi networks.

Non-Wi-Fi sources of RFI include lighting and low-power RF devices like Bluetooth, wireless phones, and microwaves. In general these devices can work nicely with 802.11 networks, but too many devices, especially devices too close to 802.11 equipment, can cause problems. The only way to eliminate this type of interference is to shut down or move the devices.

When it comes to 802.11-based interference, we are looking mainly at other WAPs generating signals that interfere with ours. The most common problem is that the limited number of 2.4-GHz channels and their natural overlap makes it easy to form overlapped channels.

A few years ago you could jump from one channel to another, using the classic channels 1, 6, or 11 in the United States, but today the most common method is to simply abandon the 2.4-GHz channel by avoiding 802.11g. The fix to interference (other than avoiding RF reflective surfaces) is to scan for RF sources using some form of RF scanner, such as a *spectrum analyzer*. We measure RFI with the *signal-to-noise ratio (SNR)*, essentially comparing the signal strength and the overall interference in the space. Figure 14-39 shows the popular AirMagnet Wi-Fi Analyzer Pro reporting SNR. Use a channel that's not overwhelmed.

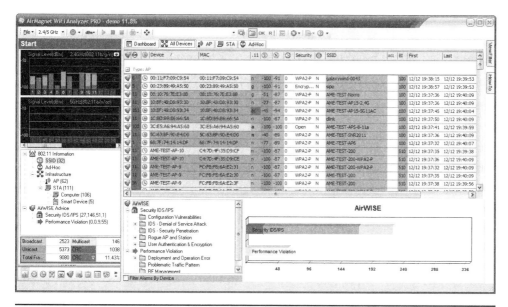

Figure 14-39 SNR on AirMagnet

Weird Connection

There are a number of situations where devices are connected to a wireless network and run at a good speed, but something is wrong—in some cases, dangerously wrong from a security perspective. Let's look at a few of these situations.

Open Networks

Open (non-encrypted) 802.11 networks are the bane of users and administrators. The two biggest challenges are how to avoid unintentionally logging into an open network with an SSID identical to one you have in another location, and how to provide security in an open network environment.

It's very common for your wireless device to access open networks with WAPs that use manufacturer default SSID names such as Linksys or D-Link. The danger with these is that bad guys know that most wireless devices, once they have created a profile to connect to one of these default, open SSIDs, will then automatically connect to them again should they ever see one—and bad guys love to use this as a tool to attack these devices.

The second issue with any open wireless is that all of the data is transferred in the clear. It's easy for bad guys to listen in on your transmissions. The only way to avoid this is either to use a VPN or to use a Web browser add-on, like HTTPS Everywhere, that tries to connect you via HTTPS to every Web page.

Wrong SSID

It's easy to access the wrong SSID. Some 802.11 clients are notorious for moving their list of discovered SSIDs in such a way that you think you are clicking one SSID when you are actually accidentally clicking the wrong one. The only fix to this is to practice diligence when logging onto a new SSID. For example, who hasn't seen SSIDs such as the infamous "attwifi"? This SSID is AT&T's attempt to use all of their clients as hotspots. Sadly, it's a simple process to create an evil twin SSID (described in the upcoming section "Rogue Access Point") to mimic the attwifi SSID and get otherwise unsuspecting people to log into it.

Manually entering an SSID can obviously result in a typo. Luckily, in these cases your typo won't accidentally land you onto another SSID. You'll just get an error.

Untested Updates/Incompatibilities

802.11 is an ever-evolving standard, and manufacturers learned a long time ago to work hard to ensure their devices could evolve with the standard. This means that anyone supporting any 802.11 network is going to find themselves continually updating client firmware/software and WAP firmware. These updates are almost always good, but you need to stay aware of problems.

First, always research and test any update (especially firmware updates as they aren't too easy to reverse). Untested updates that go into your production network can potentially wreak havoc. If at all possible, run updates on a test network first.

Incompatibilities are related to untested updates in that they tend to appear at the same time an update appears. Make sure you are extremely clear on backward compatibility of different 802.11 versions. Also be aware that even in the same type of network there might be incompatibilities. A few years ago I bought what I thought was a dual-band (2.4- and 5.0-GHz) 802.11n WAP. I invested serious money in upgrading my 802.11n NICs in a few clients to accept dual band. Sadly, it wasn't until I was installing the new WAP that I read in the instructions that the WAP only supported one of the two bands at a time, and was totally incompatible with my new, expensive wireless NICs. Ouch! Too bad I didn't test the WAP before I tried to run it in my production environment.

Rogue Access Point

A *rogue access point (rogue AP)* is simply an unauthorized access point. Rogue access points have tortured every wireless network since the day Linksys came out with the first cheap wireless router back in the early 2000s. Most rogue APs aren't evil: just a user wanting to connect to the network who installs a WAP in a handy location into the wired network. Evil rogue APs are far more nefarious, acting as a backdoor to a network or a man-in-the-middle attack, grabbing user names and passwords, among other items.

The most infamous form of rogue AP is called an evil twin. An *evil twin* is a rogue AP that intentionally mimics an existing SSID in order to get people to connect to it instead of the proper WAP. Evil twins work best in unsecured networks such as those you see in airports and hotels.

War Driving and War Chalking

We need to take a moment to discuss one of those weird CompTIA Network+ topics that covers very old issues that don't really exist anymore: war driving and war chalking. A long time ago—as late as around 2005—there weren't very many wireless networks around. Nerdy types would conduct *war driving*: looking for wireless networks by using omnidirectional antennas connected to laptops using wireless sniffing programs (this was well before every OS came with a client that located SSIDs). When a network was found, the war driver would place a special chalk mark on a nearby curb or sidewalk to tell other war drivers the location of the SSID. Figure 14-40 shows some of the more common war chalks.

Figure 14-40

Sample war chalking mark with explanation

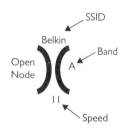

Chapter Review

Questions

1. Which wireless networking technology used the 5.0-GHz frequency range?

    A. 802.11

    B. 802.11a

    C. 802.11b

    D. 802.11g

2. Which technology enables use of a WAP without directly connecting the WAP to an AC power outlet?

    A. AES

    B. PoE

    C. Powered Wi-Fi

    D. TKIP

3. Which of the following is known as a Basic Service Set in infrastructure mode?

   A. A WAP

   B. A WPA

   C. A RADIUS server

   D. A TKIP

4. What feature enables 802.11n networks to minimize dead spots?

   A. Channel bonding

   B. FIFO

   C. MIMO

   D. Transit beamforming

5. Which of these consumer electronics may cause interference with 802.11n wireless networks?

   A. Wireless telephones

   B. Wireless televisions

   C. Cellular telephones

   D. Television remote controls

6. To achieve maximum Wi-Fi coverage in a room, where should you place the WAP?

   A. Place the WAP on the north side of the room.

   B. Place the WAP in the center of the room.

   C. Place the WAP near a convenient electrical outlet.

   D. It doesn't matter where you place the WAP.

7. What hardware enables wireless PCs to connect to resources on a wired network segment in infrastructure mode? (Select two.)

   A. An access point

   B. A router

   C. A hub

   D. A wireless bridge

8. What do you call a wireless network in infrastructure mode with more than one access point?

   A. BSS

   B. EBSS

   C. WBSS

   D. ExNet

9. What type of server supports EAP-encrypted passwords in accordance with the 802.1X standard?

   A. WAP server

   B. WEP server

   C. RADIUS server

   D. NAS server

10. Which of the following is the most secure method of wireless encryption?

   A. WEP

   B. WEP2

   C. WPA

   D. WPA2

Answers

1. **B.** 802.11a operated in the 5.0-GHz frequency range.

2. **B.** Power over Ethernet enables a WAP to use electricity from a PoE switch rather than connect to an AC power outlet directly.

3. **A.** A single wireless access point (WAP) is a Basic Service Set. WPA is a data encryption scheme. A RADIUS server provides authentication via a user name and password. TKIP is used by the WPA encryption scheme to encrypt the data.

4. **D.** Transit beamforming enables an 802.11n WAP to minimize dead spots by using multiple antennas.

5. **A.** Many wireless telephones operate in the same 2.4-GHz frequency range as 802.11n wireless networking equipment and may cause interference.

6. **B.** To achieve maximum coverage, place the WAP in the center of the room.

7. **A** and **D.** A wireless access point or wireless bridge enables you to connect wireless PCs to a wired network segment.

8. **B.** A wireless network with more than one access point is called an EBSS, or Extended Basic Service Set.

9. **C.** A RADIUS server provides authentication through a user name and password encrypted with EAP.

10. **D.** WPA2 is the most secure because it uses CCMP-AES, a 128-bit cipher that is harder to crack than the 128-bit TKIP wrapper used by WPA. Both WPA and WPA2 are stronger than WEP. WEP2 was never fully developed.

## CHAPTER 15

Virtualization and Cloud Computing

The CompTIA Network+ certification exam expects you to know how to

- 1.3 Explain the concepts and characteristics of routing and switching
- 1.7 Summarize cloud concepts and their purposes
- 2.4 Explain the purposes of virtualization and network storage technologies

To achieve these goals, you must be able to

- Describe the concepts of virtualization
- Explain why PC and network administrators have widely adopted virtualization
- Describe how virtualization manifests in modern networks
- Describe the service layers and architectures that make up cloud computing

Virtualization is the process of using powerful, special software running on a computer to create a complete environment that imitates (virtualizes) all of the hardware you'd see on a physical computer. You can install and run an operating system in this virtual environment exactly as if it were installed on its own physical computer. That *guest* environment is called a *virtual machine (VM)*. Figure 15-1 shows one such example: a system running Windows 10 using a program called Oracle VM VirtualBox to host a virtual machine running Ubuntu Linux.

This chapter explores virtualization in detail. You'll see why network professionals use virtualization and how virtualization influences the structure of modern networks. With this knowledge as a foundation, the chapter examines important concepts in cloud computing (including the role virtualization plays), how cloud computing adds value to the Internet, and how cloud networks compare to and interface with both traditional networks and each other.

Figure 15-1   VirtualBox running Linux

Historical/Conceptual

Concepts of Virtualization

Ask 100 people what the term *virtual* means and you'll get a lot of different answers. Most people define *virtual* with words like "fake" or "pretend," but these terms only begin to describe it. Let's try to zero in on virtualization using a term that hopefully you've heard: *virtual reality*. For many people, the idea of virtual reality starts with someone wearing headgear and gloves, as shown in Figure 15-2.

The headgear and the gloves work together to create a simulation of a world or environment that appears to be real, even though the person wearing them is located in a room that doesn't resemble the simulated space. Inside this virtual reality you can see the world by turning your head, just as you do in the real world. Software works with the headset's inputs to emulate a physical world. At the same time, the gloves enable you to touch and move objects in the virtual world.

To make virtual reality effective, the hardware and software need to work together to create an environment convincing enough for a human to work within it. Virtual reality doesn't have to be perfect—it has limitations—but it's pretty cool for teaching someone how to fly a plane or do a spacewalk without having to start with the real thing (Figure 15-3).

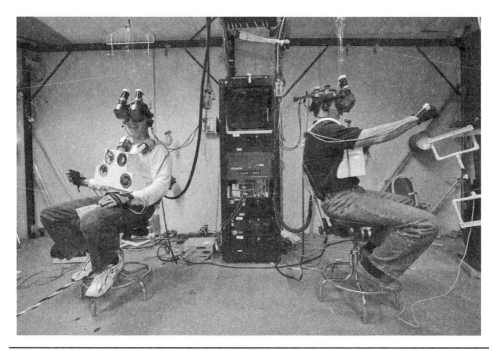

Figure 15-2   Virtual reality training (Image courtesy of NASA)

Figure 15-3   Using virtual reality to practice spacewalking (Image courtesy of NASA)

Virtualization on a computer is virtually (sorry, can't pass up the pun) the same as virtual reality for humans. Just as virtual reality creates an environment that convinces humans they're in a real environment, virtualization convinces an operating system it's running on its own hardware.

Meet the Hypervisor

Because virtualization enables one machine—called the *host*—to run multiple operating systems simultaneously, full virtualization requires an extra layer of sophisticated programming called a *hypervisor* to manage the vastly more complex interactions.

A hypervisor has to handle every input and output that the operating system would request of normal hardware. With a good hypervisor like VirtualBox you can easily add and remove virtual hard drives, virtual network cards, virtual RAM, and so on. Figure 15-4 shows the Hardware Configuration screen from VirtualBox.

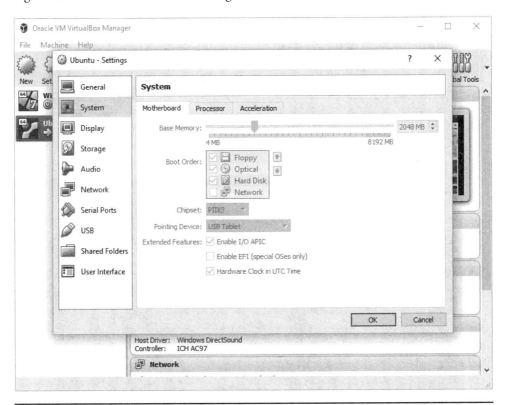

Figure 15-4   Configuring virtual hardware in VirtualBox

Virtualization even goes so far as to provide a virtualized BIOS and System Setup for every virtual machine. Figure 15-5 shows VMware Workstation virtualization software displaying the System Setup, just like you'd see it on a regular computer.

Figure 15-5
System Setup
in VMware
Workstation

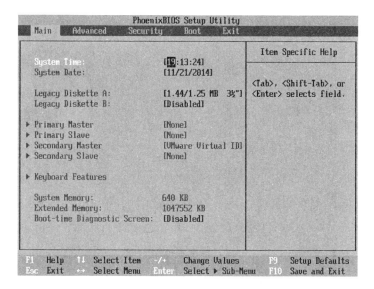

```
                        PhoenixBIOS Setup Utility
   Main    Advanced    Security    Boot    Exit

                                          Item Specific Help
     System Time:           [19:13:24]
     System Date:           [11/21/2014]
                                          <Tab>, <Shift-Tab>, or
     Legacy Diskette A:     [1.44/1.25 MB  3½"]   <Enter> selects field.
     Legacy Diskette B:     [Disabled]

   ▶ Primary Master        [None]
   ▶ Primary Slave         [None]
   ▶ Secondary Master      [VMware Virtual ID]
   ▶ Secondary Slave       [None]

   ▶ Keyboard Features

     System Memory:         640 KB
     Extended Memory:       1047552 KB
     Boot-time Diagnostic Screen:  [Disabled]


   F1   Help    ↑↓  Select Item   -/+    Change Values    F9   Setup Defaults
   Esc  Exit    ↔   Select Menu   Enter  Select ▶ Sub-Menu  F10  Save and Exit
```

NOTE   The host machine allocates real RAM and CPU time to every running virtual machine. If you want to run multiple virtual machines at the same time, make sure your host machine has plenty of CPU power and, more importantly, plenty of RAM to support all the running virtual machines.

Emulation vs. Virtualization

Virtualization takes the hardware of the host system and segments it into individual virtual machines. If you have an Intel system, a hypervisor creates a virtual machine that acts exactly like the host Intel system. It cannot act like any other type of computer. For example, you cannot make a virtual machine on an Intel system that acts like a Sony PlayStation 4. Hypervisors simply pass the code from the virtual machine to the actual CPU.

Emulation is very different from virtualization. An *emulator* is software or hardware that converts the commands to and from the host machine into an entirely different platform. Figure 15-6 shows a Super Nintendo Entertainment System emulator, Snes9X, running a game called Donkey Kong Country on a Windows system.

Desktop Virtualization

This chapter will show you a few of the ways you can perform virtualization, but before I go any further let's take the basic pieces you've learned about virtualization and put them together in one of its simplest forms. In this example, I'll use the popular VirtualBox on a Windows system and create a virtual machine running Ubuntu Linux. Clicking **New** prompts you for a name and operating system (Figure 15-7).

Click **Next** to start configuring the machine. The next step with this configuration is to determine the quantity of RAM to set aside for the VM (Figure 15-8).

Figure 15-6   Super Nintendo emulator running on Windows

The next few dialog boxes enable you to create a virtual hard drive and other settings. One of the more useful options is in Figure 15-9, where you can tell VirtualBox to dynamically size the virtual hard drive. Initially, it'll be small to save space. VirtualBox will expand the size of the file—that's all the virtual hard drive is, after all—when and if you need it.

Because virtual machines are so flexible on hardware, VirtualBox enables you to use either the host machine's optical drive or an ISO file. I'm installing Ubuntu, so I downloaded an ISO image from the Ubuntu Web site (www.ubuntu.com), and as Figure 15-10 shows, I've pointed the VirtualBox to that image once I clicked the Start option.

After you've gone through all the configuration screens, you can start using your virtual machine. You can start, stop, pause, add, or remove virtual hardware.

After the virtual machine installs, you then treat the VM exactly as though it were a real machine.

Congratulations! You've just installed a *virtual desktop*. Virtual desktops were the first type of popular virtual machines seen in the PC world.

There's a lot more to virtualization than just virtual desktops, however, but before I dive in too far, let's step back a moment and understand a very important question: Why do we virtualize?

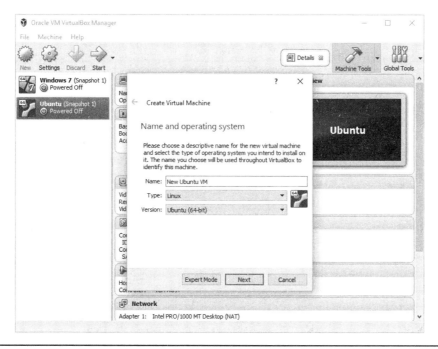

Figure 15-7 VirtualBox creating a new virtual machine

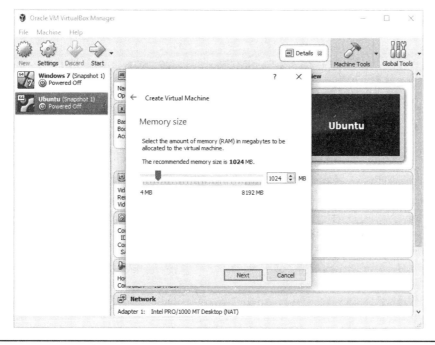

Figure 15-8 Starting the customization

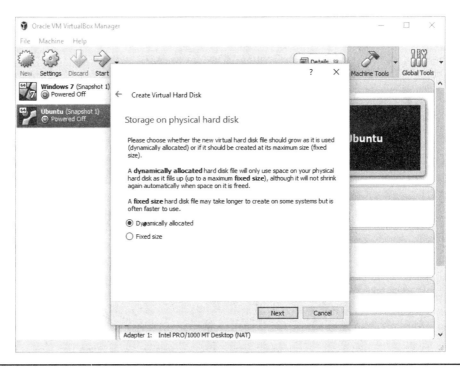

Figure 15-9 Dynamically sizing the virtual hard drive

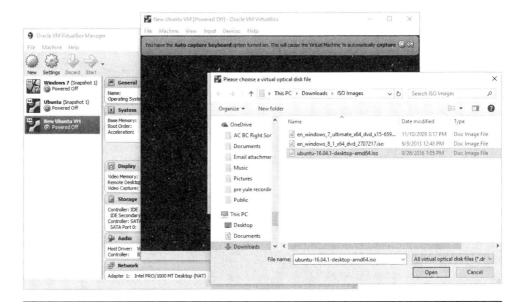

Figure 15-10 Selecting the installation media

Test Specific

Virtualization Benefits

Virtualization has taken the networking world by storm, but for those who have never seen virtualization, the big question has got to be: Why? Let's talk about the benefits of virtualization: power saving, hardware consolidation, system recovery, system duplication, and research potential. While you read this section, keep in mind two important things:

- A single hypervisor on a single system will happily run as many virtual machines as its RAM, CPU, and drive space allow. (RAM is almost always the limiting factor.)

- A virtual machine that's shut down or suspended is no more than a file or folder sitting on a hard drive.

Power Saving

Before virtualization, each server OS needed to be on a unique physical system. With virtualization, you can place multiple virtual servers on a single physical system, reducing electrical power use substantially. Rather than one machine running a Windows server and acting as a file server and DNS server, and a second machine running Linux for a DHCP server, for example, the same computer can handle both operating systems simultaneously. Apply this over an enterprise network or on a data server farm, and the savings—both in terms of dollars spent and electricity used—are tremendous.

Hardware Consolidation

Similar to power saving, why buy a high-end server, complete with multiple processors, RAID arrays, redundant power supplies, and so on, and only run a single server? With virtualization, you can easily beef up the RAM and run multiple servers on a single box.

System Recovery

The most popular reason for virtualizing is probably to keep uptime percentage as high as possible. Let's say you have a Web server installed on a single system. If that system goes down—due to hacking, malware, or so on—you need to restore the system from a backup, which may or may not be easily at hand. With virtualization, you merely need to shut down the virtual machine and reload an alternate copy of it.

A virtual machine enables you to create a *snapshot,* which saves the virtual machine's state at that moment, enabling a quick return to this state later. Snapshots are great for doing risky (or even not-so-risky) maintenance with a safety net. They aren't, however, a long-term backup strategy—each snapshot may reduce performance and should be removed as soon as the danger has passed.

System Duplication

Closely tied to system recovery, system duplication takes advantage of the fact that VMs are simply files: like any other file, they can be copied. Let's say you want to teach 20 students about Ubuntu Linux. Depending on the hypervisor you choose, you can simply install a hypervisor on 20 machines and copy a single virtual machine to all the computers. Equally, if you have a virtualized Web server and need to add another Web server (assuming your physical box has the hardware to support it), why not just make a copy of the server and power it up as well?

Research

Here's a great example that happens in my own company. I sell my popular TotalTester test banks: practice questions for you to test your skills on a broad number of certification topics. As with any distributed program, I tend to get a few support calls. Running a problem through the same OS, even down to the service pack, helps me solve it. In the pre-virtualization days, I usually had seven to ten multi-boot PCs just to keep active copies of specific Windows versions. Today, a single hypervisor enables me to support a huge number of Windows versions on a single machine (Figure 15-11)

Figure 15-11
Lots of VMs used
for research

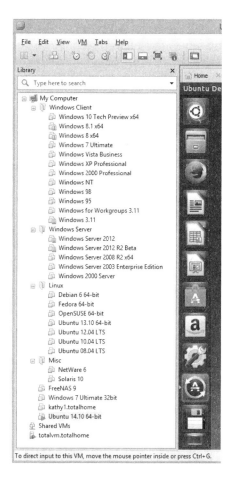

Virtualization in Modern Networks

When it comes to servers, virtualization has pretty much taken over. Many of the servers you access, particularly Web and e-mail servers, are virtualized. Like any popular technology, there are a lot of people continually working to make virtualization better. The Oracle VM VirtualBox and VMware Workstation examples shown earlier in this chapter are powerful desktop applications, but they still need to run on top of a system that's already running an operating system—the host operating system. What if you could improve performance by removing the host operating system altogether and installing nothing but a hypervisor? Well, you can! This is done all the time with another type of powerful hypervisor/OS combination called a *bare-metal* hypervisor. It's called bare metal because there's no software between it and the hardware—just bare metal. The industry also refers to this class of hypervisors as *Type-1*, and applications such as VMware Workstation as *Type-2*.

VMware's first bare-metal hypervisor, called ESX, shed the unnecessary overhead of an operating system. ESX has since been supplanted by ESXi in VMware's product lineup. ESXi is a free hypervisor that's powerful enough to replace the host operating system on a physical box, turning the physical machine into a system that does nothing but support virtual ones. ESXi, by itself, isn't much to look at; it's a tiny operating system/hypervisor that's often installed on something other than a hard drive. A host running its hypervisor from flash memory can dedicate all of its available disk space to VM storage, or even cut out the disks altogether and keep its VMs on a storage area network, which we'll discuss later in the chapter. Figure 15-12 shows how I loaded my copy of ESXi: via a small USB flash drive. The server loads ESXi off the thumb drive when I power it up, and in short order a very rudimentary interface appears where I can input essential information, such as a master password and a static IP address.

Don't let ESXi's small size fool you. It's small because it only has one job: to host virtual machines. ESXi is an extremely powerful bare-metal hypervisor.

Hypervisors

While you have many choices when it comes to desktop virtualization, your choices for real bare-metal hypervisors on Intel-based systems are limited to VMware's ESXi, Microsoft's Hyper-V, and Citrix's XenServer. These embedded hypervisors scale readily and support common features like remote VM storage, live migration, and virtual network configuration.

- **VMware Hypervisor (ESXi)**   Industry-leading ESXi has a tiny disk footprint and easily scales from a single server up to a whole data center. ESXi often pioneers new features, has wide third-party support, and has a large community of established users.

- **Microsoft Hyper-V**   Hyper-V comes with Microsoft Server and Windows 10. Microsoft is investing heavily in Hyper-V, and it has captured substantial market share from VMware. It integrates well with Microsoft's server management software and can even run Linux VMs.

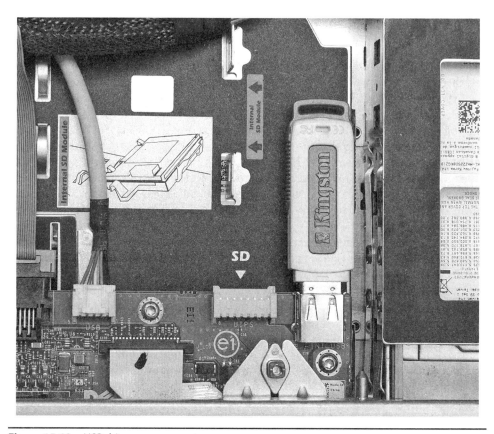

Figure 15-12 USB drive on server system

- **Citrix XenServer** Based on the open source Xen project and built on Linux, XenServer is a powerful hypervisor that serves as the foundation for massive cloud offerings (which we'll discuss later in the chapter) by Amazon, IBM, and RackSpace. While Xen lacks the market share of VMware, its open source nature, low price (or free!), and popularity with cloud providers make it worth considering.

NOTE There's another open source Linux-based hypervisor you may run into—the *Kernel-based Virtual Machine (KVM)*. The foundation of a modern OS, the kernel, handles very low-level interactions among hardware and software like task scheduling and the allotment of time and resources; as its name implies, KVM is closely integrated with Linux's kernel. While it may not be as popular as the other hypervisors, the fact that it's built into Linux means you could run into it almost anywhere.

Administering a Hypervisor

Powerful hypervisors like ESXi and Hyper-V are not administered directly at the box. Instead you use tools like VMware's vSphere Client (Figure 15-13) or Microsoft's Hyper-V Manager to create, configure, and maintain virtual machines on the host from the comfort of a client computer running this program. Once the VM is up and running, you can close the vSphere Client or Hyper-V Manager and the VM will continue to run happily on the server. For example, let's say you create a VM and install a Web server on that VM. As long as everything is running well on the Web server, you will find yourself using the vSphere Client or Hyper-V Manager only for occasional maintenance and administration.

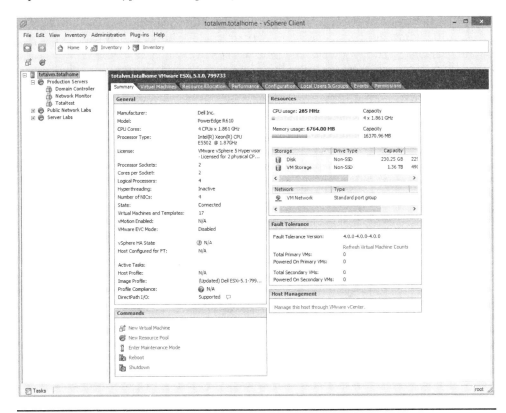

Figure 15-13   VMware vSphere Client

Scaling Virtualization

To understand the importance of virtualization fully, you need to get a handle on how it increases flexibility as the scale of an operation increases. Let's take a step back and talk about money. One of the really great things money does is give us common, easily divisible units we can exchange for the goods and services we need. When we don't have money, we have to trade goods and services to get it, and before we had money at all we had to trade goods and services for other goods and services.

Let's say I'm starving and all I have is a hammer, and you just so happen to have a chicken. I offer to build you something with my hammer, but all you really want is a hammer of your own. This might sound like a match made in heaven, but what if my hammer is actually worth at least five chickens, and you just have one? I can't give you a fifth of a hammer, and once I trade the hammer for your chicken, I can't use it to build anything else. I have to choose between going without food and wasting most of my hammer's value. If only my hammer was money.

In the same vein, suppose Mario has only two physical, non-virtualized servers; he basically has two really expensive hammers. If he uses one server to host an important site on his intranet, its full potential might go almost unused (especially since his intranet site will never land on the front page of reddit). But if Mario converts these machines into a small, centrally managed server cluster of virtual-machine hosts, he has taken a big step toward using his servers in a new, more productive way.

In this new model, Mario's servers become less like hammers and more like money. I still can't trade a fifth of my hammer for a chicken, but Mario can easily use a virtual machine to serve his intranet site and only allocate a fifth—or any other fraction—of the host's physical resources to this VM. As he adds hosts to his cluster, he can treat them more and more like a pool of common, easily divisible units used to solve problems. Each new host adds resources to the pool, and as Mario adds more and more VMs that need different amounts of resources, he increases his options for distributing them across his hosts to minimize unused resources (Figure 15-14).

Figure 15-14
No vacancy on these hosts

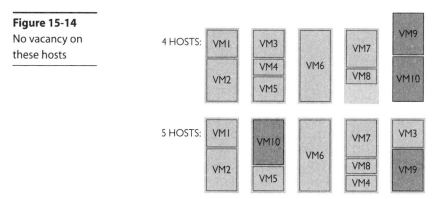

As his cluster grows, Mario is going to be able to use some really exciting developments in data storage, virtual networking, and software-defined networking to increase the flexibility and efficiency of his hardware and network.

Data Storage

Storage (hard drives, basically) tends to be either highly under- or over-utilized on individual hosts. It's common to see situations where drives sit empty in one host while another runs out of space. Equally, maintenance of drives on individual hosts is a bit of a pain: even with RAID and backups, losing a drive on a host is at best an inconvenience and at worst the loss of critical services and data.

One of the ways to overcome these two issues is to take all the storage from all the hosts and consolidate the data in a single, separate system. In this section, you're going to learn about two popular methods: SAN and NAS. Both of these technologies predate virtualized systems, but given that hypervisors can boot from removable flash media, separating storage from virtualized systems is a comfortable fit. These technologies tend to be pricey so they generally aren't worthwhile for one or two servers. As our collection of virtualized hosts begins to grow, however, moving the storage out of the host starts making sense. Let's look at SAN and NAS and see how they are used to centralize storage outside of the hosts.

Storage Area Networks   You might remember from CompTIA A+ that hard drive storage is broken up into tiny sectors, but you might not know that these sectors are also known as *blocks*. You might also remember that to access the hard drive, you have to plug it into an interface like SATA or maybe even SCSI, which your operating system uses to read and write to blocks on the disk. A *storage area network (SAN)* is a server that can take a pool of hard disks and present them over the network as any number of logical disks. The interface it presents to a client computer pretends to be a hard disk and enables the client's operating system to read and write blocks over a network.

Think of a drive accessed through the SAN as a virtual disk; much as the hypervisor convinces the operating system it runs on its own hardware, the SAN convinces the OS it is interacting with a physical hard drive. Just like with a traditional hard disk, we have to format a virtual disk before we can use it. But unlike a traditional hard disk, the virtual disk the SAN presents to us could be mapped to a number of physical drives in a number of physical locations, or even to other forms of storage.

One of the benefits of using a SAN is that, by just reading and writing at the block level, it avoids the performance costs of implementing its own file system. The SAN leaves it up to the client computers to implement their own file systems—these clients often use specialized shared file system software designed for high volume, performance, reliability, and the ability to support multiple clients using one drive.

When it comes to the infrastructure to support a SAN, there are three main choices: *Fibre Channel (FC), Internet Small Computer System Interface (iSCSI),* and *InfiniBand (IB).*

- Fibre Channel is, for the most part, its own ecosystem designed for high-performance storage. It has its own cables, protocols, and switches, all increasing the costs associated with its use. While more recent developments like *Fibre Channel over Ethernet (FCoE)* make Fibre Channel a little more flexible within a local wired network, long-distance FC is still clumsy without expensive cabling and hardware.

- iSCSI is built on top of TCP/IP, enabling devices that use the SCSI protocol to communicate across existing networks using cheap, readily available hardware. Because the existing networks and their hardware weren't built as a disk interface, performance can suffer. Part of this performance cost is time spent processing frame headers. We can ease some of the cost of moving large amounts of data around the network at standard frame size by using *jumbo frames.* Jumbo frames are usually 9000 bytes long—though technically anything over 1500 qualifies—and they reduce the total number of frames moving through the network.

• InfiniBand competes with FC and iSCSI to provide the interconnect between storage arrays and servers. IB has unique NICs and cabling. Links can (and usually are) aggregated, using four or eight connections for greater throughput.

Network Attached Storage   *Network attached storage (NAS)* is essentially a dedicated file server that has its own file system and typically uses hardware and software designed for serving and storing files. While a SAN shares a fast, low-level interface that the OS can treat just like it was a disk, the NAS—because it has its own internal file system—has to perform file-system work for all of its clients. While the simplicity and low price of a NAS make it attractive for some uses, these performance issues limit its utility in high-performance virtualization clusters.

Virtual Networking

I'll let you in on a secret: the software that runs network devices can also be run in a virtual machine. A network admin can create the virtual version of a network device on-the-fly without purchasing new hardware, or spending a Saturday at the office to move and re-cable existing hardware. These virtual networking components live on the hypervisor with the virtual servers they support. Let's take a look at the ones CompTIA wants you to know about.

Virtual Switches   Imagine for a moment that you have three virtual machines. You need all of these machines to have access to the Internet. Therefore, you need to give them all legitimate IP addresses. The physical server, however, only has a single NIC. There are two ways in which virtualization gives individual VMs valid IP addresses. The oldest and simplest way is to *bridge the NIC*. Each bridge is a software connection that passes traffic from the real NIC to a virtual one (Figure 15-15). This bridge works at Layer 2 of the OSI model, so each virtual NIC gets a legitimate, unique MAC address.

Figure 15-15
Bridged NICs

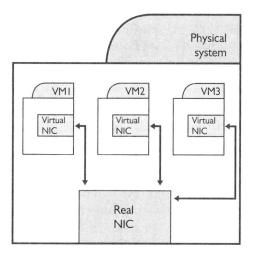

EXAM TIP There is no difference between a virtual NIC and a physical NIC, once properly configured. Virtual NICs have MAC addresses just like a physical NIC. You set up everything about a virtual NIC: IP address, subnet mask, etc., exactly as you do with a physical NIC.

The technology behind bridging NICs is a *virtual switch*, which is just software that does the same Layer 2 (Figure 15-16) switching a hardware switch does, including features like VLANs. The big difference is what it means to "plug" into the virtual switch. When the NICs are bridged, the VMs and the host's NIC are all connected to the virtual switch. In this mode, think of the NIC as the uplink port on a hardware switch. This makes virtual switches a very powerful component for networking your VMs—but just like physical networks, we need more than just Layer 2 switching. That's where virtual routers and firewalls come in.

Figure 15-16
Virtual switch

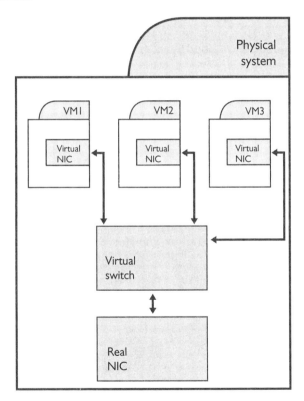

Distributed Switches Just because a switch is virtual doesn't magically prevent it from needing the same management given to a real switch. Virtual switches normally use a Web interface for configuration, just like a regular switch. Yet virtual networks grow quite quickly, even more quickly than a physical network (no waiting for a new physical switch to arrive from the store, just spin up another virtual one!). With growth comes complexity, requiring careful configuration for every new virtual switch added to existing virtual switches in a large, complex single virtual network.

The centralized installation, configuration and handling of every switch in a network is known as *distributed switching*. Every hypervisor has some form of central configuration of critical issues for switches, such as VLAN assignment and trunking.

Virtual Routers and Firewalls   Similar to how virtual machines enable us to easily reallocate computing resources when demand changes, *virtual routers* let us dynamically reconfigure networks. This lets the network keep up when VMs are moved from host to host to meet demand or improve resource use. The virtual routers are just VMs like any other; we can allocate more resources to them as traffic grows, instead of having to buy bigger, better physical routers. When it comes to firewalls, the same rules apply: *virtual firewalls* can protect servers where it would be hard, costly, or impossible to insert a physical one.

 NOTE   If you're interested in reading more about virtual routers and firewalls, a couple of interesting product lines to look at are Brocade's Vyatta vRouter and Cisco's Cloud Services Routers.

Software Defined Networking

Traditionally, hardware routers and switches were designed with two closely integrated parts: a *control plane* that makes decisions about how to move traffic, and a *data plane* that is responsible for executing those decisions. The control plane on a router, for example, is what actually speaks the routing protocols like OSPF and BGP, discussed in Chapter 7, "Routing," and builds the routing tables that it gives to the data plane. The router's data plane reads incoming packets and uses the routing table to send them to their destination.

Software defined networking (SDN) cuts the control plane of individual devices out of the picture and lets an all-knowing program called a *network controller* dictate how both physical and virtual network components move traffic through the network (Figure 15-17). SDN requires components with data planes designed to take instructions

Figure 15-17
A controller
controls traffic
to all the routers
and switches

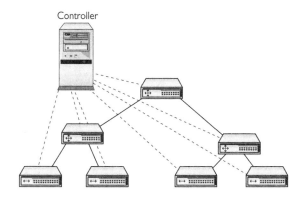

from the network controller instead of their own control plane. While it's important enough that SDN allows for a master controller, the really revolutionary idea behind SDN is that the network controller is *programmable*: we can write code that controls how the entire network will behave.

To the Cloud

While simple virtualization enabled Mario to optimize and reallocate his computing and networking resources in response to his evolving needs (as described earlier in the chapter), he can't exceed the capabilities of the hardware he owns, the networks he builds, and his ability to maintain them. Luckily, he's no longer stuck with just the hardware he owns. Because his virtual machines are just files running on a hypervisor, he can run them in *the cloud* on networks of servers worldwide. When we talk about the cloud, we're talking not just about friendly file-storage services like Dropbox or Google Drive, but also about simple interfaces to a vast array of on-demand computing resources sold by Amazon (Figure 15-18), Microsoft, and many other companies over the open Internet. The technology at the heart of these innovative services is virtualization.

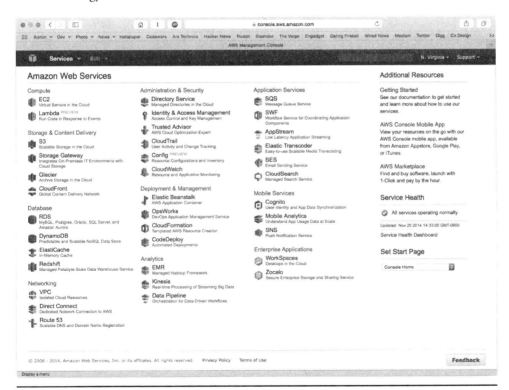

Figure 15-18 Amazon Web Services Management Console

The Service-Layer Cake

Service is the key to understanding the cloud. At the hardware level, we'd have trouble telling the difference between the cloud and the servers and networks that comprise the Internet as a whole. We use the servers and networks of the cloud through layers of software that add great value to the underlying hardware by making it simple to perform complex tasks or manage powerful hardware. As end users we generally interact with just the sweet software icing of the service-layer cake—Web applications like Dropbox, Gmail, and Facebook, which have been built atop it. The rest of the cake exists largely to support Web applications like these and their developers. In all these models, there's a strong *relationship between local and cloud resources*. The best implementations make the local/cloud software divide seamless. Let's slice it open (Figure 15-19) and start at the bottom.

Figure 15-19
A tasty three-layer cake

Infrastructure as a Service

Building on the ways virtualization allowed Mario to make the most efficient use of hardware in his local network, large-scale global *Infrastructure as a Service (IaaS)* providers use virtualization to minimize idle hardware, protect against data loss and downtime, and respond to spikes in demand. Mario can use big IaaS providers like Amazon Web Services (AWS) to launch new virtual servers using an operating system of his choice on demand (Figure 15-20) for pennies an hour. The beauty of IaaS is that you no longer need to purchase expensive, heavy hardware. You are using Amazon's powerful infrastructure as a service.

A huge number of Web sites are really more easily understood if you use the term Web applications. If you want to access Mike Meyers' videos, you go to hub.totalsem .com. This Web site is really an application (written in house) that you use to watch videos, practice simulation questions, etc. This Web application is a great tool, but as more people access the application we often need to add more capacity so you won't yell at us

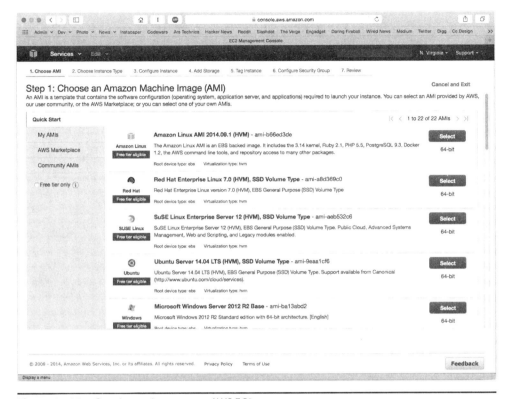

Figure 15-20 Creating an instance on AWS EC2

for a slow server. Luckily, our application is designed to run distributed across multiple servers. If we need more servers, we just add as many more virtual servers as we need. But even this is just scratching the surface. AWS (Figure 15-21) provides many of the services needed to drive popular, complex Web applications—unlimited data storage, database servers, caching, media hosting, and more—all billed by usage.

The hitch is that, while we're no longer responsible for the hardware, we are still responsible for configuring and maintaining the operating system and software of any virtual machines we create. This can mean we have a lot of flexibility to tune it for our needs, but it also requires knowledge of the underlying OS and time to manage it.

Platform as a Service

Web applications are built by programmers. Programmers do one thing really well: they program. The problem for programmers is that a Web application needs a lot more than a just programmer. To develop a Web application, we need people to manage the infrastructure: system administrators, database administrators, general network support, etc. A Web application also needs more than just hardware and an operating system. It needs

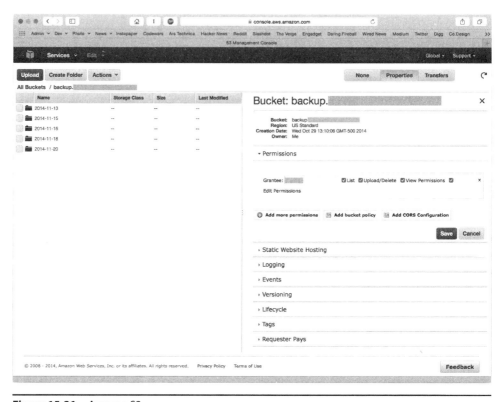

Figure 15-21   Amazon S3

development tools, monitoring tools, database tools, and potentially hundreds of other tools and services. Getting a Web application up and running is a big job.

A *Platform as a Service (PaaS)* provider gives programmers all the tools they need to deploy, administer, and maintain a Web application. They have some form of infrastructure, which could be provided by an IaaS, but on top of that infrastructure the PaaS provider builds a platform: a complete deployment and management system to handle every aspect of a Web application.

The important point of PaaS is that the infrastructure underneath the PaaS is largely invisible to the developer. The PaaS provider is aware of their infrastructure but the developer cannot control it directly, and doesn't need to think about its complexity. As far as the programmer is concerned, the PaaS is just a place to deploy and run their application.

Heroku, one of the earliest PaaS providers, creates a simple interface on top of the IaaS offerings of AWS, further reducing the complexity of developing and scaling Web applications. Heroku's management console (Figure 15-22) enables developers to increase or decrease the capacity of an application with a single slider, or easily set up add-ons that add a database, monitor your logs, track performance, and more. It could take days for a tech or developer unfamiliar with the software and services to install, configure, and integrate a set of these services with a running application; PaaS providers help cut this down to minutes or hours.

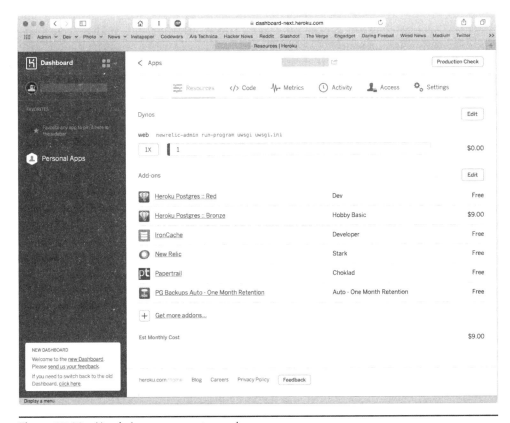

Figure 15-22   Heroku's management console

Software as a Service

Software as a Service (SaaS) sits at the top layer of the cake. This software was once fairly simple, but these days even massive applications (traditionally sold on optical discs in retail stores) are available from central online servers. The best example of modern SaaS is the Office suite from Microsoft, Office 365. Long the flagship of the retail brick-and-mortar Microsoft product line, the Office suite (Word, PowerPoint, Excel, etc.) migrated to a subscription-based online service a few years ago. In the old days, if you wanted to add Word to your new laptop, you'd buy a copy and install it from disc. These days, you pay a yearly fee to Microsoft, log into your Microsoft account, and either download Word to your laptop or just use Word Online. It's almost seamless.

Cloud Delivery Models

Organizations have differing needs and capabilities, of course, so there's no one-size-fits-all *cloud delivery model* that works for everyone. To implement cloud computing capabilities, organizations have to balance cost, control, customization, and privacy. Some organizations also have unique capacity, performance, or other needs no existing cloud provider can meet. Each organization makes its own decisions about these trade-offs, but the result is usually a cloud delivery model that can be described as public, private, community, or hybrid. Each of these models feature various *connectivity methods*, ways to access the cloud services.

Public Cloud

Most folks usually just interact with a *public cloud*, a term used to describe software, platforms, and infrastructure delivered through networks that the general public can use. When we talk about *the* cloud, this is what we mean. Out on the open, public Internet, cloud services and applications can collaborate in ways that make it easier to think of them collectively as *the cloud* than as many public clouds. The public doesn't *own* this cloud—the hardware is often owned by companies like Amazon, Google, and Microsoft—but there's nothing to stop a company like Netflix from building its Web application atop the IaaS offerings of all three of these companies at once.

The public cloud sees examples of all the *x*aaS varieties, which give specific names to these *cloud concepts*:

- Public IaaS
- Public PaaS
- Public SaaS

Private Cloud

If a business wants some of the flexibility of the cloud, needs complete ownership of its data, and can afford both, it can build an internal cloud the business actually owns—a *private cloud*. A security-minded company with enough resources could build an internal IaaS network in an onsite data center. Departments within the company could create and destroy virtual machines as needed, and develop SaaS to meet collaboration, planning, or task and time management needs all without sending the data over the open Internet. A company with these needs but without the space or knowledge to build and maintain a private cloud can also contract a third party to maintain or host it.

Again, there are private versions of each of the cloud concepts:

- Private IaaS
- Private PaaS
- Private SaaS

Community Cloud

While a community center is usually a public gathering place for those in the community it serves, a *community cloud* is more like a private cloud paid for and used by more than one organization. Community clouds aren't run by a city or state for citizens' use; the community in this case is a group of organizations with similar goals or needs. If you're a military contractor working on classified projects, wouldn't it be nice to share the burden of defending your cloud against sophisticated attackers sponsored by foreign states with other military and intelligence contractors?

Just like with the public and private cloud, there are community cloud versions of all the *x*aaS varieties:

- Community IaaS
- Community PaaS
- Community SaaS

Hybrid Cloud

Sometimes we *can* have our cake and eat it too. Not all data is crucial, and not every document is a secret. Needs that an organization can only meet in-house might be less important than keeping an application running when demand exceeds what it can handle onsite. We can build a *hybrid cloud* by connecting some combination of public, private, and community clouds, allowing communication between them. Using a hybrid cloud model can mean not having to maintain a private cloud powerful enough to meet peak demand—an application can grow into a public cloud instead of grind to a halt, a technique called *cloud bursting*. But a hybrid cloud isn't just about letting one Web application span two types of cloud—it's also about integrating services across them. Let's take a look at how Mario could use a hybrid cloud to expand his business.

Mario runs a national chain of sandwich shops and is looking into drone-delivered lunch. He'll need a new application in his private cloud to calculate routes and track drones, and that application will have to integrate with the existing order-tracking application in his private cloud. But then he'll also need to integrate it with a third-party weather application in the public cloud to avoid sending drones out in a blizzard, and a flight-plan application running in a community cloud to avoid other drones, helicopters, and aircraft (and vice versa). The sum of these integrated services and applications *is* the hybrid cloud that will power Mario's drone-delivered lunch. Like the other three clouds, the hybrid cloud sees examples of all the *x*aaS varieties, which give specific names to these cloud concepts:

- Hybrid IaaS
- Hybrid PaaS
- Hybrid SaaS

Chapter Review

Questions

1. Upgrading which component of a host machine would most likely enable you to run more virtual machines simultaneously?

    A. CPU

    B. Hard drive

    C. RAM

    D. Windows

2. What enables two VMs hosted on the same physical machine to communicate without leaving the machine itself?

    A. Virtual firewall

    B. Virtual LAN

    C. Virtual PBX

    D. Virtual switch

3. What feature lets you save a VM's state so you can quickly restore to that point?

    A. Replacement

    B. Save

    C. Snapshot

    D. Zip

4. What do you need to install a legal copy of Windows 10 into a virtual machine using VMware Workstation?

    A. A valid VM key

    B. Valid Windows 10 installation media

    C. A valid ESXi key

    D. A second NIC

5. Which of the following is an advantage of a virtual machine over a physical machine?

    A. Increased performance

    B. Hardware consolidation

    C. No backups needed

    D. Operating systems included

6. Janelle wants to start a new photo-sharing service for real pictures of Bigfoot, but doesn't own any servers. How can she quickly create a new server to run her service?

   A. Public cloud

   B. Private cloud

   C. Community cloud

   D. Hybrid cloud

7. After the unforeseen failure of her Bigfoot-picture-sharing service, bgFootr—which got hacked when she failed to stay on top of her security updates—Janelle has a great new idea for a new service to report Loch Ness Monster sightings. What service would help keep her from having to play system administrator?

   A. Software as a Service

   B. Infrastructure as a Service

   C. Platform as a Service

   D. Network as a Service

8. John has two groups of virtual machines that each need to be on their own subnet. Which of the following should he use to subnet each group of virtual machines without moving or re-cabling hardware?

   A. Virtual NIC

   B. Virtual switch

   C. Virtual router

   D. Virtual firewall

9. Which of the following would enable you to use iSCSI to read and write data over the network?

   A. Serial-attached SCSI

   B. SMB

   C. Storage area network

   D. Network attached storage

10. BigTracks is a successful Bigfoot-tracking company using an internal service to manage all of its automated Bigfoot monitoring stations. A Bigfoot migration has caused a massive increase in the amount of audio and video sent back from their stations. In order to add short-term capacity, they can create new servers in the public cloud. What model of cloud computing does this describe?

   A. Public cloud

   B. Private cloud

   C. Community cloud

   D. Hybrid cloud

Answers

1. **C.** Adding more RAM will enable you to run more simultaneous VMs. Upgrading a hard drive could help, but it's not the best answer here.

2. **D.** Hypervisors come with virtual switching capability to enable the VMs to communicate.

3. **C.** The saved state of a VM is called a snapshot. Not to be confused with a true backup.

4. **B.** You need a copy of the Windows installation media to install Windows.

5. **B.** A big benefit of virtualization is hardware consolidation.

6. **A.** Using the public cloud will enable Janelle to quickly create the servers she needs.

7. **C.** By switching to a PaaS, Janelle can concentrate on creating her service and leave the lower-level administration up to the PaaS provider.

8. **C.** A virtual router performs all the same Layer 3 tasks that its physical cousins do.

9. **C.** A storage area network uses the lower-level iSCSI protocol to present virtual disks to client machines.

10. **D.** BigTracks is creating a hybrid cloud by connecting its internal private cloud to a public cloud to expand capacity quickly.

## CHAPTER 16

Mobile Networking

The CompTIA Network+ certification exam expects you to know how to

- 1.5 Compare and contrast the characteristics of network topologies, types and technologies
- 1.6 Given a scenario, implement the appropriate wireless technologies and configurations
- 3.5 Identify policies and best practices
- 4.3 Given a scenario, secure a basic wireless network
- 4.5 Given a scenario, implement network device hardening

To achieve these goals, you must be able to

- Explain the capabilities of different mobile networking technologies
- Describe common deployment schemes for mobile devices
- Deal with sample security issues with mobile devices

Your author, being ancient in computer years, often stares at amazement at his mobile devices in terms of their built-in networking technologies. Every smartphone has cellular; that's how you make phone calls. The cheapest $35 tablet almost certainly has 802.11 Wi-Fi and Bluetooth, while even a mid-range smartphone contains as many as eight completely different network technologies for communication.

All these technologies require the attention of every security professional, in particular when mobile devices appear in an organization's infrastructure. The various network technologies give attackers multiple opportunities for wreaking havoc on the devices and maybe even to use those devices to access an organization's infrastructure. IT security requires good understanding of the network technologies, plus clear methods of managing mobile devices in the organization.

This chapter begins with an overview of all the common network technologies found on mobile devices. From there, the chapter covers several methods of managing and deploying mobile devices in the infrastructure, and then closes with a few common security scenarios that take place and how to deal with them.

Mobile Network Technologies

All of today's mobile devices are certainly powerful computers, but what makes these devices truly mobile (as opposed to little more than an electronic notebook) is wireless communication. Without the capability to communicate wirelessly with other devices, a mobile device is much less useful. Every mobile device has at least one network technology installed, enabling these devices to connect to other devices, separate networks, or the entire Internet.

Mobile devices incorporate many network technologies, from the common and well known (such as *802.11 Wi-Fi*) to the more rare and unique (such as *Z-Wave*). The proliferation of these network technologies has led to miniaturization and economies of scale, making it simple for even inexpensive devices to incorporate four or more network technologies.

 NOTE The technology advancements used in mobile devices enable almost any type of device to connect to the Internet. Light bulbs, cameras, thermostats—devices that classically would be considered "dumb"—can possess many of the same technologies seen in "smart" devices. Embedded devices that connect to the Internet and enable remote monitoring and controlling are known as *Internet of Things (IoT)* devices. Given that these devices' networking capabilities are all but identical to those of mobile devices, they'll receive occasional mention in this chapter.

Test Specific

Cellular WAN

Anyone with a smartphone these days can enjoy the convenience of using wireless cellular technology on the road. Who doesn't love firing up an Android phone or iPhone and cruising the Internet from anywhere? As cell-phone technology converges with Internet access technologies, competent techs need to understand what's happening behind the scenes. That means tackling an alphabet soup of standards.

Regardless of the standard, the voice and data used on smartphones (unless you have 802.11 wireless turned on) moves through a cellular wireless network with towers that cover the world (Figure 16-1). This is the WAN transmission medium.

Mobile data services started in the mid-1980s and, as you might imagine, have gone through a dizzying number of standards and protocols, all of which have been revised, improved, abandoned, and reworked. Instead of trying to advertise these fairly complex and intimidating technologies, the industry instead came up with the marketing term *generations*, abbreviated by a number followed by the letter *G*: 2G, 3G, and 4G.

Salespeople and TV commercials use these terms to push mobile cellular services. The generation terms aren't generally used within the industry, and certainly not at a deeply technical level. As I go through the standards you'll see on the exam and encounter in real

Figure 16-1
Cellular tower

life, I'll mention both the technical name and the generation where applicable. I'll cover five common terms here:

- GSM and EDGE
- CDMA
- HSPA+
- LTE

GSM and EDGE

The *Global System for Mobile Communications (GSM)*, the first group of networking technologies widely applied to mobile devices, relied on a type of time-division multiplexing called *time-division multiple access (TDMA)*. TDMA enabled multiple users to share the same channel more or less at the same time; and in this scenario, the switching from one user to another happened so quickly no one noticed.

NOTE There's no "C" on the end of GSM because it originally came from a French term, *Groupe Spécial Mobile*.

GSM introduced the handy *subscriber identity module (SIM)* card that is now ubiquitous in smartphones (Figure 16-2). The SIM card identifies the phone, enabling access to the cellular networks, and stores some other information (contents differ according to many factors, none relevant for this discussion).

Figure 16-2
SIM card in
phone

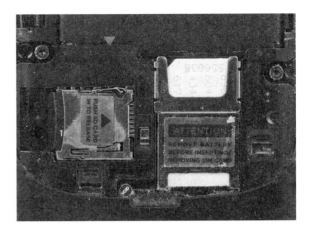

The GSM standard was considered a 2G technology. The standard continued to improve over the years, getting new names and better data speeds. One of the last of these (and one you might see on the exam) was *Enhanced Data rates for GSM Evolution (EDGE)*, which offered data speeds up to 384 Kbps.

CDMA

Code-division multiple access (CDMA) came out not long after GSM, but used a spread-spectrum form of transmission that was totally incompatible with GSM's TDMA. Rather than enabling multiple users to share a single channel by splitting the channel into time slices, spread-spectrum transmission changed the frequencies used by each user.

CDMA was considered superior to GSM, and U.S. carriers adopted CDMA *en masse*, which created some problems later since the rest of the world went GSM. Plus, CDMA lacked some key features, such as SIM cards.

NOTE The original CDMA was considered a 2G technology.

HSPA+

In the late 1990s the International Telecommunication Union (ITU) forwarded a standard called International Mobile Telecommunications-2000 (IMT-2000) to address shortcomings in mobile technology. IMT-2000 defined higher speeds, support for full-time Internet connections, and other critical functions. The standard pushed support for multimedia messaging system (MMS) (so you can send cat pictures in your text messages) and IP-based telephony.

Both GSM and CDMA improved during the late 1990s to the mid-2000s to address IMT-2000: all these improvements were marketed under probably the most confusing marketing term ever used: *3G*. Ideally, *3G* meant a technology that supported IMT-2000, although the industry was very lax in how companies used this term. (This time period is so confusing that many technologies in this period were given decimal generations to clarify the situation. One example is GSM EDGE being called 2.9G due to its lack of full IMT-2000 support.)

Evolved High-Speed Packet Access (HSPA+) was the final 3G data standard, providing theoretical speeds up to 168 Mbps, although most HSPA+ implementations rarely exceeded 10 Mbps. (Note that the CompTIA Network+ objectives list an earlier version, High-Speed Packet Access [HSPA]).

LTE

Devices and networks using *Long Term Evolution (LTE)* technology rolled out worldwide in the early 2010s and now dominate wireless services. Marketed as and now generally accepted as a true *4G* technology, LTE networks feature speeds of up to 300 Mbps download and 75 Mbps upload. All LTE services use SIM cards such as the one shown in Figure 16-3. Note the SIM size in Figure 16-3 compared to the much older SIM in Figure 16-2. The much smaller SIM in Figure 16-3 is a *nano-SIM*. The SIM in Figure 16-2 is an original, standard SIM.

Figure 16-3
Modern
nano-SIM

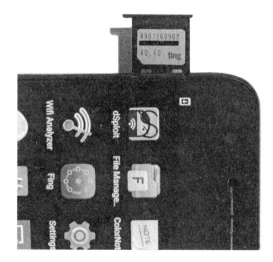

Smartphones have LTE radios built in, but it's easy to add LTE to almost any device. Need LTE on a laptop or a desktop? No problem, get an LTE NIC and just plug it into a convenient USB port (Figure 16-4).

802.11

Chapter 14 covered the 802.11 wireless standard in exhaustive detail, so there's no reason to repeat those details here. Be aware that any 802.11-capable device, even a simple IoT thermostat, suffers from all the same configuration issues discussed in Chapter 14.

There are a few aspects of how mobile devices, specifically smartphones, use 802.11 that can create issues in some situations. One issue is a wireless *hotspot*—a feature that enables a device to share its cellular WAN connection by setting up an SSID via its own 802.11 wireless. Hotspots can be dedicated devices, or simply a feature of a modern smartphone (Figure 16-5).

Figure 16-4
Cellular wireless
NIC on USB stick

Figure 16-5
Setting up
hotspot on an
Android phone

If you're one of those folks who uses a lot of data on your smartphone, it's generally a good idea to use 802.11 when available to avoid cellular WAN data use charges, but you really must be careful. Let's explore the benefits and pitfalls in more detail.

Every mobile OS maker provides features to help phones use 802.11 networks when available. These features vary dramatically between Android and iOS. Even on Android devices, the service provider might make changes to the interface as well, adding even more variance. Figure 16-6 shows some of these settings on an Android phone.

Figure 16-6
Automatic
802.11 network
connection
options on
Android

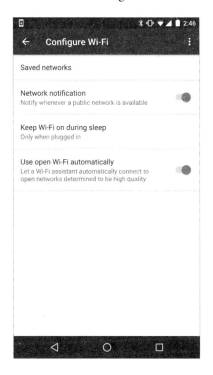

These settings, while convenient, create serious security concerns. Notice the option to connect to open (no password) networks. Open (also known as public since anyone may access them) wireless networks are very risky. Bad actors constantly monitor coffee shops, airports, and other public Wi-Fi networks, looking for ways to capture personal information. This is such a big problem today that many experts strongly recommend that you never use public Wi-Fi.

I disagree. I think you can use public Wi-Fi safely, but only if you're a wise user. Make sure to run HTTPS on all your browsers and watch for screens that don't make sense (like asking you to log in with some account that has nothing to do with what you're doing at that moment online). Most mobile operating systems provide special functions, such as requiring HTTPS Web pages or VPNs for any public connection.

Saved *wireless profiles* are also an issue in some cases. For example, many ISPs provide a standard wireless name for public access of all their access points (Xfinity and AT&T Wi-Fi are two examples). These SSIDs aren't really public, as they require logons, but attackers often create spoofed access points to get users to log in using their ISP credentials (Figure 16-7).

Figure 16-7

Fake Xfinity access page

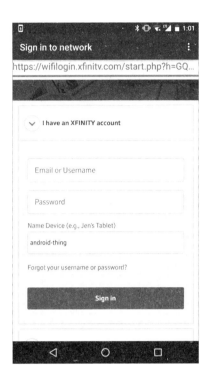

Bluetooth

Bluetooth, that wonderful technology that connects headsets to smartphones and keyboards to laptops, is a wireless networking protocol, similar to 802.11, developed to simplify connections between devices. You bring two Bluetooth-aware devices into close proximity, perform a quick pairing between the two, and they connect and work. Connected Bluetooth devices create a *personal area network (PAN)*, and security concerns apply to all the devices and communication within that PAN.

Bluetooth has two important tools to make using it more secure. First, all of today's Bluetooth devices are not visible unless they are manually set to *discovery* or *discoverable mode*. If you have a Bluetooth headset and you want to pair it to your smartphone, there is some place on the phone where you turn on this mode, as shown in Figure 16-8.

The beauty of discoverable mode is that you have a limited amount of time to make the connection, usually two minutes, before the device automatically turns it off and once again the device is no longer visible. Granted, there is radio communication between the two paired devices that can be accessed by powerful, sophisticated Bluetooth sniffers, but these sniffers are expensive and difficult to purchase, and are only of interest to law enforcement and very nerdy people.

The second tool is the requirement of using a four-digit personal identification number (PIN) during the pairing process. When one device initiates a discoverable Bluetooth device, the other device sees the request and generates a four-digit PIN. The first device must then enter that code and the pairing takes place.

Figure 16-8

Setting up discoverable mode

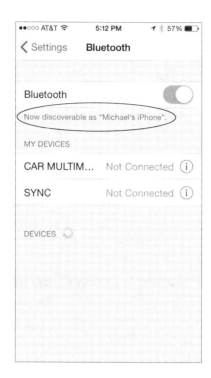

The problem with these two security tools is that they weren't required on the early generations of Bluetooth. From the time Bluetooth devices started coming out in the late 1990s up until around 2005, a number of devices skipped the discovery mode—basically just always staying in discoverable mode—or skipped the use of PINs. This foolish choice resulted in several Bluetooth attacks, two of which might show up on the CompTIA Network+ exam: Bluejacking and Bluesnarfing.

Bluejacking was the process of sending unsolicited messages to another Bluetooth device. These devices would pop up on your screen. Bluejacking wasn't considered anything more than irritating, but Bluesnarfing was another matter. *Bluesnarfing* used weaknesses in the Bluetooth standard to steal information from other Bluetooth devices. Simply adding proper use of discoverable mode as well as PINs initially stopped these attacks.

Over the years, bad actors have continued to come up with new Bluesnarfing attacks, in response to which the Bluetooth standard has been patched and updated several times. One great example of these updates was making all Bluetooth communication encrypted in Bluetooth version 4.0. This attack–patching–updating cycle continues to this day.

Assuming all your devices support Bluetooth 4.0, your Bluetooth devices are safe and robust out of the box against most attacks. But there's no such thing as a guarantee in the world of IT security. Bluetooth is a simpler technology and it's not designed to defend against aggressive, sophisticated attacks. Therefore, the only way to ensure Bluetooth security in a high-security environment is to turn it off (Figure 16-9).

Figure 16-9
Turning off
Bluetooth

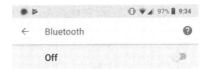

NOTE A very notable exception to the safeness (is that a word?) of Bluetooth devices is a set of security vulnerabilities published in late 2017 called *BlueBorne*. The vulnerabilities were discovered by a security company called Armis; they potentially affect more than 8 billion devices, from smartphones to tablets to cars. You won't see BlueBorne on the CompTIA Network+ exam, but you should pay attention to the tech news as this could seriously impact you and your clients in the future.

Less Common Mobile Network Technologies

Cellular WANs, 802.11, and Bluetooth are easily the dominant mobile network technologies, but there are a few alternatives that, while not as commonly used, are supported in many mobile devices. This section explores NFC, RFID, infrared, ANT+, Z-Wave, and Zigbee.

NFC

Near field communication (NFC) is a low-speed, short-range technology designed for (among other things) small-value monetary transactions. Most NFC connections consist of an NFC tag that stores private data (Figure 16-10) and some kind of NFC reader. The NFC tag is an unpowered, passive device. Bringing the NFC reader in very close proximity to the NFC tag creates an electromagnetic induction in the NFC tag, enabling the two devices to communicate using only power from the reader. This is very handy for NFC-enabled credit cards and other devices that would otherwise need batteries.

Figure 16-10
NFC tag

NOTE The fact that NFC tags are passive has a downside. A bad actor with the right reader can read every NFC-enabled card in anyone's wallet or purse, making a whole new market for metal-shielded card holders that can block a reader.

While NFC contains basic encryption, the technology relies on the short distances (<5 cm) and quick communications (hard to target with a man-in-the-middle attack) to provide security. These are acceptable when using NFC for simple data transfers, as shown in Figure 16-11, but are unacceptable for monetary transfers, because bad actors may gain access to personal information.

Figure 16-11
Transferring
a Web URL
between two
Android phones

All the popular "Tap to Pay" services such as Apple Pay and Android Pay use NFC, but add their own security protocols on top of NFC to ensure the privacy of the transaction.

RFID

Radio-frequency identification (RFID) uses the same concepts of tag and reader as NFC, but has several differences. First, RFID isn't a single standard as much as it is many standards that use the technology.

Second, different RFID standards use diverse frequencies and unique protocols. While NFC uses the 13.56-MHz band, the different RFID standards span at least six different radio bands, from as low as 120 KHz to as high as 10 GHz. RFID needs these different bandwidths to support the many different applications and environments ... which brings up the next point.

Third, RFID has much broader applications, from labeling individual parts in manufacturing, to identifying the different parts of a deep undersea structure, to labeling your pet with an injectable RFID tag. Most RFID devices have some common features:

- **Close proximity**   Devices generally communicate within 1 meter.
- **Security**   Most RFID standards include weak or no encryption.
- **Labels**   RFID tags most commonly appear inside labels, which are in turn placed on whatever component (box, part, device) needs to be queried.

RFID tags are much easier to read than NFC tags; a bad actor can simply walk near the RFID tag with the right reader (as opposed to getting within 5 cm). Therefore, RFID tags tend not to hold personally identifiable information (PII).

Infrared

Infrared (IR) communication consists of a device that emits coded infrared light and a second device that reads the code and acts upon it. The most common infrared devices are the remote controls that come with TVs, tuners, and other electronic devices.

NOTE Of all the technologies discussed here, only infrared doesn't use radio waves.

Your author loves his Android phones if for no other reason than only Androids (though not all of them) come with an infrared transmitter known generically as an *IR blaster*. IR blasters can emulate any IR remote control, turning any Android into a universal remote. Since these devices only transmit simple remote-control commands, there is no risk to your mobile device. The risk is that any IR blaster can quickly take complete control of any device designed to receive those commands, making the Android the bad actor. The only real defense is to block the IR receivers.

EXAM TIP Wireless network technologies such as Bluetooth, NFC, and IR are designed to make a single point-to-point connection at very short ranges. Bluetooth may go as far as 100 meters for the most powerful Bluetooth connections, for example; NFC devices drop that to as little as 5 cm. Any connections used by Bluetooth, NFC, or infrared are called *personal area networks (PANs)*—as mentioned earlier—to reflect their shorter distances and point-to-point nature.

ANT+

Adaptive Network Technology (ANT+) is a low-speed, low-power networking technology that, similarly to NFC, consists of a passive ANT device and an ANT reader. ANT was developed to fix a problem with alternatives like 802.11 or Bluetooth. 802.11 and Bluetooth are powerful wireless tools, but both of these technologies require rather chatty, relatively power-hungry devices. Bluetooth isn't nearly as power hungry or as fast as Wi-Fi, but when you have very small devices such as heart-rate monitors, even Bluetooth uses too much power.

Garmin introduced the proprietary ANT protocol around 2007 for low-power sensors that don't send a lot of data and that often go for extended periods of time without transferring data (like a heart-rate monitor that's used at most once a week). You'll also see ANT-capable exercise bicycles and treadmills. (Yes, ANT is popular in health clubs!)

ANT isn't as common as many other network technologies. Apple devices lack an ANT radio; roughly two-thirds of Android devices have them. If you're using, for example, an ANT heart-rate monitor and you want to use it with your iPhone, you need an ANT USB dongle to talk to your ANT device.

The latest version of ANT is called ANT+. ANT/ANT+ is a superb protocol that's incredibly low powered and has enough bandwidth for many devices. ANT is encrypted with AES, so hacking isn't an issue (yet).

Z-Wave and Zigbee

Home automation—the process of controlling lights, thermostats, cameras, even a washer and dryer remotely—is an ever-growing industry. While *wired* home automation has been around for a while, connecting smart devices *wirelessly* is a much newer concept.

Using wireless technology for home automation has many challenges. First are the huge number of IoT devices that a modern home might potentially use, from thermostats to washing machines to power outlets and light bulbs. Secondly, homes, unlike offices, are filled with small rooms, narrow staircases, and other obstacles that make regular radio-based wireless difficult. Yet demand for home automation is strong, and two competing technologies, Z-Wave and Zigbee, are in direct, head-to-head competition in wireless home automation. Z-Wave is a proprietary standard (with an open API for programmers), while Zigbee is a completely open standard. Both use a mesh networking topology to facilitate communication in homes, yet both also have hubs that act as the network interconnect.

Deployment Models

Organizations that choose to use mobile devices must create some methods of getting those devices into their employees' hands. This isn't a matter of simply purchasing devices for each person. Users have strong opinions about their devices; the whole Android versus iOS debate alone is a huge issue. To deal with these challenges, there are specific deployment models to help define how organizations approach the use of mobile devices by employees. This section explores BYOD, COBO, COPE, and CYOD, then looks at general on-boarding and off-boarding procedures.

 EXAM TIP The CompTIA Network+ objectives mention only the BYOD deployment model, not COBO, COPE, or CYOD, so expect a question or two on BYOD. I've included the other models here because they're common in the real world.

BYOD

Bring your own device (BYOD) deployment uses employees' existing mobile devices for use by the corporation. The company installs their applications on employees' mobile devices. Employees install their corporate e-mail accounts on their personal devices. BYOD requires tight controls and separation of employee personal data from corporate data.

COBO

In a *corporate-owned business only (COBO)* deployment model, the corporation owns all the devices. The corporation issues mobile devices to employees. The corporation is solely responsible for the maintenance of the devices, the applications, and the data.

COBO is very rigid—nothing but company-approved software is used on the issued mobile devices. This is often a challenge as it requires employees to carry both the corporate device and their own device.

COPE

Corporate-owned, personally-enabled (COPE) is almost identical to COBO in that the organization issues mobile devices. With COPE, however, employees are presented with a whitelist of preapproved applications that they may install.

CYOD

An organization offering *choose your own device (CYOD)* options provides employees free choice within a catalog of mobile devices. The organization retains complete control and ownership over the mobile devices, although the employees can install their own apps on the mobile devices.

On-Boarding and Off-Boarding

Regardless of the deployment model that an organization chooses, it needs some method of verifying that new mobile devices appearing in the organization's infrastructure are secure and safe to use within the organization. This procedure is known as *on-boarding*. As mobile devices leave the control of the organization, those same devices must be confirmed to no longer store any proprietary applications or data, a process called *off-boarding*.

On-Boarding

On-boarding takes place in several ways, but one common practice is to require any previously unfamiliar mobile device accessing an internal 802.11 network to go through a series of checks and scans. While exactly which checks and scans take place varies depending on the deployment model, a typical BYOD on-boarding process may include the following:

- A sign-on page requiring a user name and password
- An authorization page describing all applicable policies to which the user must agree
- A malware scan of the device
- An application scan of the device

Off-Boarding

Mobile devices move out of organizations just as often as they move in, for various reasons. A person quits and intends to take their phone with them. Mobile devices get old and are due for replacement. A device that uses tablets for controls switches from iPads to Android tablets. Whatever the case, it's important that every outgoing device goes through an inspection (sometimes manual, sometimes automatic) that deletes proprietary applications as well as any data that the organization doesn't want out in the world.

Scenarios

Mobile networking technologies present organizations with several opportunities to enhance IT security beyond what is possible with non-mobile networking technologies. Let's look at three networking technologies unique to mobile networks and devices and IoT devices and see how organizations can leverage them to enhance IT security:

- Geofencing
- Locating and disabling lost mobile devices
- Hardening IoT devices

Geofencing

Geofencing is the process of using a mobile device's built-in GPS capabilities and mobile networking capabilities to set geographical constraints on where the mobile device can be used. Geofencing works in several ways, and the CompTIA Network+ exam objectives certainly use "given a scenario" language when mentioning geofencing in the objectives.

An example scenario is that an organization uses very high-security mobile devices that must never be taken outside the large campus. The organization installs a geofencing application on each device. If any device goes outside very specific GPS ranges, the device will notify the administrator via one or more methods.

 NOTE Geofencing is often used in anti-theft applications that will also silently turn on cameras and microphones as well as lock the system.

Locating and Disabling Lost Mobile Devices

Losing a mobile device by accident or theft is never fun, but losing a corporate device, potentially filled with private and proprietary information, is an event that requires quick action on the part of the organization. Generally, the organization should follow at least the following steps if a mobile device is lost or stolen:

1. Report the loss and possible data breach to the appropriate person or group in the organization.
2. Locate and attempt to recover the device if it has a functional tool enabled, such as Find My iPhone.
3. Remote wipe the device if there is a functional tool.
4. Define any encryption on the device so that any old keys, signatures, or certificates are marked as lost/stolen.
5. Disable all accounts associated with the phone (carrier, apps, sign-in, etc.).
6. Reissue new device with all apps installed and generate new keys for any encryption (for example, BitLocker).

Try This!

Location Services

It might come as a surprise, but many folks leave their mobile devices ... somewhere and then frantically search for them an hour or two later. Typically, the device is found in a car or backpack, and moment of panic is over. If you don't discover the missing device during a quick search, however, you can turn to the location services most devices have to try to locate it.

That begs the question, how good are these location services *today*? Will Apple's Find My iPhone tell you which room in your house you left the iPhone? How about Android or Windows Phone services? I don't have the answers, because these services are improving all the time. So try this!

Hand your phone or other mobile device to a family member or very trusted friend. Try different locations, both near and far from the location of the computer you'll use to log into the location services (such as iCloud for Apple iOS devices, or Google or Microsoft accounts for their respective devices). Do the services just (approximately) locate your device, or can you remotely lock it too?

Hardening IoT Devices

Hardening IoT devices decreases the danger of loss or downtime on the devices and increases the protection of personal information and company data. Generally, hardening means to keep the devices current (software and firmware), use physical security precautions, and apply internal security options.

Consider a scenario in which an organization uses many 802.11 PTZ (pan/tilt/zoom) cameras to monitor secure areas throughout three locations. These cameras are on the one and only SSID in each location. Each SSID uses WPA2 PSK encryption. Due to location, these cameras must use 802.11 for communication. All cameras must be accessible not only in each location but also in headquarters. Your job as a consultant is to provide a list of actions the organization should take to harden these cameras. Here's a list of actions you should consider:

- Place all cameras in their own SSID.
- Put all the camera feeds on their own VLAN.
- Use a very long PSK.
- Set up routine queries for camera firmware updates from the manufacturer.
- Use user name ACLs to determine who may access the cameras.

Chapter Review

Questions

1. Which cellular WAN technology introduced the concept of the SIM card?

   A. CDMA

   B. GSM

   C. EDGE

   D. LTE

2. GSM, EDGE, and LTE all use which of the following? (Select two.)

   A. SIM cards

   B. CDMA

   C. TDMA

   D. NFC

3. A thermostat that you can control remotely with an app on your smartphone would certainly fit under which of the following?

   A. TDMA

   B. BYOD

   C. Bluetooth

   D. IoT

4. You can reduce the vulnerability of your cell phone when automatically connecting to open SSIDs by:

   A. Requiring HTTPS

   B. Disabling WPA

   C. Forgetting all wireless networks

   D. Requiring SSH

5. Which of the following does a classic hotspot require? (Select two.)

   A. Bluetooth

   B. 802.11

   C. Cellular WAN

   D. NFC

6. In order to pair to another Bluetooth device, it must be set into
_____ mode.

   A. PIN

   B. Discoverable

   C. Master

   D. Pair

7. A Bluetooth PIN code is at least _____ digits long.

   A. 3

   B. 4

   C. 6

   D. 8

8. NFC tags are always:

   A. Passive

   B. Encoded

   C. Spherical

   D. Magnetic

9. All tap-to-pay services use which networking technology?

   A. 802.11

   B. Bluetooth

   C. ANT+

   D. NFC

10. A TV remote control most likely uses which of the following network
technologies?

   A. RFID

   B. NFC

   C. Infrared

   D. Bluetooth

11. Which of the following probably uses the least power?

   A. ANT+

   B. RFID

   C. Bluetooth

   D. 802.11

12. In which deployment model does the company own all devices, issue whichever device it chooses to a given employee, and retain control of which apps are installed?

A. BYOD

B. COBO

C. COPE

D. CYOD

Answers

1. **B.** Global System for Mobile (GSM) introduced the SIM card.

2. **A, C.** GSM, Enhanced Data rates for GSM Evolution (EDGE), and Long Term Evolution (LTE) all use SIM cards and time-division multiple access (TDMA).

3. **D.** Many devices in the smart home are part of the Internet of Things.

4. **A.** Requiring HTTPS can reduce the vulnerability of cell phones when connecting to open wireless networks.

5. **B, C.** Classic hotspots require both 802.11 and cellular WAN access.

6. **B.** Bluetooth devices need to be in discoverable mode to pair.

7. **B.** Bluetooth PINs are four digits long.

8. **A.** Near field communication (NFC) tags are always passive.

9. **D.** Tap-to-pay services use NFC.

10. **C.** TV remotes typically use infrared technology.

11. **A.** ANT+ is miserly with power use.

12. **B.** In the corporate-owned business-only (COBO) model, the company owns and controls all devices absolutely.

Building a Real-World Network

The CompTIA Network+ certification exam expects you to know how to

- 1.3 Explain the concepts and characteristics of routing and switching
- 1.5 Compare and contrast the characteristics of network topologies, types and technologies
- 2.2 Given a scenario, determine the appropriate placement of networking devices on a network and install/configure them
- 2.3 Explain the purposes and use cases for advanced networking devices
- 3.1 Given a scenario, use appropriate documentation and diagrams to manage the network
- 3.2 Compare and contrast business continuity and disaster recovery concepts
- 3.5 Identify policies and best practices
- 4.6 Explain common mitigation techniques and their purposes

To achieve these goals, you must be able to

- Explain the concepts of basic network design
- Describe unified communication features and functions
- Describe the function and major components of an ICS/SCADA network

A network tech with solid practical knowledge can handle just about any networking environment. You've seen so far in this book the processes and technologies for working with local area networks (LANs) and connecting to wide area networks (WANs). You've dealt with wired and wireless networks. And you've delved into the intricacies of TCP/IP.

This chapter lays out yet another kind of network, a medium-sized space spanning multiple buildings, in this case a *campus area network (CAN)*. Plus, it looks at the technologies that help organizations communicate and operate effectively in both commercial and industrial settings.

Here's the scenario we'll use in this chapter to describe a CAN. A company—the Bayland Widgets Corporation (BWC)—has just successfully crowd-funded to build and market its latest and greatest widget. They've gone from a startup operating in cafés to an established company operating in a new campus that has three buildings (Figure 17-1). One is the commercial office, where the sales and managerial staffs operate. The second is a factory space for building the new widget. The final building is the warehouse and shipping facility.

Figure 17-1

The new campus

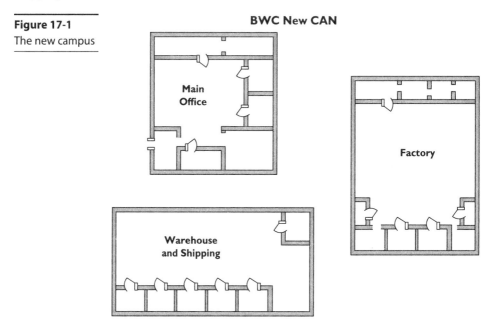

So unroll your eyes and buckle up. We've got a lot of great stuff to cover here.

The commercial space houses the primary servers, but a fiber-based network connects all three buildings, all of which have communications equipment installed. Plus, the factory and warehouse have robots and other mechanical systems that need computer-based controls.

The discussion in this chapter starts with network design, then turns to the gear used for the unified communication systems that bind all the buildings together. The chapter wraps up with a look at the industrial control systems, such as SCADA, that run the factory and warehouse portions.

Although some of the topics go beyond the current CompTIA Network+ exam, these are real-world networking scenarios in which any network tech might find himself or herself working. Plus, we'll hit a lot of exam-specific content in the process of laying out the network, including appropriate placement of wired and wireless infrastructure devices, appropriate documentation and diagrams to manage the network, and essential policies and best practices to make the network run smoothly.

So unroll your eyes and buckle up. We've got a lot of great stuff to cover here.

Test Specific

Designing a Basic Network

Designing and building a network follows similar requirements, regardless of the scope of that network. Here are seven categories to consider:

- **List of requirements**   Define the network's needs. Why are you installing this network? What primary features do you need?

- **Device types/requirements**   What equipment do you need to build this network? How should you organize the network?

- **Environment limitations**   What sort of building or buildings do you need to work with to install a network? Do you have access to the walls or ceiling?

- **Equipment limitations**   Are you using existing equipment, applications, or cabling?

- **Compatibility requirements**   What sort of compatibility issues do you have between old and new devices?

- **Wired/wireless considerations**   What type of structured cabling do you need? Does this network need wireless? How do you connect to the Internet?

- **Security considerations**   How will you deal with computer, data, and network security?

This list is workable, but leaves out a few important considerations, like costs vs. budget. Plus, although I've numbered them here, these steps might come in any order. Even though network security is in the sixth position, for example, you might make a decision concerning the firewall as early as Step 2. Don't be afraid to jump around a bit as needed to construct the network.

Let's start building the Bayland Widgets CAN using this list somewhat as a guideline. For each point, I'll use a scenario or two to consider some of the pitfalls and issues that might pop up. Later chapters cover security in detail, so I'm leaving that out of the discussion in this chapter for the most part.

Define the Network Needs

What does a CAN need in a network? In this case, because Bayland Widgets has operations, manufacturing, and shipping, things can get a little complicated. Here are the most obvious points:

- Individual offices need workstations that can do specific jobs.

- The company needs servers that can handle anything thrown at them.

- The buildings need internal cabling.

- The buildings need intermediate distribution frames (IDFs) to provide connections.

- The buildings need solid connectivity.

That seems to cover the hardware side of things, at least as far as the CAN goes. That leaves out the specific robotics or mechanical systems that handle production, warehousing, and shipping, but we can assume for now that those are all proprietary. Even if you end up working for such a company, you'd have to learn their specific systems. That's well beyond what a CompTIA Network+ tech knows right out of the box.

On the software side of things, the workstations and servers need appropriate operating systems. The network protocols need to be in place.

Once the hardware and software inside the network works, then the network needs connectivity beyond. That usually means connecting to the Internet today, though private networks within organizations continue to operate.

In the case of Bayland Widgets, on top of the standard network structures for a CAN, they need to add specific systems for unified communication and industrial controls. I'll cover those in the second and third major sections of this chapter.

Try This!

What Are *Your* Needs?

Imagine the coolest home network you've ever desired. What would that network look like? What would it do for you? Go ahead and sketch up a sample floor plan. Keep this floor plan handy for other "Try This!" sections in this chapter.

Documentation

Right here at the beginning of the network development process you should begin what will be an immediate and continual process: documentation. Every well-designed and maintained network documents every facet of that network in detail *to support configuration management.* Here are some of the areas of documentation:

- **Network diagrams** You need pretty seriously detailed diagrams that describe both the *physical* network components and the *logical* components too. We talked about diagramming way back in Chapter 5, "Installing a Physical Network," so check there for details. (For the physical, think wiring and port locations, server locations, and workstations; for the logical, think about VLANs and network segmentation.) Expect questions on logical vs. physical diagrams on the CompTIA Network+ exam.

 NOTE Cisco has extensive *diagram symbols* that pretty much everyone uses to illustrate various network components. You can download these collections in multiple formats, from PowerPoint to Visio, for example, directly from Cisco (https://www.cisco.com/c/en/us/about/brand-center/network-topology-icons.html).

- **Asset management**   The network needs a detailed list of all the software owned by the company installed on workstations and servers. This includes versions, upgrade paths, and the like. There are many good programs to facilitate this process.

- **Licensing restrictions**   As businesses and schools shift to cloud-based volume licensing programs, like Adobe Creative Cloud and Microsoft Office 365, policies and best practices need to be in place to manage those assets. If Bayland Widgets has five licenses for Creative Cloud, for example, which users and which machines have the software? How do you control who activates a license? All this needs to be documented.

- **Inventory management**   Keep good documentation about the network hardware and consumables as well. Detailed inventory management helps mitigate against devices growing legs.

- **IP address utilization**   We'll see this step later in the chapter, but I'll add a little foreshadowing here. You need to know which device—physical or virtual—has which allocated IP address.

- **Vendor documentation**   It's important to have printed or electronic versions of essential details about the hardware and software systems in use by the company. This includes up-to-date contact information for representatives of the products employed.

- **Standard operating procedures/work instructions**   I'll cover this aspect of documentation more in Chapters 18, "Managing Risk," and 19, "Protecting Your Network," but suffice it to say for here that network policies on every aspect of network behavior—from acceptable use of equipment to standards for high-grade passwords—need to be documented carefully and fully. Plus, every kind of troubleshooting scenario involving complicated systems relies on work instructions, guides for how things should function and thus a template to use for step-by-step analysis when something isn't working properly.

Network Design

Network design quantifies the equipment, operating systems, and applications used by the network. This task ties closely with the previously listed Steps 2 through 5 of designing a basic network.

You need to address the following equipment:

- Workstations
- Servers
- Equipment room
- Peripherals

Workstations

Most company workers need discrete workstations running a modern operating system, like Windows 10 or macOS. What about the clichés that office workers, accountants, salespeople, and managers prefer Windows over macOS, while the graphics people and Web developers prefer macOS over Windows? Well, sometimes clichés have more than a grain of truth. But it's also a factor of application software.

A company like Bayland Widgets will have very definite needs depending on the department. The accounting department, for example, might run Sage 50 or Quick-Books Pro, the top competing applications. If they use the former, then clients and servers should run Windows; with the latter, I'd go macOS.

The graphics folks—who do images, brochure layouts, and Web design—have it a little easier today. With Adobe Creative Cloud dominating the graphics market, application choice is easy. The fact that Creative Cloud works equally well with Windows and macOS workstations means companies can choose the platform that most enhances worker productivity. (If most of your workers grew up in Windows, in other words, choose Windows. If they all grew up with macOS, stick with macOS.)

The most entrenched platform-specific employees might be the more standard office workers, simply because Microsoft has traditionally updated Microsoft Office for the PC a year or two ahead of the macOS version.

Servers

The network needs servers. In a small company, you'd traditionally have one or two servers to handle things like network authentication, file storage and redundancy, and so on. Once you get into a bigger network, though, you'll find life easier with a more robust server solution where most (or even all) the server functions are virtualized. You can adapt the server infrastructure to accommodate multiple client types, for example, and run the necessary server functions:

- Network authentication
- Network management
- Accounting
- File management (including redundancy)
- Intranet services, such as internal Wiki and document sharing (via Microsoft SharePoint, for example)
- Development environments (for product testing, Web development, and so on)
- Software repositories (where programmers handle software development and version management)

You have a lot of flexibility here. By going virtual for some or all server resources, you can reduce your power usage and increase uptime. It's a win for everyone, including the accountants handling the bottom line.

NOTE Many small networks avoid using a full-blown file server and instead take advantage of inexpensive and reliable network attached storage (NAS) devices. Technically, an NAS device is a computer that's preconfigured to offer file storage for just about any type of client. Many NAS systems use the Common Internet File System (CIFS) configuration to create a plug and play (PnP)–type of device. Others use Network File System (NFS), Hypertext Transfer Protocol (HTTP), or File Transfer Protocol (FTP) for a similar result. These devices include features such as RAID to make storage safer.

Equipment Room

An equipment room provides a centralized core for the network. This is where the main servers live, for example, and where you implement all the features you learned about way back in Chapter 5 (proper air flow, appropriate cable management, appropriate rack systems, and so on). Documentation for the equipment room should have detailed *rack diagrams*, showing the placement and connectivity of each router, switch, and other network boxes.

Because Bayland Widgets' servers go beyond a small office/home office (SOHO) setup, the equipment room would have much greater power needs and require better *power management*. A highly populated single floor-to-ceiling rack of servers, for example, can pull upward of 40 amps of power, enough to blow any standard circuit. Many routers and other equipment will run directly on DC rather than AC. To accommodate both higher-end and standard equipment, therefore, you would run the higher-amperage circuits and then install one or more *power converters* to change from AC to DC. Many systems add robustness by installing *dual power supplies* in racked equipment and *redundant circuits* to accommodate any loss of power.

The more-demanding equipment room also demands more robust power and *battery backup*. A single, decent *uninterruptible power supply (UPS)* might adequately handle brief power fluctuations for a single rack, for example, but won't be able to deal with a serious power outage. For that kind of *power redundancy*—keeping the lights on and the servers rolling—you'd need to connect *power generators* to the equipment room, devices that burn some petroleum product to produce electricity when the main grid goes dark.

Peripherals

The peripherals—such as printers, scanners, fax machines, and so on—that a company needs to plan for and implement depend very much on what that company does in house. Bayland Widgets might produce their own brochures and fliers, for example, and thus need good, robust, color laser printers for their graphics folks. They could house the printers in a central print room or attach them at various points in the network. The capability of the printers would fluctuate according to how many and what size documents they print.

Faxing might be handled by dedicated fax machines. Or, it could be a software function installed on the machines of the folks who need to fax regularly. All these features and peripherals would need to be unique to the company. (The foosball table, for example, simply must be a peripheral in my office.)

Try This!

Your Network, Your Equipment

Continuing from the previous "Try This!" decide what equipment you want for your own home network. Surely you're going to add a home theater PC, but what about a separate media server? Do you want a computer in the kitchen? Would you like a rack in your house? Can you find a smaller rack online? Can you wall-mount it? Make a list similar to the one in this section and keep it handy for more "Try This!" sections.

Compatibility Issues

Although it doesn't necessarily apply in the scenario presented in this chapter, you need to take compatibility issues into consideration when upgrading a network in an existing space. Several issues apply. It might make huge financial sense to leave installed CAT 5e runs in place, for example, and only upgrade to CAT 6a for additional runs. The older standard can handle Gigabit Ethernet just fine, after all, and that might be sufficient for now.

If you're upgrading some systems and not others, security can become a concern. In recent years, for example, as Microsoft has pushed later, more powerful operating systems, many businesses stubbornly continue to use Windows XP or Windows 7. Upgrading some systems to Windows 10, but leaving others running the older operating systems, presents a challenge. Microsoft isn't releasing security patches for Windows XP anymore, which means Windows XP is more vulnerable by the day to hacking attacks. Windows 7 is viable as of this writing, but upgrading future-proofs user operating systems and applications.

If you find yourself having to deal with a mixed network of modern and legacy systems, you should isolate the legacy systems. Use VLANs to implement network segmentation and get those old systems out of the main network. See the discussion on implementing VLANs later in the chapter for the specifics.

These kinds of considerations vary by location and scenario, so keep the step in mind if you find yourself in an upgrade situation. (It's a helpful step to remember if you run into such scenarios on the CompTIA Network+ exam, too!)

Try This!

What's Compatible?

If you were building a new home network from scratch, which of your existing parts could work in the new network? Do you have older equipment that might have compatibility issues, like an old 100BaseT switch or router?

If you needed to use all of your old equipment, visualize your new network connecting to it and how you might get around some of these issues. Does your old printer have a way to connect to the network directly? Where would you connect your Xbox 360? What if you have older TVs? Will they work with an HDMI-equipped video card?

Create an inventory of your old equipment and jot down any compatibility issues you might imagine taking place.

Internal Connections

Now that you have an idea of your equipment and what you want to do with it, you need to get everything properly connected using structured cabling. You should also begin to install your 802.11 network. Once you connect all your equipment, you're ready to configure your internal VLANs, IP address schemes, and so on.

Structured Cabling

The structured cabling for the Bayland Widgets CAN requires a little thought to accommodate the needs of the various campus buildings. Internally, each of the three buildings can efficiently be wired with CAT 6a to all the workstations. That would provide Gigabit throughout, with all the cabling terminating in the main equipment room (Figure 17-2).

To connect the buildings, the company could use faster pipes, thus providing adequate throughput for a lot of traffic. One option is fiber running some form of 10-Gigabit Ethernet, such as 10GBaseT. The fiber connections for all three buildings would terminate at intermediate distribution frames (IDFs), one in each building. Figure 17-3 shows the IDF documentation/locations. (I'll talk about the SCADA systems in the factory later in this chapter, never fear!)

 EXAM TIP Creative companies invented methods to use unshielded twisted pair (UTP) cabling to connect runs longer than Ethernet's 100-meter limit. These devices were called *copper line drivers/repeaters*, essentially special boxes at each end of the run to manage the much amplified signal. Line drivers enabled installers to avoid using fiber, which was wildly more expensive at the time.

Figure 17-2
Cabling within
each building

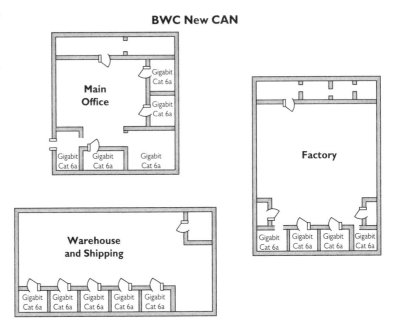

Figure 17-3
Connecting the
buildings

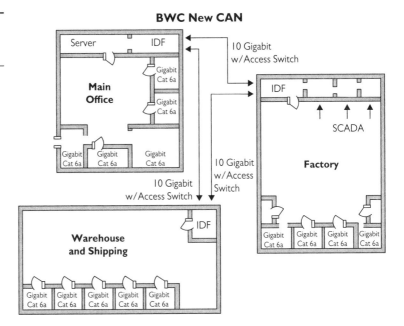

Wireless

A logical option for the Bayland Widgets CAN is to provide high-speed wireless throughout the area. Multiple 802.11ac units should be installed within each building and outside as well, all controlled by a central (or unified) wireless controller (Figure 17-4). This controller would in turn connect to the primary equipment room to provide connectivity with the wired networks.

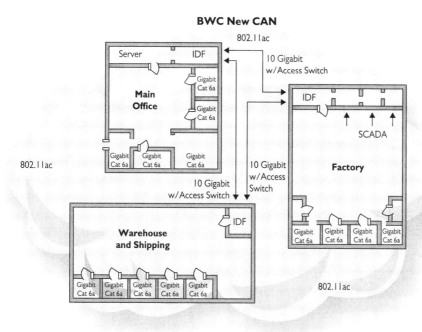

Figure 17-4   Implementing wireless

VLANs

To provide a properly segmented network, the various departments and components in the CAN need to be placed into unique *virtual local area networks (VLANs)*. As you'll recall from Chapter 11, "Advanced Networking Devices," VLANs provide much better control over the network, with security and optimized performance.

Some of the VLANs are based on department. The *quality assurance (QA)* lab doesn't need access to all the same resources as the accounting folks, and vice versa, right? The *testing lab* tests software and firmware and has very different needs than other departments.

But take the network segmentation a step further and also create unique VLANs for network services. The wireless network will get its own VLAN, for example, plus we could split it into multiple VLANs to provide support for *separate private/public networks*. That way visitors will get access to what they need, but not to important internal systems.

We haven't talked about the phone connections (that's the next part of this chapter), but they'll invariably have their own VLAN. The same is true of the industrial control systems that take care of the internal functions of the factory and warehouse. This gets complicated fast!

Set Up the Network IP Address Scheme

Long before you start plugging in RJ-45s, you need to decide on your internal IP addressing scheme. For most SOHO networks, this means picking an arbitrary, unique, internal private IP network ID and then preassigning static IP addresses to servers and WAPs. Plus, pick a DHCP server and preassign DHCP scope IP address ranges.

Try This!

Setting Up an IP Address Scheme

Now it's your turn to set up your dream home network's IP address scheme. List all of the IP address assignments for your network just like you did for Bayland Widgets. Here are the big questions: Which computers get static addresses and which get DHCP? What would you use for a DHCP server?

Setting up the IP addressing scheme beforehand saves you a lot of time and effort once you start installing the systems. Be sure to make multiple copies of this scheme. Print out a copy and put it in the equipment room. Put a copy in your network documentation.

External Connections

No network is an island anymore. At the very least, Bayland Widgets needs an ISP so folks can Google and update their Facebook pages—err, I mean, get work done online. In a SOHO network like some of the ones you've seen earlier in this book, you don't have to deal with many of the issues you'd see in larger networks. A typical home-type ISP (fiber or cable) should be more than enough for a SOHO network in terms of bandwidth.

On the other hand, Bayland Widgets needs to be connected to the Internet all the time (or pay the price in lost business), so the company should consider a couple of options. First would be to have two ISPs, with the second ISP as a fallback in case the primary ISP fails. Another option is to pay up for a highly robust service like a metro Ethernet line.

A *metro Ethernet* connection is usually a dedicated fiber line from the ISP to an office. By using Ethernet rather than one of the remote connectivity options (like SONET or MPLS that you read about in Chapter 13), the installation is less expensive and syncs with the local network more easily.

Regardless of the service used, the location of the main distribution frame (MDF) should be reflected in the documentation for the network. This documentation is also important for the telephone exchanges Bayland Widgets is installing in the next section.

Try This!

What's Available in Your Building?

Home networks won't have a preexisting ISP. You need to determine which ISPs provide service in your neighborhood. Fortunately, there are several great Web sites designed to help you see what you can get. Try this one: https://broadbandnow .com.

Enter your ZIP code (sorry—USA only). Even if you already have an Internet connection at your house, see if you can find a better deal than the one you have. How much money can you save per month?

Unified Communication

Some years ago, TCP/IP-based communications began to replace the traditional PBX-style phone systems in most organizations. This switch enabled companies to minimize wire installation and enabled developers to get more creative with the gear. Technologies such as *Voice over IP (VoIP)* made it possible to communicate by voice right over an IP network, even one as big as the Internet. Today, TCP/IP communications encompass a range of technologies, including voice, video, and messaging. On the cutting edge (led by Cisco) is the field of *unified communication (UC)*. Rather than going old school, Bayland Widgets will implement UC throughout their CAN.

It Started with VoIP

Early VoIP systems usually required multiple cables running to each drop to accommodate the various services offered. Figure 17-5 shows a typical workstation VoIP phone that connects to a drop consisting of two RJ-45 connections, one for data and the other exclusively for VoIP.

These drops would often even go to their own separate switches, and from there into separate *VoIP gateways* that would interface with old-school PBX systems or directly into the telephone network if the latter used *VoIP PBX*. These are the typical purposes and use case scenarios for *computer telephony integration (CTI)*.

 EXAM TIP   Many VoIP systems, such as Skype, are complete Internet services that rely on nothing more than software installed on computers and the computers' microphone/speakers. All of the interconnections to the PSTN are handled in the cloud. While very popular for individuals, these systems, called *unified voice services*, are often considered unacceptable in office environments where people want a more classic "phone experience."

Figure 17-5
Workstation drop

As you'll recall from Chapter 13, "Remote Connectivity," virtually all VoIP systems use the *Real-time Transport Protocol (RTP)* on TCP ports 5004 and 5005, as well as the *Session Initiation Protocol (SIP)* on TCP ports 5060 and 5061. This first-generation VoIP setup that required a separate wired network gave people pause. There really wasn't a critical need for physical separation of the data and the VoIP network, nor did these early VoIP systems handle video conferencing and text messaging. This prompted Cisco to develop and market its Unified Communications family of products.

Unified Communication Features

Of course, VoIP isn't the only communication game in town. As organizations were implementing VoIP, they realized a number of additional communications tasks would benefit from centralized management. Enter unified communication, which adds various additional services to the now-classic VoIP. These services include

- Presence information
- Video conferencing/real-time video
- Fax
- Messaging
- Collaborate tools/workflow

Along with some other real-time communication-oriented tools, these are categorized as *real-time services (RTS)*.

Most of these services should be fairly self-explanatory, but I'd like to elaborate on two of them. *Presence information services* simply refers to technologies that enable users to show they are present for some form of communication. Think of presence as a type of flag that tells others that you are present and capable of accepting other forms of communication (such as a video conference). See Figure 17-6.

Figure 17-6
Presence at work

It's also very important to differentiate between video conferencing and real-time video. *Video teleconferencing (VTC)* is the classic, multicast-based presentation where one presenter pushes out a stream of video to any number of properly configured and authorized multicast clients. These clients do not have a way (normally) to respond via video.

Real-time video, in contrast, enables bidirectional communication via unicast messages. Real-time video offers both video and audio to communicate. Figure 17-7 compares the two types of video communication. Note that unicast traffic enables multiple unique signals.

UC Network Components

A typical UC network consists of three core components: UC devices, UC servers, and UC gateways. Let's take a quick peek at each of these.

A *UC device* is what we used to call the VoIP telephone. In a well-developed UC environment, the UC device handles voice, video, and more (Figure 17-8).

A *UC server* is typically a dedicated box that supports any UC-provided service. In small organizations this might be a single box, but in larger organizations there will be many UC servers. UC servers connect directly to every UC device on the LAN. It's not uncommon to see all the UC servers (as well as the rest of the UC devices) on a separate VLAN.

A *UC gateway* is an edge device, sometimes dedicated but often nothing more than a few extra services added to an existing edge router. That router interfaces with remote UC gateways as well as with PSTN systems and services.

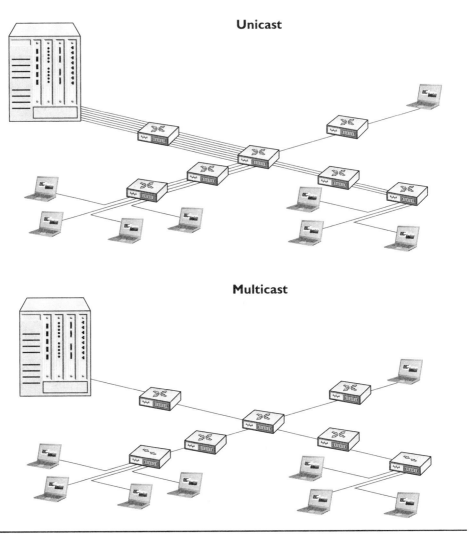

Figure 17-7   Multicast vs. unicast

UC Protocols

Unified communication leans heavily on SIP and RTP protocols, but can also use H.323 or MGCP. *H.323* is the most commonly used video presentation protocol (or *codec*), and it runs on TCP port 1720. *Media Gateway Control Protocol (MGCP)* is designed from the ground up to be a complete VoIP or video presentation connection and session controller; in essence, taking over all the work from VoIP the SIP protocol used to do and all the work from video presentation done by H.323. MGCP uses TCP ports 2427 and 2727.

Figure 17-8
Cisco Unified
IP Phone

SIP Trunking

Several companies offer cloud-based IC management solutions that use SIP to provide services. Called *SIP trunking*, the service can connect PBX systems from multiple locations seamlessly over the Internet via virtual connections called *SIP trunks*.

VTC and Medianets

All forms of communication over IP networks have some degree of sensitivity to disruption and slowdowns, but video teleconferencing is particularly susceptible. No one wants to sit in on a video conference that continually stops and jitters due to a poor or slow Internet connection. Medianets help to eliminate or reduce this problem. A *medianet* is a network of (typically) far-flung routers and servers that provide—via *quality of service (QoS)* and other tools—sufficient bandwidth for VTC. Plus, medianets work with UC servers (or sometimes by themselves) to distribute video conferences.

Medianets can be wildly complex or very simple. A medianet could be two gateway routers with enough QoS smarts to open bandwidth for active VTCs as soon as they are detected. A medianet could be a huge multinational company with its own group of high-powered edge routers, spanning the globe with an MPLS-based VLAN, working with UC servers to support tens of thousands of voice and video conversations going on continually throughout its organization.

The CompTIA Network+ exam covers only a few rudimentary aspects of medianets, especially concentrating on a few protocols, so we don't need to dive too deeply. One aspect that the CompTIA Network+ exam does cover that is not too interesting is an early adoption of VTC using an ancient technology called ISDN.

ISDN vs. IP/SIP

Many organizations using VTC still rely on products based on the old *Integrated Services Digital Network (ISDN)* service that we discussed in Chapter 13. ISDN offers 128-Kbps bandwidth, which seems very slow by modern standards. But by using multiple ISDN channels, a special VTC over ISDN standard called *H.320* combined with aggressive compression enabled the VTC industry to roll out a number of not-too-shabby VTC systems all over the world. These were not based on IP addresses (so you couldn't connect via the Internet—which was OK back then because there wasn't an Internet), but they worked pretty well given the times.

With the Internet now dominant and IP/SIP-based VTC the norm, ISDN-based VTC is being replaced fairly quickly these days by high-speed Internet connections. However, it's important enough that CompTIA wants you to understand that ISDN-based VTC is still out there; and ISDN's 128-Kbps speed can be a real challenge to integrate into a typical high-speed Ethernet network.

QoS and Medianets

Medianets are all about the quality of service. But this isn't the simple QoS that you learned about back in Chapter 11. VTC is the ultimate real-time application and it needs a level of QoS for performance that very few other applications need.

When we talk about QoS for medianets, we need to develop the concept of *differentiated services (DiffServ)*. DiffServ is the underlying architecture that makes all the QoS stuff work. The cornerstone of DiffServ is two pieces of data that go into every IP header on every piece of data: DSCP and ECN. DSCP stands for *differentiated services code point* and ECN stands for *explicit congestion notification*. These two comprise the differentiated services field (Figure 17-9).

Figure 17-9
DS field

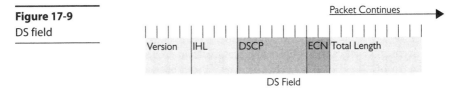

The first six bits are DSCP, making a total of eight classes of service. A *class of service (CoS)* is just a value you may use (think of it like a group) to apply to services, ports, or whatever your QoS device might use. Figure 17-10 shows a sample from my home router. My router has four QoS priority queues and I can assign a CoS to every port.

ECN is a two-bit field where QoS-aware devices can place a "congestion encountered" signal to other QoS-aware devices. The following four values may show in that field:

- **00**   Not QoS aware (default)
- **01**   QoS aware, no congestion
- **10**   QoS aware, no congestion
- **11**   QoS aware, congestion encountered

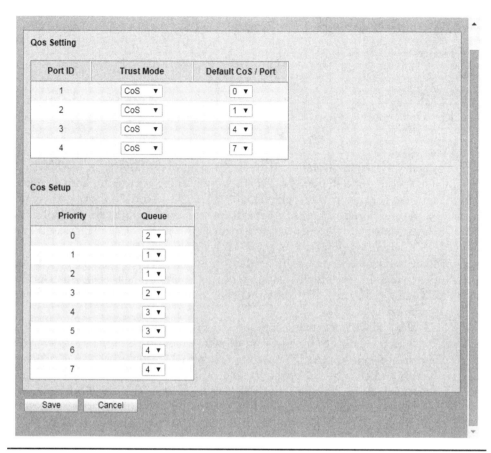

Figure 17-10 CoS settings on router

ICS

Pretty much any industry that makes things, changes things, or moves things is filled with equipment to do the jobs that have to be done. From making mousetraps to ice cream, any given industrial plant, power grid, or pipeline is filled with stuff that needs to be monitored and stuff that needs to be controlled.

Here are some examples of things to monitor:

- Temperature
- Power levels
- Fill quantity
- Illumination
- Mass

And these are some examples of the things to control:

- Heaters
- Voltage
- Pumps
- Retractable roofs
- Valves

For Bayland Widgets, it's all about the robots that control the factory, the machines that help automate packing and shipping, and the air-conditioning controls for both buildings.

In the early days of automation, you might have a single person monitoring a machine that produced something. When the temperature hit a certain point, for example, that person—the *operator*—might open a valve or turn a knob to make changes and keep the machine functioning properly. As machines became more complex, the role of the operator likewise changed. He or she needed to monitor more functions and, sometimes, more machines. Eventually, computers were brought in to help manage the machines. The overall system that monitors and controls machines today is called an *industrial control system (ICS)*.

The ICS isn't a new concept. It's been around for over 100 years using technology such as telescopes and horns to monitor and using mechanisms and pneumatics to control from a distance. But ICSs really started to take off when computers combined with digital monitors and controls. Over the last few years many ICSs have taken on more and more personal-computer aspects such as Windows- or Linux-based operating systems, Intel-style processors, and specialized PCs. Today, ICS is moving from stand-alone networks to interconnect with the Internet, bringing up serious issues for security. Competent network techs know the basic ICS variations and the components that make up those systems.

DCS

An ICS has three basic components: input/output (I/O) functions on the machine, a controller, and the interface for the operator. Input and output work through sensors and actuators. *Sensors* monitor things like temperature, for example, and the *actuator* makes changes that modify that temperature. The *controller*, some sort of computer, knows enough to manage the process, such as "keep the temperature between 50 and 55 degrees Fahrenheit." The operator watches some kind of monitor—the *interface*—and intervenes if necessary (Figure 17-11). Let's scale this up to a factory and add a little more complexity.

What if you have multiple machines that accomplish a big task, like in a factory that produces some finished product? The new widget at Bayland Widgets, for example, is produced in stages, with the machine at each stage needing monitoring and control. In the early days of computers, when computers were really expensive, the controller was a single computer. All the sensors from each of the machines had to provide feedback to that single controller. The controller would compute and then send signals to the various actuators to change things, managing the process. See Figure 17-12.

Figure 17-11

A simple ICS

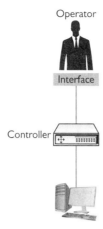

Operator

Interface

Controller

Figure 17-12

An early computer-assisted ICS

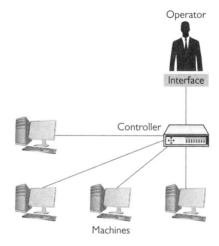

Operator

Interface

Controller

Machines

As computing power went up and costs when down, it made much more sense to put smaller controllers directly on each machine, to distribute the computing load. This is a *distributed control system (DCS)*.

In a modern DCS, each of the local controllers connects (eventually) to a centralized controller—called the *ICS server*—where global changes can be made managed (Figure 17-13). Operators at the ICS server for Bayland Widgets, for example, could direct the controllers managing the robots to change production from green widgets to blue widgets.

Operators interact with controllers through a control or computer called a *human machine interface (HMI)*. Early HMIs were usually custom-made boxes with gauges and switches. Today, an HMI is most likely a PC running a custom, touch-screen interface (Figure 17-14). It's important to appreciate that HMIs are not general purpose. You wouldn't run Microsoft Office on an HMI, even if the PC on which it is built is capable of such things. It's very common for an HMI to show a single interface that never changes.

Figure 17-13
A simple DCS

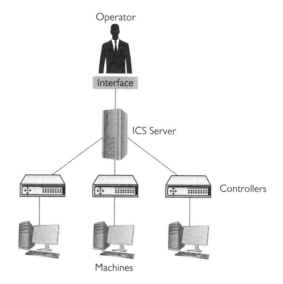

Figure 17-14
SIMATIC HMI
Basic Panel with
a touch screen
(© Siemens AG
2014, All rights
reserved)

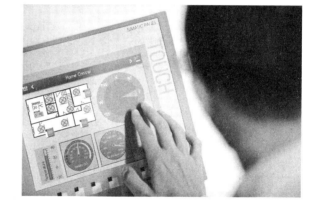

PLC

A DCS makes sense for a process that requires a continuous flow. The sensors provide real-time feedback to the controllers; the controllers are sophisticated enough to keep the machines functioning properly, making changes via the actuators. In a process that follows specific, ordered steps, in contrast, a different kind of system would make more sense.

A classic *programmable logic controller (PLC)* is a computer that controls a machine according to a set of ordered steps (Figure 17-15). Take for example a machine that produces cakes. Each step in the process of producing a cake follows a certain pattern (add ingredients, mix, bake, etc.) that has to go in order and in the proper timing. The PLC monitors sensors (like timers and oven temperatures) and tells the machine when to do the next step in the process.

Figure 17-15
Siemens SIMATIC
S7-1500 PLC
(© Siemens AG
2014, All rights
reserved)

NOTE ICS predates Ethernet and the TCP/IP protocols, but the predominance of Ethernet and TCP/IP has created a number of ICS solutions that use Ethernet and TCP/IP instead of proprietary cabling systems and communication protocols. If you were going to build an ICS from scratch today, odds are good that you would use Ethernet as your interconnection of choice.

SCADA

A *supervisory control and data acquisition (SCADA)* system is a subset of ICS. Generally, a SCADA system has the same basic components as a DCS, but differs in two very important ways. First, a SCADA system is designed for large-scale, distributed processes such as power grids, pipelines, and railroads. Second, due to the distance involved, a SCADA system must function with the idea that remote devices may or may not have ongoing communication with the central control.

Remote Terminal Unit

In general, a SCADA system is going to be a DCS using servers, HMIs, sensors, and actuators. The big difference is the replacement of controllers with devices called *remote terminal units (RTUs)*. RTUs provide the same function as a controller but have two major differences. First, an RTU is designed to have some amount of autonomy in case it loses connection with the central control. Second, an RTU is designed to take advantage of some form of long-distance communication such as telephony, fiber optic, or cellular WANs (Figure 17-16). As you might imagine, the fear of interception is a big deal with SCADA systems these days, so let's discuss the need for network segmentation on a bigger scale than previously described in the chapter.

Figure 17-16
Substation
Automation and
RTUs (© Siemens
AG 2014, All
rights reserved)

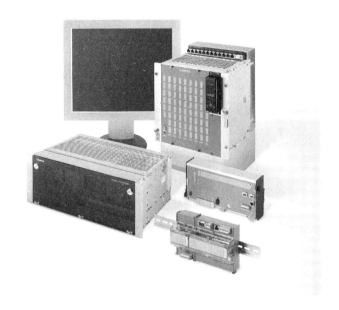

Network Segmentation

It's pretty easy to say that a network failure isn't a happy occurrence. On the lowest end, losing your network in your home is going to make someone very unhappy when they can't watch the latest episode of *Orange Is the New Black* on Netflix. Taking it to the other extreme, many ICSs are incredibly crucial for the needs of everyday living. From the DCSs that run an oil refinery to the SCADA systems keeping our electrical infrastructure up and running, the potential downside of a catastrophic failure is far worse than that of missing a show!

Security isn't the only reason we segment networks. We also reduce network congestion and limit network problems through segmentation. We segment to optimize performance. We segment to be in compliance with standards, laws, or best practices. We also segment for easier troubleshooting.

 EXAM TIP Network segmentation is done for security, performance optimization, load balancing, and compliance.

One of the best tools to help us understand network segmentation is the OSI seven-layer model, in particular the first three layers:

- **Layer 1 (Physical)** Physically separating your network from every other network. This is also known as an *air gap*.

- **Layer 2 (Data Link)** Separating a physically connected network into separate broadcast domains. Think VLANs here.

- **Layer 3 (Network)**   Separating broadcast domains by using different subnets or blocking IP routes.

- **Above Layer 3**   VPNs, separate SSIDs, separate Windows domains, virtualization

The CompTIA Network+ covers a number of situations where network segmentation is important.

Segmentation and Industrial Control Systems

All forms of ICS are by definition closed networks. A *closed network* is any network that strictly controls who and what may connect to it. However, there are two places where we begin to see connectivity. In many SCADA systems, it is very convenient to use public wireless networks to connect RTUs, and, in some cases, we connect SCADA servers to the Internet to provide intranet access. The biggest single line of defense for these two scenarios are virtual private network connections. It's impossible to find any form of SCADA/ICS that doesn't use a VPN in the cases where it must be open to the public Internet.

Chapter Review

Questions

1. When designing a basic network, which of the following are factors to consider? (Select two.)

    A. Ease of use

    B. List of requirements

    C. Equipment limitations

    D. Cost of installation

2. Which of the following is a unique server function?

    A. Network login

    B. High graphics speed

    C. Large amounts of RAM

    D. Network authentication

3. What standard is used by most NAS devices, enabling them to connect easily to almost any network?

    A. VLAN

    B. SIP

    C. RTU

    D. CIFS

4. Adding a generator to a server room is an example of what?

    A. Power conversion

    B. Power redundancy

    C. UPS

    D. Load balancing

5. H.323 uses which TCP port number?

    A. 5004

    B. 5060

    C. 2427

    D. 1720

6. The RTP protocol runs on top of which protocol?

    A. UC server

    B. SIP

    C. MGCP

    D. H.323

7. Which of the following devices would most likely be a UC gateway?

    A. VoIP telephone

    B. Desktop running Windows server

    C. Managed switch

    D. Router

8. What is a medianet's primary tool to ensure bandwidth for VTC?

    A. MPLS

    B. RTU

    C. QoS

    D. ISDN

9. The centerpiece of any ICS will be what?

    A. Sensors

    B. PLCs

    C. ICS server

    D. HMI

10. Which of the following differentiates a PLC from a DCS controller?

    A. Sequential control

    B. Sensors

    C. Operator

    D. Actuator

Answers

1. **B** and **C.** The objectives list seven categories. The two listed here are a list of requirements and equipment limitations.

2. **D.** Of the options listed, the only one that specifically applies to servers is network authentication.

3. **D.** A NAS device uses the Common Internet File System to connect easily to almost any network.

4. **B.** A generator provides power redundancy.

5. **D.** H.323 uses TCP port 1720.

6. **B.** RTP runs on top of the Session Initiation Protocol (SIP).

7. **D.** A UC gateway is most likely a router.

8. **C.** Quality of service enables medianets to ensure bandwidth for video teleconferencing.

9. **C.** The centerpiece of any ICS is the ICS server.

10. **A.** A PLC traditionally uses ordered steps to control a machine.

## CHAPTER 18

Managing Risk

The CompTIA Network+ certification exam expects you to know how to

- 1.4 Given a scenario, configure the appropriate IP addressing components
- 3.1 Given a scenario, use appropriate documentation and diagrams to manage the network
- 3.2 Compare and contrast business continuity and disaster recovery concepts
- 3.3 Explain common scanning, monitoring and patching processes and summarize their expected outputs
- 3.5 Identify policies and best practices
- 4.6 Explain common mitigation techniques and their purposes
- 5.2 Given a scenario, use the appropriate tool

To achieve these goals, you must be able to

- Describe the industry standards for risk management
- Discuss contingency planning
- Examine safety standards and actions

Companies need to manage risk, to minimize the dangers posed by internal and external threats. They need policies in place for expected dangers and also procedures established for things that will happen eventually. This is contingency planning. Finally, every company needs proper safety policies. Let's look at all three facets of managing risk.

Test Specific

Risk Management

IT *risk management* is the process of how organizations deal with the bad things (let's call them attacks) that take place on their networks. The entire field of IT security is based on the premise that somewhere, at some time, something will attack some part of your network. The attack may take as many forms as your paranoia allows: intentional, unintentional, earthquake, accident, war, meteor impact ... whatever.

What do we do about all these attacks? You can't afford to build up a defense for every possible attack—nor should you need to, for a number of reasons. First, different attacks have different probabilities of taking place. The probability of a meteor taking out your server room is very low. There is, however, a pretty good chance that some clueless user will eventually load malware on their company-issued laptop. Second, different attacks/ potential problems have different impacts. If a meteor hits your server room, you're going to have a big, expensive problem. If a user forgets his password, it's not a big deal and is easily dealt with.

The CompTIA Network+ certification covers a number of issues that roughly fit under the idea of risk management. Let's run through each of these individually.

NOTE One of the scariest attacks is a data breach. A *data breach* is any form of attack where secured data is taken or destroyed. The many corporate database hacks we've seen over the last few years—databases containing information about user passwords, credit card information, and other personal identification—are infamous examples of data breaches.

Security Policies

A *security policy* is a written document that defines how an organization will protect its IT infrastructure. There are hundreds of different security policies, but for the scope of the CompTIA Network+ certification exam we only need to identify just a few of the most common ones. These policies include internal and external ones that affect just about every organization.

NOTE The CompTIA Network+ exam, is in my opinion, way too light in its coverage of security policies. The CompTIA Security+ exam does a much better job, but even it is a bit slim. Check out the Wikipedia entry for "security policy" to discover the many types of security policies in use today.

Acceptable Use Policy

The *acceptable use policy (AUP)* defines what is and what is not acceptable to do on an organization's computers. It's arguably the most famous of all security policies as this is one document that pretty much everyone who works for any organization is required to read, and in many cases sign, before they can start work. The following are some provisions contained in a typical acceptable use policy:

- **Ownership** Equipment and any proprietary information stored on the organization's computers are the property of the organization.
- **Network Access** Users will access only information they are authorized to access.
- **Privacy/Consent to Monitoring** Anything users do on the organization's computers is not private. The organization will monitor what is being done on computers at any time.

- **Illegal Use**   No one may use an organization's computers for anything that breaks a law. (This is usually broken down into many subheadings, such as introducing malware, hacking, scanning, spamming, and so forth.)

> **NOTE**   Many organizations require employees to sign an acceptable use policy, especially if it includes a consent to monitoring clause.

Network Access Policies

Companies need a policy that defines who can do what on the company's network. The *network access policy* defines who may access the network, how they may access the network, and what they can access. Network access policies may be embedded into policies such as VPN policy, password policy, encryption policy, and many others, but they need to be in place. Let's look at a couple specifically called out on the CompTIA Network+ exam objectives.

- **Privileged user agreement policy**   A privileged user has access to resources just short of those available to administrators. Anyone granted one of those accounts should know the policies on what he or she can access without escalating a permission request. (This sort of policy also reflects on standard employee management of *role separation*, where users might have privileged access, but only to content that fits in their role in the company.)

- **Password policy**   Password policies revolve around strength of password and rotation frequency (how often users have to change their passwords, password reuse, and so on.) See "Training" later in this chapter for details.

- **Data loss prevention policy**   Data loss prevention (DLP) can mean a lot of things, from redundant hardware and backups, to access levels to data. A DLP policy takes into consideration many of these factors and helps minimize the risk of loss or theft of essential company data.

- **Remote access policy**   A remote access policy (like the VPN policy mentioned a moment ago) enforces rules on how and when and from what device users can access company resources from remote locations. A typical restriction might be no access from an open wireless portal, for example.

Policies reinforce an organization's IT security. Policies help define what equipment is used, how data is organized, and what actions people take to ensure the security of an organization. Policies tell an organization how to handle almost any situation that might arise (such as disaster recovery, covered later in this chapter).

Externally Imposed Policies

Government laws and regulations impose policies on organizations. There are rules restricting what a company employee can bring with him or her to a conference in another country, for example. There are security policies that provide *international export controls* that restrict what technology—including hardware and software—can be exported.

The *licensing restrictions* on most commercial software allow users to travel with that software to other countries. Microsoft sells worldwide, for example, so visiting Beijing in the spring with the Microsoft Office 365 suite installed on your laptop is no big deal. Commercial encryption software, on the other hand, generally falls into the forbidden-for-foreign-travel list.

Data affected by laws, such as health information spelled out in the Health Insurance Portability and Accountability Act of 1996 (HIPAA), should not be stored on devices traveling to other countries. Often such data requires special *export licenses*.

Most organizations devote resources to comply with externally imposed policies. Just about every research university in the United States, for example, has export control officers who review all actions that risk crossing federal laws and regulations. It's a really huge subject that the CompTIA Network+ only lightly touches.

Adherence to Policies

Given the importance of policies, it's also imperative for an organization to adhere to its policies strictly. This can often be a challenge. As technologies change, organizations must review and update policies to reflect those changes.

Try This!

Checking Out Real-World Security Policies

Security policies can be interesting, so try this! Go to the SANS institute Web site and check out all of their free, cool, sample security policies:

https://www.sans.org/security-resources/policies

Change Management

An IT infrastructure is an ever-changing thing. Applications are updated, operating systems change, server configurations adjust; change is a tricky part of managing an infrastructure. Change needs to happen, but not at the cost of losing security. The process of creating change in your infrastructure in an organized, controlled, safe way is called *change management.*

Change management usually begins with a *change management team*. This team, consisting of people from all over your organization, is tasked with the job of investigating, testing, and authorizing all but the simplest changes to your network.

Changes tend to be initiated at two levels: strategic-level changes, typically initiated by management and major in scope (for example, we're going to switch all the servers from Windows to Linux); and infrastructure-level changes, typically initiated by a department by making a request to the change management team. The CompTIA Network+ exam stresses the latter type of change, where *you* are the person who will go before the change management team. Let's go over what to expect when dealing with change management.

Initiating the Change

The first part of many change processes is a request from a part of the organization. Let's say you're in charge of IT network support for a massive art department. There are over 150 graphic artists, each manning a powerful macOS workstation. The artists have discovered a new graphics program that they claim will dramatically improve their ability to do what they do. After a quick read of the program's features on its Web site, you're also convinced that this a good idea. It's now your job to make this happen.

Create a *change request*. Depending on the organization, this can be a highly official document or, for a smaller organization, nothing more than a detailed e-mail message. Whatever the case, you need to document the reason for this change. A good change request will include the following:

- **Type of change**   Software and hardware changes are obviously part of this category, but this could also encompass issues like backup methods, work hours, network access, workflow changes, and so forth.

- **Configuration procedures**   What is it going to take to make this happen? Who will help? How long will it take?

- **Rollback process**   If this change in some way makes such a negative impact that going back to how things were before the change is needed, what will it take to roll back to the previous configuration?

- **Potential impact**   How will this change impact the organization? Will it save time? Save money? Increase efficiency? Will it affect the perception of the organization?

- **Notification**   What steps will be taken to notify the organization about this change?

Dealing with the Change Management Team

With your change request in hand, it's time to get the change approved. In most organizations, change management teams meet at fixed intervals, so there's usually a deadline for you to be ready at a certain time. From here, most organizations will rely heavily on a well-written change request form to get the details. The *approval process* usually consists of considering the issues listed in the change request, but also management approval and funding.

Making the Change Happen

Once your change is approved, the real work starts. Equipment, software, tools, and so forth must be purchased. Configuration teams need to be trained. The change committee must provide an adequate *maintenance window*: the time it will take to implement and thoroughly test the coming changes. As part of that process, the committee must *authorize downtime* for systems, departments, and so on. Your job is to provide *notification of the change* to those people who will be affected, if possible providing alternative workplaces or equipment.

Documenting the Change

The ongoing and last step of the change is *change management documentation*. All changes must be clearly documented, including but not limited to:

- Network configurations, such as server settings, router configurations, and so on
- Additions to the network, such as additional servers, switches, and so on
- Physical location changes, such as moved workstations, relocated switches, and so on

Patching and Updates

It's often argued whether applying patches and updates to existing systems fits under change management or regular maintenance. In general, all but the most major patches and updates are really more of a maintenance issue than a change management issue. But, given the similarity of patching to change management, it seems that here is as good a place as any to discuss patching.

 EXAM TIP CompTIA calls regularly updating operating systems and applications to avoid security threats *patch management*.

When we talk about patching and updates, we aren't just talking about the handy tools provided to us by Microsoft Windows or Ubuntu Linux. Almost every piece of software and firmware on almost every type of equipment you own is subject to patching and updating: printers, routers, wireless access points, desktops, programmable logic controllers (PLCs) … everything needs a patch or update now and then.

What Do We Update?

In general, specific types of updates routinely take place. Let's cover each of these individually, starting with the easiest and most famous, operating system (OS) updates.

OS updates are easily the most common type of update. Individuals install automatic updates on their OSs with impunity, but when you're updating a large number of systems, especially critical nodes like servers, it's never a good idea to apply all OS updates without a little bit of due diligence beforehand. Most operating systems provide some method of network server-based patching, giving administrators the opportunity to test first and then distribute patches when they desire.

All systems use device drivers, and they are another part of the system we often need to patch. In general, we only apply *driver updates* to fix an incompatibility, incorporate new features, or repair a bug. Since device drivers are only present in systems with full-blown operating systems, all OS-updating tools will include device drivers in their updates. Many patches will include feature changes and updates, as well as security vulnerability patches.

Feature changes/updates are just what they sound like: adding new functionality to the system. Remember back in the old days when a touchscreen phone only understood a single touch? Then some phone operating system came out to provide multi-touch. Competitors responded with patches to their own phone OSs that added the multi-touch feature.

All software of any complexity has flaws. Hardware changes, exposing flaws in the software that supports that hardware; newer applications create unexpected interactions; security standards change over time. All of these factors mean that responsible companies patch their products after they release them. How they approach the patching depends on scope: *major vs. minor updates* require different actions.

When a major vulnerability to an OS or other system is discovered, vendors tend to respond quickly by creating a fix in the form of a *vulnerability patch*. If the vulnerability is significant, that patch is usually made available as soon as it is complete. Sometimes, these high-priority security patches are even pushed to the end user right away.

Less significant vulnerabilities get patched as part of a regular patch cycle. You may have noticed that on the second Wednesday of each month, Microsoft-based computers reboot. Since October of 2003, Microsoft has sent out patches that have been in development and are ready for deployment on the second Tuesday of the month. This has become known as *Patch Tuesday*. These patches are released for a wide variety of Microsoft products, including operating systems, productivity applications, utilities, and more.

Firmware updates are far less common than software updates and usually aren't as automated (although a few motherboard makers might challenge this statement). In general, firmware patching is a manual process and is done in response to a known problem or issue. Keep in mind that firmware updates are inherently risky, because in many cases it's difficult to recover from a bad patch.

How to Patch

In a network environment, patching is a routine but critical process. Here are a few important steps that take place in almost every scenario of a network patch environment:

- **Research** As a critical patch is announced, it's important to do some research to verify that the patch is going to do what you need it to do and that people who have already installed the patch aren't having problems.

- **Test** It's always a good idea to test a patch on a test system when possible.

- **Configuration backups** Backing up configurations is critical, especially when backing up firmware. The process of backing up a configuration varies from platform to platform, but almost all PCs can back up their system setups, and switches and routers have well-known "backup-config" style commands.

A single system may have many patches over time. When necessary, you might find yourself having to perform a *downgrade* or *rollback* of the patch, returning to a patch that is one or two versions old. This is usually pretty easy on PCs because OSs track each update. With firmware, the best way to handle this is to track each upgrade and keep a separate copy for each patch in case a downgrade/rollback is needed.

NOTE Patches, whether major or minor, require thorough testing before techs or administrators apply them to clients throughout the network. Sometimes, though, a hot fix might slip through to patch a security hole that then breaks other things inadvertently. In those cases, by following good patch management procedures, you can roll back—the Windows terminology—or downgrade by removing the patch. You can then push an upgrade when a better patch is made available.

Training

End users are probably the primary source of security problems for any organization. We must increase *end user awareness and training* so they know what to look for and how to act to avoid or reduce attacks. Training users is a critical piece of managing risk. While a formal course is preferred, it's up to the IT department to do what it can to make sure users have an understanding of the following:

- **Security policies** Users need to read, understand, and, when necessary, sign all pertinent security policies.
- **Passwords** Make sure users understand basic password skills, such as sufficient length and complexity, refreshing passwords regularly, and password control. Traditional best practices for complexity, for example, use a minimum length of 8 characters—longer is better—with a combination of upper- and lowercase letters, numbers, and nonalphanumeric symbols, like !, $, &, and so on. Management should insist on new passwords every month, plus not allow users to reuse a password for a period of a year or more

EXAM TIP The best-password practices listed here are what you're going to see on the CompTIA Network+ N10-007 exam. Don't miss those questions. Nevertheless…

   In 2017, the National Institute of Standards and Technologies released revised password guidelines that flip the traditional best practices on their head. Gone is the need for multiple types of characters—they're too easy to crack. Gone is the regular rotation requirement (and thus reuse restrictions). What they've added is that you check a suggested password against the very long lists of passwords already in the cracking software. See Chapter 19 for more on password cracking techniques.

- **System and workplace security** Make sure users understand how to keep their workstations secure through screen locking and not storing written passwords in plain sight.
- **Social engineering** Users need to recognize typical social-engineering tactics and know how to counter them.
- **Malware** Teach users to recognize malware attacks and train them to deal with them.

Points of Failure

System failures happen; that's not something we can completely prevent. The secret to dealing with failures is to avoid a *single point of failure*: one system that, if it fails, will bring down an entire process, workflow, or, worse yet, an entire organization.

It's easy to say, "Oh, we will just make two of everything!" (This would create *redundancy* where needed.) But you can't simply make two of everything. That would create far too much unnecessary hardware and administration. Sure, redundancy is fairly easy to do, but the trick is to determine where the redundancy is needed to avoid single points of failure without too much complexity, cost, or administration. We do this process by identifying two things: critical assets and critical nodes.

Critical Assets

Every organization has assets that are critical to the operation of the organization. A bakery may have one PLC-controlled oven, a sales group might have a single database, or a Web server rack might only be connected to the Internet through one ISP. The process of determining critical assets is tricky and is usually a senior management process.

Critical Nodes

Unlike critical assets, critical nodes are very much unique to IT equipment: servers, routers, workstations, printers, and so forth. Identifying critical nodes is usually much clearer than identifying critical assets because of the IT nature of critical nodes and the fact that the IT department is always going to be painfully aware of what nodes are critical. Here are a few examples of critical nodes:

- A file server that contains critical project files
- A single Web server
- A single printer (assuming printed output is critical to the organization)
- An edge router

High Availability

Once you have identified the critical nodes in your network, it's important to ensure they keep working without interruption or downtime; in other words, to make sure critical systems have *high availability (HA)*. Core to building high availability into a network is *failover*, the ability for backup systems to detect when a master has failed and then to take over.

How does all the network traffic know to use the backup system? That's where the idea of a virtual IP comes in. A *virtual IP* is a single IP address shared by multiple systems. If that sounds a lot like what Network Address Translation (NAT) does, well, you're right. The public IP address on NATed networks is a common implementation of a virtual IP, but virtual IPs are not limited to NAT. The way servers can fail over without dropping off the network is for all the servers in the cluster to accept traffic from a single, common IP—this common address is considered a virtual IP.

Building with high availability in mind extends to more than just servers; default gateway routers are another critical node that can be protected by adding redundant backups. The two protocols used to provide this redundancy are the open standard *Virtual Router Redundancy Protocol (VRRP)* and the Cisco proprietary *Hot Standby Router Protocol (HSRP)*. The nice thing about VRRP and HSRP is that, conceptually, they both perform the same function. They take multiple routers and gang them together into a single virtual router with a single virtual IP address that clients use as a default gateway.

NOTE VRRP and HSRP do *not* provide *load balancing*, where multiple machines work together to share operational work. With these protocols, only one router is active at a time. You definitely get fault tolerance though.

Redundancy

Redundancy is an important factor in maintaining the organization's ability to continue operations after a disaster. This means the organization must maintain redundant systems, equipment, data, and even personnel. It also may mean the organization maintains redundant facilities, such as alternate processing sites (see "Business Continuity" later in the chapter for more details). Redundant processes are also important, since critical data or equipment (or even public infrastructure, such as power) may be unavailable, forcing the business to come up with *alternative business practices* for conducting its mission.

An organization can achieve redundancy in systems and data in several different ways, or usually in a combination of several ways at once. Redundancy is strongly related to the concept of *fault tolerance*, which is the ability of the system to continue to operate in the event of a failure of one of its components. Redundant systems, as well as the components they comprise, contribute to fault tolerance. Two ways to provide for both redundancy and fault tolerance include *clustering* and *load balancing*, terms that are usually associated with servers, data storage, and networking equipment (such as clustered firewalls or proxy servers), but that could be applied to a variety of assets and services. Data redundancy can also be provided by backups, which can be restored in the event of an emergency.

Clustering, in the traditional sense, means to have multiple pieces of equipment, such as servers, connected, which appear to the user and the network as one logical device, providing data and services to the organization. Clusters usually share high-speed networking connections as well as data stores and applications and are configured to provide redundancy if a single member of the cluster fails.

NOTE The term virtual as used in this section means something slightly different than it did in Chapter 15, "Virtualization and Cloud Computing," where it was used to describe software-only servers and networking devices. Here, virtual is about multiple routers being addressed—by the virtual IP— as a single logical router.

Standard Business Documents

Dealing with third-party vendors is an ongoing part of any organization. When you are dealing with third parties, you must have some form of agreement that defines the relationship between you and the third party. The CompTIA Network+ exam expects you to know about five specific business documents: a service level agreement, a memorandum of understanding, a multi-source agreement, a statement of work, and a nondisclosure agreement. Let's review each of these documents.

Service Level Agreement

A *service level agreement (SLA)* is a document between a customer and a service provider that defines the scope, quality, and terms of the service to be provided. In CompTIA terminology, *SLA requirements* are a common part of business continuity and disaster recovery (both covered a little later in this chapter).

SLAs are common in IT, given the large number of services provided. Some of the more common SLAs in IT are provided by ISPs to customers. A typical SLA from an ISP contains the following:

- **Definition of the service provided**   Defines the minimum and/or maximum bandwidth and describes any recompense for degraded services or downtime.

- **Equipment**   Defines what equipment, if any, the ISP provides. It also specifies the type of connections to be provided.

- **Technical support**   Defines the level of technical support that will be given, such as phone support, Web support, and in-person support. This also defines costs for that support.

Memorandum of Understanding

A *memorandum of understanding (MOU)* is a document that defines an agreement between two parties in situations where a legal contract wouldn't be appropriate. An MOU defines the duties the parties commit to perform for each other and a time frame for the MOU. An MOU is common between companies that have only occasional business relations with each other. For example, all of the hospitals in a city might generate an MOU to take on each other's patients in case of a disaster such as a fire or tornado. This MOU would define costs, contacts, logistics, and so forth.

Multi-source Agreement

Manufacturers of various network hardware agree to a *multi-source agreement (MSA)*, a document that details the interoperability of their components. For example, two companies might agree that their gigabit interface converters (GBICs) will work in Cisco and Juniper switches.

Statement of Work

A *statement of work (SOW)* is in essence a legal contract between a vendor and a customer. An SOW defines the services and products the vendor agrees to supply and the time frames in which to supply them. A typical SOW might be between an IT security company and a customer. An SOW tends to be a detailed document, clearly explaining what the vendor needs to do. Time frames must also be very detailed, with milestones through the completion of the work.

Nondisclosure Agreement

Any company with substantial intellectual property will require new employees—and occasionally even potential candidates—to sign a nondisclosure agreement (NDA). An NDA is a legal document that prohibits the signer from disclosing any company secrets learned as part of his or her job.

Security Preparedness

Preparing for incidents is the cornerstone of managing risk. If you decide to take the next logical CompTIA certification, the CompTIA Security+, you'll find an incredibly detailed discussion of how the IT security industry spends inordinate amounts of time and energy creating a secure IT environment. But for the CompTIA Network+ certification, there are two issues that come up: vulnerability scanning and penetration testing.

Vulnerability Scanning

Given the huge number of vulnerabilities out there, it's impossible for even the most highly skilled technician to find them by manually inspecting your infrastructure. The best way to know your infrastructure's vulnerabilities is to run some form of program—a *vulnerability scanner*—that will inspect a huge number of potential vulnerabilities and create a report for you to then act upon.

There is no single vulnerability scanner that works for every aspect of your infrastructure. Instead, a good network tech will have a number of utilities that work for their type of network infrastructure. Here are a few of the more popular vulnerability scanners and where they are used.

Microsoft Baseline Security Analyzer (MBSA) is designed to test individual systems. It's getting a little old, but still does a great job of testing one Microsoft Windows system for vulnerabilities.

Nmap is a *port scanner*, a software tool for testing a network for vulnerabilities. *Port scanning* queries individual nodes, looking for open or vulnerable ports and creating a report. Actually, it might be unfair to say that Nmap is *only* a port scanner, as it adds other useful tools. Written by Gordon Lyon, Nmap is very popular, free, and well maintained. Figure 18-1 shows sample output from Nmap, Zenmap GUI version.

When you need to perform more serious vulnerability testing, it's common to turn to more aggressive and powerful comprehensive testers. There are plenty out there, but two dominate the field: Nessus and OpenVAS. *Nessus* (Figure 18-2), from Tenable Network Security, is arguably the first truly comprehensive vulnerability testing tool and has been around for almost two decades. Nessus is an excellent, well-known tool. Once free to everyone, Nessus is still free for home users, but commercial users must purchase a subscription.

OpenVAS is an open source fork of Nessus that is also extremely popular and, in the opinion of many security types, superior to Nessus.

You need to be careful not to use the term *vulnerability scanning* to mean "just running some program to find weaknesses." Vulnerability scanning is only a small part of a more strategic program called *vulnerability management*, an ongoing process of identifying vulnerabilities and dealing with them. The tools we use are a small but important part of the overall process.

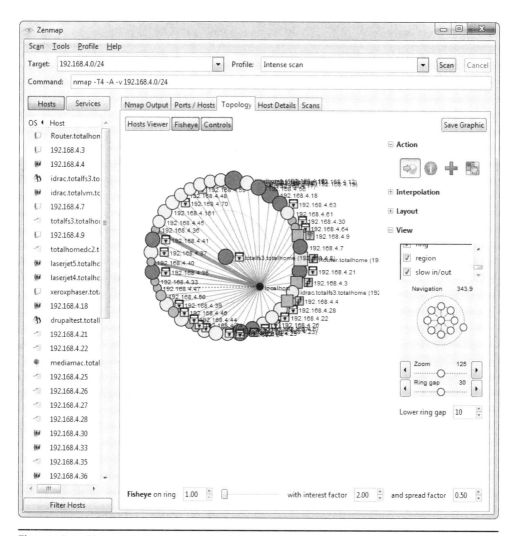

Figure 18-1 Nmap output

Penetration Testing

Once you've run your vulnerability tools and hardened your infrastructure, it's time to see if your network can stand up to an actual attack. The problem with this is that you don't want *real* bad guys making these attacks. You want to be attacked by a "white hat" hacker, who will find the existing vulnerabilities and exploit them to get access. Instead of hurting your infrastructure or stealing your secrets, this hacker reports findings so that you can further harden your network. This is called *penetration testing (pentesting)*.

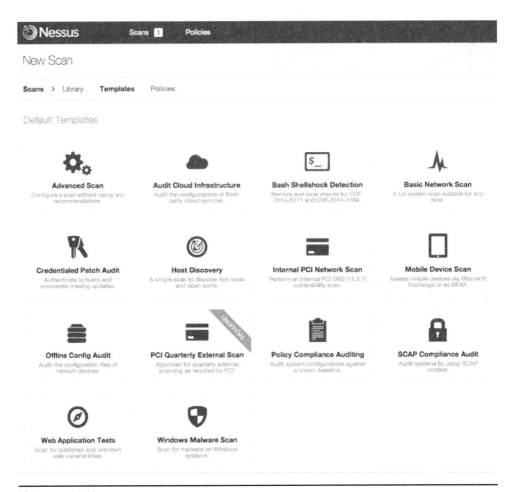

Figure 18-2 Nessus output

NOTE A legal pentest requires lots of careful documentation that defines what the pentester is to test, the level of testing, time frames, and documentation.

Unlike vulnerability testing, a good pentest requires a skilled operator who understands the target and knows potential vulnerabilities. To that end, there are a number of tools that make this job easier. Two examples are Aircrack-ng and Metasploit.

Aircrack-ng is an open source tool for pentesting pretty much every aspect of wireless networks. It's powerful, relatively easy to use (assuming you understand 802.11 wireless networks in great detail), and completely free.

Metasploit is a unique, open source tool that enables the pentester to use a massive library of attacks as well as tweak those attacks for unique penetrations. Metasploit is the go-to tool for vulnerability testing. You simply won't find a professional in this arena who does not use Metasploit. Metasploit isn't pretty, so many people use the popular Armitage GUI front end to make it a bit easier (Figure 18-3).

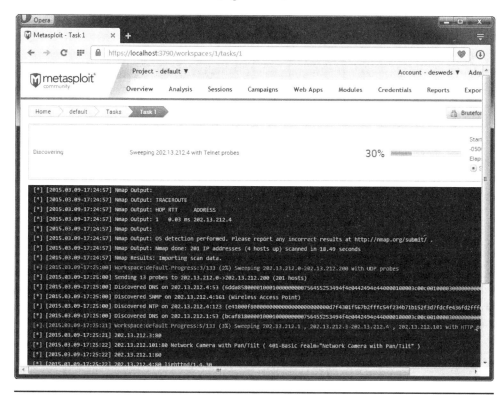

Figure 18-3 Metasploit output

There are also a number of highly customized Linux-based tools that incorporate many tools into a single bootable drive. One of the most famous packages is Kali Linux. It's hard to find a good security person who doesn't have a bootable Kali Linux USB drive.

Contingency Planning

Despite the best efforts of competent techs, there will be times when the integrity of an infrastructure is compromised—an *incident*. Incidents can and will vary in size and scope, from something as simple as an attack that was caught and stopped to something serious such as a data breach or a hurricane wiping out a data center. Whatever the case, organizations should develop a set of *contingency plans*—documents about how to limit damage and recover quickly—to respond to these incidents.

The CompTIA Network+ exam covers several aspects of contingency planning that we can divide into three groups based on the severity and location of the incident: incident response, disaster recovery, and business continuity. Incidents that take place within the organization that can be stopped, contained, and remediated without outside resources are handled by *incident response* planning. If an incident can no longer be contained, causing significant damage or danger to the immediate infrastructure, it is covered under *disaster recovery*. Last, if the disaster requires actions offsite from the primary infrastructure, it is under the jurisdiction of *business continuity*.

While related but not directly connected to contingency planning, we have forensics. Let's hit all these, but keep in mind that this is only the lightest touch on these very complex aspects of contingency planning. The goal of the CompTIA Network+ certification is only to introduce you to these concepts so that you progress to the next level (hopefully CompTIA Security+).

Incident Response

The cornerstone of incident response is the incident response team—usually one or more trained, preassigned *first responders* with policies in place for what to do. Depending on the type of event, the team may be responsible for things like: deciding whether it qualifies as an incident the team should address, ignore, or escalate; evaluating the scope and cause of the issue; preventing further disruption; resolving the cause; restoring order to affected systems; and identifying ways to prevent a recurrence. Most incidents are handled at this level. Organizations will have detailed *incident response policies* that will guide the actions of the team in various incident scenarios. However, if an incident is so vast that the incident response team cannot stop, contain, or remediate it, disaster recovery comes into play.

Disaster Recovery

Disaster recovery is a critical part of contingency planning that deals directly with recovering your primary infrastructure from a disaster. A *disaster* is an event that disables or destroys substantial amounts of infrastructure, such as a hurricane or flood.

Disaster recovery starts with an organization developing a *disaster recovery plan*. An organization considers likely disasters and creates plans for how to deal with them. The actual plans vary by the type of disaster, but there are a few concepts you'll find in just about every situation.

First there is a *disaster recovery team*, whose goal is to get the IT infrastructure up and running at the primary business location(s). One of the big jobs here is creating data backups and making sure those backups are available quickly in the face of any negative event. Any company prepared for a disaster has one or more *backup* copies—or *snapshots*—of essential data. The backed-up files comprise an *archive* of important data that the disaster recovery team can retrieve in case of some disaster.

In the early days of computing, such a backup was done via specific backup software onto some form of magnetic tape. Tape was cheap compared to hard drive space and was easy to move from one location to another. Backups followed fairly specific rotations, so that most of the essential data was always up to date in multiple locations.

Tape is slow and old these days, but hard drives and Internet connections are cheap and fast. Backups roll to removable hard drives and/or directly up into the *cloud*.

 NOTE I don't mean to make it sound as though tape backups are no longer used. They are. Many tape solutions still fully support the traditional backups as well, which are discussed next.

Traditional Data Backup Techniques

The goal of backing up data is to ensure that when a system dies, there will be an available, recent copy you can use to restore the system. You could simply back up the complete system at the end of each day—or whatever interval you feel is prudent to keep the backups fresh—but complete backups can be a tremendous waste of time and materials. Instead of backing up the entire system, take advantage of the fact that not all of the files will be changed in any given period; much of the time you only need to back up what's changed since your last backup.

Traditional backups use a file attribute called the archive bit to perform backups. The following backup types are most often supported: full, incremental, and differential.

- In a *full backup*, every file selected is backed up, and the archive bit is turned off for every file backed up. This is the standard "back it all up" option.

- An *incremental backup* includes only files with the archive bit turned on. In other words, it copies only the files that have been changed since the last full or incremental backup. This backup turns off the archive bits.

- A *differential backup* copies all the files that have been changed since the last full backup. It doesn't turn off the archive bits.

 EXAM TIP Be sure you know the types of backups, including which ones change the archive bits and which ones do not.

Most companies do a big weekly full backup, followed by incremental or differential backups at the end of every business day.

Notice that a differential backup is a cumulative backup. Because the archive bits are not set, it keeps backing up *all* changes since the last full backup. This means the backup files will get progressively larger throughout the week (assuming a standard weekly normal backup). The incremental backup, by contrast, only backs up files changed since the last full or incremental backup. Each incremental backup file will be relatively small and also totally different from the previous backup file.

The bottom line on incremental vs. differential is this. Incremental requires less storage space, but restoring from backup takes longer than differential. Differential requires more storage space but requires only two steps to restore from backup: restore the full backup, then restore the differential for that week.

Backup Plan Assessments

A proper assessment of a backup plan records how much data might by lost and how long it would take to restore. A *recovery point objective (RPO)* is the state of the backup when the data is recovered—in essence, how much data will be lost if a backup is used. Most restored systems have some amount of lost data based on when the last backup took place. Real-time backups, which are really just redundant servers, are the exception. The *recovery time objective (RTO)* is the amount of time needed to restore full functionality from when the organization ceases to function.

The CompTIA Network+ objectives directly refer to two hardware-specific disaster recovery items, MTBF and MTTR. I'll throw MTTF into the middle just for fun. Here's the scoop on these concepts.

The *mean time between failures (MTBF)* factor, which typically applies to hardware components, represents the manufacturer's best guess (based on historical data) regarding how much time will pass between major failures of that component. This assumes that more than one failure will occur, which means that the component will be repaired rather than replaced. Organizations take this risk factor into account because it may affect likelihood and impact of the risks associated with critical systems.

The *mean time to failure (MTTF)* factor indicates the length of time a device is expected to last in operation. In MTTF, only a single, definitive failure will occur and will require that the device be replaced rather than repaired.

Lastly, the *mean time to recovery (MTTR)* is the amount of time it takes for a hardware component to recover from failure.

Disaster recovery handles everything from restoring hardware to backups, but only at the primary business location. Anything that requires moving part of the organization's business offsite until recovery is complete is a part of business continuity.

Business Continuity

When the disaster disables, wipes out, floods, or in some other way prevents the primary infrastructure from operating, the organization should have a plan of action to keep the business going at remote sites. The planning and processes necessary to make this happen are known as business continuity (BC). Organizations plan for this with *business continuity planning (BCP)*. Good BCP will deal with many issues, but one of the more important ones—and one that must be planned well in advance of a major disaster—is the concept of backup sites.

Every business continuity plan includes setting up some form of secondary location that enables an organization to continue to operate should its primary site no longer function. We tend to break these secondary sites into three different types: cold, warm, and hot.

- A *cold site* is a location that consists of a building, facilities, desks, toilets, parking—everything that a business needs … except computers. A cold site will generally take more than a few days to bring online.

- A *warm site* is the same as a cold site, but adds computers loaded with software and functioning servers—a complete hardware infrastructure. A warm site lacks current data and may not have functioning Internet/network links. Bringing this site up to speed may start with activating your network links, and it most certainly requires loading data from recent backups. A warm site should only take a day or two to bring online.

- A *hot site* has everything a warm site does, but also includes very recent backups. It might need just a little data restored from a backup to be current, but in many cases a hot site is a complete duplicate of the primary site. A proper hot site should only take a few hours to bring online.

Business continuity isn't just about backup sites, but this aspect is what the CompTIA Network+ exam focuses on. Another term related to continuity planning is *succession planning*: identifying people who can take over certain positions (usually on a temporary basis) in case the people holding those critical positions are incapacitated or lost in an incident.

Forensics

Computer forensics is the science of gathering, preserving, and presenting evidence stored on a computer or any form of digital media that is presentable in a court of law. Computer forensics is a highly specialized science, filled with a number of highly specialized skills and certifications. Three of the top computer forensic certifications are the Certified Forensic Computer Examiner (CFCE), offered by the International Association of Computer Investigative Specialists (IACIS); the Certified Computer Examiner (CCE) certification, from the International Society of Forensic Computer Examiners (ISFCE); and the GIAC Certified Forensic Analyst (GCFA), offered by the Global Information Assurance Certification (GIAC) organization. Achieving one of these challenging certifications gets you well on your way to a great career in forensics.

The CompTIA Network+ exam doesn't expect you to know all there is to know about computer forensics, but instead wants you, as the typical technician, to understand enough of forensics that you know what to do in the rare situation where you find yourself as the first line of defense.

In general, CompTIA sees you as either the first responder or the technician responsible for supporting the first responder. The first responder in a forensic situation is the person or robot whose job is to react to the notification of a computer crime by determining the severity of the situation, collecting information, documenting findings and actions, and providing the information to the proper authorities. In a perfect world, a first responder has a toolbox of utilities that enables him or her to capture the state of the system without disturbing it. At the very least they need to secure the state of the media (mainly hard drives) as well as any volatile memory (RAM) in a way that removes all doubt of tampering either intentionally or unintentionally.

 NOTE One of the first mistakes any first responder can make is to turn off or reboot a computer. There's a very hot debate in the forensics community about what to do when you have to seize devices. Most experts say to pull the plug.

Like so many aspects of computer security, there isn't a single school of thought on how exactly you should do computer forensics. There are, however, a number of basic attitudes and practices that every school of thought share, especially at the very basic level covered by the CompTIA Network+ exam.

In general, when you are in a situation where you are the first responder, you need to

- Secure the area
- Document the scene
- Collect evidence
- Interface with authorities

Secure the Area

The first step for a first responder is to secure the area. In most cases someone in authority has determined the person or persons who are allegedly responsible and calls you in to react to the incident. As a first responder, your job is to secure the systems involved as well as secure the immediate work areas.

The main way you secure the area is by your presence at the scene. If possible, you should block the scene from prying eyes or potential disturbance. If it's an office, lock the door, define the area of the scene, and mark it off in some way if possible.

Keep in mind that an incident is rarely anything as exciting (or scary) as catching a user committing a felony! In most cases an incident involves something as simple as trying to determine if a user introduced malware into a system or if a user was playing World of Warcraft during work hours. In these cases it's often easy to do your job. Simply observe the system and, if you identify an issue, provide that information in house. The rules for forensics still apply. If, however, you're responding to one of the more scary scenarios, it's important for you as a first responder to understand when you need to *escalate* an issue. Given that *you* were called in to react to a particular incident, most escalation situations involve you discovering something more serious than you expected.

Document the Scene

Once you have secured the area, it's time to *document the scene*. You need to preserve the state of the equipment and look for anything that you might need to inspect forensically.

 NOTE It's always a good idea to use a camera to document the state of the incident scene, including taking pictures of the operating state of computers and switches and the location of media and other devices.

While it's obvious you'll want to locate computers, switches, WAPs, and routers, be sure to take copious notes, paying particular attention to electronic media. Here are a few items you will want to document:

- Smartphones
- Optical media

- External hard drives
- Thumb drives
- Cameras
- VoIP phones

Collect Evidence

With the scene secured and documented, it's time to start the *evidence/data collection*. The moment you take something away from an incident scene or start to handle or use any devices within the incident scene, there is a chance that your actions could corrupt the evidence you are collecting. You must handle and document all evidence in a very specific manner. *Chain of custody*, as the name implies, is the paper trail of who has accessed or controlled a given piece of evidence from the time it is initially brought into custody until the incident is resolved. From the standpoint of a first responder, the most important item to keep in mind about chain of custody is that you need to document what you took under control, when you did it, what you did to it, and when you passed it to the next person in line.

From a strict legal standpoint, the actual process of how you obtain evidence and collect data is a complex business usually left to certified forensic examiners. In general it boils down to using specialized utilities and tools, many of which are unique for the type of data you are retrieving. The tools used also differ depending on different OSs, platforms, and the personal tastes of the examiners. Every forensic examiner has a number of these tools in his or her unique forensic toolkit.

If you need to transport any form of evidence, make sure to document for chain of custody as well as inventory. In other words, make a list of who has what equipment/evidence at any one time. Pack everything carefully. You don't want a dropped case to destroy data! If you are transporting evidence, don't leave the evidence at any time. Delay your lunch break until after you hand the evidence over to the next person! Follow the proper procedures for *data transport* to avoid any problems with the evidence.

The end result of your forensics is a *forensics report*. In general, this is where you report your findings, if any. A good forensics report will include the following:

- Examiner's name and title
- Examiner's qualifications
- Objective for the forensics
- Any case or incident numbers
- Tools used
- Where the examination took place
- Files found
- Log file output
- Screen snapshots

There are two places where the forensic reports (and forensic evidence) might be used: legal holds and electronic discovery. A *legal hold* is the process of an organization preserving and organizing data in anticipation of or in reaction to a pending legal issue. For example, a company might discover that your forensic report includes findings of criminal activity that requires reporting to the authorities. In that case the data and the reports must be preserved in such a way that, should a legal authority want access to that data, they can reasonably access it. *Electronic discovery* (or e-discovery) is the process of actually requesting that data and providing it in a legal way.

Safety

Managing risk to employee physical health falls into three broad categories: electrical safety, physical/installation safety, and emergency procedures. Most companies of any size implement clear *safety procedures and policies* to keep employees intact and functioning. Let's wrap up this chapter with a discussion of these topics.

Electrical Safety

Electrical safety in a networking environment covers several topics: the inherent danger of electricity, grounding, and static.

As you'll recall from Science 101, electricity can shock you badly, damage you, or even kill you. Keep the networking closet or room clear of clutter. Never use frayed cords. Use the same skills you use to avoid getting cooked by electricity in everyday life.

It is very important with networking to use properly grounded circuits. This is more a data safety issue than a personal safety issue. Poorly grounded circuits can create a *ground loop*—where a voltage differential exists between two parts of your network. This can cause data to become unreadable. Improper grounding also exposes equipment to more risk from power surges.

Electrostatic discharge (ESD)—the passage of a static electrical charge from one item to another—can damage or destroy computing equipment. It's important to wear a properly connected anti-ESD wrist strap when replacing a NIC or doing anything inside a workstation (Figure 18-4).

Figure 18-4
Anti-ESD wrist
strap

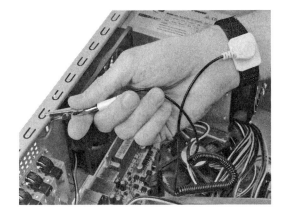

The risks from ESD get a lot smaller when you stop opening up computing machines. Routers, switches, and other networking boxes are enclosed and thus protected from technician ESD. Even when you insert a module in a router or switch, the rack is metal and protected and the box should be attached to the rack and thus grounded too.

Physical/Installation Safety

IT techs live in a dangerous world. We're in constant danger of tripping, hurting our backs, and getting burned by hot components. You also need to keep in mind what you wear (in a safety sense). Let's take a moment to discuss these physical safety issues and what to do about them.

If you don't keep organized, hardware technology will take over your life. Figure 18-5 shows a corner of my office, a painful example of a cable "kludge."

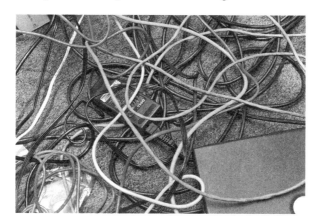

Figure 18-5
Mike's cable kludge

Cable messes such as these are dangerous tripping hazards. While I may allow a mess like this in my home office, all cables in a business environment are carefully tucked away behind computer cases, run into walls, or placed under cable runners. If you see a cable that is an obvious tripping hazard, contact the person in charge of the building to take care of it immediately. The results of ignoring such hazards can be catastrophic (see Figure 18-6).

Another physical safety issue is lifting equipment. Computers, printers, routers—everything we use—all seem to come to us in heavy boxes. Remember never to lift with your back; lift with your legs, and always use a hand truck if available. You are never paid enough to risk your own well-being. Lifting is an important consideration in an important part of a network tech's life: working with racks.

Rack Installation and Maintenance

Installing components into a rack isn't too challenging of a process. Standard 19-inch equipment racks are designed to accept a tremendous amount of abuse, making it sometimes far too easy for people to use them in ways where failure is almost a guarantee. In general, you need to keep in mind three big areas when using rack-mounted equipment: power, mounting, and environment.

Figure 18-6
What a long,
strange trip it's
been.

Power

Rack-mounted equipment has a number of special power needs. At an absolute minimum, start with a proper power source. A single small rack can get away with a properly grounded, 20-amp dedicated circuit. Larger installations will require larger, sometimes dedicated power transformers supplied by the local power grid.

 NOTE Different rack manufacturers have specific rules and standards for rack electrical grounding. Refer to the installation instructions and consider hiring professional installers when placing your racks.

When you get down to individual racks, it's always a good idea to provide each rack with its own rack-mounted UPS. You then connect every device to that UPS. If you're using power converters, always use a single power converter per rack.

Mounting

Installing gear into a safe, electrically sound, stable rack is a well-established process. For components that connect directly to a rack, such as switches, routers, and patch panels, hold them in place and secure them with four screws (Figure 18-7). The chassis are designed to support the weight of the devices.

Figure 18-7 Directly connected device in rack

Racks come in a number of styles, including enclosed, open frame, and "goal post." Best practices call for the rack to be secured to the surrounding facility structure to prevent movement or an off-balance situation from becoming a network disaster.

Bigger devices connect to the rack via a rail system. The standard procedure here is to install the rail system in the rack using locking brackets (Figure 18-8). Then install the device into the rail or tray.

Figure 18-8
Securing the rail system

Follow standard safety practices when installing gear, especially if you use power tools. *Tool safety* means, for example: use the properly sized screwdriver head; wear safety goggles when cutting wires; don't use a band saw to miter joints. The usual practices will both get you through any exam question and keep you safe in the workplace.

Environment

Racks with servers, switches, routers, and such go into closets or server rooms and they dump heat. The environment within this space must be monitored and controlled for both temperature and humidity. Network components work better when cool rather than hot.

The placement of a rack should *optimize the airflow* in a server area. All racks should be placed so that components draw air in from a shared cool row and then exhaust the hot air into a hot row.

The *heating, ventilation, and air conditioning (HVAC)* system should be optimized to recirculate and purify the hot air into cool air in a continuous flow. What's the proper temperature and humidity level? The ideal for the room, regardless of size, is an average temperature of 68 degrees Fahrenheit and ~50% humidity. A proper *fire suppression system*—one that can do things like detect fire, cut power to protect sensitive equipment, displace oxygen with fire-suppressing gasses, alert relevant staff, and activate sprinklers in a pinch—is an absolute must for any server closet or room. You need to get any electrical spark out quickly to minimize server or data loss.

Finally, follow the guidelines in the *material safety data sheet (MSDS)* for the racks and network components to determine best practices for recycling and so forth. An MSDS, as you'll recall from both your CompTIA A+ studies and from previous chapters, details how you should deal with just about any component, including information on replacement parts, recycling, and more.

Emergency Procedures

A final step in managing risk in any company is to have proper *emergency procedures* in place before the emergencies happen. Here are five essential aspects that should be covered:

- Building layout
- Fire escape plan
- Safety/emergency exits
- Fail open/fail close
- Emergency alert system

Exit plans need to cover *building layout*, *fire escape plans*, and the locations of *emergency exits*. Exit signs should be posted strategically so people can quickly exit in a real emergency.

Secured spaces, such as server rooms, need some kind of default safety mechanism in case of an emergency. Locked doors need to *fail open*—doors default to open in case of emergency—or *fail closed*—doors lock in case of emergency.

Finally, nothing beats a properly loud *emergency alert system* blaring away to get people moving quickly. Don't forget to have annual fire drills and emergency alert mixers to make certain all employees know what they need to know.

Chapter Review

Questions

1. Which item should be found in a security policy?

   A. Acceptable use policy

   B. Emergency exit plan

   C. Service level agreement

   D. Instruction on how to fill out a change request form

2. Through what mechanism is a change to the IT structure initiated?

   A. Users make a change to their environment, then report the result to the change management team.

   B. A user requests funding for a change to upper management, then submits a requisition to the change management team to source and purchase new equipment.

   C. Users submit a change request to the change management team.

   D. The change management team issues a proposed change to users in the organization, then evaluates the responses.

3. Users need training from the IT department to understand which of the following?

   A. How to troubleshoot lost network connections

   B. How to secure workstations with screen-locking and password-security techniques

   C. How to send e-mail to the change management team

   D. How to check their network connection

4. When is a memorandum of understanding used?

   A. As part of a legal contract

   B. As part of a statement of work (SOW)

   C. When a service level agreement (SLA) expires

   D. When a legal contract is not appropriate

5. The best way to know the vulnerabilities of an IT infrastructure is to run what?

   A. A system-wide antivirus scanner

   B. Cable certifier

   C. Critical asset scanner

   D. Vulnerability scanner

6. What is succession planning?

   A. Identifying personnel who can take over certain positions in response to an incident

   B. The career path by which employees of an organization can grow through the ranks

   C. The selection of failover servers in the event of a catastrophic server failure

   D. The selection of failover routers in the event of a catastrophic router failure

7. During and after a change to the IT infrastructure, what must be done?

   A. Downtime must be scheduled.

   B. New equipment must be installed.

   C. Operating systems must be patched.

   D. The changes must be documented.

8. What is the job of a first responder?

   A. Investigate data on a computer suspected to contain crime evidence.

   B. React to the notification of a computer crime.

   C. Power off computers suspected of being used in criminal activity.

   D. Wipe the drives of computers suspected of being used in criminal activity.

9. When working inside equipment, what should Jane do?

   A. Ensure that the equipment is secured to the rack with four screws.

   B. Wear a properly connected anti-ESD wrist strap.

   C. Have a fire extinguisher nearby and review its proper use.

   D. Wear safety goggles and fire retardant gloves.

10. The placement of a rack should optimize what?

    A. Airflow

    B. HVAC

    C. MSDS

    D. Emergency procedures

Answers

1. **A.** An acceptable use policy is a typical item found in a security policy.

2. **C.** Users submit a change request to the change management team to effect a change to an IT structure.

3. **B.** Typical user training includes how to secure workstations with screen-locking and password-security techniques.

4. **D.** A memorandum of understanding is used when a legal contract is not appropriate.

5. **D.** Run a vulnerability scanner to find weaknesses in an IT infrastructure.

6. **A.** Identifying personnel who can take over certain positions in response to an incident is essential in succession planning.

7. **D.** When changing an IT infrastructure, always document the changes.

8. **B.** A first responder reacts to the notification of a computer crime.

9. **B.** Jane should almost always wear a properly connected anti-ESD wrist strap when working inside equipment.

10. **A.** Figure out the proper airflow when placing a rack.

## CHAPTER 19

Protecting Your Network

The CompTIA Network+ certification exam expects you to know how to

- 1.3 Explain the concepts and characteristics of routing and switching
- 2.2 Given a scenario, determine the appropriate placement of networking devices on a network and install/configure them
- 2.3 Explain the purposes and use cases for advanced networking devices
- 4.1 Summarize the purposes of physical security devices
- 4.2 Explain authentication and access controls
- 4.4 Summarize common networking attacks
- 4.5 Given a scenario, implement network device hardening
- 4.6 Explain common mitigation techniques and their purposes
- 5.5 Given a scenario, troubleshoot common network service issues

To achieve these goals, you must be able to

- Discuss common security threats in network computing
- Discuss common vulnerabilities inherent in networking
- Describe methods for hardening a network against attacks
- Explain how firewalls protect a network from threats

The very nature of networking makes networks vulnerable. A network must allow multiple users to access serving systems. At the same time, the network must be protected from harm. Doing so is a big business and part of the whole risk management issue touched on in Chapter 18, "Managing Risk." This chapter concentrates on threats, vulnerabilities, network hardening, and firewalls.

Test Specific

Network Threats

A network *threat* is any form of *potential* attack against your network. Don't think only about Internet attacks here. Sure, hacker-style threats are real, but there are so many others. A threat can be a person sneaking into your offices and stealing passwords, or an ignorant employee deleting files they should not have access to in the first place. Natural disasters, like earthquakes, fires, floods, and crazed squirrels, are also threats.

Just by reading the word "potential" you should know that this list could go on for pages. This section includes a list of common network threats. CompTIA does not include all of these in the Network+ N10-007 objectives (because they're covered in CompTIA A+ or Security+), but I've included them here to give a real-world sense of scope:

- Spoofing
- Packet/protocol abuse
- Zero-day attack
- ARP cache poisoning
- Denial of service (with a lot of variations on a theme)
- Man-in-the-middle
- Session hijacking
- Brute force
- Compromised system
- Insider threat/malicious employee
- VLAN hopping
- Administrative access control
- Malware
- Social engineering
- And more!

It's quite a list, so let's get started.

Spoofing

Spoofing is the process of pretending to be someone or something you are not by placing false information into your packets. Any data sent on a network can be spoofed. Here are a few quick examples of commonly spoofed data:

- Source MAC address and IP address, to make you think a packet came from somewhere else
- E-mail address, to make you think an e-mail came from somewhere else
- Web address, to make you think you are on a Web page you are not on
- User name, to make you think a certain user is contacting you when in reality it's someone completely different

Generally, spoofing isn't so much a threat as it is a tool to make threats. If you spoof my e-mail address, for example, that by itself isn't a threat. If you use my e-mail address to pretend to be me, however, and to ask my employees to send to you their user names and passwords for network login? That's clearly a threat. (And also a waste of time; my employees would *never* trust me with their user names and passwords.)

One of the more aggressive spoofing attacks targets DNS servers, the backbone of network naming on all of our networks today. In *DNS cache poisoning*, an attacker targets a DNS server to query an evil DNS server instead of the correct one. The server can in turn tell the target DNS server spoofed DNS information. The DNS server will cache that spoofed information, spreading it to hosts and possibly other servers.

 EXAM TIP The CompTIA Network+ exam objectives refer to DNS cache poisoning as simply DNS poisoning. Expect to see the shortened term on the exam.

To prevent DNS cache poisoning, the typical use case scenario is to add *Domain Name System Security Extensions (DNSSEC)* for domain name resolution.

All the DNS root and top-level domains (plus hundreds of thousands of other DNS servers) use DNSSEC.

Packet/Protocol Abuse

No matter how hard the Internet's designers try, it seems there is always a way to take advantage of a protocol by using it in ways it was never meant to be used. Anytime you do things with a protocol that it wasn't meant to do and that abuse ends up creating a threat, this is *protocol abuse*. A classic example involves the Network Time Protocol (NTP).

The Internet keeps time by using NTP servers. Without NTP providing accurate time for everything that happens on the Internet, anything that's time sensitive would be in big trouble.

Here's what happened. No computer's clock is perfect, so NTP is designed for each NTP server to have a number of peers. *Peers* are other NTP servers that one NTP server can compare its own time against to make sure its clock is accurate. Occasionally a person running an NTP server might want to query the server to determine what peers it uses. The command used on just about every NTP server to submit queries is called *ntpdc*. The ntpdc command puts the NTP server into interactive mode so that you can then make queries to the NTP server. One of these queries is called *monlist*. The monlist query asks the NTP server about the traffic going on between itself and peers. If you query a public NTP server with `monlist`, it generates a lot of output:

```
$ ntpdc -c monlist fake.timeserver5.org
remote address          port local address       count m ver rstr avgint  lstint
================================================================================
time.apple.com          123 192.168.4.78            13 4   4    1d0    319     399
ntp.notreal.com         123 46.3.129.78           1324 4   4      1      0       0
123.212.32.44           123 32.42.77.82              0 0   0      0      0       0

<a few hundred more lines here>

ntpdc>
```

A bad guy can hit multiple NTP servers with the same little command—with a spoofed source IP address—and generate a ton of responses from the NTP server to that source IP. Enough of these requests will bring the spoofed source computer—now called the target or victim—to its knees. We call this a DoS attack (covered a bit later), and it's a form of protocol abuse.

If that's not sinister enough, hackers can also use evil programs that inject unwanted information into packets in an attempt to break another system. We call these *malformed packets*. Programs such as Scapy give you the capability to custom-form (or should we say malform?) packets and send them to anyone. You can use this to exploit a server that isn't designed to handle such attacks. What will happen if you send a DHCP request packet into which you have placed totally incorrect information in the Options field? What, you didn't know DHCP request packets have options? That's OK, most techs don't know that, but the guy doing this to your DHCP server is hoping that when your DHCP reads the request it will break the server somehow: giving root access, shutting down the DHCP server, whatever. This is an exploit created by packet abuse.

Zero-Day Attacks

The *way* (software or methods) an exploit takes advantage of a vulnerability is called an *attack surface*. The timeframe in which a bad guy can exploit a vulnerability in an attack surface before patches are applied to prevent the exploit is called an *attack window*. New attacks using vulnerabilities that haven't yet been identified (and fixed) are called *zero-day attacks*.

ARP Cache Poisoning

ARP cache poisoning attacks target the ARP caches on hosts and switches. As we saw back in Chapter 6, "TCP/IP Basics," the process and protocol used in resolving an IP address to an Ethernet MAC address is called Address Resolution Protocol (ARP).

Every node on a TCP/IP network has an *ARP cache* that stores a list of known IP addresses and their associated MAC addresses. On a Windows system you can see the ARP cache using the `arp -a` command. Here's part of the result of typing `arp -a` on my system:

```
C:\Users\Mike>arp -a
Interface: 202.13.212.205 --- 0xc
  Internet Address      Physical Address      Type
  202.13.212.1          d0-d0-fd-39-f5-5e     dynamic
  202.13.212.100        30-05-5c-0d-ed-c5     dynamic
  202.13.212.101        00-02-d1-08-df-8d     dynamic
  202.13.212.208        00-22-6b-a0-a2-9b     dynamic
```

If a device wants to send an IP packet to another device, it must encapsulate the IP packet into an Ethernet frame on wired LANs. If the sending device doesn't know the destination device's MAC address, it sends a special broadcast called an *ARP request*. In turn, the device with that IP address responds with a unicast packet to the requesting device. Figure 19-1 shows a Wireshark capture of an ARP request and response.

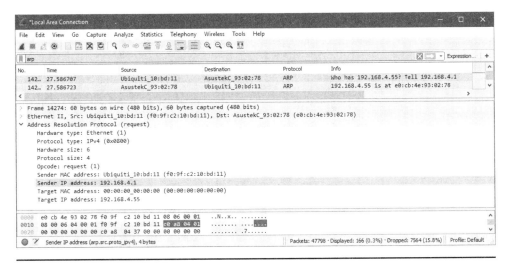

Figure 19-1 ARP request and response

The problem with ARP is that there is no security. Any device that can get on a LAN can wreak havoc with ARP requests and responses. For example, ARP enables any device at any time to announce its MAC address without first getting a request. Additionally, ARP has a number of very detailed but relatively unused specifications. A device can just declare itself to be a "router." How that information is used is up to the writer of the software used by the device that hears this announcement. More than a decade ago, ARP poisoning caused a tremendous amount of trouble.

Poisoning in Action

Here's how an ARP cache poison attack works. Figure 19-2 shows a typical tiny network with a gateway, a switch, a DHCP server, and two clients. Assuming nothing has recently changed with the computers' IP addresses, each system's ARP cache should look something like Figure 19-3. (ARP caches don't store computer names, but I've added them for clarity.)

If a bad actor can get inside the network (like plugging into an unused Ethernet port), using the proper tools, he can send false ARP frames that each computer reads, placing evil data into their ARP caches (which is why this is called ARP cache poisoning). See Figure 19-4.

Once the poisoning starts, the evil computer can perform a man-in-the-middle attack, reading every packet going through it, as shown in Figure 19-5 (which shows the evil computer with its own ISP connection, although it could also use the gateway's connection as well).

Dynamic ARP Inspection and DHCP Snooping

Clearly, we'd like to avoid this type of attack. Cisco's *Dynamic ARP Inspection (DAI)* technology in switches keeps track of ARP information, compiling a list of known good, identifiable IP and MAC addresses (Figure 19-6).

Figure 19-2
Our happy
network

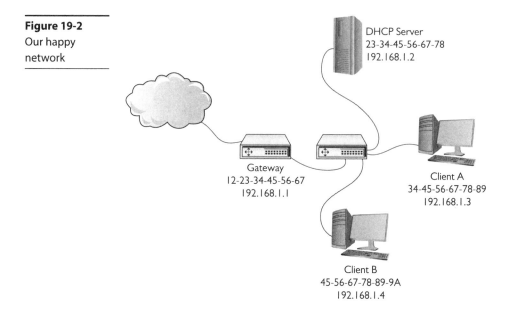

DHCP Server
23-34-45-56-67-78
192.168.1.2

Gateway
12-23-34-45-56-67
192.168.1.1

Client A
34-45-56-67-78-89
192.168.1.3

Client B
45-56-67-78-89-9A
192.168.1.4

Figure 19-3
Each computer's
ARP cache
should look
about the same.

ARP Cache

Name	MAC	IP
Gateway	12-23-34-45-56-67	192.168.1.1
DHCP	23-34-45-56-67-78	192.168.1.2
Client A	34-45-56-67-78-89	192.168.1.3
Client B	45-56-67-78-89-9A	192.168.1.4

I'm the gateway!
Here are my
MAC and IP
addresses!

EVIL COMPUTER
FE-ED-DC-CB-BA-A9
192.168.1.100

Name	MAC	IP
Gateway	FE-ED-DC-CB-BA-A9	192.168.1.100
DHCP	23-34-45-56-67-78	192.168.1.2
Client A	34-45-56-67-78-89	192.168.1.3
Client B	45-56-67-78-89-9A	192.168.1.4

Hey! Where did
all my Internet
traffic go?

Gateway
12-23-34-45-56-67
192.168.1.1

Figure 19-4   Every system's ARP cache is now poisoned.

Figure 19-5
ARP cache
poisoning
enables a man-
in-the-middle
attack.

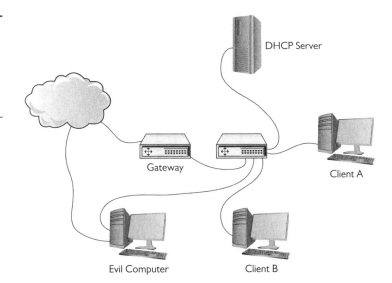

Figure 19-6
DAI database

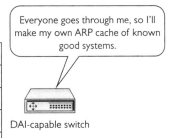

Everyone goes through me, so I'll make my own ARP cache of known good systems.

DAI-capable switch

Known Good Systems

Name	MAC	IP
Gateway	12-23-34-45-56-67	192.168.1.1
DHCP	23-34-45-56-67-78	192.168.1.2
Client A	34-45-56-67-78-89	192.168.1.3
Client B	45-56-67-78-89-9A	192.168.1.4

Now if an ARP poisoner suddenly decides to attack this network, the DAI-capable switch notices the unknown ARP commands and blocks them (Figure 19-7).

DHCP snooping is like DAI—in fact, they share the same database—in that it creates a list of MAC addresses for all of a network's known DHCP servers and clients. If an unknown MAC address starts sending DHCP server messages, the DHCP snoop–capable switch will block that device, stopping all unauthorized DHCP traffic and sending some form of alarm to the appropriate person.

EXAM TIP   Implementing Dynamic ARP Inspection (DAI) and DHCP snooping enhances *switch port protection*, a key network hardening technique. On a terminology side note, CompTIA uses *switch port* (two words), but many techs and some documentation use *switchport* (one word). It's the same thing.

Denial of Service

Hundreds of millions of servers on the Internet provide a multitude of different services. Given the amount of security now built in at so many different levels, it's more difficult

Figure 19-7

DAI in action

I'm the gateway! Here are my MAC and IP addresses!

Uh, no. I don't know your MAC... BLOCKED!!!

EVIL COMPUTER
FE-ED-DC-CB-BA-A9
192.168.1.100

DAI-capable Switch

than ever for a bad guy to cripple any one particular service by exploiting a weakness in the servers themselves. So what's a bad guy (or gal, group, or government) to do to shut down a service he doesn't like, even if he is unaware of any exploits on the target servers? Why, denial of service, of course!

A *denial of service (DoS)* attack is a targeted attack on a server (or servers) that provides some form of service on the Internet (such as a Web site), with the goal of making that site unable to process any incoming server requests. DoS attacks come in many different forms. The simplest example is a *physical attack*, where a person physically attacks the servers. Bad guys could go to where the servers are located and shut them down or disconnect their Internet connections, in some cases permanently. Physical DoS attacks are good to know for the exam, but they aren't very common unless the service is very small and served in only a single location.

The most common form of DoS is when a bad guy uses his computer to flood a targeted server with so many requests that the service is overwhelmed and ceases functioning. These attacks are most commonly performed on Web and e-mail servers, but any Internet service's servers can be attacked via some DoS method.

The secret to a successful DoS attack is to send as many packets as quickly as possible to the victim. Not only do bad guys want to send a lot of packets, they want the packets to contain some kind of request that the target server must process as long as possible. The aspect of a DoS attack that makes a server do a lot of processing and responding is called *amplification*, thus the term for this attack is an *amplified DoS attack*. A simple `monlist` command to an NTP server, like we discussed earlier, generates a big response from the server.

Internet-service servers are robust devices, designed to handle a massive number of requests per second. These robust servers make it tricky for a single bad guy at a single computer to send enough requests to slow them down. Far more menacing, and far more common than a simple DoS attack, are *distributed denial of service (DDoS)* attacks. A DDoS uses hundreds, thousands, or even millions of computers under the control of a single operator to launch a coordinated attack. DDoS operators don't own these computers, but instead use malware (discussed later) to take control of computers. A single computer under the control of an operator is called a *zombie* or *bot*. A group of computers under the control of one operator is called a *botnet*.

NOTE Zombified computers aren't always immediately obvious. DDoS operators often wait weeks or months after a computer's been infected to take control of it.

To take control of your network's computers, someone has to install malware on the computer. Again, anti-malware, training, and procedures will keep your computers safe from zombification (as long as they aren't bitten by an already zombified computer).

The goal of a botnet operator conducting a DDoS attack is to send as many amplified requests as possible, but botnets are only one way to do this. Another tactic used in DDoS attacks is to send requests with the target server's IP address as the source IP address to otherwise normally operating servers, such as DNS or NTP servers. This is called *reflection* or a *reflective DDoS attack*. These servers then send massive numbers of amplified responses to the target. Such a huge increase in the number of packets—a *traffic spike*— will bring the target down.

Deauthentication Attack

A *deauthentication (deauth) attack*—a form of DoS attack—targets 802.11 Wi-Fi networks specifically by sending out a frame that kicks a wireless client off its current WAP connection. A rogue WAP nearby presents a great and often automatic alternative option for connection. The rogue WAP connects the client to the Internet and then proceeds to collect data from that client.

The deauth attack targets a specific Wi-Fi frame called a deauthentication frame, normally used by a WAP to kick an unauthorized WAP off its network. The attacker flips this narrative on its head, using the good disconnect frame for evil purposes. (And here you thought only wired networks got all the love from DoS attacks.) Refer to Chapter 14, "Wireless Networking," to refresh your memory on Wi-Fi security.

 NOTE A *friendly* or *unintentional DoS attack* is just as it's named: a system is brought down unintentionally. The most common form of friendly DoS occurs on a super-busy server: an organization's infrastructure isn't strong enough to keep up with legitimate demand. This is very common on the Web when a popular site makes a reference to a small site or someone mentions the small site on a radio or TV program, resulting in a massive increase in traffic to the small site. This unintentional DoS attack goes by many names, such as *slashdotting* or the *Reddit hug of death*.

Man-in-the-Middle

In a *man-in-the-middle* attack, an attacker taps into communications between two systems, covertly intercepting traffic thought to be only between those systems, reading or in some cases even changing the data and then sending the data on. A classic man-in-the-middle attack would be a person using special software on a wireless network to make all the clients think his laptop is a WAP. He could then listen in on that wireless network, gathering up all the conversations and gaining access to passwords, shared keys, or other sensitive information. Man-in-the-middle attacks are commonly perpetrated using ARP poisoning.

Session Hijacking

Somewhat similarly to man-in-the-middle attacks, *session hijacking* tries to intercept a valid computer session to get authentication information. Unlike man-in-the-middle attacks, session hijacking only tries to grab authentication information, not necessarily listening in like a man-in-the-middle attack.

Brute Force

Brute force is an attack where a threat agent guesses every permutation of some part of data. Most of the time the term "brute force" refers to an attempt to crack a password, but the term applies to other attacks. You can brute force a search for open ports, network IDs, user names, and so on. Pretty much any attempt to guess the contents of some kind of data field that isn't obvious (or is hidden) is considered a brute force attack.

Physical/Local Access

Not all threats to your network originate from faraway bad guys. There are many threats that lurk right in your LAN, inside your network. This is a particularly dangerous place as these threats don't need to worry about getting past your network edge defenses such as firewalls or WAPs. You need to watch out for problems with hardware, software, and, worst of all, the people who are on your LAN.

Compromised System

Like any technology, computers can and will fail—usually when you can least afford for it to happen. Hard drives crash, servers lock up, the power fails—it's all part of the joy of working in the networking business. Because of this, you need to create redundancy in areas prone to failure (like installing backup power in case of electrical failure) and perform those all-important data backups. Beyond that, the idea is to deploy redundant hardware to provide *fault tolerance*. Take advantage of technologies like redundant array of inexpensive disks (RAID) to spread data across multiple drives. Buy a server case with multiple power supplies, or add a second NIC.

Insider Threats

The greatest hackers in the world will all agree that being inside an organization, either physically or by access permissions, makes evildoing much easier. Malicious employees are a huge threat because of their ability to directly destroy data, inject malware, and initiate attacks. These are collectively called *insider threats*.

Trusted and Untrusted Users   A worst-case scenario from the perspective of security is *unsecured access to private resources*. A couple of terms come into play here. There are trusted users and untrusted users. A *trusted user* is an account that has been granted specific authority to perform certain or all administrative tasks. An *untrusted user* is just the opposite; an account that has been granted no administrative powers.

Trusted users with poor password protection or other security leakages can be compromised. Untrusted users can be upgraded "temporarily" to accomplish a particular task and then forgotten. Consider this situation: A user accidentally copied a bunch of files to several shared network repositories. The administrator does not have time to search for and delete all of the files. The user is granted deletion capability and told to remove the unneeded files. Do you feel a disaster coming? The newly created trusted user could easily remove the wrong files. Careful management of trusted users is the simple solution to these types of threats.

Every configurable device, like a multilayer switch, has a default password and default settings, all of which can create an inadvertent insider threat if not addressed. People sometimes can't help but be curious. A user might note the IP address of a switch on his network, for example, and run Telnet or SSH "just to see." Because it's so easy to get the default passwords/settings for devices with a simple Google search, that information is available to the user. One change on that switch might mean a whole lot of pain for the network tech or administrator who has to fix things.

Dealing with such authentication issues is pretty straightforward. Before bringing any system online, change any default accounts and passwords. This is particularly true for administrative accounts. Also, disable or delete any "guest" accounts (make sure you have another account created first!).

Malicious Users Much more worrisome than accidental accesses to unauthorized resources are *malicious users* who consciously attempt to access, steal, or damage resources. Malicious users or *actors* may represent an external or internal threat.

What does a malicious user want to do? If they are intent on stealing data or gaining further access, they may try *packet sniffing*. This is difficult to detect, but as you know from previous chapters, encryption is a strong defense against sniffing. One of the first techniques that malicious users try is to probe hosts to identify any open ports. There are many tools available to poll all stations on a network for their up/down status and for a list of any open ports (and, by inference, all closed ports too). Angry IP Scanner and nmap are great tools for troubleshooting hosts, but can be used for these types of malevolent activities.

Having found an open port, another way for a malicious user to gain information and additional access is to probe a host's open ports to learn details about running services. This is known as *banner grabbing*. For instance, a host may have a running Web server installed. Using a utility like nmap or Netcat, a malicious user can send an invalid request to port 80 of the server. The server may respond with an error message indicating the type and version of Web server software that is running. With that information, the malicious actor can then learn about vulnerabilities of that product and continue their pursuit. The obvious solution to port scanning and banner grabbing is to not run unnecessary services (resulting in an open port) on a host and to make sure that running processes have current security patches installed.

In the same vein, a malicious user may attempt to exploit known vulnerabilities of certain devices attached to the network. MAC addresses of Ethernet NICs have their first 24 bits assigned by the IEEE. This is a unique number assigned to a specific manufacturer and is known as the *organizationally unique identifier (OUI)*, sometimes called the vendor ID. By issuing certain messages such as broadcasted ARP frames, a malicious user can collect all of the OUI numbers of the wired and wireless nodes attached to a network or subnetwork. Using common lookup tools, the malicious user can identify devices by OUI numbers assigned to particular manufacturers. The past few years have seen numerous DDoS attacks using zombified Internet of Things (IoT) devices, such as security cameras.

VLAN Hopping

An older form of attack that still comes up from time to time is called *VLAN hopping*. The idea behind VLAN hopping is to take a system that's connected to one VLAN and, by abusing VLAN commands to the switch, convince the switch to change your switchport connection to a trunk link.

Administrative Access Control

All operating systems and many switches and routers come with some form of *access control list (ACL)* that defines what users can do with a device's shared resources. An access control might be a file server giving a user read-only privileges to a particular folder, or a firewall only allowing certain internal IP addresses to access the Internet. ACLs are everywhere in a network. In fact, you'll see more of them from the standpoint of a firewall later in this chapter.

Every operating system—and many Internet applications—are packed with administrative tools and functionality. You need these tools to get all kinds of work done, but by the same token, you need to work hard to keep these capabilities out of the reach of those who don't need them.

NOTE The CompTIA Network+ exam does not test you on the details of file system access controls. In other words, don't bother memorizing details like NTFS permissions, but do appreciate that you have fine-grained controls available.

Make sure you know the *administrative accounts* native to Windows (administrator), Linux (root), and macOS (root). You must carefully control these accounts. Clearly, giving regular users administrator/root access is a bad idea, but far more subtle problems can arise. I once gave a user the Manage Documents permission for a busy laser printer in a Windows network. She quickly realized she could pause other users' print jobs and send her print jobs to the beginning of the print queue—nice for her but not so nice for her co-workers. Protecting administrative programs and functions from access and abuse by users is a real challenge and one that requires an extensive knowledge of the operating system and of users' motivations.

NOTE Administering your super accounts is only part of what's called *user account control*. See "Controlling User Accounts" later in this chapter for more details.

Malware

The term *malware* defines any program or code (macro, script, and so on) that's designed to do something on a system or network that you don't want to have happen. Malware comes in many forms, such as viruses, worms, macros, Trojan horses, rootkits, adware, and spyware. We'll examine all these malware flavors in this section. Stopping malware, by far the number one security problem for just about everyone, is so important that we'll address that topic in its own section later in this chapter, "Anti-malware Programs."

Crypto-malware/Ransomware

Crypto-malware uses some form of encryption to lock a user out of a system. Once the crypto-malware encrypts the computer, usually encrypting the boot drive, in most cases the malware then forces the user to pay money to get the system decrypted. When any form of malware makes you pay to get the malware to go away, we call that malware *ransomware*. If a crypto-malware uses a ransom, we commonly call it *crypto-ransomware*.

Crypto-ransomware is one of the most troublesome malwares today, first appearing around 2012 and still going strong. Zero-day variations of crypto-malware, with names such as CryptoWall or WannaCry, are often impossible to clean.

 NOTE Most crypto-malware propagates via a Trojan horse. See the upcoming "Trojan Horse" section for more information.

Virus

A *virus* is a program that has two jobs: to replicate and to activate. *Replication* means it makes copies of itself, often as code stored in boot sectors or as extra code added to the end of executable programs. A virus is not a stand-alone program, but rather something attached to a host file, kind of like a human virus. *Activation* is when a virus does something like erase the boot sector of a drive. A virus only replicates to other applications on a drive or to other drives, such as flash drives or optical media. It does not replicate across networks. Plus, a virus needs human action to spread.

Worm

A *worm* functions similarly to a virus, though it replicates exclusively through networks. A worm, unlike a virus, doesn't have to wait for someone to use a removable drive to replicate. If the infected computer is on a network, a worm will immediately start sending copies of itself to any other computers it can locate on the network. Worms can exploit inherent vulnerabilities in program code, attacking programs, operating systems, protocols, and more. Worms, unlike viruses, do not need host files to infect.

Macro

A *macro* is any type of virus that exploits application macros to replicate and activate. A *macro* is also programming within an application that enables you to control aspects of the application. Macros exist in any application that has a built-in macro language, such as Microsoft Excel, that users can program to handle repetitive tasks (among other things).

Logic Bomb

A *logic bomb* is code written to execute when certain conditions are met, usually with malicious intent. A logic bomb could be added to a company database, for example, to start deleting files if the database author loses her job. Or, the programming could be added to another program, such as a Trojan horse.

Trojan Horse

A *Trojan horse* is a piece of malware that looks or pretends to do one thing while, at the same time, doing something evil. A Trojan horse may be a game, like poker, or a free screensaver. The sky is the limit. The more "popular" Trojan horses turn an infected computer into a server and then open TCP or UDP ports so a remote user can control the infected computer. They can be used to capture keystrokes, passwords, files, credit card information, and more. Trojan horses do not replicate.

Rootkit

For a virus or Trojan horse to succeed, it needs to come up with some method to hide itself. As awareness of malware has grown, anti-malware programs make it harder to find new locations on a computer to hide. A *rootkit* takes advantage of very low-level operating system functions to hide itself from all but the most aggressive of anti-malware tools. Worse, a rootkit, by definition, gains privileged access to the computer. Rootkits can strike operating systems, hypervisors, and even firmware.

Adware/Spyware

There are two types of programs that are similar to malware in that they try to hide themselves to an extent. *Adware* is a program that monitors the types of Web sites you frequent and uses that information to generate targeted advertisements, usually pop-up windows. Many of these programs use Adobe Flash. Adware isn't, by definition, evil, but many adware makers use sneaky methods to get you to use adware, such as using deceptive-looking Web pages ("Your computer is infected with a virus—click here to scan NOW!"). As a result, adware is often considered malware. Some of the computer-infected ads actually install a virus when you click them, so avoid these things like the plague.

Spyware is a function of any program that sends information about your system or your actions over the Internet. The type of information sent depends on the program. A spyware program will include your browsing history. A more aggressive form of spyware may send keystrokes or all of the contacts in your e-mail. Some spyware makers bundle their product with ads to make them look innocuous. Adware, therefore, can contain spyware.

Social Engineering

A considerable percentage of attacks against your network fall under the heading of *social engineering*—the process of using or manipulating people inside the networking environment to gain access to that network from the outside. The term "social engineering" covers the many ways humans can use other humans to gain unauthorized information. This unauthorized information may be a network login, a credit card number, company customer data—almost anything you might imagine that one person or organization may not want a person outside of that organization to access.

Social engineering attacks aren't considered hacking—at least in the classic sense of the word—although the goals are the same. Social engineering is where people attack an organization through the people in the organization or physically access the organization to get the information they need.

The most classic form of social engineering is the telephone scam in which someone calls a person and tries to get him or her to reveal his or her user name/password combination. In the same vein, someone may physically enter your building under the guise of having a legitimate reason for being there, such as a cleaning person, repair technician, or messenger. The attacker then snoops around desks, looking for whatever he or she has come to find (one of many good reasons not to put passwords on your desk or monitor). The attacker might talk with people inside the organization, gathering names, office numbers, or department names—little things in and of themselves, but powerful tools when combined later with other social engineering attacks.

These old-school social engineering tactics are taking a backseat to a far more nefarious form of social engineering: phishing.

 CAUTION   All these attacks are commonly used together, so if you discover one of them being used against your organization, it's a good idea to look for others.

Phishing

In a *phishing* attack, the attacker poses as some sort of trusted site, like an online version of your bank or credit card company, and solicits you to update your financial information, such as a credit card number. You might get an e-mail message, for example, that purports to be from PayPal telling you that your account needs to be updated and provides a link that looks like it goes to http://www.paypal.com. Upon clicking the link, however, you end up at a site that resembles the PayPal login but is actually http://100.16.49.21/2s82ds.php, a phishing site.

Physical Intrusion

You can't consider a network secure unless you provide some physical protection to your network. I separate physical protection into two different areas: protection of servers and protection of clients.

Server protection is easy. Lock up your servers to prevent physical access by any unauthorized person. Large organizations have special server rooms, complete with card-key locks and tracking of anyone who enters or exits. Smaller organizations should at least have a locked closet. While you're locking up your servers, don't forget about any network switches! Hackers can access networks by plugging into a switch, so don't leave any switches available to them.

Physical server protection doesn't stop with a locked door. One of the most common mistakes made by techs is to walk away from a server while still logged in. Always log off from your server when you're not actively managing the server. As a backup, add a password-protected screensaver (Figure 19-8).

Figure 19-8

Applying a password-protected screensaver to a server

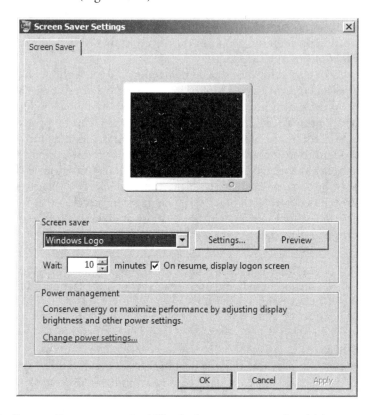

Locking up all of your client systems is difficult, but your users should be required to perform some physical security. First, all users should lock their computers when they step away from their desks. Instruct them to press the WINDOWS KEY-L combination to perform the lock. Hackers take advantage of unattended systems to get access to networks.

Second, make users aware of the potential for dumpster diving and make paper shredders available. Last, tell users to mind their work areas. It's amazing how many users leave passwords readily available. I can go into any office, open a few desk drawers, and invariably find little yellow sticky notes with user names and passwords. If users must write down passwords, tell them to put them in locked drawers!

NOTE A Windows PC should be locked down when it's not actively being used. The simplest thing to teach your users to do is to press the WINDOWS KEY-L combination when they get up from their desks. The effects from the key combination vary according to both the version of Windows and whether a system is a member of a workgroup or domain, but all will require the user to log in to access his or her account (assuming the account is password protected in the first place, of course!).

Common Vulnerabilities

If a threat is an action that threat agents do to try to compromise our networks, then a *vulnerability* is a potential weakness in our infrastructure that a threat might exploit. Note that I didn't say that a threat will take advantage of the vulnerability: only that the vulnerability is a weak place that needs to be addressed.

 EXAM TIP Look for comparison questions on zero-day attacks and other exploits vs. vulnerabilities.

Some vulnerabilities are obvious, such as connecting to the Internet without an edge firewall or not using any form of account control for user files. Other vulnerabilities are unknown or missed, and that makes the study of vulnerabilities very important for a network tech. This section explores a few common vulnerabilities.

 NOTE If you want to get an idea as to the depth of vulnerabilities, check out the Common Vulnerabilities and Exposures (CVE) database hosted by MITRE Corporation here: https://cve.mitre.org/.

Unnecessary Running Services

A typical system running any OS is going to have a large number of important programs running in the background, called *services*. Services do the behind-the-scenes grunt work that users don't need to see, such as wireless network clients and DHCP clients. There are client services and server services.

As a Windows user, I've gotten used to seeing zillions of services running on my system, and in most cases I can recognize only about 50 percent of them—and I'm good at this! In a typical system, not all these services are necessary, so you should *disable unneeded network services*.

From a security standpoint, there are two reasons it's important not to run any unnecessary services. First, most OSs use services to listen on open TCP or UDP ports, potentially leaving systems open to attack. Second, bad guys often use services as a tool for the use and propagation of malware.

The problem with trying not to run unnecessary services is the fact that there are just so many of them. It's up to you to research services running on a particular machine to determine if they're needed or not. It's a rite of passage for any tech to review the services running on a system, going through them one at a time. Over time you will become familiar with many of the built-in services and get an eye for spotting the ones that just don't look right. There are tools available to do the job for you, but this is one place where you need skill and practice.

Closing unnecessary services closes TCP/UDP ports. Every operating system has some tool for you to see exactly what ports are open. Figure 19-9 shows an example of the `netstat` command in macOS.

```
●  ●  ●                ⌂ michaels@mediamac-2: ~ — ~ — zsh — 90×41

michaels@mediamac-2 ~                                                    [9:45:48]
> $ netstat -n
Active Internet connections
Proto Recv-Q Send-Q  Local Address          Foreign Address        (state)
tcp4       0   1238  192.168.4.78.17500     192.168.4.53.9941      ESTABLISHED
tcp4     262      0  192.168.4.78.17500     192.168.4.27.59229     ESTABLISHED
tcp4       0      0  192.168.4.78.62253     192.168.4.36.17500     ESTABLISHED
tcp4       0      0  192.168.4.78.62252     192.168.4.42.17500     ESTABLISHED
tcp4       0      0  192.168.4.78.62251     192.168.4.53.17500     ESTABLISHED
tcp4       0      0  192.168.4.78.62250     192.168.4.35.17500     ESTABLISHED
tcp4       0      0  192.168.4.78.62249     192.168.4.57.17500     ESTABLISHED
tcp4       0      0  192.168.4.78.62248     23.23.249.59.443       ESTABLISHED
tcp4       0      0  192.168.4.78.62245     108.160.165.138.443    ESTABLISHED
tcp4       0      0  192.168.4.78.62211     72.246.57.9.80         ESTABLISHED
tcp4       0      0  192.168.4.78.62210     23.205.120.9.80        ESTABLISHED
tcp4       0      0  192.168.4.78.62201     23.205.120.32.80       ESTABLISHED
tcp4       0      0  192.168.4.78.62200     23.205.120.32.80       ESTABLISHED
tcp4       0      0  192.168.4.78.62199     216.38.160.128.80      ESTABLISHED
tcp4       0      0  192.168.4.78.62197     173.194.115.45.80      ESTABLISHED
tcp4       0      0  192.168.4.78.62194     216.38.160.130.80      ESTABLISHED
tcp4       0      0  192.168.4.78.62191     173.194.115.45.80      ESTABLISHED
tcp4       0      0  192.168.4.78.62183     173.194.115.96.443     ESTABLISHED
tcp4       0      0  192.168.4.78.62170     74.125.227.188.80      ESTABLISHED
tcp4       0      0  192.168.4.78.62169     173.194.115.97.443     ESTABLISHED
tcp4       0      0  192.168.4.78.62161     173.194.115.57.443     ESTABLISHED
tcp4       0      0  192.168.4.78.62160     173.194.115.98.443     ESTABLISHED
tcp4       0      0  192.168.4.78.62150     173.194.115.96.80      ESTABLISHED
tcp4       0      0  192.168.4.78.62145     193.182.8.59.4070      ESTABLISHED
tcp4       0      0  127.0.0.1.62107        127.0.0.1.62109        ESTABLISHED
tcp4       0      0  127.0.0.1.62109        127.0.0.1.62107        ESTABLISHED
tcp4       0      0  127.0.0.1.62105        127.0.0.1.62106        ESTABLISHED
tcp4       0      0  127.0.0.1.62106        127.0.0.1.62105        ESTABLISHED
tcp4      85      0  192.168.4.78.62102     50.57.203.128.443      CLOSE_WAIT
tcp4       0      0  192.168.4.78.62048     54.243.247.94.443      ESTABLISHED
tcp4       0      0  127.0.0.1.3705         127.0.0.1.60713        ESTABLISHED
tcp4       0      0  127.0.0.1.60713        127.0.0.1.3705         ESTABLISHED
tcp4       0      0  127.0.0.1.3705         127.0.0.1.60712        ESTABLISHED
tcp4       0      0  127.0.0.1.60712        127.0.0.1.3705         ESTABLISHED
tcp4       0      0  192.168.4.78.60542     108.160.167.175.80     ESTABLISHED
tcp4       0      0  192.168.4.78.60529     192.168.4.19.445       ESTABLISHED
```

Figure 19-9   netstat in action

EXAM TIP   Closing ports can lead to a common network service issue, that of *blocked TCP/UDP ports*. A typical scenario you might need to troubleshoot at a client level is a newly installed Internet-aware application (like a game) that can't access the Internet. Blocked ports—by an overly zealous tech or user—can block network access.

A similar scenario on the server side can occur when one tech blocks ports and doesn't properly document his or her actions. Another tech wouldn't necessarily know the ports are blocked and could look to other issues when confronted with an application that can't access the network.

Unpatched/Legacy Systems

Unpatched systems—including operating systems and firmware—and legacy systems present a glaring security threat. You need to deal with such problems on live systems on your network. When it comes to unpatched OSs, well, patch or isolate them! There's a number of areas in the book that touch on proper patching, so we won't go into more detail here.

Unpatched firmware presents a little more of a challenge. Most firmware never needs to be or gets patched, but once in a while you'll run into devices that have a discovered flaw or security hole. These you'll need to patch.

 EXAM TIP Look for questions on hardening network systems that discuss disabling unnecessary systems, patching and upgrades for software, and upgrading firmware.

The process of patching device firmware varies from device to device, so you'll need to do some research on each. In general, you'll download a patch from the manufacturer and run it on the device. Make sure you have good power before you start the patch. If something goes wrong in the update, you'll brick whatever device you're trying to patch. There's no undo or patch rollback with firmware, so patch only when necessary.

Legacy systems are a different issue altogether. By *legacy* we mean systems that are no longer supported by the OS maker and are no longer patched. In that case you need to consider the function of the system, update if possible, and if not possible, you need to isolate the legacy systems behind some type of firewall that will give them the support they need. Equally, you need to be extremely careful about adding any software or hardware to the systems as doing so might create even more vulnerabilities.

Most companies and institutions have policies and best practices in place for dealing with legacy systems. Every computing device has a *system life cycle*, from shiny and new, to patched and secure, to "you're still using that old junk?"

System life cycle policies address *asset disposal* with the concept of reuse, repurpose, recycle. You shouldn't just throw old gear in the trash. Your old switches and routers might be perfect for a hungry non-profit's network. Donate and take a tax write-off. Repurpose older WAPs as simple bridges for devices that don't need high speed, for example, like printers and multifunction devices. Deal with anything that stored data by putting it through a shredder and tossing the remains in metal recycling.

Unencrypted Channels

The open nature of the Internet has made it fairly common for us to *use secure protocols* or channels such as VPNs, SSL/TLS, and SSH. It never ceases to amaze me, however, how often people use *unencrypted channels*—especially in the most unlikely places. It was only a few years ago I stumbled upon a tech using Telnet to do remote logins into a very critical router for an ISP.

In general, look for the following insecure protocols and unencrypted channels:

- Using Telnet instead of SSH for remote terminal connections.
- Using HTTP instead of HTTPS on Web sites.
- Using insecure remote desktops like VNC.
- Using any insecure protocol in the clear. Run them through a VPN!

Cleartext Credentials

Older protocols offer a modicum of security—you often need a valid user name and password, for example, when connecting to a File Transfer Protocol (FTP) server. The problem with such protocols (FTP, Telnet, POP3) is that user names and passwords are sent from the user to the server in cleartext. Credentials can be captured and, because they're not encrypted, *cleartext credentials* can be readily discovered.

There are many other places where cleartext turns up, such as in third-party applications and improperly configured applications that would normally have encrypted credentials.

The problem with third-party applications using cleartext credentials is that there's no way for you to know if they do so or not. Luckily, we live in a world filled with people who run packet sniffers on just about everything. These vulnerabilities are often discovered fairly quickly and reported. Most likely, you'll get an automatic patch.

The last place where cleartext credentials can still come through is poor configuration of applications that would otherwise be well protected. Almost any remote control program has some form of "no security" level setting. This might be as obvious as a "turn off security" option or it could be a setting such as Password Authentication Protocol (PAP) (which, if you recall, means cleartext passwords). The answer here is understanding your applications and knowing ahead of time how to configure the application to ensure good encryption of credentials.

RF Emanation

Radio waves can penetrate walls, to a certain extent, and accidental spill, called *RF emanation*, can lead to a security vulnerability. Avoid this by placing some form of filtering between your systems and the place where the bad guys are going to be using their super high-tech Bourne Identity spy tools to pick up on the emanations.

To combat these emanations, the U.S. National Security Agency (NSA) developed a series of standards called *TEMPEST*. TEMPEST defines how to shield systems and manifests in a number of different products, such as coverings for individual systems, wall coverings, and special window coatings. Unless you work for a U.S. government agency, the chance of you seeing TEMPEST technologies is pretty small.

Hardening Your Network

Once you've recognized threats and vulnerabilities, it's time to start applying security hardware, software, and processes to your network to prevent bad things from happening. This is called *hardening* your network. Let's look at three aspects of network hardening: physical security, network security, and host security.

Physical Security

There's an old saying: "The finest swordsman in all of France has nothing to fear from the second finest swordsman in all of France." It means that they do the same things and know the same techniques. The only difference between the two is that one is a little better than the other. There's a more modern extension of the old saying that says: "On the other hand, the finest swordsman in all of France can be defeated by a kid with a rocket launcher!" Which is to say that the inexperienced, when properly equipped, can and will often do something totally unexpected.

Proper security must address threats from the second finest swordsman as well as the kid. We can leave no stone unturned when it comes to hardening the network, and this begins with physical security. Physical threats manifest themselves in many forms, including property theft, data loss due to natural damage such as fire or natural disaster, data loss due to physical access, and property destruction resulting from accident or sabotage.

Let's look at physical security as a two-step process. First, prevent and control access to IT resources to appropriate personnel. Second, track the actions of those authorized (and sometimes unauthorized) personnel.

Prevention and Control

The first thing we have to do when it comes to protecting the network is to make the network resources accessible only to personnel who have a legitimate need to fiddle with them. Start with the simplest approach: a *lock*. Locking the door to the *network closet* or equipment room that holds servers, switches, routers, and other network gear goes a long way in protecting the network. Key control is critical here and includes assigning keys to appropriate staff, tracking key assignments, and collecting the keys when they are no longer needed by individuals who move on. This type of access must be guarded against circumvention by ensuring policies are followed regarding who may have or use the keys. The administrator who assigns keys should never give one to an unauthorized person without completing the appropriate procedures and paperwork.

Locking down servers within the server room with unique keys adds another layer of physical security to essential devices. Additionally, all modern server chassis come with *tamper detection* features that will log in the motherboard's nonvolatile RAM (NVRAM) if the chassis has been opened. The log will show chassis intrusion with a date and time. And it's not just the server room (and resources with it) that we need to lock up. How about the front door? There are a zillion stories of thieves and saboteurs coming in through the front (or sometimes back) door and making their way straight to the corporate treasure chest. A locked front door can be opened by an authorized person, and an unauthorized person can attempt to enter through that already opened door, what's called *tailgating*. While it is possible to prevent tailgating with policies, it is only human nature to "hold the door" for that person coming in behind you. Tailgating is especially easy to do when dealing with large organizations in which people don't know everyone else. If the tailgater dresses like everyone else and maybe has a badge that looks right, he or she probably won't be challenged. Add an armload of gear, and who could blame you for helping that person by holding the door?

There are a couple of techniques available to foil a tailgater. The first is a *security guard*. Guards are great. They get to know everyone's faces. They are there to protect assets and can lend a helping hand to the overloaded, but authorized, person who needs in. They are multipurpose in that they can secure building access, secure individual room and office access, and perform facility patrols. The guard station can serve as central control of security systems such as video surveillance and key control. Like all humans, security guards are subject to attacks such as social engineering, but for flexibility, common sense, and a way to take the edge off of high security, you can't beat a professional security guard or two.

For areas where an entry guard is not practical, there is another way to prevent tailgating called a mantrap. A *mantrap* is an entryway with two successive locked doors and a small space between them providing one-way entry or exit. After entering the first door, the second door cannot be unlocked until the first door is closed and secured. Access to the second door may be a simple key or may require approval by someone else who watches the trap space on video. Unauthorized persons remain trapped until they are approved for entry, let out the first door, or held for the appropriate authorities.

Brass keys aren't the only way to unlock a door. This is the 21st century, after all. Twenty-five years ago, I worked in a campus facility with a lot of interconnected buildings. Initial access to buildings was through a security guard and then we traveled between the buildings with connecting tunnels. Each end of the tunnels had a set of sliding glass doors that kind of worked like the doors on the starship *Enterprise*. We were assigned *badges* with built-in radio frequency ID (RFID) chips. As we neared a door, the RFID chip was queried by circuitry in the door frame called a *proximity reader*, checked against a database for authorization, and then the door slid open electromechanically.

It was so cool and so fast that people would jog the hallways during lunch hours and not even slow down for any of the doors. A quarter century later, the technology has only gotten better. The badges in the old days were a little larger than a credit card and about three times as thick. Today, the RFID chip can be implanted in a small, unobtrusive *key fob*, like the kind you use to unlock your car.

 EXAM TIP *Smart cards* today use microprocessor circuitry to enable authentication, among other things. They can certainly be used to gain access, but also to make transactions and more.

If there is a single drawback to all of the physical *door access controls* mentioned so far, it is that access is generally governed by something that is in the possession of someone who has authorization to enter a locked place. That something may be a key, a badge, a key fob with a chip, or some other physical token. The problem here, of course, is that these items can be given or taken away. If not reported in a timely fashion, a huge security gap exists.

To move from the physical possession problem of entry access, physical security can be governed by something that is known only to authorized persons. A code or password that is assigned to a specific individual for a particular asset can be entered on an alphanumeric *keypad* that controls an electric or electromechanical door lock. There is a similar door lock mechanism called a cipher lock. A *cipher lock* is a door unlocking system that uses a door handle, a latch, and a sequence of mechanical push buttons. When the buttons are pressed in the correct order, the door unlocks and the door handle works. Turning the handle opens the latch or, if you pressed the wrong order of buttons, clears the unlocking mechanism so you can try again. Care must be taken by staff who are assigned a code to protect that code.

This knowledge-based approach to access control may be a little better than a possession-based system because information is more difficult to steal than a physical token. However, poor management of information can leave an asset vulnerable. Poor management includes writing codes down and leaving the notes easily accessible. Good password/code control means memorizing information where possible or securing written notes about codes and passwords.

Well-controlled information is difficult to steal, but it's not perfect because sharing information is so easy. Someone can loan out his or her password to a seemingly trustworthy friend or co-worker. While most times this is probably not a real security risk, there is always a chance that there could be disastrous results. Social engineering or overtrusting can cause someone to share a private code or password. Systems should be established to reassign codes and passwords regularly to deal with the natural leakage that can occur with this type of security.

 EXAM TIP All this talk about intangible asset control, like passwords, doesn't mean you should ignore tangible asset control. Many companies employ RFID and other electronic devices as *asset tracking tags* for inventory control purposes. Plus they'll use low-tech physical security tools like special stickers or zip ties for *tamper detection* in its most basic use of the term.

The best way to prevent loss of access control is to build physical security around a key that cannot be shared or lost. *Biometric* access calls for using a unique physical characteristic of a person to permit access to a controlled IT resource. Doorways can be triggered to unlock using fingerprint readers, facial recognition cameras, voice analyzers, retinal blood vessel scanners, or other, more exotic characteristics. While not perfect, biometrics represent a giant leap in secure access. For even more effective access control, *multifactor authentication* can be used, where access is granted based on more than one access technique. For instance, in order to gain access to a secure server room, a user might have to pass a fingerprint scan and have an approved security fob.

Let me point out something related to all of this door locking and unlocking technology. Physical asset security is important, but generally not as important as the safety of people. Designers of these door-locking systems must take into account safety features such as what happens to the state of a lock in an emergency like a power failure or fire. Doors with electromechanical locking controls can respond to an emergency condition and lock or unlock automatically, respectively called *fail close* or *fail open*. Users and occupants of facilities should be informed about what to expect in these types of events.

Monitoring

Okay, the physical assets of the network have been secured. It took guards, locks, passwords, eyeballs, and a pile of technology. Now, the only people who have access to IT resources are those who have been carefully selected, screened, trained, and authorized. The network is safe, right? Maybe not. You see, here comes the old problem again: people are human. Humans make mistakes, humans can become disgruntled, and humans can be tempted. The only real solution is heavily armored robots with artificial intelligence and bad attitudes. But until that becomes practical, maybe what we need to do next is to ensure that those authorized people can be held accountable for what they do with the physical resources of the network.

Enter video surveillance. With *video surveillance* of facilities and assets, authorized staff can be monitored for mistakes or something more nefarious. Better still, our kid with a rocket launcher (remember him?) can be tracked and caught after he sneaks into the building.

Let's look at two video surveillance concepts. *Video monitoring* entails using remotely monitored visual systems and covers everything from identifying a delivery person knocking on the door at the loading dock, to looking over the shoulder of someone working on the keyboard of a server. *IP cameras* and *closed-circuit televisions (CCTVs)* are specific implementations of video monitoring. CCTV is a self-contained, closed system in which video cameras feed their signal to specific, dedicated monitors and storage devices. CCTV cameras can be monitored in real time by security staff, but the monitoring location is limited to wherever the video monitors are placed. If real-time monitoring is not required or viewing is delayed, stored video can be reviewed later as needed.

 EXAM TIP Many small office/home office (SOHO) video surveillance systems rely on *motion detection systems* that start and stop recordings based on actions caught by the camera(s). This has the advantage of saving a lot of storage space, hopefully only catching the bad guys on film when they're breaking into your house or stealing your lawn gnomes.

IP cameras have the benefit of being a more open system than CCTV. IP video streams can be monitored by anyone who is authorized to do so and can access the network on which the cameras are installed. The stream can be saved to a hard drive or network storage device. Multiple workstations can simultaneously monitor video streams and multiple cameras with ease.

Network Security

Protecting network assets is more than a physical exercise. Physically speaking, we can harden a network by preventing and controlling access to tangible network resources through things like locking doors and video monitoring. Next we will want to protect our network from malicious, suspicious, or potential threats that might connect to or access the network. This is called *access control* and it encompasses both physical security and network security. In this section we look at some technologies and techniques to implement network access control, including user account control, edge devices, posture assessment, persistent and non-persistent agents, guest networks, and quarantine networks.

Controlling User Accounts

A user account is just information: nothing more than a combination of a user name and password. Like any important information, it's critical to control who has a user account and to track what these accounts can do. Access to user accounts should be restricted to the assigned individuals (no sharing, no stealing), and those accounts should have permission to access only the resources they need, no more. This control over what a legitimate account can do is called the *principle of least privilege* approach to network security and is, by far, the most common approach used in networks.

Tight control of user accounts helps prevent unauthorized access or improper access. *Unauthorized access* means a person does something beyond his or her authority to do. *Improper access* occurs when a user who shouldn't have access gains access through some means. Often the improper access happens when a network tech or administrator makes a mistake.

Disabling unused accounts is an important first step in addressing these problems, but good user account control goes far deeper than that. One of your best tools for user account control is to implement groups. Instead of giving permissions to individual user accounts, give them to groups; this makes keeping track of the permissions assigned to individual user accounts much easier.

Figure 19-10 shows an example of giving permissions to a group for a folder in Windows Server. Once a group is created and its permissions are set, you can then add user accounts to that group as needed. Any user account that becomes a member of a group automatically gets the permissions assigned to that group.

Figure 19-11 shows an example of adding a user to a newly created group in the same Windows Server system.

You should always put user accounts into groups to enhance network security. This applies to simple networks, which get local groups, and to domain-based networks, which get domain groups. Do not underestimate the importance of properly configuring both local groups and domain groups.

Groups are a great way to get increased complexity without increasing the administrative burden on network administrators because all network operating systems combine permissions. When a user is a member of more than one group, which permissions does he or she have with respect to any particular resource?

In all network operating systems, the permissions of the groups are *combined*; this results in the *effective permissions* the user has to access a given resource. Let's use an

Figure 19-10

Giving a group
permissions
for a folder in
Windows

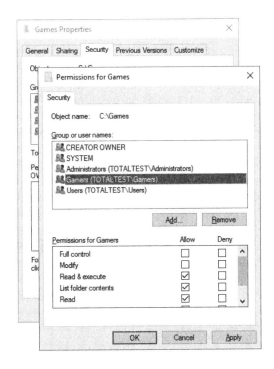

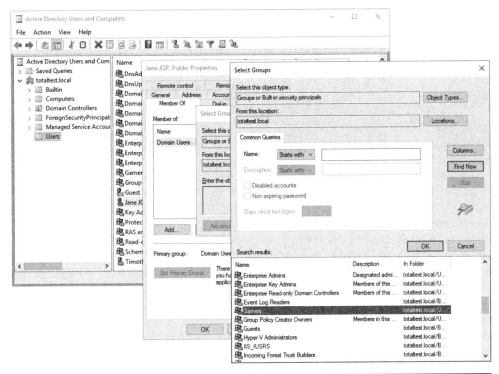

Figure 19-11   Adding a user to a newly created group

example from Windows Server. If Timmy is a member of the Sales group, which has List Folder Contents permission to a folder, and he is also a member of the Managers group, which has Read and Execute permissions to the same folder, Timmy will have List Folder Contents *and* Read and Execute permissions to that folder.

Combined permissions can also lead to *conflicting permissions*, where a user does not get access to a needed resource because one of his groups has Deny permission to that resource. Deny always trumps any other permission.

Watch out for *default* user accounts and groups—they can grant *improper access* or secret *backdoor access* to your network! All network operating systems have a default Everyone group, and it can easily be used to sneak into shared resources. This Everyone group, as its name implies, literally includes anyone who connects to that resource. Some versions of Windows give full control to the Everyone group by default. All of the default groups—Everyone, Guest, Users—define broad groups of users. Never use them unless you intend to permit all those folks to access a resource. If you use one of the default groups, remember to configure it with the proper permissions to prevent users from doing things you don't want them to do with a shared resource!

All of these groups only do one thing for you: they enable you to keep track of your user accounts. That way you know resources are only available for users who need those resources, and users only access the resources you want them to use.

Before I move on, let me add one more tool to your kit: diligence. Managing user accounts is a thankless and difficult task, but one that you must stay on top of if you want to keep your network secure. Most organizations integrate the creating, disabling/enabling, and deleting of user accounts with the work of their human resources folks. Whenever a person joins, quits, or moves, the network admin is always one of the first to know!

The administration of permissions can become incredibly complex—even with judicious use of groups. You now know what happens when a user account has multiple sets of permissions to the same resource, but what happens if the user has one set of permissions to a folder and a different set of permissions to one of its subfolders? This brings up a phenomenon called *inheritance*. I won't get into the many ways different network operating systems handle inherited permissions. Luckily for you, the CompTIA Network+ exam doesn't test you on all the nuances of combined or inherited permissions—just be aware they exist. Those who go on to get more advanced certifications, on the other hand, must become extremely familiar with the many complex permutations of permissions.

Edge

Access control can be broadly defined as exactly what it sounds like: one or more methods to govern or limit entry to a particular environment. Historically, this was accomplished and enforced with simply communicated rules and policies and human oversight. As systems grew in size and sophistication, it became possible to enforce the governing rules using automated technology, relieving managers to focus on other tasks. These control technologies began their developmental life as a central control system with peripheral actuators.

Let me show you what I mean. Take the example of the *Star Trek*–like security door system I talked about in the "Physical Security" section a little while ago. That system worked by having a computer with a database of doors, staff, and a decision matrix. Because it controlled many doors, it was centrally located and had wires running to and from it to every controlled door on the campus. Each door had two peripherals installed: a proximity reader with a status indicator, and a door open/close actuator. The proximity reader would read the data from the RFID chip carried by someone and send the data over a sometimes very long data cable to the control computer.

The computer would take the data and the door identifier and check to see it the data was valid, current, and authorized to pass through the door. If it did not meet authorization criteria, a data signal was sent back down the data line to cause a red LED to blink on the proximity reader. Of course, the door would not open. If all of the criteria were met for authorization, a good signal was sent down the data line to make a green LED glow, and power was sent down the line to operate the door actuator.

We've talked about the benefits of this system, so let's look at a few drawbacks. First, the system was proprietary. As systems like these were introduced, competition stymied any effort to create industry standards. Central control meant that large, powerful boxes had to be developed as central controllers. Expandability became an issue as controllers maxed out the number of security doors they could support. Finally, the biggest problem was the large amount of cabling needed to support large numbers of doors and potentially great distances from the central controller. The problem was made worse when facilities had to retrofit non-secure doors for secure ones.

A lot of time and technology has passed since those days. Today's automated secure entry systems take advantage of newer technologies by leveraging existing network wiring. By using IP traffic and Power over Ethernet (PoE), the entire system can usually run over the existing wiring. Applications and protocols have been standardized so they can run on existing server hardware.

Also contributing to the simplification and standardization of these security systems are edge devices. An *edge* device is a piece of hardware that has been optimized to perform a task. Edge devices work in coordination with other edge devices and controllers.

The primary defining characteristic of an edge device is that it is installed closer to a client device, such as a workstation or a security door, than to the core or backbone of a network. In this instance, a control program that tracks entries, distributes and synchronizes copies of databases, and tracks door status can be run on a central server. In turn, it communicates with edge devices. The edge devices keep a local copy of the database and make their own decisions about whether or not a door should be opened.

Posture Assessment

Network access control (NAC) is a standardized approach to verify that a node meets certain criteria before it is allowed to connect to a network. Many product vendors implement NAC in different ways. Network Admission Control (also known as NAC) is Cisco's version of network access control.

Cisco's NAC can dictate that specific criteria must be met before allowing a node to connect to a secure network. Devices that do not meet the required criteria can be shunted with no connection or made to connect to another network. The types of criteria that can be checked are broad ranging and can be tested for in a number of ways. For the purposes of this text, we are mostly concerned about verifying that a device attempting to connect is not a threat to network security.

Cisco uses *posture assessment* as one of the tools to implement NAC. Posture assessment is a feature of certain advanced Cisco network appliances. A switch or router that has posture assessment enabled and configured will query network devices to confirm that they meet minimum security standards before being permitted to connect to the production network.

Posture assessment includes checking things like type and version of anti-malware, level of QoS, and type/version of operating system. Posture assessment can perform different checks at succeeding stages of connection. Certain tests can be applied at the initial physical connection. After that, more checks can be conducted prior to logging in. Prelogin assessment may look at the type and version of operating system, detect whether keystroke loggers are present, and check whether the station is real or a virtual machine. The host may be queried for digital certificates, anti-malware version and currency, whether the machine is real or virtual, and a large list of other checks.

If everything checks out, the host will be granted a connection to the production network. If posture assessment finds a deficiency or potential threat, the host can be denied a connection or connected to a non-production network until it has been sufficiently upgraded.

Persistent and Non-persistent Agents

How does a host respond to a posture assessment query? Like a lot of things, the answer depends on the environment. Let's focus on a workstation to answer this question. A workstation requires something called an *agent* to answer a posture assessment query. An *agent* is a process or program running within the computer that scans the computer to create an inventory of configuration information, resources, and assets. When the workstation attempts to connect to the network through a posture assessment–enabled device, it is the agent that answers the security query.

Agents come in two flavors. The first is a small scanning program that, once installed on the computer, stays installed and runs every time the computer boots up. These agents are composed of modules that perform a thorough inventory of each security-oriented element in the computer. This type of agent is known as a *persistent agent*. If there is no agent to respond to a posture assessment query, the node is not permitted to connect to the production network.

Sometimes a computer needs to connect to a secure network via a Web site portal. Some portals provide VPN access to a corporate network, while others provide a less-robust connection. In either case, it is important that these kinds of stations meet the appropriate security standards before they are granted access to the network, just as a dedicated, onsite machine must. To that end, a posture assessment is installed at the endpoint. The endpoint in this instance is the device that actually creates a secure attachment to the production network. At the workstation, a small agent that scans only for the queried conditions is downloaded and run. If the query is satisfied that the station needing access is acceptable, connection is granted and the node can access the production network. When the node disconnects from the network and leaves the portal site, the agent is released from memory. This type of agent is known as a *non-persistent agent.*

It is worthwhile to note a couple of things here that, while not necessarily critical to the CompTIA Network+ exam, can be useful to know in the real world. First, the Cisco network admission control process does not consist solely of the posture assessment module in an edge device and the node agent. There is also the Cisco *Access Control Server (ACS).* It is within this program/process/server that the actual decision to admit or deny a node is made. From there, the ACS directs the edge access device to allow a connection or to implement a denial or redirect. There are additional components and configurations required to create a complete network access control system.

Also useful to know is that Cisco is not the only player in town (although they are decidedly the biggest in this arena) and using an agent is not the only way to check a node for security compliance. To paraphrase Shakespeare: "There are more things in heaven and earth, Horatio … and they aren't all workstations." There are tablets, smartphones, other bring-your-own devices (BYOD), switches, printers, and plenty of other things that can connect to a network. For this reason, there needs to be a flexible, cross-platform method of checking for node security before granting access to a secure network. For these platforms, an 802.1X supplicant, in the form of either an agent or a client, can be installed in the device. You'll remember 802.1X from Chapter 10, "Securing TCP/IP."

Further, a number of vendors have implemented *agent-less* posture assessment capability. Using a variety of techniques, hosts can be checked for things like a device fingerprint (set of characteristics that uniquely identifies a particular device), a CVE ID, or other agent-less responses. These techniques are easily implemented on a large variety of platforms and they work in a wide array of network environments.

Whether a station responds to a posture assessment query with or without an agent, the result is still one of three options: clearance into the network, connection denied, or redirect to a non-production network. Let's talk about those non-production networks.

Guest Networks and Quarantine Networks

It may be desirable for an organization to provide a connection to the Internet as a service to visitors and clients. Envision a coffee shop that welcomes its patrons to check e-mail on their portable devices while enjoying an iced latte with two pumps of white cacao mocha. As you turn on your laptop to scan for Wi-Fi networks, two SSIDs appear. One SSID is labeled CustomerNet and the other is called CorpNet. Some might try to hack into CorpNet, but clearly the intent is for consumers to attach to CustomerNet and gain access to the Internet through that connection. The CustomerNet network is an example of a *guest network.*

A guest network can contain or allow access to any resource that management deems acceptable to be used by non-secure hosts that attach to the guest network. Those resources might include an Internet connection, a local Web server with a company directory or catalog, and similar assets that are nonessential to the function of the organization.

In the preceding example, access to the guest network results from a user selecting the correct SSID. More in line with the goals of this book would be a scenario where a station attempts to connect to a network but is refused access because it does not conform to an acceptable level of security. In this case, the station might be assigned an IP address that only enables it to connect to the guest network. If the station needs access to the production network, the station could be updated to meet the appropriate security requirements. If it only requires the resources afforded by the guest network, then it's good to go.

Whenever a node is *denied* a connection to the production network, it is considered to be quarantined. It is common practice for suspicious nodes or nodes with active threats detected to be denied a connection or sent to a *quarantine network*.

So let's put it all together. An organization may have a multitude of production networks, a guest network, and a quarantine network. Who gets to go where? Stations that pass a profile query performed by an edge device with posture assessment features can connect to a production network. From there, access to the various networks and resources is determined by privileges granted to the login credentials.

If a station does not pass the posture query but does not appear to pose a threat, it will likely be connected to the guest network. Stations with active malware or that display a configuration that is conducive to hacking will be quarantined with no connection or connected to a quarantine network.

Device Hardening

Proper network hardening requires implementing device hardening. Many of the hardening techniques and best practices discussed for network access and server security apply to switches, routers, and network appliances. Let's look at five topics.

Network devices come with default credentials, the username and password that enables you to log into the device for configuration. *Changing default credentials* should be the first step in hardening a new device. As with any other system, *avoiding common passwords* adds security.

Keep network devices up to date. That means upgrading firmware, patching and updating as necessary to close any security gaps exposed over time.

Services on network devices like routers include common things, like Telnet and HTTP access; and also things you don't normally see, like TCP and UDP small services, debugging and testing tools that primarily use ports 20 and lower. If enabled, these services can be used to launch DoS and other attacks. All modern Cisco devices have these disabled; Cisco's hardening rules insist on *disabling unnecessary services*.

Using secure protocols hardens network devices. Don't use Telnet to access a managed switch or router, for example, but use SSH so that the communication is encrypted.

Disabling unused ports on network devices enhances port security for access control. This includes standard IP ports and device ports, both physical and virtual for the latter.

 EXAM TIP Attackers can use *traffic floods*—excessive or malformed packets—to conduct DoS attacks on networks and hosts, targeting vulnerable switches through their switch ports. Better switches today employ *flood guards* to detect and block excessive traffic. This enhances *switch port protection*.

Host Security

The first and last bastion of defense for an entire infrastructure's security is at the individual hosts. It's the first bastion for preventing dangerous things that users do from propagating to the rest of the network. It's the last bastion in that anything evil coming from the outside world must be stopped here.

We've talked about local security issues several times in this book and even in this chapter. User accounts and strong passwords, for example, obviously provide a first line of defense at the host level. So let's look at another aspect of host security: malware prevention and recovery.

Malware Prevention and Recovery

The only way to protect your PC permanently from getting malware is to disconnect it from the Internet and never permit any potentially infected software to touch your precious computer. Because neither scenario is likely these days, you need to use specialized anti-malware programs to help stave off the inevitable assaults. Even with the best anti-malware tools, there are times when malware still manages to strike your computer. When you discover infected systems, you need to know how to stop the spread of the malware to other computers, how to fix infected computers, and how to remediate (restore) the system as close to its original state as possible.

Malware Prevention   If your PC has been infected by malware, you'll bump into some strange things before you can even run an anti-malware scan. Like a medical condition, malware causes unusual symptoms that should stand out from your everyday computer use. You need to become a PC physician and understand what each of these symptoms means.

Malware's biggest strength is its flexibility: it can look like anything. In fact, a lot of malware attacks can feel like normal PC "wonkiness"—momentary slowdowns, random one-time crashes, and so on. Knowing when a weird application crash is actually a malware attack is half the battle.

A slow PC can mean you're running too many applications at once or you've been hit with malware. How do you tell the difference? In this case, it's the frequency. If it's happening a lot, even when all of your applications are closed, you've got a problem. This goes for frequent lockups, too. If Windows starts misbehaving (more than usual), run your anti-malware application right away.

Malware, however, doesn't always jump out at you with big system crashes. Some malware tries to rename system files, change file permissions, or hide files completely. Most of these issues are easily caught by a regular anti-malware scan, so as long as you remain vigilant, you'll be okay.

NOTE   While it's not necessarily a malware attack, watch out for hijacked e-mail accounts, too, belonging either to you or to someone you know. Hackers can hit both e-mail clients and Webmail users. If you start receiving some fishy (or phishy) e-mail messages, change your Web-based e-mail password or scan your PC for malware.

Some malware even fights back, defending itself from your many attempts to remove it. If your Windows Update feature stops working, preventing you from patching your PC, you've most likely got malware. If other tools and utilities throw up an "Access Denied" road block, you've got malware. If you lose all Internet connectivity, either the malware is stopping you or removing the malware broke your connection. In this case, you might need to reconfigure your Internet connection: reinstall your NIC and its drivers, reboot your router, and so on.

Even your browser and anti-malware applications can turn against you. If you type in one Web address and end up at a different site than you anticipated, a malware infection might have overwritten your hosts file and thus automatically changed the DNS resolver cache. Most browser redirections point you to phishing scams or Web sites full of free downloads (that are, of course, covered in malware). In fact, some free anti-malware applications are actually malware—what techs call a *rogue anti-malware* program. You can avoid these rogue applications by sticking to the recommended lists of anti-malware software found online.

Watch for security alerts in Windows, either from Windows' built-in security tools or from your third-party anti-malware program. Windows 10 includes a tool called Security and Maintenance (see Figure 19-12). (Windows 7 calls this Action Center.) You don't actually configure much using these applets; they just tell you whether or not you are protected. These tools place an icon and pop up a notification in the notification area whenever Windows detects a problem.

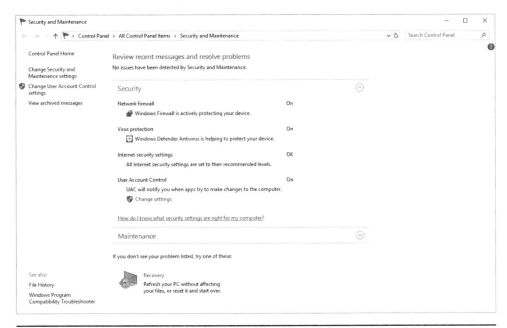

Figure 19-12 Windows 10 Security and Maintenance

Symptoms of a Compromised System   A system hit by malware will eventually show the effects, although in any number of ways. The most common symptoms of malware on a *compromised system* are general sluggishness and random crashes. In some cases, Web browsers might default to unpleasant or unwanted Web sites. Frequently, compromised systems increase network outflow a lot.

If you get enough compromised systems in your network, especially if those systems form part of a botnet or DDoS attack force, your network will suffer. The amount of traffic specifically doing the bidding of the malware on the systems can hog network bandwidth, making the network sluggish.

Watch for *top talkers*—systems with very high network output—and a network that doesn't seem nearly as fast as the specs say it should be. Monitor employee complaints about sluggish machines or poor network performance carefully and act as soon as you think you might have infected systems. You need to deal with malware—hopefully catching it before it strikes, but dealing with it swiftly when it does. Let's go there next.

Dealing with Malware   You can deal with malware in several ways: anti-malware programs, training and awareness, patch management, and remediation.

At the very least, every computer should run an anti-malware program. If possible, add an appliance that runs anti-malware programs against incoming data from your network. Also remember that an anti-malware program is only as good as its updates—keep everyone's definition file (explained a bit later) up to date with, literally, nightly updates! Users must be trained to look for suspicious ads, programs, and pop-ups, and understand that they must not click these things. The more you teach users about malware, the more aware they'll be of potential threats. Your organization should have policies and procedures in place so everyone knows what to do if they encounter malware. Finally, a good tech maintains proper incident response records to see if any pattern to attacks emerges. He or she can then adjust policies and procedures to mitigate these attacks.

EXAM TIP   One of the most important malware mitigation procedures is to keep systems under your control patched and up to date through proper patch management. Microsoft does a very good job of putting out bug fixes and patches as soon as problems occur. Microsoft isn't perfect, and sometimes new exploits are found in the patches they release. Still, at the end of the day, a patched system will likely be more secure than an unpatched one. If your systems aren't set up to update automatically, then perform manual updates regularly.

Anti-malware Programs   An *anti-malware program* such as a classic *antivirus* program protects your PC in two ways. It can be both sword and shield, working in an active seek-and-destroy mode and in a passive sentry mode. When ordered to seek and destroy, the program scans the computer's boot sector and files for viruses and, if it finds any, presents you with the available options for removing or disabling them. Anti-malware programs can also operate as *virus shields* that passively monitor a computer's activity, checking for viruses only when certain events occur, such as a program executing or a file being downloaded.

NOTE The term *antivirus* is becoming obsolete (as are *anti-spyware* and similar terms). Viruses are only a small component of the many types of malware. Many people continue to use the term as a synonym for anti-malware.

Anti-malware programs use different techniques to combat different types of malware. They detect boot sector viruses simply by comparing the drive's boot sector to a standard boot sector. This works because most boot sectors are basically the same. Some anti-malware programs make a backup copy of the boot sector. If they detect a virus, the programs use that backup copy to replace the infected boot sector. Executable viruses are a little more difficult to find because they can be on any file in the drive. To detect executable viruses, the anti-malware program uses a library of signatures. A *signature* is the code pattern of a known virus. The anti-malware program compares an executable file to its library of signatures. There have been instances where a perfectly clean program coincidentally held a virus signature. Usually, the anti-malware program's creator provides a patch to prevent further alarms.

Anti-malware software comes in multiple forms today. First is the classic *host-based anti-malware* that is installed on individual systems. Host-based anti-malware works beautifully, but is hard to administer when you have a number of systems. An alternative used in larger networks is *network-based anti-malware*. In this case a single anti-malware server runs on a number of systems (in some cases each host has a small client). These network-based programs are much easier to update and administer.

Last is *cloud/server-based anti-malware*. These servers store the software on a remote location (in the cloud or on a local server), but it's up to each host to access the software and run it. This has the advantage of storing nothing on the host system and making updating easier, but suffers from lack of administration as it's still up to the user on each host to run the anti-malware program.

EXAM TIP Expect a question on the CompTIA Network+ exam that addresses the *security implications/considerations* of malware and cloud resources. Who is responsible for security, the provider or the customer? Framed this way, a typical correct answer puts cloud resource security on the provider, not the customer. The customer is responsible for host security.

Firewalls

Firewalls are devices or software that protect an internal network from unauthorized access by acting as a filter. That's right; all a firewall does is filter traffic that flows through its ports. Firewalls are essential tools in the fight against malicious programs on the Internet.

The most basic job of the firewall is to look at each packet and decide based on a set of *rules* whether to *block* or *allow* the traffic. This traffic can be either *inbound traffic*, packets coming from outside the network, or *outbound traffic*, packets leaving the network.

Types of Firewalls

Firewalls come in many different forms. The types covered in this section are the common ones CompTIA wants you to be familiar with.

Software vs. Hardware Firewalls

The *network-based firewall* is often implemented in some sort of *hardware appliance* or is built into the router that is installed between the LAN and the wilds of the Internet. Most network techs' first encounter with a network-based firewall is the *SOHO firewall* built in to most consumer-grade routers. These firewalls form the first line of defense, providing protection for the whole network. While they do a great job of protecting whole networks, they can't provide any help if the malicious traffic is originating from inside the network itself. That is why we have host-based firewalls.

A *host-based firewall* is a software firewall installed on a "host" that provides firewall services for just that machine. A great example of this type of firewall is the Windows Firewall/Windows Defender Firewall (Figure 19-13) that has shipped with every version of Windows since XP. This makes the host-based firewall probably one of the most common types of firewalls you will encounter in your career as a network tech.

Figure 19-13   Windows Defender Firewall in Windows 10

Advanced Firewall Techniques and Features

Knowing that a firewall can live in the network or on a host is all well and good, but firewalls are very sophisticated these days and you should be familiar with the features that separate a modern firewall from a dumb *packet filter*. One of the first modern techniques added to firewalls is *stateful inspection*, or the capability to tell if a packet is part of an existing connection. In other words, the firewall is aware of the packet's state, as it relates to other packets.

This is an upgrade to the older *stateless inspection* model where the firewall looked at each packet fresh, with no regard to the state of the packet's relation to any other packet.

Building on the stateful firewall, firewalls that are *application/context aware* operate at Layer 7 of the OSI model and filter based on the application or service that originated the traffic. This makes context-aware firewalls invaluable in stopping port-hopping applications such as BitTorrent from overloading your network.

Next-Generation Firewalls   A *next-generation firewall (NGFW)* functions at multiple layers of the OSI model to tackle traffic no traditional firewall can filter alone. A Layer 3 firewall can filter packets based on IP addresses, for example. A Layer 5 firewall can filter based on port numbers. Layer 7 firewalls understand different application protocols and can filter on the contents of the application data. An NGFW handles all of this and more.

Unified Threat Management   Finally, modern, dedicated security appliances implement *unified threat management (UTM)*, marrying traditional firewalls with other security services, such as network-based IPS, load balancing, and more. (CompTIA uses the term *UTM appliance* to describe appliances that implement UTM.) UTM mitigates aggressive attacks such as *advanced persistent threats (APTs)*—organized, ongoing attacks on a specific entity. (A good example of an APT is a terrorist organization trying to hack into government security agency computers.)

Implementing and Configuring Firewalls

Now that you have a solid understanding of what a firewall is and how it works, let's delve into the details of installing and configuring a hardware firewall on a network. We'll start with the now familiar Bayland Widgets network and their gateway (Figure 19-14).

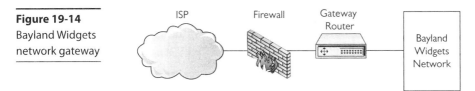

Figure 19-14
Bayland Widgets
network gateway

The location of the firewall in the Bayland Widgets network is one of the most common locations for a firewall. By placing the firewall between the trusted internal network and the Internet, it can see all the traffic flowing between the two networks. This also means that the firewall's performance is critical for our connection speed. If the firewall becomes overloaded, it can easily bring a 1-Gbps Internet connection down to 100 Mbps or slower speeds—yikes! In this case, Bayland Widgets has chosen a powerful Cisco ASA security appliance to provide the firewall.

Physically installing a firewall is just like installing other networking equipment such as routers and switches. The entry-level or SOHO models usually have a fixed number of ports, often with a fixed-purpose function (like dedicated ports for WAN traffic). Enterprise-grade hardware (typically supporting 200+ users) often is built around the idea of a flexible function that supports having cards added for different interface types and that can be reconfigured as the network changes. Once the hardware is plugged in, it's time to start configuring your firewall's settings.

Restricting Access via ACLs

Modern firewalls come with a massive number of features, and configuring them can be a daunting task for any network tech. But at its core, configuring a firewall is about defining which traffic can flow and which traffic shall not pass. This rule often takes the form of an *access control list (ACL)*, a rule applied to an interface that allows or *denies* traffic based on things like source or destination IP addresses. ACLs can restrict access to network resources.

NOTE A basic ACL can be thought of as a stateless firewall. In fact, many of the early firewalls were just ACLs on routers.

Now that we know what an ACL is, let's take a look at one that you might find on a Cisco router or firewall:

```
access-list 10 deny 10.11.12.0 0.0.0.255
access-list 10 permit any
```

That looks rather cryptic at first glance, but what it's doing is very simple. The beginning of the first line, `access-list 10`, tells IOS that we want to create an ACL and its number is 10 (back in the day, IOS ACLs only had numbers, not names). The end of the first line, `deny 10.11.12.0 0.0.0.255`, is the actual rule we want the firewall to apply. In this case, it means deny all traffic from the 10.11.12.0/24 subnet.

That's all well and good; any traffic coming from the 10.11.12.0/24 subnet will be dropped like a bad habit. But what's up with that second line, `access-list 10 permit any`? Well, that's there because of a very important detail about ACLs: they have an *implicit deny any*, or *automatically deny any packets that don't match a rule*. So in this case, if we stopped after the first line, no traffic would get through because we don't have a rule that explicitly permits it! So to make our ACL be a firewall instead of a brick wall, the last rule in this list will permit through any traffic that wasn't dropped by the first rule.

Once the ACL has been created, it must be assigned to an interface to be of any use. One interesting feature of ACLs is that they don't just get plugged in to an interface. You must specify the rules that apply to each *direction* the traffic flows. Traffic flowing through an interface can be thought of as either *inbound*, traffic entering from the network, or *outbound*, traffic flowing from the firewall out to the network. This is an important detail because you can and often want to have different rules for traffic entering and leaving through an interface.

SIM Check out the excellent Chapter 19 "Implicit Deny" Show! over at **http://totalsem.com/007**. It's a good tool for reviewing filtering techniques.

ACLs are but one method for configuring a firewall. While they may seem primitive, we've only scratched the surface of what they can do. More advanced ACLs provide the interface to many of the advanced stateful features of a modern firewall. But don't discount the simple ones we've looked at here. They are still very important in modern network security, providing the critical filtering to keep traffic flowing where it should and, maybe more importantly, from flowing where it shouldn't.

EXAM TIP   Firewalls and other advanced networking devices offer all sorts of filtering. *Web filtering*, for example, enables networks to block specific Web site access. In contrast, *content filtering* enables administrators to filter traffic based on specific signatures or keywords (such as profane language). *IP filtering* blocks specific IP address traffic; *port filtering* blocks traffic on specific ports. All of these filtering options are fairly standard network hardening techniques.

The CompTIA Network+ objectives use adjectives applied to devices to describe these filtering options. They're pretty straightforward. A *content filter* is an advanced networking device that implements content filtering.

DMZ and Firewall Placement

The use of a single firewall between the network and the ISP in the example shown in Figure 19-14 is just one approach to firewall placement. That configuration works well in simple networks or when you want strong isolation between all clients on the inside of the firewall. But what happens when we have servers, like a Web server, that need less restricted access to the Internet? That's where the concepts of the DMZ and internal/external firewalls come in.

A *demilitarized zone (DMZ)* is a network segment carved out by normally two routers—with firewalls—to provide a special place (a zone) on the network for any servers that need to be publicly accessible from the Internet. By definition, a DMZ uses *network segmentation* as a mitigation technique against attacks on the network.

NOTE   A *bastion host* is simply a machine that is fully exposed to the Internet. It sits outside any firewalls, or in a DMZ that is configured to provide no filtering of Internet traffic. Because a designation of bastion host is based on placement within the network, any unprotected machine can be considered a bastion host. In fact, you can think of the firewall as a bastion host!

The most common DMZ design is to create a DMZ by using two routers with firewalls to create a perimeter network. With a perimeter network (Figure 19-15), the two firewalls carve out areas with different levels of trust. The firewall that sits between the perimeter network and the Internet is known as an *external firewall*. It protects the public servers from known Internet attacks, but still allows plenty of traffic through to the public-facing servers.

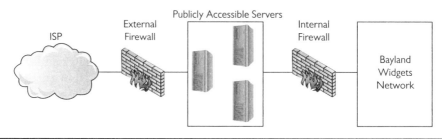

Figure 19-15   Tasty firewall sandwich

These servers are still publicly accessible, though, and are still more vulnerable to attack and takeover. That's acceptable for the public-facing servers, but the light protection afforded by the external firewall is unacceptable for internal systems. That's where the *internal firewall* comes in; it sits between the perimeter network and the trusted network that houses all the organization's private servers and workstations. The internal firewall provides extremely strong ACLs to protect internal servers and workstations.

Honeypots and Honeynets

As described, firewalls are bidirectional "filter" systems that can prevent access into a network or out of a network. It's a good system, but nothing is foolproof. Any high-value network resource provides sufficient motivation for a nefarious actor to work through the hoops to get at your goodies. Remember that malicious hackers have three primary weapons to gain access to computer assets: expertise, time, and money (to pay others with more expertise and to buy time).

To protect our network from expert hackers with too much time on their hands, we layer roadblocks to exhaust their time. We upgrade those roadblocks, and add more where practical, to defeat a hacker's expertise. We can also use something from our own arsenal that works in conjunction with our roadblocks: a detour.

Have you ever seen one of those sports-type movies where a ragtag team of misfits is playing a pro team? In the beginning of the game the pros are beating the brains out of the misfits. Then, when the misfits have had enough of a drubbing, the captain calls a play to "Let 'em through." The bad guy comes through and gets a pasting or two of his own. The network security equivalents to "Let 'em through" are honeypots and honeynets.

Now, "letting them through" is about choices. A network administrator may elect to make access to honeypots and honeynets an easy thing. Or, the network administrator may lay them out as a reward to a hacker after breaking through the normal protection barriers. This is a choice that depends on a lot of variables. In either case, a *honeypot* is a computer that presents itself as a sweet, tempting target to a hacker but, in reality, is a decoy. Honeypots can be as simple as a "real" network machine with decoy files in it. A text file called PASSWORDS.TXT with fake contents makes for an enticing objective.

Of course, there are much more sophisticated products that can run on a computer as a program or within a virtual machine. These products can mimic all of the features of a real computer asset, including firewalls and other roadblocks to keeping a hacker occupied and wasting time on a resource that will yield no value in the end.

Scale up a honeypot to present a complete network as a decoy and you have a *honeynet*. A honeynet, like a honeypot, could be built by constructing an actual network, but that wouldn't be very cost effective. Honeynets can run on a single computer or within a virtual machine and can look like a simple network or a vast installation.

Honeypots and honeynets are useful tools not just in their diversionary value, but in that they can also monitor and report the characteristics of attacks that target them.

When deploying honeypots and honeynets, it is critical that they be segmented from any live or production networks. Pure isolation is the ideal goal. Network segmentation can be achieved by creating a disconnected network or assigning them to an isolated VLAN.

Troubleshooting Firewalls

The firewalls used in modern networks are essential and flexible tools that are critical for securing our networks. Yet, this flexibility means a *misconfigured firewall* becomes more likely, and with it the threat of a security breach. You should be familiar with a couple of issues that can crop up, *incorrect ACL settings* and *misconfigured applications*.

When troubleshooting firewalls, a common place for misconfigurations to pop up is in the ACLs. Because of implicit deny, all nonmatching traffic is blocked by default. So if a newly installed firewall refuses to pass any traffic, check to see if it's missing the *permit any* ACL rule.

The other source of firewall misconfigurations you should know about concerns applications. With firewalls, "application" means two different things depending on whether you are configuring a network-based firewall or a host-based firewall.

With a network-based firewall, "application," in most situations, can be read as "protocol." Because ACLs on modern firewalls can use protocols as well as addresses and ports, a careless entry blocking an application/protocol can drop access to an entire class of applications on the network.

With a host-based firewall, "application" has its traditional meaning. A host-based firewall is aware of the actual applications running on the machine it's protecting, not just the traffic's protocol. With this knowledge, the firewall can be configured to grant or deny traffic to individual applications, not just protocols, ports, or addresses. When dealing with *incorrect host-based firewall settings* here, symptoms are most likely to pop up when an application has been accidentally added to the deny list. When this happens, the application will no longer be able to communicate with the network. Fortunately, on a single system the fix is easy: open the firewall settings, look for the application's name or executable, and change the deny to allow.

Chapter Review

Questions

1. A hacker who sends an e-mail but replaces his return e-mail address with a fake one is _____ the e-mail address.

   A. hardening

   B. malware

   C. spoofing

   D. emulating

2. Which of the following is a tool to prevent ARP cache poisoning?

   A. DHCP

   B. DAI

   C. Edge firewall

   D. DNS snooping

3. A computer compromised with malware to support a botnet is called a _____.

   A. zombie

   B. reflection

   C. DDoS

   D. locked node

4. The goal of this aspect of a DoS attack is to make the attacked system process each request for as long as possible.

   A. reflection

   B. rotation

   C. destruction

   D. amplification

5. A user's machine is locked to a screen telling her she must call a number to unlock her system. What kind of attack is this?

   A. DDoS

   B. Logic bomb

   C. Ransomware

   D. Worm

6. An attack where someone tries to hack a password using every possible password permutation is called what?

   A. Man-in-the-middle

   B. Spoofing

   C. Rainbow table

   D. Brute force

7. Which Windows utility displays open ports on a host?

   A. netstat

   B. ping

   C. ipconfig

   D. nbtstat

8. Which of the following protocols are notorious for cleartext passwords? (Select two.)

   A. SSH

   B. Telnet

   C. HTTPS

   D. POP3

9. The NSA's TEMPEST security standards are used to combat which risk?

   A. RF emanation

   B. Spoofing

   C. DDoS

   D. Malware

10. Bob is told by his administrator to go to www.runthisantimalware.com and click the "Run the program" button on that site to check for malware. What form of anti-malware delivery is this called?

    A. Host-based

    B. Network-based

    C. Cloud-based

    D. FTP-based

Answers

1. **C.** This is a classic example of spoofing.

2. **B.** Cisco Dynamic ARP Inspection (DAI) is designed to help prevent ARP cache poisoning.

3. A. All of the compromised systems on a botnet are called zombies.

4. D. The goal of amplification is to keep the targeted server as busy as possible.

5. C. Ransomware attacks can be brutal, demanding money to unlock *your* content.

6. D. Brute force uses every possible permutation and is often used in password cracking.

7. A. Only netstat shows all open ports on a Windows system.

8. B and **D.** Both Telnet and POP3 use cleartext passwords.

9. A. TEMPEST is designed to reduce RF emanation using enclosures, shielding, and even paint.

10. C. The fact that he is going to a Web site shows this is cloud-based.

## CHAPTER 20

Network Monitoring

The CompTIA Network+ certification exam expects you to know how to

- 3.1 Given a scenario, use appropriate documentation and diagrams to manage the network
- 3.3 Explain common scanning, monitoring and patching processes and summarize their expected outputs
- 5.2 Given a scenario, use the appropriate tool
- 5.3 Given a scenario, troubleshoot common wired connectivity and performance issues

To achieve these goals, you must be able to

- Explain how SNMP works
- Describe network monitoring tools
- Discuss a scenario that uses management and monitoring tools

A modern network doesn't behave properly without regular or irregular intervention from network technicians. Techs need to install network management tools and then deploy other tools to monitor, troubleshoot, and optimize networks over time. Because IP networks dominate today, we have a standard set of free tools to accomplish these goals.

This chapter looks first at network management tools, then examines the monitoring tools available and in common use. The chapter finishes with scenarios that call for deploying specific tools, analyzing their output, and fixing problems. For that final section, we'll revisit the Bayland Widgets Corporation and their campus area network (CAN) first discussed back in Chapter 17, "Building a Real-World Network."

Test Specific

SNMP

A quick Google search for **network monitoring tools** finds literally hundreds of products out there, ranging from complex and expensive to simple and free (Figure 20-1). One thing most of them have in common is the underlying protocol that enables them to work. The *Simple Network Management Protocol (SNMP)* is the de facto network

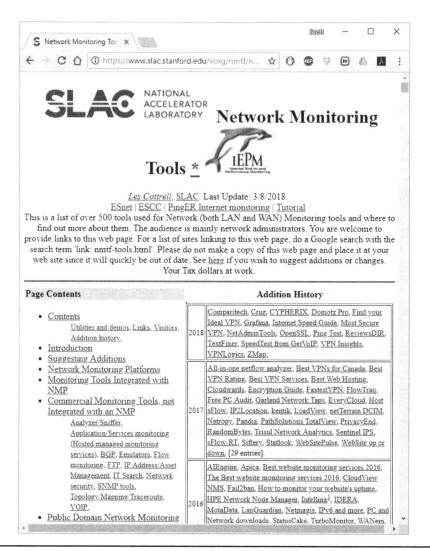

Figure 20-1   Massive list of network monitoring tools maintained by the SLAC National Accelerator Laboratory

management protocol for TCP/IP networks (and it comes dragging in a truckload full of jargon terms to describe the various components).

An SNMP system—which creates a *managed network*—consists of at least three components:

- SNMP manager
- Managed devices
- Management information bases

The *SNMP manager* requests and processes information from the *managed devices.* The SNMP manager runs specialized software called a *network management station (NMS).* Managed devices run specialized software called *agents.* Managed device types include workstations, printers, video cameras, routers, switches, and more. Figure 20-2 illustrates the basic SNMP hardware.

Figure 20-2
SNMP
components

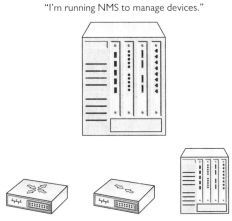

"I'm running NMS to manage devices."

"We run agent software to respond to the NMS."

The kind of information the SNMP manager can monitor from managed devices varies a lot, primarily because SNMP is an *extensible protocol,* meaning it can be adapted to accommodate different needs. Developers can create software that queries pretty much any aspect of a managed device, from current CPU load on a workstation to how much paper is left in a printer. SNMP uses *management information bases (MIBs)* to categorize the data that can be queried (and subsequently analyzed).

EXAM TIP The CompTIA Network+ objectives use the term *SNMP monitors,* under which you'll find the term *MIB.* This is shorthand for the various tools that use SNMP for monitoring network devices, plus the MIBs that inform those monitoring tools about what can be monitored on a specific device. This whole chapter discusses monitoring tools, many of which go hand in hand with SNMP. MIBs are a huge part of SNMP monitoring, though they are not monitoring tools in and of themselves. Got it?

Once set up properly, an SNMP managed network runs regular queries to managed devices and then gathers that information in a format usable by SNMP operators. We need to add a little more jargon to go through the steps of the process.

An SNMP system has up to eight core functions (depending on the version of SNMP), of which four merit discussion here: Get, Response, Set, and Trap. The common term for each of these functions is *protocol data unit (PDU).*

NOTE An SNMP PDU is not related to the PDU discussed earlier with OSI. It's the typical tech sector practice of repurposing an excellent term.

When an SNMP manager wants to query an agent, it sends a *Get* request, such as *GetRequest* or *GetNextRequest*. An agent then sends a *Response* with the requested information. Figure 20-3 illustrates the typical SNMP process.

Figure 20-3
Simple SNMP process

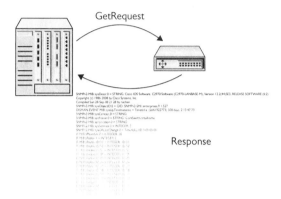

An NMS can tell an agent to make changes to the information it queries and sends, called *variables*, through a *Set* PDU, specifically *SetRequest*.

An agent can solicit information from an NMS with the *Trap* PDU. An agent can send a *Trap* with or without prior action from the SNMP manager, at least from SNMPv2 to the current SNMPv3.

I've just dropped a lot of jargon on you, so here's a scenario that will make the process and terms a little more understandable. The Bayland Widgets art department has a high-end color laser printer for producing brochures (Figure 20-4). Their CompTIA

Figure 20-4
The Bayland Widgets art department printer

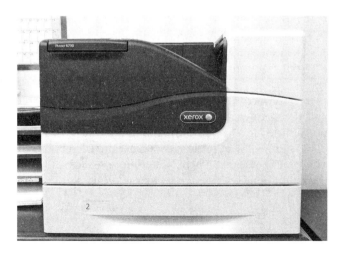

Network+ certified technicians maintain that laser printer, meaning they replace toner cartridges, change paper, and install the printer maintenance kits. (They're also CompTIA A+ certified, naturally!)

To manage this printer, nicknamed "Kitty," the techs use an SNMP network management system. At regular intervals, the NMS sends a *GetRequest* to the printer agent about the number of pages printed. According to the *Response* sent from the printer agent to the NMS, the techs can determine if the printer needs maintenance (that is, if it's at the point in its usage cycle where the printer maintenance kit parts need to be replaced).

At irregular intervals, the printer agent has to tell the techs that the printer is out of toner or out of paper. Although this information could come from the Get/Response interaction, it makes more sense that it come from the printer agent without a query. Kitty needs to yell "Help!" when she's out of toner. Otherwise the techs have to deal with irate artists, and that's just never going to be pretty. Kitty yells for help by sending a *Trap* to the NMS. Figure 20-5 illustrates the interaction.

Figure 20-5

Trap in action

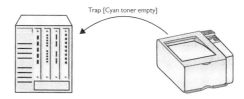

Trap [Cyan toner empty]

SNMP systems can use many additional utilities developed over the years. Some can automate various tasks. The *snmpwalk* utility, for example, tells the SNMP manager to perform a series of Get commands.

The BWC network techs don't sit at the SNMP manager, waiting for Kitty the printer to send messages about toner or ink. Instead, the manager software has the *event management* capability to send *alerts*: *notifications* directly sent to the techs when their intervention is required. These notifications can have a variety of forms. When the SNMP system was initially rolled out, one snarky manager suggested using text messages via *Short Message Service (SMS) alerts* that would cause techs' smartphones to meow upon receipt. That idea was nixed pretty early in favor of *e-mail alerts* (without any lolcat pictures attached).

SNMP has (as of this writing) three major versions. SNMP version 1 (SNMPv1) appeared in three requests for proposals (RFPs) all the way back in 1988. SNMPv2 was a relatively minor tweak to version 1. SNMPv3 added additional security with support for encryption and robust authentication, plus it provided features to make administering a large number of devices easier.

SNMP uses User Datagram Protocol (UDP) ports 161 and 162 for nonsecure communication. The NMS receives/listens on port 162. The agent receives/listens on port 161. When security is added via Transport Layer Security (TLS) the standard ports used are 10162 and 10161, respectively.

 EXAM TIP SNMP managers listen on UDP ports 162 or 10162 (with TLS). Agents listen on ports 161 or 10161 (with TLS).

Monitoring Tools

The biggest trick to monitoring a network is to start by appreciating that even the smallest network has a dizzying amount of traffic moving through it every second. Even more, this traffic is moving through all kinds of different aspects of the network, from individual interfaces coming from a single NIC in a system to everything moving through a massive router on the edge of your infrastructure.

 SIM   Check out the Chapter 20 "SNMP Monitoring" Show! and Click! sims at **http://totalsem.com/007**. The pair offer a great, practical introduction to SNMP tools.

To be able to do the monitoring, the troubleshooting, and the optimizing necessary to keep our networks in top shape, we need the right monitoring tools at the right places looking for the right things. There are hundreds of different monitoring tools available, but for the scope of the CompTIA Network+ exam, we can break them down into four major types: packet sniffers, protocol analyzers, interface monitors, and performance monitors.

Packet Sniffers

A *packet sniffer* (or just *sniffer*) is a program—a software tool—that queries a network interface and collects (captures) packets in a file called (surprisingly) a *capture file*. These programs might sit on a single computer, or perhaps on a router or a dedicated piece of hardware. The typical scenario for their use is one where network access/probing by a bad actor is suspected.

Packet sniffers need to capture all the packets they can, so it's typical for them to connect to an interface in *promiscuous mode* or, in the case of a switch, a *mirrored port*. This ensures they get as much data as possible. They run silently and transparently in the background.

Packet sniffers are essential information-gathering tools, but we also need a tool to enable analysis of the captured packets. For this reason, you don't really see packet sniffers as a stand-alone product. Instead, they are usually packaged with a protocol analyzer (see next section).

Protocol Analyzers

A *protocol analyzer* is a program that processes capture files from packet sniffers and analyzes them based on our monitoring needs. (You'll also hear the tool referred to as *packet analyzer*, though the exam uses the former term.) A good protocol analyzer can filter and sort a capture file based on almost anything and create an output to help us do monitoring properly. In other words, a protocol analyzer performs *packet/traffic analysis*. A typical question a protocol analyzer might answer is "What is the IP and MAC address of the device sending out DHCP Offer messages and when is it doing this?"

NOTE Various names are used to describe utilities that analyze packets: *packet sniffer*, *packet analyzer*, *protocol analyzer*, and *network analyzer*. There's so much overlap here! That can be attributed to the fact that so many protocol analyzers come with sniffers as well. Bottom line, don't rely on the name of the monitoring tool to determine all it can do. Read the tech specs.

Protocol Analyzing with Wireshark

There are plenty of protocol analyzers available out there, but you'd be hard pressed to find a network administrator/technician/whatever who isn't familiar with the powerful and free *Wireshark*. It was originally written by Gerald Combs, who still maintains the program with the help of hundreds of contributors. Wireshark is the perfect prototype of a protocol analyzer.

Try This!

Play Along with Wireshark

It's never too late to learn how to use protocol analyzers, so try this! Download a copy of Wireshark (www.wireshark.org) and just play. There's no danger to doing so, and it's actually a lot of fun!

The default Wireshark screen has become the standard most other protocol analyzers are based on. You select an interface to begin the capture and let the capture begin (Figure 20-6).

When you stop the capture, you'll see something like Figure 20-7. Wireshark's screen breaks into three parts. The top part is a numbered list of all the packets in the capture file, showing some of the most important information. The second part is a very detailed breakdown of the packet that is currently highlighted in the top pane. The bottom pane is the hex representation and the ASCII representation of whatever part of the second pane is detailed.

The downside to a capture is that Wireshark is going to grab everything unless you filter the capture or filter the capture file after the capture. In many cases you'll find yourself doing both. Figure 20-8 shows a filter added to a capture file to only show DHCP packets.

Note that the filter doesn't actually say "DHCP." Wireshark uses the term *bootp* because it follows the same structure as its predecessor. All the other Wireshark filters use the acronym you'd expect today, such as dns, ssh, http, and so on.

Packet Flow Monitoring with NetFlow

Packet flow monitoring, accomplished with a set of tools related to general packet sniffers and analyzers, tracks traffic flowing between specific source and destination devices. Cisco developed the concept of packet flow monitoring and subsequently included it in routers and switches. The primary tool is called *NetFlow*.

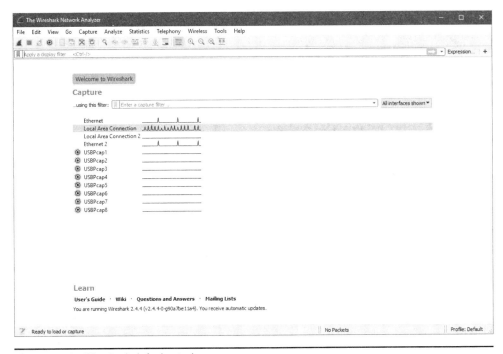

Figure 20-6 Wireshark default window

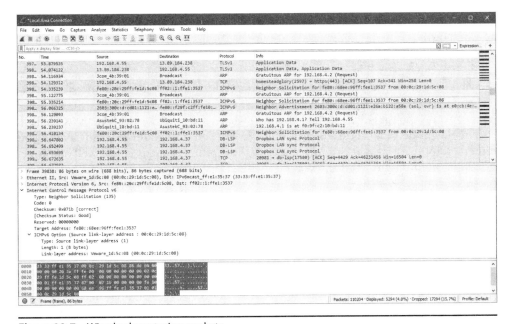

Figure 20-7 Wireshark capturing packets

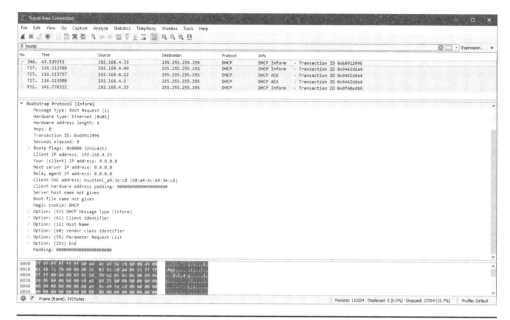

Figure 20-8 Wireshark filter

NetFlow has been around for quite a while and has evolved into a powerful tool that just about every Cisco house uses. NetFlow is similar to SNMP, but different. NetFlow is based on the idea of flows that you define to track the type of traffic you wish to see.

A single *flow* is a flow of packets from one specific place to another. Each of these flows is then cached in a *flow cache*. A single entry in a flow cache normally contains information such as destination and source addresses, destination and source ports, the source on the device running that flow, and total number of bytes of that flow.

Analyzing the flow data enables administrators to build a clear picture of the volume and flow of traffic on the network. This in turn enables them to optimize the network (by adding capacity where needed or other options).

NOTE To use NetFlow you must enable NetFlow on that device. If the device doesn't support NetFlow, you can use stand-alone probes that can monitor maintenance ports on the unsupported device and send the information to the NetFlow collector.

Most of the heavy lifting of NetFlow is handled by the *NetFlow collectors*. NetFlow collectors store information from one or more devices' NetFlow caches, placing it into a table that can then be analyzed by NetFlow analysis tools.

There are many different companies selling different tools, and which tool you should choose is often a matter of features and cost. Figure 20-9 shows a screenshot of a popular tool called LiveAction.

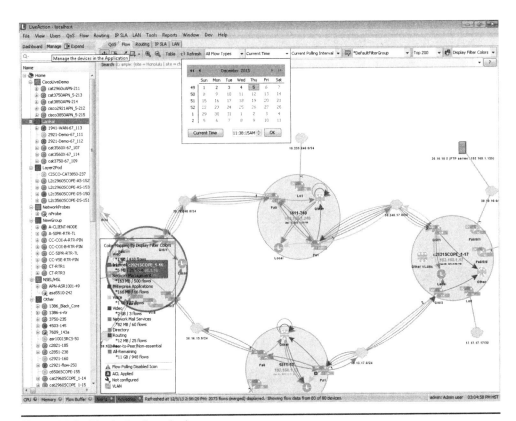

Figure 20-9   LiveAction in action!

Cisco's NetFlow started the idea of traffic flows that can then be collected and analyzed. Just about every other form of competing flow-monitoring concept (names like sFlow, NetStream, and IPFIX) builds on the idea of the flow.

Interface Monitors

If you want to know how hard your network is working, turn to an interface monitor. *Interface monitors* track the bandwidth and utilization of one or more interfaces on one or more devices. Think of them as the traffic monitors for your network. A typical question you might ask an interface monitor is "How hard is the Gigabit Ethernet port 17 on our backbone switch working right now, in megabits per second?"

Interface monitors track the quantity and utilization of traffic through a physical port or ports on a single device. Interface monitoring will consist of, among other items, the following *metrics* (performance and use option numbers):

- **Bandwidth/throughput**   At what speed is the port set to run? What duplex is the port running?

- **Utilization**   How much of the total bandwidth of the port is being used?

- **Packet drops**   A port will drop a packet for one of two reasons: an error or a discard.

- **Error rate**   How many packets per second are errors? A port treats a packet as erroneous if the packet is malformed or unreadable.

- **Discards**   How many frames are discarded per second? A *discard* is when a port intentionally drops a well-formed frame. A discard is not an error. There are many reasons for a port to discard a frame. If a port is trunking VLANs 1 and 2 and it gets a frame for VLAN 3, the port will discard the packet.

- **Interface resets**   Is the interface being reset at any time? If so, how often is this taking place?

Interface monitors started as manufacturer-specific tools, and although there are plenty of interface monitors that work on just about any platform, the manufacturer-specific ones are still very common.

The Cisco Network Assistant (CNA) software enables you to monitor Cisco routers and switches. Figure 20-10 shows the percent of utilization for a specific port on a Cisco switch. Figure 20-11 shows the packet drops and errors on that same port.

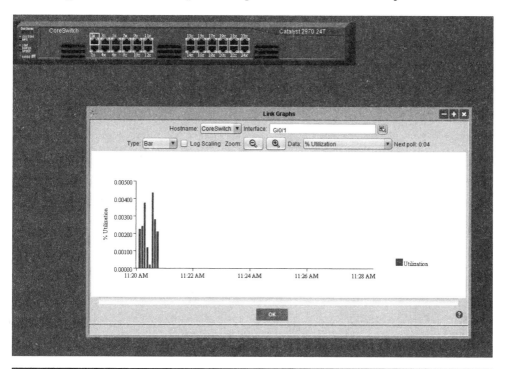

Figure 20-10   Percent of utilization of switch port 1

Contrast Figure 20-11 with Figure 20-12 showing CNA examining switch port 13 for drops and errors. That's a misbehaving port!

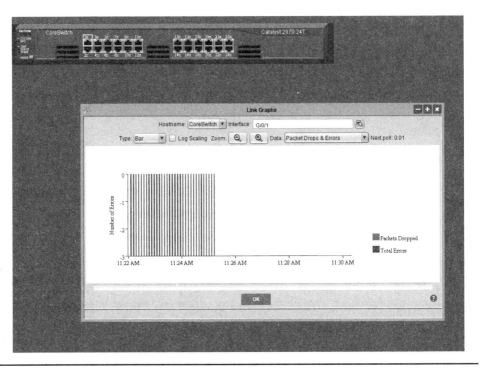

Figure 20-11   Hmm…looks pretty clean

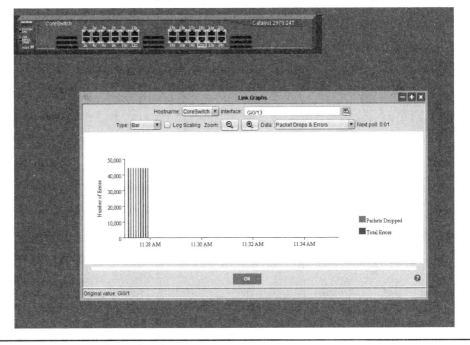

Figure 20-12   Ouch. That's a lot of errors!

NOTE Limiting the description of CNA to an "interface monitor" completely sells the software short. It can monitor individual ports on a switch, but you can use the program to set up, manage, maintain, and troubleshoot all the functions of the switch. It's much more powerful a tool than just an interface monitor.

Performance Monitors

A *performance monitor* tracks the performance of some aspect of a system over time and lets you know when things aren't normal. Performance monitors are usually tied to a particular operating system or application, as the performance monitoring requires very detailed understanding of the low-level aspects of the system. A typical question you might ask a performance monitor is "How many hits per hour occurred on my Web server over the last two weeks?"

The two most common performance monitoring tools are Windows Performance Monitor (PerfMon) and syslog (found in macOS and Linux). Although they perform the same job, I want to introduce both tools to you because they do that job very differently ... and use very different terms to describe the same things. As we next look at certain aspects that are common to any good performance monitor, I'll use the terminology for both tools.

This section explores the processes and expected outputs for log reviewing and reviewing baselines. We'll start with definitions of logs and then move into the active processes of reviewing.

NOTE The term *performance monitor* is not an industry term but instead just a handy way to discuss several utilities with similar functions that you should know. Also, PerfMon is a unique Linux tool for performance monitoring. It just happens to share the same name as Windows Performance Monitor.

Logs

Performance monitors use system log files to track performance over time. *Logs* store information about the performance of some particular aspect of a system. Different programs refer to the monitored aspect with different terms. Performance Monitor calls them *counters*; syslog calls them *facilities*. A log file might record the percentage of utilization over time of a specific Ethernet port, for example, or the average throughput of a network connection.

Baselines

The only way to know when a problem is brewing on your network is to know how things perform when all's well with the network. Part of any proper performance monitor is the facility to create a *baseline*: a log of performance indicators such as CPU usage, network utilization, and other values to give you a picture of your network and servers when they are working correctly. A major change in these values can point to problems on a server or the network as a whole.

A typical scenario for baselines is for techs and administrators to create and use appropriate documentation and diagrams for how the network optimally performs. They use this information to manage the network over time. The CompTIA Network+ exam objectives use the phrase *network configuration and performance baselines* to describe the documentation and diagrams needed in this process.

All operating systems come with some form of baseline tools. Performance Monitor is the common tool used to create a baseline on Windows systems.

Log Management

Any system that generates electronic log files has two issues. First, is security. Log files are important for the information they provide. Second, is maintenance. Log files are going to continue to grow until they fill the mass storage they are stored on. The job of providing proper security and maintenance for log files is called *log management*.

Logs often contain private or sensitive data and thus must be protected. Access to active logs must be carefully controlled. It's very common to give read access rights only to specific users, to make sure only the correct users have access to the log files. In many cases it's not uncommon for the logging application to have only write access to the files—it's not a good idea to give root access to critical log files.

Generally, log files by default simply grow until they fill the space they are stored on. To prevent this, it's common to make log files *cyclical*—when a file grows to a certain size, it begins to cycle. *Cycling* just means that as a new record appears in the file, the oldest record in the file is deleted. It's also common for log files to be re-created on a time basis. Depending on the utility, you can set a new log file to be created daily, weekly, hourly—whatever is most convenient for the administrators. These files can then be backed up.

There are many laws today that require retention of log files for a certain period of time. It's important to check with your legal department to see if any files need to be kept longer than your standard backup time frames.

Putting It All Together

Up to this point in the chapter, we've looked at management and monitoring tools as distinct things, easy to label and easy to differentiate. And in a small office/home office network, that kind of simplicity makes sense. If you have a Windows-based network with a single server running Windows Server, then of course you'd use Windows Performance Monitor to baseline and monitor your network over time. The CompTIA Network+ competencies lead to this modular thinking as well. Once you scale up past the one-server network, though, things get a lot more … *chaotic* isn't quite the right word … *nuanced* is better. Let's take a look.

Scenario: Monitoring and Managing

This scenario revisits the Bayland Widgets CAN and applies the network managing and monitoring tools to see how their techs would use these tools to manage, monitor, maintain, and troubleshoot their network.

Figure 20-13 shows the BWC campus layout with its three main buildings. The main office has servers and various individual offices. The factory houses the robots and control systems that produce the company's widgets. The warehouse and shipping building does exactly as it's named.

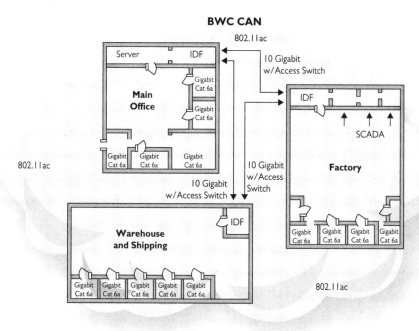

Figure 20-13 Diagram of Bayland Widgets' campus area network

Internally, each building is wired with Gigabit Ethernet. In addition, the buildings interconnect with 10-Gigabit fiber into access switches. Add onto that a campus-wide Wi-Fi network (802.11ac) and, not pictured, the router that gives them access to the Internet.

Since we're talking about managing and monitoring the whole network here, let's list all the types of networked devices:

- Routers (wired and wireless)
- Switches
- Wireless access points
- Servers
- Workstations
- Printers
- Phones

Note that I've left out the industrial control systems that run the factory and shipping automation. Plus, I've left out the security systems and other essential components of a functional CAN. This list focuses on the core networking devices that a CompTIA Network+ tech would encounter.

Modern networking tools enable skilled network administrators to manage networks as complex at Bayland Widgets' network fairly easily, after those tools have been set up properly. The tools used must be customized for the network. Plus, the various tools aren't really interchangeable. Just like you wouldn't use a hammer when you need to turn a screw, you wouldn't use a protocol analyzer when you want to check toner levels in a laser printer.

Bayland Widgets could dedicate an area in the main office as a *network operations center (NOC)*, a centralized location for techs and administrators to manage all aspects of the network. From that NOC, they could use various programs on the SNMP-managed network to query devices. A *graphing* program could create graphs and diagrams that display any set of the data received.

Graphing programs like *Cacti* would show everything about specific switches, for example, to determine utilization of that switch in many aspects—that is, how well it handles its current work load. Figure 20-14 shows Cacti with four graphs depicting network device CPU utilization, memory usage, traffic (bandwidth usage) on the WAN interface, and traffic to the file server.

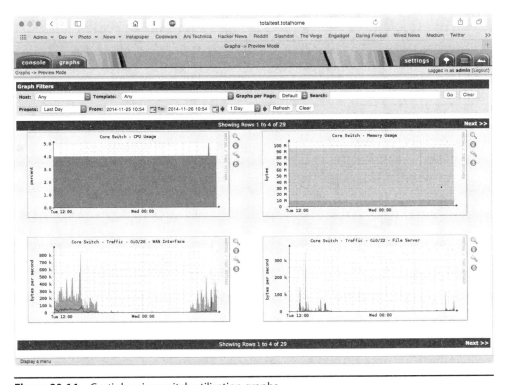

Figure 20-14   Cacti showing switch utilization graphs

With a different query, Cacti can graph available storage on a file server (Figure 20-15), or wireless channel utilization.

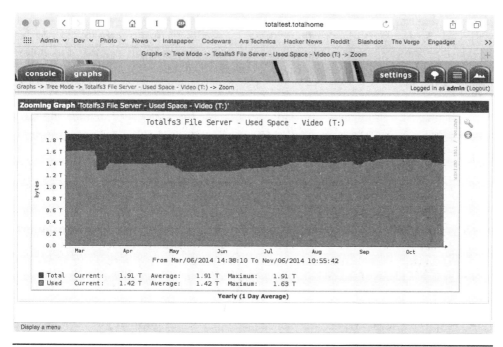

Figure 20-15   Cacti showing file server storage utilization graph

Cycling through the various network monitoring tools enables network administrators to see very quickly if a specific server or other device has problems. They could analyze the campus Wi-Fi network with a Wi-Fi analyzer and spot a problematic WAP. Going a little further up the food chain, BWC could add Nagios Network Analyzer to their network toolboxes and, after proper configuration, have that system proactively send alerts via SMS or e-mail when problem areas were detected. If the *link status*—signifying how good the connection is between two systems—between the two access servers connecting the main office and the factory goes red, that's a whole different level of priority than if Kitty the art printer runs low on toner, right?

EXAM TIP   Programs like Cacti enable you to see very quickly essential facts about your network hardware. You can see available storage, network device CPU usage, network device memory usage, and more. With wireless-aware tools, you can quickly spot problems with wireless channel usage or channel saturation. These tools are a tech's friend!

Each type of tool discussed in this chapter enables the network team at BWC to monitor and analyze all aspects of the network. The SNMP system offers very specific information about managed devices, enabling techs to respond to problems.

Performance monitoring software enables the BWC techs to create baselines when the network is functioning correctly. In a scenario where complaints about network performance come in from one portion of the network (Accounting, for example), that same software can be used to compare current network performance with the historical, normal performance. If there's a discrepancy, the techs can turn to other tools—packet flow analyzers and interface monitors—to figure out if the issue is excess traffic, failing devices, failing interfaces on a device, or an overworked *bottleneck* (a spot where traffic slows precipitously).

Network analyzers and packet flow analyzers can discover the busiest machines on the network, potentially sources of overall network slowdowns. *Top talkers* are the computers sending the most data, whereas *top listeners* are the ones receiving the most. If BWC is worried about a malware problem, finding that the computer assigned to Joe in Accounting is the top talker might track down that spam infestation.

The network techs turn to a packet sniffer/analyzer tool when they need to go deep into the traffic. Here's an example of when Wireshark might be the tool to start. BWC wants to move the network to IPv6 and turn off all IPv4 traffic. Turning off IPv4 on a test machine would be a good check on how ready the network is for IPv6. We did that the other day in my office, for example, and found that the test machine couldn't see anything on the network at all. Running Wireshark enabled us to see if the router was sending out IPv6 router advertisements with DNS. When we confirmed that information, the next step was more old-fashioned. Had we misconfigured the test workstation's IPv6 settings?

Accomplished techs use a variety of managing and monitoring tools to maintain a healthy network. Use each type of tool when that tool is appropriate. Often, you'll need to use multiple tools during a longer troubleshooting scenario.

SIEM

The Bayland Widgets people could use an approach called *security information and event management (SIEM)* to monitor and manage their network. SIEM is an industry-standard term, but there are many products of various types that are marketed as SIEM solutions. SIEM is a mashup of two processes: security event management (SEM) and security information management (SIM).

As the name would imply, SIEM is a two-part process that begins with the security event monitoring component. SEM is based on real-time monitoring of security events. The SEM framework calls for monitoring the entire enterprise, often through edge devices at monitor points, then saving the logged events to a location that supports single viewpoint review and analysis of the events. In addition to active event monitoring, another task of SEM is to collect and centralize otherwise disparately located security and event logs.

Once logs are created and saved, the second part of SIEM, security information management, kicks in: here, the log files are reviewed and analyzed by automated and human interpreters.

One place SIEM comes into play is with *file integrity monitoring (FIM)*, checking for changes in all sorts of aspects of files. These include

- Attributes and file size
- Configuration values
- Content
- Credentials
- Hash values
- Privileges and security settings

Any changes discovered could indicate that an attack has occurred or is happening right now. The verification process compares a baseline or known good copy of the file with the current file, checking for differences.

SIEM systems are complex solution suites that are found in large, enterprise environments. Depending on the organization, they may be self-implemented and managed or may be administered under contract by a vendor in the form of a managed security service provider (MSSP).

Chapter Review

Questions

1. Which PDU does an SNMP manager use to query agents?

   A. Get

   B. Response

   C. Set

   D. Trap

2. In an SNMP managed network, which software does a managed device run?

   A. Agent

   B. NMS

   C. SNMP manager

   D. MIB

3. How does an SNMP managed system categorize data that can be queried?

   A. QoS

   B. MIBs

   C. PDUs

   D. UDP

4. An SNMP manager listens on which port when used with TLS?

   A. 161

   B. 162

   C. 10161

   D. 10162

5. Jason is concerned about the communication between two workstations and wants to capture and analyze that traffic to see if anything illicit is going on. Which tool would best serve his needs?

   A. Interface monitor

   B. Packet flow monitor

   C. Packet sniffer

   D. Performance monitor

6. Where does a packet sniffer put information it collects?

   A. Answer file

   B. Capture file

   C. Pocket file

   D. Sniffer file

7. An analysis of a network shows a lot of traffic on one machine on port 161. What kind of machine is it?

   A. Managed device

   B. SNMP manager

   C. PDU

   D. MIB

8. What should you create when a network is running correctly?

   A. Answer file

   B. Capture file

   C. MIB

   D. Baseline

9. Bart has a choice of tools to view his managed network, but he primarily wants to see graphs of various types of data, such as the overall traffic and the current capacities of the file servers. Which tool offers him the best option?

   A. Cacti

   B. CNA

   C. NetFlow

   D. Wireshark

10. What tool enables you to compare current network performance with correctly functioning network performance?

   A. Baseline monitor

   B. Packet flow monitor

   C. Packet sniffer

   D. Performance monitor

Answers

1. **A.** SNMP managers use Get PDUs to query agents.

2. **A.** Managed devices run agent software.

3. **B.** SNMP managed systems use management information bases to categorize data to be queried.

4. **D.** An SNMP manager listens on port 10162 when used with TLS.

5. **B.** Jason would use packet flow monitoring software to monitor the flow between two devices.

6. **B.** Packet sniffers put information in capture files.

7. **A.** Managed devices listen on port 161.

8. **D.** Create a baseline so you can compare network performance later on.

9. **A.** Cacti is a great graphing tool.

10. **D.** A performance monitor enables you to compare current network performance with a baseline.

## CHAPTER 21

Network Troubleshooting

The CompTIA Network+ certification exam expects you to know how to

- 1.3 Explain the concepts and characteristics of routing and switching
- 5.1 Explain the network troubleshooting methodology
- 5.2 Given a scenario, use the appropriate tool
- 5.3 Given a scenario, troubleshoot common wired connectivity and performance issues
- 5.5 Given a scenario, troubleshoot common network service issues

To achieve these goals, you must be able to

- Describe appropriate troubleshooting tools and their functions
- Analyze and discuss the troubleshooting process
- Resolve common network issues

Have you ever seen a tech walk up to a network and seem to know all the answers, effortlessly typing in a few commands and magically making the system or network work? I've always been intrigued by how they do this. Observing such techs over the years, I've noticed that they tend to follow the same steps for similar problems—looking in the same places, typing the same commands, and so on.

When someone performs a task the same way every time, I figure they're probably following a plan. They understand what tools they have to work with, and they know where to start and what to do second and third and fourth until they find the problem.

This chapter's lofty goal is to consolidate my observations on how these "übertechs" fix networks. I'll show you the primary troubleshooting tools and help you formulate a troubleshooting process and learn where to look for different sorts of problems. Then you'll apply this knowledge to resolve common network issues.

Test Specific

Troubleshooting Tools

While working through the process of finding a problem's cause, you sometimes need tools. These tools are the software and hardware tools that provide information about your network and enact repairs. I covered a number of tools already: hardware tools like cable testers and crimpers and software utilities like ping and tracert. The trick is knowing when and how to use these tools to solve your network problems.

 CAUTION No matter what the problem, always consider the safety of your data first. Ask yourself this question before performing any troubleshooting action: "Can what I'm about to do potentially damage my data?"

Almost every new networking person I teach will, at some point, ask me: "What tools do I need to buy?" My answer shocks them: "None. Don't buy a thing." It's not so much that you don't need tools, but rather that different networking jobs require wildly different tools. Plenty of network techs never crimp a cable. An equal number never open a system. Some techs do nothing all day but pull cable. The tools you need are defined by your job.

This answer is especially true with software tools. Almost all the network problems I encounter in established networks don't require me to use any tools other than the classic ones provided by the operating system. I've fixed more network problems with ping, for example, than with any other single tool. As you gain skill in this area, you'll find yourself hounded by vendors trying to sell you the latest and greatest networking diagnostic tools. You may like these tools. All I can say is that I've never needed a software diagnostics tool that I had to purchase.

Hardware Tools

In multiple chapters in this book, you've read about tools used to configure a network. These *hardware tools* include cable testers, TDRs, OTDRs, certifiers, voltage event recorders, protocol analyzers, cable strippers, multimeters, tone probes/generators, and punchdown tools. Some of these tools can also be used in troubleshooting scenarios to help you eliminate or narrow down the possible causes of certain problems. Let's review the tools as listed in the CompTIA Network+ exam objectives (plus a couple I think you should know).

 EXAM TIP Read this section! The CompTIA Network+ exam is filled with repair scenarios, and you must know what every tool does and when to use it.

Cable Testers, TDRs, and OTDRs

The vast majority of cabling problems occur when the network is first installed or when a change is made. Once a cable has been made, installed, and tested, the chances of it failing are pretty small compared to all of the other network problems that might take place. If you're having trouble connecting to a resource or experiencing performance problems after making a connection, a bad cable likely isn't the culprit. Broken cables don't make intermittent problems, and they don't slow down data. They make permanent disconnects.

Network techs define a "broken" cable in numerous ways. First, a broken cable might have an *open circuit*, where one or more of the wires in a cable simply don't connect from one end of the cable to the other. The signal lacks *continuity*. Second, a cable might have a *short*, where one or more of the wires in a cable connect to another wire in the cable. (Within a normal cable, no wires connect to other wires.)

Third, a cable might have a *wire map problem*, where one or more of the wires in a cable don't connect to the proper location on the jack or plug. This can be caused by improperly crimping a cable, for example. Fourth, the cable might experience *crosstalk*, where the electrical signal bleeds from one wire pair to another, creating interference.

Fifth, a broken cable might pick up *noise*, spurious signals usually caused by faulty hardware or poorly crimped jacks. Finally, a broken cable might have *impedance mismatch*. Impedance is the natural electrical resistance of a cable. When cables of different types—think thickness, composition of the metal, and so on—connect and the flow of electrons is not uniform, it can cause a unique type of electrical noise, called an *echo*.

 EXAM TIP The CompTIA Network+ exam objectives use the terms *open/short*. More commonly, techs would refer to these issues as *open circuits* and *short circuits*.

Network technicians use three different devices to deal with broken cables. *Cable testers* can tell you if you have a continuity problem or if a wire map isn't correct (Figure 21-1). *Time domain reflectometers (TDRs)* and *optical time domain reflectometers (OTDRs)* can tell you where the break is on the cable (Figure 21-2). A TDR works with copper cables

Figure 21-1
Typical cable
tester

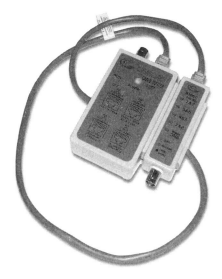

Figure 21-2
An EXFO AXS-100 OTDR (photo courtesy of EXFO)

and an OTDR works with fiber optics, but otherwise they share the same function. If a problem shows itself as a disconnect and you've first checked easier issues that would manifest as disconnects, such as loss of permissions, an unplugged cable, or a server shut off, then think about using these tools.

Certifiers

Certifiers test a cable to ensure that it can handle its rated amount of capacity. When a cable is not broken but it's not moving data the way it should, turn to a certifier. Look for problems that cause a cable to underperform. A bad installation might increase crosstalk, attenuation, or interference. A certifier can pick up an impedance mismatch as well. Most of these problems show up at installation, but running a certifier to eliminate cabling as a problem is never a bad idea. Don't use a certifier for disconnects, only slowdowns. All certifiers need some kind of *loopback adapter* on the other end of the cable run to provide termination and return of a signal. A loopback adapter is a small device with a single port.

Light Meter

The extremely transparent fiber-optic cables allow light to shine but have some inherent impurities in the glass that can reduce light transmission. Dust, poor connections, and light leakage can also degrade the strength of light pulses as they travel through a fiber-optic run. To measure the amount of light loss, technicians use an *optical power meter*, also referred to as a *light meter* (see Figure 21-3).

EXAM TIP The CompTIA Network+ exam objectives use the term *light meter*. The more accurate term in this context is either *power meter* or *optical power meter*. You may see any of these terms on the exam.

Figure 21-3
Fiberlink® 6650
Optical Power
Meter (photo
courtesy of
Communications
Specialties, Inc.)

The light meter system uses a high-powered source of light at one end of a run and a calibrated detector at the other end. This measures the amount of light that reaches the detector.

Voltage Quality Recorder/Temperature Monitor

Networks need the proper temperature and adequate power, but most network techs tend to view these issues as outside of the normal places to look for problems. That's too bad, because both heat and power problems invariably manifest themselves as intermittent problems. Look for problems that might point to heat or power issues: server rooms that get too hot at certain times of the day, switches that fail whenever an air conditioning system kicks on, and so on. You can use a *voltage quality recorder* and a *temperature monitor* to monitor server rooms over time to detect and record issues with electricity or heat, respectively. They're great for those "something happened last night" types of issues.

Cable Strippers/Snips

A *cable stripper* or *snip* (Figure 21-4) helps you to make UTP cables. You'll need a crimping tool (a *crimper*) as well. You don't need these tools to punch down 66- or 110-blocks. You would use a punchdown tool for that (as described in a bit).

Multimeters

Multimeters test voltage (both AC and DC), resistance, and continuity. They are the unsung heroes of cabling infrastructures because no other tool can tell you how much voltage is on a line. They are also a great fallback for continuity testing when you don't have a cable tester handy.

Figure 21-4
A cable stripping
and crimping
tool

 NOTE There's an old adage used by carpenters and other craftspeople that goes, "Never buy cheap tools." Cheap tools save you money at the beginning, but they often break more readily than higher-quality tools and, more importantly, make it harder to get the job done. This adage definitely applies to multimeters! You might be tempted to go for the $10 model that looks pretty much like the $25 model, but chances are the leads will break or the readings will lie on the cheaper model. Buy a decent tool, and you'll never have to worry about it.

Tone Probes and Tone Generators

Tone probes and their partners, *tone generators*, have only one job: to help you locate a particular cable. You'll never use a tone probe without a tone generator.

Punchdown Tools

Punchdown tools (Figure 21-5) put UTP wires into 66- and 110-blocks. The only time you would use a punchdown tool in a diagnostic environment is a quick repunch of a connection to make sure all the contacts are properly set.

Figure 21-5
A punchdown
tool in action

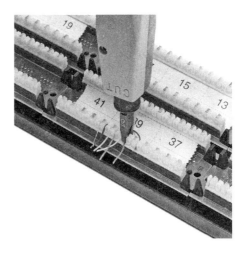

Try This!

Shopping Spree

As more and more people have networks installed in their homes, the big-box hardware stores stock an increasing number of network-specific tools. Everybody loves shopping, right? So try this! Go to your local hardware store—big box, like Home Depot or Lowes, if there's one near you—and check out their tools. What do they offer? Write down prices and features and compare with what your classmates found.

Software Tools

Make the CompTIA Network+ exam (and real life) easier by separating your software tools into two groups: those that come built into every operating system and those that are third-party tools. Typical built-in tools are tracert/traceroute, ipconfig/ifconfig/ip, arp, ping, arping, pathping, nslookup/dig, route, and netstat/ss. Third-party tools fall into the categories of packet sniffers, port scanners, throughput testers, and looking glass sites.

Try This!

Playing Along in Windows

This section contains many command-line tools that you've seen earlier in the book in various places. Now is a great time to refresh your memory about how each one works, so after I review each command, run it yourself. Then type `help` followed by the command to see the available switches for that command. Run the command with some of the switches to see what they do. Running the command is more fun than just reading about it; plus, you'll solidify the knowledge you need to master.

The CompTIA Network+ exam tests your ability to recognize the output from all of the built-in tools (except arping and ss). Take some time to memorize example outputs from all of these tools.

tracert/traceroute

The *traceroute* utility (the command in Windows is *tracert*) is used to trace all of the routers between two points. Use traceroute to diagnose where the problem lies when you have problems reaching a remote system. If a traceroute stops at a certain router, you know the problem is either the next router or the connections between them.

When sending a traceroute, it's important to keep a significant difference between Windows and UNIX/Linux/Cisco systems in mind. Windows tracert sends only ICMP packets, while UNIX/Linux/Cisco traceroute can send either ICMP packets or UDP datagrams, but sends UDP datagrams by default. Because many routers block ICMP packets, if your traceroute fails from a Windows system, running it on a Linux or UNIX system may return more complete results.

Here's sample `traceroute` output:

```
Tracing route to adsl-208-190-121-38.dsl.hstntx.swbell.net

[208.190.121.38] over a maximum of 30 hops:

  1     1 ms      <1 ms      1 ms     Router.totalhome
[192.168.4.1]

  2    38 ms      41 ms     70 ms    adsl-208-190-121-
38.dsl.hstntx.swbell.net [208.190.121.38]
```

The traceroute command defaults to IPv4, but also functions well in an IPv6 network. In Windows, use the command with the –6 switch: *tracert –6*. In UNIX/Linux, use *traceroute6* (or traceroute –6 in some variants of Linux).

ipconfig/ifconfig/ip

The *ipconfig* (Windows), *ifconfig* (macOS and UNIX), and *ip* (Linux) utilities tell you almost anything you want to know about a computer's IP settings. Make sure you know that typing `ipconfig` alone only gives basic information. Typing `ipconfig /all` gives detailed information (like DNS servers and MAC address).

Here's sample `ipconfig` output:

```
Ethernet adapter Main:

   Connection-specific DNS Suffix   . :
   IPv6 Address. . . . . . . . . . . : 2001:470:bf88:1:fc2d:aeb2:99d2:e2b4
   Temporary IPv6 Address. . . . . . : 2001:470:bf88:1:5e4:c1ef:7b30:ddd6
   Link-local IPv6 Address . . . . . : fe80::fc2d:aeb2:99d2:e2b4%8
   IPv4 Address. . . . . . . . . . . : 192.168.4.27
   Subnet Mask . . . . . . . . . . . : 255.255.255.0
   Default Gateway . . . . . . . . . : fe80::223:4ff:fe8c:b720%8
                                       192.168.4.1

Tunnel adapter Local Area Connection* 6:

Media State . . . . . . . . . . . . : Media disconnected
Connection-specific DNS Suffix  . . :
```

And here's sample `ifconfig` output:

```
lo0: flags=8049<UP,LOOPBACK,RUNNING,MULTICAST> mtu 16384
        options=3<RXCSUM,TXCSUM>
        inet6 ::1 prefixlen 128
        inet 127.0.0.1 netmask 0xff000000
        inet6 fe80::1%lo0 prefixlen 64 scopeid 0x1
        nd6 options=1<PERFORMNUD>
```

```
gif0: flags=8010<POINTOPOINT,MULTICAST> mtu 1280
stf0: flags=0<> mtu 1280
en0: flags=8863<UP,BROADCAST,SMART,RUNNING,SIMPLEX,MULTICAST> mtu 1500
        options=10b<RXCSUM,TXCSUM,VLAN_HWTAGGING,AV>
        ether 3c:07:54:7a:d4:d8
        inet6 fe80::3e07:54ff:fe7a:d4d8%en0 prefixlen 64 scopeid 0x4
        inet 192.168.4.78 netmask 0xffffff00 broadcast 192.168.4.255
        inet6 2601:e::abcd:3e07:54ff:fe7a:d4d8 prefixlen 64 autoconf
        inet6 2601:e::abcd:b84e:9fad:3add:c73b prefixlen 64 autoconf temporary
        nd6 options=1<PERFORMNUD>
        media: autoselect (1000baseT <full-duplex,flow-control>)
        status: active
```

And finally, here's Linux's `ip addr` output:

```
1: lo: <LOOPBACK,UP,LOWER_UP> mtu 65536 qdisc noqueue state UNKNOWN group default
    link/loopback 00:00:00:00:00:00 brd 00:00:00:00:00:00
    inet 127.0.0.1/8 scope host lo
      valid_lft forever preferred_lft forever
    inet6 ::1/128 scope host
      valid_lft forever preferred_lft forever
2: eth0: <BROADCAST,MULTICAST,UP,LOWER_UP> mtu 1500 qdisc pfifo_fast state UNKNOWN
group default qlen 1000
    link/ether 00:0c:29:e0:b2:85 brd ff:ff:ff:ff:ff:ff
    inet 192.168.4.19/24 brd 192.168.4.255 scope global eth0
      valid_lft forever preferred_lft forever
    inet6 2601:e:0:abcd:8cfb:6220:ec23:80a/64 scope global temporary dynamic


      valid_lft 86221sec preferred_lft 14221sec
    inet6 2601:e:0:abcd:20c:29ff:fee0:b285/64 scope global dynamic
      valid_lft 86221sec preferred_lft 14221sec
    inet6 fe80::20c:29ff:fee0:b285/64 scope link
      valid_lft forever preferred_lft forever
```

SIM   You get three for the price of one with sims in this chapter! Check out the Chapter 21, "Who Made That NIC" sims at **http://totalsem.com/007**. You'll find a Show!, a Click!, and a Challenge! on the subject that will help you solidify the usefulness of the tools for your technician's toolbox.

arp

Computers use the Address Resolution Protocol (ARP) utility to resolve IP addresses to MAC addresses. As the computer learns various MAC addresses on its LAN, it jots them down in the ARP table. When Computer A wants to send a message to Computer B, it determines B's IP address and then checks the ARP table for a corresponding MAC address.

The *arp* utility enables you to view and change the ARP table on a computer. Here's sample output from `arp -a`:

```
Interface: 192.168.4.57 --- 0xc
  Internet Address      Physical Address      Type
    192.168.4.1         b8-9b-c9-7d-e7-76     dynamic
    192.168.4.2         00-87-b6-7e-ae-23     dynamic
```

```
192.168.4.8          67-ab-cc-aa-fe-ed     dynamic
192.168.4.12         23-b5-94-17-d7-33     dynamic
192.168.4.13         4b-4b-4c-4d-4e-46     dynamic
192.168.4.14         55-55-55-55-55-55     dynamic
```

EXAM TIP   The ARP table functions at Layer 3, mapping IP addresses to MAC addresses. The ARP table therefore would be stored on a Layer 3 device. A *MAC address table*, in contrast, maps MAC addresses to ports, and thus lives on a Layer 2 device, a switch.

ping, pathping, and arping

The *ping* utility uses Internet Message Control Protocol (ICMP) packets to query by IP address or by name. It works across routers, so it's generally the first tool used to check if a system is reachable. Unfortunately, many devices block ICMP packets, so a failed ping doesn't always point to an offline system.

The ping utility defaults to IPv4, but also functions well in an IPv6 network. In Windows, use the command with the –6 switch: *ping –6*. In UNIX/Linux, use *ping6*.

Here's sample `ping` output:

```
Pinging 192.168.4.19 with 32 bytes of data:
Reply from 192.168.4.19: bytes=32 time<1ms TTL=64
Reply from 192.168.4.19: bytes=32 time<1ms TTL=64
Reply from 192.168.4.19: bytes=32 time<1ms TTL=64
Reply from 192.168.4.19: bytes=32 time<1ms TTL=64

Ping statistics for 192.168.4.19:
    Packets: Sent = 4, Received = 4, Lost = 0 (0% loss),
Approximate round trip times in milli-seconds:
    Minimum = 0ms, Maximum = 0ms, Average = 0ms
```

If `ping` doesn't work, you can try *arping*, which uses ARP frames instead of ICMP packets. The only downside to arping is that ARP frames do not cross routers because they only consist of frames, and never IP packets, so you can only use arping within a broadcast domain. Windows does not have arping. UNIX and UNIX-like systems, on the other hand, support the arping utility.

Next is sample `arping` output:

```
ARPING 192.168.4.27 from 192.168.4.19 eth0
Unicast reply from 192.168.4.27 [00:1D:60:DD:92:C6]   0.875ms
Unicast reply from 192.168.4.27 [00:1D:60:DD:92:C6]   0.897ms
Unicast reply from 192.168.4.27 [00:1D:60:DD:92:C6]   0.924ms
Unicast reply from 192.168.4.27 [00:1D:60:DD:92:C6]   0.977ms
```

EXAM TIP   The ping command has the word `Pinging` in the output. The arping command has the word `ARPING`. You'll see ping on the CompTIA Network+ exam; you won't see arping.

The ping and traceroute utilities are excellent examples of *connectivity software*, applications that enable you to determine if a connection can be made between two computers.

Microsoft has a utility called *pathping* that combines the functions of ping and traceroute and adds some additional functions.

Here is sample `pathping` output:

```
Tracing route to xeroxpaser.totalhome [182.168.4.17]
Over a maximum 30 hops:
  0  local-PC.totalhome [192.168.4.53]
  1  xrxphsr.totalhome [192.168.4.17]
Computing statistics for 25 seconds...
            Source to Here    This Node/Link
Hop  RTT    Lost/Sent - Pct   Lost/Sent - Pct Address
  0                                           local-PC.totalhome [192.168.4.53]
                              0/ 100 - 0%   :
  1   0ms     0/ 100 - 0%    0/ 100 - 0%  xrxphsr.totalhome [192.168.4.17]
Trace complete
```

nslookup/dig

The *nslookup* (all operating systems) and *dig* (macOS/UNIX/Linux) utilities help diagnose DNS problems. These tools are very powerful, but the CompTIA Network+ exam won't ask you more than basic questions, such as how to use them to see if a DNS server is working. When working on Windows systems, the nslookup utility is your only choice by default. On macOS/UNIX/Linux systems, you should prefer the dig utility. Both utilities will help in troubleshooting your DNS issues, but dig provides more verbose output by default. You need to be comfortable working with both utilities when troubleshooting modern networks.

Following is an example of the `dig` command:

```
dig mx totalsem.com
```

This command says, "Show me all the MX records for the totalsem.com domain."

Here's the output for that `dig` command:

```
; <<>> DiG 9.5.0-P2 <<>> mx totalsem.com
;; global options:  printcmd
;; Got answer:
;; ->>HEADER<<- opcode: QUERY, status: NOERROR, id: 6070
;; flags: qr rd ra; QUERY: 1, ANSWER: 3, AUTHORITY: 0, ADDITIONAL: 1
;; QUESTION SECTION:
;totalsem.com.                   IN      MX
;; ANSWER SECTION:
totalsem.com.  86400  IN  MX  10
mx1c1.megamailservers.com.
totalsem.com.  86400            IN      MX     100
mx2c1.megamailservers.com.
totalsem.com.  86400            IN      MX     110
mx3c1.megamailservers.com.
```

 EXAM TIP Running the networking commands several times will help you memorize the functions of the commands as well as the syntax. The CompTIA Network+ exam is also big on the switches available for various commands, such as `ipconfig /all`.

mtr

My Traceroute (mtr) is a dynamic (keeps running) equivalent to traceroute. Windows does not support mtr.

Here's a sample of `mtr` output:

```
                                    My traceroute   [v0.73]
totaltest (0.0.0.0)
Keys:  Help  Display mode  Restart statistics  Order of fields  quit
                              Packets             Pings
Host                         Loss%  Snt  Last   Avg  Best  Wrst StDev
1. Router.totalhome           0.0%   5   0.8   0.8   0.7   0.9   0.1
2. adsl-208-190-121-38.dsl.hstntx.s  0.0%  4  85.7  90.7  69.5 119.2  21.8
```

route

The *route* utility enables you to display and edit the local system's routing table. To show the routing table, just type **route print** or **netstat -r**.

Here's a sample of `route print` output:

```
===========================================================================
Interface List


8 ...00 1d 60 dd 92 c6 ...... Marvell 88E8056 PCI-E Ethernet Controller
1 ........................ Software Loopback Interface 1
===========================================================================
IPv4 Route Table
===========================================================================
Active Routes:
Network Destination        Netmask          Gateway       Interface  Metric
0.0.0.0                    0.0.0.0      192.168.4.1   192.168.4.27      10
127.0.0.0                255.0.0.0        On-link        127.0.0.1     306
127.0.0.1          255.255.255.255        On-link        127.0.0.1     306
127.255.255.255    255.255.255.255        On-link        127.0.0.1     306
169.254.0.0              255.255.0.0       On-link     192.168.4.27     286
169.254.214.185    255.255.255.255        On-link  169.254.214.185     276
169.254.255.255    255.255.255.255        On-link     192.168.4.27     266
192.168.4.0          255.255.255.0        On-link     192.168.4.27     266
192.168.4.27       255.255.255.255        On-link     192.168.4.27     266
192.168.4.255      255.255.255.255        On-link     192.168.4.27     266
224.0.0.0                240.0.0.0        On-link        127.0.0.1     306
224.0.0.0                240.0.0.0        On-link  169.254.214.185     276
224.0.0.0                240.0.0.0        On-link     192.168.4.27     266
255.255.255.255    255.255.255.255        On-link        127.0.0.1     306
255.255.255.255    255.255.255.255        On-link  169.254.214.185     276
255.255.255.255    255.255.255.255        On-link     192.168.4.27     266
===========================================================================
Persistent Routes:

None
```

netstat and ss

The *netstat* utility displays information on the current state of all the running IP processes on a system. It shows what sessions are active and can also provide statistics based on ports or protocols (TCP, UDP, and so on). Typing **netstat** by itself only shows current sessions. Typing **netstat -r** shows the routing table (100 percent identical to route print). If you want to know about your current sessions, netstat is the tool to use.

Here's sample netstat output:

```
Active Connections

  Proto    Local Address           Foreign Address         State
  TCP      127.0.0.1:27015         MikesPC:51090           ESTABLISHED
  TCP      127.0.0.1:51090         MikesPC:27015           ESTABLISHED
  TCP      127.0.0.1:52500         MikesPC:52501           ESTABLISHED
  TCP      192.168.4.27:54731      72-165-61-141:27039     CLOSE_WAIT
  TCP      192.168.4.27:55080      63-246-140-18:http      CLOSE_WAIT
  TCP      192.168.4.27:56126      acd4129913:https        ESTABLISHED
  TCP      192.168.4.27:62727      TOTALTEST:ssh           ESTABLISHED
  TCP      192.168.4.27:63325      65.54.165.136:https     TIME_WAIT
  TCP      192.168.4.27:63968      209.8.115.129:http      ESTABLISHED
```

Windows still comes with netstat, but the ss utility has completely eclipsed it on the Linux side. The ss utility is faster and more powerful than netstat. Unlike netstat, however, you won't find ss on the CompTIA Network+ exam. Here's sample output from ss, filtered to show only TCP connections:

```
State        Recv-Q Send-Q    Local Address:Port       Peer Address:Port
CLOSE-WAIT   28     0         10.0.2.15:52161          91.189.92.24:https
CLOSE-WAIT   28     0         10.0.2.15:46117          91.189.92.11:https
ESTAB        0      0         10.0.2.15:55542          74.125.239.40:http
```

 EXAM TIP The *iptables* utility in Linux enabled command-line control over IPv4 *tables*, rules that determine what happens with an IPv4 packet when it encounters a firewall. The CompTIA Network+ exam objectives reference this utility, though it was superseded in 2014 by *nftables*. Expect a question on iptables on the exam; assume you'll work with nftables in the real world.

Packet Sniffer/Protocol Analyzer

A *packet sniffer*, as you'll recall from Chapter 20, intercepts and logs network packets. You have many choices when it comes to packet sniffers. Some sniffers come as programs you run on a computer, while others manifest as dedicated hardware devices. Most packet sniffers come bundled with a *protocol analyzer,* the tool that takes the sniffed information and figures out what's happening on the network. Arguably, the most popular GUI packet sniffer and protocol analyzer is *Wireshark* (Figure 21-6). You've already seen Wireshark in the book, but here's a screen to jog your memory.

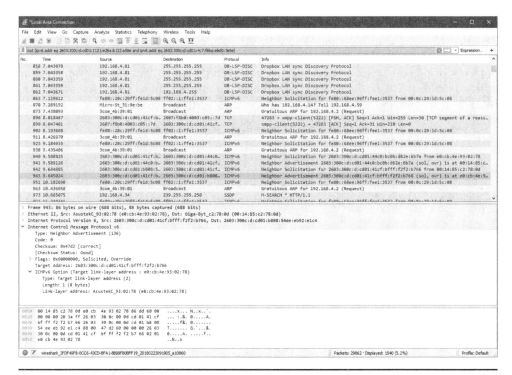

Figure 21-6 Wireshark in action

 EXAM TIP Sometimes a GUI tool like Wireshark won't work because a server has no GUI installed. In situations like this, *tcpdump* is the go-to choice. This great command-line tool not only enables you to monitor and filter packets in the terminal, but can also create files you can open in Wireshark for later analysis. Even better, it's installed by default on most UNIX/Linux systems.

Port Scanners

As you'll recall from back in Chapter 18, "Managing Risk," a *port scanner* is a program that probes ports on another system, logging the state of the scanned ports. These tools are used to look for unintentionally opened ports that might make a system vulnerable to attack. As you might imagine, they also are used by hackers to break into systems.

The most famous of all port scanners is probably the powerful and free *Nmap*. Nmap was originally designed to work on UNIX systems, so Windows folks used alternatives like Angry IP Scanner by Anton Keks (Figure 21-7). Nmap has been ported to just about every operating system these days, however, so you can find it for Windows.

Figure 21-7
Angry IP Scanner

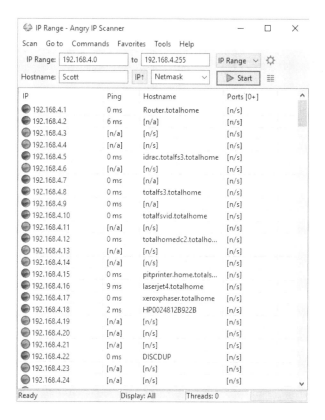

Throughput Testers

Throughput testers enable you to measure the data flow in a network. Which tool is appropriate depends on the type of network throughput you want to test. Most techs use one of several *speed-test sites* for checking an Internet connection's throughput, such as Mega-Path's Speakeasy Speed Test (Figure 21-8): www.speakeasy.net/speedtest. The CompTIA Network+ exam objectives refer to throughput testers as *bandwidth speed testers*.

Looking Glass Sites

Sometimes you need to perform a ping or traceroute from a location outside of the local environment. *Looking glass sites* are remote servers accessible with a browser that contain common collections of diagnostic tools such as ping and traceroute, plus some Border Gateway Protocol (BGP) query tools.

Most looking glass sites allow you to select where the diagnostic process will originate from a list of locations, as well as the target destination, which diagnostic, and sometimes the version of IP to test. A Google search for "looking glass sites" will provide a large selection from which to choose.

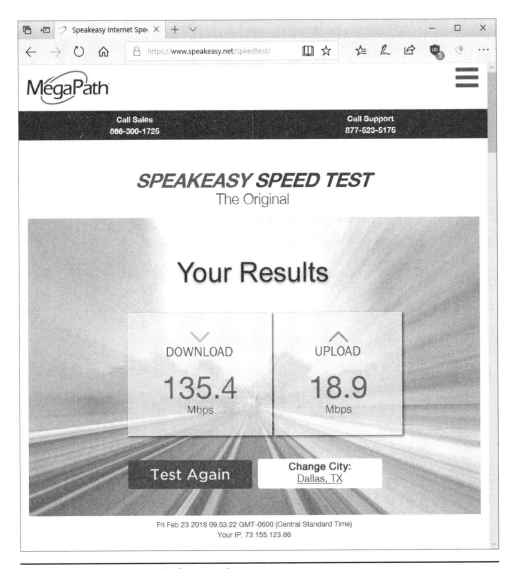

Figure 21-8   Speed Test results from Speakeasy

The Troubleshooting Process

Troubleshooting is a dynamic, fluid process that requires you to make snap judgments and act on them to try and make the network go. Any attempt to cover every possible scenario here would be futile at best, and probably also not in your best interest. If an exhaustive listing of all network problems is impossible, then how do you decide what to do and in what order?

Before you touch a single console or cable, you should remember two basic rules. For starters, to paraphrase the Hippocratic Oath, "First, do no harm." If at all possible, don't make a network problem bigger than it was originally. This is a rule I've broken thousands of times, and you will too.

But if I change the good doctor's phrase a bit, it's possible to formulate a rule you can actually live with: "First, do not trash the data!" My gosh, if I had a dollar for every megabyte of irreplaceable data I've destroyed, I'd be rich! I've learned my lesson, and you should learn from my mistakes.

The second rule is: "Always make good backups!" Computers can be replaced; data that is not backed up is, at best, expensive to recover and, at worst, gone forever.

No matter how complex and fancy, any troubleshooting process can be broken down into simple steps. Having a sequence of steps to follow makes the entire troubleshooting process simpler and easier, because you have a clear set of goals to achieve in a specific sequence.

The CompTIA Network+ exam objectives contain a detailed troubleshooting methodology that provides a good starting point for our discussion. Here are the basic steps in the troubleshooting process:

1. Identify the problem.

   a. Gather information.

   b. Duplicate the problem, if possible.

   c. Question users.

   d. Identify symptoms.

   e. Determine if anything has changed.

   f. Approach multiple problems individually.

2. Establish a theory of probable cause.

   a. Question the obvious.

   b. Consider multiple approaches:

      i. Top-to-bottom/bottom-to-top OSI model

      ii. Divide and conquer

3. Test the theory to determine the cause.

   a. Once the theory is confirmed, determine the next steps to resolve the problem.

   b. If the theory is not confirmed, reestablish a new theory or escalate.

4. Establish a plan of action to resolve the problem and identify potential effects.

5. Implement the solution or escalate as necessary.

6. Verify full system functionality and, if applicable, implement preventative measures.

7. Document findings, actions, and outcomes.

Identify the Problem

First, *identify the problem*. That means grasping the true problem, rather than what someone tells you. A user might call in and complain that he can't access the Internet from his workstation, for example, which could be the only problem. But the problem could also be that the entire wing of the office just went down and you've got a much bigger problem on your hands. You need to gather information, duplicate the problem (if possible), question users, identify symptoms, determine if anything has changed on the network, and approach multiple problems individually. Following these steps will help you get to the root of the problem.

Gather Information, Duplicate the Problem, Question Users, and Identify Symptoms

Gather information about the situation. If you are working directly on the affected system and not relying on somebody on the other end of a telephone to guide you, you will *identify symptoms* through your observation of what is (or isn't) happening.

If you're troubleshooting over the telephone (always a *joy*, in my experience), you will need to *question users*. These questions can be *close-ended*, which is to say there can only be a yes-or-no-type answer, such as, "Can you see a light on the front of the monitor?" You can also ask *open-ended* questions, such as, "What have you already tried in attempting to fix the problem?"

The type of question you ask at any given moment depends on what information you need and on the user's knowledge level. If, for example, the user seems to be technically oriented, you will probably be able to ask more close-ended questions because they will know what you are talking about. If, on the other hand, the user seems to be confused about what's happening, open-ended questions will allow him or her to explain in his or her own words what is going on.

One of the first steps in trying to determine the cause of a problem is to understand the extent of the problem. Is it specific to one user or is it network-wide? Sometimes this entails trying the task yourself, both from the user's machine and from your own or another machine.

For example, if a user is experiencing problems logging into the network, you might need to go to that user's machine and try to use his or her user name to log in. In other words, try to *duplicate the problem*. Doing this tells you whether the problem is a user error of some kind, as well as enables you to see the symptoms of the problem yourself. Next, you probably want to try logging in with your own user name from that machine, or have the user try to log in from another machine.

In some cases, you can ask other users in the area if they are experiencing the same problem to see if the issue is affecting more than one user. Depending on the size of your network, you should find out whether the problem is occurring in only one part of your company or across the entire network.

What does all of this tell you? Essentially, it tells you how big the problem is. If nobody in an entire remote office can log in, you may be able to assume that the problem is the network link or router connecting that office to the server. If nobody in any office can log in, you may be able to assume the server is down or not accepting logins. If only that one user in that one location can't log in, the problem may be with that user, that machine, or that user's account.

EXAM TIP Eliminating variables is one of the first tools in your arsenal of diagnostic techniques.

Determine If Anything Has Changed

Determine if anything has changed on the network recently that might have caused the problem. You may not have to ask many questions before the person using the problem system can tell you what has changed, but, in some cases, establishing if anything has changed can take quite a bit of time and involve further work behind the scenes. Here are some examples of questions to ask:

- "What exactly was happening when the problem occurred?"
- "Has anything been changed on the system recently?"
- "Has the system been moved recently?"

Notice the way I've tactfully avoided the word *you*, as in "Have *you* changed anything on the system recently?" This is a deliberate tactic to avoid any implied blame on the part of the user. Being nice never hurts, and it makes the whole troubleshooting process more friendly.

You should also *internally* ask yourself some isolating questions, such as "Was that machine involved in the software push last night?" or "Didn't a tech visit that machine this morning?" Note you will only be able to answer these questions if *your* documentation is up to date. Sometimes, isolating a problem may require you to check system and hardware logs (such as those stored by some routers and other network devices), so make sure you know how to do this.

EXAM TIP Avoid aggressive or accusatory questions when trying to get information from a user.

Approach Multiple Problems Individually

If you encounter a complicated scenario, with various machines off the network and potential server room or wiring problems, break it down. *Approach multiple problems individually* to sort out root causes. Methodically tackle them and you'll eventually have a list of one or more problems identified. Then you can move on to the next step.

Establish a Theory of Probable Cause

Once you've identified one or more problems, try to figure out what could have happened. In other words, *establish a theory of probable cause*. Just keep in mind that a *theory is not a fact*. You might need to chuck the theory out the window later in the process and establish a revised theory.

This step comes down to experience—or good use of the support tools at your disposal, such as your knowledge base. You need to select the most *probable* cause from all the *possible* causes, so the solution you choose fixes the problem the first time. This may not always happen, but whenever possible, you want to avoid spending a whole day stabbing in the dark while the problem snores softly to itself in some cozy, neglected corner of your network.

Don't forget to *question the obvious*. If Bob can't print to the networked printer, for example, check to see that the printer is plugged in and turned on.

Consider multiple approaches when tackling problems. This will keep you from locking your imagination into a single train of thought. You can use the OSI seven-layer model as a troubleshooting tool in several ways to help with this process. Here's a scenario to work through.

Martha can't access the database server to start her workday. The problem manifests this way: She opens the database client on her computer, then clicks on recent documents, one of which is the current project that management has assigned to her team. Nothing happens. Normally, the database client will connect to the database that resides on the server on the other side of the network.

Try a *top-to-bottom* or *bottom-to-top OSI model* approach to the problem. Sometimes it pays to try both. Here are some ideas on how this might help.

7	Application	Could there be a problem with the API that enables the database application to connect to the database server? Sure.
6	Presentation	Could there be a problem with encryption between the application and the database server? Maybe, but Martha would probably see an error message rather than nothing.
5	Session	Could a database authentication failure be preventing access? Again, this could be the problem, but Martha would probably see an error message here as well.
4	Transport	Perhaps extreme traffic on the network could block an acknowledgment segment? This seems a bit of a reach, but worth considering.
3	Network	Someone might have changed the IP address of the database server.
2	Data Link	The MAC address of the database server or Martha's machine might be blacklisted.
1	Physical	A disconnected cable or dead NIC can make for a bad day.

You might imagine the reverse model in some situations. If the network was newly installed, for example, running through some of the basic connectivity at Layers 1 and 2 might be a good first approach.

Another option for tackling multiple options is to use the *divide and conquer* approach.

On its face, divide and conquer appears to be a compromise between top-to-bottom OSI troubleshooting and bottom-to-top OSI troubleshooting. But it's better than a compromise. If we arbitrarily always perform top-to-bottom troubleshooting, we'll waste a lot of time at Layers 7 through 3 to troubleshoot Data Link layer and Physical layer issues.

Divide and conquer is a time saver that comes into play as part of developing a theory of probable cause. As you gather information for troubleshooting, a general sense of where the problem lies should manifest. Place this likely cause at the appropriate layer of the OSI model and begin to test the theory and related theories at that layer. If the theory bears out, follow the appropriate troubleshooting steps. If the theory is wrong, move up or down the OSI model with new theories of probable causes.

Test the Theory to Determine Cause

With the third step, you need to *test the theory to determine the cause* but do so without changing anything or risking any repercussions. If you have determined that the probable cause for Bob not being able to print is that the printer is turned off, go look. If that's the case, then you should plan out your next step to resolve the problem. Do not act yet! That comes next.

If the theory is not confirmed, you need to *reestablish a new theory or escalate the problem.* Go back to step two and determine a new probable cause. Once you have another idea, test it.

The reason you should hesitate to act at this third step is that you might not have permission to make the fix or the fix might cause repercussions you don't fully understand yet. For example, if you walk over to the print server room to see if the printer is powered up and online and find the door padlocked, that's a whole different level of problem. Sure, the printer is turned off, but management has done it for a reason. In this sort of situation, you need to escalate the problem.

To *escalate* has two meanings: either to inform other parties about a problem for guidance or to pass the job off to another authority who has control over the device/issue that's most probably causing the problem. Let's say you have a server with a bad NIC. This server is used heavily by the accounting department, and taking it down may cause problems you don't even know about. You need to inform the accounting manager to consult with them. Alternatively, you'll come across problems over which you have no control or authority. A badly acting server across the country (hopefully) has another person in charge to whom you need to hand over the job.

Regardless of how many times you need to go through this process, you'll eventually reach a theory that seems right. *Once the theory is confirmed, determine the next steps you need to take to resolve the problem.*

Establish a Plan of Action and Identify Potential Effects

By this point, you should have some ideas as to what the problem might be. It's time to "look before you leap" and *establish a plan of action to resolve the problem.* An action plan defines how you are going to fix this problem. Most problems are simple, but if the problem is complex, you need to write down the steps. As you do this, think about what else might happen as you go about the repair. *Identify the potential effects* of the actions you're about to take, especially the unintended ones. If you take out a switch without a replacement switch at hand, the users might experience excessive downtime while you hunt for a new switch and move them over. If you replace a router, can you restore all the old router's settings to the new one or will you have to rebuild from scratch?

Implement the Solution or Escalate as Necessary

Once you think you have isolated the cause of the problem, you should decide what you think is the best way to fix it and then *implement the solution*, whether that's giving advice over the phone to a user, installing a replacement part, or adding a software patch. Or, if the solution you propose requires either more skill than you possess at the moment or falls into someone else's purview, *escalate as necessary* to get the fix implemented.

If you're the implementer, follow these guidelines. All the way through implementation, try only one likely solution at a time. There's no point in installing several patches at once, because then you can't tell which one fixed the problem. Similarly, there's no point in replacing several items of hardware (such as a hard disk and its controller cable) at the same time, because then you can't tell which part (or parts) was faulty.

As you try each possibility, always *document* what you do and what results you get. This isn't just for a future problem either—during a lengthy troubleshooting process, it's easy to forget exactly what you tried two hours before or which thing you tried produced a particular result. Although being methodical may take longer, it will save time the next time—and it may enable you to pinpoint what needs to be done to stop the problem from recurring at all, thereby reducing future call volume to your support team—and as any support person will tell you, that's definitely worth the effort!

Then you need to test the solution. This is the part everybody hates. Once you think you've fixed a problem, you should try to make it happen again. If you can't, great! But sometimes you will be able to re-create the problem, and then you know you haven't finished the job at hand. Many techs want to slide away quietly as soon as everything seems to be fine, but trust me on this, it won't impress your customer when her problem flares up again 30 seconds after you've left the building—not to mention that you get the joy of another two-hour car trip the next day to fix the same problem, for an even more unhappy client!

In the scenario where you are providing support to someone else rather than working directly on the problem, you should have *her* try to re-create the problem. This tells you whether she understands what you have been telling her and educates her at the same time, lessening the chance that she'll call you back later and ask, "Can we just go through that one more time?"

 EXAM TIP   Always test a solution before you walk away from the job!

Verify Full System Functionality and Implement Preventative Measures

Okay, now that you have changed something on the system in the process of solving one problem, you must think about the wider repercussions of what you have done. If you've replaced a faulty NIC in a server, for instance, will the fact that the MAC address has changed (remember, it's built into the NIC) affect anything else, such as the logon security controls or your network management and inventory software? If you've installed a patch on a client PC, will this change the default protocol or any other default settings that may affect other functionality? If you've changed a user's security settings, will this affect his or her ability to access other network resources? This is part of testing your solution to make sure it works properly, but it also makes you think about the impact of your work on the system as a whole.

Make sure you *verify full system functionality*. If you think you fixed the problem between Martha's workstation and the database server, have her open the database while you're still there. That way you don't have to make a second tech call to resolve an outstanding issue. This saves time and money and helps your customer do his or her job better. Everybody wins.

Also at this time, if applicable, *implement preventative measures* to avoid a repeat of the problem. If that means you need to educate the user to do or not do something, teach him or her tactfully. If you need to install software or patch a system, do it now.

Document Findings, Actions, and Outcomes

It is *vital* that you *document findings, actions, and outcomes* of all support calls, for two reasons: First, you're creating a support database to serve as a knowledge base for future reference, enabling everyone on the support team to identify new problems as they arise and know how to deal with them quickly, without having to duplicate someone else's research efforts. Second, documentation enables you to track problem trends and anticipate future workloads, or even to identify a particular brand or model of an item, such as a printer or a NIC, that seems to be less reliable or that creates more work for you than others. Don't skip this step—it *really* is essential!

 EXAM TIP Memorize these problem analysis steps:

1. Identify the problem.

    a. Gather information.

    b. Duplicate the problem, if possible.

    c. Question users.

    d. Identify symptoms.

    e. Determine if anything has changed.

    f. Approach multiple problems individually.

2. Establish a theory of probable cause.

    a. Question the obvious.

    b. Consider multiple approaches:

        i. Top-to-bottom/bottom-to-top OSI model

        ii. Divide and conquer

3. Test the theory to determine cause.

    a. Once theory is confirmed, determine next steps to resolve problem.

    b. If theory is not confirmed, reestablish new theory or escalate.

4. Establish a plan of action to resolve the problem and identify potential effects.

5. Implement the solution or escalate as necessary.

6. Verify full system functionality and, if applicable, implement preventative measures.

7. Document findings, actions, and outcomes.

Resolving Common Network Service Issues

Network problems fall into several basic categories, and most of these problems you or a network tech in the proper place can fix. Fixing problems at the workstation, work area, or server is a network tech's bread and butter. The same is true of connecting to resources on the LAN. Problems connecting to a WAN can often be resolved at the local level, but sometimes need to get escalated. The knowledge from the previous chapters combined with the tools and methods you've learned in this chapter should enable you to fix just about any network!

There are a couple of stumbling blocks when it comes to resolving network issues. First, at almost any level of problem, the result—as far as the end user is concerned—is the same. He or she can't access resources beyond the local machine. Whether a user tries to access the local file server or do a Google search, if the attempt fails, "the network is down!" You need to fall back on the most important question a tech can ask: What can cause this problem? Then methodically work through the troubleshooting steps and tools to narrow possibilities. Let's look at a scenario to illustrate the narrowing process.

"We Can't Access Our Web Server in Istanbul!"

Everyone in the local office appears to have full access to local and Internet Web sites. No one, however, can reach a company-operated server at a particular remote site in Istanbul. There has been a recent change to the firewall configuration, so it is up to technician Terry to determine if the firewall change is the culprit or if the problem lies elsewhere.

Terry has come up with three possible theories: the remote server is down, the remote site is inaccessible, or the local firewall is preventing communication with the server. He elects to test his theories with the "quickest to test" approach. His first test is to confirm that all of the local office workstations cannot reach the remote server. Using different hosts, he uses the ping and ping6 utilities. First he pings localhost to confirm the workstation has a working IP stack, then he attempts to ping the remote server and gets no response. Next, he tries the tracert and traceroute utilities on the different hosts. Traceroute shows a functional path to the router that connects the remote office to the Internet, but does not get a response from the server.

So far, everything seems to confirm that the local office cannot get to the remote server. Just to be able to say he tried everything, Terry runs the mtr utility from a Linux box and lets it run for an extended time. At the same time, he runs the pathping utility from a

Windows computer. Neither utility can contact the server. He tries all of these utilities on some other company resources and Internet sites and has no problems connecting.

Confident that the reported symptom is confirmed, Terry puts in a call to the remote site to ask about the status. The virtual PBX sends Terry to voicemail for every extension that he calls. This could point to a network disconnection at the site or to everyone being out of the office there. Since it is 3:00 A.M. at the remote site, Terry does not have a clear answer.

The next quick test to perform is to see if the site is reachable from outside of the local office. This will confirm or eliminate his theory of a local *incorrect host-based firewall settings* issue.

Terry sits down at a computer and searches on Google for a looking glass site. He selects one from the results list and browses to the site. Once in the site, he selects the location of a source router to perform a diagnostic test, and then he selects the type of test to run; in this case, he chooses a ping test. He enters the target server address of the company remote server and submits the test parameters. After a moment, the looking glass server sends a set of pings, none of which receives a response. He tries the test from a few other source router locations and gets the same results.

To complete his tests, Terry uses the looking glass site to ping some additional hosts at the remote site and is pleased to discover that they are all reachable. Now Terry knows that the site is accessible, so it must be that the server is down. When the office opens, he will contact the technician there and offer whatever help and information that he can. In the meantime, he informs the rest of the organization of the server's status.

Narrowing the problem to a single source—an apparently down server—doesn't get all the way to the bottom of the problem (although it certainly helps!). What could cause an unresponsive server?

- Local power outage, like a blown circuit breaker
- Failed NIC on the server
- Network cable disconnected
- Improper network configuration on the server
- A changed patch cable location in the rack
- Failed component in the server
- Server shutdown
- A whole lot of other possibilities

Let's look at some of the problems from a hands-on view first, then move to LAN and WAN issues.

Hands-On Problems

Hands-on problems refer to things that you can fix at the workstation, work area, or server. These include physical problems and configuration problems.

A *power failure* or *power anomalies*, such as dips and surges, can make a network device unreachable. We've addressed the fixes for such issues a couple of times already in this book: manage the power to the network device in question and install an uninterruptible power supply (UPS).

A *hardware failure* can certainly make a network device unreachable. Fall back on your CompTIA A+ training for troubleshooting. Check the link lights on the NIC. Try another NIC if the machine seems functional in every other aspect. Ping the localhost.

Pay attention to link lights when you have a "hardware failure." The *network connection LED status indicators*—link lights—can quickly point to a connectivity issue. Try known good cables/NICs if you run into this issue.

Hot-swappable *transceivers* (which you read about way back in Chapter 4, "Modern Ethernet") can go bad. The key when working with small form-factor pluggable (SFP) or the much older gigabit interface converter (GBIC) transceivers is that you need to check both the media and the module. In other words, a seemingly *bad SFP/GBIC* could be *the cable connected to it or the transceiver.* As with other hardware issues, try known-good components to troubleshoot.

Outside invisible forces can cause problems with copper cabling. You've read about electromagnetic interference (EMI) and radio frequency interference (RFI) previously in the book. *EMI and RFI can disrupt signaling on a copper cable*, especially with the very low voltages used today on those cables. These are crazy things to troubleshoot.

An interference problem might manifest in a scenario like this one. John can use e-mail on his laptop successfully over the company's wireless network. When he plugs in at his desk in his cubicle, however, e-mail messages just don't get through.

Typically, you'd test everything before suspecting EMI or RFI causing this problem. Test the NIC on the laptop by plugging into a known-good port. You'd use a cable tester on the cable. You'd check for continuity between the port in his office to the switch. You'd glance at the cabling certification documents to see that yes, the cable worked when installed.

Only then might a creative tech at her wit's end notice the recently installed, high-powered WAP on the wall outside Tom's office. RFI strikes!

If the installation is new and unproven, a perfectly fine network device might be unreachable because of *interface errors*, meaning that the installer didn't install the wall jack correctly. The resulting *incorrect termination* might be a mismatched standard (568A rather than 568B, for example). The cable from the wall to the workstation might be bad or might be a *crossover* cable rather than *straight-through* cable. That's an *incorrect cable type*, according to the CompTIA Network+ objectives. Try another cable.

Aside from obvious physical problems, other hands-on problems you can fix manifest as some sort of misconfiguration. An *incorrect IP configuration*, such as setting a PC to a static IP address that's not on the same network ID as other resources, would result in a "dead-to-me" network. A similar fate would result from inputting *incorrect default gateway IP address* information. The same is true with an *incorrect netmask setting*—that is, the subnet mask isn't accurate. The system will go nowhere, fast.

The fix for these sorts of problems should be pretty obvious to you at this point. Go into the network configuration for the device and put in correct numbers. Figure 21-9 shows TCP/IP settings for a Windows Server machine.

Figure 21-9
TCP/IP settings in
Windows Server

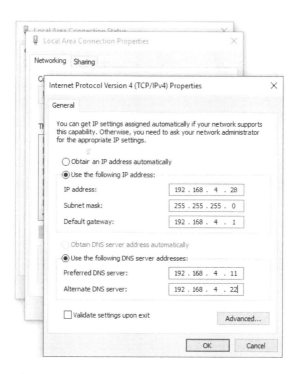

Some problems you can fix at the local machine don't point to messed-up hardware or invalid settings, but reflect the current mix of wired and wireless networks in the same place. Here's a scenario that applies to Windows versions *before* Windows 10. Tina has a wireless network connection to the Internet. She gets a shiny new printer with an Ethernet port, but with no Wi-Fi capability. She wants to print from both her PC and her laptop, so she creates a small LAN: a couple of Ethernet cables and a switch. She plugs everything in, installs drivers, and all is well. She can print from both machines. Unfortunately, as soon as she prints, her Internet connection goes down.

The funny part is that the Internet connection didn't go anywhere, but her *simultaneous wired/wireless connections* created a network failure. The wired and wireless NICs can't actually operate simultaneously and, by default, the wired connection takes priority in the order in which devices are accessed by network services.

To fix this problem, open **Network Connections** in the Control Panel. Press the ALT key to activate the menu bar, then select **Advanced | Advanced Settings** (Figure 21-10). Change the connection priority in the Advanced Settings options by selecting the one Tina wants to take priority and clicking the up arrow to move it up the list.

EXAM TIP Windows 10 does not have this simultaneous wired/wireless connection issue at all, so the problem is irrelevant as long as your clients have updated computers. You'll most likely only see this issue in an exam question.

Figure 21-10
Network
Connections
Advanced
Settings

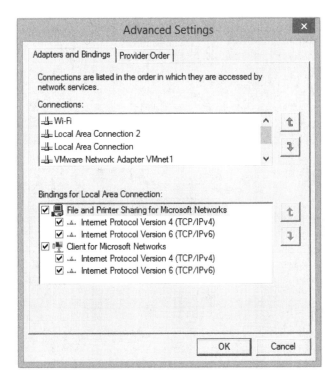

LAN Problems

Incorrect configuration of any number of options in devices can stop a device from accessing resources over a LAN. These problems can be simple to fix, although tracking down the culprit can take time and patience.

One of the most obvious errors occurs when you're duplicating machines and using static IP addresses. As soon as you plug in the duplicated machine with its *duplicate IP address*, the network will howl. No two computers can have the same IP address on a broadcast domain. The fix for the problem—after the face-palm—is to change the IP address on the new machine either to an unused static IP or to DHCP.

A related issue comes from *duplicate MAC addresses*, something that can happen when working with virtual machines or, rarely, as a result of a manufacturing error. The effect is the same as duplicate IP addresses. Either put the devices on different VLANs or swap out NICs to avoid duplication.

An *expired IP address* can cause a system not to connect. Release/renew to obtain a proper IP address from the DHCP server. If the DHCP server's scope of IP addresses has been claimed, that release/renew won't work. You'll get an error that points to an *exhausted DHCP scope*. The only fix for this is to make changes at the DHCP server.

EXAM TIP CompTIA continues to include *duplex/speed mismatch* as a common network issue, although that's not how networks work today. Every NIC, switch, and router features autosensing and autonegotiating ports. You plug two devices in and, as long as they're not otherwise misconfigured, they'll run at the same speed—most likely at full duplex.

It's important to note that if the speeds on the two NICs are mismatched, the link will not come up, but if it's just the duplex that's mismatched, the link will come up but the connection will be erratic. Look for this "common error" on the exam, but not in the real world.

Client Misconfigurations

Most clients will use DHCP for IP address, subnet mask, and default gateway settings. With manual configuration, on the other hand, errors can creep in and cause a device to fail to connect to network resources. A typical scenario is with a bring your own device (BYOD) environment, where an employee will bring in a manually configured laptop—that he didn't remember was tuned to his home network—and complain about not being able to access the LAN or the Internet.

Anything that doesn't match the LAN settings will cause a client to fail to connect. An IP address that doesn't match the subnet, for example, will bring no love. An error in the subnet mask settings—an *incorrect netmask* issue in CompTIA speak—will stop client access cold. A DNS server setting that's not accurate can cause name resolution failure. If the default gateway address is incorrect—an *incorrect gateway* issue—then there's no Internet for the client.

Server Misconfigurations

Misconfigurations of server settings can block all or some access to resources on a LAN. *Misconfigured DHCP* settings on a host above can cause problems, but they will be limited to the host. If these settings are misconfigured on the DHCP server, however, many more machines and people can be affected. A *misconfigured DNS* server might direct hosts to incorrect sites or no sites at all. It might appear as an *unresponsive service* and just do nothing. Misconfigured DNS settings on a client results in *names not resolving* and causes the network to appear to be down for the user.

You'll be clued into such misconfiguration by using ping and other tools. If you can ping a file server by IP address but not by name, this points to *DNS issues*. Similarly, if a computer fails in *discovering neighboring devices/nodes*, like connecting to a networked printer, DHCP or DNS misconfiguration can be the culprit. To fix the issue, go into the network configuration for the client or the server and find the misconfigured settings.

Adding VLANs

When you add VLANs into the network mix, all sorts of fun network issues can crop up. As an example, suppose Bill has a 24-port managed switch segmented into four VLANs, one for each group in the office: Management, Sales, Marketing, and Development (Figure 21-11).

Figure 21-11
Bill's VLAN
assignments

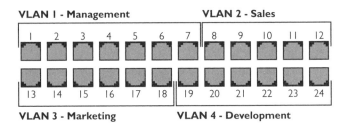

Bill thought he'd assigned six ports to each VLAN when he set up the switch, but by mistake he assigned seven ports to VLAN 1 and only five ports to VLAN 2. Merrily plugging in the patch cables for each group of users, Bill gets called up by his boss asking why Cindy over in Sales suddenly can see resources reserved for management. This obviously points to an *interface misconfiguration* that resulted in a *VLAN mismatch*.

Similarly, after fixing his initial mistake and getting the VLANs set up properly, Bill needs to plug the right patch cables into the right ports. If he messes up and plugs the patch cable for Cindy's computer into a VLAN 1 port, the intrepid salesperson would again have access to the management resources. Such *cable placement errors* show up pretty quickly and are readily fixed. Keep proper records of patch cable assignments and plug the cables into the proper ports.

Link Aggregation Problems

Ethernet networks (traditionally) don't scale easily. If you have a Gigabit Ethernet connection between the main switch and a very busy file server, that connection by definition can handle up to 1 Gbps bandwidth. If that connection becomes saturated, the only way to bump up the bandwidth cap on that single connection would be to upgrade both the switch and the server NIC to the next higher Ethernet standard, 10-Gigabit Ethernet. That's a big jump and an expensive one, plus it's an upgrade of 1000 percent! What if you needed to bump bandwidth up by only 20 percent?

The scaling issue became obvious early on, so manufacturers came up with ways to use multiple NICs in tandem to increase bandwidth in smaller increments, what's called *link aggregation* or *NIC teaming*. Numerous protocols enable two or more connections to work together simultaneously, such as the vendor-neutral IEEE 802.3ad specification *Link Aggregation Control Protocol (LACP)* and the Cisco-proprietary *Port Aggregation Protocol (PAgP)*. Let's focus on the former for a common network issue scenario.

To enable LACP between two devices, such as the switch and file server just noted, each device needs two or more interconnected network interfaces configured for LACP. When the two devices interact, they will make sure they can communicate over multiple physical ports at the same speeds and form a single logical port that takes advantage of the full combined bandwidth (Figure 21-12).

Figure 21-12
LACP

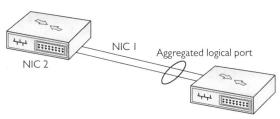

Those ports can be in one of two modes: active or passive. *Active* ports want to use LACP and send special frames out trying to initiate creating an aggregated logical port. *Passive* ports wait for active ports to initiate the conversation before they will respond.

So here's the common network error with LACP setups. An aggregated connection set to active on both ends (*active-active*) automatically talks, negotiates, and works. One set to active on one end and passive on the other (*active-passive*) will talk, negotiate, and work. But if you set both sides to passive (passive-passive), neither will initiate the conversation and LACP will not engage. Setting both ends to passive when you want to use LACP is an example of *NIC teaming misconfiguration*.

NIC teaming provides many more benefits than just increasing bandwidth, such as redundancy. You can team two NICs in a logical unit, but set them up with one NIC as the primary—*live*—and the second as the hot spare—*standby*. If the first NIC goes down, the traffic will automatically flow through the second NIC. In a simple network setup for redundancy, you'd make one connection live and the other as standby on each device. Switch A has a live and a standby, Switch B has a live and a standby, and so on.

The key here is that multicast traffic to the various devices needs to be enabled on every device through which that traffic might pass. If Switch C doesn't play nice with multicast and it's connected to Switch B, this can cause multicast traffic to stop. One "fix" for this in a Cisco network is to turn off a feature called IGMP snooping, which is enabled by default on Cisco switches. IGMP snooping is normally a good thing, because it helps the switches keep track of devices that use multicast and filter traffic away from devices that don't.

The problem with turning off IGMP snooping is that the switches won't map and filter multicast traffic. Instead of only sending to the devices that are set up to receive multicast, the switches will treat multicast messages as broadcast messages and send them to everybody. This is a NIC teaming misconfiguration that can seriously degrade network performance.

A better fix would be to send a couple of network techs to change settings on Switch C and make it send multicast packets properly.

Time Issues

Most devices these days rely on the NIST time servers on the Internet to regulate time. Every once in a while (like on the CompTIA Network+ exam), you'll see a scenario where machines, isolated from the Internet (and thus removed from a time server), will get out of sync. This can result in *incorrect time* issues that stop services from working properly. Did I mention that this is rare?

WAN Problems

Problems that stop users from accessing content across a WAN, like the Internet, can originate at the local machine, switches within the LAN, routers that interconnect the WAN, switches within the distant network, and the distant machine itself. As you might infer from the opening scenario, some of these common network problems you can fix, and some you cannot. We discussed many remote connectivity problems and solutions way back in Chapter 13, so I won't rehash them here.

This section starts with router configuration issues, issues with ISPs and frame sizes, problems with misconfigured multi-layer network appliances, issues with certificates, and company security policies. The following sections go into bigger problems that require escalation. The chapter wraps up with end-to-end connectivity.

Router Problems

Routers enable networks to connect to other networks, which you know well by now. Problems with routers simply make those connections not work. (Recall that physical problems with routers or router interface modules were covered in Chapter 8 and Chapter 13.) Loss of power or a bad module can certainly wreck a tech's day, but the fixes are pretty simple: provide power or replace the module.

Router configuration issues can be a bit trickier. The ways to mess up a router are many. You can specify the wrong routing protocol, for example, or misconfigure the right routing protocol.

An access control list (ACL) might include addresses to block that shouldn't be blocked or allow access to network resources for nodes that shouldn't have it. *Incorrect ACL settings* can lead to *blocked TCP/UDP ports* that shouldn't be blocked. A misconfiguration can lead to *missing IP routes* so that some destinations just aren't there for users.

Improperly configured routers aren't going to send packets to the proper destination. The symptoms are clear: every system that uses the misconfigured router as a default gateway is either not able to get packets out or not able to get packets in, or sometimes both. Web pages don't come up, FTP servers suddenly disappear, and e-mail clients can't access their servers. In these cases, you need to verify first that everything in your area of responsibility works. If that is true, then escalate the problem and find the person responsible for the router.

 EXAM TIP As you'll recall from Chapter 18, if you want to prevent downtime due to a failure on your default gateway, you should consider implementing *Virtual Router Redundancy Protocol (VRRP)* or, if you are a Cisco shop, *Hot Standby Router Protocol (HSRP)*.

One excellent tool for determining a router problem beyond your LAN is tracert/traceroute.

Run `traceroute` to your default gateway. (You can also use ping to check connectivity.) If that fails, you know you have a local issue and can potentially do something about it. If the traceroute comes back positive, run it to a site on the Internet. A solid connection should return something like Figure 21-13. A failed route will return a failed response.

ISPs and MTUs

I discussed the maximum transmission unit (MTU) in Chapter 7, "Routing." Back in the dark ages (before Windows Vista), Microsoft users often found themselves with terrible connection problems because IP packets were too big to fit into certain network protocols. The largest Ethernet packet is 1500 bytes, so some earlier versions of Windows set their MTU size to a value less than 1500 to minimize the fragmentation of packets.

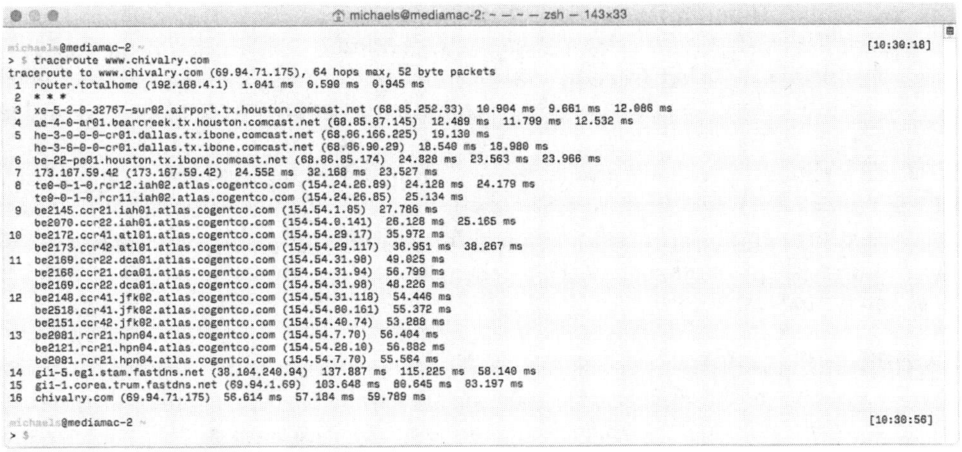

```
●  ●  ●                          ⬆ michaels@mediamac-2: ~ — ~ — zsh — 143×33
michaels@mediamac-2 ~                                                                          [10:30:18]
> $ traceroute www.chivalry.com
traceroute to www.chivalry.com (69.94.71.175), 64 hops max, 52 byte packets
 1  router.totalhome (192.168.4.1)  1.041 ms  0.590 ms  0.945 ms
 2  * * *
 3  xe-5-2-0-32767-sur02.airport.tx.houston.comcast.net (68.85.252.33)  10.904 ms  9.661 ms  12.006 ms
 4  ae-4-0-ar01.bearcreek.tx.houston.comcast.net (68.85.87.145)  12.489 ms  11.799 ms  12.532 ms
 5  he-3-0-0-0-cr01.dallas.tx.ibone.comcast.net (68.86.166.225)  19.130 ms
    he-3-6-0-0-cr01.dallas.tx.ibone.comcast.net (68.86.90.29)  18.540 ms  18.980 ms
 6  be-22-pe01.houston.tx.ibone.comcast.net (68.86.85.174)  24.828 ms  23.563 ms  23.966 ms
 7  173.167.59.42 (173.167.59.42)  24.552 ms  32.168 ms  23.527 ms
 8  te0-0-1-0.rcr12.iah02.atlas.cogentco.com (154.24.26.89)  24.128 ms  24.179 ms
    te0-0-1-0.rcr11.iah02.atlas.cogentco.com (154.24.26.85)  25.134 ms
 9  be2145.ccr21.iah01.atlas.cogentco.com (154.54.1.85)  27.706 ms
    be2070.ccr22.iah01.atlas.cogentco.com (154.54.0.141)  26.128 ms  25.165 ms
10  be2172.ccr41.atl01.atlas.cogentco.com (154.54.29.17)  35.972 ms
    be2173.ccr42.atl01.atlas.cogentco.com (154.54.29.117)  36.951 ms  38.267 ms
11  be2169.ccr22.dca01.atlas.cogentco.com (154.54.31.98)  49.025 ms
    be2168.ccr21.dca01.atlas.cogentco.com (154.54.31.94)  56.799 ms
    be2169.ccr22.dca01.atlas.cogentco.com (154.54.31.98)  48.226 ms
12  be2148.ccr41.jfk02.atlas.cogentco.com (154.54.31.118)  54.448 ms
    be2518.ccr41.jfk02.atlas.cogentco.com (154.54.80.161)  55.372 ms
    be2151.ccr42.jfk02.atlas.cogentco.com (154.54.40.74)  53.288 ms
13  be2021.rcr21.hpn04.atlas.cogentco.com (154.54.7.70)  56.404 ms
    be2121.rcr21.hpn04.atlas.cogentco.com (154.54.28.10)  56.882 ms
    be2001.rcr21.hpn04.atlas.cogentco.com (154.54.7.70)  55.564 ms
14  gi1-5.eg1.stam.fastdns.net (38.104.240.94)  137.887 ms  115.225 ms  58.140 ms
15  gi1-1.corea.trum.fastdns.net (69.94.1.69)  103.648 ms  80.645 ms  83.197 ms
16  chivalry.com (69.94.71.175)  56.614 ms  57.184 ms  59.789 ms

michaels@mediamac-2 ~                                                                          [10:30:56]
> $
```

Figure 21-13   Good connection

The problem cropped up when you tried to connect to a technology other than Ethernet, such as DSL. Some DSL carriers couldn't handle an MTU size greater than 1400. When your network's packets are so large that they must be fragmented to fit into your ISP's packets, we call it an *MTU mismatch*.

As a result, techs would tweak their MTU settings to improve throughput by matching up the MTU sizes between the ISP and their own network. This usually required a manual registry setting adjustment.

Around 2007, *Path MTU Discovery (PMTU)*, a method to determine the best MTU setting automatically, was created. PMTU works by adding a new feature called the "Don't Fragment (DF) flag" to the IP packet. A PMTU-aware operating system can automatically send a series of fixed-size ICMP packets (basically just pings) with the DF flag set to another device to see if it works. If it doesn't work, the system lowers the MTU size and tries again until the ping is successful. Imagine the hassle of incrementing the MTU size manually. That's the beauty of PMTU—you can automatically set your MTU size to the perfect amount.

Unfortunately, PMTU runs under ICMP; most routers have firewall features that, by default, are configured to block ICMP requests, making PMTU worthless. This is called a *PMTU* or *MTU black hole*. If you're having terrible connection problems and you've checked everything else, you need to consider this issue. In many cases, going into the router and turning off ICMP blocking in the firewall is all you need to do to fix the problem.

Appliance Problems

Many of the boxes that people refer to as "routers" contain many features, such as routing, Network Address Translation (NAT), switching, an intrusion detection system (IDS), a firewall, and more. These complex boxes, such as the *Cisco Adaptive Security Appliance (ASA)*, are called *network appliances*.

One common issue with network appliances is technician error. By default, for example, NAT rules take precedence over an appliance's routing table entries. If the tech fails to set the NAT rule order correctly, traffic that should be routed to go out one interface—like to the DMZ network—can go out an *incorrect interface*—like to the inside network.

Users on the outside would expect a response from something but instead get nothing, all because of a NAT *interface misconfiguration*.

The fix for such problems is to set up your network appliance correctly. Know the capabilities of the network appliance and the relationships among its services. Examine rules and settings carefully.

Certificate Problems

SSL/TLS certificates have expiration dates and companies need to maintain them properly. If you get complaints from clients that the company Web site is giving their browsers *untrusted SSL certificate* errors, chances are that the certificate has expired. The fix for that is pretty simple—update the certificate.

Company Security Policy

Implemented company security policies can make routine WAN connectivity actions completely fail. Here's a scenario.

Mike is the head of his company's IT department and he has a big problem: the amount of traffic running between the two company locations is on a dedicated connection and is blowing his bandwidth out of the water! It's so bad that data moving between the two offices will often drop to a crawl four to five times per day. Why are people using so much bandwidth?

As he inspects the problem, Mike realizes that the sales department is the culprit. Most of the data is composed of massive video files the sales department uses in their advertising campaign. He needs to make some security policy decisions. First, he needs to set up a throttling policy that defines in terms of megabits per second the maximum amount of bandwidth any single department can use per day. Second, he needs to add a *blocking policy*. If anyone goes over this limit, the company will block all traffic of that type for a certain amount of time (one hour). Third, he needs to update his company's *fair access policy* or *utilization limits* security policies to reflect these new limits. This lets employees, especially those pesky sales folks, know what the new rules are.

Beyond Local—Escalate

No single person is truly in control of an entire Internet-connected network. Large organizations split network support duties into very skill-specific areas: routers, cable infrastructure, user administration, and so on. Even in a tiny network with a single network support person, problems will arise that go beyond the tech's skill level or that involve equipment the organization doesn't own (usually it's their ISP's gear). In these situations, the tech needs to identify the problem and, instead of trying to fix it on his or her own, escalate the issue.

In network troubleshooting, problem escalation should occur when you face a problem that falls outside the scope of your skills and you need help. In large organizations, escalation problems have very clear procedures, such as who to call and what to document. In small organizations, escalation often is nothing more than a technician realizing that he or she needs help. The CompTIA Network+ exam objectives define some classic networking situations that CompTIA feels should be escalated. Here's how to recognize broadcast storms, switching loops, routing problems, and proxy ARP.

Broadcast Storms

A *broadcast storm* is the result of one or more devices sending a nonstop flurry of broadcast frames on the network. The first sign of a broadcast storm is when every computer on the broadcast domain suddenly can't connect to the rest of the network. There are usually no clues other than network applications freezing or presenting "can't connect to …" types of error messages. Every activity light on every node is solidly on. Computers on other broadcast domains work perfectly well.

The trick is to isolate; that's where escalation comes in. You need to break down the network quickly by unplugging devices until you can find the one causing trouble. Getting a packet analyzer to work can be difficult, but at least try. If you can scoop up one packet, you'll know what node is causing the trouble. The second the bad node is disconnected, the network returns to normal. But if you have a lot of machines to deal with and a bunch of users who can't get on the network yelling at you, you'll need help. Call a supervisor to get support to solve the crisis as quickly as possible.

Switching Loops

Also known as a *bridging loop*, a *switching loop* is when you connect and configure multiple switches together in such a way that causes a circular path to appear. Switching loops are rare because all switches use the Spanning Tree Protocol (STP), but they do happen. The symptoms are identical to a broadcast storm: every computer on the broadcast domain can no longer access the network.

The good part about switching loops is that they rarely take place on a well-running network. Someone had to break something, and that means someone, somewhere is messing with the switch configuration. Escalate the problem, and get the team to help you find the person making changes to the switches.

Proxy ARP

Proxy ARP is the process of making remotely connected computers truly act as though they are on the same LAN as local computers. Proxy ARP is done in a number of different ways, with a Virtual Private Network (VPN) as the classic example. If a laptop in an airport connects to a network through a VPN, that computer takes on the network ID of your local network. In order for all of this to work, the VPN concentrator needs to allow some very LAN-type traffic to go through it that would normally never get through a router. ARP is a great example. If your VPN client wants to talk to another computer on the LAN, it has to send an ARP request to get the IP address. Your VPN device is designed to act as a proxy for all that type of data.

Almost all proxy ARP problems take place on the VPN concentrator. With misconfigured proxy ARP settings, the VPN concentrator can send what looks like a denial of service (DoS) attack on the LAN. (A DoS attack is usually directed at a server exposed on the Internet, like a Web server. See Chapter 19, "Protecting Your Network," for more details on these and other malicious attacks.) If your clients start receiving a large number of packets from the VPN concentrator, assume you have a proxy ARP problem and escalate by getting the person in charge of the VPN to fix it.

End-to-End Connectivity

The *end-to-end principle* meant originally that applications and work should happen only at the endpoints in a network. In the early days of networking, this made a lot of sense. Connections weren't always fully reliable and thus were not good for real-time activity. So the work should get done by the computers at the ends of a network connection. The Internet was founded on the end-to-end principle.

With modern networks like the Internet, the end-to-end concept has had to evolve. Clearly, anything you do over the Internet goes through many different machines. So, perhaps end-to-end means that the intermediary devices simply don't change the essential data in packets that flow through them.

Add in today, though, the fact that plenty of intermediaries want to do a lot of things to your data as it flows through their devices. Thieves want to steal information. Merchants want to sell you things. Advertisers want to intrude on your monitor. Government agencies want to control what you can see or do, or simply want to monitor what you do for later, perhaps benign purposes. Other intermediaries help create trust bonds between your computer and a secure site so that e-commerce can function.

That dynamic between the fundamental principle of work only happening on the ends of the connection and all the intermediaries facilitating, pilfering, or punctuating is the current state of the Internet. It's the basic tension between ISP companies that want to build in tiered profit structures and the consumers and creators who want Net Neutrality.

As a common issue, *end-to-end connectivity* refers to connecting users with essential resources within a smaller network, such as a LAN or a private WAN. In such a scenario, the job of the tech is to ensure connections happen fully. Make sure the proper ports are open on an application server. Make sure the right people have the right permissions to access resources and that white list and black list ACLs are set up correctly.

Troubleshooting Is Fun!

The art of network troubleshooting can be a fun, frolicsome, and frequently frustrating feature of your network career. By applying a good troubleshooting methodology and constantly increasing your knowledge of networks, you too can develop into a great troubleshooting artist. Developing your artistry takes time, naturally, but stick with it.

Begin the training. Use the Force. Learn new stuff, document problems and fixes, talk to other network techs about similar problems. Every bit of knowledge and experience you gain will make things that much easier for you when crunch time comes and a network disaster occurs—and as any experienced network tech can tell you, it will occur, even on the most robust network.

Chapter Review

Questions

1. When should you use a cable tester to troubleshoot a network cable?

   A. When you have a host experiencing a very slow connection

   B. When you have an intermittent connection problem

   C. When you have a dead connection and you suspect a broken cable

   D. When you are trying to find the correct cable up in the plenum

2. What are tone probes and tone generators used for?

   A. Locating a particular cable

   B. Testing the dial tone on a PBX system

   C. A long-duration ping test

   D. As safety equipment when working in crawl spaces

3. What does `nslookup` do?

   A. Retrieves the name space for the network

   B. Queries DNS for the IP address of the supplied host name

   C. Performs a reverse IP lookup

   D. Lists the current running network services on localhost

4. What is Wireshark?

   A. Protocol analyzer

   B. Packet sniffer

   C. Packet analyzer

   D. All of the above

5. What will the command `route print` return on a Windows system?

   A. The results of the last tracert

   B. The gateway's router table

   C. The routes taken by a concurrent connection

   D. The current system's route table

6. When trying to establish symptoms over the phone, what kind of questions should you ask of a novice or confused user?

    A. You should ask open-ended questions and let the user explain the problem in his or her own words.

    B. You should ask detailed, close-ended questions to try and narrow down the possible causes.

    C. Leading questions are your best choice for pointing the user in the right direction.

    D. None; ask the user to bring the machine in because it is useless to troubleshoot over the phone.

7. While you are asking the user problem-isolating questions, what else should you be doing?

    A. Asking yourself if there is anything on your side of the network that could be causing the problem.

    B. Nothing; just keep asking the user questions.

    C. Using an accusatory tone with the user.

    D. Playing solitaire.

8. Which command shows you detailed IP information, including DNS server addresses and MAC addresses?

    A. `ipconfig`

    B. `ipconfig -a`

    C. `ipconfig /all`

    D. `ipconfig /dns`

9. What is the last step in the troubleshooting process?

    A. Implementing the solution

    B. Testing the solution

    C. Documenting the solution

    D. Closing the help ticket

10. One of your users calls you with a complaint that he can't reach the site www.google.com. You try and access the site and discover you can't connect either but you can ping the site with its IP address. What is the most probable culprit?

    A. The workgroup switch is down.

    B. Google is down.

    C. The gateway is down.

    D. The DNS server is down.

Answers

1. **C.** Cable testers can only show that you have a broken or poorly wired cable, not if the cable is up to proper specification.

2. **A.** Tone probes are only used for locating individual cables.

3. **B.** The `nslookup` command queries DNS and returns the IP address of the supplied host name.

4. **D.** All of the above; Wireshark can sniff and analyze all the network traffic that enters the computer's NIC.

5. **D.** The `route print` command returns the local system's routing table.

6. **A.** With novice or confused users, ask open-ended questions so the user can explain the problem in his or her own words.

7. **A.** Ask yourself if anything could have happened on your side of the network.

8. **C.** `ipconfig /all` displays detailed IP configuration information.

9. **C.** Documenting the solution is the last and, in many ways, the most important step in the troubleshooting process.

10. **D.** In this case, the DNS system is probably at fault. By pinging the site with its IP address, you have established that the site is up and your LAN and gateway are functioning properly.

Objective Map: CompTIA Network+

Topic	Chapter(s)	Page(s)
1.0 Networking Concepts		
1.1 Explain the purposes and uses of ports and protocols.		
Protocols and ports		
SSH 22	8, 10	290, 376
DNS 53	9	308
SMTP 25	8	291
SFTP 22	10	383
FTP 20, 21	8	295
TFTP 69	8	299
TELNET 23	8	286
DHCP 67, 68	8	266
HTTP 80	8	281
HTTPS 443	8	285
SNMP 161	10	384
RDP 3389	13	488
NTP 123	8, 10	266, 385
SIP 5060, 5061	13	490
SMB 445	9	305
POP 110	8	291
IMAP 143	8	291
LDAP 389	10	385
LDAPS 636	10	385
H.323 1720	13	490
Protocol Types		
ICMP	8	267
UDP	8	265

Topic	Chapter(s)	Page(s)
Types		
LAN	4, 13	96, 447
WLAN	14	503
MAN	13	468
WAN	13	447
CAN	17	599–600
SAN	15	565–566
PAN	16	586, 590
Technologies that facilitate the Internet of Things (IoT)		
Z-Wave	16	591
Ant+	16	590–591
Bluetooth	16	586–588
NFC	16	588–589
IR	16	590
RFID	16	589–590
802.11	16	583–586

1.6 Given a scenario, implement the appropriate wireless technologies and configurations.

802.11 standards		
a	14	508
b	14	507
g	14	508–509
n	14	509
ac	14	510
Cellular		
GSM	16	581–582
TDMA	16	582
CDMA	16	582
Frequencies		
2.4GHz	14	507, 508, 509, 537
5.0GHz	14	508, 537

Topic	Chapter(s)	Page(s)
SSL/TLS/DTLS	11	395
Site-to-site	11	394
Client-to-site	11	394
RDP	13	488–489
SSH	8, 10, 13	287–290, 376–378, 489
VNC	13	489
Telnet	8	286–290
HTTPS/management URL	11	398
Remote file access		
FTP/FTPS	8, 10	295–299, 383
SFTP	10	383
TFTP	8	299
Out-of-band management	11	398
Modem	11	398
Console router	11	398
3.5 Identify policies and best practices.		
Privileged user agreement	18	629
Password policy	18	629
On-boarding/off-boarding procedures	16	592
Licensing restrictions	17	630
International export controls	18	629
Data loss prevention	18	629
Remote access policies	18	629
Incident response policies	18	642
BYOD	16	591
AUP	18	628–629
NDA	18	638
System life cycle	19	673
Asset disposal	19	673
Safety procedures and policies	18	648–651

Topic	Chapter(s)	Page(s)
Rogue DHCP server	6	212
Untrusted SSL certificate	21	754
Incorrect time	21	751
Exhausted DHCP scope	21	749
Blocked TCP/UDP ports	19	752
Incorrect host-based firewall settings	19	745
Incorrect ACL settings	19	752
Unresponsive service	21	749
Hardware failure	21	746

Create Your Study Plan

Congratulations on completing the Network+ Assessment test on Training Hub! You should now take the time to analyze your results with these two objectives in mind:

- Identifying the resources you should use to prepare for the CompTIA Network+ exam
- Identifying the specific topics you should focus on in your preparation

Review Your Overall Score

Use the following table to help you gauge your overall readiness for the CompTIA Network+ exam based on the number of questions you answered correctly on the Net+ Assessment test.

Number of Answers Correct	Recommended Course of Study
0–26	Spend a significant amount of time reviewing the corresponding chapters from this book to make sure you understand the topics completely.
27–39	Review your scores in the specific Exam Domains shown in the next table to identify the particular areas that require your focused attention, and then use this book to review that material.
40–50	Use this book to refresh your knowledge and prepare yourself mentally for the actual exam.

Review Your Score by CompTIA Network+ Exam Domain

Domain	Weight	Number of Questions in Assessment Test	High Priority for Additional Study	Medium Priority for Additional Study	Low Priority for Additional Study
1.0 Network Concepts	23 percent	12	0–6 correct	7–9 correct	10–12 correct
2.0 Infrastructure	18 percent	9	0–5 correct	6–7 correct	8–9 correct
3.0 Network Operations	17 percent	8	0–4 correct	5–6 correct	7–8 correct
4.0 Network Security	20 percent	10	0–5 correct	6–8 correct	9–10 correct
5.0 Network Troubleshooting and Tools	22 percent	11	0–6 correct	7–9 correct	10–11 correct

About the Online Content

This book comes complete with

- A video from author Mike Meyers introducing the CompTIA Network+ certification exam

- TotalTester Online customizable practice exam software with more than 100 practice exam questions

- More than 20 sample simulations from Total Seminars' TotalSims

- More than an hour of video training episodes from Mike Meyers' CompTIA Network+ Certification series

- Links to a collection of Mike's favorite tools and utilities for network troubleshooting

System Requirements

The current and previous major versions of the following desktop Web browsers are recommended and supported: Chrome, Edge, Firefox, and Safari. These browsers update frequently and sometimes an update may cause compatibility issues with the TotalTester Online or other content hosted on the Training Hub. If you run into a problem using one of these browsers, please try using a different Web browser until the problem is resolved.

Your Total Seminars Training Hub Account

To get access to the online content, you will need to create an account on the Total Seminars Training Hub. Registration is free and you will be able to track all your online content using your account.

Single User License Terms and Conditions

Online access to the digital content included with this book is governed by the McGraw-Hill Education License Agreement outlined next. By using this digital content you agree to the terms of that license.

Access   To register and activate your Total Seminars Training Hub account, simply follow these easy steps.

1. Go to **hub.totalsem.com/mheclaim**.

2. To register and create a new Training Hub account, enter your email address, name, and password. No further information (such as credit card number) is required to create an account.

3. If you already have a Total Seminars Training Hub account, select "Log in" and enter your email and password.

4. Enter your Product Key: `6966-tj45-zfg9`

5. Click to accept the user license terms.

6. Select or deselect the Send special offers option.

7. Click "Register and Claim" to create your account. You will be taken to the Training Hub and have access to the content for this book.

Duration of License   Access to your online content through the Total Seminars Training Hub will expire one year from the date the publisher declares the book out of print.

Your purchase of this McGraw-Hill Education product, including its access code, through a retail store is subject to the refund policy of that store.

Neither McGraw-Hill Education nor its licensors shall be liable to any subscriber or to any user or anyone else for any inaccuracy, delay, interruption in service, error or omission, regardless of cause, or for any damage resulting therefrom.

In no event will McGraw-Hill Education or its licensors be liable for any indirect, special or consequential damages, including but not limited to, lost time, lost money, lost profits or good will, whether in contract, tort, strict liability or otherwise, and whether or not such damages are foreseen or unforeseen with respect to any use of the McGraw-Hill Education content.

TotalTester Online

TotalTester Online provides you with a simulation of the CompTIA Network+ exam. Exams can be taken in Practice Mode or Exam Mode. Practice Mode provides an assistance window with hints, references to the book, explanations of the correct and incorrect answers, and the option to check your answer as you take the test. Exam Mode provides a simulation of the actual exam. The number of questions, the types of questions, and the time allowed are intended to be an accurate representation of the exam environment. The option to customize your quiz allows you to create custom exams from selected domains or chapters, and you can further customize the number of questions and time allowed.

To take a test, follow the instructions provided in the previous section to register and activate your Total Seminars Training Hub account. When you register you will be taken to the Total Seminars Training Hub. From the Training Hub Home page, select **Network+ (N10-007) Sample** from the list of "Your Topics" on the Home page. Click the TotalTester tab. You can then select the option to customize your quiz and begin testing yourself in Practice Mode or Exam Mode. All exams provide an overall grade and a grade broken down by domain.

Assessment Test

In addition to the sample exam questions, the TotalTester also includes a CompTIA Network+ pre-assessment test to help you assess your understanding of the topics before reading the book. To launch the pre-assessment test, click **Network+ Assessment**. The Network+ pre-assessment test is 50 questions and runs in Exam mode. When you complete the test, you can review the questions with answers and detailed explanation by clicking **See Detailed Results**. Once you've completed the Assessment test, refer to Appendix B, "Create Your Study Plan," to get a recommended study plan based on your results.

TotalSims for Network+

 From your Total Seminars Training Hub account, select **Network+ (N10-007) Sample** from the list of "Your Topics" on the Home page. Click the TotalSims tab. The simulations are organized by chapter, and there are over 20 free simulations available for reviewing topics referenced in the book, with an option to purchase access to the full TotalSims for Network+ (N10-007) with over 120 simulations.

Mike's Video Training

Over an hour of training videos, starring Mike Meyers, are available for free. Select **Network+ (N10-007) Sample** from the list of "Your Topics" on the Home page. Click the TotalVideos tab. Along with access to the videos, you'll find an option to purchase Mike's complete video training series.

Playing the Mike Meyers Introduction Video

You can watch the video introduction to the CompTIA Network+ exam from Mike online. Select **Network+ (N10-007) Sample** from the list of "Your Topics" on the Home page. Click the Resources tab, and then select the **Mike Meyers Network+ Intro** button.

Mike's Cool Tools

Mike loves freeware/open source networking tools! Access the utilities mentioned in the text by selecting **Network+ (N10-007) Sample** from the list of "Your Topics" on the Home page. Click the Resources tab, and then select **Mike's Cool Tools**.

Technical Support

For questions regarding the TotalTester software or operation of the Training Hub, visit **www.totalsem.com** or e-mail **support@totalsem.com**.

For questions regarding book content, e-mail **hep_customer-service@mheducation .com**. For customers outside the United States, e-mail **international_cs@mheducation.com**.

3G Third-generation wireless data standard for cell phones and other mobile devices. 3G matured over time until Evolved High-Speed Packet Access (HSPA+) became the final wireless 3G data standard. It transferred at theoretical maximum speeds up to 168 megabits per second (Mbps), although real-world implementations rarely passed 10 Mbps.

4G Most popularly implemented as Long Term Evolution (LTE), a wireless data standard with theoretical download speeds of 300 Mbps and upload speeds of 75 Mbps.

4to6 Internet connectivity technology that encapsulates IPv4 traffic into an IPv6 tunnel to get to an IPv6-capable router.

6in4 An IPv6 tunneling standard that can go through IPv4 Network Address Translation (NAT).

6to4 An IPv6 tunneling protocol that doesn't require a tunnel broker. It is generally used to directly connect two routers because it normally requires a public IPv4 address.

8 position 8 contact (8P8C) Four-pair connector used on the end of network cable. Erroneously referred to as an RJ-45 connector.

10 Gigabit Ethernet (10 GbE) A very fast Ethernet designation, with a number of fiber-optic and copper standards.

10Base2 The last true bus-standard network where nodes connected to a common, shared length of coaxial cable.

10BaseFL Fiber-optic implementation of Ethernet that runs at 10 Mbps using baseband signaling. Maximum segment length is 2 km.

10BaseT An Ethernet LAN designed to run on UTP cabling. Runs at 10 Mbps and uses baseband signaling. Maximum length for the cabling between the NIC and the hub (or the switch, the repeater, and so forth) is 100 m.

10GBaseER/10GBaseEW A 10 GbE standard using 1550-nm single-mode fiber. Maximum cable length up to 40 km.

10GBaseLR/10GBaseLW A 10 GbE standard using 1310-nm single-mode fiber. Maximum cable length up to 10 km.

10GBaseSR/10GBaseSW A 10 GbE standard using 850-nm multimode fiber. Maximum cable length up to 300 m.

10GBaseT A 10 GbE standard designed to run on Cat 6a UTP cabling. Maximum cable length of 100 m.

66 block Patch panel used in telephone networks; displaced by 110 blocks in networking.

100BaseFX An Ethernet LAN designed to run on fiber-optic cabling. Runs at 100 Mbps and uses baseband signaling. Maximum cable length is 400 m for half-duplex and 2 km for full-duplex.

100BaseT An Ethernet LAN designed to run on UTP cabling. Runs at 100 Mbps, uses baseband signaling, and uses two pairs of wires on Cat 5 or better cabling.

100BaseT4 An Ethernet LAN designed to run on UTP cabling. Runs at 100 Mbps and uses four-pair Cat 3 or better cabling. Made obsolete by 100BaseT.

100BaseTX The technically accurate but little-used name for 100BaseT.

110 block Also known as a *110-punchdown block*, a connection gridwork used to link UTP and STP cables behind an RJ-45 patch panel.

110-punchdown block The most common connection used on the back of an RJ-45 jack and patch panels.

110-punchdown tool *See* punchdown tool.

802 committee The IEEE committee responsible for all Ethernet standards.

802.1X A port-authentication network access control mechanism for networks.

802.3 (Ethernet) *See* Ethernet.

802.3ab The IEEE standard for 1000BaseT.

802.3z The umbrella IEEE standard for all versions of Gigabit Ethernet other than 1000BaseT.

802.11 *See* IEEE 802.11.

802.11a A wireless standard that operates in the frequency range of 5 GHz and offers throughput of up to 54 Mbps.

802.11ac A wireless standard that operates in the frequency range of 5 GHz and offers throughput of up to 1 Gbps.

802.11a-ht Along with the corresponding 802.11g-ht standard, technical terms for mixed mode 802.11a/802.11g operation. In mixed mode, both technologies are simultaneously supported.

802.11b The first popular wireless standard, operates in the frequency range of 2.4 GHz and offers throughput of up to 11 Mbps.

802.11g   Older wireless standard that operates on the 2.4-GHz band with a maximum throughput of 54 Mbps. Superseded by 802.11n.

802.11g-ht   Along with the corresponding 802.11a-ht standard, technical terms for mixed mode 802.11a/802.11g operation. In mixed mode, both technologies are simultaneously supported.

802.11i   A wireless standard that added security features.

802.11n   An 802.11 standard that increases transfer speeds and adds support for multiple in/multiple out (MIMO) by using multiple antennas. 802.11n can operate on either the 2.4- or 5-GHz frequency band and has a maximum throughput of 400 Mbps. Superseded by 802.11ac.

802.16   *See* IEEE 802.16.

1000BaseCX   A Gigabit Ethernet standard using unique copper cabling, with a 25-m maximum cable distance.

1000BaseLX   A Gigabit Ethernet standard using single-mode fiber cabling, with a 5-km maximum cable distance.

1000BaseSX   A Gigabit Ethernet standard using multimode fiber cabling, with a 220- to 500-m maximum cable distance.

1000BaseT   A Gigabit Ethernet standard using Cat 5e/6 UTP cabling, with a 100-m maximum cable distance.

1000BaseTX   Short-lived gigabit-over-UTP standard from TIA/EIA. Considered a competitor to 1000BaseT, it was simpler to implement but required the use of Cat 6 cable.

1000BaseX   An umbrella Gigabit Ethernet standard. Also known as *802.3z*. Comprises all Gigabit standards with the exception of 1000BaseT, which is under the 802.3ab standard.

A records   DNS records that map host names to their IPv4 addresses.

AAA (Authentication, Authorization, and Accounting)   *See* Authentication, Authorization, and Accounting (AAA).

AAAA records   DNS records that map host names to their IPv6 addresses.

absorption   Quality of some building materials (such as brick, sheetrock, and wood) to reduce or eliminate a Wi-Fi signal.

acceptable use policy   A document that defines what a person may and may not do on an organization's computers and networks.

access control   All-encompassing term that defines the degree of permission granted to use a particular resource. That resource may be anything from a switch port to a particular file to a physical door within a building.

access control list (ACL) A clearly defined list of permissions that specifies what actions an authenticated user may perform on a shared resource.

Access Control Server (ACS) Cisco program/process/server that makes the decision to admit or deny a node based on posture assessment. From there, the ACS directs the edge access device to allow a connection or to implement a denial or redirect.

access port Regular port in a switch that has been configured as part of a VLAN. Access ports are ports that hosts connect to. They are the opposite of a trunk port, which is only connected to a trunk port on another switch.

Active Directory A form of directory service used in networks with Windows servers. Creates an organization of related computers that share one or more Windows domains.

activity light An LED on a NIC, hub, or switch that blinks rapidly to show data transfers over the network.

ad hoc mode A wireless networking mode where each node is in direct contact with every other node in a decentralized free-for-all. Ad hoc mode is similar to the *mesh topology*.

Adaptive Network Technology (ANT+) A low-speed, low-power networking technology; used in place of Bluetooth for connecting devices, such as smart phones and exercise machines.

Address Resolution Protocol (ARP) A protocol in the TCP/IP suite used with the command-line utility of the same name to determine the MAC address that corresponds to a particular IP address.

administrative accounts Specialized user accounts that have been granted sufficient access rights and authority to manage specified administrative tasks. Some administrative accounts exist as a default of the system and have all authority throughout the system. Others must be explicitly assigned the necessary powers to administer given resources.

ADSL (asymmetric digital subscriber line) *See* asymmetric digital subscriber line (ADSL).

Advanced Encryption Standard (AES) A block cipher created in the late 1990s that uses a 128-bit block size and a 128-, 192-, or 256-bit key size. Practically uncrackable.

adware A program that monitors the types of Web sites you frequent and uses that information to generate targeted advertisements, usually pop-up windows.

agent In terms of posture assessment, refers to software that runs within a client and reports the client's security characteristics to an access control server to be approved or denied entry to a system.

agent-less In terms of posture assessment, refers to a client that has its posture checked and presented by non-permanent software, such as a Web app program, that executes as part of the connection process. Agent-less software does not run directly within the client but is run on behalf of the client.

aggregation   A router hierarchy in which every router underneath a higher router always uses a subnet of that router's existing routes.

air gap   The act of physically separating a network from every other network.

Aircrack-ng   An open source tool for penetration testing many aspects of wireless networks.

alert   Proactive message sent from an SNMP manager as a result of a trap issued by an agent. Alerts may be sent as e-mail, SMS message, voicemail, or other avenue.

algorithm   A set of rules for solving a problem in a given number of steps.

allow   Permission for data or communication to pass through or to access a resource. Specific allowances through a firewall are called *exceptions*.

American Registry for Internet Numbers (ARIN)   A Regional Internet Registry (RIR) that parcels out IP addresses to large ISPs and major corporations in North America.

amplification   The aspect of a DoS attack that makes a server do a lot of processing and responding.

amplified DoS attack   The type of DoS attack that sends a small amount of traffic to a server, which produces a much larger response from the server that is sent to a spoofed IP address, overwhelming a victim machine.

Angled Physical Contact (APC)   Fiber-optic connector that makes physical contact between two fiber-optic cables. It specifies an 8-degree angle to the curved end, lowering signal loss. APC connectors have less connection degradation from multiple insertions compared to other connectors.

anti-malware program   Software that attempts to block several types of threats to a client including viruses, Trojan horses, worms, and other unapproved software installation and execution.

antivirus   Software that attempts to prevent viruses from installing or executing on a client. Some antivirus software may also attempt to remove the virus or eradicate the effects of a virus after an infection.

anycast   A method of addressing groups of computers as though they were a single computer. Anycasting starts by giving a number of computers (or clusters of computers) the same IP address. Advanced routers then send incoming packets to the closest of the computers.

Apache HTTP Server   An open source HTTP server program that runs on a wide variety of operating systems.

Application layer   *See* Open Systems Interconnection (OSI) seven-layer model.

application log   Tracks application events, such as when an application opens or closes. Different types of application logs record different events.

Application Programming Interface (API) Shared functions, subroutines, and libraries that allow programs on a machine to communicate with the OS and other programs.

application/context aware Advanced feature of some stateful firewalls where the content of the data is inspected to ensure it comes from, or is destined for, an appropriate application. Context-aware firewalls look both deeply and more broadly to ensure that the data content and other aspects of the packet are appropriate to the data transfer being conducted. Packets that fall outside these awareness criteria are denied by the firewall.

approval process One or more decision makers consider a proposed change and the impact of the change, including funding. If the change, the impact, and the funding are acceptable, the change is permitted.

archive The creation and storage of retrievable copies of electronic data for legal and functional purposes.

archive bit An attribute of a file that shows whether the file has been backed up since the last change. Each time a file is opened, changed, or saved, the archive bit is turned on. Some types of backups turn off the archive bit to indicate that a good backup of the file exists on tape.

Area ID Address assigned to routers in an OSPF network to prevent flooding beyond the routers in that particular network. *See also* Open Shortest Path First (OSPF).

areas Groups of logically associated OSPF routers designed to maximize routing efficiency while keeping the amount of broadcast traffic well managed. Areas are assigned a 32-bit value that manifests as an integer between 0 and 4294967295 or can take a form similar to an IP address, for example, "0.0.0.0."

ARP *See* Address Resolution Protocol (ARP).

ARP cache poisoning A man-in-the-middle attack, where the attacker associates his MAC address with someone else's IP address (almost always the router), so all traffic will be sent to him first. The attacker sends out unsolicited ARPs, which can either be requests or replies.

arping A command used to discover hosts on a network, similar to ping, but that relies on ARP rather than ICMP. The arping command won't cross any routers, so it will only work within a broadcast domain. *See also* Address Resolution Protocol (ARP) and ping.

asset disposal Reusing, repurposing, or recycling computing devices that follows system life cycle policies in many organizations.

asset management Managing each aspect of a network, from documentation to performance to hardware.

asymmetric digital subscriber line (ADSL) A fully digital, dedicated connection to the telephone system that provides download speeds of up to 9 Mbps and upload speeds of up to 1 Mbps.

asymmetric-key algorithm An encryption method in which the key used to encrypt a message and the key used to decrypt it are different, or asymmetrical.

Asynchronous Transfer Mode (ATM) A network technology that runs at speeds between 25 and 622 Mbps using fiber-optic cabling or Cat 5 or better UTP.

attenuation The degradation of signal over distance for a networking cable.

authentication A process that proves good data traffic truly came from where it says it originated by verifying the sending and receiving users and computers.

Authentication, Authorization, and Accounting (AAA) A security philosophy wherein a computer trying to connect to a network must first present some form of credential in order to be authenticated and then must have limitable permissions within the network. The authenticating server should also record session information about the client.

Authentication Server (AS) In Kerberos, a system that hands out Ticket-Granting Tickets to clients after comparing the client hash to its own. *See also* Ticket-Granting Ticket (TGT).

authoritative DNS servers DNS servers that hold the IP addresses and names of systems for a particular domain or domains in special storage areas called *forward lookup zones*. They also have *reverse lookup zones*.

authoritative name servers Another name for authoritative DNS servers. *See* authoritative DNS servers.

authorization A step in the AAA philosophy during which a client's permissions are decided upon. *See also* Authentication, Authorization, and Accounting (AAA).

Automatic Private IP Addressing (APIPA) A networking feature in operating systems that enables DHCP clients to self-configure an IP address and subnet mask automatically when a DHCP server isn't available.

Autonomous System (AS) One or more networks that are governed by a single protocol, which provides routing for the Internet backbone.

back up To save important data in a secondary location as a safety precaution against the loss of the primary data.

backup Archive of important data that the disaster recovery team can retrieve in case of some disaster.

backup designated router (BDR) A second router set to take over if the designated router fails. *See also* designated router (DR).

backup generator An onsite generator that provides electricity if the power utility fails.

badge A card-shaped device used for authentication; something you have, a possession factor.

bandwidth   A piece of the spectrum occupied by some form of signal, whether it is television, voice, fax data, and so forth. Signals require a certain size and location of bandwidth to be transmitted. The higher the bandwidth, the faster the signal transmission, thus allowing for a more complex signal such as audio or video. Because bandwidth is a limited space, when one user is occupying it, others must wait their turn. Bandwidth is also the capacity of a network to transmit a given amount of data during a given period.

bandwidth saturation   When the frequency of a band is filled to capacity due to the large number of devices using the same bandwidth.

bandwidth speed tester   Web sites for measuring an Internet connection throughput, both download and upload speeds.

banner grabbing   When a malicious user gains access to an open port and uses it to probe a host to gain information and access, as well as learn details about running services.

baseband   Digital signaling that has only one signal (a single signal) on the cable at a time. The signals must be in one of three states: one, zero, or idle.

baseline   Static image of a system's (or network's) performance when all elements are known to be working properly.

basic NAT   A simple form of NAT that translates a computer's private or internal IP address to a global IP address on a one-to-one basis.

Basic Rate Interface (BRI)   The basic ISDN configuration, which consists of two *B* channels (which can carry voice or data at a rate of 64 Kbps) and one *D* channel (which carries setup and configuration information, as well as data, at 16 Kbps).

Basic Service Set (BSS)   In wireless networking, a single access point servicing a given area.

Basic Service Set Identifier (BSSID)   Naming scheme in wireless networks.

baud   One analog cycle on a telephone line.

baud rate   The number of bauds per second. In the early days of telephone data transmission, the baud rate was often analogous to bits per second. Due to advanced modulation of baud cycles as well as data compression, this is no longer true.

Bearer channel (B channel)   A type of ISDN channel that carries data and voice information using standard DS0 channels at 64 Kbps.

bidirectional (BiDi) transceiver   Full-duplex fiber-optic connector that relies on wave division multiplexing (WDM) to differentiate wave signals on a single fiber, creating single-strand fiber transmission.

biometric   Human physical characteristic that can be measured and saved to be compared as authentication in granting the user access to a network or resource. Common biometrics include fingerprints, facial scans, retinal scans, voice pattern recognition, and others.

biometric devices   Devices that scan fingerprints, retinas, or even the sound of the user's voice to provide a foolproof replacement for both passwords and smart devices.

Bit Error Rate Test (BERT)   An end-to-end test that verifies a T-carrier connection.

block   Access that is denied to or from a resource. A block may be implemented in a firewall, access control server, or other secure gateway. *See also* allow.

block cipher   An encryption algorithm in which data is encrypted in "chunks" of a certain length at a time. Popular in wired networks.

blocks   Contiguous ranges of IP addresses that are assigned to organizations and end users by IANA. Also called *network blocks*.

Bluejacking   The process of sending unsolicited messages to another Bluetooth device.

Bluesnarfing   Use of weaknesses in the Bluetooth standard to steal information from other Bluetooth devices.

BNC connector   A connector used for 10Base2 coaxial cable. All BNC connectors have to be locked into place by turning the locking ring 90 degrees.

BNC coupler   Passive connector used to join two segments of coaxial cables that are terminated with BNC connectors.

bonding   Two or more NICs in a system working together to act as a single NIC to increase performance.

Bootstrap Protocol (BOOTP)   A component of TCP/IP that allows computers to discover and receive an IP address from a DHCP server prior to booting the OS. Other items that may be discovered during the BOOTP process are the IP address of the default gateway for the subnet and the IP addresses of any name servers.

Border Gateway Protocol (BGP-4)   An exterior gateway routing protocol that enables groups of routers to share routing information so that efficient, loop-free routes can be established.

botnet   A group of computers under the control of one operator, used for malicious purposes. *See also* zombie.

bottleneck   A spot on a network where traffic slows precipitously.

bounce   A signal sent by one device taking many different paths to get to the receiving systems.

bps (bits per second)   A measurement of how fast data is moved across a transmission medium. A Gigabit Ethernet connection moves 1,000,000,000 bps.

bridge   A device that connects two networks and passes traffic between them based only on the node address, so that traffic between nodes on one network does not appear on the other network. For example, an Ethernet bridge only looks at the MAC address.

Bridges filter and forward frames based on MAC addresses and operate at Layer 2 (Data Link layer) of the OSI seven-layer model.

bridge loop A negative situation in which bridging devices (usually switches) are installed in a loop configuration, causing frames to loop continuously. Switches using Spanning Tree Protocol (STP) prevent bridge loops by automatically turning off looping ports.

bridged connection An early type of DSL connection that made the DSL line function the same as if you snapped an Ethernet cable into your NIC.

bridging loop A physical wiring of a circuitous path between two or more switches, causing frames to loop continuously. Implementing Spanning Tree Protocol (STP) in these devices will discover and block looped paths.

bring your own device (BYOD) A trend wherein users bring their own network-enabled devices to the work environment. These cell phones, tablets, notebooks, and other mobile devices must be easily and securely integrated and released from corporate network environments using on-boarding and off-boarding technologies.

broadband Analog signaling that sends multiple signals over the cable at the same time. The best example of broadband signaling is cable television. The zero, one, and idle states exist on multiple channels on the same cable. *See also* baseband.

broadcast A frame or packet addressed to all machines, almost always limited to a broadcast domain.

broadcast address The address a NIC attaches to a frame when it wants every other NIC on the network to read it. In TCP/IP, the general broadcast address is 255.255.255.255. In Ethernet, the broadcast MAC address is FF-FF-FF-FF-FF-FF.

broadcast domain A network of computers that will hear each other's broadcasts. The older term *collision domain* is the same but rarely used today.

broadcast storm The result of one or more devices sending a nonstop flurry of broadcast frames on the network.

browser A software program specifically designed to retrieve, interpret, and display Web pages.

brute force A type of attack wherein every permutation of some form of data is tried in an attempt to discover protected information. Most commonly used on password cracking.

buffer A component of a fiber-optic cable that adds strength to the cable.

building entrance Location where all the cables from the outside world (telephone lines, cables from other buildings, and so on) come into a building.

bus topology A network topology that uses a single bus cable that connects all of the computers in a line. Bus topology networks must be terminated to prevent signal reflection.

business continuity planning (BCP)   The process of defining the steps to be taken in the event of a physical corporate crisis to continue operations. Includes the creation of documents to specify facilities, equipment, resources, personnel, and their roles.

butt set   Device that can tap into a 66- or 110-punchdown block to see if a particular line is working.

byte   Eight contiguous bits, the fundamental data unit of personal computers. Storing the equivalent of one character, the byte is also the basic unit of measurement for computer storage. Bytes are counted in powers of two.

CAB files   Short for "cabinet files." These files are compressed and most commonly used during Microsoft operating system installation to store many smaller files, such as device drivers.

cable certifier   A very powerful cable testing device used by professional installers to test the electrical characteristics of a cable and then generate a certification report, proving that cable runs pass TIA/EIA standards.

cable drop   Location where the cable comes out of the wall at the workstation location.

cable modem   A bridge device that interconnects the cable company's DOCSIS service to the user's Ethernet network. In most locations, the cable modem is the demarc.

cable stripper   Device that enables the creation of UTP cables.

cable tester   A generic name for a device that tests cables. Some common tests are continuity, electrical shorts, crossed wires, or other electrical characteristics.

cable tray   A device for organizing cable runs in a drop ceiling.

cache   A special area of RAM that stores frequently accessed data. In a network there are a number of applications that take advantage of cache in some way.

cached lookup   The list kept by a DNS server of IP addresses it has already resolved, so it won't have to re-resolve an FQDN it has already checked.

cache-only DNS servers (caching-only DNS servers)   DNS servers that do not have any forward lookup zones. They resolve names of systems on the Internet for the network, but are not responsible for telling other DNS servers the names of any clients.

caching engine   A server dedicated to storing cache information on your network. These servers can reduce overall network traffic dramatically.

Cacti   Popular network graphing program.

campus area network (CAN)   A network installed in a medium-sized space spanning multiple buildings.

canonical name (CNAME)   Less common type of DNS record that acts as a computer's alias.

captive portal   A Wi-Fi network implementation used in some public facilities that directs attempts to connect to the network to an internal Web page for that facility; generally used to force terms of service on users.

capture file   A file in which the collected packets from a packet sniffer program are stored.

card   Generic term for anything that you can snap into an expansion slot.

carrier sense multiple access with collision avoidance (CSMA/CA)   *See* CSMA/CA (Carrier Sense Multiple access with Collision avoidance).

carrier sense multiple access with collision detection (CSMA/CD)   *See* CSMA/CD (carrier sense multiple access with collision detection).

Cat 3   Category 3 wire, a TIA/EIA standard for UTP wiring that can operate at up to 16 Mbps.

Cat 5   Category 5 wire, a TIA/EIA standard for UTP wiring that can operate at up to 100 Mbps.

Cat 5e   Category 5e wire, a TIA/EIA standard for UTP wiring with improved support for 100 Mbps using two pairs and support for 1000 Mbps using four pairs.

Cat 6   Category 6 wire, a TIA/EIA standard for UTP wiring with improved support for 1000 Mbps; supports 10 Gbps up to 55 meters.

Cat 6a   Category 6a wire, a TIA/EIA standard for UTP wiring with support for 10 Gbps up to 100 meters.

Cat 7   Category 7 wire, a standard (unrecognized by TIA) for UTP wiring with support for 10+ Gbps at 600 MHz max. frequency.

category (Cat) rating   A grade assigned to cable to help network installers get the right cable for the right network technology. Cat ratings are officially rated in megahertz (MHz), indicating the highest-frequency bandwidth the cable can handle.

CCITT (Comité Consutatif Internationale Téléphonique et Télégraphique)   European standards body that established the V standards for modems.

CCMP-AES   A 128-bit block cipher used in the IEEE 802.11i standard.

central office   Building that houses local exchanges and a location where individual voice circuits come together.

certificate   A public encryption key signed with the digital signature from a trusted third party called a *certificate authority (CA)*. This key serves to validate the identity of its holder when that person or company sends data to other parties.

certifier A device that tests a cable to ensure that it can handle its rated amount of capacity.

chain of custody A document used to track the collection, handling, and transfer of evidence.

Challenge Handshake Authentication Protocol (CHAP) A remote access authentication protocol. It has the serving system challenge the remote client, which must provide an encrypted password.

Challenge-Response Authentication Mechanism-Message Digest 5 (CRAM-MD5) A tool for server authentication in SMTP servers.

change management The process of initiating, approving, funding, implementing, and documenting significant changes to the network.

change management documentation A set of documents that defines procedures for changes to the network.

change management team Personnel who collect change requests, evaluate the change, work with decision makers for approval, plan and implement approved changes, and document the changes.

change request A formal or informal document suggesting a modification to some aspect of the network or computing environment.

channel A portion of the wireless spectrum on which a particular wireless network operates. Setting wireless networks to different channels enables separation of the networks.

channel bonding Wireless technology that enables wireless access points (WAPs) to use two channels for transmission.

channel overlap Drawback of 2.4-GHz wireless networks where channels shared some bandwidth with other channels. This is why only three 2.4-GHz channels can be used in the United States (1, 6, and 11).

Channel Service Unit/Digital Service Unit (CSU/DSU) *See* CSU/DSU (Channel Service Unit/Data Service Unit).

chat A multiparty, real-time text conversation. The Internet's most popular version is known as Internet Relay Chat (IRC), which many groups use to converse in real time with each other.

checksum A simple error-detection method that adds a numerical value to each data packet, based on the number of data bits in the packet. The receiving node applies the same formula to the data and verifies that the numerical value is the same; if not, the data has been corrupted and must be re-sent.

choose your own device (CYOD) Deployment model where corporate employees select among a catalog of approved mobile devices.

cipher   A series of complex and hard-to-reverse mathematics run on a string of ones and zeroes in order to make a new set of seemingly meaningless ones and zeroes.

cipher lock   A door unlocking system that uses a door handle, a latch, and a sequence of mechanical push buttons.

ciphertext   The output when cleartext is run through a cipher algorithm using a key.

circuit switching   The process for connecting two phones together on one circuit.

Cisco IOS   Cisco's proprietary operating system.

cladding   The part of a fiber-optic cable that makes the light reflect down the fiber.

class license   Contiguous chunk of IP addresses passed out by the Internet Assigned Numbers Authority (IANA).

class of service (CoS)   A prioritization value used to apply to services, ports, or whatever a quality of service (QoS) device might use.

classful   Obsolete IPv4 addressing scheme that relied on the original class blocks, such as Class A, Class B, and Class C.

classless   IPv4 addressing scheme that does not rely on the original class blocks, such as Class A, Class B, and Class C.

Classless Inter-Domain Routing (CIDR)   The basis of allocating and routing classless addresses, not restricting subnet masks to /8, /16, or /24, which classful addressing did. *See also* subnetting.

classless subnet   A subnet that does not fall into the common categories such as Class A, Class B, and Class C.

cleartext   *See* plaintext.

cleartext credentials   Any login process conducted over a network where account names, passwords, or other authentication elements are sent from the client or server in an unencrypted fashion.

client   A computer program that uses the services of another computer program; software that extracts information from a server. Your autodial phone is a client, and the phone company is its server. Also, a machine that accesses shared resources on a server.

client/server   A relationship in which client software obtains services from a server on behalf of a user.

client/server application   An application that performs some or all of its processing on an application server rather than on the client. The client usually only receives the result of the processing.

client/server network   A network that has dedicated server machines and client machines.

client-to-site A type of VPN connection where a single computer logs into a remote network and becomes, for all intents and purposes, a member of that network.

closed-circuit television (CCTV) A self-contained, closed system in which video cameras feed their signal to specific, dedicated monitors and storage devices.

cloud computing Using the Internet to store files and run applications. For example, Google Docs is a cloud computing application that enables you to run productivity applications over the Internet from your Web browser.

cloud/server based Remote storage and access of software, especially anti-malware software, where it can be singularly updated. This central storage allows users to access and run current versions of software easily, with the disadvantage of it not running automatically on the local client. The client must initiate access to and launching of the software.

cloud/server-based anti-malware Remote storage and access of software designed to protect against malicious software where it can be singularly updated.

clustering Multiple pieces of equipment, such as servers, connected, which appear to the user and the network as one logical device, providing data and services to the organization for both redundancy and fault tolerance.

coarse wavelength division multiplexing (CWDM) An optical multiplexing technology in which a few signals of different optical wavelength could be combined to travel a fairly short distance.

coaxial cable A type of cable that contains a central conductor wire surrounded by an insulating material, which in turn is surrounded by a braided metal shield. It is called coaxial because the center wire and the braided metal shield share a common axis or centerline.

code-division multiple access (CDMA) Early cellular telephone technology that used spread-spectrum transmission. Obsolete.

cold site A location that consists of a building, facilities, desks, toilets, parking, and everything that a business needs except computers.

collision The result of two nodes transmitting at the same time on a multiple access network such as Ethernet. Both frames may be lost or partial frames may result.

collision domain *See* broadcast domain.

collision light A light on some older NICs that flickers when a network collision is detected.

command A request, typed from a terminal or embedded in a file, to perform an operation or to execute a particular program.

Common Internet File System (CIFS) The protocol that NetBIOS used to share folders and printers. Still very common, even on UNIX/Linux systems.

community cloud   A private cloud paid for and used by more than one organization.

compatibility issue   When different pieces of hardware or software don't work together correctly.

compatibility requirements   With respect to network installations and upgrades, requirements that deal with how well the new technology integrates with older or existing technologies.

complete algorithm   A cipher and the methods used to implement that cipher.

computer forensics   The science of gathering, preserving, and presenting evidence stored on a computer or any form of digital media that is presentable in a court of law.

concentrator   A device that brings together at a common center connections to a particular kind of network (such as Ethernet) and implements that network internally.

configuration management   A set of documents, policies, and procedures designed to help you maintain and update your network in a logical, orderly fashion.

configuration management documentation   Documents that define the configuration of a network. These would include wiring diagrams, network diagrams, baselines, and policy/procedure/configuration documentation.

configurations   The settings stored in devices that define how they are to operate.

connection   A term used to refer to communication between two computers.

connectionless   A type of communication characterized by sending packets that are not acknowledged by the destination host. UDP is the quintessential connectionless protocol in the TCP/IP suite.

connectionless communication   A protocol that does not establish and verify a connection between the hosts before sending data; it just sends the data and hopes for the best. This is faster than connection-oriented protocols. UDP is an example of a connectionless protocol.

connection-oriented   Network communication between two hosts that includes negotiation between the hosts to establish a communication session. Data segments are then transferred between hosts, with each segment being acknowledged before a subsequent segment can be sent. Orderly closure of the communication is conducted at the end of the data transfer or in the event of a communication failure. TCP is the only connection-oriented protocol in the TCP/IP suite.

connection-oriented communication   A protocol that establishes a connection between two hosts before transmitting data and verifies receipt before closing the connection between the hosts. TCP is an example of a connection-oriented protocol.

console port   Connection jack in a switch used exclusively to connect a computer that will manage the switch.

content filter An advanced networking device that implements content filtering, enabling administrators to filter traffic based on specific signatures or keywords (such as profane language).

content switch Advanced networking device that works at least at Layer 7 (Application layer) and hides servers behind a single IP.

contingency plan Documents that set out how to limit damage and recover quickly from an incident.

contingency planning The process of creating documents that set out how to limit damage and recover quickly from an incident.

continuity The physical connection of wires in a network.

continuity tester Inexpensive network tester that can only test for continuity on a line.

convergence Point at which the routing tables for all routers in a network are updated.

copy backup A type of backup similar to normal or full, in that all selected files on a system are backed up. This type of backup does *not* change the archive bit of the files being backed up.

core The central glass of the fiber-optic cable that carries the light signal.

corporate-owned business only (COBO) Deployment model where the corporation owns all the mobile devices issued to employees. Employees have a whitelist of preapproved applications they can install.

cost An arbitrary metric value assigned to a network route with OSFP-capable routers.

counter A predefined event that is recorded to a log file.

CRC (cyclic redundancy check) A mathematical method used to check for errors in long streams of transmitted data with high accuracy.

crimper Also called a *crimping tool*, the tool used to secure a crimp (or an RJ-45 connector) onto the end of a cable.

crossover cable A specially terminated UTP cable used to interconnect routers or switches, or to connect network cards without a switch. Crossover cables reverse the sending and receiving wire pairs from one end to the other.

cross-platform support Standards created to enable terminals (and now operating systems) from different companies to interact with one another.

crosstalk Electrical signal interference between two cables that are in close proximity to each other.

crypto-malware Malicious software that uses some form of encryption to lock a user out of a system. *See also* ransomware.

CSMA/CA (carrier sense multiple access with collision avoidance)   Access method used only on wireless networks. Before hosts send out data, they first listen for traffic. If the network is free, they send out a signal that reserves a certain amount of time to make sure the network is free of other signals. If data is detected in the air, the hosts wait a random time period before trying again. If there are no other wireless signals, the data is sent out.

CSMA/CD (carrier sense multiple access with collision detection)   Obsolete access method that older Ethernet systems used in wired LAN technologies, enabling frames of data to flow through the network and ultimately reach address locations. Hosts on CSMA/CD networks first listened to hear if there is any data on the wire. If there was none, they sent out data. If a collision occurred, then both hosts waited a random time period before retransmitting the data. Full-duplex Ethernet completely eliminated CSMA/CD.

CSU/DSU (Channel Service Unit/Data Service Unit)   A piece of equipment that connects a T-carrier leased line from the telephone company to a customer's equipment (such as a router). It performs line encoding and conditioning functions, and it often has a loopback function for testing.

customer-premises equipment (CPE)   The primary distribution box and customer-owned/managed equipment that exists on the customer side of the demarc.

cyclic redundancy check (CRC)   *See* CRC (cyclic redundancy check).

daily backup   Also called a *daily copy backup*, makes a copy of all files that have been changed on that day without changing the archive bits of those files.

daisy-chain   A method of connecting together several devices along a bus and managing the signals for each device.

data backup   The process of creating extra copies of data to be used in case the primary data source fails.

Data Encryption Standard (DES)   A symmetric-key algorithm developed by the U.S. government in the 1970s and formerly in use in a variety of TCP/IP applications. DES used a 64-bit block and a 56-bit key. Over time, the 56-bit key made DES susceptible to brute-force attacks.

Data Link layer   *See* Open Systems Interconnection (OSI) seven-layer model.

Data Over Cable Service Interface Specification (DOCSIS)   The unique protocol used by cable modem networks.

datagram   A connectionless transfer unit created with User Datagram Protocol designed for quick transfers over a packet-switched network.

datagram TLS (DTLS) VPN   A virtual private network solution that optimizes connections for delay-sensitive applications, such as voice and video.

DB-9   A 9-pin, D-shaped subminiature connector, often used in serial port connections.

DB-25   A 25-pin, D-shaped subminiature connector, typically use in parallel and older serial port connections.

dead spot   A place that should be covered by the network signal but where devices get no signal.

deauthentication (deauth) attack   A form of DoS attack that targets 802.11 Wi-Fi networks specifically by sending out a frame that kicks a wireless client off its current WAP connection. A rogue WAP nearby presents a stronger signal, which the client will prefer. The rogue WAP connects the client to the Internet and then proceeds to intercept communications to and from that client.

decibel (dB)   A measurement of the quality of a signal.

dedicated circuit   A circuit that runs from a breaker box to specific outlets.

dedicated line   A telephone line that is an always open, or connected, circuit. Dedicated telephone lines usually do not have telephone numbers.

dedicated server   A machine that does not use any client functions, only server functions.

de-encapsulation   The process of stripping all the extra header information from a packet as the data moves up a protocol stack.

default   A software function or operation that occurs automatically unless the user specifies something else.

default gateway   In a TCP/IP network, the IP address of the router that interconnects the LAN to a wider network, usually the Internet. This router's IP address is part of the necessary TCP/IP configuration for communicating with multiple networks using IP.

Delta channel (D channel)   A type of ISDN line that transfers data at 16 Kbps.

demarc   A device that marks the dividing line of responsibility for the functioning of a network between internal users and upstream service providers. Also, *demarcation point*.

demarc extension   Any cabling that runs from the network interface to whatever box is used by the customer as a demarc.

demilitarized zone (DMZ)   A lightly protected or unprotected subnet network positioned between an outer firewall and an organization's highly protected internal network. DMZs are used mainly to host public address servers (such as Web servers).

demultiplexer   Device that can extract and distribute individual streams of data that have been combined together to travel along a single shared network cable.

denial of service (DoS)   An effort to prevent users from gaining normal use of a resource. *See also* denial of service (DoS) attack.

denial of service (DoS) attack   An attack that floods a networked server with so many requests that it becomes overwhelmed and ceases functioning.

dense wavelength division multiplexing (DWDM)   An optical multiplexing technology in which a large number of optical signals of different optical wavelength could be combined to travel over relatively long fiber cables.

designated router (DR)   The main router in an OSPF network that relays information to all other routers in the area.

destination port   A fixed, predetermined number that defines the function or session type in a TCP/IP network.

device driver   A subprogram to control communications between the computer and some peripheral hardware.

device ID   The last six digits of a MAC address, identifying the manufacturer's unique serial number for that NIC.

device types/requirements   With respect to installing and upgrading networks, these determine what equipment is needed to build the network and how the network should be organized.

DHCP four-way handshake (DORA)   DHCP process in which a client gets a lease for an IPv4 address—Discover, Offer, Request, and Ack.

DHCP lease   Created by the DHCP server to allow a system requesting DHCP IP information to use that information for a certain amount of time.

DHCP relay   A router process that, when enabled, passes DHCP requests and responses across router interfaces. In common terms, DHCP communications can cross from one network to another within a router that has DHCP relay enabled and configured.

DHCP scope   The pool of IP addresses that a DHCP server may allocate to clients requesting IP addresses or other IP information like DNS server addresses.

DHCP snooping   Switch process that monitors DHCP traffic, filtering out DHCP messages from untrusted sources. Typically used to block attacks that use a rogue DHCP server.

dial-up lines   Telephone lines with telephone numbers; they must dial to make a connection, as opposed to a dedicated line.

differential backup   Similar to an incremental backup in that it backs up the files that have been changed since the last backup. This type of backup does not change the state of the archive bit.

differentiated services (DiffServ)   The underlying architecture that makes quality of service (QoS) work.

dig (domain information groper)   *See* domain information groper (dig).

digital signal 1 (DS1)   The signaling method used by T1 lines, which uses a relatively simple frame consisting of 25 pieces: a framing bit and 24 channels. Each DS1 channel holds a single 8-bit DS0 data sample. The framing bit and data channels combine to make 193 bits per DS1 frame. These frames are transmitted 8000 times/sec, making a total throughput of 1.544 Mbps.

digital signal processor (DSP)   *See* DSP (digital signal processor).

digital signature   An encrypted hash of a private encryption key that verifies a sender's identity to those who receive encrypted data or messages.

digital subscriber line (DSL)   A high-speed Internet connection technology that uses a regular telephone line for connectivity. DSL comes in several varieties, including asymmetric (ADSL) and symmetric (SDSL), and many speeds. Typical home-user DSL connections are ADSL with a download speed of up to 9 Mbps and an upload speed of up to 1 Kbps.

dipole antenna   The standard straight-wire antenna that provides most omnidirectional function.

direct current (DC)   A type of electric circuit where the flow of electrons is in a complete circle.

directional antenna   An antenna that focuses its signal more toward a specific direction; as compared to an omnidirectional antenna that radiates its signal in all directions equally.

direct-sequence spread-spectrum (DSSS)   A spread-spectrum broadcasting method defined in the 802.11 standard that sends data out on different frequencies at the same time.

disaster recovery   The means and methods to recover primary infrastructure from a disaster. Disaster recovery starts with a plan and includes data backups.

discretionary access control (DAC)   Authorization method based on the idea that there is an owner of a resource who may at his or her discretion assign access to that resource. DAC is considered much more flexible than mandatory access control (MAC).

disk mirroring   Process by which data is written simultaneously to two or more disk drives. Read and write speed is decreased but redundancy, in case of catastrophe, is increased. Also known as *RAID level 1. See also* duplexing.

disk striping   Process by which data is spread among multiple (at least two) drives. It increases speed for both reads and writes of data, but provides no fault tolerance. Also known as *RAID level 0.*

disk striping with parity   Process by which data is spread among multiple (at least three) drives, with parity information as well to provide fault tolerance. The most commonly implemented type is RAID 5, where the data and parity information is spread across three or more drives.

dispersion Diffusion over distance of light propagating down fiber cable.

distance vector Set of routing protocols that calculates the total cost to get to a particular network ID and compares that cost to the total cost of all the other routes to get to that same network ID.

distributed control system (DCS) A small controller added directly to a machine used to distribute the computing load.

Distributed Coordination Function (DCF) One of two methods of collision avoidance defined by the 802.11 standard and the only one currently implemented. DCF specifies strict rules for sending data onto the network media. *See also* Point Coordination Function (PCF).

distributed denial of service (DDoS) Multicomputer assault on a network resource that attempts, with sheer overwhelming quantity of requests, to prevent regular users from receiving services from the resource. Can also be used to crash systems.

distributed switching The centralized installation, configuration, and handling of every switch in a virtualized network.

DLL (dynamic link library) A file of executable functions or data that can be used by a Windows application. Typically, a DLL provides one or more particular functions, and a program accesses the functions by creating links to the DLL.

DNS cache poisoning An attack that adds or changes information in a DNS server to point host names to incorrect IP addresses, under the attacker's control. When a client requests an IP address from this DNS server for a Web site, the poisoned server hands out an IP address of an attacker, not the legitimate site. When the client subsequently visits the attacker site, malware is installed.

DNS domain A specific branch of the DNS name space. Top-level DNS domains include .com, .gov, and .edu.

DNS forwarding DNS server configuration that sends (forwards) DNS requests to another DNS server.

DNS resolver cache A cache used by Windows DNS clients to keep track of DNS information.

DNS root servers The highest in the hierarchy of DNS servers running the Internet.

DNS server A system that runs a special DNS server program.

DNS tree A hierarchy of DNS domains and individual computer names organized into a tree-like structure, the top of which is the root.

document A medium and the data recorded on it for human use; for example, a report sheet or book. By extension, any record that has permanence and that can be read by a human or a machine.

documentation A collection of organized documents or the information recorded in documents. Also, instructional material specifying the inputs, operations, and outputs of a computer program or system.

domain A term used to describe a grouping of users, computers, and/or networks. In Microsoft networking, a domain is a group of computers and users that shares a common account database and a common security policy. For the Internet, a domain is a group of computers that shares a common element in their DNS hierarchical name.

domain controller A Microsoft Windows Server system specifically configured to store user and server account information for its domain. Often abbreviated as "DC." Windows domain controllers store all account and security information in the *Active Directory* domain service.

domain information groper (dig) Command-line tool in non-Windows systems used to diagnose DNS problems.

Domain Name System (DNS) A TCP/IP name resolution system that resolves host names to IP addresses, IP addresses to host names, and other bindings, like DNS servers and mail servers for a domain.

domain users and groups Users and groups that are defined across an entire network domain.

door access controls Methodology to grant permission or to deny passage through a doorway. The method may be computer-controlled, human-controlled, token-oriented, or many other means.

dotted decimal notation Shorthand method for discussing and configuring binary IP addresses.

download The transfer of information from a remote computer system to the user's system. Opposite of *upload*.

drive duplexing *See* duplexing.

drive mirroring The process of writing identical data to two hard drives on the same controller at the same time to provide data redundancy.

DS0 The digital signal rate created by converting analog sound into 8-bit chunks 8000 times a second, with a data stream of 64 Kbps. This is the simplest data stream (and the slowest rate) of the digital part of the phone system.

DS1 The signaling method used by T1 lines, which uses a relatively simple frame consisting of 25 pieces: a framing bit and 24 channels. Each DS1 channel holds a single 8-bit DS0 data sample. The framing bit and data channels combine to make 193 bits per DS1 frame. These frames are transmitted 8000 times/sec, making a total throughput of 1.544 Mbps.

DSL Access Multiplexer (DSLAM)   A device located in a telephone company's central office that connects multiple customers to the Internet.

DSL modem   A device that enables customers to connect to the Internet using a DSL connection. A DSL modem isn't really a modem—it's more like an ISDN terminal adapter—but the term stuck, and even the manufacturers of the devices now call them DSL modems.

DSP (digital signal processor)   A specialized microprocessor-like device that processes digital signals at the expense of other capabilities, much as the floating-point unit (FPU) is optimized for math functions. DSPs are used in such specialized hardware as high-speed modems, multimedia sound cards, MIDI equipment, and real-time video capture and compression.

dual stack   Networking device, such as a router or PC, that runs both IPv4 and IPv6.

duplexing   Also called *disk duplexing* or *drive duplexing*, similar to mirroring in that data is written to and read from two physical drives for fault tolerance. In addition, separate controllers are used for each drive, for both additional fault tolerance and additional speed. Considered RAID level 1. *See also* disk mirroring.

dynamic addressing   A way for a computer to receive IP information automatically from a server program. *See also* Dynamic Host Configuration Protocol (DHCP).

Dynamic ARP Inspection (DAI)   Cisco process that updates a database of trusted systems. DAI then watches for false or suspicious ARPs and ignores them to prevent ARP cache poisoning and other malevolent efforts.

Dynamic DNS (DDNS)   A protocol that enables DNS servers to get automatic updates of IP addresses of computers in their forward lookup zones, mainly by talking to the local DHCP server.

Dynamic Host Configuration Protocol (DHCP)   A protocol that enables a DHCP server to set TCP/IP settings automatically for a DHCP client.

dynamic link library (DLL)   *See* DLL (dynamic link library).

dynamic multipoint VPN (DMVPN)   A virtual private network solution optimized for connections between multiple locations directly.

dynamic NAT (DNAT)   Type of Network Address Translation (NAT) in which many computers can share a pool of routable IP addresses that number fewer than the computers.

dynamic port numbers   Port numbers 49152–65535, recommended by the IANA to be used as ephemeral port numbers.

dynamic routing   Process by which routers in an internetwork automatically exchange information with other routers. Requires a dynamic routing protocol, such as OSPF or RIP.

dynamic routing protocol   A protocol that supports the building of automatic routing tables, such as OSPF or RIP.

E1   The European counterpart of a T1 connection that carries 32 channels at 64 Kbps for a total of 2.048 Mbps—making it slightly faster than a T1.

E3   The European counterpart of a T3 line that carries 16 E1 lines (512 channels), for a total bandwidth of 34.368 Mbps—making it a little bit slower than an American T3.

EAP-TLS (Extensible Authentication Protocol with Transport Layer Security)   A protocol that defines the use of a RADIUS server as well as mutual authentication, requiring certificates on both the server and every client.

EAP-TTLS (Extensible Authentication Protocol with Tunneled Transport Layer Security)   A protocol similar to *EAP-TLS* but only uses a single server-side certificate.

edge device   A hardware device that has been optimized to perform a task in coordination with other edge devices and controllers.

edge router   Router that connects one Autonomous System (AS) to another.

effective permissions   The permissions of all groups combined in any network operating system.

electromagnetic interference (EMI)   Interference from one device to another, resulting in poor performance in the device's capabilities. This is similar to having static on your TV while running a hair dryer, or placing two monitors too close together and getting a "shaky" screen.

electronic discovery   The process of requesting and providing electronic and stored data and evidence in a legal way.

electrostatic discharge (ESD)   *See* ESD (electrostatic discharge).

e-mail (electronic mail)   Messages, usually text, sent from one person to another via computer. E-mail can also be sent automatically to a large number of addresses, known as a *mailing list*.

e-mail alert   Notification sent by e-mail as a result of an event. A typical use is a notification sent from an SNMP manager as a result of an out-of-tolerance condition in an SNMP managed device.

e-mail client   Program that runs on a computer and enables a user to send, receive, and organize e-mail.

e-mail server   Also known as a *mail server*, a server that accepts incoming e-mail, sorts the e-mail for recipients into mailboxes, and sends e-mail to other servers using SMTP.

emulator   Software or hardware that converts the commands to and from the host machine to an entirely different platform. For example, a program that enables you to run Nintendo games on your PC.

encapsulation   The process of putting the packets from one protocol inside the packets of another protocol. An example of this is TCP/IP encapsulation in Ethernet, which places TCP/IP packets inside Ethernet frames.

encryption   A method of securing messages by scrambling and encoding each packet as it is sent across an unsecured medium, such as the Internet. Each encryption level provides multiple standards and options.

endpoint   In the TCP/IP world, the session information stored in RAM. *See also* socket.

endpoints   Correct term to use when discussing the data each computer stores about the connection between two computers' TCP/IP applications. *See also* socket pairs.

end-to-end principle   Early network concept that originally meant that applications and work should happen only at the endpoints in a network, such as in a single client and a single server.

Enhanced Data rates for GSM Evolution (EDGE)   Early cellular telephone technology that used a SIM card; obsolete.

Enhanced Interior Gateway Routing Protocol (EIGRP)   Cisco's proprietary hybrid protocol that has elements of both distance vector and link state routing.

enhanced small form-factor pluggable (SFP+)   Fiber-optic connector used in 10 GbE networks.

environment limitations   With respect to building and upgrading networks, refers to the degree of access to facilities and physical access to physical infrastructure. The type of building or buildings must be considered. Access to the walls and ceilings will factor in the construction of the network.

environmental monitor   Device used in telecommunications rooms that keeps track of humidity, temperature, and more.

ephemeral port   In TCP/IP communication, an arbitrary number generated by a sending computer that the receiving computer uses as a destination address when sending a return packet.

ephemeral port number   *See* ephemeral port.

equipment limitations   With respect to installing and upgrading networks, the degree of usage of any existing equipment, applications, or cabling.

equipment rack   A metal structure used in equipment rooms to secure network hardware devices and patch panels. Most racks are 19" wide. Devices designed to fit in such a rack use a height measurement called *units*, or simply *U*.

ESD (electrostatic discharge)   The movement of electrons from one body to another. ESD is a real menace to PCs because it can cause permanent damage to semiconductors.

Ethernet   Name coined by Xerox for the first standard of network cabling and protocols. Ethernet is based on a bus topology. The IEEE 802.3 subcommittee defines the current Ethernet specifications.

Ethernet over Power (EoP)   The IEEE 1901 standard, also known as *HomePlug HD-PLC*, provides high-speed home networking through the building's existing power infrastructure.

evil twin   An attack that lures people into logging into a rogue access point that looks similar to a legitimate access point.

Evolved High-Speed Packet Access (HSPA+)   The final wireless 3G data standard, transferring theoretical maximum speeds up to 168 Mbps, although real-world implementations rarely passed 10 Mbps.

executable viruses   Viruses that are literally extensions of executables and that are unable to exist by themselves. Once an infected executable file is run, the virus loads into memory, adding copies of itself to other EXEs that are subsequently run.

Exim   E-mail server for every major platform; fast and efficient.

exit plan   Documents and diagrams that identify the best way out of a building in the event of an emergency. It may also define other procedures to follow.

Extended Service Set (ESS)   A single wireless access point servicing a given area that has been extended by adding more access points.

Extended Service Set Identifier (ESSID)   An SSID applied to an Extended Service Set as a network naming convention.

Extended Unique Identifier, 48-bit (EUI-48)   The IEEE term for the 48-bit MAC address assigned to a network interface. The first 24 bits of the EUI-48 are assigned by the IEEE as the organizationally unique identifier (OUI).

Extended Unique Identifier, 64-bit (EUI-64)   The last 64 bits of the IPv6 address, which are determined based on a calculation based on a device's 48-bit MAC address.

Extensible Authentication Protocol (EAP)   Authentication wrapper that EAP-compliant applications can use to accept one of many types of authentication. While EAP is a general-purpose authentication wrapper, its only substantial use is in wireless networks.

external connections   A network's connections to the wider Internet. Also a major concern when setting up a SOHO network.

external data bus (EDB)   The primary data highway of all computers. Everything in your computer is tied either directly or indirectly to the EDB.

external firewall   The firewall that sits between the perimeter network and the Internet and is responsible for bearing the brunt of the attacks from the Internet.

external network address A number added to the MAC address of every computer on an IPX/SPX network that defines every computer on the network; this is often referred to as a *network number*.

external threats Threats to your network through external means; examples include virus attacks and the exploitation of users, security holes in the OS, or weaknesses of the network hardware itself.

fail close Defines the condition of doors and locks in the event of an emergency, indicating that the doors should close and lock.

fail open Defines the condition of doors and locks in the event of an emergency, indicating that the doors should be open and unlocked.

FAQ (frequently asked questions) Common abbreviation coined by BBS users and spread to Usenet and the Internet. This is a list of questions and answers that pertains to a particular topic, maintained so that users new to the group don't all bombard the group with similar questions. Examples are "What is the name of the actor who plays *X* on this show, and was he in anything else?" or "Can anyone list all of the books by this author in the order that they were published so that I can read them in that order?" The common answer to this type of question is "Read the FAQ!"

far-end crosstalk (FEXT) Crosstalk on the opposite end of a cable from the signal's source.

Fast Ethernet Nickname for the 100-Mbps Ethernet standards. Originally applied to 100BaseT.

fault tolerance The capability of any system to continue functioning after some part of the system has failed. RAID is an example of a hardware device that provides fault tolerance for hard drives.

F-connector A screw-on connector used to terminate small-diameter coaxial cable such as RG-6 and RG-59 cables.

FDDI (Fiber Distributed Data Interface) *See* Fiber Distributed Data Interface (FDDI).

Federal Communications Commission (FCC) In the United States, regulates public airwaves and rates PCs and other equipment according to the amount of radiation emitted.

Fiber Distributed Data Interface (FDDI) Older technology fiber-optic network used in campus-sized installations. It transfers data at 100 Mbps and uses a token bus network protocol over a ring topology.

fiber-optic cable A high-speed physical medium for transmitting data that uses light rather than electricity to transmit data and is made of high-purity glass fibers sealed within a flexible opaque tube. Much faster than conventional copper wire.

Fibre Channel (FC)   A self-contained, high-speed storage environment with its own storage arrays, cables, protocols, cables, and switches. Fibre Channel is a critical part of storage area networks (SANs).

file hashing   When the download provider hashes the contents of a file and publishes the resulting message digest.

file server   A computer designated to store software, courseware, administrative tools, and other data on a local or wide area network (WAN). It "serves" this information to other computers via the network when users enter their personal access codes.

File Transfer Protocol (FTP)   A set of rules that allows two computers to talk to one another as a file transfer is carried out. This is the protocol used when you transfer a file from one computer to another across the Internet.

fire ratings   Ratings developed by Underwriters Laboratories (UL) and the National Electrical Code (NEC) to define the risk of network cables burning and creating noxious fumes and smoke.

firewall   A device that restricts traffic between a local network and the Internet.

FireWire   An IEEE 1394 standard to send wide-band signals over a thin connector system that plugs into TVs, VCRs, TV cameras, PCs, and so forth. This serial bus developed by Apple and Texas Instruments enables connection of 60 devices at speeds ranging from 100 to 800 Mbps.

first responder   The person or robot whose job is to react to the notification of a possible computer crime by determining the severity of the situation, collecting information, documenting findings and actions, and providing the information to the proper authorities.

flat name space   A naming convention that gives each device only one name that must be unique. NetBIOS uses a flat name space. TCP/IP's DNS uses a hierarchical name space.

flat-surface connector   Early fiber-optic connector that resulted in a small gap between fiber-optic junctions due to the flat grind faces of the fibers. It was replaced by Angled Physical Contact (APC) connectors.

flood guard   Technology in modern switches that can detect and block excessive traffic.

flow   A stream of packets from one specific place to another.

flow cache   Stores sets of flows for interpretation and analysis. *See also* flow.

forensics report   A document that describes the details of gathering, securing, transporting, and investigating evidence.

forward lookup zone   The storage area in a DNS server to store the IP addresses and names of systems for a particular domain or domains.

forward proxy server   Server that acts as middleman between clients and servers, making requests to network servers on behalf of clients. Results are sent to the proxy server, which then passes them to the original client. The network servers are isolated from the clients by the forward proxy server.

FQDN (fully qualified domain name)   *See* fully qualified domain name (FQDN).

fractional T1 access   A service provided by many telephone companies wherein customers can purchase a number of individual channels in a T1 line in order to save money.

frame   A defined series of binary data that is the basic container for a discrete amount of data moving across a network. Frames are created at Layer 2 of the OSI model.

frame check sequence (FCS)   A sequence of bits placed in a frame that is used to check the primary data for errors.

Frame Relay   An extremely efficient data transmission technique used to send digital information such as voice, data, LAN, and WAN traffic quickly and cost-efficiently to many destinations from one port.

FreeRADIUS   Free RADIUS server software for UNIX/Linux systems.

freeware   Software that is distributed for free with no license fee.

frequency division multiplexing (FDM)   A process of keeping individual phone calls separate by adding a different frequency multiplier to each phone call, making it possible to separate phone calls by their unique frequency range.

frequency mismatch   Problem in older wireless networks with manual settings where the WAP transmitted on one channel and a wireless client was set to access on a different channel.

frequency-hopping spread-spectrum (FHSS)   A spread-spectrum broadcasting method defined in the 802.11 standard that sends data on one frequency at a time, constantly shifting (or *hopping*) frequencies.

frequently asked questions (FAQ)   *See* FAQ (frequently asked questions).

FUBAR   Fouled Up Beyond All Recognition.

full backup   Archive created where every file selected is backed up, and the archive bit is turned off for every file backed up.

full-duplex   Any device that can send and receive data simultaneously.

fully meshed topology   A mesh network where every node is directly connected to every other node.

fully qualified domain name (FQDN)   The complete DNS name of a system, from its host name to the top-level domain name. Textual nomenclature to a domain-organized resource. It is written left to right, with the host name on the left, followed by any hierarchical subdomains within the top-level domain on the right. Each level is separated from any preceding or following layer by a dot (.).

gain   The strengthening and focusing of radio frequency output from a wireless access point (WAP).

gateway router   A router that acts as a default gateway in a TCP/IP network.

general logs   Logs that record updates to applications.

geofencing   The process of using a mobile device's built-in GPS capabilities and mobile networking capabilities to set geographical constraints on where the mobile device can be used.

Get (SNMP)   A query from an SNMP manager sent to the agent of a managed device for the status of a management information base (MIB) object.

giga   The prefix that generally refers to the quantity 1,073,741,824. One gigabyte is 1,073,741,824 bytes. With frequencies, in contrast, giga- often refers to one billion. One gigahertz is 1,000,000,000 hertz.

Gigabit Ethernet   *See* 1000BaseT.

gigabit interface converter (GBIC)   Modular port that supports a standardized, wide variety of gigabit interface modules.

gigabyte   1024 megabytes.

global routing prefix   The first 48 bits of an IPv6 unicast address, used to get a packet to its destination. *See also* network ID.

Global System for Mobile (GSM)   Early cellular telephone networking standard; obsolete.

global unicast address   A second IPv6 address that every system needs in order to get on the Internet.

grandfather, father, son (GFS)   A tape rotation strategy used in data backups.

graphing   Type of software that creates visual representations and graphs of data collected by SNMP managers.

greenfield mode   One of three modes used with 802.11n wireless networks wherein everything is running at higher speed.

ground loop   A voltage differential that exists between two different grounding points.

Group Policy   A feature of Windows Active Directory that allows an administrator to apply policy settings to network users *en masse*.

Group Policy Object (GPO)   Enables network administrators to define multiple rights and permissions to entire sets of users all at one time.

groups   Collections of network users who share similar tasks and need similar permissions; defined to make administration tasks easier.

guest   In terms of virtualization, an operating system running as a virtual machine inside a hypervisor.

guest network   A network that can contain or allow access to any resource that management deems acceptable to be used by insecure hosts that attach to the guest network.

H.320   A standard that uses multiple ISDN channels to transport video teleconferencing (VTC) over a network.

H.323   A VoIP standard that handles the initiation, setup, and delivery of VoIP sessions.

hackers   People who break into computer systems. Those with malicious intent are sometimes considered *black hat* hackers and those who do so with a positive intent (such as vulnerability testing) are regularly referred to as *white hat* hackers. Of course, there are middle-ground hackers: *gray hats*.

half-duplex   Any device that can only send or receive data at any given moment.

hardening   Applying security hardware, software, and processes to your network to prevent bad things from happening.

hardware appliance   Physical network device, typically a "box" that implements and runs software or firmware to perform one or a multitude of tasks. Could be a firewall, a switch, a router, a print server, or one of many other devices.

hardware tools   Tools such as cable testers, TDRs, OTDRs, certifiers, voltage event recorders, protocol analyzers, cable strippers, multimeters, tone probes/generators, butt sets, and punchdown tools used to configure and troubleshoot a network.

hash   A mathematical function used in cryptography that is run on a string of binary digits of any length that results in a value of some fixed length.

HDMI Ethernet Channel (HEC)   Ethernet-enabled HDMI ports that combine video, audio, and data on a single cable.

header   First section of a frame, packet, segment, or datagram.

heating, ventilation, and air conditioning (HVAC)   All of the equipment involved in heating and cooling the environments within a facility. These items include boilers, furnaces, air conditioners and ducts, plenums, and air passages.

hex (hexadecimal)   Hex symbols based on a numbering system of 16 (computer shorthand for binary numbers), using 10 digits and 6 letters to condense zeroes and ones to binary numbers. Hex is represented by digits 0 through 9 and alpha *A* through *F*, so that 09h has a value of 9, and 0Ah has a value of 10.

hierarchical name space   A naming scheme where the full name of each object includes its position within the hierarchy. An example of a hierarchical name is www.totalseminars.com, which includes not only the host name, but also the domain name. DNS uses a hierarchical name space scheme for fully qualified domain names (FQDNs).

high availability (HA)   A collection of technologies and procedures that work together to keep an application available at all times.

high-speed WAN Internet cards   A type of router expansion card that enables connection to two different ISPs.

history logs   Logs that track the history of how a user or users access network resources, or how network resources are accessed throughout the network.

home automation   The process of remotely controlling household devices, such as lights, thermostats, cameras, and washer and dryer.

home page   Either the Web page that your browser is set to use when it starts up or the main Web page for a business, organization, or person. Also, the main page in any collection of Web pages.

honeynet   The network created by a honeypot in order to lure in hackers.

honeypot   An area of a network that an administrator sets up for the express purpose of attracting a computer hacker. If a hacker takes the bait, the network's important resources are unharmed and network personnel can analyze the attack to predict and protect against future attacks, making the network more secure.

hop   The passage of a packet through a router.

hop count   An older metric used by RIP routers. The number of routers that a packet must cross to get from a router to a given network. Hop counts were tracked and entered into the routing table within a router so the router could decide which interface was the best one to forward a packet.

horizontal cabling   Cabling that connects the equipment room to the work areas.

host   A single device (usually a computer) on a TCP/IP network that has an IP address; any device that can be the source or destination of a data packet. Also, a computer running multiple virtualized operating systems.

host ID   The portion of an IP address that defines a specific machine in a subnet.

host name   An individual computer name in the DNS naming convention.

host-based anti-malware   Anti-malware software that is installed on individual systems, as opposed to the network at large.

host-based firewall   A software firewall installed on a "host" that provides firewall services for just that machine, such as Windows Firewall.

hostname   Command-line tool that returns the host name of the computer it is run on.

hosts file The predecessor to DNS, a static text file that resides on a computer and is used to resolve DNS host names to IP addresses. Automatically mapped to a host's DNS resolver cache in modern systems. The hosts file has no extension.

host-to-host Type of VPN connection in which a single host establishes a link with a remote, single host.

host-to-site Type of VPN connection where a host logs into a remote network as if it were any other local resource of that network.

hot site A complete backup facility to continue business operations. It is considered "hot" because it has all resources in place, including computers, network infrastructure, and current backups, so that operations can commence within hours after occupation.

hotspot A wireless access point that is connected to a cellular data network, typically 4G. The device can route Wi-Fi to and from the Internet. Hotspots can be permanent installations or portable. Many cellular telephones have the capability to become a hotspot.

HTML (Hypertext Markup Language) An ASCII-based script-like language for creating hypertext documents like those on the World Wide Web.

HTTP over SSL (HTTPS) A secure form of HTTP in which hypertext is encrypted by Transport Layer Security (TLS) before being sent onto the network. It is commonly used for Internet business transactions or any time where a secure connection is required. The name reflects the predecessor technology to TLS called Secure Sockets Layer (SSL). *See also* Hypertext Transfer Protocol (HTTP) *and* Secure Sockets Layer (SSL).

hub An electronic device that sits at the center of a star topology network, providing a common point for the connection of network devices. In a 10BaseT Ethernet network, the hub contains the electronic equivalent of a properly terminated bus cable. Hubs are rare today and have been replaced by switches.

human machine interface (HMI) In a distributed control system (DCS), a computer or set of controls that exists between a controller and a human operator. The human operates the HMI, which in turn interacts with the controller.

hybrid cloud A conglomeration of public and private cloud resources, connected to achieve some target result. There is no clear line that defines how much of a hybrid cloud infrastructure is private and how much is public.

hybrid topology A mix or blend of two different topologies. A star-bus topology is a hybrid of the star and bus topologies.

hypertext A document that has been marked up to enable a user to select words or pictures within the document, click them, and connect to further information. The basis of the World Wide Web.

Hypertext Markup Language (HTML) *See* HTML (Hypertext Markup Language).

Hypertext Transfer Protocol (HTTP)   Extremely fast protocol used for network file transfers on the World Wide Web.

Hypertext Transfer Protocol over SSL (HTTPS)   Protocol to transfer hypertext from a Web server to a client in a secure and encrypted fashion. Uses Transport Layer Security (TLS) rather than Secure Sockets Layer (SSL) to establish a secure communication connection between hosts. It then encrypts the hypertext before sending it from the Web server and decrypts it when it enters the client. HTTPS uses port 443.

hypervisor   In virtualization, a layer of programming that creates, supports, and manages a virtual machine. Also known as a *virtual machine manager (VMM)*.

ICS (industrial control system)   A centralized controller where the local controllers of a distributed control system (DCS) meet in order for global changes to be made.

ICS (Internet Connection Sharing)   Also known simply as *Internet sharing*, the technique of enabling more than one computer to access the Internet simultaneously using a single Internet connection. When you use Internet sharing, you connect an entire LAN to the Internet using a single public IP address.

ICS server   Unit in a distributed control system (DCS) that can be used to manage global changes to the controllers.

IEEE (Institute of Electrical and Electronics Engineers)   The leading standards-setting group in the United States.

IEEE 802.2   IEEE subcommittee that defined the standards for Logical Link Control (LLC).

IEEE 802.3   IEEE subcommittee that defined the standards for CSMA/CD (a.k.a. *Ethernet*).

IEEE 802.11   IEEE subcommittee that defined the standards for wireless.

IEEE 802.14   IEEE subcommittee that defined the standards for cable modems.

IEEE 802.16   A wireless standard (also known as *WiMAX*) with a range of up to 30 miles.

IEEE 1284   The IEEE standard for the now obsolete parallel communication.

IEEE 1394   IEEE standard for FireWire communication.

IEEE 1905.1   Standard that integrates Ethernet, Wi-Fi, Ethernet over power lines, and Multimedia over Coax (MoCA).

IETF (Internet Engineering Task Force)   The primary standards organization for the Internet.

ifconfig   A command-line utility for Linux servers and workstations that displays the current TCP/IP configuration of the machine, similar to ipconfig for Windows systems. The newer command-line utility, ip, is replacing ifconfig on most systems.

IMAP (Internet Message Access Protocol)   An alternative to POP3. Currently in its fourth revision, IMAP4 retrieves e-mail from an e-mail server like POP3, but has a number of features that make it a more popular e-mail tool. IMAP4 supports users creating folders on the e-mail server, for example, and allows multiple clients to access a single mailbox. IMAP uses TCP port 143.

impedance   The amount of resistance to an electrical signal on a wire. It is used as a relative measure of the amount of data a cable can handle.

implicit deny   The blocking of access to any entity that has not been specifically granted access. May also be known as *implicit deny any*. An example might be a whitelist ACL. Any station that is not in the whitelist is implicitly denied access.

in-band management   Technology that enables managed devices such as a switch or router to be managed by any authorized host that is connected to that network.

inbound traffic   Packets coming in from outside the network.

incident   Any negative situation that takes place within an organization.

incident response   Reaction to any negative situations that take place within an organization that can be stopped, contained, and remediated without outside resources.

incremental backup   Backs up all files that have their archive bits turned on, meaning they have been changed since the last backup. This type of backup turns the archive bits off after the files have been backed up.

Independent Basic Service Set (IBSS)   A basic unit of organization in wireless networks formed by two or more wireless nodes communicating in ad hoc mode.

Independent Computing Architecture (ICA)   Citrix technology that defined communication between client and server in remote terminal programs.

industrial control system (ICS)   *See* ICS (industrial control system).

infrared (IR)   Line-of-sight networking technology that uses light pulses on the non-visible (to humans) spectrum.

Infrastructure as a Service (IaaS)   Providing servers, switches, and routers to customers for a set rate. IaaS is commonly done by large-scale, global providers that use virtualization to minimize idle hardware, protect against data loss and downtime, and respond to spikes in demand. *See also* cloud computing.

infrastructure mode   Mode in which wireless networks use one or more wireless access points to connect the wireless network nodes centrally. This configuration is similar to the *star topology* of a wired network.

inheritance   A method of assigning user permissions, in which folder permissions flow downward into subfolders.

insider threats   Potential for attacks on a system by people who work in the organization.

Institute of Electrical and Electronics Engineers (IEEE) *See* IEEE (Institute of Electrical and Electronics Engineers).

insulating jacket The external plastic covering of a fiber-optic cable.

Integrated Services Digital Network (ISDN) *See* ISDN (Integrated Services Digital Network).

integrity Network process that ensures data sent to a recipient is unchanged when it is received at the destination host.

interface identifier (interface ID) The second half (64 bits) of an IPv6 address, unique to a host.

interface monitor A program that tracks the bandwidth and utilization of one or more interfaces on one or more devices in order to monitor traffic on a network.

interframe gap (IFG) A short, predefined silence originally defined for CSMA/CD; also used in CSMA/CA. Also known as an *interframe space (IFS)*.

interframe space (IFS) *See* interframe gap (IFG).

intermediate distribution frame (IDF) The room where all the horizontal runs from all the work areas on a given floor in a building come together.

Intermediate System to Intermediate System (IS-IS) Protocol similar to, but not as popular as, OSPF, but with support for IPv6 since inception.

internal connections The connections between computers in a network.

internal firewall The firewall that sits between the perimeter network and the trusted network that houses all the organization's private servers and workstations.

internal network A private LAN, with a unique network ID, that resides behind a router.

internal threats All the things that a network's own users do to create problems on the network. Examples include accidental deletion of files, accidental damage to hardware devices or cabling, and abuse of rights and permissions.

Internet Assigned Numbers Authority (IANA) The organization originally responsible for assigning public IP addresses. IANA no longer directly assigns IP addresses, having delegated this to the five Regional Internet Registries. *See also* Regional Internet Registries (RIRs).

Internet Authentication Service (IAS) Popular RADIUS server for Microsoft environments.

Internet Connection Sharing (ICS) *See* ICS (Internet Connection Sharing).

Internet Control Message Protocol (ICMP)   A TCP/IP protocol used to handle many low-level functions such as error reporting. ICMP messages are usually request and response pairs such as echo requests and responses, router solicitations and responses, and traceroute requests and responses. There are also unsolicited "responses" (advertisements) which consist of single packets. ICMP messages are connectionless.

Internet Corporation for Assigned Names and Numbers (ICANN)   Entity that sits at the very top of the Internet hierarchy, with the authority to create new top-level domains (TLDs) for use on the Internet.

Internet Engineering Task Force (IETF)   *See* IETF (Internet Engineering Task Force).

Internet Group Management Protocol (IGMP)   Protocol that routers use to communicate with hosts to determine a "group" membership in order to determine which computers want to receive a multicast. Once a multicast has started, IGMP is responsible for maintaining the multicast as well as terminating at completion.

Internet Information Services (IIS)   Microsoft's Web server program for managing Web servers.

Internet layer   In the TCP/IP model, the layer that deals with the Internet Protocol, including IP addressing and routers.

Internet Message Access Protocol Version 4 (IMAP4)   *See* IMAP (Internet Message Access Protocol).

Internet of Things (IoT)   The billions of everyday objects that can communicating with each other, specifically over the Internet. These include smart home appliances, automobiles, video surveillance systems, and more.

Internet Protocol (IP)   The Internet standard protocol that handles the logical naming for the TCP/IP protocol using IP addresses.

Internet Protocol Security (IPsec)   Network layer encryption protocol.

Internet Protocol version 4 (IPv4)   Protocol in which addresses consist of four sets of numbers, each number being a value between 0 and 255, using a period to separate the numbers (often called *dotted decimal* format). No IPv4 address may be all 0s or all 255s. Examples include 192.168.0.1 and 64.176.19.164.

Internet Protocol version 6 (IPv6)   Protocol in which addresses consist of eight sets of four hexadecimal numbers, each number being a value between 0000 and ffff, using a colon to separate the numbers. No IP address may be all 0s or all ffffs. An example is fe80:ba98:7654:3210:0800:200c:00cf:1234.

Internet Small Computer System Interface (iSCSI)   A protocol that enables the SCSI command set to be transported over a TCP/IP network from a client to an iSCSI-based storage system. iSCSI is popular with storage area network (SAN) systems.

interVLAN routing   A feature on some switches to provide routing between VLANs.

intranet   A private TCP/IP network inside a company or organization.

Intra-Site Automatic Tunnel Addressing Protocol (ISATAP)   An IPv6 tunneling protocol that adds the IPv4 address to an IPv6 prefix.

intrusion detection system (IDS)/intrusion prevention system (IPS)   An application (often running on a dedicated IDS box) that inspects incoming packets, looking for active intrusions. The difference between an IDS and an IPS is that an IPS can react to an attack.

ip   Linux terminal command that displays the current TCP/IP configuration of the machine; similar to Windows' ipconfig and macOS's ifconfig.

IP   *See* Internet Protocol (IP).

IP address   The numeric address of a computer connected to a TCP/IP network, such as the Internet. IPv4 addresses are 32 bits long, written as four octets of 8-bit binary. IPv6 addresses are 128 bits long, written as eight sets of four hexadecimal characters. IP addresses must be matched with a valid subnet mask, which identifies the part of the IP address that is the network ID and the part that is the host ID.

IP Address Management (IPAM)   Software that includes at a minimum a DHCP server and a DNS server that are specially designed to work together to administer IP addresses for a network.

IP addressing   The processes of assigning IP addresses to networks and hosts.

IP camera   Still-frame or video camera with a network interface and TCP/IP transport protocols to send output to a network resource or destination.

IP filtering   A method of blocking packets based on IP addresses.

IP helper   Command used in Cisco switches and routers to enable, disable, and manage internetwork forwarding of certain protocols such as DHCP, TFTP, Time Service, TACACS, DNS, NetBIOS, and others. The command is technically `ip helper-address`.

ipconfig   A command-line utility for Windows that displays the current TCP/IP configuration of the machine; similar to macOS's ifconfig and UNIX/Linux's ip.

IPsec VPN   A virtual private networking technology that uses IPsec tunneling for security.

IRC (Internet Relay Chat)   An online group discussion. Also called *chat*.

ISDN (Integrated Services Digital Network)   The CCITT (Comité Consutatif Internationale Téléphonique et Télégraphique) standard that defines a digital method for telephone communications. Originally designed to replace the current analog telephone systems. ISDN lines have telephone numbers and support up to 128-Kbps transfer rates. ISDN also allows data and voice to share a common phone line. Never very popular, ISDN is now relegated to specialized niches.

ISP (Internet service provider)   An institution that provides access to the Internet in some form, usually for a fee.

IT (information technology)   The business of computers, electronic communications, and electronic commerce.

Java   A network-oriented programming language invented by Sun Microsystems (acquired by Oracle) and specifically designed for writing programs that can be safely downloaded to your computer through the Internet and immediately run without fear of viruses or other harm to your computer or files. Using small Java programs (called *applets*), Web pages can include functions such as animations, calculators, and other fancy tricks.

jitter   A delay in completing a transmission of all the frames in a message; caused by excessive machines on a network.

jumbo frames   Usually 9000 bytes long, though technically anything over 1500 bytes qualifies, these frames make large data transfer easier and more efficient than using the standard frame size.

just a bunch of disks (JBOD)   An array of hard drives that are simply connected with no RAID implementations.

K-   Most commonly used as the suffix for the binary quantity 1024. For instance, 640K means 640 × 1024 or 655,360. Just to add some extra confusion to the IT industry, *K* is often misspoken as "kilo," the metric value for 1000. For example, 10KB, spoken as "10 kilobytes," means 10,240 bytes rather than 10,000 bytes. Finally, when discussing frequencies, K means 1000. So, 1 KHz = 1000 kilohertz.

kbps (kilobits per second)   Data transfer rate.

Kerberos   An authentication standard designed to allow different operating systems and applications to authenticate each other.

Key Distribution Center (KDC)   System for granting authentication in Kerberos.

key fob   Small device that can be easily carried in a pocket or purse or attached to a key ring. This device is used to identify the person possessing it for the purpose of granting or denying access to resources such as electronic doors.

key pair   Name for the two keys generated in asymmetric-key algorithm systems.

keypad   The device in which an alphanumeric code or password that is assigned to a specific individual for a particular asset can be entered.

kilohertz (KHz)   A unit of measure that equals a frequency of 1000 cycles per second.

LAN (local area network)   A group of PCs connected together via cabling, radio, or infrared that use this connectivity to share resources such as printers and mass storage.

last mile The connection between a central office and individual users in a telephone system.

latency A measure of a signal's delay.

layer A grouping of related tasks involving the transfer of information. Also, a particular level of the OSI seven-layer model, for example, Physical layer, Data Link layer, and so forth.

Layer 2 switch Any device that filters and forwards frames based on the MAC addresses of the sending and receiving machines. What is normally called a "switch" is actually a "Layer 2 switch."

Layer 2 Tunneling Protocol (L2TP) A VPN protocol developed by Cisco that can be run on almost any connection imaginable. LT2P has no authentication or encryption but uses IPsec for all its security needs.

Layer 3 switch Also known as a *router*, filters and forwards data packets based on the IP addresses of the sending and receiving machines.

LC (local connector) A duplex type of small form factor (SFF) fiber connector, designed to accept two fiber cables. *See also* local connector (LC).

LED (light emitting diode) Solid-state device that vibrates at luminous frequencies when current is applied.

leeching Using another person's wireless connection to the Internet without that person's permission.

legacy mode One of three modes used with 802.11n wireless networks where the wireless access point (WAP) sends out separate packets just for legacy devices.

legal hold The process of an organization preserving and organizing data in anticipation of or in reaction to a pending legal issue.

light leakage The type of interference caused by bending a piece of fiber-optic cable past its maximum bend radius. Light bleeds through the cladding, causing signal distortion and loss.

light meter An optical power meter used by technicians to measure the amount of light lost through light leakage in a fiber cable.

lights-out management Special "computer within a computer" features built into better servers, designed to give you access to a server even when the server itself is shut off.

Lightweight Access Point Protocol (LWAPP) Protocol used in wireless networks that enables interoperability between thin and thick clients and WAPs.

Lightweight Directory Access Protocol (LDAP) A protocol used to query and change a database used by the network. LDAP uses TCP port 389 by default.

Lightweight Extensible Authentication Protocol (LEAP)   A proprietary EAP authentication used almost exclusively by Cisco wireless products. LEAP is an interesting combination of MS-CHAP authentication between a wireless client and a RADIUS server.

line tester   A device used by technicians to check the integrity of telephone wiring. Can be used on a twisted-pair line to see if it is good, dead, or reverse wired, or if there is AC voltage on the line.

link aggregation   Connecting multiple NICs in tandem to increase bandwidth in smaller increments. *See also* NIC teaming.

Link Aggregation Control Protocol (LACP)   IEEE specification of certain features and options to automate the negotiation, management, load balancing, and failure modes of aggregated ports.

Link layer   In the TCP/IP model, any part of the network that deals with complete frames.

link light   An LED on NICs, hubs, and switches that lights up to show good connection between the devices. Called the *network connection LED status indicator* on the CompTIA Network+ exam.

link segments   Segments that link other segments together but are unpopulated or have no computers directly attached to them.

link state   Type of dynamic routing protocol that announces only changes to routing tables, as opposed to entire routing tables. Compare to distance vector routing protocols. *See also* distance vector.

link status   A network analyzer report on how good the connection is between two systems.

link-local address   The address that a computer running IPv6 gives itself after first booting. The first 64 bits of a link-local address are always FE80::/64.

Linux   The popular open source operating system, derived from UNIX.

list of requirements   A list of all the things you'll need to do to set up your SOHO network, as well as the desired capabilities of the network.

listening port   A socket that is prepared to respond to any IP packets destined for that socket's port number.

LMHOSTS file   A static text file that resides on a computer and is used to resolve NetBIOS names to IP addresses. The LMHOSTS file is checked before the machine sends a name resolution request to a WINS name server. The LMHOSTS file has no extension.

load balancing   The process of taking several servers and making them look like a single server, spreading processing and supporting bandwidth needs.

local   Refers to the computer(s), server(s), and/or LAN that a user is physically using or that is in the same room or building.

local area network (LAN)   *See* LAN (local area network).

local authentication   A login screen prompting a user to enter a user name and password to log into a Windows, macOS, or Linux computer.

local connector (LC)   One popular type of small form factor (SFF) connector, considered by many to be the predominant fiber connector. While there are several labels ascribed to the "LC" term, it is most commonly referred to as a *local connector. See also* LC (local connector).

Local Exchange Carrier (LEC)   A company that provides local telephone service to individual customers.

local user accounts   The accounts unique to a single Windows system. Stored in the local system's registry.

localhost   The hosts file alias for the loopback address of 127.0.0.1, referring to the current machine.

lock   In this context, a physical device that prevents access to essential assets of an organization, such as servers, without a key.

log   Information about the performance of some particular aspect of a system that is stored for future reference. Logs are also called *counters* in Performance Monitor or *facilities* in syslog.

log management   The process of providing proper security and maintenance for log files to ensure the files are organized and safe.

logic bomb   Code written to execute when certain conditions are met, usually with malicious intent.

logical address   A programmable network address, unlike a physical address that is burned into ROM.

logical addressing   As opposed to physical addressing, the process of assigning organized blocks of logically associated network addresses to create smaller manageable networks called subnets. IP addresses are one example of logical addressing.

Logical Link Control (LLC)   The aspect of the NIC that talks to the operating system, places outbound data coming "down" from the upper layers of software into frames, and creates the FCS on each frame. The LLC also deals with incoming frames by processing those addressed to the NIC and erasing ones addressed to other machines on the network.

logical network diagram   A document that shows the broadcast domains and individual IP addresses for all devices on the network. Only critical switches and routers are shown.

logical topology   A network topology defined by signal paths as opposed to the physical layout of the cables. *See also* physical topology.

Long Term Evolution (LTE)   Better known as 4G, a wireless data standard with theoretical download speeds of 300 Mbps and upload speeds of 75 Mbps.

looking glass site   Web site that enables a technician to run various diagnostic tools from outside their network.

loopback adapter   *See* loopback plug.

loopback address   Sometimes called the localhost, a reserved IP address used for internal testing: 127.0.0.1.

loopback plug   Network connector that connects back into itself, used to connect loopback tests.

loopback test   A special test often included in diagnostic software that sends data out of the NIC and checks to see if it comes back.

MAC (media access control) address   Unique 48-bit address assigned to each network card. IEEE assigns blocks of possible addresses to various NIC manufacturers to help ensure that each address is unique. The Data Link layer of the OSI seven-layer model uses MAC addresses for locating machines.

MAC address filtering   A method of limiting access to a wireless network based on the physical addresses of wireless NICs.

MAC filtering   *See* MAC address filtering.

MAC reservation   IP address assigned to a specific MAC address in a DHCP server.

MAC-48   The unique 48-bit address assigned to a network interface card. This is also known as the *MAC address* or the *EUI-48*.

macro   A specially written application macro (collection of commands) that performs the same functions as a virus. These macros normally autostart when the application is run and then make copies of themselves, often propagating across networks.

mailbox   Special holding area on an e-mail server that separates out e-mail for each user.

main distribution frame (MDF)   The room in a building that stores the demarc, telephone cross-connects, and LAN cross-connects.

maintenance window   The time it takes to implement and thoroughly test a network change.

malicious user   A user who consciously attempts to access, steal, or damage resources.

malware   Any program or code (macro, script, and so on) that's designed to do something on a system or network that you don't want to have happen.

man in the middle   A hacking attack where a person inserts him- or herself into a conversation between two others, covertly intercepting traffic thought to be only between those other people.

managed device   Networking devices, such as routers and advanced switches, that must be configured to use.

managed network   Network that is monitored by the SNMP protocol consisting of SNMP managed devices, management information base (MIB) items, and SNMP manager(s).

managed switch   *See* managed device.

management information base (MIB)   SNMP's version of a server. *See* Simple Network Management Protocol (SNMP).

mandatory access control (MAC)   A security model in which every resource is assigned a label that defines its security level. If the user lacks that security level, they do not get access.

mantrap   An entryway with two successive locked doors and a small space between them providing one-way entry or exit. This is a security measure taken to prevent tailgating.

manual tunnel   A simple point-to-point connection between two IPv6 networks. As a tunnel, it uses IPsec encryption.

material safety data sheet (MSDS)   Document that describes the safe handling procedures for any potentially hazardous, toxic, or unsafe material.

maximum transmission unit (MTU)   Specifies the largest size of a data unit in a communications protocol, such as Ethernet.

MB (megabyte)   1,048,576 bytes.

MD5 (Message-Digest Algorithm Version 5)   A popular hashing function.

mean time between failures (MTBF)   A factor typically applied to a hardware component that represents the manufacturer's best guess (based on historical data) regarding how much time will pass between major failures of that component.

mean time to recovery (MTTR)   The estimated amount of time it takes to recover from a hardware component failure.

Mechanical Transfer Registered Jack (MT-RJ)   The first type of small form factor (SFF) fiber connector, still in common use.

Media Access Control (MAC)   The part of a NIC that remembers the NIC's own MAC address and attaches that address to outgoing frames.

media converter   A device that lets you interconnect different types of Ethernet cable.

Media Gateway Control Protocol (MGCP)   A protocol that is designed to be a complete VoIP or video presentation connection and session controller. MGCP uses TCP ports 2427 and 2727.

medianet   A network of far-flung routers and servers that provides sufficient bandwidth for video teleconferencing (VTC) via quality of service (QoS) and other tools.

mega-   A prefix that usually stands for the binary quantity 1,048,576. One megabyte is 1,048,576 bytes. One megahertz, however, is 1,000,000 hertz. Sometimes shortened to *meg*, as in "a 286 has an address space of 16 megs."

memorandum of understanding (MOU)   A document that defines an agreement between two parties in situations where a legal contract is not appropriate.

mesh topology   Topology in which each computer has a direct or indirect connection to every other computer in a network. Any node on the network can forward traffic to other nodes. Popular in cellular and many wireless networks.

Metasploit   A unique tool that enables a penetration tester to use a massive library of attacks as well as tweak those attacks for unique penetrations.

metric   Relative value that defines the "cost" of using a particular route.

metro Ethernet   A metropolitan area network (MAN) based on the Ethernet standard.

metropolitan area network (MAN)   Multiple computers connected via cabling, radio, leased phone lines, or infrared that are within the same city. A perfect example of a MAN is the Tennessee city Chattanooga's gigabit network available to all citizens, the Chattanooga Gig.

MHz (megahertz)   A unit of measure that equals a frequency of 1 million cycles per second.

Microsoft Baseline Security Analyzer (MBSA)   Microsoft-designed tool to test individual Windows-based PCs for vulnerabilities.

MIME (Multipurpose Internet Mail Extensions)   A standard for attaching binary files, such as executables and images, to the Internet's text-based mail (24-Kbps packet size).

Miredo   An open source implementation of Teredo for Linux and some other UNIX-based systems. It is a NAT-traversal IPv6 tunneling protocol.

mirroring   Also called *drive mirroring*, reading and writing data at the same time to two drives for fault-tolerance purposes. Considered *RAID level 1*.

mixed mode   Also called *high-throughput*, or *802.11a-ht/802.11g-ht*, one of three modes used with 802.11n wireless networks wherein the wireless access point (WAP) sends special packets that support older standards yet can also improve the speed of those standards via 802.

modal distortion A light distortion problem unique to multimode fiber-optic cable.

model A simplified representation of a real object or process. In the case of networking, models represent logical tasks and subtasks that are required to perform network communication.

modem (modulator-demodulator) A device that converts both digital bit streams into analog signals (modulation) and incoming analog signals back into digital signals (demodulation). Most commonly used to interconnect telephone lines to computers.

modulation techniques The various multiplexing and demultiplexing technologies and protocols, both analog and digital.

modulator-demodulator (modem) *See* modem (modulator-demodulator).

monlist A query that asks an NTP server about the traffic between itself and peers.

motion detection system A feature of some video surveillance systems that starts and stops recordings based on actions caught by the camera(s).

mounting bracket Bracket that acts as a holder for a faceplate in cable installations.

MS-CHAP Microsoft's dominant variation of the CHAP protocol, uses a slightly more advanced encryption protocol.

MTU (maximum transmission unit) *See* maximum transmission unit (MTU).

MTU black hole When a router's firewall features block ICMP requests, making MTU worthless.

MTU mismatch The situation when your network's packets are so large that they must be fragmented to fit into your ISP's packets.

multicast Method of sending a packet in which the sending computer sends it to a group of interested computers.

multicast addresses A set of reserved addresses designed to go from one system to any system using one of the reserved addresses.

multifactor authentication A form of authentication where a user must use two or more factors to prove his or her identity; for example, some sort of physical token that, when inserted, prompts for a password.

multilayer switch A switch that has functions that operate at multiple layers of the OSI seven-layer model.

multilink PPP A communications protocol that logically joins multiple PPP connections, such as a modem connection, to aggregate the throughput of the links.

multimeter A tool for testing voltage (AC and DC), resistance, and continuity.

multimode   Type of fiber-optic cable with a large-diameter core that supports multiple modes of propagation. The large diameter simplifies connections, but has drawbacks related to distance.

multimode fiber (MMF)   Type of fiber-optic cable that uses LEDs.

multiple in/multiple out (MIMO)   A feature in 802.11 WAPs that enables them to make multiple simultaneous connections.

multiplexer   A device that merges information from multiple input channels to a single output channel.

Multiprotocol Label Switching (MPLS)   A router feature that labels certain data to use a desired connection. It works with any type of packet switching (even Ethernet) to force certain types of data to use a certain path.

multisource agreement (MSA)   A document that details the interoperability of network hardware from a variety of manufacturers.

multiuser MIMO (MU-MIMO)   Feature of 802.11ac networking that enables a WAP to broadcast to multiple users simultaneously.

MX records   Records within DNS servers that are used by SMTP servers to determine where to send mail.

My Traceroute (mtr)   Terminal command in Linux that dynamically displays the route a packet is taking. Similar to traceroute.

name resolution   A method that enables one computer on the network to locate another to establish a session. All network protocols perform name resolution in one of two ways: either via *broadcast* or by providing some form of *name server*.

name server   A computer whose job is to know the name of every other computer on the network.

NAT (Network Address Translation)   *See* Network Address Translation (NAT).

NAT translation table   Special database in a NAT router that stores destination IP addresses and ephemeral source ports from outgoing packets and compares them against returning packets.

NAT64   A transition mechanism that embeds IPv4 packets into IPv6 packets for network traversal.

native VLAN   The specified VLAN designation that will be assigned to all untagged frames entering a trunk port in a switch.

nbtstat   A command-line utility used to check the current NetBIOS name cache on a particular machine. The utility compares NetBIOS names to their corresponding IP addresses.

near field communication (NFC)   A low-speed, short-range networking technology designed for (among other things) small-value monetary transactions.

near-end crosstalk (NEXT)   Crosstalk at the same end of a cable from which the signal is being generated.

neighbor advertisement   IPv6 packet sent in response to a multicast neighbor solicitation packet.

neighbor discovery   *See* Neighbor Discovery Protocol (NDP).

Neighbor Discovery Protocol (NDP)   IPv6 protocol that enables hosts to configure automatically their own IPv6 addresses and get configuration information like routers and DNS servers.

neighbor solicitation   IPv6 process of finding a MAC address of a local host, given its IPv6 address.

Nessus   Popular and extremely comprehensive vulnerability testing tool.

NetBEUI (NetBIOS Extended User Interface)   Microsoft's first networking protocol, designed to work with NetBIOS. NetBEUI is long obsolesced by TCP/IP. NetBEUI did not support routing.

NetBIOS (Network Basic Input/Output System)   A protocol that operates at the Session layer of the OSI seven-layer model. This protocol creates and manages connections based on the names of the computers involved.

NetBIOS name   A computer name that identifies both the specific machine and the functions that machine performs. A NetBIOS name consists of 16 characters: the first 15 are an alphanumeric name, and the 16th is a special suffix that identifies the role the machine plays.

NetBIOS over TCP/IP (NetBT)   A Microsoft-created protocol that enables NetBIOS naming information to be transported over TCP/IP networks. The result is that Microsoft naming services can operate on a TCP/IP network without the need for DNS services.

NetBIOS/NetBEUI   *See* NetBEUI; *see also* NetBIOS.

NetFlow   The primary tool used to monitor packet flow on a network.

NetFlow collector   Component process of NetFlow that captures and saves data from a NetFlow-enabled device's cache for future NetFlow analysis.

netstat   A universal command-line utility used to examine the TCP/IP connections open on a given host.

network   A collection of two or more devices interconnected by telephone lines, coaxial cables, satellite links, radio, and/or some other communication technique. A computer *network* is a group of computers that are connected together and communicate with one another for a common purpose. Computer networks support "people and organization" networks, users who also share a common purpose for communicating.

network access control (NAC) Control over information, people, access, machines, and everything in between.

network access policy Rules that define who can access the network, how it can be accessed, and what resources of the network can be used.

network access server (NAS) System that controls the modems in a RADIUS network.

Network Address Translation (NAT) A means of translating a system's IP address into another IP address before sending it out to a larger network. NAT manifests itself by a NAT program that runs on a system or a router. A network using NAT provides the systems on the network with private IP addresses. The system running the NAT software has two interfaces: one connected to the network and the other connected to the larger network.

The NAT program takes packets from the client systems bound for the larger network and translates their internal private IP addresses to its own public IP address, enabling many systems to share a single IP address.

network appliance Feature-packed network box that incorporates numerous processes such as routing, Network Address Translation (NAT), switching, intrusion detection systems, firewall, and more.

Network as a Service (NaaS) The act of renting virtual server space over the Internet. *See also* cloud computing.

network attached storage (NAS) A dedicated file server that has its own file system and typically uses hardware and software designed for serving and storing files.

network blocks Also called *blocks*, contiguous ranges of IP addresses that are assigned to organizations and end users by IANA.

network closet An equipment room that holds servers, switches, routers, and other network gear.

network design The process of gathering together and planning the layout for the equipment needed to create a network.

network diagram An illustration that shows devices on a network and how they connect.

network ID A number used in IP networks to identify the network on which a device or machine exists.

network interface A device by which a system accesses a network. In most cases, this is a NIC or a modem.

network interface card (NIC) Traditionally, an expansion card that enables a PC to link physically to a network. Modern computers now use built-in NICs, no longer requiring physical cards, but the term "NIC" is still very common.

network interface unit (NIU)   Another name for a demarc. *See* demarc.

Network layer   Layer 3 of the OSI seven-layer model. *See also* Open Systems Interconnection (OSI) seven-layer model.

Network Management Software (NMS)   Tools that enable you to describe, visualize, and configure an entire network.

network management station (NMS)   SNMP console computer that runs the SNMP manager software.

network map   A highly detailed illustration of a network, down to the individual computers. A network map will show IP addresses, ports, protocols, and more.

network name   Another name for the *Service Set Identifier (SSID)*.

network operations center (NOC)   A centralized location for techs and administrators to manage all aspects of a network.

network prefix   The first 64 bits of an IPv6 address that identifies the network.

network protocol   Special software that exists in every network-capable operating system that acts to create unique identifiers for each system. It also creates a set of communication rules for issues like how to handle data chopped up into multiple packets and how to deal with routers. TCP/IP is the dominant network protocol today.

network segmentation   Separating network assets through various means, such as with VLANs or with a DMZ, to protect against access by malicious actors.

network share   A shared resource on a network.

network technology   The techniques, components, and practices involved in creating and operating computer-to-computer links.

network threat   Any number of things that share one essential feature: the potential to damage network data, machines, or users.

Network Time Protocol (NTP)   Protocol that gives the current time.

network topology   Refers to the way that cables and other pieces of hardware connect to one another.

network-based anti-malware   A single source server that holds current anti-malware software. Multiple systems can access and run the software from that server. The single site makes the software easier to update and administer than anti-malware installed on individual systems.

network-based firewall   Firewall, perhaps implemented in a gateway router or as a proxy server, through which all network traffic must pass inspection to be allowed or blocked.

newsgroup   The name for a discussion group on Usenet.

next hop   The next router a packet should go to at any given point.

next-generation firewall (NGFW)   Network protection device that functions at multiple layers of the OSI model to tackle traffic no traditional firewall can filter alone.

NFS (Network File System)   A TCP/IP file system–sharing protocol that enables systems to treat files on a remote machine as though they were local files. NFS uses TCP port 2049, but many users choose alternative port numbers. Though still somewhat popular and heavily supported, NFS has been largely replaced by Samba/CIFS. *See also* Samba *and* Common Internet File System (CIFS).

NIC teaming   Connecting multiple NICs in tandem to increase bandwidth in smaller increments. *See also* link aggregation.

Nmap   A network utility designed to scan a network and create a map. Frequently used as a vulnerability scanner.

node   A member of a network or a point where one or more functional units interconnect transmission lines.

noise   Undesirable signals bearing no desired information and frequently capable of introducing errors into the communication process.

non-discovery mode   A setting for Bluetooth devices that effectively hides them from other Bluetooth devices.

non-persistent agent   Software used in posture assessment that does not stay resident in client station memory. It is executed prior to login and may stay resident during the login session but is removed from client RAM when the login or session is complete. The agent presents the security characteristics to the access control server, which then decides to allow, deny, or redirect the connection.

nonrepudiation   Not being able to deny having sent a message.

normal backup   A full backup of every selected file on a system. This type of backup turns off the archive bit after the backup.

ns (nanosecond)   A billionth of a second. Light travels a little over 11 inches in 1 ns.

NS records   Records that list the authoritative DNS servers for a domain.

nslookup   A very handy tool that advanced techs use to query DNS servers.

NTFS (NT File System)   A file system for hard drives that enables object-level security, long filename support, compression, and encryption. NTFS 4.0 debuted with Windows NT 4.0. Later Windows versions continue to update NTFS.

NTFS permissions   Groupings of what Microsoft calls special permissions that have names like Execute, Read, and Write, and that allow or disallow users certain access to files.

NTLDR   A Windows NT/2000/XP/2003 boot file. Launched by the MBR or MFT, NTLDR looks at the BOOT.INI configuration file for any installed operating systems.

ntpdc A command that puts the NTP server into interactive mode in order to submit queries.

object A group of related counters used in Windows logging utilities.

OEM (Original Equipment Manufacturer) Contrary to the name, does not create original hardware, but rather purchases components from manufacturers and puts them together in systems under its own brand name. Dell, Inc. and Gateway, Inc., for example, are for the most part OEMs. Apple, Inc., which manufactures most of the components for its own Mac-branded machines, is not an OEM. Also known as *value-added resellers (VARs)*.

off-boarding The process of confirming that mobile devices leaving the control of the organization do not store any proprietary applications or data.

offsite The term for a virtual computer accessed and stored remotely.

Ohm rating Electronic measurement of a cable's or an electronic component's impedance.

omnidirectional antenna Technology used in most WAPs that send wireless signals in all directions equally.

on-boarding The process of verifying that new mobile devices appearing in the organization's infrastructure are secure and safe to use within the organization.

onsite The term for a virtual computer stored at your location.

open port *See* listening port.

Open Shortest Path First (OSPF) An interior gateway routing protocol developed for IP networks based on the shortest path first or *link state algorithm*.

open source Applications and operating systems that offer access to their source code; this enables developers to modify applications and operating systems easily to meet their specific needs.

Open Systems Interconnection (OSI) An international standard suite of protocols defined by the International Organization for Standardization (ISO) that implements the OSI seven-layer model for network communications between computers.

Open Systems Interconnection (OSI) seven-layer model An architecture model based on the OSI protocol suite, which defines and standardizes the flow of data between computers. The following lists the seven layers:

- **Layer 1** The *Physical layer* defines hardware connections and turns binary into physical pulses (electrical or light). Cables operate at the Physical layer.
- **Layer 2** The *Data Link layer* identifies devices on the Physical layer. MAC addresses are part of the Data Link layer. Switches operate at the Data Link layer.

- **Layer 3** The *Network layer* moves packets between computers on different networks. Routers operate at the Network layer. IP operates at the Network layer.

- **Layer 4** The *Transport layer* breaks data down into manageable chunks with TCP, at this layer. UDP also operates at the Transport layer.

- **Layer 5** The *Session layer* manages connections between machines. Sockets operate at the Session layer.

- **Layer 6** The *Presentation layer*, which can also manage data encryption, hides the differences among various types of computer systems.

- **Layer 7** The *Application layer* provides tools for programs to use to access the network (and the lower layers). HTTP, SSL/TLS, FTP, SMTP, DNS, DHCP, and IMAP are all examples of protocols that operate at the Application layer.

OpenSSH   A series of secure programs developed by the OpenBSD organization to fix the limitation of Secure Shell (SSH) of only being able to handle one session per tunnel.

operating system (OS)   The set of programming that enables a program to interact with the computer and provides an interface between the PC and the user. Examples are Microsoft Windows 10, Apple macOS, and SUSE Linux.

operator   In a distributed control system, the operator is a human who runs the computer-controlled resources through a human machine interface. *See also* human machine interface (HMI).

Optical Carrier (OC)   Specification used to denote the optical data carrying capacity (in Mbps) of fiber-optic cables in networks conforming to the SONET standard. The OC standard is an escalating series of speeds, designed to meet the needs of medium-to-large corporations. SONET establishes OCs from 51.8 Mbps (OC-1) to 39.8 Gbps (OC-768).

optical power meter   Device that measures light intensity of light pulses within or at the terminal ends of fiber-optic cables.

optical time domain reflectometer (OTDR)   Tester for fiber-optic cable that determines continuity and reports the location of cable breaks.

organizationally unique identifier (OUI)   The first 24 bits of a MAC address, assigned to the NIC manufacturer by the IEEE.

orthogonal frequency-division multiplexing (OFDM)   A spread-spectrum broadcasting method that combines the multiple frequencies of DSSS with FHSS's hopping capability.

OS (operating system)   *See* operating system (OS).

oscilloscope   A device that gives a graphical/visual representation of signal levels over a period of time.

OSPF (Open Shortest Path First)   *See* Open Shortest Path First (OSPF).

outbound traffic   Packets leaving the network from within it.

out-of-band management   Method to connect to and administer a managed device such as a switch or router that does not use a standard network-connected host as the administrative console. A computer connected to the console port of a switch is an example of out-of-band management.

overlay tunnel   Enables two IPv6 networks to connect over an IPv4 network by encapsulating the IPv6 packets within IPv4 headers, transporting them across the IPv4 network, then de-encapsulating the IPv6 data.

packet   Basic component of communication over a network. A group of bits of fixed maximum size and well-defined format that is switched and transmitted as a complete whole through a network. It contains source and destination address, data, and control information. *See also* frame.

packet analyzer   A program that reads the capture files from packet sniffers and analyzes them based on monitoring needs.

packet filtering   A mechanism that blocks any incoming or outgoing packet from a particular IP address or range of IP addresses. Also known as *IP filtering*.

packet sniffer   A tool that intercepts and logs network packets.

pad   Extra data added to an Ethernet frame to bring the data up to the minimum required size of 64 bytes.

partially meshed topology   A mesh topology in which not all of the nodes are directly connected.

passive optical network (PON)   A fiber architecture that uses a single fiber to the neighborhood switch and then individual fiber runs to each final destination.

password   A series of characters that enables a user to gain access to a file, a folder, a PC, or a program.

Password Authentication Protocol (PAP)   The oldest and most basic form of authentication and also the least safe because it sends all passwords in cleartext.

patch antenna   Flat, plate-shaped antenna that generates a half-sphere beam; used for broadcasting to a select area.

patch cables   Short (2 to 5 foot) UTP cables that connect patch panels to switches.

patch management   The process of regularly updating operating systems and applications to avoid security threats.

patch panel   A panel containing a row of female connectors (ports) that terminate the horizontal cabling in the equipment room. Patch panels facilitate cabling organization and provide protection to horizontal cabling. *See also* vertical cross-connect.

Path MTU Discovery (PMTU)   A method for determining the best MTU setting that works by adding a new feature called the "Don't Fragment (DF) flag" to the IP packet.

path vector   Routing protocol in which routers maintain path information. This information gets updated dynamically. *See* Border Gateway Protocol (BGP-4).

pathping   Command-line tool that combines the features of the ping command and the tracert/traceroute commands.

payload   The primary data that is sent from a source network device to a destination network device.

PBX (private branch exchange)   A private phone system used within an organization.

peer-to-peer (P2P)   A network in which each machine can act as either a client or a server.

peer-to-peer mode   *See* ad hoc mode.

penetration testing (pentesting)   An authorized, network hacking process that will identify real-world weaknesses in network security and document the findings.

Performance Monitor (PerfMon)   The Windows logging utility.

peripherals   Noncomputer devices on a network; for example, fax machines, printers, or scanners.

permanent DoS (PDoS)   An attack that damages a targeted machine, such as a router or server, and renders that machine inoperable.

permissions   Sets of attributes that network administrators assign to users and groups that define what they can do to resources.

persistent agent   In network access control systems, a small scanning program that, once installed on the computer, stays installed and runs every time the computer boots up. Composed of modules that perform a thorough inventory of each security-oriented element in the computer.

persistent connection   A connection to a shared folder or drive that the computer immediately reconnects to at logon.

personal area network (PAN)   The network created among Bluetooth devices such as smartphones, tablets, printers, keyboards, mice, and so on.

phishing   A social engineering technique where the attacker poses as a trusted source in order to obtain sensitive information.

physical address   An address burned into a ROM chip on a NIC. A MAC address is an example of a physical address.

Physical Contact (PC) connector   Family of fiber-optic connectors that enforces direct physical contact between two optical fibers being connected.

Physical layer   *See* Open Systems Interconnection (OSI) seven-layer model.

physical network diagram   A document that shows all of the physical connections on a network. Cabling type, protocol, and speed are also listed for each connection.

physical topology   The manner in which the physical components of a network are arranged.

ping (packet internet groper)   A small network message sent by a computer to check for the presence and response of another system. Also, a command-line utility to check the "up/down" status of an IP addressed host. A ping uses ICMP packets. *See also* Internet Control Message Protocol (ICMP).

ping –6   A command-line utility to check the "up/down" status of an IP addressed host. The "–6" switch included on the command line, using the Windows version of ping, specifies that the host under test has an IPv6 address.

ping6   Linux command-line utility specifically designed to ping hosts with an IPv6 address.

plain old telephone service (POTS)   *See* public switched telephone network (PSTN).

plaintext   Also called *cleartext*, unencrypted data in an accessible format that can be read without special utilities.

platform   Hardware environment that supports the running of a computer system.

Platform as a Service (PaaS)   A complete deployment and management system that gives programmers all the tools they need to administer and maintain a Web application. *See also* cloud computing.

plenum   Usually a space between a building's false ceiling and the floor above it. Most of the wiring for networks is located in this space. Plenum is also a fire rating for network cabling.

plenum-rated cable   Network cable type that resists burning and does not give off excessive smoke or noxious fumes when burned.

Point Coordination Function (PCF)   A method of collision avoidance defined by the 802.11 standard but has yet to be implemented. *See also* Distributed Coordination Function (DCF).

point-to-multipoint topology   Topology in which one device communicates with more than one other device on a network.

Point-to-Point Protocol (PPP)   A protocol that enables a computer to connect to the Internet through a dial-in connection and to enjoy most of the benefits of a direct connection. PPP is considered to be superior to the Serial Line Internet Protocol (SLIP) because of its error detection and data compression features, which SLIP lacks, and the capability to use dynamic IP addresses.

Point-to-Point Protocol over Ethernet (PPPoE) A protocol that was originally designed to encapsulate PPP frames into Ethernet frames. Used by DSL providers to force customers to log into their DSL connections instead of simply connecting automatically.

point-to-point topology Network topology in which two computers are directly connected to each other without any other intervening connection components such as hubs or switches.

Point-to-Point Tunneling Protocol (PPTP) A protocol that works with PPP to provide a secure data link between computers using encryption.

pointer record (PTR) A record that points IP addresses to host names. *See also* reverse lookup zone.

polyvinyl chloride (PVC) A material used for the outside insulation and jacketing of most cables. Also a fire rating for a type of cable that has no significant fire protection.

port (logical connection) In TCP/IP, 16-bit numbers between 0 and 65535 assigned to a particular TCP/IP process or application. For example, Web servers use port 80 (HTTP) to transfer Web pages to clients. The first 1024 ports are called *well-known ports*. They have been pre-assigned and generally refer to TCP/IP processes and applications that have been around for a long time.

port (physical connector) In general, the portion of a computer through which a peripheral device may communicate, such as video, USB, serial, and network ports. In the context of networking, the jacks found in computers, switches, routers, and network-enabled peripherals into which network cables are plugged.

Port Address Translation (PAT) The most commonly used form of Network Address Translation, where the NAT uses the outgoing IP addresses and port numbers (collectively known as a socket) to map traffic from specific machines in the network. *See also* Network Address Translation (NAT).

port aggregation A method for joining two or more switch ports logically to increase bandwidth.

port authentication Function of many advanced networking devices that authenticates a connecting device at the point of connection.

port blocking Preventing the passage of any TCP segments or UDP datagrams through any ports other than the ones prescribed by the system administrator.

port bonding The logical joining of multiple redundant ports and links between two network devices such as a switch and storage array.

port filtering *See* port blocking.

port forwarding Preventing the passage of any IP packets through any ports other than the ones prescribed by the system administrator.

port mirroring   The capability of many advanced switches to mirror data from any or all physical ports on a switch to a single physical port. Useful for any type of situation where an administrator needs to inspect packets coming to or from certain computers.

port number   Number used to identify the requested service (such as SMTP or FTP) when connecting to a TCP/IP host. Some example server port numbers include 80 (HTTP), 21 (FTP), 25 (SMTP), 53 (DNS), and 67 (DHCP).

port scanner   A program that probes ports on another system, logging the state of the scanned ports.

port scanning   The process of querying individual nodes, looking for open or vulnerable ports and creating a report.

Post Office Protocol Version 3 (POP3)   One of the two protocols that receive e-mail from SMTP servers. POP3 uses TCP port 110. Old and obsolete, this protocol was replaced by IMAP.

PostScript   A language defined by Adobe Systems, Inc., for describing how to create an image on a page. The description is independent of the resolution of the device that will create the image. It includes a technology for defining the shape of a font and creating a raster image at many different resolutions and sizes.

posture assessment   Process by which a client presents its security characteristics via an agent or agent-less interface to an access control server. The server checks the characteristics and decides whether to grant a connection, deny a connection, or redirect the connection depending on the security compliance invoked.

power converter   Device that changes AC power to DC power.

Power over Ethernet (PoE)   A standard that enables wireless access points (WAPs) to receive their power from the same Ethernet cables that transfer their data.

power redundancy   Secondary source of power in the event that primary power fails. The most common redundant power source is an uninterruptible power supply (UPS).

power users   A user account that has the capability to do many, but not all, of the basic administrator functions.

PPP (Point-to-Point Protocol)   *See* Point-to-Point Protocol (PPP).

PPPoE (PPP over Ethernet)   *See* Point-to-Point Protocol over Ethernet (PPPoE).

preamble   A 7-byte series of alternating ones and zeroes followed by a 1-byte *start frame delimiter*, always precedes a frame. The preamble gives a receiving NIC time to realize a frame is coming and to know exactly where the frame starts.

prefix delegation   An IPv6 router configuration that enables it to request an IPv6 address block from an upstream source, then to disseminate it to local clients.

prefix length   The IPv6 term for subnet mask. In most cases, it's /64.

Presentation layer   *See* Open Systems Interconnection (OSI) seven-layer model.

primary (master) DNS server   The name server where records are added, deleted, and modified. The primary DNS server sends copies of this zone file to secondary (slave) DNS servers in a process known as a zone transfer.

primary lookup zone   A *forward lookup zone* stored in a text file. *See also* forward lookup zone.

Primary Rate Interface (PRI)   A type of ISDN that is actually just a full T1 line carrying 23 B channels.

primary zone   A *forward lookup zone* that is managed within and by the authoritative DNS server.

private cloud   Software, platforms, and infrastructure that are delivered via the Internet and are made available to the general public.

private IP addresses   Groups of IP addresses set aside for internal networks; Internet routers block these addresses, such as 10.*x.x.x* /8, 172.(16–31).*x.x* /16, and 192.168. (0–255).*x* /24.

private port numbers   *See* dynamic port numbers.

program   A set of actions or instructions that a machine is capable of interpreting and executing. Used as a verb, it means to design, write, and test such instructions.

programmable logic controller (PLC)   A computer that controls a machine according to a set of ordered steps.

promiscuous mode   A mode of operation for a NIC in which the NIC processes all frames that it sees on the cable.

prompt   A character or message provided by an operating system or program to indicate that it is ready to accept input.

proprietary   Term used to describe technology that is unique to, and owned by, a particular vendor.

Protected Extensible Authentication Protocol (PEAP)   An authentication protocol that uses a password function based on MS-CHAPv2 with the addition of an encrypted TLS tunnel similar to *EAP-TLS*.

protocol   An agreement that governs the procedures used to exchange information between cooperating entities; usually includes how much information is to be sent, how often it is sent, how to recover from transmission errors, and who is to receive the information.

protocol analyzer   A tool that monitors the different protocols running at different layers on the network and that can give Application, Session, Network, and Data Link layer information on every frame going through a network.

protocol data unit (PDU) Specialized type of command and control packet found in SNMP management systems (and others).

protocol stack The actual software that implements the protocol suite on a particular operating system.

protocol suite A set of protocols that are commonly used together and operate at different levels of the OSI seven-layer model.

proximity reader Sensor that detects and reads a token that comes within range. The polled information is used to determine the access level of the person carrying the token.

proxy ARP The process of making remotely connected computers act as though they are on the same LAN as local computers.

proxy server A device that fetches Internet resources for a client without exposing that client directly to the Internet. Most proxy servers accept requests for HTTP, FTP, POP3, and SMTP resources. The proxy server often caches, or stores, a copy of the requested resource for later use.

PSTN (public switched telephone network) *See* public switched telephone network (PSTN).

public cloud Software, platforms, and infrastructure delivered through networks that the general public can use.

public switched telephone network (PSTN) Also known as *plain old telephone service (POTS)*, the most common type of phone connection, which takes your sounds, translated into an analog waveform by the microphone, and transmits them to another phone.

public-key cryptography A method of encryption and decryption that uses two different keys: a public key for encryption and a private key for decryption.

public-key infrastructure (PKI) The system for creating and distributing digital certificates using sites like Comodo, Symantec, or GoDaddy.

punchdown tool A specialized tool for connecting UTP wires to a 110-block. Also called a *110-punchdown tool*.

PVC-rated cable Type of network cable that offers no special fire protection; burning produces excessive smoke and noxious fumes.

quad small form-factor pluggable (QSFP) BiDi fiber-optic connector used in 40GBase networks.

quality of service (QoS) Policies that control how much bandwidth a protocol, PC, user, VLAN, or IP address may use.

quarantine network Safe network to which are directed stations that either do not require or should not have access to protected resources.

raceway   Cable organizing device that adheres to walls, making for a much simpler, though less neat, installation than running cables in the walls.

rack monitoring system   Set of sensors in an equipment closet or rack-mounted gear that can monitor and alert when an out-of-tolerance condition occurs in power, temperature, and/or other environmental aspects.

radio frequency interference (RFI)   The phenomenon where a Wi-Fi signal is disrupted by a radio signal from another device.

Radio Grade (RG) ratings   Ratings developed by the U.S. military to provide a quick reference for the different types of coaxial cables.

RADIUS server   A system that enables remote users to connect to a network service.

ransomware   Crypto-malware that uses some form of encryption to lock a user out of a system. Once the crypto-malware encrypts the computer, usually encrypting the boot drive, in most cases the malware then forces the user to pay money to get the system decrypted.

real-time processing   The processing of transactions as they occur, rather than batching them. Pertaining to an application, processing in which response to input is fast enough to affect subsequent inputs and guide the process, and in which records are updated immediately. The lag from input time to output time must be sufficiently small for acceptable timeliness. Timeliness is a function of the total system: missile guidance requires output within a few milliseconds of input, whereas scheduling of steamships requires a response time in days. Real-time systems are those with a response time of milliseconds; interactive systems respond in seconds; and batch systems may respond in hours or days.

Real-time Transport Protocol (RTP)   Protocol that defines the type of packets used on the Internet to move voice or data from a server to clients. The vast majority of VoIP solutions available today use RTP.

real-time video   Communication that offers both audio and video via unicast messages.

reassembly   The process where a receiving system verifies and puts together packets into coherent data.

recovery point objective (RPO)   The state of the backup when the data is recovered. It is an evaluation of how much data is lost from the time of the last backup to the point that a recovery was required.

recovery time objective (RTO)   The amount of time needed to restore full functionality from when the organization ceases to function.

Reddit hug of death   The massive influx of traffic on a small or lesser-known Web site when it is suddenly made popular by a reference from the media. *See also* Slashdotting.

redundant array of independent [or inexpensive] disks [or devices] (RAID)   A way to create a fault-tolerant storage system. RAID has six levels. Level 0 uses byte-level striping and provides no fault tolerance. Level 1 uses mirroring or duplexing. Level 2 uses bit-level striping. Level 3 stores error-correcting information (such as parity) on a separate disk and data striping on the remaining drives. Level 4 is level 3 with block-level striping. Level 5 uses block-level and parity data striping.

reflection   Used in DDoS attacks, requests are sent to normal servers as if they had come from the target server. The response from the normal servers are reflected to the target server, overwhelming it without identifying the true initiator.

reflective DDoS   *See* reflection.

refraction   Bending of radio waves when transmitted through glass.

regedit.exe   A program used to edit the Windows registry.

Regional Internet Registries (RIRs)   Entities under the oversight of the Internet Assigned Numbers Authority (IANA), which parcels out IP addresses.

registered jack (RJ)   Type of connector used on the end of telephone and networking cables. *See* RJ-11 *and* RJ-45, *respectively.*

registered ports   Port numbers from 1024 to 49151. The IANA assigns these ports for anyone to use for their applications.

regulations   Rules of law or policy that govern behavior in the workplace, such as what to do when a particular event occurs.

remote   Refers to the computer(s), server(s), and/or LAN that cannot be physically used due to its distance from the user.

remote access   The capability to access a computer from outside a building in which it is housed. Remote access requires communications hardware, software, and actual physical links.

remote access server (RAS)   Refers to both the hardware component (servers built to handle the unique stresses of a large number of clients calling in) and the software component (programs that work with the operating system to allow remote access to the network) of a remote access solution.

Remote Authentication Dial-In User Service (RADIUS)   An AAA standard created to support ISPs with hundreds if not thousands of modems in hundreds of computers to connect to a single central database. RADIUS consists of three devices: the RADIUS server that has access to a database of user names and passwords, a number of network access servers (NASs) that control the modems, and a group of systems that dial into the network.

Remote Copy Protocol (RCP)   Provides the capability to copy files to and from the remote server without the need to resort to FTP or Network File System (NFS, a UNIX form of folder sharing). RCP can also be used in scripts and shares TCP port 514 with RSH.

Remote Desktop Protocol (RDP)   A Microsoft-created remote terminal protocol.

Remote Installation Services (RIS)   A tool introduced with Windows 2000 that can be used to initiate either a scripted installation or an installation of an image of an operating system onto a PC.

remote login (rlogin)   Program in UNIX that enables you to log into a server remotely. Unlike Telnet, rlogin can be configured to log in automatically.

remote shell (RSH)   Allows you to send single commands to the remote server. Whereas rlogin is designed to be used interactively, RSH can be easily integrated into a script.

remote terminal   A connection on a faraway computer that enables you to control that computer as if you were sitting in front of it and logged in. Remote terminal programs all require a server and a client. The server is the computer to be controlled. The client is the computer from which you do the controlling.

remote terminal unit (RTU)   In a SCADA environment, has the same functions as a controller plus additional autonomy to deal with connection loss. It is also designed to take advantage of some form of long-distance communication.

repeater   A device that takes all of the frames it receives on one Ethernet segment and re-creates them on another Ethernet segment. Repeaters operate at Layer 1 (Physical) of the OSI seven-layer model. They do not check the integrity of the Layer 2 (Data Link) frame so they may repeat incorrectly formed frames. They were replaced in the early 1980s by bridges which perform frame integrity checking before repeating a frame.

replication   A process where multiple computers might share complete copies of a database and constantly update each other.

resistance   The tendency for a physical medium to impede electron flow. It is classically measured in a unit called *ohms*. *See also* impedance.

resource   Anything that exists on another computer that a person wants to use without going to that computer. Also an online information set or an online interactive option. An online library catalog and the local school lunch menu are examples of information sets. Online menus or graphical user interfaces, Internet e-mail, online conferences, Telnet, FTP, and Gopher are examples of interactive options.

Response   Answer from an agent upon receiving a Get protocol data unit (PDU) from an SNMP manager.

reverse lookup zone   A DNS setting that resolves IP addresses to FQDNs. In other words, it does exactly the reverse of what DNS normally accomplishes using forward lookup zones.

reverse proxy server   A connectivity solution that gathers information from its associated servers and shares that information to clients. The clients don't know about the servers behind the scenes. The reverse proxy server is the only machine with which they interact.

RF emanation   The transmission, intended or unintended, of radio frequencies. These transmissions may come from components that are intended to transmit RF, such as a Wi-Fi network card, or something less expected, such as a motherboard or keyboard. These emanations may be detected and intercepted, posing a potential threat to security.

RG-6   A grade of coaxial cable used for cable television and modern cable modem Internet connections. RG-6 has a characteristic impedance of 75 ohms.

RG-58   A grade of small-diameter coaxial cable used in 10Base2 Ethernet networks. RG-58 has a characteristic impedance of 50 ohms.

RG-59   A grade of coaxial cable used for cable television and early cable modem Internet connections. RG-59 has a characteristic impedance of 75 ohms.

ring topology   A network topology in which all the computers on the network attach to a central ring of cable.

RIP (Routing Information Protocol)   The first version of RIP, which had several shortcomings, such as a maximum hop count of 15 and a routing table update interval of 30 seconds, which was a problem because every router on a network would send out its table at the same time.

RIPv2   The second version of RIP. It fixed many problems of RIP, but the maximum hop count of 15 still applies.

riser   Fire rating that designates the proper cabling to use for vertical runs between floors of a building.

risk management   The process of how organizations evaluate, protect, and recover from threats and attacks that take place on their networks.

Rivest Cipher 4 (RC4)   A streaming symmetric-key algorithm.

Rivest, Shamir, Adleman (RSA)   *See* RSA (Rivest, Shamir, Adleman).

RJ (registered jack)   Connectors used for UTP cable on both telephone and network connections.

RJ-11   Type of connector with four-wire UTP connections; usually found in telephone connections.

RJ-45   Type of connector with eight-wire UTP connections; usually found in network connections and used for 10/100/1000BaseT networking.

roaming   A process where clients seamlessly change wireless access point (WAP) connections, depending on whichever WAP has the strongest signal covered by the broadcast area.

rogue access point (rogue AP)   An unauthorized wireless access point (WAP) installed in a computer network.

rogue DHCP server An unauthorized DHCP server installed in a computer network.

role-based access control (RBAC) The most popular authentication model used in file sharing, defines a user's access to a resource based on the roles the user plays in the network environment. This leads to the idea of creation of groups. A group in most networks is nothing more than a name that has clearly defined accesses to different resources. User accounts are placed into various groups.

rollback The process of downgrading—undoing—a recently applied patch or updated.

ROM (read-only memory) The generic term for nonvolatile memory that can be read from but not written to. This means that code and data stored in ROM cannot be corrupted by accidental erasure. Additionally, ROM retains its data when power is removed, which makes it the perfect medium for storing BIOS data or information such as scientific constants.

root directory The directory that contains all other directories.

rootkit A Trojan horse that takes advantage of very low-level operating system functions to hide itself from all but the most aggressive of anti-malware tools.

route A command that enables a user to display and edit the local system's routing table.

route redistribution Occurs in a multiprotocol router. A multiprotocol router learns route information using one routing protocol and disseminates that information using another routing protocol.

router A device that connects separate networks and forwards a packet from one network to another based only on the network address for the protocol being used. For example, an IP router looks only at the IP network number. Routers operate at Layer 3 (Network) of the OSI seven-layer model.

router advertisement A router's response to a client's router solicitation, also sent at regular intervals, that gives the client information to configure itself (prefix, prefix length, and more).

router solicitation In IPv6, a query from a host to find routers and get information to configure itself.

Routing and Remote Access Service (RRAS) A special remote access server program, originally only available on Windows Server, on which a PPTP endpoint is placed in Microsoft networks.

Routing Information Protocol (RIP) *See* RIP (Routing Information Protocol) *and* RIPv1.

routing loop A situation where interconnected routers loop traffic, causing the routers to respond slowly or not respond at all.

routing table A list of paths to various networks required by routers. This table can be built either manually or automatically.

RS-232 The recommended standard (RS) upon which all serial communication takes place on a PC.

RSA (Rivest, Shamir, Adleman) An improved asymmetric cryptography algorithm that enables secure digital signatures.

run A single piece of installed horizontal cabling.

Samba An application that enables UNIX systems to communicate using Server Message Blocks (SMBs). This, in turn, enables them to act as Microsoft clients and servers on the network.

SC connector Fiber-optic connector used to terminate single-mode and multimode fiber. It is characterized by its push-pull, snap mechanical coupling, known as "stick and click." Commonly referred to as *subscriber connector*, *standard connector*, and sometimes, *square connector*.

scalability The capability to support network growth.

scanner A device that senses alterations of light and dark. It enables the user to import photographs, other physical images, and text into the computer in digital form.

secondary (slave) DNS server Authoritative DNS server for a domain. Unlike a primary (master) DNS server, no additions, deletions, or modifications can be made to the zones on a secondary DNS server, which always gets all information from the primary DNS server in a process known as a zone transfer.

secondary lookup zone A backup lookup zone stored on another DNS server. *See also* forward lookup zone.

secondary zone A backup of a primary zone. It is used to provide fault tolerance and load balancing. It gets its information from the primary zone and is considered authoritative. *See also* primary zone.

Secure Copy Protocol (SCP) One of the first SSH-enabled programs to appear after the introduction of SSH. SCP was one of the first protocols used to transfer data securely between two hosts and thus might have replaced FTP. SCP works well but lacks features such as a directory listing.

Secure Hash Algorithm (SHA) A popular cryptographic hash.

Secure Shell (SSH) A terminal emulation program that looks exactly like Telnet but encrypts the data. SSH has replaced Telnet on the Internet.

Secure Sockets Layer (SSL) A protocol developed by Netscape for transmitting private documents over the Internet. SSL worked by using a public key to encrypt sensitive data. This encrypted data was sent over an SSL connection and then decrypted at the receiving end using a private key. Deprecated in favor of TLS.

security   A network's resilience against unwanted access or attack.

security considerations   In network design and construction, planning how to keep data protected from unapproved access. Security of physical computers and network resources is also considered.

security guard   Person responsible for controlling access to physical resources such as buildings, secure rooms, and other physical assets.

security information and event management (SIEM)   A two-part process consisting of security event monitoring (SEM), which performs real-time monitoring of security events, and security information management (SIM), where the monitoring log files are reviewed and analyzed by automated and human interpreters.

security log   A log that tracks anything that affects security, such as successful and failed logons and logoffs.

security policy   A set of procedures defining actions employees should perform to protect the network's security.

segment   The bus cable to which the computers on an Ethernet network connect.

segmentation   In a TCP/IP network, the process of chopping requested data into chunks that will fit into a packet (and eventually into the NIC's frame), organizing the packets for the benefit of the receiving system, and handing them to the NIC for sending.

sequential   A method of storing and retrieving information that requires data to be written and read sequentially. Accessing any portion of the data requires reading all the preceding data.

server   A computer that shares its resources, such as printers and files, with other computers on the network. An example of this is a Network File System server that shares its disk space with a workstation that has no disk drive of its own.

Server Message Block (SMB)   *See* SMB (Server Message Block).

server-based network   A network in which one or more systems function as dedicated file, print, or application servers, but do not function as clients.

service level agreement (SLA)   A document between a customer and a service provider that defines the scope, quality, and terms of the service to be provided.

Service Set Identifier (SSID)   A 32-bit identification string, sometimes called a *network name*, that's inserted into the header of each data packet processed by a wireless access point.

services   Background programs in an operating system that do the behind-the-scenes grunt work that users don't need to interact with on a regular basis.

session   A networking term used to refer to the logical stream of data flowing between two programs and being communicated over a network. Many different sessions may be emanating from any one node on a network.

session hijacking   The interception of a valid computer session to get authentication information.

Session Initiation Protocol (SIP)   A signaling protocol for controlling voice and video calls over IP. SIP competes with H.323 for VoIP dominance.

Session layer   *See* Open Systems Interconnection (OSI) seven-layer model.

session software   Handles the process of differentiating among various types of connections on a PC.

Set   The PDU with which a network management station commands an agent to make a change to a management information base (MIB) object.

share level security   A security system in which each resource has a password assigned to it; access to the resource is based on knowing the password.

share permissions   Permissions that only control the access of other users on the network with whom you share your resource. They have no impact on you (or anyone else) sitting at the computer whose resource is being shared.

shareware   Software that is protected by copyright, but the copyright holder allows (encourages!) you to make and distribute copies, under the condition that those who adopt the software after preview pay a fee. Derivative works are not allowed, and you may make an archival copy.

shell   Generally refers to the user interface of an operating system. A shell is the command processor that is the actual interface between the kernel and the user.

shielded twisted pair (STP)   A cabling for networks composed of pairs of wires twisted around each other at specific intervals. The twists serve to reduce interference (also called *crosstalk*). The more twists, the less interference. The cable has metallic shielding to protect the wires from external interference. *See also* unshielded twisted pair (UTP) for the more commonly used cable type in modern networks.

short circuit   Allows electricity to pass between two conductive elements that weren't designed to interact together. Also called a *short*.

Short Message Service (SMS) alert   A proactive message regarding an out-of-tolerance condition of an SNMP managed device sent as an SMS text.

Shortest Path First   Networking algorithm for directing router traffic. *See also* Open Shortest Path First (OSPF).

signal strength   A measurement of how well your wireless device is connecting to other devices.

signaling topology   Another name for logical topology. *See* logical topology.

signature   Specific pattern of bits or bytes that is unique to a particular virus. Virus scanning software maintains a library of signatures and compares the contents of scanned files against this library to detect infected files.

Simple Mail Transfer Protocol (SMTP)   The main protocol used to send electronic mail on the Internet.

Simple Network Management Protocol (SNMP)   A set of standards for communication with network devices (switches, routers, WAPs) connected to a TCP/IP network. Used for network management.

single point of failure   One component or system that, if it fails, will bring down an entire process, workflow, or organization.

single sign-on   A process whereby a client performs a one-time login to a gateway system. That system, in turn, takes care of the client's authentication to any other connected systems for which the client is authorized to access.

single-mode fiber (SMF)   Fiber-optic cables that use lasers.

site survey   A process that enables you to determine any obstacles to creating the wireless network you want.

site-to-site   A type of VPN connection using two Cisco VPN concentrators to connect two separate LANs permanently.

Slashdotting   The massive influx of traffic on a small or lesser-known Web site when it is suddenly made popular by a reference from the media. *See also* Reddit hug of death.

small form factor (SFF)   A description of later-generation, fiber-optic connectors designed to be much smaller than the first iterations of connectors. *See also* local connector (LC) *and* Mechanical Transfer Registered Jack (MT-RJ).

small form-factor pluggable (SFP)   A Cisco module that enables you to add additional features to its routers.

small office/home office (SOHO)   *See* SOHO (small office/home office).

smart card   Device (such as a credit card) that you insert into your PC or use on a door pad for authentication.

smart device   Device (such as a credit card, USB key, etc.) that you insert into your PC in lieu of entering a password.

smart jack   Type of network interface unit (NIU) that enables ISPs or telephone companies to test for faults in a network, such as disconnections and loopbacks.

SMB (Server Message Block)   Protocol used by Microsoft clients and servers to share file and print resources.

SMTP (Simple Mail Transfer Protocol)   *See* Simple Mail Transfer Protocol (SMTP).

smurf   A type of hacking attack in which an attacker floods a network with ping packets sent to the broadcast address. The trick that makes this attack special is that the return address of the pings is spoofed to that of the intended victim. When all the computers on the network respond to the initial ping, they send their response to the intended victim.

smurf attack   *See* smurf.

snap-ins   Small utilities that can be used with the Microsoft Management Console.

snapshot   A tool that enables you to save an extra copy of a virtual machine as it is exactly at the moment the snapshot is taken.

sneakernet   Saving a file on a portable medium and walking it over to another computer.

sniffer   Diagnostic program that can order a NIC to run in promiscuous mode. *See also* promiscuous mode.

snip   *See* cable stripper.

SNMP (Simple Network Management Protocol)   *See* Simple Network Management Protocol (SNMP).

SNMP manager   Software and station that communicates with SNMP agents to monitor and manage management information base (MIB) objects.

snmpwalk   SNMP manager PDU that collects management information base (MIB) information in a tree-oriented hierarchy of a MIB object and any of its subordinate objects. The snmpwalk command queries the object and then automatically queries all of the objects that are subordinated to the root object being queried.

social engineering   The process of using or manipulating people inside the networking environment to gain access to that network from the outside.

socket   A combination of a port number and an IP address that uniquely identifies a connection.

socket pairs   *See* endpoints.

software   Programming instructions or data stored on some type of binary storage device.

Software as a Service (SaaS)   Centralized applications that are accessed over a network. *See also* cloud computing.

software defined networking (SDN)   Programming that allows a master controller to determine how network components will move traffic through the network. Used in virtualization.

SOHO (small office/home office)   Refers to a classification of networking equipment, usually marketed to consumers or small businesses, which focuses on low price and ease of configuration. SOHO networks differ from enterprise networks, which focus on flexibility and maximum performance.

SOHO firewall   Firewall, typically simple, that is built into the firmware of a SOHO router.

solid core   A cable that uses a single solid wire to transmit signals.

SONET (Synchronous Optical Network)   An American fiber carrier standard for connecting fiber-optic transmission systems. SONET was proposed in the mid-1980s and is now an ANSI standard. SONET defines interface standards at the Physical layer of the OSI seven-layer model.

Source Address Table (SAT)   A table stored by a switch, listing the MAC addresses and port of each connected device.

Spanning Tree Protocol (STP)   A protocol that enables switches to detect and prevent bridge loops automatically.

speed-test site   A Web site used to check an Internet connection's throughput, such as www.speakeasy.net/speedtest.

split pair   A condition that occurs when signals on a pair of wires within a UTP cable interfere with the signals on another wire pair within that same cable.

spoofing   A security threat where an attacker makes some data seem as though it came from somewhere else, such as sending an e-mail with someone else's e-mail address in the sender field.

spyware   Any program that sends information about your system or your actions over the Internet.

SQL (Structured Query Language)   A language created by IBM that relies on simple English statements to perform database queries. SQL enables databases from different manufacturers to be queried using a standard syntax.

SRV record   A generic DNS record that supports any type of server.

SSH File Transfer Protocol (SFTP)   A replacement for FTP released after many of the inadequacies of SCP (such as the inability to see the files on the other computer) were discovered.

SSID broadcast   A wireless access point feature that announces the WAP's SSID to make it easy for wireless clients to locate and connect to it. By default, most WAPs regularly announce their SSID. For security purposes, some entities propose disabling this broadcast.

SSL (Secure Sockets Layer) *See* Secure Sockets Layer (SSL).

SSL VPN A type of VPN that uses SSL encryption. Clients connect to the VPN server using a standard Web browser, with the traffic secured using SSL. The two most common types of SSL VPNs are SSL portal VPNs and SSL tunnel VPNs.

ST connector Fiber-optic connector used primarily with 2.5-mm, single-mode fiber. It uses a push on, then twist-to-lock mechanical connection commonly called stick-and-twist although ST actually stands for straight tip.

star topology A network topology in which all computers in the network connect to a central wiring point.

star-bus topology A hybrid of the star and bus topologies that uses a physical star, where all nodes connect to a single wiring point (such as a hub) and a logical bus that maintains the Ethernet standards. One benefit of a star-bus topology is *fault tolerance*.

start frame delimiter (SFD) One-byte section of an Ethernet packet that follows the preamble and precedes the Ethernet frame.

start of authority (SOA) record DNS record that defines the primary name server in charge of the forward lookup zone.

stateful (DHCP) Describes a DHCPv6 server that works very similarly to an IPv4 DHCP server, passing out IPv6 addresses, subnet masks, and default gateways as well as optional items like DNS server addresses.

stateful filtering/stateful inspection A method of filtering in which all packets are examined as a stream. Stateful devices can do more than allow or block; they can track when a stream is disrupted or packets get corrupted and act accordingly.

stateless (DHCP) Describes a DHCPv6 server that only passes out information like DNS servers' IP addresses, but doesn't give clients IPv6 addresses.

stateless filtering/stateless inspection A method of filtering where the device that does the filtering looks at each IP packet individually, checking the packet for IP addresses and port numbers and blocking or allowing accordingly.

statement of work (SOW) A contract that defines the services, products, and time frames for the vendor to achieve.

static addressing The process of assigning IP addresses by manually typing them into client computers.

static NAT (SNAT) A type of Network Address Translation (NAT) that maps a single routable IP address to a single machine, allowing you to access that machine from outside the network.

static routes   Entries in a router's routing table that are not updated by any automatic route discovery protocols. Static routes must be added, deleted, or changed by a router administrator. Static routes are the opposite of dynamic routes.

static routing   A process by which routers in an internetwork obtain information about paths to other routers. This information must be supplied manually.

storage   A device or medium that can retain data for subsequent retrieval.

storage area network (SAN)   A server that can take a pool of hard disks and present them over the network as any number of logical disks.

STP (Spanning Tree Protocol)   *See* Spanning Tree Protocol (STP).

straight-through cable   UTP or STP cable segment that has the wire and pin assignments at one end of the cable match the wire and same pin assignments at the other end. Straight-through cables are used to connect hosts to switches and are the connective opposite of crossover cables.

stranded core   A cable that uses a bundle of tiny wire strands to transmit signals. Stranded core is not quite as good a conductor as solid core, but it will stand up to substantial handling without breaking.

stream cipher   An encryption method that encrypts a single bit at a time. Popular when data comes in long streams (such as with older wireless networks or cell phones).

stripe set   Two or more drives in a group that are used for a striped volume.

structured cabling   Standards defined by the Telecommunications Industry Association/Electronic Industries Alliance (TIA/EIA) that define methods of organizing the cables in a network for ease of repair and replacement.

STS overhead   Carries the signaling and protocol information in Synchronous Transport Signal (STS).

STS payload   Carries data in Synchronous Transport Signal (STS).

subnet   Each independent network in a TCP/IP internetwork.

subnet ID   Portion of an IP address that identifies bits shared by all hosts on that network.

subnet mask   The value used in TCP/IP settings to divide the IP address of a host into its component parts: network ID and host ID.

subnetting   Taking a single class of IP addresses and chopping it into multiple smaller groups.

subscriber identity module (SIM) card   Small storage device used in cellular phones to identify the phone, enable access to the cellular network, and store information such as contacts.

succession planning   The process of identifying people who can take over certain positions (usually on a temporary basis) in case the people holding those critical positions are incapacitated or lost in an incident.

supervisory control and data acquisition (SCADA)   A system that has the basic components of a distributed control system (DCS), yet is designed for large-scale, distributed processes and functions with the idea that remote devices may or may not have ongoing communication with the central control.

supplicant   A client computer in a RADIUS network.

switch   A Layer 2 (Data Link) multiport device that filters and forwards frames based on MAC addresses.

switch port protection   Various methods to help modern switches deal with malicious software and other threats. Includes technologies such as flood guards.

switching loop   When you connect multiple switches together in a circuit causing a loop to appear. Better switches use Spanning Tree Protocol (STP) to prevent this.

symmetric DSL (SDSL)   Type of DSL connection that provides equal upload and download speed and, in theory, provides speeds up to 15 Mbps, although the vast majority of ISPs provide packages ranging from 192 Kbps to 9 Mbps.

symmetric-key algorithm   Any encryption method that uses the same key for both encryption and decryption.

synchronous   Describes a connection between two electronic devices where neither must acknowledge (ACK) when receiving data.

Synchronous Digital Hierarchy (SDH)   European fiber carrier standard equivalent to SONET.

Synchronous Optical Network (SONET)   *See* SONET (Synchronous Optical Network).

Synchronous Transport Signal (STS)   Signal method used by SONET. It consists of the STS payload and the STS overhead. A number is appended to the end of STS to designate signal speed.

system life cycle   Description of typical beginning and end of computing components. Handling such devices at the end includes system life cycle policies and asset disposal.

system log   A log file that records issues dealing with the overall system, such as system services, device drivers, or configuration changes.

System Restore   A Windows utility that enables you to return your PC to a recent working configuration when something goes wrong. System Restore returns your computer's system settings to the way they were the last time you remember your system working correctly—all without affecting your personal files or e-mail.

T connector   A three-sided, tubular connector found in 10Base2 Ethernet networking. The connector is in the shape of a *T* with the "arms" of the *T* ending with a female BNC connector and the "leg" having a male BNC connector. The T connector is used to attach a BNC connector on a host between two cable segments.

T1   A leased-line connection capable of carrying data at 1,544,000 bps.

T1 line   The specific, shielded, two-pair cabling that connects the two ends of a T1 connection.

T3 line   A leased-line connection capable of carrying data at 44,736,000 bps.

tailgating   When an unauthorized person attempts to enter through an already opened door.

tamper detection   A feature of modern server chasses that will log in the mother-board's nonvolatile RAM (NVRAM) if the chassis has been opened. The log will show chassis intrusion with a date and time. Alternatively, the special stickers or zip ties that break when a device has been opened.

TCP segment   The connection-oriented payload of an IP packet. A TCP segment works on the Transport layer.

TCP three-way handshake   A three-packet conversation between TCP hosts to establish and start a data transfer session. The conversation begins with a SYN request by the initiator. The target responds with a SYN response and an ACK to the SYN request. The initiator confirms receipt of the SYN ACK with an ACK. Once this handshake is complete, data transfer can begin.

tcpdump   A command-line packet sniffing tool.

TCP/IP model   An architecture model based on the TCP/IP protocol suite, which defines and standardizes the flow of data between computers. The following lists the four layers:

- **Layer 1**   The *Link layer (Network Interface layer)* is similar to OSI's Data Link and Physical layers. The Link layer consists of any part of the network that deals with frames.

- **Layer 2**   The *Internet layer* is the same as OSI's Network layer. Any part of the network that deals with pure IP packets—getting a packet to its destination—is on the Internet layer.

- **Layer 3**   The *Transport layer* combines the features of OSI's Transport and Session layers. It is concerned with the assembly and disassembly of data, as well as connection-oriented and connectionless communication.

- **Layer 4**   The *Application layer* combines the features of the top three layers of the OSI model. It consists of the processes that applications use to initiate, control, and disconnect from a remote system.

TCP/IP suite The collection of all the protocols and processes that make TCP over IP communication over a network possible.

telecommunications room A central location for computer or telephone equipment and, most importantly, centralized cabling. All cables usually run to the telecommunications room from the rest of the installation.

telephony The science of converting sound into electrical signals, moving those signals from one location to another, and then converting those signals back into sounds. This includes modems, telephone lines, the telephone system, and any products used to create a remote access link between a remote access client and server.

Telnet A program that enables users on the Internet to log onto remote systems from their own host systems.

temperature monitor Device for keeping a telecommunications room at an optimal temperature.

TEMPEST The NSA's security standard that is used to combat radio frequency (RF) emanation by using enclosures, shielding, and even paint.

Temporal Key Integrity Protocol (TKIP) *See* TKIP-RC4.

Teredo A NAT-traversal IPv6 tunneling protocol, built into Microsoft Windows.

Terminal Access Controller Access Control System Plus (TACACS+) A proprietary protocol developed by Cisco to support Authorization, Authentication, and Accounting (AAA) in a network with many routers and switches. It is similar to RADIUS in function, but uses TCP port 49 by default and separates AAA, and accounting into different parts.

terminal adapter (TA) The most common interface used to connect a computer to an ISDN line.

terminal emulation Software that enables a PC to communicate with another computer or network as if it were a specific type of hardware terminal.

termination Endpoint in a network segment. *See* demarc.

TFTP (Trivial File Transfer Protocol) *See* Trivial File Transfer Protocol (TFTP).

thick AP A wireless access point that is completely self-contained with a full set of management programs and administrative access ways. Each thick AP is individually managed by an administrator who logs into the WAP, configures it, and logs out.

thin AP A wireless access point with minimal configuration tools installed. Instead, it is managed by a central controller. An administrator can manage a large number of thin APs by logging into the central controller and performing management tasks on any thin APs from there.

Thinnet   Trade name for 10Base2 Ethernet technology. Thinnet is characterized by the use of RG-58 coaxial cable segments and BNC T connectors to attach stations to the segments.

threat   Any form of potential attack against a network.

TIA/EIA (Telecommunications Industry Association/Electronics Industry Association)   The standards body that defines most of the standards for computer network cabling. Many of these standards are defined under the TIA/EIA 568 standard.

TIA/EIA 568A   One of two four-pair UTP crimping standards for 10/100/1000BaseT networks. Often shortened to T568A. The other standard is *TIA/EIA 568B*.

TIA/EIA 568B   One of two four-pair UTP crimping standards for 10/100/1000BaseT networks. Often shortened to T568B. The other standard is *TIA/EIA 568A*.

TIA/EIA 606   Official methodology for labeling patch panels.

Ticket-Granting Ticket (TGT)   Sent by an Authentication Server in a Kerberos setup if a client's hash matches its own, signaling that the client is authenticated but not yet authorized.

time division multiplexing (TDM)   The process of having frames that carry a bit of every channel in every frame sent at a regular interval in a T1 connection.

time domain reflectometer (TDR)   Advanced cable tester that tests the length of cables and their continuity or discontinuity, and identifies the location of any discontinuity due to a bend, break, unwanted crimp, and so on.

TKIP-RC4   The extra layer of security that Wi-Fi Protected Access (WPA) adds on top of Wired Equivalent Privacy (WEP); uses RC4 for cipher initialization.

TLS (Transport Layer Security)   *See* Transport Layer Security (TLS).

tone generator   *See* toners.

tone probe   *See* toners.

toners   Generic term for two devices used together—a tone generator and a tone locator (probe)—to trace cables by sending an electrical signal along a wire at a particular frequency. The tone locator then emits a sound when it distinguishes that frequency. Also referred to as *Fox and Hound*.

top listener   Host that receives the most data on a network.

top talker   Host that sends the most data on a network.

top-level domain (TLD) names   Peak of the hierarchy for naming on the Internet; these include the .com, .org, .net, .edu, .gov, .mil, and .int names, as well as international country codes such as .us, .eu, etc.

top-level domain servers   A set of DNS servers—just below the root servers—that handle the top-level domain names, such as .com, .org, .net, and so on.

topology   The pattern of interconnections in a communications system among devices, nodes, and associated input and output stations. Also describes how computers connect to each other without regard to how they actually communicate.

tracert (also traceroute)   A command-line utility used to follow the path a packet takes between two hosts.

tracert –6 (also traceroute6)   A command-line utility that checks a path from the station running the command to a destination host. Adding the –6 switch to the command line specifies that the target host uses an IPv6 address. tracerout6 is a Linux command that performs a traceroute to an IPv6 addressed host.

traffic analysis   Tools that chart a network's traffic usage.

traffic shaping   Controlling the flow of packets into or out of the network according to the type of packet or other rules.

traffic spike   Unusual and usually dramatic increase in the amount of network traffic. Traffic spikes may be the result of normal operations within the organization or may be an indication of something more sinister.

trailer   The portion of an Ethernet frame that is the frame check sequence (FCS).

transceiver   The device that transmits and receives signals on a cable.

Transmission Control Protocol (TCP)   Part of the TCP/IP protocol suite, operates at Layer 4 (Transport) of the OSI seven-layer model. TCP is a connection-oriented protocol.

Transmission Control Protocol/Internet Protocol (TCP/IP)   A set of communication protocols developed by the U.S. Department of Defense that enables dissimilar computers to share information over a network.

transmit beamforming   A multiple-antenna technology in 802.11n WAPs that helps get rid of dead spots.

Transport layer   *See* Open Systems Interconnection (OSI) seven-layer model.

Transport Layer Security (TLS)   A robust update to SSL that works with almost any TCP application.

Trap   Out-of-tolerance condition in an SNMP managed device.

Trivial File Transfer Protocol (TFTP)   A protocol that transfers files between servers and clients. Unlike FTP, TFTP requires no user login. Devices that need an operating system, but have no local hard disk (for example, diskless workstations and routers), often use TFTP to download their operating systems.

Trojan horse   A virus that masquerades as a file with a legitimate purpose, so that a user will run it intentionally. The classic example is a file that runs a game, but also causes some type of damage to the player's system.

trunk port   A port on a switch configured to carry all data, regardless of VLAN number, between all switches in a LAN.

trunking   The process of transferring VLAN data between two or more switches.

trusted user   An account that has been granted specific authority to perform certain or all administrative tasks.

tunnel   An encrypted link between two programs on two separate computers.

tunnel broker   In IPv6, a service that creates the actual tunnel and (usually) offers a custom-made endpoint client for you to use, although more advanced users can often make a manual connection.

Tunnel Information and Control (TIC) protocol   One of the protocols that sets up IPv6 tunnels and handles configuration as well as login.

Tunnel Setup Protocol (TSP)   One of the protocols that sets up IPv6 tunnels and handles configuration as well as login.

twisted pair   Twisted pairs of cables, the most overwhelmingly common type of cabling used in networks. The two types of twisted pair cabling are UTP (unshielded twisted pair) and STP (shielded twisted pair). The twists serve to reduce interference, called *crosstalk*; the more twists, the less crosstalk.

two-factor authentication   A method of security authentication that requires two separate means of authentication; for example, some sort of physical token that, when inserted, prompts for a password. Also called *multifactor authentication*.

TXT record   Freeform type of DNS record that can be used for anything.

type   Part of an Ethernet frame that describes/labels the frame contents.

U (unit)   *See* unit (U).

UART (Universal Asynchronous Receiver/Transmitter)   *See* Universal Asynchronous Receiver/Transmitter (UART).

UC device   One of three components of a UC network, it is used to handle voice, video, and more.

UC gateway   One of three components of a UC network, it is an edge device used to add extra services to an edge router.

UC server   One of three components of a UC network, it is typically a dedicated box that supports any UC-provided service.

UDP (User Datagram Protocol)   *See* User Datagram Protocol (UDP).

UDP datagram   A connectionless networking container used in UDP communication.

Ultra Physical Contact (UPC) connector   Fiber-optic connector that makes physical contact between two fiber-optic cables. The fibers within a UPC are polished extensively for a superior finish and better junction integrity.

UNC (Universal Naming Convention)   Describes any shared resource in a network using the convention *<server name>**<name of shared resource>*.

unencrypted channel   Unsecure communication between two hosts that pass data using cleartext. A Telnet connection is a common unencrypted channel.

unicast   A message sent from one computer to one other computer.

unicast address   A unique IP address that is exclusive to a single system.

unidirectional antenna   An antenna that focuses all of its transmission energy in a single, relatively narrow direction. Similarly, its design limits its ability to receive signals that are not aligned with the focused direction.

unified communication (UC)   A system that rolls many different network services into one. Instant messaging (IM), telephone service, and video conferencing are a few examples.

unified threat management (UTM)   A firewall that is also packaged with a collection of other processes and utilities to detect and prevent a wide variety of threats. These protections include intrusion detection systems, intrusion prevention systems, VPN portals, load balancers, and other threat mitigation apparatus.

unified voice services   Complete self-contained Internet services that rely on nothing more than software installed on computers and the computers' microphone/speakers to provide voice telecommunication over the Internet. All of the interconnections to the public switched telephone network (PSTN) are handled in the cloud.

uninterruptible power supply (UPS)   A device that supplies continuous clean power to a computer system the whole time the computer is on. Protects against power outages and sags. The term *UPS* is often used mistakenly when people mean stand-by power supply or system (SPS).

unit (U)   The unique height measurement used with equipment racks; 1 U equals 1.75 inches.

Universal Asynchronous Receiver Transmitter (UART)   A device inside a modem that takes the 8-bit-wide digital data and converts it into 1-bit-wide digital data and hands it to the modem for conversion to analog data. The process is reversed for incoming data.

UNIX   A popular computer software operating system used on many Internet host systems.

unsecure protocol   Also known as an *insecure protocol*, transfers data between hosts in an unencrypted, clear text format. If these packets are intercepted between the communicating hosts, their data is completely exposed and readable.

unshielded twisted pair (UTP)   A popular cabling for telephone and networks composed of pairs of wires twisted around each other at specific intervals. The twists serve to reduce interference (also called *crosstalk*). The more twists, the less interference. The cable has *no* metallic shielding to protect the wires from external interference, unlike its cousin, *STP*. 10BaseT uses UTP, as do many other networking technologies. UTP is available in a variety of grades, called categories, as defined in the following:

- **Category 1 UTP**   Regular analog phone lines, not used for data communications
- **Category 2 UTP**   Supports speeds up to 4 Mbps
- **Category 3 UTP**   Supports speeds up to 16 Mbps
- **Category 4 UTP**   Supports speeds up to 20 Mbps
- **Category 5 UTP**   Supports speeds up to 100 Mbps
- **Category 5e UTP**   Supports speeds up to 100 Mbps with two pairs and up to 1000 Mbps with four pairs
- **Category 6 UTP**   Improved support for speeds up to 10 Gbps
- **Category 6a UTP**   Extends the length of 10-Gbps communication to the full 100 meters commonly associated with UTP cabling

untrusted user   An account that has been granted no administrative powers.

uplink port   Port on a switch that enables you to connect two switches together using a straight-through cable.

upload   The transfer of information from a user's system to a remote computer system. Opposite of *download*.

URL (uniform resource locator)   An address that defines the type and the location of a resource on the Internet. URLs are used in almost every TCP/IP application. An example HTTP URL is http://www.totalsem.com.

Usenet   The network of UNIX users, generally perceived as informal and made up of loosely coupled nodes, that exchanges mail and messages. Started by Duke University and UNC-Chapel Hill. An information cooperative linking around 16,000 computer sites and millions of people. Usenet provides a series of "news groups" analogous to online conferences.

user   Anyone who uses a computer. You.

user account   A container that identifies a user to the application, operating system, or network, including name, password, user name, groups to which the user belongs, and other information based on the user and the OS or NOS being used. Usually defines the rights and roles a user plays on a system.

User Datagram Protocol (UDP)   A protocol used by some older applications, most prominently TFTP (Trivial FTP), to transfer files. UDP datagrams are both simpler and smaller than TCP segments, and they do most of the behind-the-scenes work in a TCP/IP network.

user profile   A collection of settings that corresponds to a specific user account and may follow the user, regardless of the computer at which he or she logs on. These settings enable the user to have customized environment and security settings.

user-level security   A security system in which each user has an account, and access to resources is based on user identity.

UTP coupler   A simple, passive, double-ended connector with female connectors on both ends. UTP couplers are used to connect two UTP cable segments together to achieve longer length when it is deemed unnecessary or inappropriate to use a single, long cable.

V standards   Standards established by CCITT for modem manufacturers to follow (voluntarily) to ensure compatible speeds, compression, and error correction.

V.92 standard   The current modem standard, which has a download speed of 57,600 bps and an upload speed of 48 Kbps. V.92 modems have several interesting features, such as Quick Connect and Modem On Hold.

variable   Value of an SNMP management information base (MIB) object. That value can be read with a Get PDU or changed with a Set PDU.

variable-length subnet masking (VLSM)   *See* Classless Inter-Domain Routing (CIDR).

vertical cross-connect   Main patch panel in a telecommunications room. *See also* patch panel.

very-high-bit-rate DSL (VDSL)   The latest form of DSL with download and upload speeds of up to 100 Mbps. VDSL was designed to run on copper phone lines, but many VDSL suppliers use fiber-optic cabling to increase effective distances.

video surveillance   Security measures that use remotely monitored visual systems that include IP cameras and closed-circuit televisions (CCTVs).

video teleconferencing (VTC)   The classic, multicast-based presentation where one presenter pushes out a stream of video to any number of properly configured and properly authorized multicast clients.

View   The different displays found in Performance Monitor.

virtual firewall   A firewall that is implemented in software within a virtual machine in cases where it would be difficult, costly, or impossible to install a traditional physical firewall.

virtual IP   A single IP address shared by multiple systems. This is commonly the single IP address assigned to a home or organization that uses NAT to have multiple IP stations on the private side of the NAT router.

virtual local area network (VLAN)   A common feature among managed switches that enables a single switch to support multiple logical broadcast domains. Not only is VLAN support a common feature of managed switches but VLAN installations take advantage of this feature and are very common today.

virtual machine (VM)   A virtual computer accessed through a class of programs called a hypervisor or virtual machine manager. A virtual machine runs *inside* your actual operating system, essentially enabling you to run two or more operating systems at once.

virtual machine manager (VMM)   *See* hypervisor.

Virtual Network Computing (VNC)   A terminal emulation program.

virtual PBX   Software that functionally replaces a physical PBX telephone system.

virtual private network (VPN)   A network configuration that enables a remote user to access a private network via the Internet. VPNs employ an encryption methodology called *tunneling*, which protects the data from interception.

virtual router   A router that is implemented in software within a virtual machine. The scalability of a virtual machine makes it easy to add capacity to the router when it is needed. Virtual routers are easily managed and are highly scalable without requiring the purchase of additional network hardware.

virtual switch   Special software that enables virtual machines (VMs) to communicate with each other without going outside of the host system.

Virtual Trunking Protocol (VTP)   A proprietary Cisco protocol used to automate the updating of multiple VLAN switches.

virus   A program that can make a copy of itself without your necessarily being aware of it. All viruses carry some payload that may or may not do something malicious.

virus definition or data files   Enables the virus protection software to recognize the viruses on your system and clean them. These files should be updated often. Also called *signature files*, depending on the virus protection software in use.

virus shield   Anti-malware program that passively monitors a computer's activity, checking for viruses only when certain events occur, such as a program executing or a file being downloaded.

VLAN hopping   Older technique to hack a switch to change a normal switch port from an access port to a trunk port. This allows the station attached to the newly created trunk port to access different VLANs. Modern switches have preventative measures to stop this type of abuse.

VLAN pooling   Used in wireless networking, a setup where multiple VLANs share a common domain. The multiple VLANs are used to keep broadcast traffic to manageable levels. Wireless clients are randomly assigned to different VLANs. Their common domain enables them all to be centrally managed.

VLAN Trunking Protocol (VTP)   Cisco proprietary protocol to automate the updating of multiple VLAN switches.

Voice over IP (VoIP)   Using an IP network to conduct voice calls.

VoIP gateway   Interface between a traditional switched telephone network and a VoIP service provider.

VoIP PBX   A private branch exchange that uses VoIP instead of the traditional switched telephone circuits.

volt (V)   Unit of measurement for voltage.

voltage   The pressure of the electrons passing through a wire.

voltage quality recorder   Tracks voltage over time by plugging into a power outlet.

VPN concentrator   The new endpoint of the local LAN in L2TP.

VPN tunnel   A connection over the Internet between a client and a server; the VPN tunnel enables the client to access remote resources as if they were local, securely.

vulnerability   A potential weakness in an infrastructure that a threat might exploit.

vulnerability management   The ongoing process of identifying vulnerabilities and dealing with them.

vulnerability scanner   A tool that scans a network for potential attack vectors.

WAN (wide area network)   A geographically dispersed network created by linking various computers and LANs over long distances, generally using leased phone lines. There is no firm dividing line between a WAN and a LAN.

warm boot   A system restart performed after the system has been powered and operating. This clears and resets the memory, but does not stop and start the hard drive.

warm site   Facility with all of the physical resources, computers, and network infrastructure to recover from a primary site disaster. A warm site does not have current backup data and it may take a day or more to recover and install backups before business operations can recommence.

wattage (watts or W)   The amount of amps and volts needed by a particular device to function.

wavelength   In the context of laser pulses, the distance the signal has to travel before it completes its cyclical oscillation and starts to repeat. Measured in nanometers, wavelength can be loosely associated with colors.

Web server   A server that enables access to HTML documents by remote users.

Web services   Applications and processes that can be accessed over a network, rather than being accessed locally on the client machine. Web services include things such as Web-based e-mail, network-shareable documents, spreadsheets and databases, and many other types of cloud-based applications.

well-known port numbers   Port numbers from 0 to 1204 that are used primarily by client applications to talk to server applications in TCP/IP networks.

wide area network (WAN)   *See* WAN (wide area network).

Wi-Fi   The most widely adopted wireless networking type in use today. Technically, only wireless devices that conform to the extended versions of the 802.11 standard—802.11a, b, g, n, and ac—are Wi-Fi certified.

Wi-Fi analyzer   *See* wireless analyzer.

Wi-Fi Protected Access (WPA)   A wireless security protocol that addresses weaknesses and acts as an upgrade to WEP. WPA offers security enhancements such as dynamic encryption key generation (keys are issued on a per-user and per-session basis), an encryption key integrity-checking feature, user authentication through the industry-standard Extensible Authentication Protocol (EAP), and other advanced features that WEP lacks.

Wi-Fi Protected Access 2 (WPA2)   An update to the WPA protocol that uses the Advanced Encryption Standard algorithm, making it much harder to crack.

Wi-Fi Protected Setup (WPS)   Automated and semi-automated process to connect a wireless device to a WAP. The process can be as simple as pressing a button on the device or pressing the button and then entering a PIN code.

WiMAX   *See* 802.16.

Windows domain   A group of computers controlled by a computer running Windows Server, which is configured as a domain controller.

Windows Firewall/Windows Defender Firewall   The firewall that has been included in Windows operating systems since Windows XP; originally named Internet Connection Firewall (ICF) but renamed in XP Service Pack 2.

Windows Internet Name Service (WINS)   A name resolution service that resolves NetBIOS names to IP addresses.

WINS proxy agent   A Windows Internet Name Service (WINS) relay agent that forwards WINS broadcasts to a WINS server on the other side of a router to keep older systems from broadcasting in place of registering with the server.

wire scheme   *See* wiring diagram.

Wired Equivalent Privacy (WEP)   A wireless security protocol that uses a 64-bit encryption algorithm to scramble data packets.

wired/wireless considerations   The planning of structured cabling, determining any wireless requirements, and planning access to the Internet when building or upgrading networks.

wireless access point (WAP)   Connects wireless network nodes to wireless or wired networks. Many WAPs are combination devices that act as high-speed hubs, switches, bridges, and routers, all rolled into one.

wireless analyzer   Any device that finds and documents all wireless networks in the area. Also known as a *Wi-Fi analyzer*.

wireless bridge   Device used to connect two wireless network segments together, or to join wireless and wired networks together in the same way that wired bridge devices do.

wireless controller   Central controlling device for thin client WAPs.

wireless LAN (WLAN)   A complete wireless network infrastructure serving a single physical locale under a single administration.

wireless network   *See* Wi-Fi.

wireless survey tool   A tool used to discover wireless networks in an area; it also notes signal interferences.

wiremap   Extensive network testing using a better cable tester.

Wireshark   A popular packet sniffer.

wiring diagram   A document, also known as a *wiring schematic*, that usually consists of multiple pages and that shows the following: how the wires in a network connect to switches and other nodes, what types of cables are used, and how patch panels are configured. It usually includes details about each cable run.

wiring schematic   *See* wiring diagram.

work area   In a basic structured cabling network, often simply an office or cubicle that potentially contains a PC attached to the network.

Workgroup   A convenient method of organizing computers under Network/My Network Places in Windows operating systems.

workstation   A general-purpose computer that is small and inexpensive enough to reside at a person's work area for his or her exclusive use.

worm   A very special form of virus. Unlike other viruses, a worm does not infect other files on the computer. Instead, it replicates by making copies of itself on other systems on a network by taking advantage of security weaknesses in networking protocols.

WPA2-Enterprise   A version of WPA2 that uses a RADIUS server for authentication.

WWW (World Wide Web)   A vast network of servers and clients communicating through the Hypertext Transfer Protocol (HTTP). Commonly accessed using graphical Web-browsing software such as Microsoft Internet Explorer and Google Chrome.

X.25   The first generation of packet-switching technology, it enables remote devices to communicate with each other across high-speed digital links without the expense of individual leased lines.

Yost cable   Cable used to interface with a Cisco device.

zero-configuration networking (zeroconf)   Automatically generated IP addresses when a DHCP server is unreachable.

zero-day attack   New attack that exploits a vulnerability that has yet to be identified.

Zigbee   Wireless home automation control standard.

zombie   A single computer under the control of an operator that is used in a botnet attack. *See also* botnet.

Z-Wave   Wireless home automation control standard.

INDEX